THE NEW
BOOK OF KNOWLEDGE

I
volume
9

THE NEW
BOOK OF
KNOWLEDGE

Grolier

INCORPORATED
NEW YORK

I, the ninth letter in the English alphabet, is a descendant of the ancient Phoenician and Hebrew letter *yod* and the Greek letter *iota*.

In Phoenician speech the letter *yod* usually had the sound of a semiconsonant that the Phoenicians pronounced like the Y in the word "yellow." It also had a vowel sound, pronounced "ee" as in the word "see." The word *yod* probably meant "hand," and many language scholars believe that an earlier version of the letter may have represented a hand or the palm of a hand. *Yod* looked like this:

When the Greeks adopted the Phoenician alphabet, they renamed the letter *iota* and changed it from a semiconsonant to a vowel. The Greeks pronounced the *iota* like the I in the word "marine." In early Greek writing the letter had a zigzag shape similar to the Phoenician letter. Eventually, however, the letter took on a straighter form, and by 403 B.C. it looked like this:

The Romans learned the Greek alphabet from the Etruscans, who ruled in Rome from the end of the 7th to the end of the 6th century B.C. But in the Roman alphabet the I sometimes stood for an I vowel sound, sometimes for a Y consonant. The Y sound of the letter eventually passed into a J sound similar to the sound heard in the word "jewel"—so the letter I was used for the sound of J, too. The I still had this double use when the Romans gave their alphabet to the nations of western Europe. It continued to be used for both sounds in English until the 17th century, when I and J became two separate letters.

The small letter *i* is simply a shortened form of the capital. Originally it had no mark over it. But a dash appears over the letter in some manuscripts of about the 11th century. In these old handwritten manuscripts the letters were often extremely small and squeezed tightly together. When the *i* consisted of a single small stroke of the pen, it could easily be confused with other letters. For example, the word "minimum" looked like this:

minimum

By placing a dash over the letter, medieval scribes found that both the *i* and the other letters were easier to read. Later, printers followed the example of the scribes but changed the dash to the round dot that we are accustomed to seeing today.

In English we usually pronounce the letter I by opening the lips and placing the tongue behind the lower front teeth. The main sounds of the letter in English are the "short" I, as in the word "wit," and the "long" I, as in the word "tide." In all the western European languages, the I is pronounced "ee," as in the word "meet." Almost all English words with this sound, such as "machine" or "casino," have been taken from foreign languages. The English I is also sometimes pronounced like a Y, as in the word "onion," or like the U in "turtle," as in the word "stir."

The letter I also serves as a word referring to the speaker, as in "I am John Smith." In English grammar it is the first person singular pronoun.

In a series I stands for the ninth member in the way that A, B, and C stand for first, second, and third. In chemistry I stands for the element iodine.

The letter I is also found in many abbreviations. On maps it often stands for "island." In many organization names, such as ITU (International Typographical Union), it stands for the word "international."

Reviewed by MARIO PEI
Columbia University

See also ALPHABET.

IBSEN, HENRIK (1828–1906)

Henrik Ibsen, Norwegian poet and playwright, influenced the literature of all nations. He was born on March 20, 1828, in Skien, Norway. His father was a well-to-do merchant but he lost his fortune when Henrik was 8, and the family moved to a little farm. The change affected Henrik deeply. He hated the "middle-class" school he had to attend in place of a university preparatory school. At home he did not play with the other children but locked himself into a room to read. He was talented at painting and good, too, at building things, at performing magic tricks, and at putting on puppet shows.

When he was 15, he went to the small town of Grimstad to be an apprentice in a druggist's shop. The pay was so small that he could afford little clothing or food. He read, wrote poetry, and studied Latin, hoping to pass the university entrance exams. A friend sent one of his poems to a paper, and it was published. Later another friend paid for the publication of Henrik's first play, *Catilina* (1850).

Henrik left Grimstad for Christiania (now Oslo) in 1850 and took the university exams, but his grades in Greek and arithmetic were not good enough. For 9 months he and two friends published a liberal, satirical weekly. His play *The Warrior's Barrow* was performed successfully that winter, and he was asked to compose a prologue for a musical festival benefiting the Norwegian Theater in Bergen. When the famous violinist Ole Bull, founder of the theater, heard the prologue, he appointed Ibsen theater poet and stage manager. Ibsen's practical experience in Bergen has been equaled by few other playwrights— perhaps only by Shakespeare and Molière.

Ibsen's first popular success was *The Feast at Solhaug* in 1856. The next year he was asked to direct the Norwegian Theater in Christiania. He married Susannah Thoresen in 1858. Their only child, Sigurd, was born in 1859. The theater went bankrupt in 1862, and Ibsen borrowed from his friends in order to keep on writing. The success of *The Pretenders* in 1863 brought him a government grant to travel abroad. He began *Brand* in Ariccia, Italy. After its publication in 1866, the Norwegian government granted Ibsen a lifelong pension. Before the grant went into effect, however, Ibsen's extreme poverty and an attack of malaria drove him nearly to suicide.

Ibsen wrote about Norway but he could not live there. He was bitter about his countrymen's lack of understanding of his work. He lived instead in Italy and Germany. The German youth idolized him. His plays were the sensations of every season. *The Pillars of Society* (1877) played in five Berlin theaters simultaneously in 1878. *A Doll's House* (1879) provoked violent discussions. Great actresses played its heroine, Nora, in all the capitals of the world. Public performances of *Ghosts* (1881) were forbidden in Germany, but *An Enemy of the People* (1882) became the most talked-about play of the year. The unhappy ending of *Hedda Gabler* (1890) was denounced.

Ibsen's seriousness of purpose, his close observation of the life around him, and the infinite pains he took to rewrite increased his powers with every play. He never ceased being an inspiration to young dramatists. His plays fall into three groups: (1) poetic, idealistic dramas, such as the romantic *Peer Gynt* (1867); (2) plays that attempted to reform social conditions; the greatest of these, *Ghosts* (1881), inspired the naturalistic problem play in all modern literatures; and (3) psychological dramas that were studies of single individuals; the first of these, *The Wild Duck* (1884), was a pioneer of the modern symbolical play. All the plays have as their theme the conflict between the moral ideals of the individual and the moral conventions and traditions of society. Ibsen believed that the individual should remain true to himself under all circumstances.

In 1891 Ibsen returned to Norway to live—Christiania's most distinguished citizen. Two of his last works—*The Master Builder* (1892) and *When We Dead Awaken* (1899)—are largely autobiographical. He died on May 23, 1906. His monument in Oslo bears no name or inscription. It simply has a carving of a miner's hammer, symbol of a man who dug ever deeper into human experience.

Ibsen's poem "The Miner" says:

> Hammer blow on hammer blow,
> Till the lamp of life burns low!

Reviewed by REGINALD L. COOK
Middlebury College

ICE

Everyone knows that water is important in our lives. Without liquid water we could not live. Water also occurs naturally as a solid called ice (and as a gas, water vapor). Ice, too, is important in our lives.

We usually think of ice as something used to cool beverages in summer, but it has other important uses. For example, we use it to keep food from spoiling.

Ice can also be dangerous. Ice in a frozen harbor can crush the hulls of ships. Floating islands of ice—the great icebergs of the North Atlantic—have sunk many ships and caused much loss of life. And you know how dangerous icy roads can be.

▶ THE SCIENCE OF ICE

Scientists study ice for many reasons. The most important reason is that $\frac{1}{10}$ of the land area of our planet is covered with ice. Then, too, more than $\frac{1}{3}$ of the world's people come in contact with snow and ice each year.

Whether ice takes the form of an ice cube or of a mountain glacier, it has the same properties. Ice forms by the same process in a refrigerator, in a puddle in your backyard, or at the North Pole. So this article will start its discussion of ice with refrigerators and end up with glaciers and the great Antarctic ice sheet.

Freezing and Melting

To understand ice, you must first understand something about heat. One of the most important scientific laws states that heat always flows from warm objects and places to cooler objects and places. The difference between a refrigerator tray full of water and the same tray full of ice cubes is heat. If enough heat flows out of the water, it turns into ice.

When you put the ice-cube tray into the freezing compartment, its surroundings are cooler than the water. Heat begins to flow out of the water. Soon the temperature is lowered to a point where ice starts to form. If the cooling continues, the water turns into a solid piece of ice. When you raise the temperature

HEAT FLOWS FROM WARMER OBJECTS AND PLACES TO COOLER OBJECTS AND PLACES

ICE CUBES FORM AS HEAT FLOWS FROM WATER IN TRAY TO COOLER SURROUNDINGS

ICE CUBES MELT AS HEAT FLOWS INTO THEM FROM WARMER LIQUID

POND FREEZES AS HEAT FLOWS FROM POND WATER TO COOLER AIR

POND THAWS AS HEAT FLOWS FROM WARMER AIR INTO ICE

of the surroundings, heat starts to flow back into the ice and ice changes back into a liquid.

At sea level, with ice made from pure water, melting always takes place at the same temperature—32 degrees Fahrenheit. In fact, 32 degrees is defined as the **melting point of ice** at normal atmospheric pressure, which is the term scientists use to describe air pressure at sea level.

A piece of ice at a temperature below its melting point is dry. You can add heat to the ice by placing it in a warm room. The temperature of the ice rises quickly to 32 degrees, and the ice begins to melt. All the while that the piece of ice is melting, heat flows into the ice. But the temperature doesn't change. It remains at 32 degrees until all the ice is melted. The heat that goes into the ice and melts it without changing the temperature is called **latent heat**. "Latent" means "hidden."

Changing the Freezing Point with Chemicals

The melting point of ice (or the freezing point of water) is generally given as 32 degrees. However, the temperature at which water starts to turn into ice can vary, depending on certain conditions.

For example, if the water is very pure (and does not contain any dust particles), it can be cooled to 0 degrees or lower before it freezes. It must be kept very still, however. Water in this state is said to be **supercooled**.

To freeze supercooled water, all that is necessary is to drop in a few particles of dirt. Ice crystals begin to form at once. In fact, a good hard shake will cause supercooled water to turn into ice. When supercooled water freezes, the temperature goes up to 32 degrees and stays there until freezing is completed.

Adding chemicals to water can also change its freezing point. A good example is the antifreeze used in car radiators where winters are cold. A mixture of equal parts of antifreeze and water will not freeze until the temperature goes down to 40 degrees below zero. And that is 72 degrees below the normal freezing point of water.

Common salt is a chemical used to change the melting point of ice. Adding salt to ice lowers its melting point, which is another way of saying that it lowers the freezing point. That is why salt is used to melt the ice on roads and sidewalks. A mixture of 1 part salt to 8 parts ice starts to melt at 20 degrees. Thus, if the air temperature is 25 degrees, this ice will melt although pure ice would not. Water from the sea contains dissolved salt, and does not freeze until the temperature drops to about 28 degrees.

The Physics of Ice-Skating

If the pressure on ice is increased, its melting point is lowered. And that is why ice skates work. When you are on ice skates, all the weight of your body is concentrated on a

HOW DOES AN ICE SKATE GLIDE ON ICE?

To demonstrate the physics of ice-skating, you need an ice cube, a soda-pop bottle, about 12 inches of thin wire, and two pencils. Wrap 3 inches of one end of the wire tightly around one pencil. Wrap the other end of the wire around the other pencil. Place the ice cube on the mouth of the bottle. Holding one pencil in each hand, place the wire across the ice cube and apply a steady downward push on the pencils. In a few moments the wire will cut all the way through the ice, yet the ice cube remains in one piece. How can this be? Pressure lowers the melting point of the ice directly under the wire, so the wire moves through the cube. As the wire passes through, the water behind it freezes into ice again, for the pressure is removed. Something similar happens when you skate. Your weight causes a thin layer of ice to melt directly under the skate blade. You glide forward on a thin film of water. When the skate has passed and the pressure is removed, the water freezes into ice again.

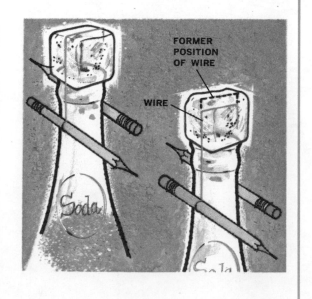

FORMER POSITION OF WIRE

WIRE

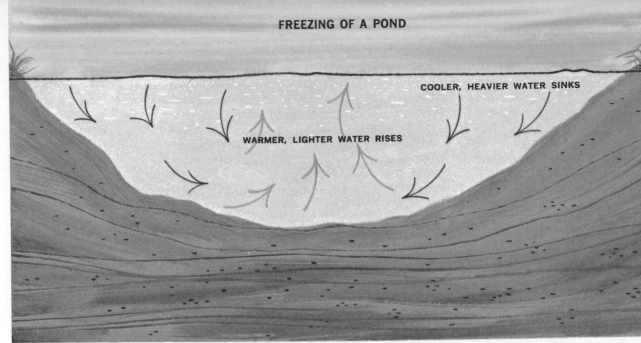

COOLER, HEAVIER WATER SINKS

WARMER, LIGHTER WATER RISES

Water, heaviest at 39 degrees Fahrenheit, sinks and pushes warmer water to surface. Circulation continues until all water is 39 degrees. When further cooled, water becomes lighter, and pond starts to freeze at surface.

very small area of ice right under the edge of the skates. Because pressure is built up, the melting point of the ice under the blade is lowered. The ice melts, and a very thin layer of water is formed between the ice and your skate. This acts as a lubricant, making the surface more slippery. As soon as you move forward the pressure is removed. The melting point then returns to 32 degrees and the film of water freezes again.

A close look at ice cubes will show you many other important physical properties of ice. Ice is hard, and it is transparent (except when it contains air bubbles). Ice floats on water. That means that ice weighs less than an equal volume (amount) of water. Air-free ice floats on fresh water with about $9/10$ of its volume under water. Salt water is denser (heavier) than fresh water. So objects float higher in salt water than they do in fresh. New icebergs contain air bubbles, and thus they float in the sea with about $4/5$ of their volume under water.

Because most of the ice is hidden, icebergs are a great danger to ships. In April, 1912, the *Titanic,* the largest ship afloat at that time, sank in the North Atlantic after colliding with an iceberg. Some 1,500 people were lost. Soon afterward an International Ice Patrol was set up. Its job is to report on the southward movement of icebergs. The United States Coast Guard keeps a record of icebergs and broadcasts their location to ships at sea.

▶ ICE IN NATURE

Ice forms on the earth's surface in two ways. It may form by the freezing of water or it may start as snow that slowly changes into ice.

Ice from Water

Let's take the case of a small pond and see what happens as it freezes. During the summer the water becomes warmer. It absorbs heat from the sun, and it is in contact with the warm air. As winter approaches, the air temperature drops. The water then loses heat to the air, and its temperature falls.

To understand what happens next, you have to know another fact about water. It is heaviest at 39 degrees. At temperatures higher or lower than 39 degrees it is lighter.

As the surface of the pond cools to 39 degrees the water on the top becomes heavier and sinks to the bottom. In sinking, it pushes warmer, lighter water up from below. The new surface water cools, sinks, and pushes more bottom water to the surface. This circulation continues until all of the pond is at 39 degrees.

When all the water is at 39 degrees, further

cooling of the surface water only makes it lighter. So it stays at the surface. As a result, the pond starts to freeze at the surface, while the water at the bottom remains at 39 degrees.

(Because water is heavier than ice, plant and animal life can survive in the water at the bottom. If ice were heavier than water, ponds and lakes would freeze from the bottom. Few living things would survive in them.)

Ice from Snow

The other way that ice forms in nature is from snow. In most places where winter snows fall, temperatures later climb high enough to melt all of the snow that has fallen. In very high mountain areas and in the polar regions this is not the case. In those regions some of the winter snow remains at the end of the summer. Because some snow remains unmelted each year, the thickness of snow in these areas gradually increases over the years.

Snow falls in beautiful six-sided shapes. New-fallen snow is full of air bubbles. Light and fluffy, it is only $\frac{1}{5}$ to $\frac{1}{10}$ as heavy as water. But as it lies on the ground the new-fallen snow changes slowly. For one thing, the weight of the snow on top presses on the snow nearer the bottom. Also, the snow crystals become more and more rounded and are packed together. This, too, makes the snow denser. Even where there is no melting, as in most of Antarctica, the snow after 1 year increases to twice its original density. This packed-down snow is called **firn**.

By the time the firn has been buried for several hundred years and is 200 feet or so deep, it is about four times as dense as new-fallen snow. In this dense snow the air bubbles no longer join together, and the material is now called ice.

In areas where there is some melting, the density of snow increases much faster. This is so because some of the water from the melting trickles down through the rest of the snow and fills the air spaces between snow crystals. Later it refreezes and makes ice.

▶ RIVERS OF ICE

Apart from its low temperature, an ice cube from the refrigerator appears to be a perfectly ordinary solid object. Ice, however, has some unusual properties. Suppose a very thick piece of ice—say 200 feet thick—is placed on a level surface. It will gradually spread out sideways. This movement is called **creep** or **flow**. We can refer to the **flow of ice** in much the same way that we talk about the flow of water.

The Flow of Ice

The effects of ice flow can be seen even in a small piece. If an ice cube is placed between two metal plates and the plates are pushed toward each other, the ice will be squeezed out sideways. The rate of flow is very small with such small forces. But if the force is increased, the rate of flow increases rapidly.

The same thing happens in nature. As you know, the depth of snow may increase from year to year, and the snow gradually changes into ice. While the ice is thin, it remains almost motionless. When the ice becomes 200 to 300 feet thick, the force produced by the weight of ice above causes the ice at the bottom to flow. Normally it flows downhill, carrying the upper layers of ice with it. When a whole mass of ice moves slowly downhill, we call it a **glacier**.

Each year thousands of icebergs break off from glaciers and drift through the North Atlantic. The largest icebergs in this photograph are probably about 100 yards across.

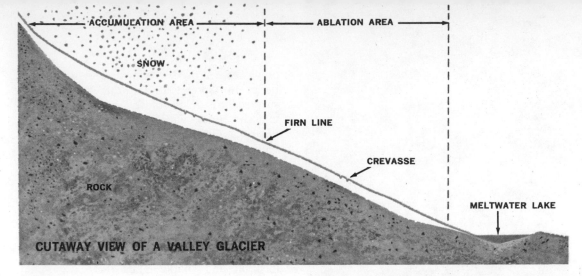

SNOW

FIRN LINE

CREVASSE

ROCK

MELTWATER LAKE

CUTAWAY VIEW OF A VALLEY GLACIER

Glaciers

Glaciers are found at present in the regions around the North and South poles and in mountainous areas elsewhere. Near the equator in South America and in Kenya in Africa, some of the mountains are high enough (15,000 feet or more) for the average air temperature to be well below freezing point. Thus there are glaciers in equatorial lands as well as in cold ones. Of course, for glaciers to form at all, snow must fall. A few places in Antarctica have no glaciers simply because very little snow falls.

Ablation

As the ice in the glacier flows downhill to warmer altitudes the amount of melting increases. (Water from such melting is called melt water.) Some of the melt water may soak into the glacier and refreeze. The rest either flows off the glacier in streams or evaporates into the air. These processes, by which ice is lost from the glacier, are called **ablation**.

Some glaciers reach the sea and melt when they come in contact with the warmer seawater. **Calving**, the name used when large icebergs break off a glacier and float away, is also a form of ablation.

Accumulation

Now let's take a look at a glacier in a mountainous area. High up in the mountains the amount of new snow and ice added each year is greater than the amount lost by melting and evaporation. This upper part of the glacier is called the **accumulation area**.

Farther down the mountain, ablation is greater than accumulation of snow. This part of the glacier is the **ablation area**.

At some level on the glacier, summer melting just balances the winter's accumulation of snow. This level is called the **firn line**. Above the firn line the glacier's surface is permanently snow-covered. Below it the surface is ice in the summer and snow in the winter.

Of course, the firn line may not stay at the same level from year to year. Unusually heavy snowfalls for a number of years will move the firn line down the glacier. Several years of unusually warm summer temperatures will move it up the glacier.

Sometimes a glacier may reach a point where snow accumulation all over it is the same as the total amount of ablation. The thickness and the length of the glacier then stay the same from year to year. All that the glacier does is to move the ice down the mountain to a level where it melts. With most glaciers the movement is only a few hundred feet each year, but a few move very much faster than this.

Crevasses

It is very rare for a glacier to flow down a perfectly smooth valley. Valleys usually have "steps" and hollows in them. Frequently the width of a valley varies from one place to another.

As a glacier flows over a step or hollow the ice near the surface is stretched, and it may crack. These cracks in the glacier are called **crevasses**. They are one of the greatest dangers in crossing glaciers and ice sheets. Explorers, scientists, and skiers have fallen into these great cracks.

In summer the snow on the lower parts of glaciers melts, and so the crevasses can be

Crevasse in glacier near top of Mt. Olympus, Washington.

crevasses are usually not more than 150 feet deep. In Greenland and the Antarctic the surface ice is much colder. There the crevasses may be much wider and much deeper. In northeast Greenland scientists have measured crevasses that were 120 feet wide. In the Antarctic some crevasses are known to be more than 200 feet deep.

Classifying Glaciers

Scientists divide glaciers into groups according to their temperature—as temperate or cold. Or they may group glaciers according to location and shape. Thus there are valley glaciers, ice caps, ice sheets, and ice shelves. Some of these types of glaciers are illustrated in the diagrams.

Unanswered Questions About Glaciers

There are many problems connected with these smaller glaciers. Scientists still do not know how a glacier moves over its bed. In some places where two glaciers start from the same area of accumulating snow, scientists have found that one glacier is getting longer while the other is growing shorter. But they do not know why.

▶ EARTH'S GREAT ICE SHEETS

At present about 10 percent of the earth's land is covered with ice. At other times in the earth's history there has been less ice than now. At times there has been more—much more.

seen and avoided. In winter crevasses may be covered by a layer of snow deep enough to hide them but not strong enough to support a man. In the accumulation area crevasses are almost always snow-covered. There the danger of a serious accident is always present.

On glaciers in the mountainous regions of the temperate and tropical zones of the earth,

KINDS OF GLACIERS

ICE CAP

GLACIERS

ROCK

ICE SHEET

ICE SHELF (CUTAWAY VIEW)

WATER

VALLEY GLACIER

The Ice Ages

For a few periods lasting for thousands of years large areas of the continents were buried deeply under sheets of ice. These times are referred to as **ice ages**. Scientists think that during our planet's history at least four ice ages have covered large parts of the earth with great sheets of ice.

The most recent ice age started about 3,000,000 years ago. During this age the ice advanced four times, and each time melted back. When the ice advanced, large parts of North America and Europe were buried under thousands of feet of ice. These ice sheets disappeared about 6,000 years ago. The only ones left are those covering Greenland and Antarctica, and no one knows whether they will melt away or grow larger.

The Greenland and Antarctic ice sheets contain nearly all of the land ice on the earth's surface. Most of the rest is on the islands north of Canada, in Iceland, and in Spitsbergen.

▶THE GREENLAND ICE SHEET

Greenland is about the size of the United States east of the Mississippi. More than ⅘ of the island is covered with ice. The ice-free areas are on the coasts in the southwest and the far north. The surface of the ice sheet rises to about 8,000 feet in altitude in the north and south and to about 10,000 feet in the center of this large island.

For many hundreds of years the Greenland

The Greenland ice sheet covers an area of over 700,000 square miles.

Eskimo traveled by sled over the edges of the ice sheet, moving from one coastal settlement to another. The first man to cross the island over the ice sheet was a great Norwegian explorer, Fridtjof Nansen. In 1888 he and five companions traveled by sled from the east coast, over the inland ice, to the southwest coast. Since then many explorers and scientists

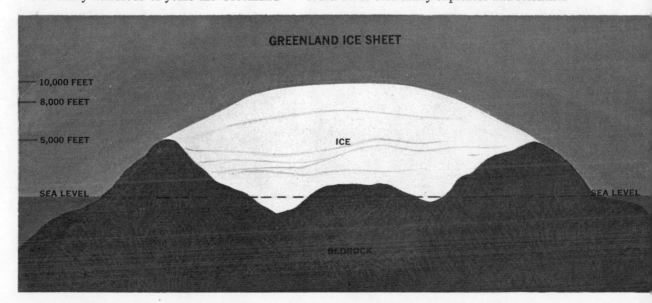

GREENLAND ICE SHEET

10,000 FEET
8,000 FEET
5,000 FEET
ICE
SEA LEVEL
SEA LEVEL
BEDROCK

have crossed the ice sheet. A few hardy scientists have even spent the winter on it. Hardy they were because they recorded temperatures as low as 88 degrees below zero.

Measuring the Depth of Greenland's Ice Sheet

The thickness of the Greenland ice sheet was first measured by German scientists in 1930. They set off explosives in holes drilled a few feet down into the ice. The force of the explosion compressed (squeezed) the ice nearby. The compression set up shock waves that traveled in all directions. Waves traveling through the surface layers of ice were detected by microphones spread out on the ice. Other waves went down through the ice. The solid rock beneath the ice reflected the waves to the surface, where the microphones detected them.

Mathematics tells us that Rate times Time equals Distance. The scientists knew the distance the waves had traveled at the surface and the time taken. So they could easily figure out the rate, or speed, at which the waves traveled through ice. Knowing rate and time, they could then work out the distance the waves had traveled between the surface of the ice and the rock below. This gave them the thickness of the ice.

The Germans found that the ice near the edge of the ice sheet was about 5,000 feet thick. It was even thicker in the middle of south Greenland.

Since World War II, French, British, and American scientists have made ice measurements. In some parts of Greenland the ice is more than 10,000 feet thick. In many areas the bottom of the ice is well below sea level.

(A fast, easy way of measuring ice thickness has been used recently. A plane flies over the ice sending out bursts, or "pulses," of radio waves. The waves pass through the ice and are reflected by the underlying rock. Instruments in the plane measure the time it takes the waves to return to the plane.)

The land in the middle of Greenland is pushed down into the earth's crust by the great weight of ice. If the ice were removed, the land would rise about 3,000 feet.

If the ice on Greenland did melt, the level of all the oceans would rise about 20 feet. Parts of many seaports, including London and New York, would be flooded as a result.

The Greenland ice sheet melts more slowly than snow and new ice accumulate. Thus the ice sheet continues to flow down to the sea in many places. In many other places glaciers from the inland ice flow through the coastal

Drill brings up ice core from more than 2 miles under polar ice cap.

Scientists in a forest clearing measure snow depth and water content.

Wind pressure and ocean currents shape ice into boulderlike form.

mountains to the sea. There they break up to form icebergs. Some icebergs are carried south by currents into the North Atlantic.

Measuring Snow Accumulation

Snow accumulation is measured in two ways. The easiest is to erect poles and to measure the snow as it piles up against the poles. The other method is to dig pits or to drill into the ice and remove cores of it. Then the snow layers can be studied. The coring method works particularly well in Greenland.

The air temperature there rises to at least 32 degrees for a few days each summer, except on the highest parts of the inland ice. The surface snow melts slightly. Then it refreezes, forming a layer of crystals that are rounded and cemented together.

These clearly marked layers enable scientists to measure the accumulation of snow for each year. One core, 4,400 feet long, provided samples all the way through the ice. The bottom ice was more than 75,000 years old. Careful study of the core showed the scientists how temperatures had varied through these 75,000 years.

Scientists can now measure with fair accuracy the total yearly accumulation of snow on the Greenland ice sheet. They also know the amount of melting around the edges. But how much ice is lost each year in the form of icebergs is still something of a mystery.

▶ THE ANTARCTIC ICE SHEET

Antarctica is 1½ times as large as the United States. All of this continent, except some small areas, is covered with ice.

In western Antarctica the ice sheet rises to about 7,500 feet above sea level. In the deepest part of the ice sheet the ice measures more than 13,000 feet. The rock beneath this great mass of ice is more than 8,000 feet below sea level in one area. If the ice were to disappear, the coastal part of western Antarctica would become a series of islands.

In eastern Antarctica the shape of the land at the bottom of the ice is less well known. The surface of the ice rises to about 13,000 feet above sea level. In the areas where explorations have been made, the bottom of the ice is found to be 2,000 feet below sea level.

After years of making measurements, scientists can estimate the total volume of ice in Antarctica. If it all melted, sea levels the world over would rise about 150 feet.

An ice cave, carved out of glacier ice by meltwater streams.

Ice Shelves

Large ice shelves fringe the coasts of Antarctica. The largest are the Ross and the Filchner ice shelves. Both are as big as the state of Texas.

The ice of the shelves floats on the sea, but it is not formed by the freezing of seawater. Shelf ice forms from the glaciers that spread seaward from the inland parts of the continent. The 1,000-foot-thick ice of the Ross Shelf moves northward at speeds of up to 4,000 feet a year.

Ice Islands

Sometimes the front of an ice shelf breaks off into the ocean, forming huge flat-topped icebergs. One such iceberg, discovered in 1927, was 100 miles long and 100 miles wide. This great ice island stood 130 feet high in the water. Altogether it must have been more than 600 feet thick. Antarctic icebergs are formed far from the usual shipping lanes and melt long before they can drift into them.

Questions About the Antarctic Ice Sheet

Scientists who study the Antarctic ice sheet still are not sure whether the amount of ice in Antarctica is growing bigger or smaller. Snow accumulation there is very difficult to measure. In some large areas the yearly snowfall amounts to only a few inches. One strong blizzard can blow away a whole year's accumulation before it can be measured.

Nearly all of the ice lost from the Antarctic continent is in the form of icebergs. So far no one can even make a good guess about the amount lost each year.

▶ WHY SCIENTISTS STUDY ICE

There are many reasons why scientists study ice, both in the laboratory and where it occurs naturally. The study of the way ice forms in rivers and on the sea is important in designing dams and harbors and for navigation in northern areas. There are other reasons, too—and some are ones that you could hardly guess. For example, the study of ice can help to explain the behavior of metal. Metals "flow" or "creep" much as ice does, but much more slowly.

In some ways it is easier to study ice by experiments on glaciers and ice shelves than by experiments on small pieces of ice in the laboratory. Some of the other reasons for studying glaciers have been mentioned. Scientists still know very little about the way glaciers change the surface of the land they move over. Also, details of how glaciers respond to changes in climate are still a mystery.

Finally, and most important of all, man is naturally curious about his home planet. At present we know almost as much about the surface of the moon as we do about the Antarctic continent.

COLIN BULL
The Ohio State University

See also ICE AGES.

ICE AGES

Ice ages are times when thick sheets of ice have spread over large parts of the continents. The ice sheets form when glaciers of high mountains and polar regions grow to great size. Slowly, over hundreds and hundreds of years, the glaciers reach out. They cover the land with sheets of ice that may be several thousand feet thick.

During the earth's history there have been several ice ages. The last one, often called the Ice Age, began at least 3,000,000 years ago. At least four times during the Ice Age great sheets of ice advanced over the land. Each time they melted and drew back.

The last advance ended about 18,000 years ago. At that time a large part of North America was covered by ice. The ice reached as far south as the site of New York City today. Areas of Northern Europe and Asia were also partly covered by ice, but not so heavily as North America. Then the ice began to disappear. Some of it evaporated directly into the air, and some melted. About 6,000 years ago the continents of the Northern Hemisphere were once more almost free of ice.

But Antarctica and Greenland did not lose their ice. Both of these large regions are still covered by ice sheets between 1 and 2 miles thick. This fact raises an important question: Has the Ice Age really ended, or will glaciers advance again?

Clearly, man needs an answer to that question. During each spread of ice, world conditions changed greatly. Air and ocean temperatures fell by tens of degrees Fahrenheit. Places that are now the sites of great cities were completely ice-covered. Other areas, now deserts, were well-watered and covered with plant life. And with great quantities of water trapped in glaciers on the land, sea levels fell hundreds of feet.

Those were just a few of the great changes that affected the earth during the advances of ice. The advances are called **glacial stages**. Each glacial stage was followed by an **interglacial stage**. This was a warmer time, after the ice melted and before the next glacial stage.

Was the last glacial stage the end of the Ice Age? Or are we living in an interglacial interval that will be followed by another glacial stage? Before scientists can answer such questions, they must discover what causes ice ages. This is one of the great, baffling problems of science.

In trying to solve this problem, scientists concentrate on the most recent ice age. This is the one that can best be studied.

▶ THE PLEISTOCENE ICE AGE

The cause of the Ice Age is hidden in climates of the past. To discover what past climates were like, when they changed, and how, scientists turn to the records left in rocks.

Our planet is believed to be approximately 5,000,000,000 (billion) years old. Rocks—and the fossils of past life in them—give scientists a fairly clear record of the kinds of life that existed during the past 1,000,000,000 years. Rocks more than 1,000,000,000 years old have very few fossils. And these fossils have been changed so much by heat, pressure, and wearing away that they cannot be read clearly. Thus, scientists know little about climates and life during the first 4,000,000,000 years of the earth's history.

Scientists have divided the earth's history into several major time divisions. Each division is marked by certain kinds of rock and fossils and is given a name. We are living in the time division known as the Pleistocene epoch, which began about 1,000,000 years ago. During this time a series of severe glacial stages occurred. Although the Ice Age began earlier, it is sometimes called the Pleistocene Ice Age.

Past Climates and the Ice Age

Scientists learn much about past climates from the places where fossils of ancient plants and animals are found. For example, the fossil remains of certain fruit trees (such as fig trees) and many forms of sea animals (such as corals) are now found in the ancient rocks of such regions as Iceland, Spitzbergen, Alaska, and Antarctica.

At the present time such plants and animals as these are found only in tropical and near-tropical regions. This leads scientists to think that warm climates covered most of the earth for many hundreds of millions of years. Then about 60,000,000 years ago world climate became steadily colder until the Ice Age began.

When ice melts, material under glacier is left behind, forming smooth, egg-shaped mounds called drumlins (*left*), and smooth, cone-shaped hills called kames (*right*).

Above left: Debris left behind by retreating glacier at Glacier Bay, Alaska. Above right: Kettles—holes in the ground—are formed when knobs of ice under glacial debris melt. Below: Minnesota landscape shows long, snakelike ridges called eskers, formed by piled-up material left by retreating glacier.

▶THE TRACKS OF GLACIERS

Just as warm climates left records in the kinds of fossils found in rock, so the glaciers left their marks upon the earth. There are several kinds of these marks. Each tells us that great sheets of ice once covered the land.

Glacial Till

When a glacier grows, it gouges boulders, stones, mud, and sand out of the earth and carries them along. When the glacier melts, it drops this material. Thus, the presence of such material shows where a glacier has been.

For the most part, the rock that covers the continents was formed by the hardening of sand or mud. Rock of this kind is called sedimentary rock. It is found in fairly even layers. Each layer is made up of particles that are all about the same size.

The rock deposited by glaciers is very

different. It is made of a mixture of sand, mud, boulders, and cobbles (rounded stones). These materials are not found in layers but are mixed. Many of the larger cobbles and boulders have one or more flat sides that developed when the ice dragged these loose rocks over the solid bedrock beneath. Many of the rock particles were also grooved and scratched in the dragging process. All this material picked up and deposited by glacial ice is called **glacial till**. Till is a sure clue that glacial ice was once present.

Glacial Erosion

Another way of telling where ice sheets existed is to look for the marks that

Above: Road cut reveals glacial till, a scattered mixture of various materials picked up and deposited by glacier. Below: Strongly layered sedimentary rock, formed by hardening of sand or mud, differs sharply from unlayered glacial till.

A glacier in British Columbia molded this valley into a smooth U-shaped form, typical of valleys once occupied by glaciers.

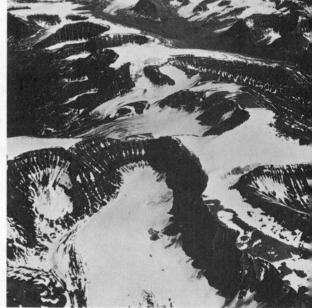

Above left: Glaciers scratch and polish rocks lying in their path. Above right: Photo taken 10,000 feet over Greenland mountains shows cirques—bowl-shaped holes formed by glaciers.

glaciers have left on the rocks that were beneath them. Glacial ice moves very slowly. As it moves, it scours the soil cover from much of the land. Loose rock particles are picked up and carried along in the bottom of the ice. These both polish and scratch the solid rock surface over which the glacier moves. In mountain country the bedrock is carved by moving ice into various special forms that no other force in nature can create. This is known as **glacial erosion**.

▶ MAPPING THE ICE AGES

Scientists can map the parts of the earth that were covered by ice during the ice ages. They make an outline of the regions with glacial till and glacial erosion. In North America the last great ice sheet stopped its southward advance in a line running roughly across the northern United States. In Europe the southern limit extended through southern England, Holland, Germany, and the northern edge of the Carpathian Mountains into Siberia.

Yet some places that were ice-covered do not show any signs of till or glacial erosion. Here there is another way to tell that thick ice once covered the land, but this is not easy to do without careful observation.

The clue is an ancient, sandy, shell-covered beach that lies many hundreds of feet above sea level. Such beaches were first formed when a sheet of ice thousands of feet thick covered a large land area. The ice, which weighed millions to billions of tons, caused the land to sink. When the ice disappeared, the land rose slowly back to its original level. This took thousands of years.

Imagine a strip of land along a coastline that has been pressed down under a great ice sheet. When the ice melted, waves formed a beach and washed shells up on the beach. When the land was uplifted, this beach rose slowly to its present level, many hundreds of feet above the ocean. Such ancient beaches are found on coastlines and islands all around the Arctic region.

Hudson Bay, the region of North America where the ice was thickest, was pushed down the most. When the ice melted, the ocean flowed into this great depression. Since that time thousands of years ago, the floor of Hudson Bay has been rising. The bay is becoming more and more shallow. Some day Hudson Bay may become dry land.

▶ HOW THE ICE AGES WERE DISCOVERED

How did scientists find out that the ice, which had disappeared thousands of years ago, was ever present?

The beginning of this scientific detective story goes back about 150 years. For a long time before that, geologists had been trying to explain some very curious rocks that seemed much out of place.

Normally boulders and rock particles in soil match the bedrock beneath. But here and there throughout the Northern Hemisphere, there are boulders—often very large ones— that are made of rock quite different from the rest of the rock in regions where they are

Rock deposited by glacier perches in unlikely spot on California mountain. Samples of such rocks—called erratic boulders—show that they differ from rocks of surrounding areas.

found. The mismatched boulders, called **erratics** or **wanderers**, could not have broken off from the rock beneath. Therefore, they must have been moved by a force, such as gravity, floods, waves, or wind.

All of these forces can move rocks. But none could have moved the very large erratics over the wide area in which they are found. Also, erratics are often found perched in very strange positions, where neither wind nor gravity could have put them. And whatever force moved the erratics also moved and left behind great blankets of the mixed rock called glacial till.

Ridges of rock, such as those in Alaska, are deposited at the end of a glacier as it retreats. Such ridges are called terminal (end) moraines.

Photo of glacier in mountains of Switzerland shows lateral (side) moraines, ridges of mixed materials that form along the sides of a glacier.

Ice Can Move Rocks

The idea that ice carried erratics and till was first suggested in the early part of the 1800's by two Swiss scientists named J. Venetz and Jean de Charpentier. These two men had studied glaciers in the Alps and were convinced that ice—and ice alone—could account for the erratics. Being solid, ice can carry all kinds and sizes of material on its surface and in its interior.

But erratics were found hundreds and even thousands of miles away from present-day mountain glaciers. If the idea proposed by the two Swiss was true, it meant that glacial ice must have moved great distances from the mountains or from the cold regions in the far north. In the case of glaciers that began high in the mountains, the ice must have spread like a large apron over the valley floors, which are now much too warm for snow to accumulate very thickly. In places where there are no high mountains, the ice must have started hundreds or thousands of miles away in the colder regions of high latitudes. All of this was hard to believe when the idea first came out.

The theory was not accepted until final proof that glaciers could move was produced by another Swiss scientist, Louis Agassiz. To this imaginative man science owes the whole idea of the great Ice Age.

Agassiz knew that he had to study the present before he could understand the past. He journeyed into the Alps because glaciers could still be found there.

He proved that the glaciers of the Alps actually moved. And then he proved that the ice of the Alpine glaciers carried huge amounts of rock. The rock carried by glaciers can be found piled up at the ends and sides of glaciers as ridges of mixed materials. Such ridges are called **moraines**.

Then Agassiz was able to show that the moraines near glaciers look just like many others found in regions where there is no ice. The only way to explain the erratics and moraines was to assume that at one time in the earth's past history vast regions had been covered by ice. By showing that glaciers can move and carry rock, Agassiz demonstrated that ice ages had taken place in the past and that much of the land had lain under a great blanket of ice.

▶ HOW GLACIERS DEVELOP AND MOVE

There are two types of glaciers: **alpine**, or **valley, glaciers** and **continental glaciers**, or **ice sheets**. Alpine glaciers are found in the valleys of high mountains where the average temperature throughout the year is quite low. If the altitude is high enough and the climate cold enough, enough snow may fall during the winter months to last all through the summer. During the following winter still more snow can accumulate. Much of it, too, will last without disappearing in the summer. In this way a permanent, ever-thickening **snowfield** forms at the head of the valley.

With the increase in the thickness of the snow, the pressure on top changes the deeper

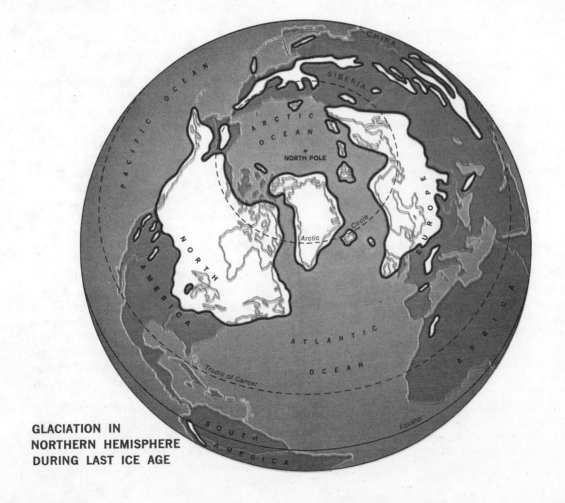

GLACIATION IN NORTHERN HEMISPHERE DURING LAST ICE AGE

snow into ice. When the snow and ice reach a certain thickness, the entire mass is pulled by the force of gravity, and it begins to move slowly down the valley. The long tongue of ice moving away from the snowfield is called the valley, or alpine, glacier.

Today alpine glaciers are found only in high mountains. But during the generally colder climate of the Ice Age, alpine glaciers also formed at lower altitudes.

Continental glaciers, or ice sheets, covered far larger areas of the world, including places where much of the world's population now lives. Alpine glaciers could, and still do, develop in any region as long as the mountain is high enough. In fact, there are some glaciers in the high mountains of Central Africa and South America near the equator. But continental glaciers, which covered the broad, low areas of the continents, began only in the polar regions.

Ice sheets began to develop when the winter snows in polar lands did not disappear the following summer. Each year a little more permanent snow piled up, until the snow was many feet deep. The pressure of the snow on top changed the deeper snow into ice.

When the thickness of the ice reached several hundred feet, the pressure under the thickest part of the ice sheet squeezed the ice toward the thinner margins. This is the way the great ice sheets of the past moved over the lands, bulldozing away the rocks and trees in their paths. The motion may have been very slow—possibly only inches a day—but little could withstand the force of the moving ice.

▶ THE GLACIAL AND INTERGLACIAL STAGES

During the Ice Age the ice sheets advanced and withdrew at least four times.

The discovery that not one but several ice sheets covered the Northern Hemisphere is another bit of scientific detection. The evidence is found both on the land and in the sea. The study of glaciation began with Agassiz on the land. The study of the ocean bottom did not really begin in earnest until the mid-1900's.

On the continents Agassiz, followed by others who learned from him, began to chart the regions that had been covered by ice. They did this mostly by locating the large areas of glacial till left behind by continental ice sheets.

In many regions, especially near the edges of the former glaciers, scientists found that till sometimes occurred in two or more layers— one on top of the other.

When scientists studied these layers of overlapping till, they made a startling discovery: the layers had formed many thousands of years apart. Thus, there must have been more than one glacial period.

Till and Gumbotil

The scientists made that discovery because the lower half of a layer of till is usually a mixture of soil, rock, sand, and gravel. The upper half, which has been exposed to weather and the chemical action of plants, is different in color and appearance from the lower portion. The lower part is said to be **fresh till**, unchanged from glacial times. The upper part is said to be decayed and is called **gumbotil**. Sometimes scientists found two or more layers of till. Each had a lower portion of fresh till and a decayed upper zone of gumbotil.

The gumbotil could have been formed only by the process called **weathering**. This is an important natural process in which the chemical elements in the air and the action of plants cause decay of rock material. The rusting of iron and the change of granite into clay are good examples of this process. The greater the depth of the weathered layer, the longer the exposure to the air must have been.

A deep layer of gumbotil means that the till itself lay uncovered to the natural elements for many thousands of years. A layer of fresh till on top of a layer of gumbotil means that a more recent glacial stage carried a new layer of till with its advancing ice and dropped it on the older layer.

By piecing together information of this kind, scientists learned that from four to eight glacial stages took place during the Pleistocene epoch. Each stage is named for the place where its deposits were first examined and recognized. Scientists used the names of regions in the United States or Europe because good examples of each of the stages occur there.

One problem in the study of the Ice Age is the strong scouring, or eroding, effect of glaciers on the land. Each new ice sheet removes deposits and forms left by the earlier

PLEISTOCENE ICE AGE

STAGE	UNITED STATES DESCRIPTION	EUROPEAN DESCRIPTION
(Fourth Interglacial?)	(Recent)	
Fourth Glacial stage	Wisconsin	Würm
Third Interglacial	Sangamon	Riss-Würm
Third Glacial stage	Illinoian	Riss
Second Interglacial	Yarmouth	Mindel-Riss
Second Glacial stage	Kansan	Mindel
First Interglacial	Aftonian	Günz-Mindel
First Glacial stage	Nebraskan	Günz

ones. Therefore scientists know the events of the last (Wisconsin, or Würm) glacial stage best of all. In fact, most of what has been learned of the earlier glacial stages comes from studies of till deposits near the margins of former ice sheets. There the deposits of older ice ages were not always reached and were not covered or destroyed by later ones.

▶ ICE AGE IN THE OCEANS

The oceans preserve the natural record of the past better than the land. This occurs because the surface of the land is continually worn and eroded by water and ice. The ocean bottom, however, is a much less active place. Scientists have found places on the ocean floor where no important shifting of sand and mud has occurred for countless ages. From these regions they obtain the very best scientific evidence that world climates have changed in the past. Some of the sediment for scientific study comes from depths greater than 20,000 feet.

Oceanographers (scientists who study the seas) use ships fitted with many instruments made specially to take samples of sediments from the depths of the oceans. One way is to drop over the side of a ship a long, hollow steel tube or pipe a few inches in diameter and as long as 100 feet. The tube has several tons of lead weight attached to the top end. The tube is dropped with its open end pointing downward. A wire cable to pull it up is connected to the top. When the tube hits bottom, the lead weight drives it deep into the bed of the ocean.

When the tube is pulled up, it contains a long cylinder of sediment. This is carefully removed and studied layer by layer. These **cores** of sediment often contain a collection of microscopic shells. Among these shells are the skeletons of tiny one-celled animals called **foraminifera** or sometimes just **forams**, for short. These small creatures have been present in the sea for hundreds of millions of years.

There are two ways in which climate changes of the past can be learned from the study of foram shells in the rock cores.

There are several kinds of forams. Some live in cold water, some in warm. Scientists have learned how to tell them apart. Cores of sediment formed during an ice age show changes from warm-water forams (indicating interglacial stages) to cold-water forams (indicating glacial stages).

The climate changes recorded by the alternating layers of warm-water and cold-water

Shells of tiny one-celled animals called foraminifera.

forams found in deep-sea sediment cores match quite well with the evidence found on land. Together, both sets of evidence prove that several successive glacial stages occurred.

However, this method tells only that changes from warm to cold and back to warm took place. About 1950, a way was found to learn what the actual water temperature was when the forams were alive. To use this method, scientists must analyze the shells of the forams in order to learn the different kinds of oxygen present.

There are two kinds of oxygen in the air we breathe. One kind is heavier than the other. The lighter, more common kind is called O^{16}. The heavier, rarer kind is O^{18}. The ocean water also contains tremendous amounts of oxygen. Most of it is O^{16}, but there is also a little of the heavier O^{18}.

The shells of foraminifera are made of a chemical that contains much oxygen. The oxygen is absorbed from seawater. As the water becomes warmer, more of the heavier oxygen is absorbed. As it becomes colder, more of the lighter kind is used by the forams. The amount of each type of oxygen that is taken up by the growing foraminifera also depends on how salty the seawater is.

Scientists can set up a scale that gives clues to the temperature of the water in the past. Both the temperature and the salt content of the ocean water changed as the glaciers on land grew or melted. When a scientist is studying a deep-sea core he carefully notes the amounts of O^{16} and O^{18} found in the forams at different levels in the core. The comparison of these amounts (that is, the ratio of O^{16} to O^{18}) tells him about the number of glaciations that occurred on land.

▶THE TIMETABLE OF THE ICE AGES

To understand the cause of ice ages and to predict new ones, scientists must know when the ice ages began. They must know how long glacial and interglacial stages lasted.

A good beginning has been made.

Varves Help Tell Glacial Time

The earliest way of telling "glacial time" was by studying special kinds of sediments called **varves**. A varve is made up of two layers of sediment, one thicker than the other. The sediment was deposited in a lake that was once next to a glacier.

During the summer, when glacial ice melted rapidly, a thick layer of mud and coarse material was carried to the lake. In the following winter only a very thin layer of fine, dark material formed. This was then covered by a thick summer layer the following year, and so on. Each pair of layers is called a varve.

One varve stands for 1 year of glacial time. Scientists count the number of varves that piled up in an old glacial lake. This tells them how long a particular glacier remained in the same place. And from the thickness of the varves, they know whether the melting was fast or slow. This, in turn, tells whether the climate was warm or cold in the year that the varve was deposited.

The varves from a glacial deposit in one region can be compared to varves in another region. The number of varves in each deposit—and their thickness—can be matched. This shows whether a glacier was present at the same time over a large region.

Although varves tell scientists how many years glaciers lasted in one place, they do not tell how long ago glaciers covered the land. For this, another method is used. It is called dating by radioactive decay of carbon.

Radioactive Carbon Dating Method

Radioactivity is the process in which chemical elements decay, changing into other elements. For example, uranium is radioactive; over a long period of time it decays into lead. One special kind of carbon, carbon-14 (C^{14}), is also radioactive. It slowly decays to nitrogen-14 (N^{14}).

The carbon dioxide in the air is made up of oxygen and carbon. Most of the carbon is carbon-12 (C^{12}), but a small part of it is radioactive C^{14}. Plants use carbon dioxide in making their food and so take in some C^{14}. Most animals eat plants or eat other animals that eat plants so that all living things contain carbon-14.

When the plants or animals die, they may become fossils. The radioactive C^{14} in the fossils slowly decays to nitrogen. As time goes on, less and less C^{14} remains in the fossils. By comparing the amounts of C^{14} and C^{12} in a fossil, scientists can tell when it died.

If a glacier overran a forest, they can tell when the trees died and thus when the ice moved into the region.

In a fossil older than 50,000 years, there is too little C^{14} left to be measured accurately. Therefore, scientists cannot use this method to date glacial events that took place more than 50,000 years ago. However, scientists have learned some important facts by the radioactive dating method. Using it they found that:

The great ice sheets on the continents of Europe and North America began to retreat about 18,000 years ago.

The oceans began to get warmer about 13,000 years ago.

The last of the Pleistocene ice sheets disappeared from Canada about 6,000 years ago.

Glacial Dating from Deep-Sea Sediments

To learn about older glacial time, scientists studied cores of deep-sea sediments more than 50,000 years old. They know the rate at which mud and clay fall to the bottom of the ocean. The thickness of the sediment tells them the age of the layers of mud and clay.

Most sediment on the ocean floor far from land is mud, clay, and sand. But pebbles and pieces of broken rock have been found in cores of these sediments. About the only way such pieces of rock can get so far from land is by melting out of an iceberg. (Icebergs are floating masses of ice that break off glaciers.) The age of a sediment in which the pebbles and rock are found tells how long ago certain glacial changes took place.

One clue to the Ice Age is a deep-sea core from the southern Indian Ocean. Pebbles deep within the core must have floated in icebergs from Antarctica about 3,000,000 years ago. In Antarctica itself a lava flow at least 10,000,000 years old lies over rocks covered with glacial scratches. These finds, and similar ones in Alaska, suggest that the Ice Age in the northernmost and southernmost parts of the earth began at least 10,000,000 years ago. However, the changes of the glacial-to-interglacial stages began less than 1,000,000 years ago.

▶THE CAUSE OF THE GREAT ICE AGE

What caused the Pleistocene Ice Age? And why were there several glacial stages, with warm stages in between?

Scientists take samples of rock and other materials from the ocean floor.

That is one of the great mysteries of science. It has not yet been solved, although many theories have been suggested.

Theories About the Sun's Energy

Ice ages were times when the climate became colder. And so many scientists have tried to account for this through changes in the energy of the sun reaching the earth's surface. Some scientists think there are actual changes in the amount of energy given off by the sun from time to time. This could cause the earth's climate to become colder or warmer. Repeated ice ages could result.

Other scientists think the amount of energy sent out by the sun remains about the same. They say something happens to sunlight before it reaches the earth, and this causes climate changes. One suggestion is that dust from huge volcanic eruptions could fill the air and cut off large amounts of sunlight from the earth.

Another idea is that changes in the amount of carbon dioxide in the air would cause great changes in climate. Sunlight heats the earth's surface. The surface radiates some of the heat back into space in the form of invisible infrared light. The carbon dioxide in the atmosphere absorbs the radiation, so the air is warmed. If there is much carbon dioxide, the air will be kept warm. With less carbon dioxide, the air will be cooler. So changes in the amount of carbon dioxide in the air would change world temperatures.

Still another theory relates climate changes to changes in the distance between the earth and the sun and in the tilt of the earth's axis. One scientist showed that changes in temperature could be expected to repeat themselves in tens of thousands of years. That is, a long period of cold climate would be followed by a long period of warm climate and so on.

None of these theories explains why the earth cooled off enough to cause the first of the Pleistocene ice stages. They only explain changes in climate after the ice stages had begun.

▶ **THE EWING-DONN THEORY**

In 1956 two American scientists, Maurice Ewing and William L. Donn, proposed a new theory to explain the cause of the Pleistocene Ice Age and the glacial stages.

Scientists know that the material of the earth's interior is in layers. The heaviest material is in the center. The outer layers are made up of lighter rock. Imagine an orange with its skin loosened from the fruit. The skin could slide around the fruit. Ewing and Donn think one of the outer layers of the Earth can slip around the interior in the same way.

It is also known that there is a slow sliding movement of great layers, or plates, of crustal rock beneath the sea. These plates carry the continents along, in a movement called **continental drift**.

According to the Ewing-Donn theory, the Pacific Ocean was once where the North Pole is now. The South Indian Ocean was at the South Pole. Most of the region around the equator was ocean. Because the poles and the equator were located in the oceans, water flowed freely between them. The constant mixing of warm water with cold kept the polar regions from ever becoming very cold. The mixing of the waters could also explain the warm climate over most of the earth during the hundreds of millions of years when there were no glaciers.

Not long before the Ice Age began, the continued shifting of an outer layer carried the Arctic Ocean to the North Pole and the continent of Antarctica to the South Pole. The continents drifted to very nearly their present locations. The map on page 19 shows that the Northern Hemisphere looked very much then as it does now.

The movement of the poles and the drifting of the continents separated the Arctic and Antarctic regions from the rest of the world. You can see that the Arctic Ocean is almost landlocked, except for a passageway between Greenland and Norway. Antarctica is a great landmass in the South Pole region. Very little warm water from near the equator can get to the polar regions. Thus they have become very cold. The Ewing-Donn theory states that the Ice Age began soon after the poles became landlocked and cold.

This theory explains Pleistocene glacial and interglacial stages in an altogether new way. It says that ice sheets begin to build up on continents in the Arctic region when the Arctic Ocean is free of ice. At such a time, evaporation from the ocean adds a great deal of moisture to the air. Snow falls and glaciers begin. Ice sheets cannot get started when the Arctic Ocean is covered with ice most of the year, for there would be too little moisture in the polar air. The air is very dry, and hardly any snow falls. An ice-covered Arctic Ocean brings about an interglacial stage.

Ewing and Donn think it is cold enough in the far north to keep most of the Arctic ice from melting at present. Ice covers much of that ocean most of the year. They say, therefore, that we are now in an interglacial stage of the Pleistocene Ice Age. If the Arctic ice cover melts, a new glacial stage will begin. Glacial and interglacial stages will follow as long as the poles are in their present landlocked positions.

WILLIAM L. DONN
Lamont-Doherty Geological Observatory of
Columbia University

See also ICE; OCEANOGRAPHY; RADIOACTIVE DATING.

ICEBERGS

Icebergs are mountains of freshwater ice floating in the ocean. They are huge chunks broken off from the great masses of land ice called glaciers. Some icebergs are only a few hundred feet long; others may be miles long. Some float about 10 feet above the surface of the water; many tower up 100 to 300 feet.

Most of the icebergs in the Northern Hemisphere come from Greenland. Icebergs of the Southern Hemisphere come from Antarctica.

▶ HOW ICEBERGS ARE FORMED

Almost all of Greenland and Antarctica are covered by glaciers the year round. So are some parts of Alaska. The glaciers may be thousands of feet thick. Their front ends—or tongues—reach down to the ocean. At the coast the tips of the tongues break off and become icebergs. This process of iceberg formation is called **calving**.

When calving occurs, a loud cracking noise fills the air. Sometimes a low rumbling can be heard for hours before the ice actually breaks away. People close enough can hear the hissing of air as it escapes from bubbles bursting in the ice along the break.

Glaciers calve all year round. Just as many icebergs break off in winter as in summer. In the winter, however, their passageway to the open sea is often jammed with masses of frozen seawater. Icebergs pile up behind this jam of sea ice. In the spring, when the ice block is broken, a whole fleet of icebergs may sail out toward the open ocean.

▶ ICEBERGS TRAVEL WITH OCEAN CURRENTS

Icebergs drift with ocean currents. The map shows the currents of the North Atlantic. It also shows the paths taken by icebergs that calve off from Greenland glaciers.

Icebergs from the eastern coast of Greenland drift southward. They are carried by the Greenland Current, which then swings them

Most of an iceberg is hidden under the water.

often enter the lanes used by ships crossing the Atlantic Ocean.

▶ HOW ICEBERGS MELT

An iceberg starts to break up almost as soon as it is afloat. Cracks appear and become filled with water from ice that melts during the day. When this meltwater freezes at night, it expands and widens the cracks. The ice is weakened, and pieces of the iceberg break off and float away. The iceberg becomes smaller and smaller. Most icebergs melt completely within a few days of entering the Gulf Stream.

▶ DANGER AHEAD!

An iceberg is a beautiful and awesome sight. Most icebergs are shining white or light blue. The tops of many North Atlantic icebergs are carved into weird shapes. From a distance they sometimes look like floating castles with spires and turrets gleaming against the sky.

But an iceberg is a danger to ships at sea. This is because most of its ice—$6/7$ to $7/8$ of its mass—is hidden underneath the water. When a large iceberg is sighted from a ship, no one can tell how far the ice extends under the water. The ship may be rammed by hidden ice and sunk. The only sure safety from iceberg damage is to sail away from the iceberg.

northward around the tip of the island. Part of the way up the coast the icebergs are caught in the cold Labrador Current and carried southward toward Newfoundland.

On the way, most of the icebergs become grounded among the many islands and bays along the Labrador coast. The others float on toward the open sea. Off Newfoundland they are caught by a warm current from the south called the Gulf Stream. Icebergs that do not ground and remain in the Labrador current

Arrows mark the routes that icebergs take as they drift into the Atlantic Ocean.

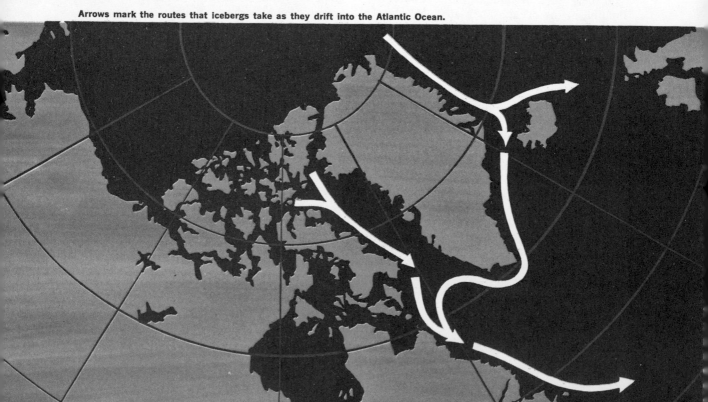

A U.S. Coast Guard ship of the International Ice Patrol investigates an iceberg near Greenland. The iceberg will be charted so that ships can avoid it.

In a thick fog, during a storm, or on a dark night icebergs are particularly dangerous because they are hard to see from a distance. The ocean around the Grand Banks of Newfoundland is the world's most dangerous iceberg area because this is a place of dense fog. April, May, and June are the "iceberg months" in this region. In these months ships take a more southerly route, to avoid icebergs.

The greatest tragedy at sea due to icebergs occurred on the night of April 14, 1912. This was the sinking of the British ship *Titanic*. It was the biggest ship built up to that time. The builders said it was unsinkable. The ship was sailing from England to the United States on its first voyage when it hit an iceberg 500 miles south of Newfoundland and sank. More than 1,500 lives were lost with the *Titanic*.

International Ice Patrol

After the sinking of the *Titanic,* an international conference was called. Its purpose was to find a way to prevent such disasters. As a result of this conference, the International Ice Patrol was set up in 1913 and soon began its work.

The United States Coast Guard maintains the International Ice Patrol. Countries whose ships sail the North Atlantic contribute to the cost. The patrol usually starts its work in February and continues into July.

The International Ice Patrol has been charting icebergs in the North Atlantic shipping lanes since 1914. Twice a day the patrol transmits information by radio to ships in these shipping lanes. The information gives the location and approximate size of icebergs that have been sighted. Since the ice patrol was started, no lives have been lost because of icebergs in the patrolled area.

▶**ANTARCTIC ICEBERGS**

The icebergs of the Antarctic are formed in much the same way as those of the Arctic regions. They are usually flat-topped, and often show 300 to 400 feet above the surface of the water. Icebergs 20 to 30 miles long have often been sighted in the Antarctic region. In fact, some of the early Antarctic explorers mistook the larger icebergs for islands. Because there is little shipping in the waters where they are found, these icebergs present very little danger.

REBECCA B. MARCUS
Author, *First Book of Glaciers*
Reviewed by A. L. LONSDALE
Lieutenant Commander
United States Coast Guard

See also ICE; ICE AGES.

A "hike," with windward runner off the ice, is thrilling action. But if it is too high, the boat may capsize.

ICEBOATING

Sailing on ice is called iceboating. Iceboats are used for both pleasure sailing and competitive racing, and both are exciting. The sport requires a love of the cold winter weather. It also requires fast reflexes, common sense, and a sturdy iceboat.

Those who ride on an iceboat for the first time get a feeling of speed quite unlike anything experienced before. Iceboats skim over the ice extremely rapidly (the fastest known speed is almost 150 miles per hour). Zooming along close to the ice, without protection of canopy or windshield and with the wind in the sail driving the boat ever faster, is indeed breathtaking. Iceboat speeds exceed those of any other non-motorized vehicle.

▶ HOW ICEBOATING STARTED

Iceboating got its start some hundreds of years ago, possibly in Holland or in some country adjacent to the Baltic Sea. It started as a means of transporting people and goods across frozen rivers and bays.

In the middle of the 18th century the Dutch mounted a certain type of sailing boat on runners and used it for transportation purposes on the rivers and lakes of Holland. In Canada and in the United States iceboats were used in the Great Lakes area for transporting lumbermen and provisions during the winter. Iceboats were being built and used at Poughkeepsie on the Hudson River as far back as 1790. Their use on the Great South Bay of Long Island, New York, developed from the need for transporting supplies to the lifesaving stations on Fire Island.

The days of using iceboats for practical purposes have long since gone. Today roads and bridges exist where there were none a century and a half ago. Other forms of transportation have come into being—automobiles, trucks, airplanes, and helicopters. Progress has lifted the iceboat out of its useful role. It is now solely a pleasure craft.

Increased leisure-time use of the outdoors for recreation has resulted in an enormous growth in iceboating, especially since World War II. Unfortunately, iceboating cannot be a worldwide sport. It is limited to cold climates, where lakes, bays, and rivers freeze over in wintertime. Iceboats need ice at least 4 inches thick. And since iceboats require a lot of room because of their speed, small lakes or ponds are not adequate. Some areas that get freezing weather also get heavy snowfalls. This cancels out the possibility of iceboating. Iceboats can move through 3 or 4 inches of light snow. But once the snow is deeper or becomes crusty, iceboating has to wait for rain to wash off the snow or for a thaw that will melt it down, after which it will refreeze as ice. Cold climates that are reasonably damp without too much snow are ideal.

▶ ICEBOATS FOR PLEASURE

The first iceboat built for pleasure could have been nothing more than a box mounted on skates and propelled by some kind of sail attached to a mast. When racing iceboats became popular in the United States and Canada in the mid-19th century, the trend was to build them big, putting on all the sail they could handle. The trend today is toward small, sturdy boats with a minimum of sail.

There are two broad categories of iceboats in use today: (1) the triangular-shaped iceboat with three runners, and (2) the elliptical-shaped, rounded-bottom boat called the scooter. It is to be noted that a powered ice sled—a kind of sled structure on which a motor and airplane propeller have been mounted—is not classed as an iceboat.

The triangular-shaped, three-runner type may be further subdivided into two groups: (1) the stern-steerers (steering runner, or rudder, mounted at the tail end of the boat), and (2) the bow-steerers (steering runner mounted at the nose end of the boat). The stern-steerers came first and are a direct outgrowth of sailboats, which are all rudder-steered from the rear. Stern-steerers were the only type in use in the United States and in Canada when iceboating flourished on Lake Ontario and the Hudson River from the mid-1800's into the early 1900's.

The bow-steerer did not come along until iceboating was well established as a sport. The trend after 1920 was toward this smaller, faster, and sportier iceboat. The development brought the steering rudder up forward, reversing the triangle so that it pointed forward instead of backward. Designers also introduced the streamlining that we see in today's iceboats. The emphasis is not on size and heft but on strength, lightness, and sleekness.

There are several classes of these bow-steering iceboats. Each of them was developed for ease of handling and speed. One of the early ones was called the mosquito class. It had on its sail an emblem of a mosquito poised ready to dive onto a target. This class later became known as the skeeter class. There were soon enough of these boats in the United States and Canada to form an association called the International Skeeter Association, which currently holds annual championship regattas.

The Great South Bay scooter is in a class quite by itself. Although it is accepted in the membership of the Eastern Ice Yachting Association, it races in its own subdivisions, known as the "big scoots" and the "little scoots," according to the size. Instead of being triangular in shape and mounted on three runners, the scooter has an oval shape, with strips of metal fastened on its rounded bottom —rounded from side to side and from front to back. It has no steering rudder at all and in this respect is unique throughout the world.

Instead, it is steered by pulling in on the jib (the small sail in front of the mast). It is called amphibious because, unlike other ice-boats, when going fast enough it will ride over small areas of open water. It was developed for use on Great South Bay, where the ice, because of tidal wash, is apt to be soft, uncertain, and full of holes. These boats will readily jump over open cracks and ridges that would crash other types of iceboats.

▶ RACING

Iceboats race in established classes, and the class is set according to sail area. The Northwestern Ice Yachting Association and the Eastern Ice Yachting Association recognize these classes according to sail area:

Class A: 250 sq. ft. and over.
Class B: up to 250 sq. ft.
Class C: up to 175 sq. ft.
Class D: up to 125 sq. ft.
Class E: up to 75 sq. ft.

Race courses are established by placing markers out on the ice. The markers must be readily visible for a considerable distance. Orange is a preferred color because it can be seen clearly against ice, snow, and the shore-line. The markers can be set for a triangular course or a two-marker windward (upwind) and leeward (downwind) course. The course will be sailed either clockwise (the markers on the right as you round them) or counter-clockwise (the markers on your left). This is determined in advance, as are the number of times around the course (laps). At the start, boats line up between selected points, with their bows brought up to an imaginary line perpendicular to the wind. The boats are usually headed on the wind, with sails paid out, and all boats must be similarly headed. (This is essential if there is a heavy wind blowing.) There is an understanding by all participants as to the direction (tack) that all boats will follow immediately on takeoff. In other words, all boats must turn either to the right on a port tack or to the left on a starboard tack. If this were not done, there would be wild confusion as the boats criss-crossed one another. The starting signal is generally the lowering of a flag or arm, sometimes accompanied by the boom of a cannon. To provide maximum traction for

Iceboats lined up for the start of a race. These are all bow-steerer, Class E boats. The haze at the left is the puff from the starter's cannon.

pushing and holding, as well as for safety when walking on the ice, iceboaters wear ice creepers fitted over their shoes, which give them a grip on the ice.

When only two boats are racing, it is easy to determine the winner—the boat that comes in first or comes in first more often than the other when two or more races (heats) are sailed. When more than two boats are racing for a championship, there are usually either three or five heats, and the race is decided on a point system. The winner is the boat with the most number of points. A point is given for starting a race, a point for finishing, and a point for each boat beaten. For example, with 10 boats in a race the winner would receive 11 points; the boat coming in seventh would receive 5 points, etc. After the five heats the boat that has accumulated the highest number of points is declared the champion—and it may not be the boat coming in first the most times! The point system places a premium on durability as well as on speed. If a boat breaks down during a race, it gets a DNF (Did Not Finish) and is given only the single point for starting. A boat must finish to win any points for beating other boats.

▶ RULES AND SAFETY PRECAUTIONS

Rules have been established by the ice-boating associations, and it is important that they be adhered to, especially in racing. The rules specify what to do under a variety of quickly changing circumstances. They also give assurance of what the fellow alongside or coming at you will do. Along with rules, though, and of utmost value, is good common sense.

The speed of an iceboat makes the danger of collision great when several boats are converging on a marker, each boat striving to round it ahead of the others. For this reason you should never make any change in your direction without being sure of what you're doing and what it will do to those about you. And remember that in an iceboat you are always tacking upwind or downwind and are never running free with the wind. Generally, if you are on the starboard tack (wind coming from your right side, so that your boom is to the left), you have the right of way over boats on the port tack. If two boats are converging on the same tack, the one to windward has to give way.

"Hikes" (the windward runner raised off the ice) are thrilling and also useful. In racing, hikes allow you to use some of the wind-force that you would otherwise have to spill out of your sail. Coming gradually down out of a hike gives you the feel of control over the boat. It also gives you a sort of "downhill" momentum until you have picked up all the speed that the wind can furnish to your sail and that your boat can use. For maximum speed it is unwise to hold a hike too long. And for safety's sake it is unwise to take one up too close to the point of no return. When your hike gets dangerously high, a sharp puff of wind, the leeward runner's hitting a soft spot, or the steering fork's gouging into the ice can take you over into a capsize. A capsize is less likely with a bow-steerer than with a stern-steerer. But the consequences can be more damaging to the skipper and to his boat.

Heading into the wind is the only effective way to stop an iceboat when it is under way. Many iceboaters, however, equip their boats with hand brakes consisting of a metal or wooden bar with a metal claw at the bottom end. The handle of this bar is within ready reach. The leverage is such that the claw's gouging into the ice will assist in stopping the boat after it is headed into the wind or when you are pulling into a parking area. Great care must be taken when bringing an iceboat into an area where there are skaters or people standing about. It is best, even in light winds, to let the sail down outside the area and push the boat in.

Iceboat owners give a variety of names to their iceboats. Names such as "Sacroiliac," "Wizard," and so on, are humorous. Others, such as the name of a member of the family, are sentimental. Still others, such as "Whirlwind," "Meteorite," and "Blitzen," try to reflect the elements. Some, such as "Imp," "Phantom," or "Oomph," describe the boat's personality. Names of the great racing boats of years ago, however, are not likely to lose their place in iceboating's "Hall of Fame" to any of the boats of today. There are many fast boats, but none is so outstanding that it could be expected to take on all comers and win every time out, as boats of a century ago did. The development and copying of innovations are now so rapid that a single boat cannot expect to stay unbeaten for long. The names of great boats of the past, supreme in their day, will long be remembered: "The Scud," "Dreadnaught," "Icicle," "Robert Scott," "Wolverine," "Jack Frost," "Princess II," "Deuce," "Debutante III," and "Pirate." This is the way of iceboating.

NORWOOD C. POTTER
Former Commodore
Eastern Ice Yachting Association

ICE CREAM

The history of ice cream is a mystery. No one knows exactly how and when people began to eat it. There is one story that the Roman emperor Nero (A.D. 37–68) sent slaves to the mountains to bring back snow. The snow was served to him sweetened with honey and fruit pulp. Marco Polo (1254–1324) tasted flavored ices, too, during his famous travels in the Far East. He brought the recipes back to Italy.

Recipes for ices spread from Italy to the rest of Europe in the 1500's. The chefs of kings constantly experimented with new combinations to please their masters, and at some point cream and butter were added to the recipes for ice. The new dish was called cream ice. Cream ice, molded into amusing shapes, began to be served on the tables of kings across Europe. Louis XIV (1638–1715) surprised his court with a dessert of eggs in cups of silver and gilt. The eggs, of course, were really cream ice.

Gradually cream ice took the name it has today. One of the earliest advertisements for ice cream was put in a New York paper in 1786. The ad announced that "Ladies and gentlemen may be supplied with ice-cream every day at the City Tavern by their humble servant, Joseph Crowe." But ice cream was still not an everyday event. It was usually presented in fancy shapes at the end of dinner parties. Dolley Madison (1768–1849) was famous for her imaginative dinners, and she was the first to serve ice cream at the White House. When her guests came into the dining room, they found a table covered with delicious dishes, and in the center of the table, a huge mound of pink ice cream on a silver platter.

Ice cream was such a delicacy because it was so hard to make. At first it was beaten and then shaken by hand in a pan of salt and ice until it became firm. A freezer that was cranked by hand was developed around 1846. Making ice cream was still a chore, but cranking the freezer was much easier and faster than shaking the mixture in a pan.

"Ice-cream socials" became a popular way

Milk from the dairy cow is tested in a spotless modern dairy plant. Trained workers in laboratories test all the products that go into ice cream.

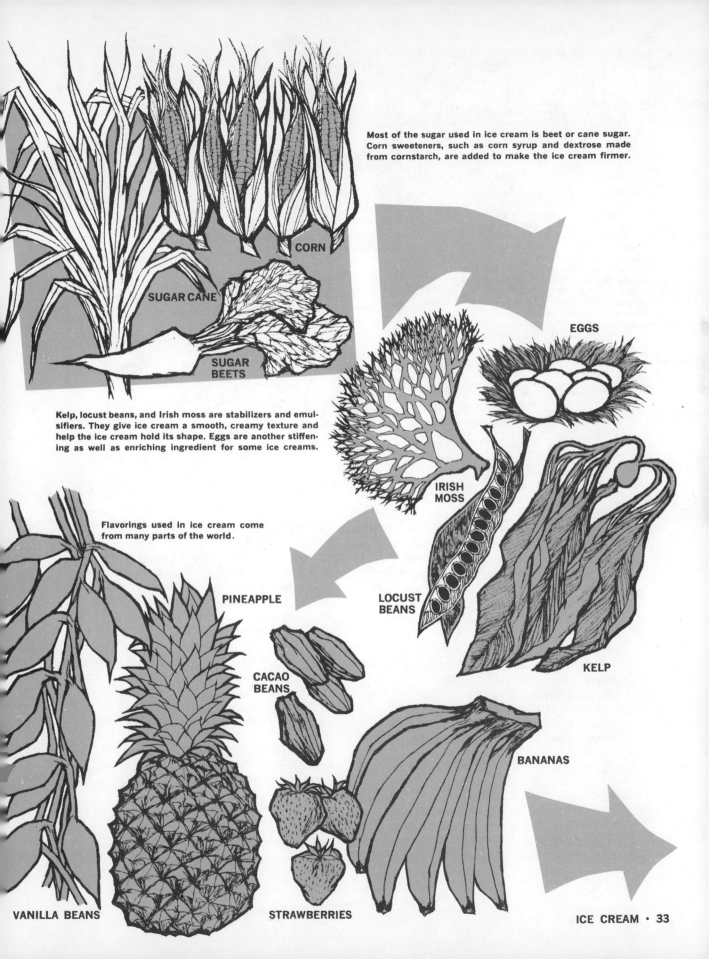

Most of the sugar used in ice cream is beet or cane sugar. Corn sweeteners, such as corn syrup and dextrose made from cornstarch, are added to make the ice cream firmer.

CORN

SUGAR CANE

SUGAR BEETS

Kelp, locust beans, and Irish moss are stabilizers and emulsifiers. They give ice cream a smooth, creamy texture and help the ice cream hold its shape. Eggs are another stiffening as well as enriching ingredient for some ice creams.

EGGS

IRISH MOSS

Flavorings used in ice cream come from many parts of the world.

PINEAPPLE

LOCUST BEANS

KELP

CACAO BEANS

BANANAS

VANILLA BEANS

STRAWBERRIES

ICE CREAM FACTORY

In the factory, ice cream mix is pasteurized, homogenized, and cooled before it is frozen. Air is whipped into the mix as it freezes to make the ice cream smooth and free from frozen lumps. Flavorings and fruit or nuts are added to the ice cream as it flows from the freezer. The ice cream is packaged while it is still soft. It finishes freezing as it travels on a conveyor belt inside a cold tunnel, where the temperature is kept below zero. From the tunnel the ice cream is loaded onto refrigerated trucks and carried to supermarkets, drugstores, restaurants, schools, and many other places.

to entertain friends. Everyone helped turn the crank of the freezer, and homemade peach or strawberry ice cream was the reward. The development of the continuous freezer in the 1920's made the manufacture of ice cream very quick and economical. It soon was easier to buy packaged ice cream than to make it at home. Eskimo pies and popsicles began to be sold at the same time.

Possibly ice-cream cones began with the World's Fair in 1893. Vendors there sold Fried Ice Cream. The ice cream was covered with a fritter batter and then quickly dipped in very hot lard or olive oil. Putting the ice cream in an already prepared cone was the next step. Today there are many novelty products, from frozen drumsticks to ice-cream pies.

▶ OTHER ICE CREAM PRODUCTS

Ice cream has many companion products. French ice cream and most frozen custard have had egg yolk added to the ice cream mix. **Ice milk** is a frozen dessert that is very much like ice cream but has less milk fat. The milk fat content in ice milk is from 2 to 7 percent. Ice cream contains about 11 percent milk fat. A new frozen product known as **mellorine-type frozen dessert** is just like ice cream, but the fat is from vegetable sources instead of milk. **Spumoni** is a frozen Italian dessert made mainly out of whipped cream.

Sherbets are another product of the industry. They are usually flavored with fruits or fruit juices and contain some milk products. The milk fat content, however, is not much more than 1 percent, but there is a high sugar content of about 30 percent. Federal standards require that a small amount of edible acid, such as citric acid, be put in the sherbet. The acid gives sherbets their tart flavor. **Ices** are similar to their first cousins, the sherbets, but no milk is added to the ices.

ROBERT H. NORTH
Executive Vice President
International Association of Ice Cream
Manufacturers

ICE HOCKEY

Ice hockey is one of the modern games played with a stick and a ball. Stick-and-ball games probably originated in Persia, the home of polo. The ancient Greeks played a kind of hockey, which was included in their Olympic Games. In 1922 a 2,400-year-old seawall was discovered in Athens. On the wall were carved pictures of youths playing a sport much like the field hockey of today. Hurley, a field sport allied to hockey, is mentioned in Irish records of A.D. 1272.

Ice hockey originated in Canada more than 100 years ago. One claim is that English soldiers played an early form of ice hockey on the frozen surface of Lake Ontario at Kingston, Ontario, as early as 1867.

Kingston and Montreal both lay claim to having had the first organized hockey leagues. Kingston certainly had one in 1885. Five years later the first regional body to promote hockey was organized and called the Ontario Hockey Association. It started with 10 teams across the province. In 1914 the Canadian Amateur Hockey Association was formed with a few thousand players.

Although Canada was the birthplace of amateur hockey, the professional game started in the United States. In the winter of 1904–05 a professional hockey league was formed at Houghton, Michigan. The National Hockey Association, parent of the National Hockey League of today, started in 1910. Until 1967 the NHL was made up of the Boston Bruins, Chicago Black Hawks, Detroit Red Wings, New York Rangers, Montreal Canadiens, and Toronto Maple Leafs. Then the Oakland Seals, Los Angeles Kings, Minnesota North Stars, Philadelphia Flyers, Pittsburgh Penguins, and St. Louis Blues were added. In 1970 and 1972 the Buffalo Sabres, Vancouver Canucks, New York Islanders, and Atlanta Flames joined the NHL. The teams are divided into two divisions: the East and the West. In 1972, the World Hockey Association was formed with teams in 12 United States and Canadian cities.

The Amateur Hockey Association of the United States was formed in New York on October 29, 1937. Originally it had four leagues with 14 teams. Today the AHAUS directs scores of leagues with hundreds of teams and thousands of registered players.

Hockey is now played in nearly 30 countries. It is governed by the International Ice Hockey Federation, which stages an annual world tournament.

▶THE AIM OF THE GAME

Hockey on ice is said to be the fastest team game in the world. It is played by two teams

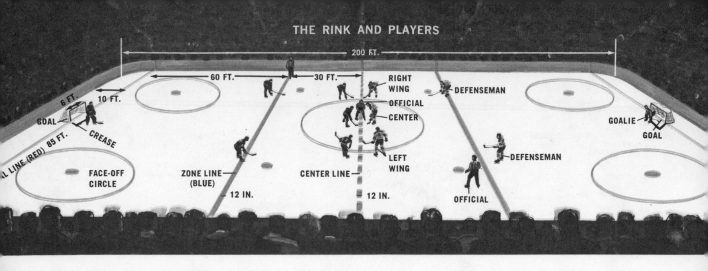

200 FT.
60 FT. — **30 FT.**
6 FT. — **10 FT.**
GOAL — CREASE
OAL LINE (RED) 85 FT.
FACE-OFF CIRCLE
ZONE LINE (BLUE)
12 IN.
CENTER LINE
12 IN.
RIGHT WING
OFFICIAL
CENTER
LEFT WING
DEFENSEMAN
DEFENSEMAN
OFFICIAL
GOALIE
GOAL

of six men in action at one time, with extra players, or substitutes, on the sidelines. Each team has the double objective of trying to put a small rubber disc, called a puck, into the opponent's net while preventing the opponent from scoring.

▶ THE HOCKEY RINK

Hockey is played in an enclosure usually 200 feet in length and 85 feet in width. The ice surface is surrounded by a wall or fence, preferably made of wood, which is not less than 3 and not more than 4 feet in height. This fence, known as the boards, is painted white on the ice surface side to make it easier to see the black puck.

Originally the rinks were covered with natural ice, but today in most standard rinks, even in cold countries such as the U.S.S.R. and Sweden, an artificial ice surface is used.

Standard ice markings used all over the world are painted on the floor of the arena before flooding. The zone lines are blue, the goal lines red. The crease is an area in front of the goal where the goalie has privileges.

▶ RINK EQUIPMENT

The goal is a metal-framed structure covered at the back with a strong netting to retain the puck. Goalpost uprights and the crossbar are of metal. The uprights are 2 inches in diameter, and they are planted firmly in the ice 6 feet apart. The crossbar is 4 feet high.

Benches to seat at least 14 players on each team are placed along the side of the rink just outside the playing area. At center ice a special bench is provided for the timekeeper and another special area is set aside for use as a penalty box.

Each rink has a gong, bell, or siren to signal the end of each period and an electric time clock in view of the spectators. Behind each goal, outside the ice surface, a special area is set aside for the goal judge, who indicates when a score is made by pressing a button that lights a red bulb at that end of the rink.

▶ PLAYING EQUIPMENT

In children's games only minimum equipment—skates, boots, and sticks—is required. Organized teams use special pants, shin guards, skates, shoulder pads, gloves, sticks, sweaters, and socks.

Sticks, made of special varieties of wood, must not exceed 53 inches in length from the heel to the end of the handle and 14¾ inches from the heel to the end of the blade.

The puck is 1 inch thick, 3 inches in

PLAYING EQUIPMENT

STICK
SHIN GUARDS
SKATES
HELMET
ELBOW PADS
PUCK
GLOVES
HIP PADS

diameter, and cannot weigh less than 5½ ounces or more than 6 ounces.

No stick blade can be more than 3 inches in height except the special stick used by the goaltender, which can be 4½ inches in height at the heel.

Speed or figure skates are barred because of the danger of injury.

Goalies are permitted to wear special pads similar to, but larger than, those worn by baseball catchers, and heavy leg guards, which must not measure more than 10 inches in width. Many goalies today wear specially molded rubber-and-plastic face masks. Jacques Plante, for many years one of the finest goalies in the world, made the use of masks popular.

Use of any gear made of metal is prohibited.

▶ THE TEAMS

Hockcy, originally playcd with seven men, changed to six-man teams nearly 50 years ago. Because of the high speed of the game and the physical demands it makes, substitutes may be used. The extra players vary from three or four in amateur games to as many as a dozen in professional matches.

The team is made up of a goalie, right and left defensemen, center, right wing, and left wing.

Each team must name one captain and two alternates. They are the only players permitted to speak to the referee about a rule interpretation, and their status is shown by the letters C or A on their sweaters.

Each team names a substitute goalie on its player list. Players may be changed at any time during a match, but no more than six men can be on the ice at any one time.

▶ REFEREES

Two systems of officiating are in use. Professional hockey and most senior amateur leagues in North America use a referee who is in charge of the game and two linesmen who signal offsides.

▶ OTHER OFFICIALS

Minor officials include goal judges and timekeepers. They are usually appointed by the home team, while the referees and linesmen are usually appointed by the league or the referee in chief.

▶ SCORING

A goal is counted each time the puck is shot into the goal or legally deflected into the goal. The game consists of three 20-minute periods with 10-minute rests between them. Goals and assists may be awarded on each score. Besides the man credited with the goal score, up to a maximum of two other players may be credited with assists on the scoring play.

▶ BASIC REQUIREMENTS

The first requirement for a hockey player is to be able to skate well, something which is overlooked more often than you might think. The higher the league, the greater the stress on skating; and it is certain that the inability to skate well enough is the one thing that can keep a player skilled in other respects from playing in the best leagues.

Stickhandling, shooting, team play, puck sense ("knowing" where the puck is, even if not in view), and a constant will to win are all very important requirements.

A good hockey player must be in top physical condition, and that means that he must obey the rules of good health and fitness at all times during the season. Because the hockey season is long and schedules, even in amateur leagues, may run almost 5 months, there is need for a good mental attitude. One of the key jobs of any coach is to keep his team mentally as well as physically fresh.

▶ BASIC TECHNIQUES

Skating. There is no limit to the amount of time that can be used to develop good skating. The average player skates about 3 miles in a regulation game, sometimes at speeds reaching 20 miles an hour.

Much of the difficulty players have with skating is a lack of proper basic instruction in the beginner stage. A hockey player must be able to start and stop quickly, turn either way, and skate backward almost as fast as he can skate forward. And he must learn to control and to "carry" the puck at the same time.

Experienced players find they can improve their skating by developing muscles through special gymnasium exercises and by regular, planned skating drills.

Shooting. Shooting is all-important in hockey. Here, too, practice is vital. Players should find out, with the help of their coaches, the proper stick "lie" and the stick weight. The lie is the angle made by the handle and blade of the stick, and it can vary greatly. It is a matter of individual preference, but it is determined to some extent by the height, weight and physical makeup of the player.

While great use is made of the slap shot in modern hockey, it is still not popular with many coaches. In this shot the puck is propelled by driving the blade of the stick against the puck almost as you might hit a golf ball. But the hands are far apart on the hockey stick, and there is less backswing. The slap shot travels at a high rate of speed, but it is very inaccurate.

Most players get better results by concentrating on a good wrist shot for both forehand and backhand drives. Here, as in every other skill, planned practice will be rewarded.

Ankle-high shots aimed at the corners of the goals are the best scoring shots. High shots aimed at the outside top corners are also in an area where the chance of scoring is very good.

The best scoring opportunity is offered in the head-on approach down the center of the ice or the slot area. Angle shots are harder to score; and the more acute the angle, the less open goal there is to shoot at.

Stickhandling. Stickhandling is moving (carrying) the puck with the stick. The more skillfully it is done, the harder it is for the opponent to take the puck away. Stickhandling is used less today as an offensive weapon, because forward passing has put more emphasis on skating, passing, and shooting than on individual skill with the puck. Stickhandling drills should be used to improve skill and teach new tricks.

Checking. Checking is primarily a defensive skill. A defender can use his body to throw an opponent off balance and make him lose the puck. Or, he can use his stick to stop an opponent's attack before it gets underway.

▶ HOW TO PLAY

To start the game, the referee drops the puck in the center spot between the sticks of the two opposing centers and gives the signal to play. This is called a face-off. Each center then tries to hit the puck out to the wings, who play it toward the goal.

SHOOTING

When a goal is scored, and at the beginning of each period, a face-off starts the game again. A face-off can also occur on one of the circles shown on the rink diagram if a foul is committed, if the puck goes out of bounds, or if the referee blows his whistle because of an offside.

If your team has speed but lacks size, plan to use speed. If you have a big, strong team, play the game at a slower pace so you can make your weight and size count in bodily contact. The speedy team tries to use quick-breaking plays in which the puck is continually "head-manned" (passed forward to the man in front). When this man sees one of his own team skate past him he tries to advance the puck again.

With a hitting team the tactics may be to cover the opponents to prevent the play pattern from forming and to slow down the skaters, making them easier to body check.

Often a team dominating the attack is the victim of the missed goal opportunity, which results in a quick-break goal for the team being pressed. Frequently these goals are a turning point in the game.

Hockey offers little chance to use set plays such as we see in football. Efforts have been made from time to time to introduce signals and prearranged combinations. The Boston Bruins of the NHL experimented with the idea at one time, but they found it would not work.

Basically the backbone of team strategy is defensive, and checking is the key to success. New coaches soon learn that almost all goals originate in a defensive mistake, and these occur most often when a team is being checked hard in its own end of the ice.

▶ PLAYING RULES

With few exceptions hockey rules are standard throughout the world.

The major differences are between the rules used in professional hockey and those in force in world amateur hockey. In the world federation no body checking is permitted beyond the red center line of the attacking team. This is the main variation from United States and Canadian rules, but it is important. It has a great effect on the character and the tempo of the game, making the International Ice

STICKHANDLING

BLOCKING

Hockey Federation contests less rough in style than those seen in North America.

Responsibility

Managers and coaches are responsible for the conduct of their players at all times.

Equipment

The game must not be delayed for the adjustment of equipment. The goalie's equipment is the sole exception to this rule.

Fouls and Penalties

There are six types of penalties—minor, bench minor, major, misconduct, match, and penalty shots.

Minor penalties (2-minute removal from the ice to the penalty box) are given for tripping, slashing with the stick, elbowing, hooking, interfering with an opponent, or delaying the game. Any stoppage in play halts the penalty time.

Bench minors are called for some breach of conduct by players or officials on the sidelines.

Major penalties (banishment from the ice for 5 minutes) are given for more serious offenses such as fighting, charging an opponent from behind, and intentionally trying to injure.

Misconduct penalties (banishment from the ice for 10 minutes) are given chiefly for abuse of officials. The player involved must sit in the penalty box, but he may be replaced on the ice. While his team loses his services, it is not required to play short-handed. Misconduct penalties may be given to players who continue to offend against the regulations. In this case the player is removed from the ice and sent to the dressing room for the remainder of the game but may be replaced on the ice.

Match penalties (banishment from the remainder of the game and automatic suspension) are rare and are usually given to a player who intentionally injures an opponent. Another player takes his place on the penalty bench and serves a major penalty term. The offending player is kept out of hockey until his case is dealt with by the league executives.

The **penalty shot** is a free shot on goal usually awarded when a player is tripped from behind when he has no one between him and the goal. All players except the penalty shoot-er and the defending goalie must stand aside. The shooter can take his shot from a distance or can skate close up to try and feint the goalie out of position before shooting.

If the defending goalie has been removed and an attacking player with no one between him and the goal is impeded by an object thrown by the opposition or is fouled from behind, a goal is awarded.

Icing the Puck

Icing the puck is the act of the defensive team in shooting the puck from its own zone to relieve pressure by the opposition. If the puck crosses the red line at the far end of the rink it is said to have been iced, and it is brought back and faced off in one of the two circles in the defending team's end of the rink.

In world amateur hockey a short-handed team is not allowed to ice the puck. However, under NHL and North American amateur rules, when a short-handed team ices the puck, play does not stop.

Offsides

An offside is a passing play where the puck is shot forward beyond the legal limits of forward passing. The position of the player's skates and not that of his stick decides whether there is an offside or not. A player is off side when both skates are over the outer edge of the blue line involved in the play. In short, it is illegal to complete a pass over the opposition's blue line.

Goal Scoring

A goal is not scored until the entire puck has crossed the goal line into the net area.

The Puck

The puck must be kept in forward motion at all times. If not, the referee calls a face-off. When the puck is lost to the referee's view, he stops play and calls a face-off.

If a second puck is thrown on the ice, play continues with the legal puck until the referee stops the game.

Play is not stopped if the puck strikes an official, but no goal can be scored by a puck deflecting into a goal off an official.

LEONARD W. TAYLOR
Associate Sports Editor
Kitchener-Waterloo Record

ICELAND

ICELAND

Iceland lies in the middle of the North Atlantic Ocean, just south of the Arctic Circle. It is considered part of Europe, though it is more than 500 miles from the coast of Scotland, and over 600 miles separate it from the mainland of Norway. In fact, Greenland, which is geographically part of North America, is only 200 miles to the west.

The Norsemen began permanent settlement of Iceland in the year 874. Little more than a century later, Icelanders founded colonies in southwestern Greenland. In the year 1000 Leif Ericson sighted the shores of the North American mainland. Thus, Iceland's geography and history made it a stepping-stone between Europe and North America.

▶ THE PEOPLE

For almost 1,000 years—from the time the island was first settled until the 20th century—time seemed to stand still in Iceland. The people lived in lonely farmhouses and tiny villages, much as their Viking ancestors had done. During the 19th and 20th centuries the way of life changed, slowly at first, then more and more quickly.

Today Iceland is a modern country with a very high standard of living. The old, dark houses of sod and stone have been replaced by well-lighted, modern buildings, usually of concrete. There are apartment houses in the larger towns. Most Icelanders, even those in rural areas, have electricity, telephones, and radios.

Much has changed but much has remained the same. Almost all of the 200,000 Icelanders are descendants of the first Norwegian settlers.

Isafjordur, the chief town on the northwest coast of Iceland.

Glima, the ancient Icelandic form of wrestling.

About 97 percent of the population is Lutheran. Lutheranism was adopted in the 16th century.

Icelandic is still like Old Norse. Icelanders can easily read works written in the 12th century, when writing began on the island. Before that time myths, family histories, and laws were memorized and passed from generation to generation by storytellers. The Eddas and sagas—as the tales are called—were written down in the 12th and 13th centuries. They are works of great beauty and are important for what they tell of the early islanders and their voyages to Greenland and North America. Recent discoveries in eastern Canada have proved that the Vikings reached America nearly 500 years before Columbus. All the clues came from the sagas.

The sagas have helped to make Iceland a country of readers. For centuries, during the long winter nights, parents read the old tales aloud to their children. Everyone learns to read and write. Children must have at least 7 years of schooling. Higher education is provided by the state at the country's only university, in Reykjavik.

▶ **THE LAND**

Iceland's wild and beautiful landscape is largely the product of fire and ice. The island was formed by the outpouring of immense amounts of glowing, fluid rock from great cracks in the ocean floor. Layer upon layer poured out, cooling and hardening into a dark-colored rock called basalt. Before the eruptions ended, a great basalt platform rose from the ocean floor. The remains of this plateau can be seen in the northwestern and eastern parts of the island, where basaltic cliffs tower 2,000 feet out of the water.

After the eruptions ended, one earthquake after another shattered the center of the island. The fires beneath Iceland have not gone out. Iceland is still one of the most active volcanic regions in the world. An area running across the island's center from southwest to northeast is part of a great rift, or crack, in the earth.

It is in Iceland's rift zone that the strangest and most jumbled landscapes are found. Here are great volcanoes such as Hekla, which has erupted more than a dozen times since the country was settled. Here are great cracks in the earth such as the Almannagja. Here are vast deserts of lava and ash, such as the Odadhahraun, covering hundreds of square miles. Here, too, are volcanoes buried in ice such as Katla.

Hot springs are found in almost all parts of the island. The first gushing spring ever seen by white men is located in the southwest. It is Geysir, which has given its name to all such springs, or geysers.

Iceland has the largest glacier (Vatnajokull) outside Greenland and the polar regions. Altogether, glaciers cover about one eighth of the island. Hundreds of square miles

---

FACTS AND FIGURES

REPUBLIC OF ICELAND is the official name of the country.

CAPITAL: Reykjavik.

LOCATION: North Atlantic Ocean. **Latitude**—63° 24′ N to 66° 32′ N. **Longitude**—13° 28′ W to 24° 32′ W.

AREA: 39,768 sq. mi.

POPULATION: 200,000 (estimate).

LANGUAGE: Icelandic.

GOVERNMENT: Republic. **Head of state**—president. **Head of government**—prime minister. **International co-operation**—United Nations, North Atlantic Treaty Organization (NATO), Council of Europe, Organization for Economic Co-operation and Development (OECD), European Free Trade Association (EFTA).

NATIONAL ANTHEM: *O Gud vors lands* ("O God of our land").

ECONOMY: Agricultural products—hay, potatoes, turnips, greenhouse crops, dairy products, mutton and other livestock products. **Industries and products**—fishing and fish processing, food processing, electrical appliances, clothing, cement, fertilizers, tourism. **Chief minerals**—no important mineral deposits. **Chief exports**—fish and fish products, mutton, wool. **Chief imports**—machinery, fuels, metals, textiles, timber, paper, cereals, automobiles. **Monetary unit**—krona.

Reykjavik, the capital of Iceland.

more are covered by constantly shifting melt-water streams that flow out from beneath them. Such features are known as outwash plains—mazes of sand, water, and quicksand. One of these, Skeidharasandur, can be crossed only by airplane.

Climate. Iceland got its name from the drift ice that was packed into the fjords of its north and east coasts by the East Greenland Current. This cold current kept icebergs in the bays almost every summer. The temperature was so low that winter snows hardly melted and grass would not grow.

The climate became warmer during the 19th century, but the East Greenland Current still has a strong influence on Iceland's weather. The north and east coasts are cooler, drier, and foggier than the south and west coasts. In the southeast, mild, moist winds from the Atlantic deposit as much as 160 inches of precipitation a year. Much of it is in the form of snow. In southern Iceland the climate is so mild that midwinter temperatures rarely go below freezing. The average summer temperature is in the low 50's.

Plant and Animal Life. Most of Iceland is a tundra and desert region where only grasses, heather, and low flowering plants grow. The only wooded areas now found in Iceland are specially protected groves and recently planted stands of spruce and pine. Many birds visit Iceland while migrating between Europe and America. Foxes, reindeer, minks, and seals are the only wild animals.

Natural Resources. Iceland has no important mineral deposits. But there are many streams and rivers that can be harnessed to produce electricity. Most hydroelectric power now comes from power plants along the Ellidaar, Sog, and Laxa rivers. There are at least a dozen steam fields in the rift zone, where steam and gases under pressure escape to the surface. Water from hot springs is used to heat the homes of many Icelanders, especially in Reykjavik.

Cities. Over 70 percent of the people live in towns, mostly along the coasts. The capital and only large city in Iceland is Reykjavik, which is the nation's chief port and center of culture, commerce, industry, and domestic air travel. Its present population is about 82,000. The next largest town, Akureyri (population 11,000), is the commercial center of the north. Keflavik, which is about 30 miles west of Reykjavik, is important because of the large NATO air base that is located there.

Fishing and fish processing are Iceland's most important industries.

▶INDUSTRIES AND PRODUCTS

Agriculture. From the time the island was first settled, almost all Icelanders were farmers. Now only about 20 percent of the people are engaged in farming. Over 90 percent of the farmers' income comes from livestock. Sheep are raised mainly for their meat. Cattle are kept to provide milk and other dairy products. Hay is the chief crop. Garden vegetables and even some tropical fruits such as bananas and oranges are grown in greenhouses heated by hot springs.

Industry. Fishing and fish processing are Iceland's most important industries. The surrounding waters are rich in cod, herring, and other valuable food fish. About 10 percent of the islanders work as fishermen. Canning factories and freezing plants are scattered along the coast and employ about 7 percent of the population.

The rest of the people are engaged in industry, commerce, communications, and various services. Most manufacturing depends on imported goods and is for home use. Cheap electricity has made it possible to build a fertilizer factory—a development of great importance to Icelandic agriculture. The island also has its own cement factory, which uses seashells for lime. In 1969 a large aluminum plant, using hydroelectric power, began operating near Reykjavik.

Communications. All telephone and telegraph systems are state-owned. Radio broadcasting is also run by the state. There are no railroads in Iceland, but buses run regularly to the chief towns and districts. Many Icelanders have cars, though most roads are still gravel-topped and narrow. Iceland's two airlines, Icelandair and Icelandic Airlines, make domestic and foreign flights.

▶GOVERNMENT

Iceland is a constitutional republic headed by a president. Executive power rests mainly with the prime minister and his cabinet. The Althing, as the legislature is called, is divided into two houses. All citizens over 21 years of age have the right to vote.

▶HISTORY

In the year 874 a Norwegian Viking chieftain named Ingolfur Arnarsson sailed near the south coast of Iceland. He threw his wooden throne into the water, vowing that he would build his home wherever it washed up on the shore. He had to hunt a long time to find it, as it had drifted to the southwestern tip of the island and deep into a bay. Ingolfur called the bay Reykjavik—the smoking bay—because of the hot springs nearby.

Ingolfur was followed by many other Norwegian chieftains, their families, and their slaves. They left Norway because they refused to swear allegiance to King Harald the Fairhaired (850?–933). In Iceland each chieftain could still be his own master.

In the summer of 930 all the chieftains and their representatives met on the plain below the Almannagja. This first all-island assembly, the Althing, passed laws, settled disputes, and gave judgments. It was the world's first democratic parliament, and Thingvellir ("the plain of the assembly") became Iceland's most sacred landmark. Here in the year 1000 the Althing voted to accept Christianity as the faith of the islanders.

In 1262 the Althing voted to recognize the King of Norway as the ruler of Iceland. In return the King promised to send several shiploads of supplies to the island each year.

Iceland ponies are useful for travel over the rugged terrain.

It was almost a matter of life or death to the Icelanders. In the nearly 400 years since the island had been settled, the forests had almost all been cut down. The climate was growing colder. The grains the Vikings had brought with them would no longer ripen. Without wood to repair ships and food to eat, the Icelanders were cut off and in danger of dying out. Freedom seemed a small price to pay for clinging to life.

When the Norwegian royal family died out in 1380, Iceland, along with Norway, came under the rule of Denmark. By 1602 Danish trade with the island was carried on under a royal monopoly, which only added to the suffering of the people. In 1783–84 the volcano Laki erupted. It seemed as though the end of the world had come for Icelanders. For 6 months dust settled over the island, poisoning the grass and killing the livestock. When the eruption ended, one fifth of the island's people had died of starvation.

But Laki's eruption was the beginning of a new age for Iceland. Denmark took pity on the islanders and in 1787 partly removed the trade monopoly. Then in the late 19th century, the development of more seaworthy ships brought the island new wealth from fishing and fish processing.

Iceland's current prosperity is largely due to World War II and the Cold War that followed it. In 1940 the island was occupied by the British to prevent Nazi Germany from seizing it. In 1941 the United States replaced Great Britain as the island's protector. The Americans built a large air base at Keflavik.

In 1944 the Icelanders proclaimed their independence from Denmark. American forces have been at Keflavik almost continuously since the war. Iceland, a charter member of the North Atlantic Treaty Organization, has no armed forces of its own. The people of the young republic are not happy to have foreign troops on their soil, but they realize that Iceland is too small and too weak to protect itself.

Iceland is strategically located on the air routes between the United States and the Soviet Union. The airplane has made Iceland a stepping-stone between Europe and North America again—a role that the island has not played since the days of the Vikings.

VINCENT MALMSTROM
Middlebury College

ICE-SKATING

Girls and boys skated on frozen lakes and streams in northern Europe more than 1,000 years ago. For skates they used animal bones ground to a smooth, flat surface. These they fastened to their feet with leather straps.

By the 17th century ice-skating had become very popular in the Netherlands, where the canals were frozen over through much of the winter. Most skates were made of wood, but some had metal blades. The Dutch who settled New Netherland in America brought their *schaatsen* ("skates") with them. Many Scots who moved to Canada and other British colonies also had skates. So skating became as popular an activity in North America as it had been in Europe.

Around 1860 steel blades appeared. These allowed skaters more freedom of movement, so that they could do difficult figures on ice. As a result, many skating clubs were formed.

With steel blades skaters could not only perform figures; they could fly over the ice faster, too. So the sport of speed skating developed.

Today many countries hold national figure-skating and speed-skating championship meets each year. There are also North American and world championship meets. The highest goal of all for amateur skaters is a title in the winter Olympics held every 4 years. International events are governed by the International Skating Union, organized in 1891.

▶ SKATING EQUIPMENT

Good ice-skating equipment consists of a pair of leather boots with steel blades that are screwed to the boots at heel and toe.

The blade of a figure skate is about ¼ inch thick. Each of the blades has an inside and an outside edge. This gives the skate a good grip on the ice. The blade is also curved, like a rocker, so only part of it touches the ice at a time. Sawlike teeth, or picks, in the curved forward end of the blade help the skater dig the toes into the ice for certain spins and jumps.

When you choose skating boots, be sure they fit snugly. For best support, lace them loosely in the toe section, then pull the laces tight from the middle of your foot to just above the ankle. Put a knot there to keep the laces tight. Then finish lacing rather loosely and tuck in the ends securely.

Wear cotton or lightweight wool socks. If you wear thick wool socks to stuff up boots that are too large, you will cut off the flow of blood and your feet will become cold. If you wear boots that fit properly, you won't be troubled with "weak ankles."

Take care of your equipment. Always wipe your boots and blades with a dry cloth after you use them. Don't walk on surfaces other than ice unless you have guards over the blades. When you put the boots away, clean and polish the leather, and go over the blades with an oily cloth to keep them from rusting.

Avoid bulky clothing. Sweaters and regular trousers are best for boys. Short, full skirts and blouses or sweaters, or simple, one-piece dresses with short, flared skirts are suitable for girls. Tights should be worn with skirts to keep the legs warm.

LEARNING TO SKATE

LEAN FORWARD
FROM WAIST

PUSH WITH FRONT
OF ONE BLADE

TAKE SHORT STEPS

AND LONG GLIDES

LEARNING TO SKATE

You may hope to become a good figure or speed skater or a hockey player, but first you must learn to straight skate.

Stand on the ice and bend your body forward slightly from the waist. Don't lean forward too much, or the teeth of your skates will trip you. Try gliding along on both feet.

Now try to push off from the front part of the blade of one skate. (But do not push off from the teeth of the blade.) Repeat this for each stroke. The stroke should be long and smooth. Bend the knee of your forward leg as you start each stroke, straightening it as you come to the end of the glide.

Once you have started, how do you stop? You can force your heels apart and point your toes together to make a snowplow position. Or, after you have become sure of yourself (not before, or you can have a bad fall), you can stop by using the ski position. To do this, raise your body for a moment and quickly turn sideways. Keep your skates side by side and lean slightly inward. Your skates will skid sideways on the ice, acting as a brake.

FIGURE SKATING

After you get the feel of straight skating, you will be ready to try figure skating. This requires considerable practice.

Each of your skates has two edges. To skate on one of these edges, you lean either out or in. Skate forward first, leaning in the direction of the outside edge, and you will find yourself swinging in a curve. Practice skating both forward and backward on the inside and the outside edges of each skate. Skating in curves, or arcs, naturally leads to skating in circles, which are the foundation of figure skating.

An important step is learning how to cut corners. If you wish to cut to the right while skating on the right foot, bring the left foot in front of the right. Shift your weight gradually until the left foot crosses over the right and touches the ice on the inside edge. The left foot now carries the weight, and the right foot can be lifted off the ice. Bring it up beside the left and shift your weight to the right foot. Bring your left foot up and cross it in front as before. Repeat these moves around a large circle and hold each edge as long as you can.

Practice crossing over backward as well as forward to both right and left.

General Body Position

Since you skate with your whole body, every part of it should be in the correct position. Your head should be up, never bent forward. Keep your arms at waist level, with the elbows in. The free leg (the one you are not skating on) should be stretched out with the knee slightly bent. As you move the free leg from a forward to backward position, do it with control, and smoothly and easily. The free foot should point downward and outward. The hands should be carried naturally, with the fingers neither spread out nor clenched.

Basic Figures

The figure eight—two circles joined at one point—is the basis for all figures. Some figures are plain circle eights, while others have turns called rockers, counters, threes, brackets, and loops.

The moves and control you develop from learning figures carry through into free skating, pair skating, and dancing.

You can skate an eight both forward and backward and on either the inside or outside edges. To begin a right forward outside eight, look in the direction you plan to go and raise your arms to waist level with the hands held out and the palms down. Stand straight, your feet in a wide V position with the heels close together and your knees bent slightly. The inside edge of your left foot does the pushing that carries you around the first circle of the eight on your right foot. The left foot does not touch the ice again after the push-off until you have completed the first circle.

To start the figure eight, bring the right foot to the instep of the left foot and let your body and head slant forward. Shift your weight from the left foot to the right (skating) foot as you push forward, and use your body weight to help you glide. Your right knee is well bent, the right shoulder forward. The left shoulder and hip are back. Your body leans forward and a little into the circle. The free foot is in back, with the toe pointed to the side.

Your right knee starts to straighten halfway around the circle, and the left foot moves down, passing close to the skating foot and then forward and up. The left shoulder also

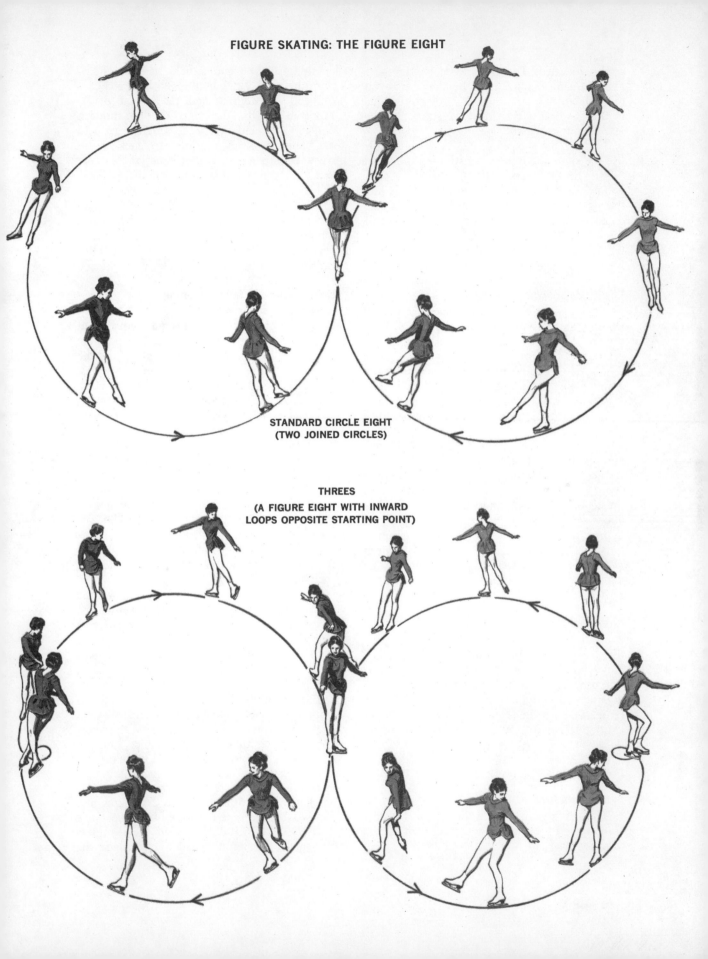

FIGURE SKATING: THE FIGURE EIGHT

STANDARD CIRCLE EIGHT
(TWO JOINED CIRCLES)

THREES

(A FIGURE EIGHT WITH INWARD
LOOPS OPPOSITE STARTING POINT)

comes forward. The right knee bends again after the midpoint, and this bending helps you to complete the circle. Your body straightens to the position it was in at the start, and the left foot touches the ice.

To start the second circle on the left foot, use the same directions, substituting the word "right" for "left" and "left" for "right."

The three is another basic figure. It is like the eight but has an inward turn in the middle of each circle, opposite the starting point of the figure. The easiest three turn is the change from the outside forward edge to the inside backward edge of the skate.

The Kinds of Figure Skating

Figure skating includes singles (a person skating alone), pairs (two persons skating together), and dance (a couple dancing together). To measure their progress, skaters take tests or enter competitions set up by the amateur skating association in their country. A panel of judges marks the skaters on a scale from 0 (which means "not skated") to 6 (which means "perfect").

In singles competitions the contestants usually skate what are called school figures (which count about 60 percent of their final score) and a free skating program set to music of their own choosing (which counts about 40 percent). Pairs do not perform figures; they only do a free skating program to music. Dancers skate to a definite pattern (compulsory dances) and sometimes skate a free dance, an original program of dance moves to music they have selected.

Clubs and Associations

Joining a local skating club will add to your fun and also help you skate better. Most clubs have group lessons or a professional teacher or both. Lessons are a must if you wish to advance and compete in figure skating. Rule books that give in detail the rules for amateur ice figure skating are available at national figure skating associations.

THERESA WELD BLANCHARD
Former United States Figure Skating Champion

▶ SPEED SKATING

Though speed skating began in Europe, Canada and the United States were among the first countries to hold national speed-skating championships. Canada held its first championship in 1887, the United States in 1891.

Speed skating reached the height of its importance with the start of the modern Winter Olympiads in 1924, which were held in Chamonix, France. In those games and in every Olympiad since that time, there were four events in speed skating: the men's 500-, 1,500-, 5,000-, and 10,000-meter events.

It was not until the 1960 Winter Olympiad at Squaw Valley, California, that a women's competition was held. In these games there were also four events: the 500-, 1,000-, 1,500-, and 3,000-meter races.

Three Types of Speed Skating

There are three distinct types of speed skating, and the techniques and equipment vary to some degree in each one. It is possible for a racer to excel in all three, but usually the skater has a preference for one or two styles. The three are (1) European, or metric double-track style, (2) outdoor, or American style, and (3) indoor style.

European Style and Scoring. European style is the most universally accepted, and it is the only one recognized for Olympic and world competitions.

In this style the course is large, 400 meters to the lap. The track is divided by a snow lane about two-thirds of the way around. The part not divided is known as the crossover side.

Only two skaters race at a time, and the skaters change lanes on the crossover side on each lap of the race.

Each skater is individually clocked, and the fastest time decides the winner as well as the other finishers in order of their respective times.

In the Olympic games each distance is a race in itself and each winner an individual champion.

The world championship and any sectional or national championship are decided by an allover point total. This is based on the average 500-meter time in each distance, and the skater with the lowest point total is champion.

For instance, if a skater races the 500 meters in 42 seconds, he receives 42 points. If he skates the 1,500 meters in 2 minutes and 30 seconds, the time is divided by three, since there are three 500 meters in the distance. This gives him another 50 points, since the time reduced to seconds is 150, which is divided by three.

The same is true of any distance. To figure points in a 3,000 meter, divide by six; in the 5,000 meter, divide by 10.

Outdoor, or American, Style and Scoring. Outdoor American style is practiced mainly in the United States and Canada, and the races are held on a slightly smaller track than that used in metric racing. This track is usually 6 laps to the mile and sometimes as small as 8 laps to the mile. Instead of only two skaters racing at once, a group of skaters compete at the same time in what is called pack or horse-race style.

The field of skaters is narrowed to a final group by eliminations known as **heats**. In each heat, at a given racing distance the first two or three leaders at the finish qualify for either a semifinal or final.

When a final race is held in a specific distance, the points are distributed as follows: 5 points for first, 3 for second, 2 for third, and 1 for fourth.

At the conclusion of a competition, the championship is awarded to the skater having the largest number of points.

Distances vary, for different age groups, from 220 yards to 5 miles.

Indoor Style and Scoring. Indoor racing is popular in many countries, mainly the United States, Canada, England, Scotland, Australia, and Japan.

Short tracks are used in indoor racing due to the confines of the building and the smaller ice surfaces. These tracks are usually from 10 to as many as 16 laps to the mile, and are narrow.

Surfaces of indoor ice vary from a normal minimum of 85 feet by 185 feet, to a large rink 125 feet by 250 feet. This accounts for the tracks varying from 10 to 16 laps to the mile.

Point scoring is done in the same way as in outdoor American-style racing.

Speed Skating Equipment

Basic equipment is the same for all speed skating, though the skates vary slightly for each style.

The competitive uniform consists of a wool or stretch-nylon jersey and lightweight wool tights. These should fit snugly but should not be constricting. The tights especially should be knit in such a manner as to be elastic.

A warm-up suit is practical, since it will keep the skater comfortable in cold weather and can be easily removed just before starting a race. It is usually made as a two-piece outfit similar to the racing uniform, but in a loose fashion. The jacket may have a zipper all the way down the front, and the pants, or bottoms, should have full-length zippers on the outside of each leg from the waist to the bottom of the pants leg.

The skates, of course, are the most important part of the equipment, and can vary in five ways: (1) blade length, (2) blade width, (3) blade radius, or "rocker" (pitch of the blade from toe to heel), (4) blade setting, and (5) "cup," or stanchion, height.

It is unwise to set definite standards, since a small person would use slightly shorter skates in all styles of racing than would a larger person.

Hard, outdoor ice requires a thin blade, but since American-style racing cuts up the ice more than European style, a slightly wider blade is necessary to prevent the blade from bending. On the larger tracks the straightaways (straight stretches) are longer; thus a longer and flatter blade will hold the stroke true. The larger the track, the wider the turn; so the skater reduces ankle strain in European style by using the lowest possible cup.

It is necessary, however, as the track becomes shorter and the turns narrower, to use a higher cup. This keeps the sole plate of the shoe from touching the ice when the skater leans on the turns. This would result in a fall and destroy the racer's chances. For the same reason the indoor-track models have the blades set on the left of both shoes, allowing a greater "lean."

The radius, or rocker, also is geared to the width of the track turn. Greater blade curve is needed for short turns, but too much curve on a skate used for outdoor racing causes the stroke to waver on the long glide on straightaways.

Technique and Strategy

The stroke is basically the same in all three styles of speed skating—pushing out to the side instead of to the back, and carrying the body over the glide foot. The knees remain

SPEED SKATING

THE START

RACER PUSHES OFF, SLOWLY INCREASES LENGTH OF STRIDE

LONG-DISTANCE RACING

LONG GLIDES, SHORT STEPS

SHORT-DISTANCE TURNING

BODY LEANS TOWARD TURN

slightly bent, and the body leans forward, but not so far as to ride forward on the blade.

The European style demands the best possible conditioning and knowledge of pace and timing. The skater should know his capabilities and be able to expend his efforts equally over each lap. Each turn of the track should be completed in the same amount of time regardless of the distance of the race. Correct form, even stroking, and good physical condition help to accomplish this.

American-style and indoor racing demand a sense of timing and position. Since the idea is to beat competitors in the same race, time is

CROSSOVER STRIDES

not so important. Short bursts of speed are often necessary to improve your position in the race and to prevent being "boxed" in a pack where it is difficult to get out and use your speed.

It is extremely important to know how to pass a competitor both on turns and straight-aways without fouling or getting knocked down.

European, American, or indoor style, speed skating is a wholesome sport for the well-conditioned athlete.

LAMAR E. OTTSEN
Chairman, Olympic Speed Skating Committee

IDAHO

The water ran furiously from one rock to another, foaming and roaring in every direction. The sound echoed through the wilderness. William Clark of the historic Lewis and Clark expedition gazed fearfully downstream. The day was August 23, 1805. Clark had planned to cross Idaho by traveling down this river. It would be a shortcut on his way to the Pacific Ocean. He turned to his Indian guide and suggested that they try to continue. Already they had come a hard 40 miles.

The guide shook his head. There was no hope of going on. William Clark turned back and searched for another route across Idaho. The raging waters of the Salmon River had blocked his way.

The Salmon is coiled in the very center of Idaho. Along its 420-mile course it roars through vast areas of wilderness land. Today a skilled boatman may travel downstream along the route that William Clark wanted to take. But only the most hardy adventurer would dare the trip upstream. For good reason the Salmon is widely known by another name, the River of No Return.

STATE FLAG.

STATE TREE: Western white pine.

STATE BIRD: Mountain bluebird.

STATE FLOWER: Syringa.

No one really knows where the word "Idaho" comes from. Some people say that it comes from a Shoshone Indian expression meaning, "It is sunup!" Others like to translate it, "Behold! The sun is coming down the mountain." Many others are sure that Idaho means "Gem of the Mountains." A Shoshone Indian would probably say the word does not come from his language. But all would agree that dawn can be a time of great beauty in Idaho's high country. The peaks of the Rockies shine like gems in the sunrise.

On the highest peaks the snow never disappears. Melting snow from the mountain snowfields supplies the many streams that flow down to the plains. These streams provide the water that makes the deserts bloom.

The lands below the snowfields and rocky crags are covered by great evergreen forests. Some of the nation's most beautiful recreational areas are found in these forests. There too are some of the few unexplored areas of the United States. The commercial forest lands support a valuable lumber industry. Mining districts also have sprung up in the midst of these forested mountain areas. One district alone—the Coeur d'Alene district —produces about half the nation's silver as well as large amounts of lead and zinc.

Most of the people in Idaho live below the

evergreen forests. They make their homes in sheltered valleys throughout the state and on the desert plateaus and plains of the south. On the plains the farmers irrigate the dry fields to grow the famous Idaho potatoes as well as sugar beets and many other crops. In some areas wheat is grown without irrigation.

Members of the Lewis and Clark expedition in 1805 were the first white men to see Idaho. By 1809 fur trappers and traders began to enter the area. Many of the names of Idaho's rivers, towns, and lakes—Coeur d'Alene, Boise, Pend Oreille Lake—show the influence of early French Canadian trappers and missionaries.

Gold, discovered in northern Idaho in 1860, brought many miners and prospectors. In the years that followed, cattlemen and lumbermen and farmers "discovered" Idaho. More recently Idaho has been discovered by skiers, hunters, hikers, and campers. Tourists by the thousands come simply to gaze at the natural wonders of the state.

▶ THE LAND

Idaho is the most northwesterly of the group of states known as Mountain States. It has an odd shape. It looks like a throne—or perhaps the boot of a sleeping giant. The top of the throne—or the toe of the boot—borders on British Columbia, Canada's mountainous province.

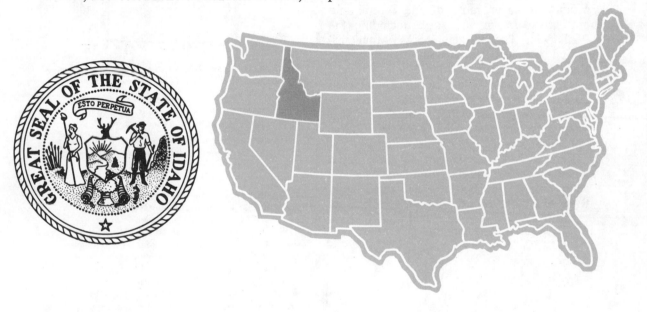

IDAHO

CAPITAL: Boise.

STATEHOOD: July 3, 1890; the 43rd state.

SIZE: 83,557 sq. mi.; rank, 13th.

POPULATION: 713,008 (1970 census); rank, 42nd.

ORIGIN OF NAME: Commonly thought to be of American Indian origin, although scholars have been unable to trace it in Indian languages.

ABBREVIATION: Ida.

NICKNAMES: Gem of the Mountains; Gem State.

STATE SONG: "Here We Have Idaho."

STATE MOTTO: *Esto perpetua* (May she [it] endure forever).

STATE SEAL: A man stands at one side of a shield, and a woman stands at the other side. The man, a miner, represents the mineral wealth of Idaho. The woman stands for justice, liberty, and the equality of women's rights. The pictures on the shield represent the Snake River, the mountains of Idaho, agriculture, and timber resources. The elk's head above the shield is a symbol of Idaho's wildlife in the upland areas. The state motto appears on a streamer above the elk's head. The sheaf of wheat and the horns of plenty below the shield stand for agricultural wealth. The single star in the lower border represents Idaho, a new light in the galaxy of states.

STATE FLAG: The state seal in color is centered on a blue field. The words "State of Idaho" appear on a red streamer beneath the seal.

The long, narrow part of northern Idaho is known as the Panhandle. In the extreme north the distance across the state from east to west is only 45 miles. In southern Idaho the east-west distance is about 300 miles. The greatest distance from north to south is almost 500 miles.

Landforms

Within the unusual outline of the state lie parts of three great natural regions of the United States—the Rocky Mountains, the Columbia Plateau, and the Basin and Range Region.

The Rocky Mountains make up the largest natural region in Idaho. The Northern Rocky Mountains cover most of the central and northern parts of the state, including the Panhandle. The Middle Rocky Mountains extend in a narrow strip along Idaho's border with Wyoming.

The mountain region includes more than 20 separate groups of mountains. In the extreme north are the Selkirk and the Cabinet mountains. The Clearwater Mountains cover the north central part of the state.

Central Idaho is known for its rugged mountains, deep canyons, high meadows, and alpine lakes. The Sawtooth and the Salmon River mountains and the Lemhi and the Lost

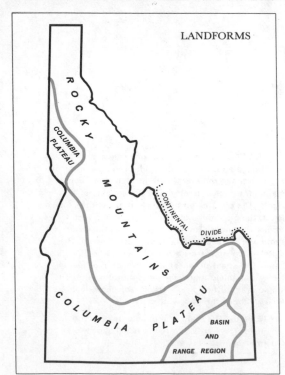

LANDFORMS

River ranges are the most important mountains of this area. The highest peaks in the state are in the Lost River Range. Borah Peak in this range is the highest point in the state.

The crests of the Bitterroot Range and the Coeur d'Alene Mountains form much of the northern boundary between Idaho and Montana. Farther south are the Beaverhead Mountains. The Continental Divide runs through the Beaverhead Mountains along part of the Idaho-Montana boundary.

Idaho's Middle Rocky Mountains include

parts of two ranges, the Teton and the Wasatch ranges. A small part of the Teton Range extends into Idaho from Wyoming. The Wasatch Range extends southward into Utah.

The Columbia Plateau is the second largest of Idaho's natural regions. It is a tableland that stretches in a wide arc across the southern and eastern parts of the state. The plateau is made up of many layers of lava. Ages ago the land in this area was very rugged. Then came a long period when volcanoes erupted and huge amounts of lava flowed from great cracks in the earth. The lava filled in canyons and buried mountains. The surface of the area is now mostly flat to rolling, but some mountainous areas remain. The Columbia Plateau is important to agriculture because its lava soils are very productive when irrigated.

The Basin and Range Region of southeastern Idaho is a continuation of the great natural desert region of the western United States. It is made up of chains of mountains separated by desert plains. The most important mountain range in this area is the Bannock Range.

Rivers and Lakes

The Snake River is Idaho's most important river. It flows in a great arc across the southern part of the state. It forms a large part of Idaho's boundary with Oregon, then turns westward into Washington. There it joins the Columbia River. Most of the state is drained by the Snake and its tributaries. These include the Salmon, Clearwater, Payette, and Boise rivers.

Most of the rivers in the Panhandle area flow toward the Columbia River. Among these are the St. Joe, Kootenai, Pend Oreille, Spokane, and Coeur d'Alene rivers. In the Basin and Range Region the principal river is the Bear. It drains into Great Salt Lake in Utah.

The mountainous uplands of Idaho are dotted with hundreds of lakes. Most of these lakes were created by melting glaciers many thousands of years ago. The two largest are Pend Oreille and Coeur d'Alene. Both are among the world's most beautiful lakes. Bear Lake in the southeastern corner of the state is shared with Utah. Idaho also has many man-made lakes. Of these the American Falls Reservoir is the largest.

Idaho's rivers have spectacular waterfalls. Shoshone Falls on the Snake River plunges 212 feet over a horseshoe rim nearly 1,000 feet wide. Upper Mesa Falls on Henrys Fork of the Snake River drops 114 feet. It is one of the most impressive falls in the state. Moyie Falls is a series of beautiful cascades on the Moyie River, a tributary of the Kootenai.

Climate

Idaho has deserts as well as areas of abundant rainfall. It has mountain peaks where the snow never melts as well as sheltered valleys where trees blossom early in the spring. Temperatures are milder in Idaho than in the states that lie east of Idaho in the Great Plains. Warm air from the Pacific Ocean comes on westerly winds to modify the climate of much of the state. The high ranges of the Continental Divide often stop blizzards and cold air that come from Canada and the Arctic regions. Lewiston on the western border of the state has a normal January temperature of 33 degrees Fahrenheit and a normal July temperature of 75 degrees. At Idaho Falls in the southeast the normal for January is 19 degrees and for July, 69 degrees.

Winter is the wettest season in most sections, and summer is the driest. The most humid parts of the state are in the Panhandle and the Rocky Mountains. Some areas there receive an average annual precipitation of more than 40 inches. The driest part of Idaho is the Snake River Plain. There the average annual precipitation is under 10 inches. At higher elevations much of the precipitation consists of snow. The lowlands, such as the Lewiston area, often receive very little snow.

Generally the growing season is longer in

Picnickers enjoy a summer day at Coeur d'Alene Lake.

the west than in the east. But in many high valleys there is no month without freezing temperatures. The main agricultural areas of the state have a growing season of 125 to 150 days. The area around Lewiston has the longest growing season—about 200 days. This is as long as the growing season in many areas of the Cotton Belt in the southeastern United States.

Natural Resources

Idaho has an abundance of natural resources. Chief among them are soils, forests, minerals, water, grazing lands, and wildlife.

Soils. Idaho has many different kinds of soils. In the mountains the soils are thin and not very fertile. Forests can thrive on these soils. On the Columbia Plateau the soils are made up of windblown materials, called loess, and lava. This kind of soil becomes very fertile when it is irrigated.

Forests. More than one third of Idaho is forested. The principal forest trees are western white pine, ponderosa pine, lodgepole pine,

and Douglas fir. Northern Idaho has the world's largest stand of western white pine—the state tree. Other important trees are the western larch, Engelmann spruce, and western red cedar. The Indians once hollowed out canoes and carved totem poles from the giant red cedar. It rivals the California redwood in size and age. Many other trees, such as the mountain maple and the Rocky Mountain ash, add to the variety and beauty of the forests.

Minerals. Minerals of commercial value are found in nearly all counties of the state. The greatest concentration of mineral wealth is in the Panhandle, particularly in the Coeur d'Alene district. Silver, lead, and zinc are the leading minerals. Other minerals include phosphates, antimony, copper, granite, sand and gravel, mercury, tungsten, vanadium, and gemstones. The phosphate deposits of southeastern Idaho are among the largest in the United States.

Water. One of Idaho's most valuable resources is the water in its rivers and streams.

Arrowrock Dam (*left*) is on the Boise River, a tributary of the Snake River, in southwestern Idaho. Arrowrock Reservoir provides water for irrigation of thousands of acres of crops around the city of Boise. Potatoes (*below*) thrive in the rich soils of the Snake River Valley. Here workers are irrigating a field near Twin Falls. Idaho is the nation's leading producer of potatoes.

Wallace (*below*), seat of Shoshone County, is a trading center for mining and lumbering. Nearby are lead, silver, and zinc mines of the Coeur d'Alene mining district.

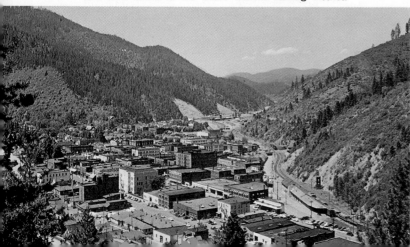

Dams on the rivers have created huge reservoirs, which store water for irrigation and hydroelectric power. The reservoirs, or man-made lakes, also make good places for recreation.

The Snake River has a series of important dams. The one farthest east is Palisades Dam. Its reservoir, which Idaho shares with Wyoming, is used for irrigation and power. Farther downstream are the American Falls Dam at American Falls and the Minidoka Dam near Rupert. Their reservoirs provide water for one of the largest irrigated areas in the United States. In the Hell's Canyon section of the Snake are the Oxbow, Brownlee, and Hell's Canyon dams. They were built to produce hydroelectric power. Other important dams in Idaho are Anderson Ranch Dam and spectacular Arrowrock Dam on the Boise River and Cascade Dam on the North Fork of the Payette River. Dworshak Dam, a more recent construction, is on the Clearwater River.

Wildlife. Many sportsmen come to Idaho to hunt and fish. Wildlife is abundant. Some of the common large animals are deer, elks, mountain goats, mountain sheep, antelope, moose, and bears. There are many smaller fur-bearing animals, such as muskrats, coyotes, weasels, raccoons, beavers, otters, and skunks. Game birds include sage hens, grouse, chukar partridge, and doves.

Idaho's lakes and streams are well-known for trout, salmon, and whitefish. Salmon breed in large numbers in the Salmon River and its tributaries. The king, or Chinook, salmon travels to the ocean, where it lives for several years. But it always swims back to the river, seeking a place to spawn and later to die.

POPULATION

TOTAL: 713,008 (1970 census). **Density—**9 persons to each square mile.

GROWTH SINCE 1870

Year	Population	Year	Population
1870	14,999	1930	445,032
1890	88,548	1950	588,637
1900	161,772	1960	667,191
1910	325,594	1970	713,008

Gain Between 1960 and 1970—6.9 percent.

CITIES: Population of Idaho's largest cities, according to the 1970 census.

City	Population	City	Population
Boise	74,990	Nampa	20,768
Pocatello	40,036	Coeur d'Alene	16,228
Idaho Falls	35,776	Caldwell	14,219
Lewiston	26,068	Moscow	14,146
Twin Falls	21,914		

▶ THE PEOPLE AND THEIR WORK

During the 1860's there were more than 20,000 people in Idaho. Many of them had arrived in 1860 to seek gold in the Orofino area. But the gold did not last long. Many of the miners left, and by 1870 the population had gone down to about 15,000. Then, late in the 1870's, Idaho began a steady growth. Railroads were built, and ranchers came to Idaho. Soon the lead and silver mines were opened. After 1900, irrigation projects changed much of the dry Snake River Plain into rich farming land. People began to arrive in large numbers from the eastern and midwestern states. Many others, especially sheep and cattle ranchers, came from the neighboring western states.

One group of sheepherders, the Basques, came to the hills of southern Idaho from Oregon. Their ancestors were from the Pyrenees of northern Spain and southwestern France. Boise is now a center for the Basques in the United States.

Idaho has a population of several thousand Indians. They belong mainly to the Coeur d'Alene (Skitswish), Kutenai, Shoshone, and Nez Percé tribes. Most of them still live in tribal communities on reservations.

Where the People Live

Idaho, like the rest of the Mountain States, is sparsely settled. Most of the people live in the rich farming lands watered by the Snake River. Other population centers are in the agricultural, mining, and tourist areas of the Panhandle.

Industries and Products

The industries and products of Idaho are closely related to its natural resources. Farming, lumbering, the tourist trade, and mining are important sources of income. Manufacturing largely involves processing the products that come from Idaho's farms and forests and mines.

Agriculture. Only three states—California, Texas, and Colorado—have more acres of irrigated land than Idaho. Idaho's irrigated land is mainly in the fertile Snake River Plain. In some parts of the state, crops can be grown without irrigation, even if there is not much rainfall. This kind of farming is called dry farming.

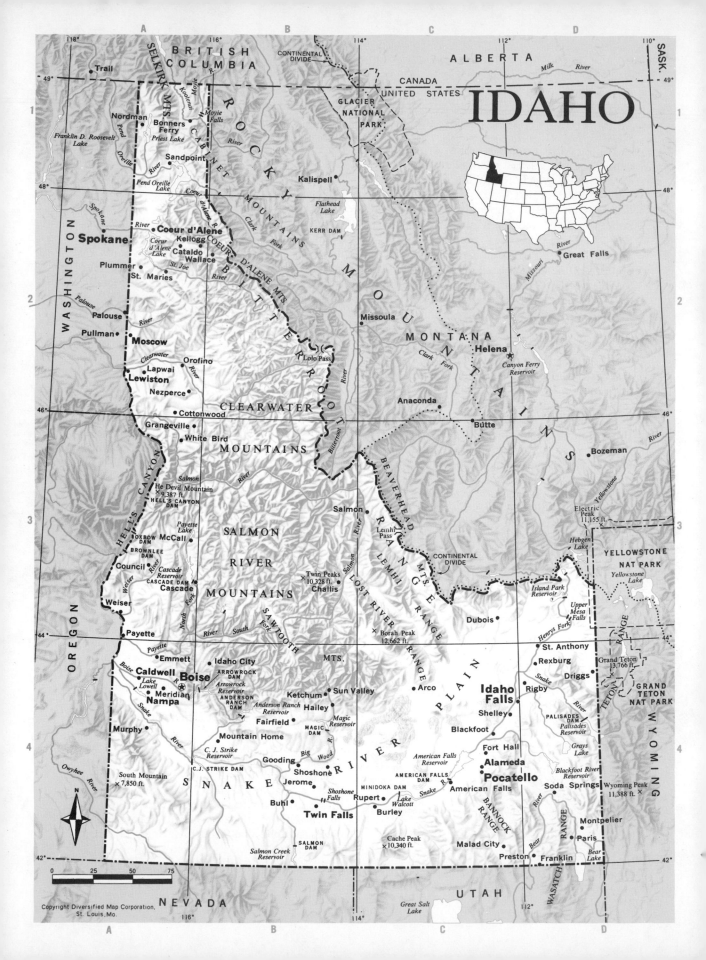

IDAHO

INDEX TO IDAHO MAP

WHAT IDAHO PRODUCES

AGRICULTURAL PRODUCTS: Cattle and calves, potatoes, milk, wheat, sugar beets, sheep and lambs, hay, barley, dry beans, dry peas.

MANUFACTURED GOODS: Frozen fruits and vegetables and other processed foods, lumber and wood products, chemicals and allied products (principally industrial chemicals).

MINERALS: Silver, phosphate rock, zinc, lead, sand and gravel, stone (principally granite and basalt), copper.

Idaho is famous for potatoes. It produces nearly one fifth of the nation's crop. Most of the potatoes are grown in the irrigated Snake River area. After potatoes, wheat is the most valuable crop. The yield per acre in Idaho is one of the highest in the nation. Wheat is grown mainly in the dry-farming area radiating north and southeast of Lewiston and in the southeastern and south central parts of the state.

Other important crops include sugar beets, dry beans, barley, alfalfa, dry peas, and onions. Apples, prunes, cherries, and other fruits are grown throughout the state, especially in the north and the southwest. Bees thrive where there are orchards or fields of alfalfa and clover. Idaho ranks high among the states as a producer of honey.

The raising of cattle and sheep has been an important occupation in Idaho since its early days. Today beef cattle and calves are a leading source of income. Grazing lands are plentiful, and irrigated fields near the grazing lands produce large amounts of hay for additional livestock feed.

Most of the dairy farms are in the irrigated southern part of the state. Milk from these farms is made into such products as dried milk, butter, cheese, and ice cream. Idaho is the leading producer of cheese in the West. Poultry farms are also located in the irrigated areas, usually near cities.

Forest Products. Lumbering is one of Idaho's oldest industries, and it remains an important industry today. The chief products of the state's forests are lumber, railroad ties, telephone poles, laths, plywood, veneer, and boxes. Sawdust is compressed and made into fireplace logs. Wood chips and other leftovers from the sawmills are made into pulp and paper.

Mining. The Coeur d'Alene district is the mining center of Idaho. The largest silver mine in the country, the Sunshine Mine, is located there. Nearby is Bunker Hill, one of the nation's largest lead mines.

Idaho ranks first in the nation in production of silver and second in zinc and lead. Only Tennessee produces more zinc than Idaho. Only Missouri produces more lead. Other metals include copper, tungsten, and vanadium. Tungsten is used in steel. It is also used for the filaments of electric light bulbs. Vanadium is a rare-earth metal used in certain kinds of steel.

Idaho also produces various nonmetallic minerals, such as phosphate rock, sand and gravel, and gemstones. It ranks high among the states in the production of phosphate. Idaho is a leading producer of abrasive garnet and pumice. Abrasive garnet is used for polishing. Pumice is a light, spongy stone thrown up by volcanoes. It is used for cleaning and polishing.

Gemstones can be found in all parts of the state. Beautiful fire opals come from Gem County near Emmett. Adams County has

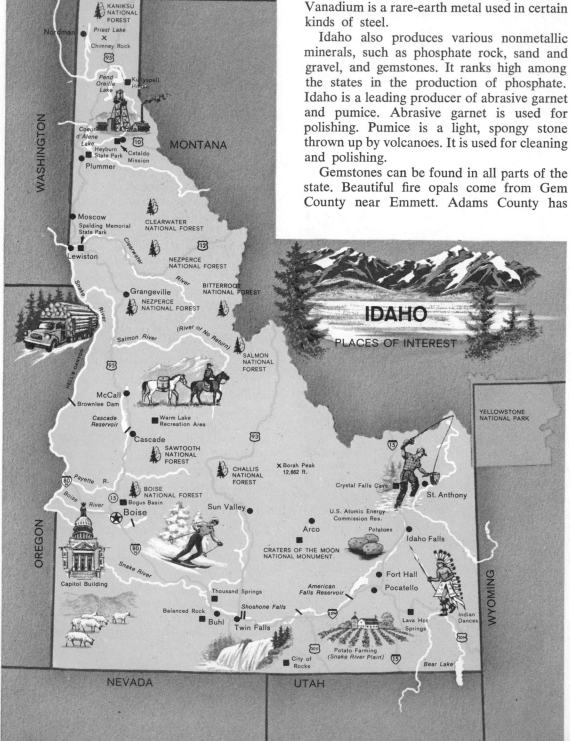

rubies, sapphires, and many pink garnets. Other areas have quartz, agates, jasper, and onyx. Some of the stones are mined commercially. But many are found by people who explore by themselves.

Manufacturing. Most of Idaho's factories are engaged in the processing of food, timber, and minerals. Two of the newest industries are potato processing and phosphate processing. Many products are made from potatoes, including dehydrated potatoes, frozen french fries, and starch. Chemicals and fertilizers are made from phosphate rock.

The Tourist Trade. At present the tourist business is one of Idaho's main sources of income. Perhaps the state is most famous for the ski center at Sun Valley, but there are numerous other areas that attract their share of visitors.

Transportation and Communication

Idaho's first railroads were built in the late 1800's. Today four transcontinental railways cross the state. These and other railways maintain more than 3,000 miles of track in the state.

Many of Idaho's highways follow the routes of old trails. U.S. Highway 10 in the Panhandle follows a wagon road built by Lieutenant John Mullan in 1861. The Lewis and Clark Highway follows the route of Lewis and Clark through Idaho. U.S. 30 follows the famous Oregon Trail. There are also several north-south highways. More than 80 places throughout the state have commercial and municipal airports.

The first newspaper to appear in Idaho was *The Golden Age,* which was published in Lewiston from 1862 to 1865. The *Idaho Statesman* has been published continuously in Boise since 1864. At present more than a dozen daily newspapers and about 70 weekly papers are published in the state. There are more than 40 radio stations and several television stations.

▶ EDUCATION

The first school in Idaho was established by missionaries in 1836. For many years afterward the only schools in the territory were study classes or private schools. Then in 1864 the territory passed an act establishing a common school system.

Schools and Colleges

A system of public education was planned in 1890 when Idaho became a state. The number of school districts grew until there were more than 1,000. In 1947 the school system was reorganized, and districts were consolidated.

The major state-supported institutions of higher learning are the University of Idaho at Moscow, Idaho State University at Pocatello, Boise State College at Boise, and Lewis-Clark Normal School at Lewiston. The University of Idaho and Idaho State have significant graduate degree programs. The junior colleges located at Coeur d'Alene, Twin Falls, and Rexburg are supported mainly by their communities or churches. Private schools located in the state include the College of Idaho at Caldwell and Northwest Nazarene College at Nampa.

Libraries and Museums

There are nearly 80 public libraries in Idaho, and bookmobiles operate in several areas. The library of the University of Idaho is the largest in the state. It contains special collections on the history of Idaho and the Pacific Northwest. Other major collections include the Atomic Energy Commission Library at Idaho Falls and the State Law Library, the State Traveling Library, and the Jerome Day Mining Library, all in Boise.

The Idaho Historical Society at Boise has a large collection of documents, relics, and costumes associated with the history of the state. Also in Boise is the Boise Gallery of Art, which features the work of Idaho artists. The Idaho State University Museum at Pocatello is known for its natural history exhibits. Other museums are mainly of local interest.

▶ PLACES OF INTEREST

Idaho is one of the most beautiful and unspoiled states in the West. Its ski slopes, fishing streams, and spectacular scenery attract people from many parts of the nation and the world.

National Areas

Idaho has 16 national forests, some of which are shared with neighboring states. Three famous primitive areas lie within Idaho's national forests. These are the Selway-

Bitterroot, the Idaho, and the Sawtooth primitive areas. These lands have not been settled or used commercially. They have no roads—only pack trails and, here and there, rough landing strips for small planes. They remain as they were before the West was settled, except that Indians no longer roam the forests. Idaho also has one national monument, the Craters of the Moon National Monument, and a small part of Yellowstone National Park.

Craters of the Moon National Monument is located near Arco in the southern part of the state. It covers 75 square miles of strange volcanic formations. The area is called Craters of the Moon because its cinder cones, craters, and weird piles of rocks look like the moon as seen through a telescope. Three periods of eruptions and lava flows produced this area. The last period probably occurred only a few hundred years ago. The Indians still have legends of a time when the hills smoked and exploded and the whole desert trembled. Today there are black caves and pits of very great depth. There are tunnels with fantastic lava formations colored in bright shades of red and blue. And there are heaps of foamlike rock as well as strange molds of trees, because the rivers of lava buried a whole forest. The monument is a dark, awesome place. But it is one of the most interesting in the United States.

Boise National Forest is one of the largest forests in Idaho. It includes many abandoned mines and ghost towns. Idaho City is one of the most famous. In the 1860's it was a gold-mining center with about 30,000 people. Today only about 200 people live there, among a few his-

toric buildings and other reminders of the early days. Part of the Sawtooth Primitive Area lies in this forest. There is a winter sports area, Bogus Basin, near Boise. Not far from Cascade is the Warm Lake Recreation Area.

Kaniksu National Forest is in northern Idaho. Parts of it are located also in Washington and Montana. Everything grows well in this forest. In the Roosevelt Grove of Ancient Cedars near Nordman are huge trees more than 800 years old. Many parts of the forest resemble a tropical garden because of the abundance of ferns, shrubs, and wild flowers. Pend Oreille and Priest lakes lie partly within the forest. Not far from Priest Lake is Chimney Rock, a steep pinnacle that was carved out by three glaciers. Mountain goats can climb this rock with ease, but it is difficult for men to scale. Besides mountain goats, there are hundreds of deer, elks, and bears.

Nezperce National Forest is in north central Idaho. On the western edge of the forest is the Hell's Canyon–Seven Devils Scenic Area of Idaho and Oregon. Hell's Canyon of the Snake River is the wildest, deepest gorge in North America. At one point its depth is almost 8,000 feet. The Seven Devils area is named for the seven sharp peaks that rise along the edge of the canyon.

State Recreation Areas

Idaho has established about 30 areas to help preserve historic places and places of natural beauty. The following list shows the variety.

The City of Rocks is a recreation area in southern Idaho. The rocks were carved from a huge granite dome by wind and water. There are shapes that resemble Oriental temples, for-

Craters of the Moon National Monument on the Snake River Plain near Arco contains many weird formations of volcanic rock.

Steam rises into the wintry air from a heated swimming pool at Sun Valley. Skiers hike along the snowy path bordering the pool.

tresses, bathtubs, dragons, chickens, and elephants. One group of spires rises 250 feet from the floor of the basin. From a distance it looks like the skyline of New York City. A legend says that a fortune is buried among five juniper trees somewhere in this huge maze of rocks.

Heyburn State Park near Plummer in northern Idaho is the largest state park. It is like a sunken garden, surrounded on all sides by lofty, forested mountains. It includes several beautiful small lakes.

Lava Hot Springs is not far from Pocatello. For centuries the Indians set aside this area as one to be shared in peace by all tribes. The park has many hot mineral springs and a remarkable pool called the Mud Bath. This pool is fed by 30 natural springs with water of varying temperatures. It is surrounded by cinder cones, black rocks, and other remains of ancient volcanic activity.

Spalding Memorial State Park near Lewiston is the site of the Lapwai Mission—Idaho's first mission and school. The park is named for the Reverend Henry Spalding and his wife, missionaries who came to the Northwest in 1836. The park contains an old Indian burial ground, monuments to the Spaldings, and historic relics.

Other Places

Idaho has many scenic and historic sites that are not part of the state or federal park systems. Some of these are recreation areas. Others are known because they are beautiful or unusual.

Balanced Rock near Buhl is one of the strangest sights in the state. The rock, 40 feet high, is shaped like a huge mushroom.

Cataldo Mission near Cataldo was started about 1850. Father Antonio Ravalli, with the help of Indians, built this unusual church. Wooden pegs were used as nails, and mud from the river was spread over the walls. The wall paintings were done with Indian dyes.

Crystal Falls Cave near St. Anthony is one of Idaho's many remarkable caves. It is a huge cavern with delicate and unusual ice formations along its corridors. It also includes a frozen river and a waterfall of ice.

Sun Valley in the Sawtooth Mountains is known around the world as a winter sports and resort area. It has been the scene of many national and international ski events. The resort is also open during the summer for many other activities.

Thousand Springs near Buhl is another strange sight. For two miles along the walls of the Snake River canyon, natural springs gush into the

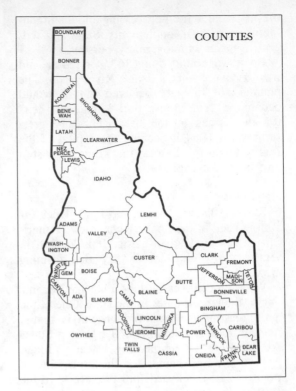

river. The springs are believed to be the outlets of underground rivers.

Annual Events

Many interesting events are held in Idaho every year. These include rodeos, harvest festivals, state fairs, and Indian dances.

February, March—Winter Sports Carnival, McCall; Harriman Cup Races, Sun Valley.

May—Apple Blossom Festival, Payette; Music Week, Boise.

July—Rodeos at Grangeville, Idaho Falls, Pocatello, and Nampa; Indian Dances (Sun, War, Owl, Rabbit, and Grass dances) at Fort Hall.

August—Western Idaho State Fair, Boise.

September—Roundup, Lewiston; Eastern Idaho State Fair, Blackfoot.

October—Spud Day Festival (after potato harvest), Shelley.

▶CITIES

Most of Idaho's largest cities are located on the Snake River or its tributaries.

Boise

The capital of Idaho is located in the Boise River valley, a rich agricultural area in the southwestern part of the state. Industries of the city include food processing and the manufacturing of farm implements. State and federal agencies employ many persons.

Boise was founded in 1863, soon after gold was discovered in the Boise River basin. The planners of the city believed that it would become a "storehouse and kitchen garden" for the mines in the area. The city grew rapidly. In 1864 it became the capital of the Idaho territory. Before that time Lewiston had been the capital.

Idaho Falls

Idaho Falls was once called Eagle Rock for a large rock in the Snake River where American eagles made their nests. It is located in southeastern Idaho in a very rich farming area.

Within recent years Idaho Falls has become one of the largest cities in the state. One of the main reasons for its rapid growth is that a nuclear research station of the United States Atomic Energy Commission is nearby. Idaho Falls is a major center for the processing of potatoes. Its stockyards are the largest in the state.

Pocatello

Pocatello was named for an Indian chief of the Bannock tribe. The city was established in 1882, when a railroad was completed to this point in southeastern Idaho. Today Pocatello is a shipping point for beef, grains, and dairy products. Its manufactured products include chemicals and cement.

Lewiston

The explorers Meriwether Lewis and William Clark camped at the junction of the Snake and the Clearwater rivers in 1805. Later a mining town was established there. It was named Lewiston in honor of Meriwether Lewis. For one year, 1863–64, Lewiston served as the first capital of the Idaho territory.

Lewiston is walled in by mountains, and it is almost 400 miles from the Pacific Ocean. Yet it is a Pacific "port" because certain kinds of vessels can come to Lewiston via the Columbia River-Snake River route. The city is the center of a grain and cattle area and of lumbering activities. One of the largest sawmills in the world is located there.

▶ **GOVERNMENT**

The constitution of the state of Idaho was adopted in 1889, about 6 months before the territory became a state. There have been many amendments to the constitution. One of these granted women the right to vote in 1896. This was 24 years before a similar amendment was made to the United States Constitution.

The executive branch of Idaho's government consists of a governor and other executive officers. Each is elected for a 4-year term. There is a governor's cabinet, consisting of several departments, such as labor, agriculture, law enforcement, and finance.

The legislature of Idaho is made up of two bodies, the Senate and the House of Representatives. There are 35 senators and 70 representatives, all elected for 2-year terms. The legislature holds annual sessions, beginning on the second Monday in January.

The highest state court in Idaho is called the Supreme Court. It is made up of five justices. The major trial courts in the state are called district courts. Supreme Court justices and district court judges are elected by the people.

▶ **FAMOUS PEOPLE**

The following are among the well-known persons whose names are associated with Idaho:

Sacagawea (1787?–1812?), known as the Bird Woman, was a Shoshone Indian guide for the Lewis and Clark expedition. She was born in Idaho, probably near Lemhi. In 1800 she was captured by Hidatsa Indians and carried to their village in North Dakota. There she was sold to a Canadian trader named Toussaint Charbonneau, who was living with the Hidatsa. Charbonneau married her. Lewis and Clark employed Charbonneau as an interpreter, with the understanding that his wife would go with him on the expedition. She made the long journey with her baby son strapped to her back. Many stories are told of the ways in which she aided the explorers, especially in obtaining help from the Shoshone.

Records of the time do not agree on the details of Sacagawea's life. Some accounts say that Sacagawea returned with her husband to the Hidatsa and that she died in North Dakota in 1812. Others say that she stayed in the Northwest with her own people and died there in 1884—at the age of almost 100 years.

George L. Shoup (1836–1904) was Idaho's last territorial governor (1889), first state governor (1890), and first United States senator (1890–1901). He served as a colonel during the Civil War. Before that time and later he was a merchant in Colorado and Montana. With other businessmen he founded Salmon, Idaho, in 1866. From that time he made his home in Idaho and worked to make it known and develop its resources. He was born in Pennsylvania.

Chief Joseph (1840–1904), a Nez Percé chief, is remembered as a brilliant military man. He led those members of his tribe who refused to recognize a treaty made in 1863. This treaty gave Nez Percé lands to the federal government and made the Nez Percé live on the Lapwai reservation in Idaho. In 1876 the government decided to enforce the treaty. Chief Joseph realized that he could not win in open battle. He decided instead to escape to Canada with his people, including many women and children. He led them on a 1,000-mile retreat through Idaho and Montana that is one of the marvels of military history. On the way he eluded and outwitted some of the best officers of the United States Army. Finally, only 30 miles from the Canadian border, he was defeated by General Nelson A. Miles.

General Miles reported that the surrender took place one morning when the sun stood at about 10 o'clock. As Chief Joseph was about to hand his rifle to the General, he raised his eyes toward the sun and said, "From where the sun now stands, I fight no more against the white man." And he kept his word. He spent the rest of his life working for the education and welfare of his people. It is thought that Chief Joseph was born in Oregon. He died at the Colville reservation in Washington.

William Edgar Borah (1865–1940), lawyer and statesman, became internationally famous during his long service as United States senator from Idaho (1907–40). He was known especially for his ability as an orator and for his independent stand on important national issues. He was born in Illinois but came to Boise in 1890 to practice law.

Well-known persons born in Idaho include sculptor Gutzon Borglum (near Bear Lake), poet Ezra Loomis Pound (Hailey), and author Vardis Fisher (Jefferson County). Author Ernest Hemingway was born in Illinois, but he spent much time hunting and fishing at Ketchum near Sun Valley. He is buried there.

▶ **HISTORY**

Various Indian tribes were living in Idaho in the early 1800's. They included the Coeur d'Alene and the Kutenai tribes in the Panhandle, the Bannock and the Shoshone in the south, and the Nez Percé in north central Idaho. All of these tribes were friendly in their first contacts with settlers. Trouble came only when settlers arrived in great numbers and began to take the land.

Discovery and Exploration

Members of the expedition of Meriwether Lewis and William Clark entered Idaho in August, 1805, by way of the Lemhi Pass. Because they could not descend the Salmon River, they left Idaho and traveled north into Montana. One month later they again entered Idaho, this time over the Lolo Pass. They made their way to the Clearwater River and traveled down this river to Lewiston. From there they went on to the Pacific.

Fur traders and trappers were next to explore Idaho. Among the first fur traders was David Thompson, representative of a British company. Thompson founded a trading post, Kullyspell House, on the shores of Pend Oreille Lake in 1809. Later other trading posts were established in the south. The first was Fort Henry, built by Andrew Henry in 1810 in the upper Snake River valley. In 1834 Nathaniel Wyeth, a Boston merchant, established Fort Hall near present-day Pocatello. Because it was located on the Oregon Trail, Fort Hall later became one of the chief trading posts of the West. Fort Boise, near the mouth of the Boise River, was also established in 1834. By 1840 most of the valuable furs had been taken from Idaho, and the traders and trappers began to disappear.

Toward the end of the fur-trading era, missionaries began to arrive. In 1836 Henry Spalding and his wife Eliza established the Lapwai Mission near what is now Lewiston.

They organized a school and taught the Indians how to farm. They also brought the first printing press to the area. A few years later, Father Pierre De Smet, a Belgian-born missionary, established a mission near what is now Cataldo. About 1850 an Italian-born missionary, Father Antonio Ravalli, was commissioned to build a church there. The Mormons attempted to establish a mission in the Lemhi Valley in 1855. But they gave up their plans because of increasing trouble with the Indians.

Settlement and Statehood

Idaho was originally part of the Oregon country—a vast area including Oregon, Washington, and a part of Canada. When Oregon became a state in 1859, Idaho was included in the Washington territory. Shortly afterward, gold was discovered in Idaho, and people came to the area by the thousands. Congress created the Idaho territory in 1863.

The first permanent settlement in Idaho was made by the Mormons at Franklin in 1860. Other permanent settlements were established at several places between 1860 and 1870. Some of these were Lewiston, Boise, and Soda Springs. Troubles with the Indian tribes were settled by the late 1870's. On July 3, 1890, Idaho became the 43rd state.

The Coeur d'Alene mining district was opened not long after Idaho became a state. While the mines were being developed, many disputes arose between the miners, unions, and mine owners. A long series of mining strikes began. In 1899 the Bunker Hill plant was dynamited by striking miners. To restore order, Governor Frank Steunenberg called in federal troops. Many miners did not approve of this action. Six years later Steunenberg was assassinated, and a famous trial followed. William E. Borah represented the state. Clarence Darrow, the best-known lawyer of his day, represented the accused assassins. One of the accused, Harry Orchard, was convicted.

Growth in Modern Times

Since the early 1900's Idaho has grown steadily. In 1902, Congress passed an act that marked the beginning of large-scale irrigation. Idaho was then able to reclaim vast areas of arid and partly arid lands. Soon agriculture became the chief source of income. Along with irrigation projects came the development of waterpower. Most recently the food- and timber-processing industries have grown remarkably, as has the tourist business.

The Future

To some extent Idaho is divided by its physical geography. Northern Idaho has many ties with the state of Washington. Southeastern Idaho has much in common with northern Utah. The Boise area and the rest of Idaho make up a unit within the state. Recently the increased use of air transportation and the improvement of highway systems have done much to join the different sections. This trend will continue, and Idaho will find it easier to develop its great resources for the benefit of the state as a whole.

HERBERT J. VENT
University of Idaho

IMPORTANT DATES

1805 Lewis and Clark expedition crossed what is now Idaho.

1809 David Thompson established Kullyspell House, a fur-trading post, on Pend Oreille Lake.

1834 Nathaniel Wyeth built Fort Hall on the Snake River in southeast Idaho.

1836 Henry Spalding founded a mission at Lapwai.

1837 First child, Eliza Spalding, born to settlers in Idaho.

1860 Gold discovered near Orofino; first permanent settlement at Franklin by the Mormons.

1863 Congress created the territory of Idaho, including Montana and part of Wyoming; Lewiston became the territorial capital.

1864 Capital moved to Boise; Montana became a separate territory.

1868 Idaho assumed its present boundaries when Wyoming became a separate territory.

1877 Nez Percé and other Indian wars began; wars ended 2 years later.

1882 Silver and lead discovered in the Coeur d'Alene district; mining began 2 years later.

1889 University of Idaho founded at Moscow.

1890 July 3, Idaho became the 43rd state.

1896 Idaho granted women the right to vote.

1906 Minidoka Dam completed, first federal reclamation project in Idaho.

1936 Sun Valley resort opened.

1947 Public school system reorganized.

1955 Arco, Idaho, became the first village in the United States to be lighted (for one hour) by atomic power.

1958 Brownlee Dam, largest power plant on the Snake River, placed in service.

1962 Lewis and Clark Highway from Lewiston to Missoula, Montana, completed and dedicated.

1963 100th anniversary of the Idaho territorial act; Idaho State College became Idaho State University.

1968 A constitutional amendment was approved providing for annual sessions of the legislature.

ILIAD

The *Iliad,* by Homer, who also composed the *Odyssey,* is the earliest and the most famous work of Greek literature. Like all epic poems, it is written in a grand style and is about heroes. Homer lived perhaps in the 8th century B.C. and told the story of events that happened 400 years earlier. He may not have written at all. Perhaps he recited his poems orally.

The *Iliad* is named after Ilium, another name for Troy. The Trojan War started when Prince Paris of Troy carried off Queen Helen of Sparta. Homer does not tell all the events of this war. He covers only a few weeks during the 10th and last year. But he uses the flashback technique, through which we see many earlier incidents. And he also gives many hints of what is to follow.

The chief hero is Achilles. Achilles becomes angry at Agamemnon, the Greek commander in chief, who takes away a prize Achilles had won. Achilles feels insulted and withdraws from the fight. Throughout most of the 24 books (or parts) of the poem, he stays brooding angrily in his tent. But he is never far from our thoughts, and we watch him become a better human being through suffering. The very first words of the poem indicate the subject. "The wrath of Achilles is my theme," the poet says.

The Trojans are winning. Agamemnon offers Achilles many gifts and begs him to rejoin the fighting. He refuses. Later he allows his good friend Patroclus to fight in his (Achilles') own armor. The Trojan Prince Hector kills Patroclus. This so angers and saddens Achilles that, at last, he does fight again. He covers himself with glory and finally kills Hector. Hector's father, King Priam, goes to Achilles and begs him to release his son's body. Achilles does, partly because Priam reminds him of his own father. This is a very moving scene.

There are other moving scenes, such as the farewell of Hector to his wife, Andromache, and son, Astyanax. The little boy is frightened by Hector's helmet with its horsehair plume, and Hector gently removes it. Homer had marvelous understanding of human relationships.

The *Iliad* is famous for its exciting battle scenes. Homer knew that war was terrible, yet it often brought out the best in men—courage and self-sacrifice.

There is also the scene on the Trojan watchtowers, when Helen appears before the old men of Troy. Old as they are, they feel that such a beautiful woman is worth all the heartbreak.

Fighting was a rather personal affair. Most of the people we hear about are noblemen, princes, and kings. Always they search for glory, while following a strict code of honor. When the Greek Diomedes is about to fight the Trojan Glaucus, they first introduce themselves. When they discover that their grandfathers were friends, they decide not to fight but to exchange their armor.

The gods constantly take sides between the parties, and they champion individuals. Achilles' mother, Thetis, persuades Zeus to help the Trojans when her son is angry. She also brings him new armor, after he has lost his through the death of Patroclus. Aphrodite carries her son Aeneas out of the battle when he is wounded by the enemy.

Some of the most humorous scenes show the gods among themselves. Often they behave just like mortals, quarreling and fighting.

The *Iliad* ends with a truce, for the burial of Hector. For the stories of what happened afterward, we must look elsewhere—to Vergil's *Aeneid,* for example, with its story of the Trojan Horse.

Homer is dramatic, noble, and realistic. We feel we know his characters. Though he was a Greek, he gives very fair treatment to the Trojans. The story moves rapidly. There are many speeches. One notable feature of Homer's style is the use of epithets. Achilles is "swift-footed." The sea is "wine-dark." Aphrodite is "laughter-loving."

As their "Bible," the *Iliad* had enormous influence on the thought of the Greeks. Alexander the Great carried a copy with him while conquering Asia. The *Iliad* also greatly influenced the world's literature, not merely epic poetry. This influence is first evident among the Greeks themselves, especially the writers of tragedy.

URSULA SCHOENHEIM
Queens College

Reviewed by GILBERT HIGHET
Columbia University

ILLINOIS

One of Illinois' famous landmarks is known by a strange name—Starved Rock. It is a huge sandstone cliff, 125 feet high, on the banks of the Illinois River near La Salle. The French explorer La Salle called it *Le Rocher*—"the Rock." The name Starved Rock is based on legends.

One legend says that about the year 1769 a band of Illinois Indians took refuge on top of the Rock. They were being pursued by a huge force of Potawatomi who wanted to avenge the death of Chief Pontiac. From their rock fortress the Illinois Indians were able to keep their enemies at bay. But hunger and thirst defeated them. Their enemies cut the cords with which they tried to lift vessels of water from the river. Finally, with true Indian courage, they died of starvation in full view of their vast hunting grounds. From that time the Rock was known as Starved Rock.

In 1911 the state bought Starved Rock and some of the surrounding land for use as a park. Starved Rock State Park was opened the following year. Today it is one of Illinois' most beautiful vacation spots.

STATE FLOWER: Meadow violet.

STATE BIRD: Eastern cardinal.

STATE TREE: Bur oak.

STATE FLAG.

Illinois, "Land of Lincoln," is a land of striking differences. It has both level prairies and wooded hills. It is one of the great agricultural states of the nation. It is also one of the leading states in manufacturing and commerce. It has large cities. Yet much of Illinois is rural and thinly populated. The extreme southern part of the state is somewhat like the Old South. The northern and central parts of Illinois reflect the hustle and bustle of huge industries and large-scale agriculture.

Illinois has been known by various names. Long ago it was known as the country of the Illinois Indians, or Illinois country. Early settlers found great stretches of grassland in the northern and central parts of the area. They called Illinois the Prairie State. Southern Illinois had another name—Egypt. It seems strange that any part of Illinois could resemble Egypt. But people say that the floodplains where the Mississippi and the Ohio rivers meet are very much like the great plain of the Nile River near Cairo, Egypt. Today the official nickname or slogan of Illinois is Land of Lincoln.

Abraham Lincoln came to Illinois when he was about 21 years of age. In 1832, 2 years after moving to the state, he ran for a seat in the General Assembly, as the state legislature is called. He lost, but already he was thinking of himself as a native Illinois man. In 1834 he ran again and won. At that time Vandalia in Fayette County was the capital of Illinois. Vandalia was a town of about 800 people, and the state house was a ramshackle building.

Lincoln and other legislators from Sangamon County wanted to see the capital moved to Springfield, the largest town in their county. The people of Vandalia became alarmed at the talk of shifting the capital. Quickly a new state house was built. The General Assembly began meeting in the new building in December, 1836. Everyone realized almost at once that it was too small.

Lincoln worked harder than ever gathering support for a bill to make Springfield the capital. In February, 1837, the bill came up for a vote. The state Senate passed it. The House was about to do so, too. But suddenly a motion to table (put off consideration of) the bill was passed by only one vote.

That night Lincoln held a meeting with his nine fellow legislators from Sangamon County. They were called the Long Nine because of their height. After the meeting they went out into the winter darkness to call on other legislators who might be won over. The next morning balloting began again. Within a week it was all over. The Long Nine had won. The capital was to be moved to Springfield, where it remains today.

At that time Abe Lincoln was only 28 years old, but he was already a skillful leader. He had shown that he could gather his forces and

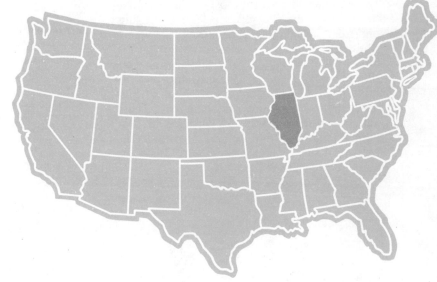

ILLINOIS

CAPITAL: Springfield.

STATEHOOD: December 3, 1818; the 21st state.

SIZE: 56,400 sq. mi.; rank, 24th.

POPULATION: 11,113,976 (1970 census); rank, 5th.

ORIGIN OF NAME: From the Indian word *Iliniwek, or illiniwek. Illini* meant "man," and the ending made the word plural. The French changed the word to Illinois.

ABBREVIATION: Ill.

NICKNAMES: Land of Lincoln (official); Prairie State.

STATE SONG: "Illinois."

STATE MOTTO: "State sovereignty, national union."

STATE SEAL: An eagle, the national emblem, is in the foreground, perched on a rock. It holds a shield in its claws. In its beak is a scroll bearing the state motto. Two dates are on the rock—1818, the year Illinois was admitted to the Union, and 1868, the year this seal was first used. The stars and stripes in the shield represent the original 13 states. The olive branch at the base of the shield is the symbol of peace. In the background the rising sun shines over the prairie.

STATE FLAG: A design much like the design on the state seal appears in color in the center of a white field. The flag is bordered in gold, and the word "Illinois" appears under the state seal emblem.

lead them to victory. A quarter of a century later he was to do that when the existence of the United States itself was threatened. He learned how in Illinois. That is why Illinois truly deserves to be called the Land of Lincoln.

▶ THE LAND

Illinois is in the north central part of the United States. The city of Cairo at the southern tip of Illinois is about 500 miles from the Gulf of Mexico. Rockford near the northern border is about 400 miles from Canada. The state is about 750 miles from the Atlantic Ocean and 1,800 miles from the Pacific.

Landforms

Glaciers that overran the area during the Ice Age helped to form most of Illinois. Like huge bulldozers the glaciers leveled off hills and filled in valleys. They carried vast quantities of earth material, which was left on the land as the ice melted. When the last glaciers disappeared, most of Illinois had become quite level. But there are many areas of hills and valleys, sharp bluffs, and bare rock. These varied surface features are included in four natural regions—the Central Lowland, the Interior Low Plateaus, the Ozark Plateaus, and the Coastal Plain.

The Central Lowland. Most of Illinois lies within a large region of the United States

THE LAND

LOCATION: Latitude—36° 58′ N to 42° 30′ N. **Longitude**—87° 30′ W to 91° 30′ W.
Wisconsin to the north, Lake Michigan on the northeast, Indiana on the east, Kentucky to the south, Missouri and Iowa on the west.

ELEVATION: Highest—Charles Mound, 1,241 ft. **Lowest**—On the Mississippi River below Cairo, 279 ft.

LANDFORMS: The Central Lowland covering most of the state; the Interior Low Plateaus, the Ozark Plateaus, and the Coastal Plain in the extreme south.

SURFACE WATERS: Major rivers—Mississippi, Ohio, Wabash, Illinois, Kaskaskia, Sangamon, Rock, Des Plaines. **Major man-made lakes**—Carlyle Reservoir, Shelbyville Reservoir, Rend, Crab Orchard, Springfield, Decatur, Bloomington. **Largest natural lakes**—Fox (in the Chain-O′-Lakes) and Calumet.

CLIMATE: Temperature—July average, from 75° F. in the north to 80° in the south; maximum above 100°. January average, from 24° in the north to 36° in the south; minimum below zero. **Precipitation**—Annual, 32–48 in.; maximum in spring and early summer. Snowfall varies from 30 in. in the north to 10 in. in the south. **Growing season**—Varies from less than 160 days in the north to more than 200 days in the south.

known as the Central Lowland. It is made up of several sections. The sections in Illinois are called the Till Plains, the Driftless Area, and the Great Lakes Plain.

The Till Plains cover most of the state. In this area glaciers from the north left thick deposits of earth material, or till. These deposits formed a flat to gently rolling surface, broken here and there by low, broad ridges. Ridges made by glaciers are called moraines.

The Driftless Area is in the extreme northwestern corner of the state. It is the only part of the Central Lowland in Illinois that was not covered and smoothed by glaciers. Long ago streams cut through the land to produce the

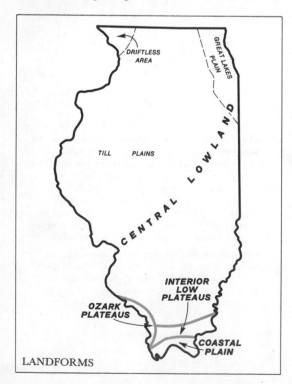

LANDFORMS

rough, hilly surface. Now streams flow in deep, V-shaped valleys. High bluffs border the floodplains of the Mississippi. Charles Mound in this area is the highest point in the state.

The Great Lakes Plain borders Lake Michigan in the northeastern part of the state. During the Ice Age this part of Illinois was the bottom of an ancient lake. Today it is a level area that dips slightly toward Lake Michigan. The land is drained by the Chicago and the Calumet rivers. These small, sluggish streams have been dredged to form ship canals. The plain is surrounded by a gently rolling wooded area called the Valparaiso Moraine.

The Interior Low Plateaus. This region of Illinois is sometimes called the Shawnee Hills. It is made up of hill lands that stretch for about 75 miles across the southern part of the state. The area is rugged and heavily forested. Streams flow in deep, narrow valleys.

The Ozark Plateaus. A very small section of the Ozark Plateaus enters Illinois from Mis-souri. It extends in a narrow strip along the Mississippi River in the southwestern part of the state. The high, scenic bluffs along the river are an important feature of this region.

The Coastal Plain. The southernmost part of Illinois lies within a great region of the United States known as the Coastal Plain. The floodplains of the Ohio, the Mississippi, and the Cache rivers meet in this part of the state. These floodplains are low and are subject to floods when the rivers rise. There are many small lakes and swampy areas in this part of the state.

Rivers and Lakes

Although it is an inland state, Illinois is somewhat like an island. Large rivers surround it to the west, south, and east. It has a 60-mile shoreline on Lake Michigan.

The Mississippi River forms the western boundary and drains 98 percent of the state. Tributaries of the Mississippi include the Illinois, the Rock, the Kaskaskia, and the

The lights of Chicago's modern skyline are reflected in the waters of Lake Michigan.

The Chicago Circle Campus of the University of Illinois.

Ohio rivers. The Ohio River provides a natural boundary in the south and the southeast. The Wabash, a large tributary of the Ohio, forms part of the eastern boundary.

The Spoon River flows into the Illinois River. It is a small river, but its valley has become famous. In the early 1900's the poet Edgar Lee Masters wrote a collection of poems called the *Spoon River Anthology*. The poems tell the story of persons who lived in the area.

Illinois' natural lakes were formed by glaciers. Many such lakes occur in the moraines north of Chicago. The best-known are Fox, Grass, and Pistakee—lakes that make up a group called Chain-O'-Lakes. Other lakes occur in the floodplains of the major rivers. Lake Peoria is really a wide place in the Illinois River.

The man-made lakes were created by dams built across some of the major rivers. These lakes are especially important in central and southern Illinois. Their main purpose is to provide water for nearby cities. They also make good places for recreation. The Crab Orchard National Wildlife Refuge is a paradise for the nature lover. It surrounds Crab Orchard Lake near Carbondale.

Climate

Illinois is in the center of the North American continent. It has a typically continental climate. The southern part of the state has hot, humid summers. The winters are cold and changeable, although temperatures are usually above freezing. Central Illinois and northern Illinois also have hot summers, but the winters are more severe than in the south.

All parts of the state get enough rain and melted snow to grow a variety of crops. Precipitation varies from 48 inches in the south to 32 inches in the area north of Chicago. Most of the precipitation comes as rain during the warm half of the year. Thunderstorms are frequent in summer, and freezing rains often fall in central Illinois in winter. Severe storms in the form of tornadoes and hailstorms occur most often in the spring. Snow covers the ground during much of the winter in northern Illinois, but the ground is free of snow for long periods in the south.

The growing season ranges from more than 200 days a year in the far south to less than 160 days in the north.

Natural Resources

The most important natural resources in Illinois are its soils, minerals, and water supplies. Others include forests, wildlife, and scenic attractions.

Soils. The soils of Illinois are among the best in the world. There are three major groups—grassland soils, forest soils, and alluvial, or floodplain, soils.

The grassland soils in central and northern

Illinois are rich and dark in color. The decay of tall grass that once grew in this area helped make the soil rich. The forest soils are yellow to brown in color. They are found mainly on the hill lands of southern and northwestern Illinois. Generally these are less fertile than grassland soils. Alluvial soils occur in the floodplains of the rivers, where sediments have been deposited. These soils vary in color and fertility. Floods are a yearly problem where there are alluvial soils.

Minerals. Illinois has a substantial amount of mineral wealth. The minerals are of three general types—the mineral fuels, the metallic minerals, and the nonmetallic, or earthy, minerals. Coal, oil, and natural gas are mineral fuels. Enormous coal-bearing formations underlie the whole southern two thirds of the state. Illinois' supply of oil will not last as long as its reserves of coal. In the 1960's coal replaced oil as the state's most valuable mineral. Small quantities of lead and zinc are found in the southern part of Illinois and in the northwest. Earthy substances of great importance are limestone, sand and gravel, fluorspar, and clay. Fluorspar is mined with lead and zinc in southern Illinois. The others are found in many parts of the state.

Water. The water resources include the rivers, lakes, and underground supplies from deep wells. All are important because they furnish water for household and industrial uses. Water resources are conserved by dams, which hold water in reservoirs until it is needed. The rivers and lakes provide water transportation and places for recreation.

Forests. Most of the forests are in the hill lands of southern Illinois. Other forested areas are found in the northwest and along most of the larger rivers. The forests supply lumber, fence posts, and firewood. They are also important as places for recreation and as a home for wildlife. The oak is the most plentiful tree, but hickory, walnut, sycamore, maple, and cottonwood are also important. Some cypress trees grow in the extreme south.

Wildlife. Illinois' wildlife includes a variety of small animals and birds. Rabbits, squirrels, quails, pheasants, ducks, and geese are numerous. Deer are found in the forests of southern and northern Illinois. Carp and catfish abound in the large rivers. The most popular game fish is the largemouth bass.

▶ THE PEOPLE AND THEIR WORK

Most of the earliest settlers of Illinois came from Kentucky, Tennessee, Virginia, and the Carolinas. They made their homes in the southern part of the state. Northern and central Illinois were settled later. People from New England and immigrants from Germany, Great Britain, and Scandinavia came to these areas between 1830 and 1850. Large numbers of Italians and Poles came to northern Illinois between 1870 and 1920. Since 1930 many people have moved to Illinois from states to the south, and this movement still goes on.

Where the People Live

More than four fifths of the people live in urban places. Over half the people live in the Chicago area. Many of the counties in southern Illinois are sparsely inhabited. The people of this area are moving to other parts of the state. Shifts in population are taking place in northern Illinois as great numbers move to the suburbs of the large cities.

Industries and Products

Agriculture was Illinois' earliest source of wealth. But for almost a century more money has come from manufacturing than from crops and livestock.

Manufacturing. Most of the manufacturing is done in northern Illinois, especially in the Chicago area. Other important industrial centers are Rockford, Peoria, Rock Island and Moline, Decatur, La Salle and Peru, Springfield, and the cities in the East St. Louis area.

The iron and steel industry of northeastern Illinois and northwestern Indiana is one of the largest in the United States. This basic industry furnishes the metals needed to make hundreds of products. Illinois has long been a leading producer of farm machinery, construction and earth-moving equipment, freight cars, diesel engines, and other transportation equipment. The many factories in the state also turn out tools and dies, electrical machinery, radio and television sets, pianos, and household appliances. Illinois is second only to New York in the printing and publishing industry.

Illinois' mines, quarries, and oil fields supply raw materials for a number of important industries. Limestone is used to manufacture cement. Millions of barrels of cement are

ILLINOIS

WISCONSIN

A · 92° · B · 91° · C · 90° · D · 89° · E · 88° · F · 87°

Janesville
Beloit
Racine
Kenosha
Zion

Dubuque
Galena
×Charles
Mound
1,241 ft.
Cedarville
Waukegan

1 · Freeport · **Rockford** · Belvidere · Woodstock · Glencoe · 1
Wilmette
Evanston
Skokie

Cedar
Rapids
Mount
Carroll
Oregon
Carpentersville
Des
Plains
Park Ridge

42° · Thomson · Elgin · Sycamore · Elmhurst · **Oak Park** · 42°
Cicero

Morrison
Dixon
De Kalb
Geneva
Wheaton
Berwyn
Chicago

Davenport
Sterling
Aurora
East Chicago
Michigan
City

2 · East
Moline · Yorkville · Gary · 2
Moline
Des
Plaines R.
Hammond

**Rock
Island**
Princeton
Ottawa
Morris
Joliet
Park
Forest

Cambridge
Peru
La Salle
Oglesby
Hennepin
Kankakee

Aledo
Kewanee

IOWA
Toulon
Streator
Kankakee
INDIANA

41° · Oquawka · Lacon · 41°
Monmouth
Galesburg
Pontiac
Watseka

Nauvoo
Lake
Peoria
Eureka
Lafayette

Carthage
Peoria
Creve Coeur
Lake
Bloomington
Paxton

3 · Canton · Pekin · **Normal** · Rantoul · 3
Lewistown
Bloomington

Macomb
Havana

Rushville
Lincoln
Clinton
Champaign
Danville

40° · Petersburg · Salt
Creek · Monticello · Urbana · 40°
Quincy
Mount
Sterling
Virginia
Decatur
Bement
Paris

Hannibal
New
Salem
Springfield⊛
Lake
Decatur
Tuscola

4 · Pittsfield · Jacksonville · Lake
Springfield · Sullivan · Charleston · Terre
Haute · 4
Winchester
Taylorville
Mattoon
Marshall

Carrollton
Shelbyville
Pana
Toledo
Hunt
Robinson

Carlinville
Hillsboro
Effingham

39° · Hardin · Vandalia · Newton · 39°
Jerseyville
Greenville
Olney
Lawrenceville

Alton
Edwardsville
Louisville

Florissant
Granite City
Carlyle
Salem
Mount
Carmel

5 · University City · **East St. Louis** · Centralia · Albion · 5
St. Louis
O'Fallon
Belleville
Fairfield

Kirkwood
Waterloo
Nashville
Mount Vernon

Prairie du
Rocher
Pinckneyville
McLeansboro
Carmi

38° · Kaskaskia · Benton · Evansville · 38°
Chester
Owensboro

Murphysboro
Marion
Harrisburg

6 · Carbondale · Crab Orchard
Lake · Shawneetown · **KENTUCKY** · 6
Cape
Girardeau
Jonesboro
Elizabethtown
Vienna
Golconda

Metropolis
Cairo
Mound
City
Paducah

7 · 37° · 37° · 7
A · 91° · B · 90° · C · 89° · D · 88° · E · 87° · F

**LAKE
MICHIGAN**

Moquoketa River
Wapsipinicon River
Mississippi River
Rock River
Fox
Des Plaines R.
Kankakee River
Tippecanoe River
Freeman
Lake

Cedar River
Illinois River
Spoon River
Mackinaw River

Des Moines River
Sangamon River

Missouri River
Salt River
Kaskaskia River
Little Wabash River
Embarras River
Wabash River
White River

Gasconade River
Mississippi River
Ohio River
Green River

Cache River
Ohio River
Kentucky
Lake

MISSOURI

Statute Miles
0 10 20 30 40 50 60

N

INDEX TO ILLINOIS MAP

produced each year in plants at Oglesby, La Salle, and Dixon. Many plants make brick, tile, and pottery from clay. Silica sand is used to manufacture glass products at Ottawa, Alton, Streator, and Chicago. Small oil refineries operate in the oil fields near Centralia, Pana, Robinson, and Lawrenceville. The large refineries are near Chicago and East St. Louis. These large plants use petroleum imported by pipelines from other states. They produce gasoline, heating oil, lubricating oils, and various chemicals.

Food processing is one of the most important industries in the Chicago area. Chicago once was the meat-packing center of the world. Although it no longer has that distinction, meat-packing is still important in Chicago as well as in East St. Louis and Peoria. Illinois is the nation's leading maker of candy, and it ranks high in production of another delicious food—ice cream. Thousands of people are employed in industries that process corn, soybeans, and other grains. Decatur is known as the soybean capital of the world because of its large soybean-processing plants.

Mining. Coal is Illinois' most important mineral. Most of the large coal mines are in western and southern Illinois. Coal is mostly used by utilities to generate electricity. Oil, second to coal in value, comes from an area southeast of Springfield. Southern Illinois produces fluorspar, which is used in metal industries and is also a source of fluoride, which is used in the drinking water of many communities.

Agriculture. Illinois ranks high among the states in agricultural production. One reason is that a large part of the total area is in farmland. Illinois also has a fortunate combination of fertile soil, level land, a climate that favors a variety of crops, and good transportation to nearby markets.

Most of the best farmland is in the glaciated areas in the northern two thirds of the state. The owner of a farm in this part of Illinois may have more than $100,000 invested in his land and machinery. Farm income is high when compared with farm incomes in most other states. As a result Illinois farmers generally have a high standard of living. But there are parts of Illinois that are not so fortunate. Much of the hill land of southern Illinois is not very productive. Here farm incomes are low.

Farmers in Illinois grow many field crops, but they are best known for grains. Illinois is the nation's leading producer of soybeans. It ranks second only to Iowa in corn. Soybeans are grown throughout most of the central and the southern parts of the state. The Corn Belt extends across central Illinois. Oats are an important crop in most of the northern two thirds of the state. Wheat is grown in the central and south sections. Other grain crops include rye, barley, buckwheat, and popcorn.

Much of the grain that is grown north and west of the Illinois River is fed to livestock. Beef cattle and hogs together make up about 40 percent of the value of all agricultural products. Dairy products are especially important in northern Illinois and around East St. Louis. Farmers in some parts of the state specialize in poultry and eggs.

WHAT ILLINOIS PRODUCES

MANUFACTURED GOODS: Construction and other kinds of machinery; processed foods, principally grain mill products, beverages, and bakery products; electrical equipment and supplies; fabricated metal products; basic steel and other primary metal products; printing and publishing matter; chemicals and allied products; transportation equipment; instruments of various kinds; stone, clay, and glass products; paper and allied products; rubber and plastic products; petroleum and coal products; apparel; furniture and fixtures.

AGRICULTURAL PRODUCTS: Corn, hogs, cattle and calves, soybeans, milk, wheat, eggs, horticultural specialties, oats, sheep and lambs, hay, sweet corn.

MINERALS: Bituminous coal, petroleum, stone, sand and gravel, cement, fluorspar, clays, zinc.

Truck farms near the large cities produce a variety of fruits and vegetables. Vegetables for canning and quick-freezing are grown in several parts of the state. Calhoun County is well known for apple orchards.

Transportation and Communication

Good transportation has helped Illinois to grow and prosper. From early days it has been easy to build roads and railroads across Illinois' level prairies. The great rivers that border the state have always provided excellent transportation by water. Today Illinois is the center of a vast network of railroads and highways, waterways, and airways.

Illinois is a leading state in railroad transportation. The railroads operate over more than 10,000 miles of main-line track. These lines extend into almost every county of the state. Chicago is the rail center of the United States. Other large railroad centers are the East St. Louis area and Peoria.

Many well-known highways cross Illinois. Among them are U.S. 66 and U.S. 40. Hundreds of miles of new federal interstate highways have been built throughout the state. Toll roads and expressways are especially important in the Chicago area.

The two largest inland water systems in the United States flank Illinois. On the northeast is the Great Lakes system, which connects with the Atlantic Ocean through the St. Lawrence Seaway. On the west is the Mississippi River, which empties into the Gulf of Mexico.

More than a century ago the state built the Illinois and Michigan Canal to link the Great Lakes with the Mississippi. This canal is not used very much today. Boats going from Lake Michigan to the Mississippi now follow the 325-mile Illinois Waterway. This waterway makes use of the Sanitary and Ship Canal in the Chicago area, the Des Plaines River, and the Illinois River. The Calumet Sag Channel is also part of the system. It links the waterway with Lake Calumet and the important industrial district of south Chicago and the surrounding area.

When the St. Lawrence Seaway was completed in 1959, Lake Michigan and the other Great Lakes became, in effect, an inland sea. Ocean vessels can now dock at Navy Pier in Chicago and at other points in the area.

Harvesting corn, Illinois' most important field crop.

Chicago is the airlines crossroads of the United States. More planes and passengers pass through O'Hare International Airport in Chicago than through any other airport in the country.

Every large town in Illinois has a newspaper and many have daily papers. Chicago's major dailies include the *Tribune, News, Sun-Times, American,* and *Today.* Other leading dailies in the state are the Bloomington *Pantagraph,* the Peoria *Journal Star,* and the *Illinois State Journal,* published at Springfield. Large cities have television stations, and many of the smaller towns have radio stations.

▶ **EDUCATION**

Before Illinois became a separate territory, it was part of a large area called the Northwest Territory. This large territory was governed under federal laws passed in 1785 and 1787. One very important provision of these laws was that land be set aside to support education in the territory and in the states that would be created from it.

Schools and Colleges

Illinois became a separate territory in 1809 and a state in 1818. In 1845 the state passed a law allowing taxes to be levied for public education. Ten years later a system of free public schools was established. Today public schools operate in more than 1,000 school districts. There are also many private and parochial schools.

Illinois has more than 80 colleges and universities and one half as many junior colleges. The University of Illinois is one of the largest state-supported universities in the nation. The main campus is situated in the cities of Urbana and Champaign. Another campus is in Chicago. Southern Illinois University at Carbondale is the second largest public university in the state. It operates a large branch campus at Edwardsville near St. Louis. Other large state universities are Northern, Eastern, Western, and Illinois State, at De Kalb, Charleston, Macomb, and Normal respectively.

Well-known private colleges and universities are the University of Chicago, De Paul University, Loyola University, and the Illinois Institute of Technology, all in Chicago, and Northwestern University in Evanston. Smaller schools include Knox College at Galesburg, Bradley University at Peoria, Illinois Wesleyan University at Bloomington, Wheaton College at Wheaton, Augustana College at Rock Island, and Millikin University at Decatur.

Libraries

More than 400 public libraries supply books to the people of Illinois. The first free public library opened in 1839. The Chicago Public Library was started after the Chicago fire in 1871. It is the largest public library in the state. The John Crerar Library in Chicago is well known for its science collections. The Newberry Library, also in Chicago, is noted for its rare books and special collections in history, music, and literature. The Illinois State Historical Library in Springfield has large collections pertaining to Abraham Lincoln, the Civil War, and state and local history.

Fine Arts and Museums

Illinois has several cultural institutions of national interest. Among them are Chicago's symphony orchestra and opera company. The following are the leading museums in the state:

The Art Institute of Chicago contains collections of French, Dutch, Italian, and American masterpieces. It is especially noted for its fine collection of French paintings from the late 1800's and early 1900's. The Art Institute has well-known art and drama schools.

The Chicago Natural History Museum has many famous exhibits, including one that shows the races of man. Other displays feature botany, zoology, and geology.

The Museum of Science and Industry in Chicago occupies a restored building of the World's Columbian Exposition of 1893. The many exhibits show science, technology, and industry at work. Visitors may operate the machines in some of the exhibits. A replica of an Illinois coal mine is one of the museum's special features.

The Illinois State Museum of Natural History and Art is in Springfield. The collections cover science, natural history, and the fine arts. The museum provides many services for the state. These include a "museumobile"—a traveling museum with more than 20 exhibits—a department that lends films and other materials to schools, and workshops for teachers and directors of small museums.

▶ PLACES OF INTEREST

Illinois has more than 80 state park areas. Some of these areas preserve historic places or places of unusual beauty. Most of them pro-

The reconstructed village of New Salem in Lincoln's New Salem State Park.

vide places for outdoor recreation. Illinois also has one national forest—the Shawnee National Forest—and numerous state and national wildlife refuges and conservation areas. Chicago and northeastern Illinois have miles of sandy beaches along Lake Michigan.

The Lincoln Trail in Illinois

The state has preserved more than a dozen places associated with Abraham Lincoln. The many persons who visit these shrines may feel that they are following in Lincoln's footsteps.

Lincoln Trail Monument near Lawrenceville stands on the site where the Lincoln family entered Illinois in 1830. The monument portrays the family, with young Abraham Lincoln walking beside the covered wagon.

Lincoln Trail Homestead State Park near Decatur preserves the site of the Lincoln family's first home in Illinois.

Lincoln's New Salem State Park near Petersburg contains the reconstructed village of New Salem. Cabins, shops, and a schoolhouse have been restored and furnished to appear as they did when Lincoln lived in the town during the 1830's. Each year Robert Sherwood's play *Abe Lincoln in Illinois* is presented in the park. The grave of Ann Rutledge is in the cemetery at the edge of Petersburg. Ann Rutledge, daughter of the innkeeper at New Salem, was said to have been engaged to Lincoln. She died at the age of 19.

Lincoln Log Cabin State Park, south of Charleston, contains the reconstructed cabin where Lincoln's father and stepmother spent the last years of their lives. Both are buried in a cemetery nearby.

Moore Home State Memorial is also near Charleston. At this home Lincoln visited his stepmother just before going to Washington for his inauguration as president.

Vandalia State House State Memorial at Vandalia preserves the building, once the state capitol, where Lincoln served as a legislator.

Bryant Cottage State Memorial in Bement is the house in which Stephen A. Douglas and Lincoln are said to have conferred about their famous debates.

Lincoln, seat of Logan County, is the only town that was named for Abraham Lincoln before he became famous. He helped plan the town and christened it with watermelon juice.

Lincoln Home State Memorial and **Lincoln Tomb State Memorial** are the most famous of the Lincoln shrines in Springfield. The home is

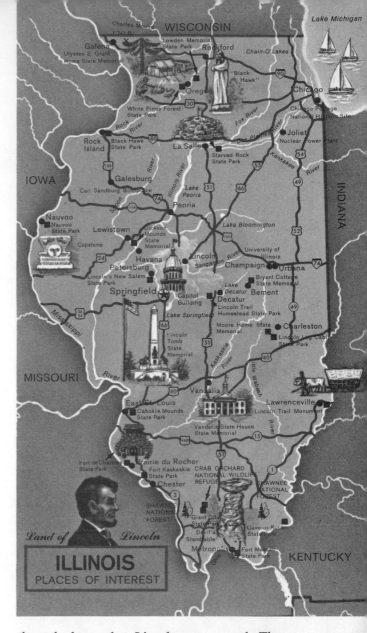

the only home that Lincoln ever owned. The tomb memorial contains the tomb of Lincoln and crypts in which Mrs. Lincoln and three of their children are buried.

Other Historic or Scenic Places

Almost everywhere in the state there are reminders of prehistoric Indians, of the early French occupation of Illinois, or of later events in Illinois' history.

Black Hawk State Park is on the Rock River near Rock Island. A museum in the park contains relics of the Sauk and the Fox Indian tribes. Each Labor Day weekend members of these tribes return to the park for a powwow.

Cave-in-Rock State Park on the Ohio River is

named for a huge cave in the river bank. The cave was once the home of prehistoric Indians. Later it was a hideaway for river pirates.

Chicago Portage National Historic Site near Chicago preserves a section of the portage discovered by Marquette and Jolliet. (A portage is an overland route between navigable waters. Boats and cargo are carried over this route.) This historic portage was used by French and American pioneers to join the waters of the Mississippi with the waters of the Great Lakes.

Dickson Mounds State Memorial is in the Spoon River valley between Lewistown and Havana. It contains an unusual display of mounds that have been excavated. More than 200 human skeletons have been uncovered in the mounds. They lie just as they were found. Other Indian mounds may be seen at **Cahokia Mounds State Park** near East St. Louis.

Fort Kaskaskia State Park near Chester includes the site of the historic fort first built by the French in 1736. The fort stood on a summit overlooking the site of Kaskaskia, first capital of Illinois. **Fort de Chartres State Park** near Prairie du Rocher and **Fort Massac State Park** near Metropolis preserve the locations of other early French forts.

Giant City State Park, south of Crab Orchard Lake, contains unusual rock formations. To the imaginative viewer these formations look like a city built of stone.

Ulysses S. Grant Home State Memorial at Galena preserves the house that the people of Galena gave to General Grant when he returned from the Civil War.

Lowden Memorial State Park on the Rock River near the city of Oregon contains a towering statue of an Indian. The sculptor, Lorado Taft, had no one Indian in mind. But many people call the statue Black Hawk after the famous Indian chief.

Nauvoo State Park near Nauvoo is the setting each September of a pageant called the Wedding of the Wine and the Cheese. The pageant is based on customs brought to Nauvoo by French settlers in 1849. These settlers introduced the growing of grapes and the making of wine. But Nauvoo's chief fame is associated with the Mormons. In 1839 Joseph Smith, founder of the Mormon Church, started a community at the town of Commerce. He renamed it Nauvoo, meaning "beautiful place." By 1845 it was the largest town in Illinois, with a population of more than 20,000. But trouble developed between the Mormons and the other townspeople. Joseph Smith and his brother were killed, and the Mormons were forced to leave Nauvoo. Today several old Mormon homes in Nauvoo are open to visitors. The history of the Mormons is included in Volume M.

Carl Sandburg Birthplace at Galesburg is the restored cottage where Carl Sandburg, famous poet and biographer of Abraham Lincoln, was born.

White Pines Forest State Park near Oregon is notable for its fine grove of white pines. It is a favorite place for fishing and camping.

Annual Events

Some of Illinois' annual events attract national or international attention. Others are of local interest.

Easter—Easter Sunrise Service at Soldier Field in Chicago; Passion Play, Zion.

Summer—Watermelon Festival, Havana; Illi-

Starved Rock, a huge sandstone cliff on the banks of the Illinois River.

nois State Fair, Springfield; International Trade Fair, Chicago.

September—Melon Day, Thomson; Festival of the Grape, Nauvoo.

November—Chrysanthemum Show, Chicago.

December—International Livestock Exposition, Chicago.

▶ CITIES

Illinois' largest cities are Chicago, Rockford, Peoria, Springfield, and Decatur, in that order. Suburbs surround all these cities and increase the size of the urban areas.

Springfield

The capital city, Springfield, is located in central Illinois. It is in the heart of the Corn Belt as well as in an important coal-mining area. Industries in the city make tractors, clocks, radio parts, flour and cereal products, and beverages. Springfield has many places associated with Abraham Lincoln—his home, law offices, church, and tomb.

Pioneers from the south settled in the area in 1818, the year Illinois became a state. The settlement was incorporated as a town in 1832. It became the state capital in 1837.

Chicago

Chicago, largest city in Illinois and second largest city in the United States, is located on the southwestern shore of Lake Michigan. An article on Chicago is included in Volume C.

The tomb of Abraham Lincoln in Springfield.

Rockford

Illinois' second largest city got its name from its location—a ford across the Rock River. Rockford was founded in 1834 and incorporated as a city in 1853. Today it is the center of an important agricultural area. It is also one of the most highly industrialized cities in the state. It manufactures machine tools, farm implements, furniture, automobile parts, hand tools, and household appliances.

Other Cities

Peoria, located on the Illinois River, is important as a transportation center. It is widely known for the manufacture of heavy earth-moving equipment. Champaign and Urbana are twin cities in the center of a rich agricultural area. Chanute Air Force Base is at nearby Rantoul. Rock Island and Moline, together with Davenport across the Mississippi River in Iowa, make up one of the nation's great centers for the manufacturing of farm machinery.

Chicago has many suburbs. Evanston, Cicero, Oak Park, Skokie, and Arlington Heights are the largest. These places share the industrial activity of the area. They are also residential suburbs.

East St. Louis has strong ties with St.

COUNTIES

Louis, Missouri. Granite City and Alton are the largest Illinois cities near East St. Louis.

GOVERNMENT

Illinois' fourth state constitution was adopted by the voters of the state in 1970. Its effective date was July 1, 1971. Earlier state constitutions were adopted in 1818, 1848, and 1870. Each constitution has provided for a government made up of three branches. Each branch has duties assigned to it by the constitution.

The General Assembly makes the laws of the state. It is composed of the House of Representatives, which has 177 members, and the Senate, which has 59 members. Representatives are elected for 2-year terms, and senators are elected for 4-year terms. The General Assembly has regular sessions every year at the State House in Springfield.

The executive branch carries out the laws of the state. It is headed by a governor, elected for a 4-year term. The governor appoints the heads of a number of state departments. Other executive officials are elected by the people themselves. They are the lieutenant governor

(the governor's running mate), secretary of state, attorney general, treasurer, and auditor of public accounts.

The judicial branch is responsible for interpreting and applying the laws. This branch is made up of the state Supreme Court and various other courts. The Illinois judiciary was modernized in the 1960's, and the 1970 constitution incorporated those reforms in most respects.

FAMOUS PEOPLE

Illinoisans who have gained fame include Indian chiefs, presidents of the United States, plowmakers, poets, and statesmen.

Black Hawk (1767–1838), a chief of the Sauk Indians, was born near Rock Island. He is known for his struggle against the westward movement of settlers. In 1832 he led the Sauk and the Fox in a revolt known as the Black Hawk War. Later Black Hawk dictated his life story to an interpreter. The book, called *Autobiography of Black Hawk,* has become a classic.

Shadrach Bond (1773–1832) came to Illinois from Maryland in 1791. He was Illinois' first territorial delegate to Congress. In 1818 he was elected the first governor of the state.

John Deere (1804–86), born in Vermont, came to Illinois in 1837 and opened a blacksmith shop. At that time the prairie farmers were using plows with iron shares, or blades. With these plows it was hard to cut through the tough prairie sod, and the soil stuck to the blades. Deere developed a new kind of plow— a plow with a steel share. This plow opened the prairies to large-scale farming.

Abraham Lincoln (1809–65), 16th president of the United States, made his home in Illinois from 1830 to 1861. A biography of Lincoln is included in Volume L.

Ulysses S. Grant (1822–85), 18th president of the United States and commander of the victorious Union armies during the Civil War, was born in Ohio. He came to Illinois in 1860 to work in his brothers' leather store at Galena. A biography of Grant appears in Volume G.

Jane Addams (1860–1935), born in Cedar-

The State House in Springfield.

ville, was a famous social worker who founded Hull House in Chicago. A biography of Jane Addams is included in Volume A.

Julius Rosenwald (1862–1932), president of Sears, Roebuck and Company and a leading developer of the mail-order business in the United States, was born in Springfield. He gave millions of dollars to education and charity.

Adlai E. Stevenson (1900–65) was governor of Illinois from 1949 to 1953 and was twice the candidate of the Democratic Party for president of the United States (1952 and 1956). His biography is included in Volume S.

Other persons well-known in government were born in Illinois or made their homes in the state. Everett Dirksen (Pekin) was minority leader of the United States Senate from 1959 until his death in 1969. Stephen A. Douglas (born in Vermont but long a resident of Illinois) and William Jennings Bryan (Salem) were orators and political leaders of earlier times. Two other well-known senators from Illinois are Paul H. Douglas (Salem), who served from 1949 to 1967, and Charles H. Percy (born in Florida), who succeeded Douglas. Biographies of Bryan and Stephen A. Douglas are included in Volumes B and D.

During the late 1800's Illinois was the home of many world-famous industrialists and civic leaders. They included meat packers Philip Armour and Gustavus Swift, mail-order merchant Aaron Montgomery Ward, and department-store owner Marshall Field. Others were George Pullman, designer and manufacturer of the railroad sleeping car, and Cyrus McCormick, developer of the reaper and manufacturer of farm machinery. All these persons were born in other states.

Many famous writers have lived in Illinois. Among those born in the state are novelists John Dos Passos (Chicago) and Ernest Hemingway (Oak Park), journalists Finley Peter Dunne and John Gunther (Chicago), and poets Vachel Lindsay (Springfield), Archibald MacLeish (Glencoe), and Carl Sandburg (Galesburg). Biographies of Hemingway and Sandburg appear in Volumes H and S.

Persons in the entertainment world who were born in Illinois include actor Ralph Bellamy (Chicago), actor and folk singer Burl Ives (Hunt), comedian Jack Benny (Waukegan), and band leader Benny Goodman (Chicago). Walt Disney, creator of Donald Duck and Mickey Mouse, was born in Chicago.

▶ HISTORY

The earliest inhabitants of Illinois were probably prehistoric Indians called mound builders. The mounds that they built have been found in several places in Illinois.

When Illinois was first explored, many different tribes of the great Algonkian family of Indians lived in the area. The Sauk, Fox, Potawatomi, and other tribes lived in northern Illinois. The Miami were in east central Illinois, and the Shawnee in the southeast. A confederation of tribes known as the Illinewek lived in the valley of the Illinois River. The Peoria, Cahokia, and Kaskaskia Indians all belonged to this confederation.

Exploration and Early Settlement

The first explorers to enter the Illinois territory were Frenchmen. In 1673 Louis Jolliet and Jacques Marquette explored part of the area. A few years later La Salle and his lieutenant, Henri de Tonti, explored much of Illinois country. They were trying to find the mouth of the Mississippi River. In 1680 La Salle founded Fort Crève Coeur near Lake Peoria. Two years later he built Fort St. Louis at Starved Rock. This fort was abandoned in 1691 or 1692, when a second Fort St. Louis was built at Peoria.

This era of exploration opened the way to more permanent settlements. The first Illinois towns were Jesuit missions or French trading posts. The most important of these settlements were Cahokia near East St. Louis, built about 1699, and Kaskaskia, built about 1703. Fort Kaskaskia, Fort de Chartres, and Fort Massac (originally spelled Massiac) were constructed to protect these settlements.

Illinois Becomes a State

In 1763 Great Britain won control of a large area that included Illinois. But because of an Indian uprising, the British could not take possession until 1765. The British ruled the area from that date until the Revolutionary War. Then in 1778 George Rogers Clark of Virginia and a group of frontiersmen called the Long Knives marched to Kaskaskia. They captured the town for Virginia in a bloodless battle. Virginia claimed the territory but turned its claim over to the federal government after the war.

In 1787 Illinois was included in a large area northwest of the Ohio River known as the Northwest Territory. When Congress created the Indiana territory in 1800, Illinois was included in that territory. In 1809 the Illinois territory was created, and Ninian Edwards became the territorial governor. Illinois was admitted to the Union as the 21st state in 1818. The first capital was Kaskaskia, and Shadrach Bond was the first governor. The capital was moved to Vandalia in 1820 and to Springfield in 1837.

IMPORTANT DATES

1673 Marquette and Jolliet explored Illinois.

1680 La Salle built Fort Crève Coeur near the present site of Peoria.

1699 French missionaries started a settlement at Cahokia near East St. Louis.

1703 The French founded Kaskaskia, 60 miles south of Cahokia.

1763 France ceded the Illinois country to the British.

1778 George Rogers Clark captured Kaskaskia and Cahokia from the British during the Revolutionary War.

1787 Ordinance of 1787 governed Illinois as part of the Northwest Territory.

1803 Fort Dearborn built at the mouth of the Chicago River.

1809 Illinois became a separate territory.

1818 December 3, Illinois admitted to the Union as the 21st state.

1832 Indians defeated in Black Hawk War and removed from Illinois.

1833 Chicago incorporated as a village.

1837 Springfield selected as the state capital.

1848 Illinois and Michigan Canal completed; first railroad entered Chicago.

1858 Lincoln and Douglas held famous debates in campaign for the United States Senate.

1860 Abraham Lincoln elected 16th president of the United States.

1889 Jane Addams founded Hull House in Chicago.

1893 World's Columbian Exposition held in Chicago.

1900 Completion of Sanitary and Ship Canal, a part of the Illinois Waterway, in the Chicago area.

1922 Opening of Calumet Sag Channel, another part of the Illinois Waterway.

1933 Century of Progress Exposition held in Chicago; Illinois Waterway to the Mississippi completed.

1942 Atomic Age began with the world's first successful nuclear chain reaction, produced at the University of Chicago.

1959 Opening of St. Lawrence Seaway.

1964 Modernization of state court system (authorized by constitutional amendment in 1962) went into effect.

1970 A new state constitution was adopted by the voters, effective in 1971.

Illinois Grows

Northern Illinois was the first part of the state to be explored. But for many years northern Illinois lagged behind southern Illinois in settlement. During most of the 1700's only a small trading post existed at the present site of Chicago. Settlement of the northern area continued to be slow until the opening of the Erie Canal in 1825. Another spur to settlement was the removal of the Indians to lands farther west.

In 1833 Chicago was a village of only 350 people. Four years later its population was about 4,000. The Illinois and Michigan Canal was started in 1836 and completed in 1848. It opened a trade route and helped Chicago and northern Illinois to grow.

East central Illinois was the last part of the state to be settled. Pioneers did not know how to deal with the tall grass and poor drainage. The lack of trees made it hard to build houses. And many people thought that if trees did not grow on the land, it was unfit for farming.

The coming of the railroads in the 1850's and the start of the Civil War changed the economy of Illinois. Farms grew bigger, and the new railroads carried the farm crops to the large cities. Grain was sold to the eastern states and to the federal government for feeding the Union armies. The Civil War also created a great demand for manufactured products. Illinois became a leader in food processing and in the manufacture of farm machinery and transportation equipment.

Farming, manufacturing, and trade all continued to develop through World War I and the 1920's. Chicago celebrated with a Century of Progress world's fair in 1933. In 1942, after the start of World War II, the first nuclear chain reaction took place at the University of Chicago. Illinois has continued to be an important atomic research center. Its industries keep on growing larger and becoming more efficient and complex.

The Future

The economic life of Illinois is founded solidly on productive farming, rich fuel deposits, and varied industry. With this solid base, Illinois is well prepared to meet the challenge of a nuclear-electronic age.

JAMES E. PATTERSON
Illinois State University

ILLUMINATED MANUSCRIPTS

Illuminated manuscripts are books that have been written and illustrated by hand. The word "illuminated" comes from *illuminare,* a Latin word that means "to light up." Some experts believe that the term was used because those who made illuminated manuscripts were trying to light up the word of God.

Illustrated books have been made throughout the ages. The ancient Egyptians made them, and, of course, they are still made by the modern printing press. But illuminated manuscripts are usually thought of as an art of the Middle Ages. This was an age when only a few people could read. The church fathers believed that pictures in a book would provide religious education to those who could not understand words. For the same reason, the beautiful churches and cathedrals of the age were also lavishly decorated.

Illuminated manuscripts were usually filled with pictures of religious events. Often the first letter of a new section was surrounded with decoration. These illustrations were called **miniatures**. They were called this partly because of their size (although many filled a whole page) but mainly because their main color was often minium, a red pigment that comes from lead. Almost all illuminated manuscripts were done in rich colors and gold.

Although most illuminated manuscripts were created in Christian monasteries, not all decorations used had religious subjects. Pages were bordered with designs that made a frame for the text. Sometimes the designs were based on flowers and plants. Often the designs were geometric patterns—circles, triangles, squares, and so forth. The patterns had nothing at all to do with the text but were created only to decorate the page.

Early in the Middle Ages, pages of manuscripts were dyed purple. Then a **scribe** wrote the text in gold or silver ink. The manuscript was given next to the **illuminator**, who decorated it with **gouache** (a kind of thick watercolor paint) and gold leaf, made by beating a piece of gold until it became thinner than paper. The pages were made of parchment, the skin of a sheep or goat.

The first beautiful illuminated manuscripts

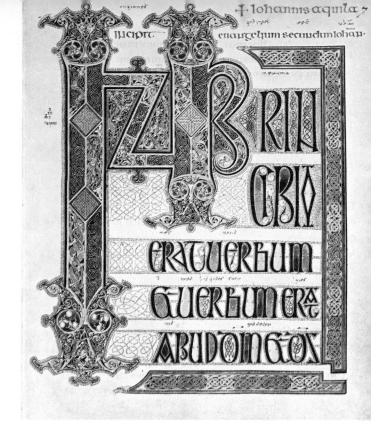

Initial page from the Lindisfarne Gospels, a manuscript made in 8th-century England. British Museum.

were probably made in the eastern part of the Roman Empire, later called the Byzantine Empire. Small groups of traveling artists, usually representing a palace or church, created these early manuscripts. Then, in the 6th century, writing rooms called **scriptoria** were built into monasteries. Monks became scribes and illuminators. At first they simply copied the old manuscripts but later they began making new books. During the following several centuries scriptoria were built in monasteries throughout Europe.

Around the middle of the 12th century, monasteries began to decline as centers of learning. They were replaced by universities. Illuminated manuscripts were then created by artists outside the church. Manuscripts were no longer copied but were created individually. Also, some people who were not church leaders began to grow richer. They wanted beautiful handmade books, but they did not want religious ones. Finally, in the 15th century, the modern printing press was invented. Woodcut illustrations that could be printed with the text replaced hand-painted pictures. There was no longer any need for illuminated manuscripts.

Above: Illumination showing Saint Luke, from the Gospel Book of Otto III, ruler of part of Germany about A.D. 1000. Bavarian State Library, Munich. Below: Illustration from *Le Cuer d'amours espris* ("The Heart of the Spirit of Love," 1457). Library, Vienne, France.

A page from a 16th-century Persian book of poems. British Museum.

Some very beautiful illuminated manuscripts were created in the Eastern world of Islam. There is little illustration in these Islamic manuscripts, however, because the religion discourages showing the human figure. Illumination of religious texts was made up of abstract ornament—designs that did not represent real people or things. Islamic artists worked mostly on **calligraphy**—the art of beautiful writing. The finest Islamic manuscripts were created in Persia between the 14th and 18th centuries. Some artists believed that it was all right to place illustrations in books that were not religious. For this reason there are many lovely illustrations in books of stories, poems, and fables.

ILLUSTRATION AND ILLUSTRATORS

Illustration is the art of telling a story with pictures. An illustrator is an artist who translates words into pictures that can be instantly understood. Illustrations have many purposes —to explain scientific facts, to describe new products in advertisements, to picture events in a story, to portray the main idea of a poem. When an illustration is successful, characters come to life and ideas are made clear.

▶ THE FIRST ILLUSTRATORS

The oldest known book containing writing and illustration was an Egyptian scroll that was made of papyrus, a part of a tall plant that grew along riverbanks. The people in the illustrations were shown in scenes of work and religious worship. The figures, always seen from a side view, were placed in rows above and below the writing.

Illustrated Parchment Books

The ancient Greeks illustrated papyrus scrolls in the style developed by the Egyptians. Then between A.D. 100 and 400, papyrus scrolls were replaced by books with pages of parchment made from the skin of goats and sheep. Gradually the style of illustration changed. Pictures were no longer fitted into small spaces, but often filled a whole page. The colored pictures illustrated stories of the Greek gods. The characters looked completely human, and the situations were drawn from real life. The Greeks and Romans illustrated plays, poems, and stories as well as scientific works on botany and astronomy.

Medieval Illustration

During the Middle Ages most books were made in monasteries. There prayer books and copies of the Bible were written and illustrated. Decoration of manuscripts with many colors and gold or silver is called **illumination**. The art of illumination flourished from the early Middle Ages until the invention of printing in the 15th century. The first letter of the first word in a new chapter was often decorated with figures. Sometimes the decoration was so detailed that a whole page was required for that one letter. There were fantastic trails of ivy, fruits, and flowers that

Woodcut illustrating fishing from *The Book of Hawking, Hunting, and Heraldry*, printed in England in 1496.

A page from Emperor Maximilian's prayer book (1515), illustrated with pen-and-ink drawings by Albrecht Dürer.

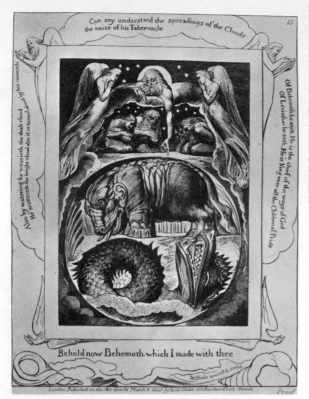

Page from *The Book of Job* (1825), which English artist William Blake designed, illustrated, and printed.

Sports of a Country Fair (1810) by Thomas Rowlandson, whose illustrations appeared in British journals.

twined from the first letter all around the margins of the pages.

Through the centuries Christian churches have been decorated with paintings of Bible stories. One of the purposes of these illustrations was to teach the lessons of Christianity to people who could not read. Illustrations in books often served the same purpose.

The Muslims did not encourage artists to illustrate the human figure in the Koran, their holy book. Beautiful gold and blue patterns decorated religious books made in Persia. Stories and poetry were illustrated with princes and princesses in fairy-tale worlds of blossoming flowers and trees. The illustrations were unshaded, and the figures showed little movement.

In China and Japan, **calligraphy** (fine writing) has always been considered as important an art as illustration. Many scrolls were illustrated.

▶ **ILLUSTRATIONS IN THE FIRST PRINTED BOOKS**

Fifteenth-century printed books were written and illustrated by the woodcut method. These religious books, first made in Germany and the Low Countries, had many illustrations and very little text because cutting pictures into the wood was easier than cutting letters. After they were printed, the illustrations were often colored by hand. The style of these pictures was still much like that of illuminated manuscripts.

A printing press with movable metal type was invented by Johann Gutenberg in Mainz, Germany, about 1440. Because the letters were reusable, a variety of books could be printed in a short period of time. Illustrations were still printed from wood blocks.

During the late 16th and 17th centuries, engravings and etchings were used for printing illustrations in books. These illustrations were elaborate and very detailed. Among the great artists of the time who did book illustration were Peter Paul Rubens (1577–1640) in Flanders, Rembrandt van Rijn (1606–99) in the Dutch republic, and Jacques Callot (1592–1635) in France.

▶ **THE 18TH AND 19TH CENTURIES**

In England, William Hogarth (1697–1764) was the most important illustrator of his time. His pictures were filled with details that described English society. For example, Hogarth attacked the many people who earned their living by flattering the rich. William Blake (1757–1827) not only wrote some of the most beautiful poems of his day but also illustrated them. He etched both the illustration and the text on the same printing plate so that the words became part of the design. He used thin, sharp lines for his strange, floating, twisting forms.

In the 19th century illustration flourished,

especially in books of stories and poetry. More than ever before, many great painters turned to illustration. In France, for example, Eugène Delacroix (1798–1863) illustrated Goethe's *Faust*.

Of all the artists who made fun of life and manners in late 18th-century England, Thomas Rowlandson (1756–1827) was among the most successful. His hearty, run-down characters were drawn with flowing, delicate lines.

Honoré Daumier (1808–79) was famous in his day for newspaper illustrations. He drew realistic pictures of life in Paris. He knew how to show the wickedness of a dishonest politician or the sweetness of a child sleeping in its mother's arms.

In the middle of the 19th century many illustrated magazines were started in the United States. Among the many fine artists who contributed to these magazines was Winslow Homer (1836–1910), whose wood engravings of the Civil War appeared in *Harper's Weekly*.

Toward the end of the century the quality and appearance of books suffered from the misuse of cheap printing methods. In England, William Morris (1834–96), the writer and designer, decided to improve book design by returning to early hand-printing processes

Above left: In 1838 George Cruikshank etched illustrations for *Oliver Twist*. Above right: *Excursion Train*, an 1864 newspaper lithograph by Honoré Daumier. Below: Winslow Homer's *The Bathe at Newport* appeared in *Harper's Weekly* in 1858.

One of many "Gibson girls." This illustration, *School Days*, is from Charles Dana Gibson's *Americans* (1900).

Captain Ahab, from a 1930 edition of Melville's *Moby Dick*, illustrated by Rockwell Kent.

such as the woodcut. His influence was felt all over Europe and continued into the 20th century.

▶ THE 20TH CENTURY

Since 1900 a few great artists have illustrated books. Sometimes artists have written their own texts. Henri Matisse wrote and illustrated *Jazz* (1947); Georges Rouault, *Circus of the Shooting Star* (1939).

Because of the rapid growth of magazines in the United States, there have been many new opportunities for illustrators. One of the most influential American magazine illustrators was Charles Dana Gibson (1867–1944). He created a "truly American girl" who was tall, pretty, and athletic. The "Gibson girl" became very popular, and American women tried to copy her simple style of dress.

The magazine illustrations by Walter Biggs (1886–1968) were of the same high quality as his fine paintings, and Edward A. Wilson (1886–   ) was an outstanding book illustrator. Rockwell Kent (1882–1971) was

known for his original book illustrations. He was able to work in a variety of media, including woodcut and pen and ink. The edition of *Moby Dick* he illustrated is a collector's classic.

Dean Cornwell (1892–1960) was known as a mural painter as well as an illustrator. His murals graced the walls of the General Motors Building, the first New York World's Fair, and the Lincoln Memorial. Cornwell's magazine and advertising illustration was notable for its careful attention to detail.

Floyd Davis (1896–1966) was one of the most effective illustrators of the period. He had a special talent for capturing the moods of his characters. Al Parker (1906–   ), who became known as the great innovator, inspired other illustrators. His active imagination could produce a new approach to layout and illustration every time he faced a new assignment. Carl Erickson (1891–1958), who signed his drawings "Eric," had an easy sense of style that made him the favorite of fashion magazines. The beautiful compositions and

Howard Pyle illustrated his *Book of Pirates* in 1921.

Walter Crane's cover for Nathaniel Hawthorne's book.

Rumpelstiltskin, a 1907 illustration by Arthur Rackham.

Kate Greenaway's Little Bo-peep from *Mother Goose* (1881).

Little Bo-peep has lost her sheep,
And can't tell where to find them;
Leave them alone, and they'll come home,
And bring their tails behind them.

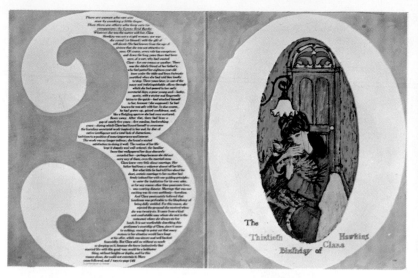

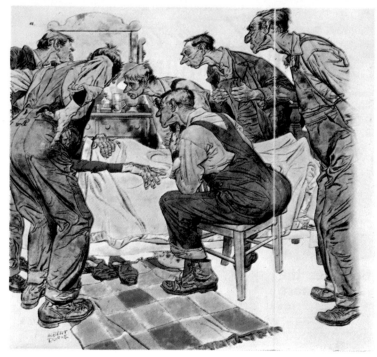

Above left: Illustration by Al Parker for a story in *McCall's* magazine (1965). Above right: Robert Peak's drawing for "The Brave One," a story in *Redbook* magazine (1962). Left: Albert Dorne illustrated "Six Greedy Loafers" in *Collier's* (1953). Below left: John Alcorn did the pictures for *Books!* (1962). Below right: "The Tree of Life," a story in *McCall's,* was illustrated with this picture by Bernie Fuchs (1965).

Harvey Schmidt's drawing for the CBS calendar (1962).

"If television can take responsibility for the way it provides a window on the world for little children... it can continue to provide the excitement of fairy stories and Westerns...without which life would be tame indeed..."

These words are excerpted from an article by Dr. Margaret Mead in TV GUIDE. The renowned anthropologist's probing and provocative study of the effect of television violence on children clearly reflects TV GUIDE's continuing interest in apprising its readers of the influence of television on their lives. Though program listings and profiles of performers are staple ingredients of the magazine, it is TV GUIDE's consistently authoritative coverage of every aspect of television that accounts for its editorial vigor. And its editorial vigor accounts for its astonishing growth— 56 regional editions now being published, advertising revenue for the first quarter of this year up 33% over the same period in 1959.

Best-selling weekly magazine in America...circulation 7,250,000

TV GUIDE

Advertisement for *TV Guide* by Austin Briggs (1960).

striking action drawings of Robert Fawcett (1903–67) won him great respect as an illustrator.

Harold von Schmidt (1893–   ) chose the western scene as his special subject. His vigorous depictions of charging Indians and saber-carrying cavalrymen made the epic story of the Old West come alive. Peter Helck (1893–   ) drew heroic illustrations of industrial America that appeared in all the leading magazines. He also delighted in making illustrations of antique cars and auto races. Jon Witcomb (1906–   ) and Coby Whitmore (1913–   ) became favorites of teen-agers because of their romantic drawings of young men and women.

The editorial and advertising art of Ben Stahl (1910–   ) had many of the characteristics of fine paintings. He successfully blended his gift for painting with the commercial demands of illustration.

Norman Rockwell (1894–   ) is surely the most beloved and most famous of all American illustrators. His work has probably been seen and appreciated by more people than that of any other illustrator in history.

In the 1950's the full impact of television was felt by magazines. They had to compete with this new form of mass entertainment. Magazine illustration developed to meet the challenge. Art directors eagerly welcomed young artists who could contribute something fresh and different. More than ever magazine and advertising art needed the touch of the fine artist. Well-established illustrators discovered that they had more freedom to do something unusual and personal.

Austin Briggs (1908–   ), who had long been a favorite with advertisers and magazine art directors, found that his seemingly casual drawing technique was in great demand. Bob Peak (1927–   ) and Bernie Fuchs (1932–   ) were able to communicate various moods. Their exciting new techniques and use of color became well-known.

The field of illustration benefited from a fresh desire on the part of art directors and editors to explore new frontiers. New color processes and technical improvements in printing made it possible for the commercial artist to realize effects that were once available only in handmade books.

Fashion drawing by Dorothy Hood (1965).

they took the bull by the horns

The whimsical creature shown above was one of a quartet of unusual ways that Mademoiselle Shoes illustrated their products in a recent advertising campaign—running only in The New Yorker. The advertisements, created by their agency, Irving Serwer Advertising, were designed to help Mademoiselle build a reputation for youthful style and craftsmanship among leading retailers and consumers. Said Irv Tober, Advertising Director of Mademoiselle: "Only The New Yorker could have handled this campaign and accomplished the desired results. Reaction to it was immediate and vigorous, with many favorable comments from important retail accounts, and widespread customer enthusiasm. The New Yorker has the atmosphere for us."

The New Yorker, No. 25 West 43rd Street, New York 36, New York • Other Advertising Offices: Chicago, San Francisco, Los Angeles, Atlanta, London

Tomi Ungerer's 1961 drawing for a Mademoiselle shoe ad.

Jonah and the whale, an illustration by Stas Pyka advertising an episode in the NBC television series Frontiers of Faith (1965).

A page from *The Witches of Venice,* written and illustrated by Beni Montresor in 1963.

Millions of Cats (1928) was written and illustrated by Wanda Gág.

One of Ernest H. Shepard's famous drawings for A. A. Milne's *Winnie-the-Pooh* (1926).

Milton Glaser illustrated Conrad Aiken's *Cats and Bats and Things with Wings* (1965). This page shows "The Goats."

▶ ILLUSTRATION OF CHILDREN'S BOOKS

It was not until the middle of the 18th century that books were written especially for children. An Englishman, Edward Lear (1812–88), wrote and illustrated limericks—light verse—and nonsense books such as *The Owl and The Pussy Cat* (1871).

The Swiss artist Rodolphe Töpffer (1799–1846) illustrated many children's books, including his *Album of Caricatures.* He also contributed to the development of the comic strip. Today much of the best and most exciting illustration is found in children's books.

ALBERT DORNE
President, Famous Artists Schools, Inc.

See also BOOKS; COMMERCIAL ART; ILLUMINATED MANUSCRIPTS.

Immigrants at Kennedy International Airport in New York.

IMMIGRATION AND EMIGRATION

The story of immigration and emigration is the story of people who leave one country to settle in another. Emigration is the departure from a country; immigration is the entry into a country. The story really began when prehistoric man first left his home in search of a better life. But modern immigration and emigration did not develop until after the discovery and settlement of the New World.

The countries of the New World have been called nations of immigrants. For when the people of Europe emigrated from their homelands to settle in lands across the seas, they became immigrants to the new countries of North and South America. Most immigration has occurred since the 1800's. Most of the people living in the so-called New World are descendants of immigrants.

▶ PROBLEMS OF ADJUSTMENT

An immigrant is called an alien by law. He is also an alien in fact, for he is a stranger in a land not his own. Often unfamiliar with the language and customs of his new country, the immigrant, particularly after 1890, usually settled in the poorer sections of a city. He was forced by ignorance to take work in industries where the worst possible conditions, wages, and hours prevailed. The immigrant was an easy prey for tricksters who promised help and then stole his money. Sometimes he was victimized by his own countrymen who had emigrated before him. Because he was poor and alien, the citizens of the new country generally viewed him with hostility and suspicion. As a result, the immigrant tended to settle among others from his country in communities that kept the old traditions.

Over the years the problems of adjustment have been eased in several ways. People have become more understanding of aliens. The immigrant himself is more aware of the conditions he is likely to meet in the new country. Working conditions have been improved, and social legislation broadened.

An important factor in immigration today has been the passage of immigration laws restricting the number of immigrants allowed to enter a particular country. A look at the history of immigration in the United States will be helpful in understanding the background of such laws.

▶ IMMIGRATION IN THE UNITED STATES

The poem by Emma Lazarus engraved on the Statue of Liberty in New York Harbor reads:

. . . "Give me your tired, your poor,
Your huddled masses yearning to breathe free,
The wretched refuse of your teeming shore.
Send these, the homeless, tempest-tost to me,
I lift my lamp beside the golden door!"

The golden door of the United States was opened to immigrants long before 1883, when this poem was written. Indeed, by that time the Congress of the United States had already passed two laws restricting immigration.

Early Immigration

In colonial times immigration was encouraged. Those who came were mostly from rural areas. They settled on the vast acres of available land and prospered. Generally familiar with the English language, these first immigrants often had the same interests as the early settlers. They came seeking political and religious freedom and greater economic opportunity, and they found these in America.

Occasionally there were protests against some immigrants, but in general, tolerance was high. Immigrants often faced great difficulty in obtaining official permission to emigrate from their homelands. At this time, however, the United States placed no legal restrictions on immigrants entering the country. The dangers of a long ocean journey, the difficulties of settling in a frontier land, trouble with the Indians, disease, famine, lack of finances—all these limited the number of people emigrating from the Old World to the New. Local laws dealing with immigrants restricted only those likely to become public charges.

Not until 1820 did the United States Government begin a careful count of the number of immigrants arriving annually. However, it is estimated that between 1790 and 1820 about 250,000 immigrants came to the United States. By 1840 the number of immigrants was nearly 1,000,000. The large majority of these were of British and Irish origin. In addition, there were significant minorities of Germans, Scandinavians, Dutch, and Swiss.

The first federal legislation dealing with immigration was passed in 1819. Nonrestrictive in character, the act required a listing of all legal arrivals. Between 1820 and 1875 there was no regulation of immigration on the part of the federal government. During this period of free immigration 9,104,034 aliens arrived in this country.

New Immigration

By about 1880 a new period in immigration was beginning. Most of the immigrants who arrived before this date were of northern and western European origin. These people were the "old immigration." The "new immigration" consisted of people from southern and eastern Europe and from Asia. It was this new wave of immigrants, with totally different cultural backgrounds and customs, that aroused fierce opposition. Agitation for restrictive legislation on immigration became intense. This led to the selective period of immigration, between 1880 and 1920. During this time Congress tried to restrict immigration by type, or category, of immigrants only, not by number of immigrants.

The first restrictive federal law, enacted on March 3, 1875, dealt with the problem of Chinese immigration. Most of the early Chi-

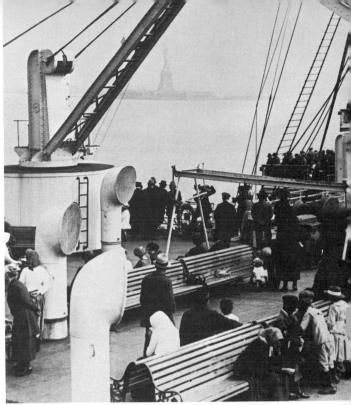

Between 1901 and 1910 nearly 9,000,000 immigrants came to the United States.

nese immigrants had been brought here for cheap labor. Their strange language and customs aroused much dislike. Also, the surplus of workers created by their presence lowered the wages paid to domestic laborers. On May 6, 1882, the Chinese Exclusion Act became law. This act suspended for 10 years all new immigration of Chinese laborers. Almost 230,000 Chinese had come to the United States between 1820 and 1880. As a result of the act of 1882, this number dropped to 61,711 between 1881 and 1890. The Chinese Exclusion Act was extended for another 10 years in 1892, and it was not until 1943 that these laws were repealed.

Restrictions against the Chinese were not the only immigration laws enacted at this time. In August, 1882, 3 months after the first Chinese Exclusion Act was enacted, Congress passed a general immigration law marking the beginning of modern immigration legislation. This act excluded as immigrants "any convict, lunatic, idiot or any person unable to take care of himself or herself without becoming a public charge." The Alien Contract Labor Law of February 26, 1885, forbade the making of labor contracts prior to the immigration of the worker. Previously, companies in the United States advertised abroad for workers, who found no jobs when they arrived. This restriction on American employers had the effect of limiting the number of workers entering the country. Despite the general restriction act of 1882 and the Alien Contract Labor Law of 1885, however, the number of Europeans coming to the United States between 1881 and 1890 was 5,246,613 —over twice the number in any previous decade. Subsequent restrictive acts, passed in 1891 and 1903, attempted to deal with this situation by enlarging the categories of immigrants to be excluded. The Alien Contract Labor Law also established a Federal Bureau of Immigration with the power to enforce these laws. As a result, immigration in the decade 1891 to 1900 fell to 3,687,564.

Increased Restrictions

But the great period of immigration was just beginning. Nearly 9,000,000 immigrants came to the United States between 1901 and 1910. An act was passed in February, 1907, that created a commission to study immigration problems. This act also enlarged the classes of immigrants to be excluded. Also in 1907 the United States concluded a "gentlemen's agreement" with Japan. This was an executive agreement that limited the number of Japanese allowed to enter the United States. The agreement was a result of the demands to extend the Chinese exclusion acts to the Japanese. Despite these restrictive measures, however, 1,285,349 immigrants came to this country in 1907.

In 1917 Congress passed an immigration act, over President Woodrow Wilson's veto, that required immigrants to be able to read and write at least one language. Religious refugees, children under 16 years, and physically handicapped immigrants were exempted from the literacy test. The act listed 33 categories of immigrants to be excluded. It remained one of the basic immigration laws until 1952. But these restrictions were generally ineffective. Between 1881 and 1890 immigrants from southern and eastern Europe accounted for 18.3 percent of the total. In the next decade the "new immigration" represented 51.9 percent. Between 1901 and 1910, 70.8 percent of all the immigrants came from southern and eastern Europe. And in

the 10 years between 1911 and 1920 the percentage was 59.

Quota Act. Finally, in 1921, Congress passed a quota law. The act was designed as a temporary measure to give Congress time to work out a new immigration policy. Under this act the quota of each foreign country was limited to a number equal to 3 percent of foreign-born people of that nationality living here in 1910. The purpose of this law was to encourage immigration from northern and western Europe and to discourage immigration from southern and eastern Europe. But in the first year covered by the act, the countries of northern and western Europe filled only 46.4 percent of their quotas, while the nations of southern and eastern Europe filled 95.3 percent.

Under the Quota Act of 1921 any immigrant who lived in a country of the Western Hemisphere for 1 year was allowed to enter the United States as a nonquota immigrant. In 1922 this requirement was changed to 5 years. Still, many otherwise inadmissible European and Asiatic aliens emigrated to Canada, Mexico, and Central or South America for the waiting period and then came to the United States.

In 1923 and 1924 the number of immigrants from northern and western Europe was more than twice the number from southern and eastern Europe. In 1924 Congress passed the National Origins Act, which prohibited Oriental immigration and changed the quota from 3 to 2 percent and the base year from 1910 to 1890, since fewer immigrants of southern or eastern European origin resided in the United States in that year. Between 1925 and 1929 the total quota for immigrants of southern and eastern European origin was 102,115. For immigrants from northern and western Europe the total was 704,995.

National Origins. The national-origins formula under the 1924 law provided that the total number of immigrants allowed to enter in any one year be limited to 164,000. The act further stated that as of July 1, 1927, the total number of immigrants entering the United States in any one year should be reduced to 150,000. The annual quota for each nationality was to be based on the number of people of that nationality living in the United States in 1920. It was not until 1929, however, that this portion of the act went into effect. The 1924 act also changed the requirement for quota exemptions from a 5-year residency in a country of the Western Hemisphere to birth in a country of the Western Hemisphere. More than these provisions, however, the Depression that began in 1929 kept many immigrants from coming to this country. Between 1931 and 1940 immigration totaled 528,431, the lowest for any decade since 1821 to 1830. In this decade more people left than entered the United States. Most of these were resident aliens from southern and eastern Europe who could not make a living under the conditions of severe economic crisis.

Developments Since World War II

With the onset of World War II the economy of the United States boomed. After the war thousands of homeless refugees crowded the ports of the United States. In 1948 Congress suspended quotas to accommodate these refugees under the Displaced Persons Act. This allowed refugees who had entered Germany, Austria, or Italy before December 22, 1945, to be charged against future quotas for their country. In 1950 the base date was extended to January 1, 1949, because it was said that the original act indirectly discriminated against Jews and Catholics.

The Refugee Relief Act of 1952 provided for a maximum of 205,000 nonquota refugee immigrants to enter the country over a 3-year period. In 1957 quota restrictions on displaced persons were lifted completely. The number of displaced persons and refugees admitted to the United States between 1946 and 1964 was about 730,000. The total number of immigrants coming to the United States between 1941 and 1964 was just under 5,000,000.

McCarran-Walter Act

The Displaced Persons and Refugee Relief acts were departures from laws usually applied to immigration and emigration. The basic law on immigration and emigration in the United States was the Immigration and Nationality Act of 1952. Known also as the McCarran-Walter Act, the law listed 31 categories of excludable aliens. These included diseased individuals, criminals, public charges, or subversives (people considered dangerous to the security of the country). A total quota on the number of immigrants entering the United States in any one year was set at 154,657, with a minimum quota for most countries guaranteed at 100 annually. Quotas varied somewhat through the years. The McCarran-Walter Act provided that the quotas available to any one country be reduced by the number of immigrants charged against future quotas under the hardship conditions stipulated in the act of 1917, the Displaced Persons and Refugee Relief acts, and any other act of Congress. But this provision was repealed in 1957.

Quota Distribution. Western Europe had the largest quota. Great Britain was allowed 65,361 immigrants yearly. Germany had a quota of 25,814. But for all of Asia the quota was 2,990; for Africa, Australia, New Guinea, and New Zealand, and several Pacific Islands, the number was 2,000.

Western European nations left much of their quotas unfilled, while countries with smaller quotas were tremendously oversubscribed. However, under the law unused quotas could not be transferred from one country to another. Each country's annual share of the total quota was based on the national-origins formula. Except for the countries in the Asia-Pacific triangle, this number equals one sixth of 1 percent of the population of the United States in 1920. Quotas for the Asia-Pacific triangle, excluding China and Japan, were set at 2,000. China's annual quota was 105; Japan's was 185.

Nonquota Immigrants. The McCarran-Walter Act provided for the immigration of certain persons without quota restrictions. These included alien wives, husbands, or unmarried children under 21 of American citizens. Citizens of Canada and independent nations of Latin America were allowed to immigrate on a nonquota basis. Congress extended nonquota status to certain groups from time to time. The Refugee Relief Act of 1953 and the Refugee-Escapee Act of 1957 were examples of this.

Although these people were not restricted by number, they were restricted by type. That is, they had to prove they were not criminals, public charges (which meant they had to have prospects of a job), subversives, or carriers of contagious diseases. Many people who were not restricted by quota but who could not fulfill the above qualifications tried to enter the country illegally.

Preferences. Preferences for immigrants were given by the United States under the 1952 act. First preference was given to those aliens "urgently needed" because of skills and training. If the immigrant met certain requirements of residency, literacy, and good character, he was eligible to become a naturalized citizen of the United States. Under the Mc-Carran-Walter Act, racial barriers were eliminated as restrictions of immigration and naturalization.

In the United States the laws concerning immigration are administered by the Immigration and Naturalization Service, which is part of the United States Department of Justice.

Present United States Immigration Law

Every president since Franklin Roosevelt has proposed changes in the immigration laws in order to open the golden door a bit wider.

On October 3, 1965, at the Statue of Liberty in New York Harbor, President Lyndon B. Johnson signed into law an immigration reform bill that eliminated the national origins quota system. The bill called for the elimination of the national origins formula, which discriminated against Asians and southern Europeans, within 3 years. The new law gives first preference for immigration to per-

sons with skills needed in the United States and to relatives of United States citizens. No more than 170,000 immigrants from the Eastern Hemisphere and 120,000 from the Western Hemisphere may enter the United States each year, with no more than 20,000 coming from any one country. Parents, husbands and wives, and minor children of citizens will be admitted without quota restriction.

▶ IMMIGRATION IN OTHER LANDS

Other nations also maintain selective immigration policies. Canada restricts immigration to people of certain nationalities, age groups, and skills. Nonquota immigration is limited to citizens and subjects of Great Britain, France, and the United States.

The number of immigrants entering Canada has varied with the economic conditions of the country. During the decade of railroad construction between 1880 and 1890, workers emigrated to Canada sometimes at the rate of 100,000 annually. In 1900 and the 10 years following, the average annual immigration was 200,000. These were the years of rapid prairie settlement in Canada. Between 1910 and 1912 more than 200,000 people left the United States for Canada. World War I stopped almost all immigration. Average immigration for the 1920's was 100,000; and for the Depression years of the 1930's, 16,000.

Since 1949 close to 1,000,000 immigrants have arrived in Israel.

More than 2,000,000 immigrants have entered Australia since 1945.

From 1941 to 1955 Canada received about 1,200,000 aliens. Many of these were refugees from World War II.

Australia. Australia is another country that has received a large number of immigrants over the years. Here, too, the number is determined by economic conditions. During the gold rush of the 1850's, immigrants came in unprecedented numbers. Between 1852 and 1861 over 500,000 more people came into the country than left it. Today about eight of every 10 immigrants come from Great Britain, according to a selective immigration policy. In general, Africans and Asians are barred from settling permanently in Australia. Quotas are increased or decreased according to economic needs. Since the end of World War II more than 2,000,000 immigrants have been admitted.

Latin America. Nearly three of every four immigrants who came to Latin America between 1946 and 1955 settled in Argentina and Brazil. Most immigrants to Argentina come from Italy, Spain, and Portugal. Most of the immigrants to Brazil are either Italian or Portuguese. Argentina encouraged immigration after the 1870's, but there have been restrictions since 1941. In 1934 Brazil passed a restrictive quota law setting a maximum total of 77,020 immigrants yearly.

Mexico and Venezuela encourage the immigration of workers. Mexico allows European countries a yearly quota of up to 1,000.

Africa. Most immigrants to Africa have settled in South Africa. Under a quota act passed in 1930 only British subjects "of pure European descent" are allowed unlimited entry. Nearly 30,000 people a year came to South Africa during the 1930's, when an economic crisis enveloped most of the world. In the 1950's the annual average was about 14,500.

Asia. Because exclusion laws kept the Chinese, Indians, and Japanese from entering other nations, these people emigrated largely to other Asian countries. Burma, Indochina, Indonesia, Malaysia, Thailand, and the Philippines received the largest number of Chinese. People from India began emigrating to Ceylon, Malaysia, Indonesia, South Africa, and Europe after the 1830's. Emigration from Japan, not allowed until 1885, has been mainly to Hawaii, Siberia, and the continental United States.

Many refugees made homeless by World War II moved to Israel. Most of these came from Europe, Asia, and Africa. Between 1948 and 1955 there were sometimes as many as 250,000 immigrants in one year.

Europe. France, Great Britain, and Germany have received the highest number of immigrants. The two world wars brought in many people looking for jobs. France received the second highest number of immigrants after World War I. The United States ranked first. Displaced persons and refugees from Eastern Europe came in droves to the west after World War II.

Many emigrants from the Republic of Ireland and the British West Indies have settled in the United Kingdom because of job opportunities. In 1968 a great controversy arose when the British Parliament passed a Commonwealth Immigrants Act that, among a number of other provisions, limited the number of Asian families with British citizenship who could enter the United Kingdom in any given year. The act was passed in the face of a major exodus of Indians and Pakistanis from the African nation of Kenya. Many of these people had been removed from government jobs in Kenya and found themselves stateless, save for their understood rights to British citizenship. Opponents of the bill said it showed racial prejudice. Those in favor of it said it was designed to avert strains on British social services and on the British economy.

Reviewed by WILLIAM J. CHUTE
Queens College (New York)

See also ALIENS; CITIZENSHIP; NATURALIZATION.

IMMUNOLOGY

Immunology is the study of how the body reacts to invasions by outside organisms and substances. The invaders might be bacteria, viruses, protozoa, fungi, animal parasites, or something else. They might be the vitally needed cells of a blood transfusion or a transplanted organ.

In reacting to these things, certain groups of the body's cells must make a kind of chemical choice. They accept what belongs to the body, and reject intruders. Getting rid of the intruders, or trying to, is called an **immune response**.

The body has a whole set of immune responses. Generally they are useful. They protect the body against disease. But sometimes these same defenses are overactive. Allergies and some other serious disorders called autoimmune (self-immune) diseases seem to be nothing more than confused immune responses. And in so-called spare-parts surgery, the body may altogether reject a transfusion, a skin graft, or a transplanted kidney.

As a result, medical scientists are doing a good deal of work to find out more about immune responses.

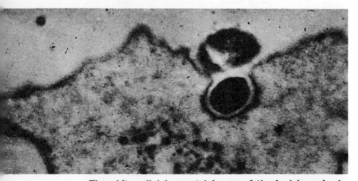

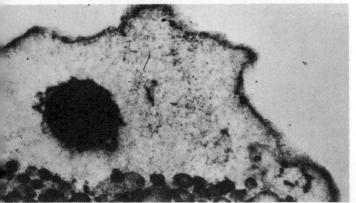

The white cell (phagocyte) is one of the body's main defenses against invading bacteria. Above: A phagocyte begins to capture two bacteria. The phagocyte flows around the bacteria and engulfs them. Below: A phagocyte with a bacterial cell it has captured.

Immune responses of the body are generally divided into two kinds. These are **native immunity** and **acquired immunity**.

▶ NATIVE IMMUNITY

Native immunity is the resistance that the body has inherited to many different organisms. People simply do not catch dog distemper, for example. Nor does a dog catch a human cold.

In the same species certain individuals are far more resistant than others to diseases. The tuberculosis bacillus, for example, is almost everywhere. Yet not every person comes down with tuberculosis, even when he is exposed to it. Scientists still do not know much about why differences like these exist.

A person's native resistance depends on the body's skin barriers, chemical agents, devouring cells, and the inflammatory process.

Man's outer skin and the mucous linings of his body entrances physically turn aside most agents of disease. The skin and mucous linings are coated with chemicals. The skin also has a layer of lactic acids and fatty acids that kill microbes.

Tears, saliva, and the nasal and intestinal secretions contain **lysozyme**. This is an enzyme, or special protein, that dissolves certain bacteria. Inside the body other proteins also kill bacteria.

The Role of White Cells

Within the body also are the **phagocytes**. These white cells swallow up unwanted things. Some circulate in the blood. Some either wander or remain fixed in the lymphoid tissues and other parts of the body. If microbes get into the body through a cut in the skin, little blood phagocytes called **polymorphonuclear** cells engulf them. Then large phagocytes called **monocytes** assemble. They swallow up any dead cells and debris as well as any remaining bacteria.

Inflammation is the response of tissue cells when hurt. The injury may come from infection, or it may come from a blow, a burn, or chemical or radiation damage. To repair the damage, the body musters a whole chain of reactions. The injured part becomes red, fevered, swollen, and sore. Inside, phagocytes have already arrived on the scene.

Meanwhile, the body is building another

ANTIBODIES ARE SPECIFIC

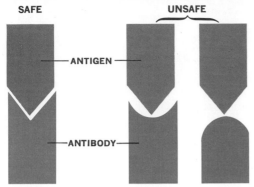

An antigen can be controlled only by a specific antibody. Other antibodies will not be effective against the antigen.

PROTECTION BY VACCINATION

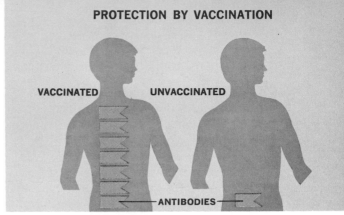

A person who is vaccinated builds up a supply of antibodies. A person who is not vaccinated has few antibodies.

strong defense—the **antibodies**. These are very large and complicated protein molecules. They appear in the blood, in the lymph, and in the body's cells.

▶ACQUIRED IMMUNITY

Acquired immunity is something a person develops himself. Native immunity gives general protection against all invaders. Acquired immunity protects against only one kind of invader.

Acquired immunity depends on the body's ability to make antibodies. This ability is inherited. But the body's own experience with an invader leads it to produce an antibody that reacts to that invader and probably to no other. The invader is called an **antigen**.

Viruses, bacteria, protozoa, fungi, and animal parasites can serve as antigens. So can toxins, the poisons produced by bacteria such as those causing diphtheria. And so can pollen and certain chemicals.

Invading antigens may enter through a cut or be breathed in or swallowed. Antibodies begin to form within a few days. They reach their greatest numbers after 2 weeks or so. When the threat is gone, some of the antibodies remain in the blood. These antibodies are important when certain diseases threaten the body again. The body makes more antibodies within a day or two. This is what happens, for example, with smallpox or measles. One attack enables a person to make enough antibodies to repel the disease a second time he is infected.

Active Immunity

Doctors take advantage of this kind of response to protect people against diseases.

They know that killed or altered antigens, when injected into a person, can cause antibodies to be produced. The antibodies then fight off the disease that the antigen causes. The person is thus protected against the disease.

Such prepared antigens are called **vaccines**. Since the vaccinated person or animal has to make his own antibodies rather than get them from somebody else, the procedure is sometimes called **active immunization**.

Active immunization is commonly used to protect people against such diseases as typhoid, typhus, cholera, plague, smallpox, yellow fever, Rocky Mountain spotted fever, diphtheria, whooping cough, tetanus, and even rabies, as well as polio. A series of several shots (injections) may be needed. Later the person may need a booster shot. Its purpose is to raise the number of antibodies in his blood.

Passive Immunity

Antibodies may be taken from one individual and given to another. To receive them in this way is to acquire **passive immunity**. For example, during pregnancy a mother's antibodies pass to her unborn child through their bloodstream connection. These antibodies give him the same immunities his mother had. The immunities last for a little while after he is born.

Anyone who has recovered from a disease has some antibodies left over. These antibodies were made to fight this specific disease. It is possible to take the antibodies from this person. The antibodies are then injected into a person who has been exposed to the same disease. The immunized person is then protected against the disease. This procedure is sometimes used against measles and infectious hepatitis.

The usual method of transferring antibodies is to take them from an animal that was deliberately given a disease. The animal then develops antibodies against the disease. The antibodies are carried in the clear part of the animal's blood. This part is known as the **serum**. Any serum used to transfer particular antibodies to someone is called an **antiserum**.

Antiserums can be used to prevent diseases such as diphtheria, measles, polio, and tetanus. They can also be used to bolster the body when it has already been exposed. For example, snake-venom antibodies are given following snakebite. And anti-anthrax serum is given after exposure to the sheep disease anthrax.

Passive immunity provides protection for only a few weeks. Active immunity may last for years or for life.

The history of a person's immunities is so well "written" into his blood that antigens can be used in the crime laboratory to tell whether a bloodstain came from one person or another.

▶ STRUCTURE OF ANTIBODIES

The molecules of antibodies, like those of typical antigens, are very large. They contain thousands of atoms. Scientists now think these molecules are shaped like fat cigars. Antibodies are made of protein. Next to water, protein is the main stuff of the body and its cells.

Antibodies, like other proteins, consist of long chains of smaller units, called amino acids. These are the protein building blocks. There are about 20 different kinds of amino acids. A typical protein chain may contain several hundred amino-acid units. These units occur one after another in a definite pattern. It is this pattern that determines the kind of protein.

Once the pattern is made, the protein chain takes on a "second-order structure," often a spiral, or helix. Next, this helix folds on itself in a complex but precise way so that each protein molecule has an intricate three-dimensional shape. Each kind of protein molecule has its own particular shape. It is this so-called third-order structure that allows it to carry out its particular job.

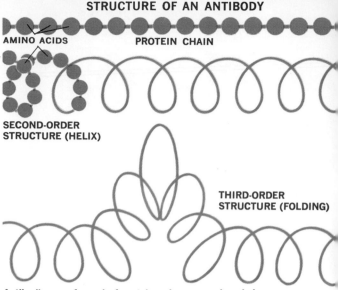

STRUCTURE OF AN ANTIBODY

AMINO ACIDS PROTEIN CHAIN

SECOND-ORDER STRUCTURE (HELIX)

THIRD-ORDER STRUCTURE (FOLDING)

Antibodies are formed of proteins—long, complex chains of amino acids. In the second-order structure the protein chain takes on the shape of a spiral. The spiral folds into the third-order structure.

All antibodies belong to a group of proteins called **globulins**. The most common globulins are found in the blood and are called **gamma globulins**. Though they are big—with a molecular weight about 10,000 times that of oxygen—their chemically active areas are known to be small. So are those of the antigen molecules. There are probably not more than two or three of these active areas on each molecule, taking up maybe 1 percent of its total surface.

▶ FORMATION OF ANTIBODIES

There are two leading theories about how antibodies are formed: the instructive theory and the selective theory.

According to the instructive theory, the shape of the antigen's active area determines the shape of its antibody. By this theory, the antigen makes its way into a cell and touches a globulin molecule. This happens just as the globulin is folding into its third-order structure. And so the antigen acts as a template, or mold, for the folding antibody. By this theory, the active areas of the antigen fit into the newly molded pockets of the antibody the way a lead soldier fits its mold or a key fits its lock.

According to the selection theory, a certain cell or group of cells in the body "knows" how to make an antibody for a certain antigen. This can be done for the thousands of possible antigens. That is because the particular cell or

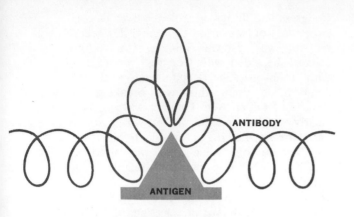

INSTRUCTIVE THEORY

According to the instructive theory, an antigen touches a globulin molecule just as the molecule is folding into a third-order structure. The globulin folds around the antigen and forms an antibody for it.

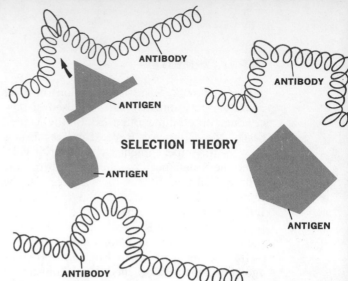

SELECTION THEORY

According to the selection theory a cell inherits the information needed to make antigen antibodies. When an antigen invades the body, it stimulates the cells to make the right antibody to react against it.

cell-family carries genetic information in its nucleus for making that antibody. When an antigen comes into the body, the antigen stimulates the multiplication of the cell-family that will react with it.

The Source of Antibodies

Where do antibodies come from? Scientists now believe that antibodies are made by certain kinds of white cells, called **plasma cells**.

Very probably the plasma cells themselves come from other white cells of the body, called **lymphocytes**. Evidence points to this. Besides, experiments with animals have shown that lymphocytes carry both antibodies and the information for making more. In these experiments the ability to produce certain antibodies—not merely the antibodies themselves—was transferred from one animal to another. This was done by simply transferring cell material that included many of the lymphocytes.

As for where lymphocytes come from, there may be a new answer to a very old question. A little-known part of the body, the **thymus gland**, seems to be their original source. The function of the thymus was poorly understood for years, partly because the gland practically disappears after childhood. Now it seems probable that in early life the thymus seeds the blood with lymphocytes. These lymphocytes settle down in other lymphoid

tissues to produce offspring. From such cells antibodies come.

▶ WHEN DO ANTIBODIES FORM?

Presumably these same early-born lymphocytes or their descendants can help the body tell "itself" apart from "non-self." The body obviously does not form antibodies against the thousands of antigens inside itself and native to it. Only in the rather rare autoimmune diseases does it make antibodies that are used against itself.

Yet it knows and reacts to something foreign. If skin is grafted from even as close a relative as a father to his son, for example, the graft will nearly always be cast off sooner or later. Unless the son's immune response is blocked by heavy doses of radiation or chemicals, his activated lymphocytes seem to carry antibodies to the very doorstep of the graft.

Recently it has been found that if an animal is injected at birth, or even before, with tissues from the embryo of another animal, it will later accept grafts from the strange animal as its own. In other words, antibody-forming mechanisms must develop very early. When the body is exposed to an antigen before these mechanisms do develop, it never makes antibodies against the antigen. This is known as **induced tolerance**.

L. D. HAMILTON, M.D.
Sloan-Kettering Institute for Cancer Research
See also ANTIBODIES AND ANTIGENS.

IMPEACHMENT

Impeachment is a legal action brought against a government official accused of misconduct or criminal offenses. In the United States the House of Representatives brings charges for impeachment by a majority vote. Then the Senate becomes a court and tries the accused official. The Chief Justice of the Supreme Court presides if the president is impeached. If the Senate, by a two-thirds majority vote, finds the impeached officer guilty, he is removed from office.

Impeachment began in England 600 years ago. Parliament impeached royal ministers it did not like. In 1621 the famous author Francis Bacon was accused by Parliament of taking bribes as lord chancellor. Another famous impeachment was that of Warren Hastings, a governor-general of India. He was found innocent in 1795 after a 7-year trial. In time, impeachments became unnecessary in England because government ministers could not remain in office without support from the House of Commons. There have been no impeachments there since 1805.

The United States Constitution says a federal official may be impeached for treason, for taking bribes, and for "high crimes and misdemeanors." But is it a "high crime" for an official to oppose the policies of the party in power? If so, impeachment would be a sword that congressmen could hold over the head of a president who disagreed with them.

The question came up when Supreme Court Justice Samuel Chase was impeached in 1804. He had been appointed by the Federalists. Later, Jeffersonians came into power, and they thought Judge Chase was blocking their policies. The House impeached Chase, but the Senate acquitted him (declared him not guilty). This decision seemed to mean that it was not an impeachable crime to oppose the party in power.

But the question exploded again over 60 years later when for the first time in American history the House impeached a president. Andrew Johnson became president when Abraham Lincoln was assassinated. The Civil War had just ended, and the country's biggest problem was reconstruction of state governments in the ruined South.

Johnson and the Republican majority in Congress had disagreed violently over Reconstruction. Johnson tried to remove his secretary of war, Edwin Stanton, from office because he sided with Congress rather than with Johnson. The Republicans said that Johnson, in doing this, was breaking the Tenure of Office Act. This act was not very clearly worded and did not provide a sound basis for impeaching a president. However, the Tenure of Office Act was used as something of an excuse by Congress. The main reason for the impeachment was that Johnson had tried to block all the efforts of Congress to make laws on questions of Reconstruction.

His trial, in 1868, lasted 2 months. In spite of all the pressure the radicals brought on other senators, 7 Republicans voted with 12 Democrats "not guilty." The vote was 35 to 19—one vote short of the two-thirds majority necessary for conviction.

The question of the impeachment of a president arose for the second time in American history in 1974 when articles of impeachment against President Richard M. Nixon were approved by the Committee on the Judiciary of the House of Representatives. The articles charged the President with obstruction of justice, abuse of power, and failure to comply with Committee subpoenas. But before the full House met to act on the impeachment charges, President Nixon resigned. A Committee report was accepted by the House of Representatives.

Impeachments have occurred infrequently in the United States, and of the federal officials impeached, few have been convicted and removed from office.

State governments, too, have impeachment power. In most states, procedures are similar to those of the federal government.

Impeachment is a built-in safeguard against bad government. It is a drastic action used only against an official whose offenses are serious. But the threat of impeachment often causes a really corrupt official to resign before charges can be brought. The power to impeach, if it is not misused, helps to protect the public against corrupt or criminal officials.

Reviewed by Eric McKitrick
Columbia University

See also JOHNSON, ANDREW; NIXON, RICHARD M.

IMPERIALISM

Imperialism is a hard word to define because it has become a term of abuse. Literally, it means the government of one people by another people. The governing country is called the mother or metropolitan country. The subject, or dependent, country or countries make up the empire of the mother country.

Imperialism may take the form of either direct or indirect control of another people. The mother country may control the trade, business, industry, or finances of the subject country. Or imperialism may be based on colonization. An example of this kind of imperialism was the settlement of North America by people from Europe. All of South America, too, was colonized, by Spain and Portugal. And in the 1600's the Dutch empire extended from the Dutch East Indies (present-day Indonesia) to islands in the Caribbean Sea. A common form of imperialism today is the satellite system of the Soviet Union.

Since the beginning of history stronger countries have conquered weaker countries and established empires. The most famous example of imperialism in ancient times is the Roman Empire. The Romans controlled much of Europe and all the lands on the Mediterranean Sea. To these areas they brought Roman law and order. They also brought the burden of heavy taxes.

When Columbus discovered America in 1492, he claimed all the land he saw for the King and Queen of Spain. Many of the explorers who followed Columbus claimed for their kings the lands they discovered. In the 16th and 17th centuries Spain, Portugal, France, the Netherlands, and England all developed empires.

During this period a nation's wealth was believed to be based on the number and riches of her colonies. It was not long before one country wanted the wealth of another. Many wars followed. By 1763 France had lost most of its American empire to England. England lost many of its first American colonies as a result of the American Revolution. In the early 1800's Spain lost her Latin-American empire. The English, with holdings in Africa and Asia, were the only people to preserve a very large empire.

After 1870 a new type of imperialism appeared. It followed the rapid increase in scientific and technical knowledge. The development of the steam engine had given rise to railroads, steamships, and industrial machinery. Steamships could carry trade anywhere in the world much faster than sailing ships. The growth of industry in Europe created a great need for raw materials from all over the world. Coal and iron were needed for making steel; cotton and wool, for making cloth. The countries of Western Europe also needed new markets outside Europe where they could sell the products of their industries. They spent large amounts of money developing markets in Asia and Africa. They set up docks, warehouses, mines, plantations, factories, railroads, and banks.

The countries of Asia and Africa did not have strong governments. They often were unable to safeguard the financial investments of Europeans. The Europeans would then move in to protect their investments.

At the same time, Europeans felt that their civilization was much better than any other. They felt that they had a duty to carry this modern civilization to the rest of the world. By 1914 the major countries of Europe had divided the world among themselves. Although imperialism inflicted much suffering on the subject peoples, it brought benefits too. These benefits included a better system of law and higher standards of health and education.

With better education the leaders of the subject peoples soon wanted their countries to be independent. At the same time it became a principle of modern society that people should govern themselves if they are able to do so. Since 1914 the British Empire, which at one time covered one quarter of the world, has given independence to most of its colonies. Since the end of World War II many Asian and African nations have gained their freedom.

Imperialism has played an important part in the movement of the peoples of the world toward one worldwide civilization. Today this movement is being further strengthened by the work of the United Nations.

Reviewed by HERMAN AUSUBEL
Columbia University

IMPETIGO. See DISEASES.

INCAS. See INDIANS OF SOUTH AMERICA.

INCOME TAX

An income tax is a tax on earnings or profits. It is paid to a government—national, state, or local—to help provide necessary public services. Thus, a citizen pays as a tax a portion of his wages or salary, and of his dividends, interest, rents, or other income. Corporations and other businesses pay income taxes on their profits.

A personal income tax is levied on the gains from employment (salary) and from investment (dividends and interest). Corporate income tax is levied on the profits made by industry. Other kinds of taxes are levied on things owned (property taxes), on goods produced or sold (excise and sales taxes), or services rendered.

In most income-tax systems, the tax is levied only on the income remaining after subtracting (1) expenses and (2) other deductions and exemptions allowed by law to the individual or to corporations.

Income-Tax History

The principle of a proportionate tax on income goes back many centuries. Ancient Greece and medieval Europe had some systems of income tax, but these were generally ineffective. It was really the English income tax, first levied about 1799, which showed this type of tax could be an important source of revenue for government and could be administered efficiently.

Countries in all parts of the world today have some form of income tax. In Canada and Great Britain about half of the national tax revenues come from income taxes. Most of the European and Asian countries and many South American countries place a tax on the income of their citizens. Australia and New Zealand also have an income tax.

The United States first levied an income tax during the Civil War. The Revenue Act of 1862 provided for levies to help finance the cost of the war. This early income tax was in many ways similar to the income tax we know today. For example, it provided for the filing of tax returns, for personal exemptions, and for some withholding of the tax at the source of income.

The law also created the agency today called the Internal Revenue Service. It is the responsibility of the Internal Revenue Service to collect the federal revenue and enforce the federal tax laws.

After the Civil War ended, government expenses dropped, and the income tax was allowed to die 10 years later. It was revived in 1894 under President Grover Cleveland's administration, but it was declared unconstitutional by the Supreme Court of the United States the next year.

Supporters of the income tax continued to press for this method of raising revenues. In 1909 legislation was passed to amend the Constitution to give Congress power to tax incomes. That same year Alabama was the first state to approve this amendment. However, the approval of three fourths of the states was necessary. It was not until 1913, when Wyoming ratified it, that the Sixteenth Amendment went into effect. It states:

"The Congress shall have power to lay and collect taxes on incomes, from whatever source derived, without apportionment among the several States, and without regard to any census or enumeration."

On October 3, 1913, Congress enacted an income-tax law. It imposed a tax on net incomes of both individuals and corporations. The basic principles of this law have continued in effect to the present. Over the years, however, there have been numerous changes in tax rates, deductions and exemptions, and other provisions. All of these provisions are contained in a document, called the Internal Revenue Code.

United States Federal Income Tax

The federal income tax is the most important source of funds for operation of the United States Government. It accounts for about three fourths of all the revenue received.

Most government-supported activities depend in large part on moneys received from the income tax. Examples of these vital activities are national defense, commerce, and education.

The Internal Revenue Service, a part of the United States Treasury Department, administers the federal income-tax law. This system is regarded as the most effective in the world. It is rated in terms of compliance (number of people filing returns), revenue produced (amount of money collected), and low cost of collection and administration.

Self-Assessment

One of the most important features of the United States income-tax law is what is called self-assessment. This means that the citizen himself figures his income, his deductions, and the amount of his tax and then makes full payment. Corporations and other businesses follow the same procedure in meeting their federal tax obligations.

Each taxpayer files a statement called a return. This gives the facts and figures of his income and deductions. Then he pays the tax he owes. In a very real sense the citizen is a partner of his government in the administration of its tax laws. He shares responsibility for making the system work.

One provision of the law is called withholding, or pay-as-you-go. This makes it easier for people to pay their federal income tax. Employers deduct, or withdraw, from each worker's salary a share of his annual income tax every payday and pay it to the government. In that way the employee pays as he earns and does not have to provide the entire amount of the tax at the end of the tax year. When he files his return, the taxpayer calculates the exact amount of tax due for the previous year. If the amount deducted during the year is more than the total amount of tax due, the taxpayer gets a refund. If not enough has been withheld, a payment must be made by the individual taxpayer to cover the difference.

About 97 percent of the tax is paid to the Internal Revenue Service voluntarily, through self-assessment and withholding. Only about 3 percent is accounted for by direct enforcement. Enforcement action is taken by the Internal Revenue Service when a taxpayer fails to file a return or to pay the correct tax.

Progressive Tax Rates

Another feature of the United States income tax is that it levies progressive, or graduated, rates. That is, persons who have higher incomes pay at higher rates than those who have smaller incomes. Under the graduated rates set by the Congress in the Revenue Act of 1969, an unmarried person pays 14 percent on the first $500 of taxable income and progressively higher rates on the rest of his income, up to 70 percent tax on portions of taxable income over $100,000. These graduated rates are lower for married taxpayers filing joint tax returns. They are also lower for an individual taxpayer who is the head of a household.

State and Local Income Taxes

While income taxes are important sources of revenue, most states and many local governments depend more on other kinds of taxes. Many local governments rely heavily on property taxes. Many state governments resort to sales taxes or taxes on such things as gasoline, alcoholic beverages, tobacco products, and so on. The federal government also taxes these items.

The first state income tax of importance was introduced by Wisconsin in 1911. By mid-1971 income taxes were levied by 39 of the 50 states.

Since the end of World War II many local governments also have adopted income taxes. In some sections of the United States citizens must pay income taxes to as many as three levels of government—federal, state, and local.

Obligation of Citizenship

The need of government for tax revenue continues—for the national defense and other programs vital to the developing nation and expanding population. These demands have kept the income tax a broadly based tax, applying to almost every citizen who receives income.

Such a tax has been administered effectively, with a high level of compliance. In the United States, for example, nearly all citizens realize and accept their obligation to pay their fair share of the costs of their government. It costs the United States less than ½ cent to collect $1 of tax revenue—the lowest tax-dollar cost in the world.

The willingness of the people to assess themselves voluntarily and to pay their correct tax when due is the heart and strength of the American tax system.

MORTIMER M. CAPLIN
Former Commissioner of Internal Revenue
See also TAXATION.

INDEPENDENCE DAY

Independence Day is a national American holiday, celebrated each year on July 4. It commemorates the adoption of the Declaration of Independence by the Continental Congress on July 4, 1776. The Declaration told the world that "these United Colonies are, and of right ought to be, free and independent states." July 4 marks, therefore, the birth of the United States of America.

The first celebration of American independence took place 4 days later in Philadelphia, where the Continental Congress was meeting. The ceremony began with a public reading of the Declaration of Independence. From the tower of the State House, now called Independence Hall, the Liberty Bell rang out. The coat of arms of the king of England was taken down. There was a parade, and cannons boomed.

John Adams, a signer of the Declaration, thought that Americans would celebrate a "great anniversary festival." In a letter to his wife he wrote, "It ought to be commemorated as the day of deliverance, by solemn acts of devotion to God Almighty. It ought to be solemnized with pomp and parade, with shows, games, sports, guns, bells, bonfires, and illuminations, from one end of this continent to the other, from this time forward forevermore."

The first anniversary was celebrated in Philadelphia the following year. It included pomp and parade, guns, bells, and bonfires. A more elaborate celebration was held there in 1788, after the new Constitution had been ratified. There was a large parade, a speech, and a dinner. During the dinner many toasts were proposed, accompanied by fanfares of trumpets and cannons. There were toasts to: "The People of the United States," "General Washington," and "The Whole Family of Mankind."

When the soldiers of the Revolutionary Army were sent home in 1783, they carried to their hometowns the idea of celebrating July 4. They would gather each year on this day to tell stories of the war to each other. The celebrations quickly spread to new towns. As people moved west during the 1800's, they spread the celebration of the Fourth to new territories as well. The first celebration on the West Coast was held in Los Angeles, California, in 1847.

It was not long before the whole country celebrated the Fourth, almost as John Adams had suggested. At sunrise all over the nation gun salutes were fired and bells rung. Flags were flown from buildings, from homes, and along the streets. Many shop windows were decorated with red, white, and blue. Churches held special services. There were parades followed by public readings of the Declaration of Independence. National songs were sung, and speeches were made.

July 4 also meant fireworks. Firecrackers could be heard all day. Rockets, sparklers, Roman candles, pinwheels, and other fireworks were set off in the evening. But there were many accidents. As many as 5,000 people were injured on one July 4 holiday. The demands for a "safe and sane Fourth" became so great that many states outlawed fireworks. Today large displays of fireworks are put on by local businesses, clubs, or communities. But these displays are given under careful controls so that they can be enjoyed in safety.

July 4 is also the beginning of summer fun. Beaches, parks, and amusement areas are filled with holiday crowds. People gather at picnics where they play softball, run races, and enjoy other games.

Many important events have taken place on July 4. The United States Military Academy at West Point was opened on July 4, 1802. Thomas Jefferson, author of the Declaration of Independence, and John Adams both died on July 4, 1826. Construction of the nation's first railroad, the Baltimore and Ohio, began on July 4, 1828. The cornerstone of the Washington Monument was laid on Independence Day, 1848. In 1903 President Theodore Roosevelt sent the first message on the new Pacific cable from California to the Philippines via Hawaii. On July 4, 1946, the United States granted independence to the Republic of the Philippines.

The first 49-star American flag, honoring the new state of Alaska, was raised on July 4, 1959. The following year (on July 4), the first 50-star flag, honoring Hawaii, was flown.

Reviewed by RICHARD B. MORRIS
Columbia University

INDEPENDENCE HALL

Independence Hall in Philadelphia is the official birthplace of the United States. It is the place where the Declaration of Independence was signed, where George Washington took command of the Continental Army, and where the Constitution was drafted. Yet it was not called Independence Hall until nearly 50 years after the American Revolution. It was first called the Pennsylvania State House.

In 1729 the city of Philadelphia offered to build a meeting house for the Pennsylvania Assembly. The colonial lawmakers had been meeting in private houses. Andrew Hamilton, a lawyer famous for his defense of freedom of the press, designed the hall. Carpenters built it on the outskirts of town, on what is now Chestnut Street. The work went slowly. In 1736 the Assembly began meeting in the unfinished Assembly Chamber. The building was not completed until the 1740's.

The First Continental Congress came to Philadelphia in September, 1774. The delegates refused the State House as a meeting place because they thought the Pennsylvania Assembly might try to influence their thinking. They chose to meet in Carpenters' Hall. But in May, 1775, the Second Continental Congress did not fear being influenced by the Assembly and decided to meet in the Assembly Chamber of the State House. There the delegates debated and drafted the Declaration of Independence. They approved the final draft on July 4, 1776. Four days later a delegate read the Declaration from a platform used for political meetings that stood in the State House Yard. That evening Philadelphians celebrated with bonfires and the ringing of bells—including the State House bell, later called the Liberty Bell.

When the British took Philadelphia during the Revolutionary War, the Continental Congress had to leave town. The British used the State House as a prison and hospital. When Congress returned in 1778, they found the hall "filthy" with "the inside torn much to pieces." After the State House was cleaned, Congress again met there. They adopted the Articles of Confederation, but the Articles did not work well. In 1787 the Constitutional Convention was held in the State House to draft a constitution.

Independence Hall in Philadelphia as it appears today.

In 1790 the national government moved from the State House to a building next door called Congress Hall. This was the nation's capital until 1800. When Philadelphia was no longer the national capital, people forgot about the State House. The wooden steeple, which had been in bad repair for many years, was removed in 1781. The hall became the Peale Museum, full of stuffed birds and snakes. In 1816 the old, neglected building was about to be torn down. But the city of Philadelphia bought the building and the square around it for $70,000.

In 1824 Philadelphia welcomed the Marquis de Lafayette. He was a hero in the United States because he had helped Washington during the Revolution. What could be a better place to honor Lafayette than the State House? The parade in the French general's honor ended with an official welcome in "Independence Chamber" (the Assembly Chamber). Many years later people began calling the building Independence Hall. A wooden steeple much like the old one was added in 1828. However, the new steeple was somewhat taller than the old one and had a four-faced clock. Otherwise the building was restored to its original appearance.

Today people come from all over the world to visit the place where the Declaration of Independence was signed. They read the famous documents and look at the restored rooms with their historic furnishings. And they see the Liberty Bell, which is now in a room on the ground floor of the tower. Independence Hall is one of the main shrines of the American Revolution.

Reviewed by M. O. ANDERSON
Superintendent
Independence National Historical Park

INDEXES AND INDEXING

The index is the key that unlocks the contents of a book. It guides the reader to the exact page on which he will find the particular information he wants. The first indexes included only general topics. Topics were not arranged in alphabetical order until the 17th century. Today a book written to provide information is considered of little value unless it is carefully indexed to show the exact location of every fact and subject and each person, place, and event discussed in its pages. Modern indexes, alphabetically arranged, are placed at the back of a book or in the final volume of some series of books.

Heading, Entry, and Subheading. The word or proper name used to indicate the subject indexed is called the heading. The heading, together with the number of the page or pages in the text on which the information is found, is called the entry. The usefulness of an index depends on the choice of the words selected as headings. These words must accurately describe the contents of the book, and they must be words that are familiar to the index user. They must be specific, logical, and definite terms that have only one meaning. There must be a separate heading for each subject mentioned in the book. Each topic must be listed under the same heading each time it appears. It cannot be scattered under different words of similar meaning.

A particular word useful in one index may be too general a term for the index of another book or too specific for a third. A bird guide will not use the heading "birds" in its index. It will list only the names of the particular species of birds it describes. The index of a world geography will not include the name of a village too small to be in the text. The index of a book on outer space written before the United States' first space flight will not list John Glenn.

If there are many references to one subject, subheadings will be used under a main heading for that subject. These bring together into one place different types of information on the subject. The subheadings identify and locate the items. In some indexes the subheadings form a kind of study guide to the topic.

Subheadings usually are placed in alphabetical order below the main heading. With this arrangement they can be seen clearly. They may be in paragraph form or one subheading to a line.

Advertising A 306–13
  magazines **M** 99
  marketing **M** 343
  newspapers **N** 86
  public relations **P** 331
  radio and television programs **R** 411
  selling **S** 262–63
  See also Propaganda

Advertising A 306–13; magazines **M** 99; marketing **M** 343; newspapers **N** 86; public relations **P** 331; radio and television programs **R** 411; selling **S** 262–63; *see also* Propaganda

Cross-References. There are two types of guideposts, called cross-references, that make all indexes easier to use. The first is the "see" reference. This directs the reader away from a term not used as an entry to the one where the information will be found. The other is the "see also" reference. It directs the reader to additional and related information that will be found in another place.

The "see" reference is necessary because different people think of the same subject in different ways. Insofar as possible, the index includes all the terms that might be used to describe a topic listed. Under each term there appears a "see" reference to the word chosen for the entry. Many things, some people, and some places are known by more than one name. Ping-Pong is a game that some people play. Others call the game table tennis. The index will include both names and use a "see" reference under the one that is not the entry.

Ping-Pong *see* Table tennis
• • •
Table tennis or Ping-Pong T 212

Samuel Langhorne Clemens and Mark Twain are two names for the same person. Some books put information about him under one name, some under the other. However, the "see" reference will show the name under which the information will be found.

Clemens, Samuel Langhorne *see* Twain, Mark
• • •
Twain, Mark (Samuel Langhorne Clemens), American writer **T** 482
  Huckleberry Finn, The Adventures of **H** 510
  Tom Sawyer, The Adventures of **T** 318

When an index is not well supplied with "see" references, it is sometimes necessary to look in several places before the term chosen for the entry can be found. If a user follows up the "see" references, he will be sure to find the information he wants.

Some words found in indexes are so closely connected that it is difficult to separate completely the information they cover. "Athletics," "Games," and "Sports" are such words. The exact information the reader wants may appear under only one of the three. A "see also" reference can be used to bring the three terms together.

> **Athletics**
>   gymnastics **G** 202
>   physical education **P** 394
>   track and field **T** 282–84
>   *See also* Games; Sports
> **Games G** 222–26
>   billiards **B** 112–13
>   bowling **B** 214–16
>   chess **C** 312–13
>   table tennis **T** 212
>   *See also* Athletics; Sports
> **Sports**
>   archery **A** 218–20
>   baseball **B** 312–16
>   golf **G** 412–14
>   skiing **S** 214–16
>   soccer **S** 220–22
>   *See also* Athletics; Games

"See also" references are also helpful in guiding the reader away from a general heading when the material he wants is listed under a specific heading.

Kinds of Indexes There are indexes to newspapers, to magazines, and to books. Some magazines publish indexes once a year or every 6 months and issue them to subscribers who request copies. The magazines *Time* and *National Geographic* are among those that do. Other indexes cover the material in many magazines. The *Readers' Guide to Periodical Literature,* published since 1900, makes available the information contained in approximately 130 popular United States magazines of general interest. It indexes articles by main subjects and by authors, but not usually by title. Published semimonthly except in July and August, its information is quickly available. There is an annual cumulation of the monthly issues. All the entries are interfiled and bound in one volume.

Other magazine indexes specialize in particular types of information. Magazines of interest to teachers are covered by the *Education Index*. Magazines of interest to farmers and to scientists concerned with the production of food are covered by the *Agricultural Index*. On the inside front cover these indexes list the magazines they include. Each has useful instructions, abbreviations, and explanations at the beginning of each volume.

The largest index to many books is the *Cumulative Book Index*. It lists by author, title, and subject practically all books printed in English. It includes as well the publisher and the price of each book. The CBI, as it is often called, is published monthly except for July, August, and December. Like the magazine indexes, it is cumulated often. The CBI, which began as the *United States Catalog,* is a part of the national bibliography, a record of book publication.

The most useful indexes to books of a particular kind are those to plays, to poetry, and to quotations. Many plays and poems are published in collections, and it is difficult to know which collection will contain a certain selection. An index to plays shows in what book each listed play can be found. A poetry index does the same thing for each poem it includes. An index to quotations makes it possible to find a passage from the writings or speeches of particular persons. It also helps in finding quotations on certain subjects.

Some indexes are never in book form but are always kept on cards. The card catalog of a library is the index of the books on its shelves. Quite a few large business offices index business letters on card files, often with mechanical sorters and electronic equipment. Some people use card files for indexing recipes and for friends' addresses.

MARY KENT GRANT
Reviewed by EDWIN B. COLBURN
Vice-President and Chief of Indexing Services
The H. W. Wilson Company

See also REFERENCE BOOKS.

INDIA

South of the Himalayas and extending to the Indian Ocean is a vast region sometimes known as the Indian subcontinent. A region rich in history, it saw the rise and fall of many great empires and kingdoms. Dominated politically by Great Britain for almost 200 years, independence came to the subcontinent in 1947, when it was partitioned into the two nations of India and Pakistan.

▶ THE PEOPLE

With a population of over 500,000,000 India is second only to China in number of people. Its average population density is more than 400 persons per square mile, in contrast to less than 60 in the United States. More than 70 percent of the people live in the country's many thousands of villages. India has some of the world's major cities—such as Calcutta, Bombay, Madras, and Delhi—and yet when

Indian women often work on construction projects.

compared to the total population of the country, relatively few people live in the cities.

Archeologists have uncovered two great cities in the Indus River valley in what was formerly northwestern India and is now West Pakistan—Harappa and Mohenjo-Daro—that may date back to 2500 B.C. The people of the Indus valley are believed to have been the earliest to live in India. Another people who have lived in India since prehistoric times are the Dravidians. They are a dark-skinned people who are known to have lived in villages and practiced farming as far back as the end of the Stone Age. Today the Dravidians make up most of the population of southern India.

The Aryans and Dravidians. The Aryans entered India a number of times beginning around 1500 B.C. They probably came from the Caucasus mountain region. The Indus valley people were either conquered or assimilated by the Aryans.

The Aryans were tall, fair of skin, with thin noses and straight black hair. The life of the Aryan people was well organized. Priests, who were also teachers, were called *Brahmans*. Rulers were known as *Kshatriya,* and businessmen were called *Vaishya*. The Dravidian group, called *Sudra* by the Aryans, worked with their hands. Marriage between *Sudras* and Aryans was not allowed.

The Aryans spread gradually throughout northern India. Their society and culture became a combination of Aryan and local elements in northern India. But southern India remained principally Dravidian. Today there still is a cultural difference between the Indo-Aryan north and the Dravidian south.

Later invasions brought to India many people of central Asian stock, as well as some Greeks and Arabs. Present-day Indians are the descendants of all these people. The dominant strain of the Indian people, however, is Aryan in origin, and racially most northern Indians are regarded as Caucasoid (white).

Religion. Nearly all the main religions of the world are represented in India. Although Hinduism is the religion of a vast majority of the people, India also has a large Mus-

lim population and a considerable number of Christians and Sikhs. Other minority religious groups include the Buddhists and Jains, with smaller communities of Parsis (Zoroastrians) and Jews.

Languages. Almost three fourths of the people of India speak Indo-Aryan languages, of which Hindi—with its related dialects—is the most important. Hindi is the official language of India. English is the second national language and is used in administration, business, and higher education. Many

STATES AND TERRITORIES

STATES: Andhra Pradesh, Assam, Bihar, Gujarat, Haryana, Himachal Pradesh, Jammu and Kashmir, Kerala, Madhya Pradesh, Manipur, Meghalaya, Tamil Nadu (Madras), Maharashtra, Mysore, Nagaland, Orissa, Punjab, Rajasthan, Tripura, Uttar Pradesh, and West Bengal.

FEDERALLY ADMINISTERED TERRITORIES: Andaman and Nicobar Islands; Arunachal Pradesh; Chandigarh; Dadra and Nagar Haveli; Delhi, Goa, Daman, and Diu; Laccadive, Minicoy, and Amindivi Islands; Mizoram; Pondicherry.

Birla Temple, a Hindu place of worship in New Delhi.

Celebration of a religious festival during the Muslim month of Muharram.

Although school is free and compulsory for all children aged 6 to 11, there is still a shortage of classrooms. Children often study outdoors in villages.

Hindi words that come from Sanskrit are similar to the European words. For example, the Hindi word *mata* is *mater* in Latin, *Mutter* in German, and *mother* in English.

There is also a large number of Urdu-speaking people in northern India. Urdu is a Hindi-based language. Its spoken form is similar to Hindi, but its script is Persian-Arabic. It is today the national language of West Pakistan.

Regional languages are used in the Indian states—for example, Bengali in West Bengal, Marathi in Maharashtra, and Punjabi in Punjab. All these are Indo-Aryan languages and are similar to Hindi.

Dravidian languages are spoken in southern India. The four important Dravidian languages are Tamil, spoken in Madras, Telugu in Andhra Pradesh, Malayalam in Kerala, and Kannada in Mysore.

Most educated Indians speak several languages. They speak their native regional language as well as Hindi and English. Hindi, the national language, is now being taught in schools to children in all parts of India.

Education. School is most important in the life of Indian boys and girls. Since India's independence in 1947, school has been free and compulsory for children between the ages of 6 and 11.

Some schools are run by the government, while others are run by private organizations or by Christian missions. The country as a whole has a large number of recognized educational institutions. But many of the village elementary schools have only one teacher, and because of the shortage of trained teachers, a large-scale expansion of schools has been difficult. Nevertheless, it is estimated that the country has more than 70,000,000 students.

Secondary-school (grades 6 to 10) education in India includes the learning of basic crafts, such as spinning and weaving, vegetable gardening, fruit preservation, carpentry, leatherwork, and domestic crafts. Educators believe that training in these skills will lead to gainful employment of students when they graduate from school. Some students go on to the higher secondary schools (grades 11 and 12) for 1 or 2 years. Students who graduate from the higher secondary schools can be admitted to one of the many universities in India.

A young girl learns to read the Hindi alphabet.

Many Indian boys leave school after grade 8 or 10, and learn the crafts of their fathers. A skilled craftsman—such as a jeweler, carpenter, or weaver with his own shop—teaches some of his sons the craft taught him by his father. One or two sons, however, may complete high school and college and become professional men, such as teachers, lawyers, or doctors.

Indian Family Life. Family ties are very strong in India. The Indian family is made up not only of a man and his wife and their children, but it also includes a large "joint family." The sons bring their wives to their parents' home and there bring up their children. Often the joint family includes grandsons and their wives and children. Daughters and granddaughters remain in the family until they get married. Then they become part of their husband's joint family. After the death of the head of a family, a very large joint family may split apart, as sons start new joint families of their own. In the joint family all the property is held together, and all able members work together to support the old and sick members of the family.

Men take care of family money matters and the family's relations with the outside world. Women manage the household. Neither men nor women interfere with each other's duties. All members of the family respect the authority of the elders, particularly of the oldest male, in outside matters. But the mother has a great deal of authority in matters affecting the running of the household.

In recent years the joint family system has begun to break up as a result of new job opportunities in the cities. Couples and their children drift off to look for jobs. Family members, however, still consider the joint family home as their center, to which they return periodically.

Most marriages are arranged by the parents of the bride and groom. Dating takes place only among the few Westernized Indians.

Children grow up in the warmth of a large family circle that consists of the mother, many aunts, and many young cousins and brothers and sisters to play with. Hindu children celebrate "Sister's Day," called Raksha Bandhan Day. A sister ties a *rakhi* (silken amulet) around the wrist of her brother for his protection, and in turn he gives her a gift.

Castes. The peculiar Indian institution of the caste system developed out of the early Aryan custom of separating people according to the work they did. Members of each caste tend to follow a common occupation. For example, servants, janitors, and other menial workers belong to the lower castes, while educators and administrators are often members of the higher castes. Families that make up a caste usually live in the same neighborhood.

The castes are hereditary social classes. An Indian born in a low-caste family cannot change his caste to a higher group by education or wealth. In fact the entire Indian social structure is rigidly restricted by the caste system.

Formerly, members of a hereditary group known as the untouchables (considered outcasts) were much discriminated against by the Hindu castes. Although they make up a very large group, the untouchables were segregated in the Indian society. But the practice of untouchability has been abolished by the Indian constitution.

Festivals. The great many Indian religious beliefs and different cultural traditions account for the large number of festivals in India.

Dasehra, one of the chief festivals of India, celebrated in September or October, symbolizes the triumph of Good over Evil. In Delhi, *Dasehra* celebrations are climaxed with the burning of giant images of legendary demons made of bamboo and papier-mâché and stuffed with firecrackers. In Mysore, a city in southern India, a parade through arch-covered streets is led by the governor of the state riding on a richly decorated elephant.

Dipavali, or the Festival of Lamps, is celebrated in October or November. All homes are lit with lamps or candles, and every town and hamlet is filled with light to show great joy.

For the Indian Muslims, *Ramzan* (*Ramadan*) *Id-al-Fitr* is the chief festival. *Ramzan,* the 9th month of the Islamic year, is observed by the Muslims as a sacred month during which they fast every day from dawn to sunset. The *Id-al-Fitr* festival marks the end of the month of *Ramzan* and is celebrated as a joyful event. People wear their best clothes, and mosques are crowded with worshipers.

Christmas is celebrated by Christians throughout India. Shops and homes take on a holiday air. In some northern Indian villages, groups of Christians sing native Christmas carols to the accompaniment of musical instruments.

The birthday anniversary of Guruanak, the founder of the Sikh religion, is celebrated with great joy, as is the birthday of Guru Gobind Singh, a Sikh religious leader.

Independence Day (August 15) is observed by people all over India with a sense of national pride, but Republic Day (January 26) celebrations in New Delhi, the capital, are the most impressive.

Homes. The types of houses vary in different parts of the country, depending on climate and the availability of building materials. A more expensive house may be built of brick with wooden doors and windows and a tile roof. The house may have many rooms or a few, and it may have one or two stories. A low-cost house is generally built of mud and straw with a thatched roof and has only one or two rooms. The majority of country houses have an interior courtyard around which the rooms are built. Sometimes there is an open court in front of the house. At night farmers keep the cattle or other animals in one of the rooms that open on the courtyard. In the courtyard women sit to prepare vegetables for cooking, children study their lessons, men have their hair cut, and peddlers bring wares to show.

In a Hindu house the kitchen is considered a sacred room. A poor man's house may not have a separate kitchen. The cooking may be done in one corner of a large room that is also used for other purposes.

The family sits on the floor mat for meals, eaten in or near the kitchen. People outside the family and members of the family who have not performed the ritual of bathing do not enter the kitchen section of the orthodox Hindu house.

In the homes of the poorer families food is cooked on a little clay stove (*chula*) in one corner of the room, or in a little alcove. Food is eaten with the tips of the fingers from a bowl or tray, and hands are washed before and after eating.

Most well-to-do families have a separate room for worship. Only after bathing and changing into a clean garment may one enter the "worship room."

The daily bath is an important ritual among Indians. A bath may be taken near a well outside the house, or at a watertap—if there is one—in the house, or in the rivers or lakes in rural areas.

Most Indian houses have little or no furniture. In northern Indian village houses, rice straw covered with a rug or carpet is the bed. In southern Indian rural houses a simple mat may serve as the bed. In cities beds with mattresses and chairs with cushions are common. In large cities, where European influence is strongest, Western-type furniture is found in Indian homes.

Indian Villages. There are hundreds of thousands of villages in India, about one for every 575 acres of cultivated land. The village is not only a center of farming activities, but it is also the center of social activities.

The appearance and size of an Indian village depends very much on its location and climate. In the western part of the Ganges Plain of northern India, villages are large and closely grouped together. In the eastern part of the plain there are scattered villages, each made up of a few homes. In the Ganges delta region of West Bengal the village is made up of small groups of houses scattered throughout the rice and jute fields and usually built on raised blocks above high flood level. In Rajasthan and the Deccan region the land is dry. Because there are only a few sources of water for each village, houses are built close together.

The size of Indian villages varies widely. Some may have only a few hundred people, while others may have several thousand inhabitants. A small village does not have a post office or shops, but some of the large villages have small shops in which matches, kerosene for lamps, salt, soap, flashlights, and other articles are sold. Generally the villagers buy and sell at nearby market towns or at the weekly market. The market is often located at the spot where bullock-cart roads from several villages meet.

The chief means of transportation in rural India is the slow-moving, two-wheeled bullock cart. It is estimated that there are millions of these bullock carts in India, although more and more villagers have begun to use bicycles for transportation.

In most of India, village houses were commonly grouped according to the caste of the people. Often at the center of the village stood a little Hindu temple or Muslim mosque.

A nearby lake, pond, or river supplies water for livestock, washing clothes, and domestic use. Drinking water comes from the village wells. The Republic of India has outlawed caste discriminations, but in the small and isolated Indian villages caste discriminations continue though on a modest scale, and social changes are slow.

The standard of living in Indian villages is very low. Per capita income of the villagers averages about $70 per year. Clothing is simple, and houses are small and crowded. Each house has only a few bare essentials, such as copper and earthenware pots for cooking, carrying water, and storing grain.

The University of Madras.

Other common household articles may be a few cotton quilts, a small box with a few clothes, and a religious picture or figure.

To bring medical care to the rural population, health centers have been established in the rural areas. Each of these centers includes a dispensary with four to six hospital beds and is staffed with a doctor and several nurses and midwives. It is estimated that there are thousands of such health centers in the country. In addition to these health centers, remote villages are served by roving health units made up of a doctor and a nurse traveling in a medical van.

India's Cities. The cities of India present contrasts of old and new architectural designs, and of the Western and the Oriental ways of life. Nowhere is this contrast more clear than between Delhi and New Delhi, the capital of India. These twin cities are situated on the west bank of the Jumna River in northwestern India. Delhi's city wall, bazaars, narrow streets, and the 17th-century Mogul imperial palace give the old city a distinctly Oriental flavor. New Delhi, on the other hand, has wide avenues, modern office buildings, a fashionable shopping center, a racetrack, a golf course, and two airports. Together, Delhi and New Delhi have a population of 2,500,000.

Agra, about 125 miles from Delhi, is known the world over as the city of the Taj Mahal. Completed in 1653 by the Mogul emperor Shah Jahan as a memorial to his queen, Mumtaz Mahal, the monument dominates the city's landscape.

Bombay, on the west coast, has the tempo of a large Western city with its giant business houses and skyscrapers. Bombay is not only the nation's major port and commercial center, but it is also a large industrial center and film capital. It has a population of about 5,000,000.

Calcutta, the hub of eastern India, is a great center of commerce and industry. About 5,000,000 people are packed into the city and its industrial suburbs. The city's museums tell much about Indian life and history. For the most part Calcutta and its suburbs are a jam-packed eyesore with groups of flimsy, one-room huts—each housing as many as 10 people. Thousands of people sleep on sidewalks.

The major city of southern India is Madras, with a population of about 2,000,000. A center of music, dance, and the fine arts, Madras gives the visitor a colorful picture of Hindu life. Hindu temples seem to be everywhere in the area around Madras. They were built between A.D. 600 and 1600, during a great period of religious art, much like the Middle Ages in Europe.

There are many different ways to travel on the narrow streets of Udaipur in Rajasthan.

▶ THE LAND

India has three major physical areas: (1) the Himalayas and their foothills; (2) the northern plains; and (3) the plateau of peninsular India.

The Himalaya Mountains. The great mountain wall of the Himalayas stretches 1,500 miles between the gorges of the Indus River on the west to those of the Brahmaputra River on the east. To the east, between India and Burma, are the Patkai and the Naga hills. At the western end of the Himalayas, beyond the Indus River, lies the Karakoram range. Of the 94 Asian peaks that are higher than 24,000 feet, all but two are in the Himalayas and the Karakoram. No other mountain ranges in the world have so many peaks of this height.

The Himalayas are a series of parallel ranges; their width varies from 100 to 150 miles. These ranges can be grouped into the Great Himalayas, the Lesser Himalayas, and the Outer Himalayas, or Siwalik ranges. In each region the southern slopes of the range are steep, while the northern slopes facing Tibet are much gentler. The northern slopes are generally covered by forests below the snow line. The southern slopes are too steep either to gather snow or to support much tree growth, except in the valleys.

The average height of the Great Himalayas

Ancient system of irrigation still in use in parts of India.

Hindu pilgrims come from all over India to bathe in the waters of the sacred Ganges River. The river is believed to have the power to purify the soul.

Bombay, on India's west coast, is the country's commercial center. Wide avenues and European-style buildings, such as Victoria Railway Station (*right*) and the Municipal Building (*left*), give the city a cosmopolitan appearance.

An Indian village nestled in the snow-covered Himalayas.

is 20,000 feet. The range contains such famous peaks as Mt. Everest (29,028 feet), highest in the world, and Kanchenjunga (28,146 feet). Because of the mountains' great heights there are only a few passes through which people can travel. These passes are situated on the main Indo-Tibetan trade route through the Chumbi Valley, northeast of the city of Darjeeling.

Few peaks of the Lesser Himalayas are higher than 15,000 feet. The ranges of the Lesser Himalayas average 50 miles in width and are interspersed with large valleys. Some of these are fertile, quite large, and of great scenic beauty. In the Lesser Himalayas there are "hill stations," or mountain resorts—such as Simla and Darjeeling—where people can escape the awful summer heat of the northern Indian plain.

The Outer Himalayas form low foothills between the Lesser Himalayas and the Indian plains. This low foothill zone is 35 miles wide but gets narrower in the east.

North Indian Plains. Between peninsular India and the Himalayas lie the alluvial plains of the Indus, Ganges, and Brahmaputra rivers. These plains, called the Indo-Gangetic lowland, stretch from the Arabian Sea to the Bay of Bengal in a great arc ranging in width from 300 miles in the west to somewhat less than 90 miles at the eastern end above the Ganges delta. Within this region lies the most productive and most densely settled section of India. As a result of the 1947 partition of the Indian subcontinent, the greater part of the Indus basin now lies within West Pakistan.

All three great rivers that water the lowland—the Indus, the Ganges, and the Brahmaputra—are supplied by permanent glaciers of the Himalayas.

The Indus River has been such an important barrier to invaders from the west that its name was given to the whole country. Industhan (or Hindustan) means the "land beyond the Indus." The source of the Indus lies in Tibet.

The headwater tributaries of the Ganges rise in the area of the Great Himalayas, between the peaks of Bandarpunch (20,720 feet) and Nanda Devi (25,645 feet). The Ganges enters the plain from the Outer Himalayas through a gorge at Hardwar, where the headwork of the Ganges Canals System is

located. The Ganges flows due east, turns south, and with the Brahmaputra River flows through East Pakistan, finally emptying into the Bay of Bengal.

The Brahmaputra River comes around the eastern end of the Himalayas through a gorge about 8,000 feet deep. It flows for nearly 700 miles through a region of tea gardens and rice fields in the Indian state of Assam. From Assam it flows south into the major jute-growing section of East Pakistan and empties into the Bay of Bengal.

Peninsular India. The peninsular plateau, or Deccan plateau, is separated from the Indo-Gangetic plain by many hills varying from 1,500 to 4,000 feet in height. On one side of the peninsula are the low, broken Eastern Ghats. The average elevation of the Eastern Ghats is about 3,000 feet, although the mountains rise in places to almost 9,000 feet.

The peninsular tableland is rocky and uneven. It extends to a number of hilly ranges in the far south that are over 4,000 feet high in some places. The northwestern part of the peninsular plateau is covered by vast lava flows. Successive lava flows created the Deccan Traps. The Traps look like giant staircases. They are actually weathered, steplike, and flat-topped basalt hills, and they are the major scenic feature of the Deccan.

The west coast of the peninsula is a land of small fishing villages, coconut palms, and spice gardens. Many ancient ports dot the coastline. In the hills a few miles inland are coffee, tea, and rubber plantations.

The peninsular plateau is crossed by the Narbada, Tapti, Cauvery, and Godavari rivers. The Narbada, Godavari, and Cauvery are—like the Ganges—sacred rivers of India. The banks of the Narbada are lined with Hindu shrines and temples. The Cauvery, also known as Dakshina Ganga, or Ganges of the South, is the second most sacred river of India—the Ganges is first. The Cauvery River has been harnessed for irrigation and hydroelectric power and supplies power to many areas of Mysore. There is much farming activity in the fertile deltas on the east coast.

The Climate. To understand the Indian climate one must understand the monsoon wind system. In the winter, when the landmass

FACTS AND FIGURES

INDIA is the official name of the country. Its ancient name was Bharat.

CAPITAL: New Delhi.

LOCATION AND SIZE: South Asia. **Latitude**—8° 04' N to 37° 18' N. **Longitude**—68° 07' E to 97° 24' E. **Area**—1,261,813 sq. mi.

PHYSICAL FEATURES: Highest point—Mt. Godwin Austen (K2) in Kashmir (28,250 ft.). **Lowest point**—Sea level. **Chief rivers**—Ganges, Indus, Brahmaputra, Beas, Sutlej, Jumna, Bhagirathi, Padma, Mahanadi, Godavari, Kistna, Cauvery, Narbada, and Tapti. **Chief mountain peaks**—Nanda Devi (25,645 ft.) and Kamet (25,447 ft.).

POPULATION: 537,000,000 (estimate).

LANGUAGE: Hindi (official), English (second official language); hundreds of other languages and dialects including Assamese, Bengali, Oriya, Gujarati, Marathi, Kashmiri, Punjabi, Tamil, Telugu, Malayalam, Kannada, Urdu.

RELIGION: Hindu, Muslim, Christian, Sikh, Jain, Buddhist, Parsi (Zoroastrian), Jewish.

GOVERNMENT: Republic. **Head of state**—president. **Head of government**—prime minister. **International co-operation**—United Nations, Commonwealth of Nations, Colombo Plan.

NATIONAL ANTHEM: *Jana-gana-mana* ("The Mind of the Multitude of the People"). First line—"Thou are the ruler of the minds of all people."

ECONOMY: Agricultural products—rice, wheat, sugarcane, cotton, tea, coffee, rubber, pepper, cardamom, coir, copra, cashew nuts, bananas, groundnuts, sesame seeds, linseed, cottonseed, rapeseed, mustard, jute, tobacco, opium, maize, millet and sorghum, chickpeas. **Industries and products**—textiles (cotton, jute, wool, silk, rayon, nylon), chemicals, iron and steel, cement, aluminum, industrial machinery and equipment, copper and brass, movies, electric motors, coal, plastics, handicrafts (shawl and carpet weaving, woodcarving and metalworking), food processing (wheat flour, rice, sugar, vegetable oil), tanning, plywood and paper, bicycles. **Chief minerals**—coal, iron ore, mica, manganese, copper, ilmenite, chrome ore, petroleum, monazite, bauxite. **Chief exports**—tea, cotton goods, jute, manganese ores, cashew kernels, raw cotton, unmanufactured tobacco, iron ore, mica, raw wool, coffee, goatskins, leather (undressed), cotton waste, coal, castor oil, refined sugar. **Chief imports**—food, raw materials, mineral fuels, chemicals, textiles, iron and steel, motor vehicles, unwrought copper, machine tools and metalworking machinery, power-generating machinery, cotton textile machinery, electrical generators. **Monetary unit**—rupee.

and therefore there is no rain over most of India in the winter. In the summer, when the landmass is warmer than the surrounding water, the monsoon wind moves deep into the subcontinent from the Bay of Bengal and the Arabian Sea. The season of the summer monsoon brings a great deal of rain.

In January there is a wide range of temperatures from north to south. The days are warm and the nights cold. The average temperature for January is less than 55 degrees Fahrenheit in the Punjab, about 60 degrees along the Ganges River, and about 75 degrees in Madras. April and May, when the sun is directly above India, are the hottest months. The average temperature for May is more than 100 degrees in northwestern India, and is over 85 degrees in the Ganges delta in east central India. The summer monsoon usually starts about the middle or end of June and is accompanied by very heavy rain and violent thunder and lightning. In most parts of India, between June and September, the summer monsoon, or southwest winds, brings rain. The winter monsoon, or northeast winds, brings rain only to the Madras coast in southeastern India.

In India, where most of the people are farmers, the amount of rain and when it falls are very important. When rainfall is very abnormal, as is often the case, there may be drought in one place and flood in another. Drought and flood lead to crop failures. Annual rainfall ranges from less than 10 inches a year in parts of the northwest to about 450 inches at Cherrapunji in Assam in the northeast. A very small percentage of the land receives over 100 inches. Calcutta on the east coast has 63 inches yearly; Delhi in the north, 25; and Bombay in the west, 71.

Natural Resources. India has many natural resources. The most important mineral-bearing area is the Chota Nagpur plateau in the east. Most of the country's coal, iron, mica, and copper comes from this region. Ilmenite and monazite, the strategic minerals, are found in the sands of the Kerala coast in southwestern India. India's supplies of manganese, ilmenite, monazite, and iron ore are among the largest in the world.

India's rivers provide the water resources for irrigation and hydroelectric power development. Underground waters also are a val-

is cooler than the surrounding water, the prevailing winds of the winter monsoon move from the Indian subcontinent toward the ocean. These land winds are generally dry, uable source of water supply for farming purposes.

India's forests cover about 190,000,000 acres. Wood from the forest is used for timber and fuel. Acetic acid, oils, methyl alcohol, and valuable drugs are extracted from wood.

Medicinal plants, essential oils, resins, waxes, dyes, and fibers are resources that are not yet being used to the best advantage.

▶ ECONOMY

Farming. India is an agricultural country. About 70 percent of the people depend on farming for their living. It is estimated that seven out of every eight village families are entirely or partly dependent on agriculture. The eighth family supports itself by trade or by supplying services to other villagers.

A large number of Indian people raise only enough to live on. Old methods of farming are still being used. Because there are few jobs available in the cities, the movement of population from farms to urban areas has been slow.

Most farmland is cut up into tiny plots. As a result farm machinery is not used to any extent. Most Indian farmers use hand labor to plant and harvest. Progress, however, is being made in modernizing farming activities. India is not always able to meet the food needs of its tremendous population. In recent years it has had to turn to surplus-grain–producing countries, such as the United States and Canada, for very large amounts of grain to meet emergency food shortages. Various public and

The bullock cart and the modern oil well show the old and the new in India.

private projects and technical assistance programs to raise food production have been started in an effort to overcome the country's problems.

India is the world's second largest producer of rice. Rice is grown in the Ganges valley and the coastal areas of peninsular India. Wheat is raised in a large area of northern and central India. Sugarcane is grown in the Ganges Plain, and cotton is grown in the southern and northwestern areas of the Deccan plateau and the Punjab. Tea, India's most important beverage, is produced in Assam in northeastern India. Coffee, rubber, pepper, and cardamom plantations are found in southern India.

Shopping in a market in rural India.

Spinning cotton thread is an important handicraft in India.

Calcutta is a major seaport. Ships from all over the world load and unload goods at its docks.

Thick coconut groves along the Kerala coast in southwestern India yield coir and copra from coconuts. Most of the country's supply of cashew nuts also comes from the southwest. Bananas are raised in the fertile soil of the east coast river deltas.

Industry. A relatively small number of Indians earn their living in large-scale factory industry. Many more work at handicrafts. Industries have increased in number since independence, under the government's five-year plans. But a lack of adequate transportation and a shortage of power, skilled labor, and capital, as well as the necessity to divert funds to food production, have held back potential industrial growth.

The manufacture of jute for use in packaging and bagging is one of India's largest industries. It is located mainly in the Calcutta area. The Indian cotton mill industry is one of the world's largest. Most mills are in Bombay and Ahmedabad, a major city of west central India. Chemicals, iron and steel, cement, and aluminum are the other main industries.

Rice, India's most important food crop, is transplanted by hand.

Right: Coconuts, an important crop of Kerala, yield coir and copra. Boats on Kerala's waterways carry coconuts to factories. Below: New roads, many built completely by hand, are being constructed throughout India. There is still, however, a shortage of paved highways and other types of allweather roads.

Above: The inspiring Taj Mahal, built in the 17th century by the Mogul emperor Shah Jahan as a tomb for his wife. Below: Worshipers bathe before an ancient Hindu temple.

GOVERNMENT

According to the constitution of 1950, the political organization of the Republic of India is based on a federal system. India has both a central government and state governments. The constitution gives the vote to all Indians, both male and female, over 21 years of age. The president and vice-president are elected for terms of 5 years by an electoral college made up of members of the national and state legislatures.

The national legislature consists of two houses. The House of the People (*Lok Sabha*), the lower house, is elected by popular vote and elects its own speaker. The Council of States (*Rajya Sabha*), the upper house, is headed by the vice-president and is composed of members elected by the state legislatures and a small number of members appointed by the president.

Following the British parliamentary system, the prime minister of India is a member of the House of the People, and he and his cabinet are responsible to the legislature. Therefore, the executive and the administrative branches of the government must keep the confidence of the legislature in order to remain in power.

▶ HISTORY

Early History. India's history goes back many centuries before the birth of Christ. Around 1500 B.C., Aryan people from the northwest of the subcontinent settled in India and built a highly developed civilization. During the following centuries the Aryans gradually spread over all of northern India. In the 6th century B.C. two great religions, Buddhism and Jainism, originated in eastern India. During the next 1,000 years Buddhism spread over most of Asia, and India became a "holy land" visited by pilgrims from far-off places. In the meantime, part of western India was conquered by Persia. Through the Persians, India came into contact with the Greek world. In 326 B.C. Alexander the Great of Macedonia invaded India but withdrew after his homesick army refused to go farther.

Hindu Kingdoms. Up until Alexander's invasion the Aryan people had been divided into many small kingdoms. Inspired by Alexander's invasion, Chandragupta Maurya, King of Magadha (modern Bihar), began to conquer the smaller kingdoms and build a large empire in northern India. He succeeded in unifying the Aryan people under a single rule. Asoka, Chandragupta's grandson, who reigned during the 3rd century B.C., was one of the great rulers of India. He initiated a policy of religious and racial tolerance.

After the death of Asoka, India again broke up into many small kingdoms. New waves of people from southwestern Asia entered the country, bringing foreign influence to northern India. In the same period several Dravidian kingdoms flourished in southern India. These kingdoms spread Indian influence to Southeast Asia, and Hindu empires were built in Cambodia, Thailand, and Indonesia.

Gupta Rulers. In the 4th century A.D. the Guptas, a new dynasty (or ruling house), came to power in northern India. The best known of the Gupta rulers was Chandragupta II, who extended his empire over all of northern India. The Gupta period was the golden age of Indian culture. Poets and artists flourished. Several great universities were established. It was during this era that the mathematical concept of zero was developed in India. Later the concept was carried by the Arabs from India to Europe.

The Gupta empire was destroyed at the end of the 5th century by the Huns, a tribe of people from central Asia. Thereafter, for more than a century, northern India was under the control of a number of local kingdoms. Finally, early in the 7th century one of the kings, Harsha, was able to unify much of northern India. But Harsha died in 647, leaving no heir to his throne. As a result, northern India was again broken up into a number of small kingdoms.

During the post-Gupta period several Dravidian kingdoms flourished in southern India. Among these, the Chola and Pallava kingdoms on the east coast were seafaring states. Their ships traded with Siam and Java and brought Hindu cultural influence to Southeast Asia.

Muslim Invasions. During the 11th century Muslim invaders from central Asia conquered northern India. They founded the sultanate (kingdom) of Delhi that dominated northern India for almost 2 centuries. In 1398 the Mongol conqueror Tamerlane invaded the Delhi Sultanate. As a result, northern India was again split into a number of kingdoms. In

the south the Hindu empire of Vijayanagar was established and flourished until 1565.

The Mogul Conquest. The political disintegration of northern India led to an invasion by still another people—the Moguls—from central Asia. Their leader, Baber, a descendant of Tamerlane and Genghis Khan, conquered northern India in 1526 and proclaimed himself the first Mogul emperor of India. His grandson Akbar, who reigned from 1556 to 1605, was one of the ablest and best-known rulers of India. Unlike other Muslim rulers, Akbar allowed people of all religions to worship as they pleased. Akbar's son Jahangir ruled from 1605 to 1627. During his reign an English ambassador sent by James I, King of England, first visited the subcontinent of India.

Mogul architecture reached its highest development during the reign of Emperor Shah Jahan (1627–58), who built the famous Taj Mahal at Agra as a tomb for his wife. Shah Jahan's successor, Aurangzeb, who ruled from 1659 to 1707, had neither the ability nor the tolerance of the former emperors. He destroyed many Hindu temples in northern India and followed a policy of extreme bigotry. The weak Mogul emperors who succeeded Aurangzeb were in no position to check invasions from the northwest. In 1739 Nadir Shah of Persia defeated Mogul armies and carried away from Delhi most of the movable wealth of the Moguls. The resulting political chaos paved the way for the spread of British power in India.

European Penetration of India. In 1498 Vasco da Gama discovered the sea route to India. Soon afterward European traders—the Portuguese, Dutch, French, and English— came to the shores of India to look for the fine cotton cloth, rare woods, jewels, silk, and spices that they had heard about. The Portuguese were the first to establish control on the west coast of India. Although the Portuguese later lost most of their Indian territories, they remained in Goa until 1961.

During the first half of the 18th century, the Dutch, French, and British set up trading settlements on the coast of India and became active rivals. In 1757 the British, under Robert Clive of the East India Company, won an important battle at Plassey by defeating the French and their local allies. Consequently the rich Ganges valley region came under the control of the British East India Company.

The British Indian Empire. The battle of Plassey laid the foundation of the East India Company's empire. The company, through war and diplomacy, continued to take over more and more Indian territory during the second half of the 18th century. Indian resentment of the British led to the Sepoy Mutiny of 1857, which was put down by the company. In the following year, the British Government took over the East India Company's Indian empire, and in 1877 Queen Victoria was proclaimed Empress of India. The political map of India remained basically the same from the time the Sepoy Mutiny was suppressed until the subcontinent was partitioned in 1947.

The Indian National Movement. The Indian national movement first began in the late 19th century and the beginning of the 20th century. The Indians wanted a constitution that would give them a greater share in governing themselves. The British proved slow in granting reforms, and the revolutionary movement grew. The Indians demanded self-government and freedom from British control. Important constitutional reforms were finally carried out by the British after World War I, but these reforms were too late to stop the tide of nationalism.

Mahatma Gandhi. Mohandas K. Gandhi (1869–1948), often called *Mahatma,* or Great Soul, became the leader of the Indian national movement. Gandhi was a Hindu, and was trained in law in England. He served twice as president of the All-India National Congress (Congress Party), formed in 1885 to work for the self-government of the Indian people. In 1919 Gandhi began to support self-rule, nonviolence, the development of native handicrafts, and the removal of "untouchability." ("Untouchability," an outgrowth of the Hindu caste system, forced millions of low-caste Hindus, called untouchables, to do the work considered undesirable by higher-caste Hindus. The untouchables, considered unclean and therefore not to be touched, were forced to live completely apart from the other castes.) Gandhi started a civil disobedience movement. He urged the Indians not to buy British goods and to reject taxation without representation.

Partition and Independence. In 1935 Britain gave India a new constitution. It provided for a bicameral federal legislature, with a council of states and an assembly. The Muslims complained, however, that the Hindu majority would gain control and thereby place Muslim religion and culture in a disadvantageous position. In 1942 the Muslims demanded a separate state of Pakistan to be formed from areas in the subcontinent that had a majority of Muslims. When all attempts to form a single government in an undivided India failed, the Indians finally agreed to the creation of the Muslim state of Pakistan. On August 15, 1947, the Indian subcontinent achieved independence, but it was partitioned into two nations, which are now the republics of India and Pakistan. After the partition of the subcontinent about 9,000,000 Hindus and Sikhs moved from Pakistan to India. The settling of these people has been a major problem for India.

In January, 1948, Gandhi, who was working toward an independent and unified India,

IMPORTANT DATES

About 2500 B.C.	Advanced civilization flourishes in the Indus valley.
About 1500 B.C.	Aryans enter India.
563 B.C.	Gautama Buddha is born.
327– 325 B.C.	India is invaded by Alexander the Great.
324 B.C.	Chandragupta Maurya founds India's first northern empire.
274– 232 B.C.	Reign of Asoka, Chandragupta's grandson, who initiates a policy of religious and racial tolerance.
100 B.C.– A.D. 225	Andhra dynasty rules central India.
320	Gupta empire in northern India is founded by Chandragupta I.
380– 413	Reign of Chandragupta II, who extends Gupta empire over all of northern India.
About 500	The Huns enter northwest India and destroy the Gupta empire.
600– 900	Pallava and Pandya dynasties flourish in southern India.
606– 647	Reign of Harsha, who unifies much of northern India.
888– 1267	Southern India is united by the Chola dynasty.
1336– 1565	Vijayanagar empire flourishes in southern India.
1398	Tamerlane invades the Delhi Sultanate, and northern India is again split into a number of kingdoms.
1498	Vasco da Gama discovers the sea route to India.
1510	Portuguese gain control of Goa on the west coast.
1526	Baber founds the Mogul empire in northern India.
1556– 1605	Reign of Akbar, Mogul emperor who extends the empire.
1612	First trading station is established by the British East India Company.
1615	English ambassador sent by James I, King of England, visits India.
1628– 1658	Reign of Shah Jahan, who builds the Taj Mahal.
1658– 1707	Reign of Aurangzeb, who follows a policy of religious intolerance. After his death Mogul empire decays.
1756	British soldiers are imprisoned in the Black Hole of Calcutta by the Nawab of Bengal.
1757	Robert Clive, of the British East India Company, defeats the Nawab of Bengal at the battle of Plassey and gains control of the Ganges valley.
1772– 1885	The British East India Company gains control of most of India.
1857– 1859	Sepoy Mutiny.
1858	British Government takes over the East India Company's Indian empire.
1877	Queen Victoria is proclaimed Empress of India.
1885	Indian National Congress is organized.
1885– 1947	Rise of the Indian independence movement.
1909	Morley-Minto reforms (Indian Councils Act) increase power of provincial legislative councils.
1914– 1918	World War I. Indian leaders support the British.
1919	British carry out constitutional reforms but cannot stop the tide of nationalism. Mohandas K. Gandhi, leader of Indian national movement, begins to support self-rule and passive resistance.
1935	Britain gives India a new constitution providing for a council of states and an assembly.
1942	Britain promises India full dominion status after war and an interim government during war. Congress Party demands immediate independence and begins civil disobedience.
1947	Indian subcontinent granted independence but partitioned into two nations—India and Pakistan. Nehru becomes Prime Minister of India. Pakistan invades Kashmir.
1948	Gandhi assassinated.
1949	United Nations arranges cease-fire in Kashmir.
1950	India proclaims itself a sovereign republic.
1961	India takes control of Goa.
1962	Fighting breaks out between India and China.
1964	Nehru dies; Shastri becomes prime minister.
1965	Indo-Pakistani conflict over Kashmir.
1966	Shastri dies; Indira Gandhi becomes prime minister.
1971	Refugees from civil war in East Pakistan cross into India; India and the Soviet Union sign 20-year friendship pact.

Pedicabs and bicycles are the chief means of transportation in Hyderabad.

was assassinated in Delhi by an extremist Hindu who blamed Gandhi for the partition of the subcontinent. Gandhi's principal lieutenant, Jawaharlal Nehru (1889–1964), became leader of India.

Before 1947 there were areas on the Indian subcontinent that were not directly governed as part of the British Empire in India. These were ruled by Indian princes and were known as princely states. In 1947 a large number of Indian princely states joined the Indian union. When Kashmir, which had not joined either India or Pakistan, was invaded by Pakistani tribesmen in the fall of 1947, the Maharaja of Kashmir, unable to resist the invasion, decided to accede to India. With the accession, it became the responsibility of India to protect Kashmir, and Indian troops were sent accordingly. In January, 1949, the United Nations arranged for a cease-fire in Kashmir between India and Pakistan. Thereafter the relations between the two countries remained tense. Hostilities broke out again in 1965.

By 1954 India had gained control of several former French settlements in the subcontinent. In 1961 Indian troops liberated Portuguese-held areas in India and thereby ended all European control in the subcontinent. India became a republic under a new constitution in 1950, but it remains a member of the Commonwealth of Nations.

Communist China has always claimed the North-East Frontier Agency and Ladakh— territories that India considers its own. An uneasy border situation has existed between China and India ever since a Chinese army entered Tibet in 1950. In 1962 the Chinese attacked India. Although a cease-fire was arranged, relations between the two countries have been strained. The fragile truce with Pakistan was broken in 1971. Following the flight into India of millions of refugees from the civil war in East Pakistan, fighting erupted between India and Pakistan. Indian troops occupied East Pakistan and helped the Bengalis form an independent state called Bangladesh. Earlier in 1971, India and the Soviet Union had signed a 20-year friendship treaty.

PRADYUMNA P. KARAN
University of Kentucky
Reviewed by INFORMATION SERVICE OF INDIA

INDIA, ART OF. See ORIENTAL ART AND ARCHITECTURE.

INDIANA

Who's a Hoosier? Anyone who comes from Indiana is a Hoosier, and the state is known as the Hoosier State. Many stories are told to explain the name. One popular explanation is that the settlers in Indiana usually yelled, "Who's hyer?" to travelers knocking at their cabin doors. In time "Who's hyer?" became Hoosier.

But scholars say that such stories are unlikely. They trace the history of the name to the dialect word "hoozer," which meant anything large of its kind or an awkward, unskilled person. It also meant any rough-and-ready frontiersman. Then it came to be applied in a good-natured way to the frontiersmen of Indiana. No one knows exactly how or why.

One of the earliest known uses of the name was in a poem, "The Hoosier's Nest," by John Finley, published in an Indianapolis newspaper in the 1830's. It told of a stranger's visit in the cabin of an Indiana settler. Later the beloved Indiana author Edward Eggleston made the name famous through his novels *The Hoosier Schoolmaster* and *The Hoosier Schoolboy,* published in the 1870's and 1880's.

STATE FLOWER: Peony.

STATE TREE: Tulip tree.

STATE BIRD: Cardinal.

STATE FLAG.

A good way to know Indiana is to know its great river—the Wabash. The early French explorers and traders called this river the Ouabache. That was the way they spelled a shortened form of the Indian name, which was thought to mean "shining white." The English changed the spelling to Wabash. Before the forests were cut down and soil was washed into the river, the Wabash did look white. It was silvery white in the summer sun and pale and milky during the winter.

The river lives in song. In the 1890's one of Indiana's native sons composed a song recalling his boyhood "on the banks of the Wabash far away." He was Paul Dresser (born Paul Dreiser), a writer and publisher of popular songs. His more famous brother, the novelist Theodore Dreiser, helped with the words. The song became the state song of Indiana and a classic of American folk music.

The Wabash River is 475 miles long. It has its source in the state of Ohio—about 10 miles east of the Indiana-Ohio border. In Indiana it flows northwestward to Huntington. Then it follows a somewhat southwesterly course across the state. The Wabash River turns directly south near the Illinois border. For the last 200 miles of its southward journey, it forms the boundary between Indiana and Illinois. The Wabash ends at the southwestern tip of Indiana. There it flows into the Ohio, which carries its waters to the Mississippi.

Many important events have taken place on or near the banks of the Wabash. The first Europeans to claim the area were the French. About 1700 they established Fort Miami at the portage connecting the Maumee River with the Little Wabash (also called Little River), where Fort Wayne now stands. Fort Vincennes was another early French post. But the French did not succeed in holding the area. They lost it to the British, who made it part of the Canadian province of Quebec.

During the Revolutionary War, George Rogers Clark captured Vincennes from the British. Its capture meant that the boundary line between the United States and Canada would be fixed at the Great Lakes rather than farther south at the Ohio River. The capture of Vincennes also opened the area to American settlers. In 1811 William Henry Harrison defeated the Indians in the battle of Tippecanoe. The battle took place near Lafayette, not far from the banks of the Wabash. New Harmony on the lower Wabash was the site of a renowned experiment in community living and education.

The Wabash River country has several things for which Indiana is famous. It has corn and hogs, limestone and coal, literature and politics. It also has busy industrial cities. But to see the busiest and most famous industrial area of Indiana, the visitor must travel to the north of the Wabash—to East Chicago, Gary,

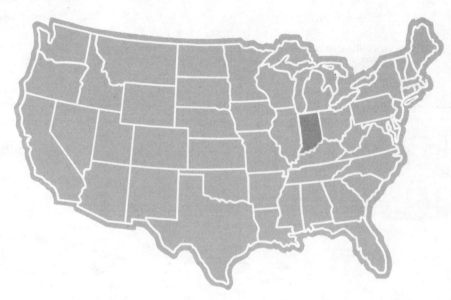

INDIANA

CAPITAL: Indianapolis.

STATEHOOD: December 11, 1816; the 19th state.

SIZE: 36,291 sq. mi.; rank, 38th.

POPULATION: 5,193,669 (1970 census); rank, 11th.

ORIGIN OF NAME: From the word "Indian" plus the *a* ending used in many geographical names.

ABBREVIATION: Ind.

NICKNAME: Hoosier State.

STATE SONG: "On the Banks of the Wabash Far Away," by Paul Dresser.

STATE MOTTO: "The Crossroads of America."

STATE SEAL: A pioneer scene shows a woodsman felling a tree to clear the land. A bison flees across the plains. The sun sets in the distance. This design appeared originally on the seal of Indiana territory. It symbolizes the westward expansion of the nation. The date in the border of the seal is the year of statehood.

STATE FLAG: Two circles of golden stars surround a burning torch, also in gold, in the center of a deep blue field. The outer circle of 13 stars stands for the original 13 states. The five stars in the lower half of the inner circle stand for the next five states admitted to the Union. The large star above the flame represents Indiana, the 19th state. The torch stands for liberty and enlightenment.

and Hammond on the shores of Lake Michigan. There is an area of great steel mills, factories, and oil refineries. At night the orange glow from the blast furnaces lights the sky for miles around.

▶ THE LAND

Indiana is located in the eastern half of the United States. It extends from the Ohio River on the south to the tip of Lake Michigan on the northwest. Average elevations throughout the state vary from 650 to 750 feet above sea level. The lowest areas are in the extreme southwest. The highest point is near the eastern border of the state.

Landforms

Ages ago most of Indiana was covered by glaciers. The areas that were smoothed by the moving ice are part of a large physical division of the United States known as the Central Lowland. The rest of Indiana—the hilly areas of the south—is part of the Interior Low Plateaus.

Central Lowland. All of northern and central Indiana lies within the Central Lowland. This region extends into many neighboring states. In Indiana it includes the Great Lakes Plain and the Till Plains.

The Great Lakes Plain covers more than 8,000 square miles in the northern part of the state. It is made up mostly of flat areas.

Glaciers leveled this part of Indiana and dug out many small lakes. In the northwest there is a nearly flat plain, which developed from the bottom of an ancient lake. This area contains many sand dunes. They line the southern and eastern shores of Lake Michigan.

The Till Plains cover most of the state— more than 20,000 square miles. In this area glaciers deposited great amounts of earth material, or till. Some of the deposits are more than 500 feet deep. Most of the land is extremely flat. But here and there the melting ice left small hills and ridges with gentle slopes. Fertile soils and level lands have made this part of the state a rich farming area.

Interior Low Plateaus. About one sixth of Indiana is included in the Interior Low Plateaus. This region extends southward into Kentucky. High hills, uneven ridges, and deep ravines make this plateau area the most rugged in the state. One of the most unusual features is the Knobs, or the "Hoosier Alps." They are hills that rise abruptly 400 to 600 feet above the surrounding land. In the central part of the region there is a limestone belt with interesting features, such as sinkholes, caves, and underground streams.

Rivers and Lakes

The Wabash and its tributaries, such as the Tippecanoe, White, and Patoka rivers, drain about two thirds of the state. Other important streams are the Kankakee in the northwest, the Maumee in the northeast, and the Whitewater in the southeast. The winding course of the Ohio River forms all of Indiana's southern boundary.

Almost every county in Indiana has a lake. Lakes are especially numerous in the northern part of the state, where there are at least 1,000. Lake Wawasee, the largest natural lake in the state, is located in this area. Indiana's man-made lakes, or reservoirs, store water for periods of drought, help to control floods, and make good places for recreation. The largest are Monroe Reservoir near Bloomington and Mansfield Reservoir near Terre Haute. Mansfield is known as the Raccoon Lake State Recreation Area.

Climate

Indiana has a humid continental climate with cold winters and hot, humid summers.

GREAT LAKES PLAIN

CENTRAL LOWLAND

TILL PLAINS

INTERIOR LOW PLATEAUS

LANDFORMS

Frequent changes in the weather are common. During the winter there are often periods of mild weather. During the summer there are cool and pleasant periods.

Normal winter temperatures range from 27 degrees Fahrenheit in the north to 34 degrees in the south. Summer temperatures average 74 degrees in the north and 78 degrees in the south.

Wet winds blowing from the Gulf of Mexico bring the state most of its rainfall. Usually the amount is several inches greater in the south than in the north. The average decreases northward because of the greater distance from the Gulf. Snowfall varies greatly from year to year. The heaviest snows are in the northwestern corner of the state. Winds blowing across Lake Michigan may bring as much as 50 inches of snow a year to this area.

The precipitation is distributed fairly evenly throughout the year. But all parts of the state have occasional droughts as well as heavy rains that cause floods. The worst droughts are in the southern hills. Floods occur throughout the state but are most common to the streams that flow into the Ohio River.

Indiana's growing season varies from 150 days to 200 days. The season is longest in the extreme southwest and along the Ohio River.

Natural Resources

Some of Indiana's natural resources, such as soils, were left by the glacial ice that spread southward during the Ice Age. Other valuable natural resources are coal and petroleum.

Soils. In much of central and northern Indiana rich, deep soils have developed from materials left by glaciers. These soils, called loams, are made up of sand, clay, and decayed plants. Since southern Indiana was never covered by glaciers, the soils in that part of the state are thin and less fertile.

Minerals. Bituminous (soft) coal and petroleum are among Indiana's valuable mineral deposits. They are found mainly in the west and the southwest. Most of the mineral resources of northern and central Indiana were left by the glaciers. Clay, sand, and gravel are contained within the thick blanket of glacial material. Indiana also has large amounts of limestone, sandstone, and gypsum.

Forests. In pioneer days the only part of Indiana without trees was the prairie land in the northwest. There were hundreds of sawmills, and the lumbering industry was very important. The original forests have been largely cut over, but thousands of acres have been replanted in trees. Hardwood timber is still a valuable natural resource, especially in the southern part of the state.

Wildlife. The bears and wildcats that once roamed Indiana's forests are gone. Animals hunted and trapped today are the small animals, such as muskrat, raccoon, mink, rabbit, and squirrel. The deer herd at present numbers more than 50,000. Fish found in the lakes and streams include bass, pickerel, pike, goggle-eye, and sunfish. Quail, pheasant, and

---

THE LAND

LOCATION: Latitude—37° 47′ N to 41° 46′ N. **Longitude**—84° 48′ W to 88° 06′ W.
Lake Michigan and Michigan to the north, Ohio to the east, Kentucky to the south, Illinois to the west.

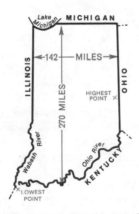

ELEVATION: Highest—Near the midpoint of the eastern border, 1,257 ft. **Lowest**—In the southwestern corner where the Wabash River flows into the Ohio River, about 320 ft.

LANDFORMS: The Central Lowland (Great Lakes Plain and Till Plains) covering most of the state; Interior Low Plateaus in the south.

SURFACE WATERS: Major rivers—Wabash, Tippecanoe, White, Kankakee, Maumee, Whitewater, and Ohio.
Largest natural lakes—Wawasee, James, Maxinkuckee, Bass. **Major man-made lakes**—Monroe, Mansfield, Geist, Morse, Cataract, Freeman, Shafer.

CLIMATE: Temperature—January average, from 27° F. in the north to 34° in the south. July average, from 74° in the north to 78° in the south. **Precipitation**—Rainfall average, 36–43 in. Snowfall varies from about 10 in. a year in the south to more than 50 in. in certain parts of the north. **Growing season**—Varies from about 150 days to 200 days.

partridge are the most common game birds. In the marshy areas in the north there are ducks, wild geese, and the great blue heron.

THE PEOPLE AND THEIR WORK

In early times the most common routes of travel funneled settlers into Indiana by way of the south. For this reason most of the early Hoosiers came from Virginia, Kentucky, Tennessee, and North Carolina. They built their homes and started farming in southern Indiana. In 1820 the population of Indiana was about 147,000. More than four fifths of this number lived in the southern one third of the state.

By 1850 a striking change had occurred. New routes of travel, especially along the Erie Canal and the Cumberland Road, were bringing settlers from the eastern states and from Europe. By that time the population of Indiana had reached almost 1,000,000. Of this number, two fifths lived in southern Indiana, two fifths in the central part of the state, and the rest in the north. During the next half-century (1850–1900) immigrants arrived in large numbers. They settled mainly in the cities of central and northern Indiana, where industry was developing. From that time on, southern Indiana lagged behind the rest of the state in population.

Where the People Live

Increasing numbers of people are moving from rural areas to the cities and larger towns. Today two thirds of the population live in cities of more than 2,500 people. The greatest gains are in northwestern Indiana. But the east central part of the state is also growing rapidly.

Industries and Products

Indiana is known for its rich farmlands and great factories. Agriculture is still important, as it was in the past. But manufacturing is the major source of income. More than one third of all Indiana's workers are employed in factories and mills.

Manufacturing. Indiana includes one of the most famous industrial districts in the world. This is the area at the base of Lake Michigan, known as the Calumet area. A large oil refinery was the first industry to come to this land of swamps and dunes. Then one of the

---

WHAT INDIANA PRODUCES

MANUFACTURED GOODS: Basic steel and other primary metal products; electrical equipment and supplies; automobile and other transportation equipment; machinery; chemical products (principally drugs); processed foods; fabricated metal products; stone, clay, and glass products; rubber and plastics products; printing and publishing matter; furniture and fixtures; petroleum products.

AGRICULTURAL PRODUCTS: Hogs, corn, soybeans, cattle and calves, milk, eggs, wheat, horticultural specialties, turkeys, tomatoes.

MINERALS: Bituminous coal, cement, stone, petroleum, sand and gravel, clays, gypsum.

---

largest steel companies in the United States built its mills there. The location was considered good because it is between the Lake Superior iron mines and the Appalachian coalfields. The poet Carl Sandburg was fascinated by the Calumet area. In a poem called "Smoke and Steel" he gives a vivid description of the huge open-hearth furnaces that burn night and day producing steel.

Factories in the Calumet area and elsewhere in the state make hundreds of products from steel, iron, and other metals. Among these products are radio and electronic equipment; electrical appliances, such as stoves and refrigerators; transportation equipment, such as railroad cars and automobile bodies and parts; and mining and farm machinery. Indiana is also a leading producer of furniture, with more than 40 cities involved in its manufacture.

Other industries make use of the agricultural and mineral products of the state. Corn and wheat are turned into flour and animal feeds. Tomatoes and other vegetables are canned. Milk from the dairy farms in the northwest is made into cheese. Limestone and clay are used in the making of cement, and fine sands in the making of glass. Dozens of products come from petroleum. Some of them are gasoline, motor oils, and chemicals.

Agriculture. For many years Indiana has been one of the leading agricultural states in the nation. The early settlers tried at first to grow such crops as cotton, tobacco, and grapes. But they soon found that most of the area was better suited to grains, such as corn and wheat.

Today the main crops are soybeans, corn, and wheat. Soybeans and corn are grown

A dairy farm in central Indiana.

One of the many open-hearth furnaces in Indiana's Calumet area, a world-famous industrial district. The furnaces burn day and night, producing steel.

mainly in west central and central Indiana. This area is in the Corn Belt, which extends across the midwestern part of the nation. Wheat is more common in the southwest and southeast.

Truck farming is important in several parts of the state. Tomatoes, potatoes, onions, and celery are among the vegetables usually grown. Only California produces more tomatoes for canning than does Indiana. Fruit crops include apples, peaches, and melons. Indiana ranks first in the nation in the production of popcorn.

At present the sale of livestock, especially hogs and cattle, and of livestock products, such as milk and eggs, brings more total income to the farmers of Indiana than the sale of cash crops.

Mining. Coal is Indiana's most important mineral. It is produced in 15 counties, mainly in the southwest. The reserves of coal are large enough to last several hundred years. Petroleum is second in importance. But geologists believe that supplies of petroleum are limited.

Indiana produces much of the building limestone used in the United States. Indiana limestone went into the construction of Rockefeller Center in New York City and the Pentagon in Washington, D.C. Limestone is also processed for use in fertilizer and in the manufacture of portland cement. Sand and gravel, which are produced in large amounts, are used mainly for road construction. Clay

is mined throughout the state. It is used in making tiles, bricks, pottery, and other products. Recently gypsum mining has become important in southwestern Indiana.

Transportation and Communication

Indiana has chosen as its official motto "The Crossroads of America." The motto refers to the many routes of travel that cross the state. Some of these routes have been of national importance since pioneer days. By the late 1830's two major roads crossed the state. The Michigan Road extended from Michigan City on Lake Michigan to Madison on the Ohio River. The Cumberland Road, or National Road, started in Maryland and extended to Illinois. It passed through central Indiana. Today U.S. 40 follows the route of this famous early road. Other leading highways are U.S. 31, U.S. 41, and the Indiana East-West Toll Road. This toll road is the westernmost link in a chain of turnpikes that connect Chicago and New York.

The first railroad in Indiana was built in Shelby County in 1834. It consisted of a few miles of track and a horse-pulled car. Today more than 20 major lines cross the state. Indianapolis is one of the nation's leading railroad centers.

Water transportation was especially important to the early settlers. In the 1830's "canal fever" struck Indiana. Hoosiers were impressed by the great success of the Erie Canal in New York. They built the Wabash and Erie

The School of Music at Indiana University.

Canal, linking Lake Erie and the Ohio River. This canal cost millions of dollars. Soon after it was completed the railroads came, and the canal was abandoned.

With the opening of the St. Lawrence Seaway in 1959, water transportation has increased in importance. Indiana has two ports on Lake Michigan—Gary and Indiana Harbor in East Chicago. Recently traffic has also increased on the Ohio River.

Most of the large cities have airports. Several airlines serve Indiana, linking it to the major cities of the United States.

Indiana's early newspapers were all weeklies. They helped to take the place of books, which were hard to get in pioneer country. Local news was usually scarce, but there was much national political news. Many of the papers had unusual or amusing names—the *Coon-Skinner,* the *Broad Axe of Freedom,* the *Grubbing Hoe of Truth.* The first newspaper was the *Indiana Gazette,* published in Vincennes in 1804. Today approximately 90 dailies and more than 200 other newspapers are published in the state.

The first radio station was started in 1922. Today Indiana has more than 150 AM and FM stations and about 15 television stations.

▶ EDUCATION

Indiana's first educational and cultural center developed in the community of New Harmony. It was founded in 1825 by Robert Owen, a British industrialist and social reformer. The town had been established earlier by a German religious leader, George Rapp. He and his followers, called Rappites, came to Pennsylvania from Germany in the early 1800's. In 1814 they started a colony on the Wabash River in southwestern Indiana. They named it Harmonie, or Harmony. About 10 years later they decided to return to Pennsylvania. Owen bought the land and named the town New Harmony. His idea was to establish a model community where the people would share everything equally. They would join in creative work in music, the theater, literature, art, and science.

Owen had the help of several well-known persons. Among the most important was William Maclure, a pioneer geologist and educator. Maclure invited other scholars to go with him to New Harmony. They arrived on a special boat that became famous as the "Boatload of Knowledge." Owen's experiment was not a success, but many of the scholars stayed in New Harmony. The town remained one of the cultural and scientific centers of the United States until the Civil War. New Harmony was made a National Historical Landmark in 1965.

Schools and Colleges

In 1816 the authors of Indiana's first constitution wrote that a system of general education was to be established "as soon as circumstances will permit." But the pioneers were too busy clearing land and planting crops to worry about schools. The next constitution, in 1851, directed the General Assembly to provide a system of common schools. From this provision came the Free School Law of 1852 —the foundation of Indiana's present public education system.

The first institution of higher education in Indiana was Vincennes University, established in 1806. Today Indiana has approximately 40 colleges and universities. The four state-supported institutions are Indiana University in Bloomington, Purdue University in Lafayette, Indiana State University in Terre Haute, and Ball State University in Muncie. Well-known private institutions of higher learning include DePauw University in Greencastle, the University of Notre Dame in Notre Dame, Butler University in Indianapolis, Valparaiso University in Valparaiso, and Wabash College in Crawfordsville.

Libraries

The library system of Indiana owes a great deal to William Maclure. In his will he gave money to establish libraries for groups of workingmen. Only one of these libraries remains today—the Working Men's Institute Library in New Harmony. Public libraries have now taken over most of the others.

The Indianapolis Public Library has a special collection of children's literature and of Indiana authors. The Indiana State Library at Indianapolis specializes in Indiana history. The oldest collection of books in the state is in the Old Cathedral Library in Vincennes.

The Arts and Museums

Since the decline of New Harmony many other cities throughout the state have become

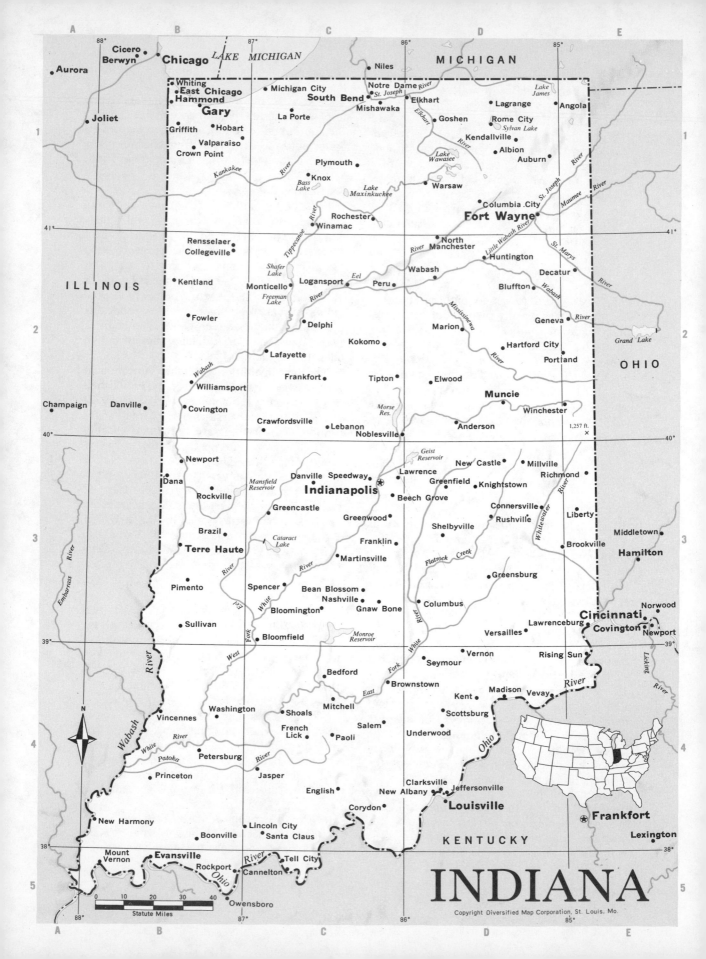

INDIANA

Statute Miles
0 10 20 30 40

MICHIGAN

ILLINOIS

OHIO

KENTUCKY

LAKE MICHIGAN

Aurora
Cicero
Berwyn
Chicago
Joliet
Whiting
East Chicago
Hammond
Gary
Griffith
Hobart
Valparaiso
Crown Point
Michigan City
La Porte
South Bend
Mishawaka
Notre Dame
St. Joseph
Niles
Elkhart
Goshen
Lagrange
Rome City
Angola
Lake James
Sylvan Lake
Kendallville
Albion
Auburn
Plymouth
Knox
Bass Lake
Lake Maxinkuckee
Lake Wawasee
Warsaw
Columbia City
Fort Wayne
St. Joseph
Maumee River
Rochester
Winamac
Rensselaer
Collegeville
Kentland
North Manchester
Huntington
Little Wabash River
Decatur
St. Marys
River
Shafer Lake
Logansport
Eel
Peru
Wabash
Bluffton
Wabash
Monticello
Freeman Lake
Fowler
Delphi
Marion
Mississinewa
Geneva
River
Grand Lake
Kokomo
Hartford City
Portland
Lafayette
Williamsport
Wabash
Covington
Frankfort
Tipton
Elwood
Muncie
Winchester
Danville
Champaign
Crawfordsville
Lebanon
Noblesville
Morse Res.
Anderson
1,257 ft.
Newport
Dana
Danville Speedway
Lawrence
New Castle
Millville
Richmond
Indianapolis
Greenfield
Knightstown
Mansfield Reservoir
Rockville
Greencastle
Beech Grove
Connersville
Rushville
Liberty
Greenwood
Shelbyville
Brazil
Cataract Lake
Franklin
Middletown
Terre Haute
Martinsville
Greensburg
Brookville
Hamilton
Whitewater River
Pimento
Spencer
Bean Blossom
Nashville
Flatrock Creek
Norwood
Sullivan
White
Bloomington
Gnaw Bone
Columbus
Cincinnati
Lawrenceburg
Covington
Newport
Bloomfield
Fork
Monroe Reservoir
Versailles
Rising Sun
Licking River
West
Vernon
Seymour
Bedford
Fork
Brownstown
Madison
Vevay
River
East
Kent
Washington
Mitchell
Scottsburg
Vincennes
Shoals
Salem
Underwood
French Lick
Paoli
White River
Petersburg
Jasper
English
Clarksville
New Albany
Jeffersonville
Princeton
Corydon
Louisville
Frankfort
Lexington
New Harmony
Lincoln City
Santa Claus
Boonville
Mount Vernon
Evansville
Rockport
Cannelton
Tell City
Ohio River
Owensboro

Embarrass River
Wabash River
Patoka River
Ohio

Tippecanoe River
Kankakee River

N

INDEX TO INDIANA MAP

centers of art, music, and the theater. Nearly 20 cities have symphony orchestras. Almost every county seat has an indoor art exhibit during the winter and an outdoor art fair in the spring. Brown County has a well-known artists' colony and a theater. Clowes Memorial Hall, at Butler University, draws major artists and performers from all over the world.

The John Herron Art Institute in Indianapolis is one of Indiana's most important art centers. It exhibits American and European paintings, sculpture, and prints. It also operates an art school. The Indianapolis Children's Museum has natural science, history, and art exhibits as well as portable displays for use in classrooms.

The Lincoln National Life Foundation in Fort Wayne houses mementos and paintings of Abraham Lincoln and his family. The Evansville Museum of Arts and Sciences in Evansville is known for its art gallery and its planetarium. The Sheldon Swope Art Gallery in Terre Haute has an unusual collection of fans, glass, silver, and pottery. It also has sculpture and paintings by contemporary American artists. The Howard National Steamboat Museum in Jeffersonville preserves the history of steamboat building. In the past, steamboats built in Jeffersonville were known on the rivers of both North and South America. Other important museums in Indiana include those established by historical societies throughout the state.

▶ PLACES OF INTEREST

Indiana's outdoor recreation is provided basically by its parks and memorials. Rivers

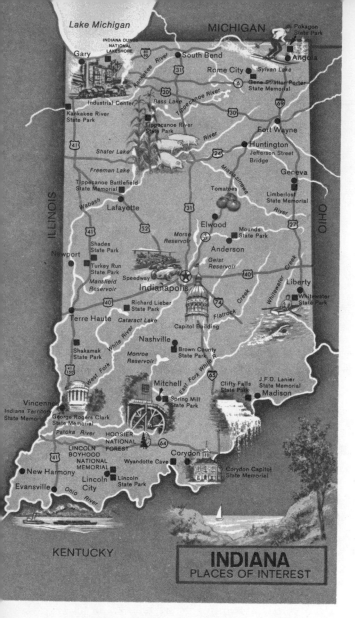

Lake Michigan

MICHIGAN

INDIANA
PLACES OF INTEREST

KENTUCKY

ILLINOIS

OHIO

Lincoln Boyhood National Memorial near Lincoln City preserves the site of Abraham Lincoln's boyhood home. It also contains the burial place of Lincoln's mother, Nancy Hanks Lincoln. She died in 1818, 2 years after the family came to Indiana from Kentucky. Next to the memorial area is **Lincoln State Park,** a wooded recreation area with an artificial lake for swimming, boating, and fishing.

Brown County State Park covers thousands of acres of rolling hills near Nashville. It is a memorial to Frank McKinney "Kin" Hubbard, the Hoosier cartoonist who created a humorous character named Abe Martin. The park is best known for the beauty of its foliage in the spring and the autumn.

Clifty Falls State Park near Madison is a park of scenic attractions—hills, valleys, waterfalls, and woodlands. Unusual features are Clifty Falls and a deep canyon where the sun can be seen only at noon.

Corydon Capitol State Memorial preserves the historic building at Corydon that was Indiana's first state capitol (1816–25).

George Rogers Clark State Memorial in Vincennes is a circular Doric temple built on the site of an old fort. Within the temple are large murals depicting Clark's conquests and the opening of the West.

Indiana Dunes National Lakeshore was established by Congress in 1966. It is located near Gary on the shores of Lake Michigan, and is known for its white beaches and its constantly shifting dunes. They are formed from sand that is swept onto the shore by waves. As the sand dries, it is whipped up by the wind and drifts into huge heaps. Many varieties of plant life are found in the park—from pine trees to flowering cactus.

Indiana Territory State Memorial in Vincennes preserves the building that served as the first capitol of Indiana territory.

J. F. D. Lanier State Memorial in Madison is a mansion overlooking the Ohio River and the hills of Kentucky. It was the home of James F. D. Lanier, a pioneer banker who helped to finance Indiana's troops during the Civil War. The mansion is famous for the beauty of its architecture and furnishings.

Limberlost State Memorial in Geneva was the home of Gene Stratton Porter during the 1890's and early 1900's. Mrs. Porter was Indiana's most popular woman author. Her cabin on Sylvan Lake near Rome City is also preserved as a state memorial.

The Mounds State Park, east of Anderson, is situated on high bluffs near the White River. The park contains nine mounds, or burial places,

and natural lakes, reservoirs, wooded campsites, hiking trails, and picnic areas afford additional enjoyment. There is one national forest, the Hoosier National Forest.

Parks and Memorials

Indiana's state park system was started in 1916 by the well-known conservationist Colonel Richard Lieber. It is considered one of the finest park systems in the United States. Today it includes more than 30 areas. They are so located that no resident of the state is more than an hour's drive from a state park or memorial. Indiana has one national memorial and a national lakeshore, which are described along with some of the state areas.

built by prehistoric inhabitants of the area. Most of the earthworks in the park are circular, although two are shaped like guitars.

Pokagon State Park near Angola is known as Indiana's winter playground. Winter sports include skating, skiing, tobogganing, and bobsledding. The park is also the home of buffalo, deer, and elk.

Spring Mill State Park near Mitchell has many scenic wonders. It includes caves, an underground river containing rare blindfish, and a restored pioneer village.

Tippecanoe Battlefield State Memorial near Lafayette is the site of the battlefield where William Henry Harrison, governor of Indiana territory, defeated the Indians.

Other Places

Indiana has many other places that attract visitors. Some are historical places. Others are known for their natural beauty. Villages such as Gnaw Bone, Bean Blossom, Rising Sun, Santa Claus, and Pimento often attract visitors simply because of their unusual names.

French Lick is a famous health resort, known for its mineral waters. It was settled in 1811. Jefferson Street Bridge in Huntington spans the Little Wabash River. Along one side of the bridge over the river, there are stores and business houses. Very old bridges of this sort exist in Europe, but the Jefferson Street Bridge is probably the only one in the United States. Wyandotte Cave near Corydon is one of the largest caverns in North America. It includes more than 20 miles of explored passageways and chambers.

Annual Events

Indiana's best-known annual event occurs on May 30. On that day people from all over the world watch the famous 500-mile automobile race at the Indianapolis Motor Speedway. Other annual events include fairs, festivals, and patriotic celebrations.

May—Memorial Day automobile race, Indianapolis; opening of Friendship Gardens, Michigan City.

June—Festival of the Golden Rain Tree, New Harmony.

August—State Fair, Indianapolis (late August and early September); State Tomato Festival, Elwood.

October—James Whitcomb Riley Memorial Program, statewide; Harvest Festival, Vincennes.

December—Indiana Day, statewide.

▶ CITIES

Indianapolis is the hub of activity in Indiana. Most of the other large cities in the state are located to the north of this hub, especially around Lake Michigan. The two largest cities to the south of Indianapolis are Terre Haute and Evansville.

Indianapolis

The capital and largest city of Indiana is located near the center of the state. The original town was called Fall Creek. In 1820 this settlement was chosen as the site for the new capital of Indiana. But the seat of government was not moved from Corydon until

Beach scene at Indiana Dunes National Lakeshore on the shores of Lake Michigan.

1825. A map of Indianapolis shows a street pattern that looks like a spider web. At the center is a circular area known as Monument Circle. It contains the 285-foot Soldiers and Sailors Monument.

Indianapolis is the banking, commercial, and agricultural center of the state. It is also a manufacturing center. Points of special interest are the World War Memorial Plaza, the state fairgrounds, and the Indianapolis Motor Speedway. Educational institutions include the Indiana University Medical Center, Butler University, and extension divisions of Indiana and Purdue universities.

Gary

Gary is located at the southern end of Lake Michigan. It was founded in 1906 by the United States Steel Corporation. Sand dunes were leveled, a river was moved, and swamps were drained to make way for factories, houses, and parks. People from many countries came to work in the mills.

Today Gary is the center of one of the world's largest steel-producing areas. Among other products made in Gary are cement, automobile parts, and clothing. A huge oil refinery is also located there.

COUNTIES

Soldiers and Sailors Monument stands in the center of Monument Circle in Indianapolis, the state capital.

Fort Wayne

Fort Wayne lies at the junction of three rivers—the St. Marys, the St. Joseph, and the Maumee. There, about the year 1700, the French founded a trading post on the site of a Miami Indian village. In 1794 General Anthony ("Mad Anthony") Wayne established Fort Wayne, one of the first American forts in Indiana.

Fort Wayne is a key railroad point and an industrial center located in a rich farming, stock-raising, and dairying area. It is also the home of Concordia Senior College, St. Francis College, and Indiana Technical College. Johnny Appleseed (John Chapman), who wandered about the countryside in pioneer times preaching and planting apple orchards, is buried in Fort Wayne.

Other Cities

Hammond, East Chicago, Gary, and Whiting form the Calumet industrial area in the extreme northwest. Michigan City, a few miles northwest of the Calumet area, is a well-known summer resort. Farther to the east is South Bend. Guided missiles are among the many products manufactured in South Bend. Elkhart, 15 miles east of South Bend, produces more than half the band instruments made in the United States. Muncie is a trade and industrial center of eastern Indiana. Two studies of life in Muncie made the city famous. These studies, by the sociologists Robert S. and Helen Merrell Lynd, were entitled *Middletown* and *Middletown in Transition.*

Terre Haute, whose name means "high land" in French, is located in an area of farms and coal mines in west central Indiana. Evansville, largest city of southern Indiana, is located on a bend of the Ohio River. It is an important manufacturing center.

▶ **GOVERNMENT**

Indiana's first state constitution, adopted in 1816, was copied largely from the constitutions of Ohio and Kentucky. The second constitution, ratified in 1851, is still in effect. With its amendments it is the law of the state.

The legislature is called the General Assembly. It is composed of two houses, the Senate and the House of Representatives. The Senate consists of 50 members, elected for 4-year terms. The House consists of 100 members, elected for 2-year terms.

The governor, the chief executive of the state, enforces the laws. He is elected for a 4-year term, and he may not succeed himself immediately.

The highest court in the state is the Supreme Court. Other courts are circuit, superior, and special courts, all commonly referred to as county courts.

▶ **FAMOUS PEOPLE**

As early as 1827 it was said that the people of Indiana were a "scribbling and a forth-putting people." Indiana has produced a long list of poets, novelists, and humorists. It has also produced statesmen, scientists, and other national leaders.

William Henry Harrison (1773–1841), ninth president of the United States, was born in Virginia. As a young man he fought the Indians in the Northwest Territory and became an important political figure there. In 1800 he was appointed the first territorial governor of Indiana. A biography of William Henry Harrison is included in Volume H.

Lewis ("Lew") Wallace (1827–1905) was a lawyer, soldier, diplomat, and author. He was born in Brookville. Wallace served as state senator. He was also an officer in the Civil War, governor of New Mexico territory, and United States minister to Turkey. But he is best known as the author of a famous novel, *Ben-Hur.* The General Lew Wallace Study in Crawfordsville attracts many visitors. It contains war relics, art objects, and Wallace's correspondence with Abraham Lincoln.

Benjamin Harrison (1833–1901), 23rd president of the United States, was a grandson of William Henry Harrison. Benjamin Harrison was born in Ohio, but he moved to Indianapolis when a young man. His long career in politics included service as a United States senator, 1881–87. A biography of Benjamin Harrison is included in Volume H.

Harvey Washington Wiley (1844–1930), a noted chemist, was born in Kent. He became a professor of chemistry at Purdue University and also state chemist of Indiana. In 1883 Wiley was appointed chief chemist of the United States Department of Agriculture. He made many important contributions to the development of scientific agriculture. He also worked for a law to protect people against impure foods and drugs. In 1906 Congress passed such a law. Wiley's achievements brought him many awards.

James Whitcomb Riley (1849–1916), born in Greenfield, is known as the Hoosier Poet. During his boyhood he often visited the county courthouse with his father. There he became familiar with the manners and speech of many kinds of people. Later he wrote about the country and the people he knew best—Indiana and the Hoosiers. Among his most famous poems are "When the Frost Is on the Punkin," "The Old Swimmin' Hole," and "The Raggedy Man."

Other native-born Indiana writers include poet William Vaughn Moody (Spencer) and authors Lloyd C. Douglas (Columbia City), Theodore Dreiser (Terre Haute), Edward Eggleston (Vevay), George Barr McCutcheon (Tippecanoe County), George Jean Nathan (Fort Wayne), Gene Stratton Porter (Wabash County), and Newton Booth Tarkington (Indianapolis). Famous humorists are George Ade (Kentland) and Frank McKinney ("Kin") Hubbard. Hubbard was born in Ohio, but he lived in Indianapolis for many years. Historian Charles Austin Beard was born in Knightstown, and journalist Ernest Taylor ("Ernie") Pyle near Dana.

Several persons who were born in Indiana or who lived there have been candidates for the presidency of the United States. Those elected were the two Harrisons and Abraham Lincoln. Eugene Victor Debs (Terre Haute), labor leader, was the Socialist candidate several times, beginning in 1900. Wendell Lewis Willkie (Elwood) was the Republican nominee in 1940.

Indiana is often called the Mother of Vice-Presidents because many Hoosiers have been nominated for the vice-presidency of the United States. The following held that office: Schuyler Colfax (1869–73, under President Ulysses S. Grant), Thomas Andrews Hendricks (March, 1885–November, 1885, under President Grover Cleveland), Charles Warren Fairbanks (1905–09, under President Theodore Roosevelt), and Thomas Riley Marshall (1913–21, under President Woodrow Wilson).

Hoosiers in the entertainment world include Richard ("Red") Skelton (Vincennes) and actor Clifton Webb (born Webb Parmelee Hollenbeck, Indianapolis). Hoagland Howard ("Hoagy") Carmichael (Bloomington) and Cole Porter (Peru) became famous for popular music.

Wilbur Wright, American pioneer in aviation, was born in Millville. A biography of Wilbur Wright and his brother Orville is included in Volume W. Inventor Elwood Haynes (Portland) pioneered in the development of the automobile. He built a horseless carriage and made the first successful test run at Kokomo on July 4, 1894. Astronaut Virgil Ivan ("Gus") Grissom was born in Mitchell.

▶ HISTORY

The first inhabitants of Indiana were the Mound Builders, who lived hundreds of years before the time of Columbus. Little is known of these prehistoric people. But from thousands of objects found in the mounds and studied by scientists, their story is unfolding. It tells of people who hunted with crude, bone-tipped spears, lived in caves, and moved continually in search of food. They used crude

pottery utensils and made beautiful stone and copper ornaments. Only recently have scientists assumed that the Mound Builders were probably Indians from whom the historic Indians may have been descended.

Before the white man came to Indiana, the area was inhabited by Miami and Potawatomi Indians. Other tribes of early days were the Delaware, Shawnee, Wyandot, and Kickapoo.

Exploration and Early Settlement

Indiana was once part of a vast French empire that extended from the mouth of the St. Lawrence to the mouth of the Mississippi. French missionaries worked to convert the Indians to Christianity. Traders charted land and water routes through the wilderness. Robert Cavelier, Sieur de La Salle, was probably the first European to explore what is now Indiana. In 1679 he entered the area near present-day South Bend.

By the early 1700's English traders from the east were seriously threatening the French in the Ohio Valley. To strengthen their position, the French established three posts in Indiana. Fort Miami was built where the city of Fort Wayne now stands. Another fort was established at the Indian village of Ouiatenon near present-day Lafayette. Post Vincennes, the largest of the three, occupied the present site of Vincennes. But the threat was not ended. Both the French and the English wanted the raw materials that America produced. Each struggled to win the Indians away from the other. Finally the English won, and the French empire in America vanished.

The English occupied Indiana for only a short time. First they tried to stop all settlement west of the Appalachian Mountains. Then, to govern this frontier land more easily, they made the area part of the Canadian province of Quebec. George Rogers Clark's expedition against the English was one of the important events of the Revolutionary War. In the winter of 1779 his small army endured great hardship in marching on Vincennes and capturing it from the English. England and the United States made peace in 1783. Indiana then belonged to the United States.

Indiana Territory

After the Revolutionary War, Indiana was part of a large area called the Northwest

Territory. It extended from Pennsylvania west to the Mississippi and from the Great Lakes south to the Ohio River. In 1800 Ohio and part of Michigan became known as the Northwest Territory. The remainder of the original Old Northwest was organized as Indiana territory. The governor was William Henry Harrison. The capital was Vincennes. Michigan territory was created in 1805 and Illinois territory in 1809, leaving Indiana with its present boundaries. In 1813 the capital of Indiana territory was moved to Corydon.

By 1809 the southern one third of the territory had been purchased from the Indians. They refused to dispose of more land. Under the able leadership of Chief Tecumseh and his brother, who was known as the Prophet, they resisted the settlers. William Henry Harrison defeated the Indians in the famous battle of Tippecanoe in November,

1811. During the War of 1812 many Indian tribes supported the British. Indian raiders attacked Fort Wayne, Fort Harrison (now Terre Haute), and the small Pigeon Roost settlement near present-day Underwood in southern Indiana. Tecumseh, who had fled to Canada, was killed fighting for the British. Indian resistance was shattered. Peace came to the land, and the Indiana territory prepared for statehood.

Statehood and Modern Times

In June, 1816, delegates met under a tree known as Constitution Elm at Corydon to prepare Indiana's first constitution. On December 11, Indiana became the 19th state. The first governor was Jonathan Jennings. As the population of central Indiana increased, everyone realized that the capital at Corydon was too far south. In 1820 a new capital was chosen. This city, Indianapolis, has served as the capital since 1825.

In the early years of statehood Indiana changed slowly from a frontier land. Beginning in the 1830's, roads, railroads, and canals were built. By 1850 immigrants were arriving in large numbers. Agriculture continued to be the leading occupation, and corn continued to be the leading crop. Corn on the cob, parched corn, corn bread, hominy, and many other corn concoctions provided the basic Hoosier food. There was little manufacturing. During the Civil War about 200,000 Hoosiers served the Union.

Indiana's early period ended with the Civil War. Industries grew rapidly after that time. Manufacturing was no longer based on the processing of raw materials from the farms and forests. After 1920 Indiana became an important steel-producing state. Its factories make a great variety of products from iron and steel.

The Future

The story of Indiana is a story of steady growth and development. Hoosiers of today expect this trend to continue. They are working to conserve Indiana's many natural resources, to produce more goods, and to provide good schools for an expanding population.

LEE GUERNSEY
DONALD B. SCHEICK
Indiana State University

IMPORTANT DATES

1679 La Salle, exploring for France, was probably the first European to enter Indiana.

1732 François Marie Bissot, Sieur de Vincennes built a fort at the present site of Vincennes.

1763 Indiana included in territory ceded to Britain by France at the end of the French and Indian War.

1779 George Rogers Clark captured Vincennes from the British during the Revolutionary War.

1787 Congress created the Northwest Territory, including Indiana.

1800 Indiana territory established, with capital at Vincennes; present-day Indiana, Illinois, Michigan, and Wisconsin were included.

1805 Indiana territory reduced in size by creation of Michigan territory; reduced further by creation of Illinois territory in 1809.

1811 Indians defeated by William Henry Harrison in the battle of Tippecanoe.

1813 Territorial capital moved to Corydon.

1816 December 11, Indiana admitted to the Union as the 19th state; Lincoln family came to Indiana from Kentucky.

1820 Indiana Seminary established at Bloomington; renamed Indiana University in 1838.

1824 Law establishing Indianapolis as state capital approved, to be effective the next year.

1851 Second (present) state constitution ratified.

1861 Indiana fought on the Union side during the Civil War.

1874 Purdue University opened to students.

1906 Steelworks built in the Lake Michigan area; Gary founded as a residence for steelworkers.

1911 First 500-mile automobile race at Indianapolis.

1959 St. Lawrence Seaway opened, giving Indiana direct access to the sea.

1966 Indiana celebrates its sesquicentennial—150 years of statehood.

1967 Richard Hatcher was elected mayor of Gary, the first black mayor in the state's history.

1971 Indianapolis celebrated the 150th anniversary of its founding.

INDIAN ART OF NORTH AND SOUTH AMERICA

Before Christopher Columbus reached the New World, the natives of North and South America had developed several different civilizations. Some Indians had formed great nations. Their cities had large temples, pyramids, and even apartment houses. Other tribes lived on a very simple level. Their way of life was like that of cavemen in the Stone Age.

Like peoples in all parts of the world, the Indians of the Americas created works of art. The more advanced tribes fashioned wide varieties of skillfully made, finely finished works. The more primitive tribes created art in simpler ways—by crudely decorating the few objects they owned.

▶ MIDDLE AMERICA

The earliest advanced civilizations were located in Middle America—Central America and Mexico. The farmers of the region made fine pottery figurines. It is likely that many of these sculptures were used in religious cere-

A stone head over 8 feet high, carved by Olmec artists before 300 B.C. Museum of Anthropology, University of Veracruz, Jalapa, Mexico.

monies intended to assure good crops. The Indian farmers of central Mexico made female figures with narrow waists, painted bodies, and elaborate hairdos. The features were delicately modeled—particularly the eyebrows, eyes, and mouths. Little stubs were used to represent arms. Some of these figurines have two heads. Pottery was usually made in simple bowl or bottle form, but many animal, bird, and fish shapes have been found. They are almost always made of well-polished black clay.

Olmec

The elaborate religious practices of Middle America began with the Olmec people, who lived near the coast of the Gulf of Mexico. Characteristic of Olmec art was a jaguar symbol. Often the features of a snarling jaguar were combined with human features. The Olmec usually carved in a bold and monumental style, creating great stone heads as tall as 8 feet. Yet these Indians were equally skilled in carving small figures out of hard jade.

Teotihuacan

Somewhat later, at the site of Teotihuacan near present-day Mexico City, an immense ceremonial center and city began to spread out over several square miles. Its great paved avenues and courtyards were lined with dozens of temples, pyramids, and palaces. The Teotihuacan pyramids were the greatest structures in all America. Hundreds of feet of walls covered with magnificent frescoes (paintings done on wet plaster) have been uncovered. The people of Teotihuacan made handsome pottery and fashioned fine jewelry of jade and other precious stones.

Maya

In Guatemala and southern Mexico the Mayan people—outstanding artists, architects, and mathematicians—achieved one of the most splendid civilizations in the New World. Having developed a form of writing, the Mayans made bark-cloth books filled with text and illustrations.

Mayan sculptors worked skillfully with stone, wood, and clay. They created natural-looking figures dressed in costumes of astonishing richness and complicated detail. Painters covered the walls and ceilings of

These colossal figures, up to 15 feet high, were built by the Toltecs, an ancient people of Middle America.

On Mexico's Yucatán peninsula are the ruins of the ancient city of Chichén Itzá.

Left: Silver doll, 7 inches high, Inca, 15th or 16th century. National Museum of Natural History, Santiago, Chile.

Above: Human skull decorated with mosaic; Aztec, 16th century(?). British Museum. Left: Nazca vase, Peru, before A.D. 700. Cummings Collection, Chicago.

Below: Paracas embroidery, approximately 2,000 years old. National Museum of Anthropology and Archeology, Lima, Peru.

ceremonial chambers with battle scenes and pictures of imaginary creatures.

Aztec

The last great Indian civilization to dominate Middle America was that of the Aztecs. Great builders, they linked their island capital, Tenochtitlan (Mexico City), to the shore with causeways. To prevent invasion, the causeways were built with removable bridges. In the center of the city was the great temple, where bloody sacrifices to the gods took place. Some statues reflect the fierceness of the Aztecs, yet other figures seem gentle. The Aztecs were excellent potters, textile weavers, feather embroiderers, stonecutters, and goldsmiths.

▶ SOUTH AMERICA

The Indians who lived in the Andes mountains and along the deserts of the Pacific coast of South America gradually developed fine skills and an advanced way of life. In the 15th century the Incas united these Indians, forming a vast empire. For technical achievement and splendor the Inca empire was rivaled in the New World only by the Maya and Aztec civilizations.

Chavin

A new religion was introduced into the central Andes as early as 1000 B.C. by the Chavin people. The major symbol of the cult was a large, fanged cat like a jaguar. Sometimes the jaguar is shown complete, but in many cases only a fanged mask or the lips and teeth are used. The jaguar features are often combined with human figures in a way that is very similar to some Olmec figures of Middle America.

Paracas

To the south a somewhat later civilization developed on the Paracas Peninsula. The Paracas people made pottery decorated with bright, glossy paints.

The Paracas people were magnificent needleworkers. Their textiles are among the oldest and most widely admired in the world. Shirts, turbans, huge capes, and other clothing were woven of alpaca wool and cotton, and then embroidered in rich colors. Large pieces required millions of stitches and perhaps years to complete. The extremely complicated designs contained representations of animals, fish, birds, and mythological beings. Most of these masterpieces served only to wrap the bodies of dead rulers. The extreme dryness of the country has preserved the cloth for over 2,000 years.

Nazca

In the first centuries of the Christian era the Paracas civilization seems to have changed gradually into the Nazca culture. The Nazca people made globe-shaped vases with two little spouts connected by a handle. They also fashioned pottery in the forms of animals and vegetables. The use of many colors was highly perfected, but the Nazca potters had little interest in sculptured form. They preferred instead to draw the features and details on pottery.

Mochica

The Mochica and Nazca cultures existed at the same time. The Mochicas also made fine pottery, although they worked very differently from the Nazca people. Colors were less important than sculptural form. Many pieces were modeled in the form of human heads or animals and vegetables. The Mochicas were also masters of metalcrafts. Their copperwork and gold jewelry inlaid with precious stones are particularly beautiful.

Tiahuanaco

After the decline of the Nazca and Mochica cultures a new civilization dominated most of the Andean region. This culture takes its name from the site of Tiahuanaco near Lake Titicaca in Bolivia. The Tiahuanaco people were fine builders and sculptors, and some immense stone structures remain from their civilization. One of these, the Gate of the Sun, was made of a single block of stone and carved with many winged, running figures.

Inca

By 1450 the Incas controlled the Andes. The Incas, inheriting many skills from the tribes they defeated, created a glorious though short-lived civilization. Inca objects were simple and well-made. In painting and weaving they used geometric designs and a few simplified human and animal forms. The Incas made countless objects of metal. Among them were tall beakers decorated with raised sculpture.

For their buildings the Incas carved huge stones—some as heavy as 200 tons. The stones were so perfectly carved that they fit together without any mortar. In places, not even a knife blade could fit between the blocks.

▶ NORTH AMERICA

The Indians of North America were not so advanced as some of those of Middle and South America. Nevertheless, North American Indians did make objects of great interest and beauty.

North Pacific Tribes

The tribes of the Pacific coast of Alaska and Canada were great fishermen. They hunted whales in great canoes that were often carved with wonderful symbolic beasts and other designs. Especially famous are the tall totem poles that North Pacific Indians erected to honor their ancestors and to symbolize their clans. Wood, horn, and soft stone were skillfully carved by the men, while the women wove fine baskets of spruce roots and blankets of mountain-goat wool. The designs range from easily recognizable versions of humans and animals to very complicated, often crowded arrangements combining parts of living creatures.

The Basket Weavers of California

Farther down the coast there were many small tribes who were outstanding basketmakers. Some of their baskets were so finely and tightly woven that they held water. One of these tribes, the Pomo Indians, wove colorful feathers and beads into their baskets. Some Indians of these tribes still weave fine baskets.

The Southwest Indians

In Arizona and New Mexico some of the Pueblo Indians built stone and adobe (unfired clay) houses, often several floors in height. These were the first "apartment houses" in the New World. The Pueblos painted their ceremonial chambers with religious symbols connected with rain and plentiful crops. Indians of the area, especially the Navajo, made paintings by pouring sands of several colors upon a smooth floor. These sand paintings were used in ceremonies, then immediately destroyed.

The Plains Indians

Many people picture all Indians as warriors dressed in beaded buckskin and wearing large, feathered war bonnets. But such items were used mostly by the Indians of the Great Plains. The objects made for and by women were decorated in a geometric fashion, and the items made by men often represented ceremonies or famous acts of courage in war.

The Plains Indians excelled in the art of drawing. They drew lively figures in thin, delicate lines on animal skins. The outlined areas were then painted in rich colors. Feather decorations were much used, and great care in design and construction was given to them. The Plains Indians, like many nomadic (wandering) peoples, made very lavish personal decorations, since their way of life allowed them to carry very few possessions.

Mound Builders

East of the Great Plains the Mound Builders made enormous artificial hills, often with supporting walls. Though early mounds appear to have been used mainly as burial places, later ones were sometimes laid out in the shapes of animals and were probably used for ceremonies. The beautifully fashioned stone objects found in the mounds include tobacco pipes carved in simplified animal shapes.

Woodland Indians

The Woodland tribes lived in the eastern United States. Among the more famous tribes were the Iroquois of New York State. They made fantastic, frightful masks carved from the wood of living trees. These masks were supposed to have the power to cure disease. Animal hair was attached to the head and eyebrows. Eyes and teeth were often made of metal that flashed in the light, making the total effect even more startling. Other masks were woven entirely from corn husks.

▶ THE EFFECT OF EUROPEAN SETTLERS

After the Europeans came to the New World, there were many changes in Indian

Above: Sioux Indian drawings by Chief Sitting Bull, celebrating some of his adventures; United States, 19th century.

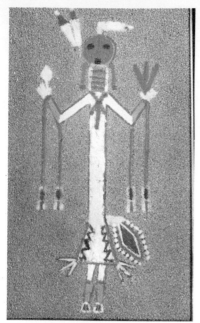

Sand painting by the Navajo Indians.

Right: A beaded basket made by the Pomo Indians of California.

life. In the Spanish colonies particularly, skilled Indians worked on grand churches and other buildings. The new materials brought by the Europeans, including metals, beads, and cloth, all had an effect on Indian art. The Indians were quick to copy some of the objects and styles of the Europeans. Glass bead embroidery replaced porcupine quill decoration on clothing. Even war clubs were fashioned in the shape of the white man's rifle.

ROBERT SONIN
The Brooklyn Museum

INDIAN BEADWORK

"Decorate your moccasins so that your feet may be as beautiful as the flowers you walk amongst."

This was one of the American Indians' ways of showing respect for Mother Earth.

Long ago the Indians decorated their garments with painted designs. They made colors with pigments of earth, grasses, clays, and berries. In time they began to make fine porcupine-quill embroidery, which they colored by boiling the quills in the paint pigments. Indians also made beads from bone, shell, or dried berries. They fashioned them into necklaces or decorations for the fringes of their garments and bags.

About 1675 the white traders brought colorful glass beads to the tribes. But it was not until about 1800 that beads reached the Plains Indians.

The earliest beads brought by the white people were called pony beads by the Indians because they were brought in by the traders' pony packtrains. Most of these beads were dark blue. Some were white and a few were a dull red color. The Indians worked them into several rows of blue, then a few rows of white, and again the blues. This type of pony beadwork continued until about 1840, when a smaller "seed" bead was brought in. The Indians still use seed beads.

Originally these beads were not very plentiful. For this reason Indian women used a combination of both quills and beads. After beads became plentiful, the Indians did less of the beautiful quillwork, using it often as an edging for sleeve bands, shoulder bands, and legging strips, which were embroidered with broad bead bands. Moccasins, too, carried this combination, but the entire top of the foot would be done in quills, with the narrow band around the foot beaded. These bead strips, or bands, were usually not more than eight beads wide.

▶ THREE TYPES OF BEADWORK USED

For some years after beads were introduced to the Indians, sinew was used in place of needles and thread for beadwork. Sinew is a tendon, or cord. The Indians generally used the long sinew found along the backbone of buffalo, deer, or elk.

After the sinew had dried, it was split into very fine, threadlike strands. Next, it was soaked to make it pliable. Then, twisting one end to make a point, the Indian woman strung a few beads on it. With a fine awl, she made a hole in the skin she was working on, pushed the sinew through, and pulled the beads up tight. So well did she do her work that not a stitch could be seen on the reverse side of the skin. She did this by splitting the thickness of the hide with the awl.

Overlay, or Spot Stitch

One of the earliest methods of applying the beads is called the overlay, or spot stitch.

By using this method, the Indian woman could curve her design, making it into either flowers or leaves or a combination of both.

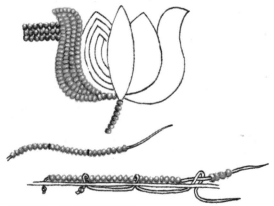

OVERLAY, OR SPOT STITCH
Draw design on the skin. Bead it by inserting sinew thread into skin and stringing beads on thread. Lay strand of beads across article you are making. To hold beads in place, sew another thread of sinew across the strand, every six to eight beads. Fill in colors within outline, row after row. Then bead in one-color background in even, horizontal lines.

Lazy Stitch

The second method used is called the lazy stitch. This type of beadwork was most often used by Western Indians. It lends itself to straight-sided, or geometric, designs, and is most often seen on fully beaded vests and pipe bags and on the tops of women's dresses.

After the Indians began to obtain cloth from the traders, they also were able to get fine bead needles, and much of the beadwork, especially that of the woodland tribes, was done on cloth.

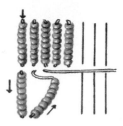

LAZY STITCH
String beads eight to a thread. Bring beads across skin in vertical position, and fasten down. Next to point where sinew is inserted, make another hole. Bring sinew up through hole, and string eight more beads. Lay these beside first row, leaving narrow space between rows, and sew in position. Continue along design, one row down and one up.

Loom Weaving

The third method is loom weaving. The earliest bead loom, used by the Ojibway women, was a bow-shaped ash branch. To each upturned end they fastened a doubled-over piece of birch bark. Through a row of holes made in these pieces they threaded the loom.

When they worked with sinew, they wove so that as the thread passed through the beads one strand passed over the loom string, the next passed under, and so on. When they used thread and needle, they strung the beads on the thread and then placed the strand under the loom threads, pushing the beads up between the strands. Next they passed the needle back through the beads, taking care this time that the needle passed across the loom strings on their upper side. The beads were then drawn up tight, and the next row was added.

This bow-type loom was easy for an Indian woman to carry with her, but at home she often used a framelike loom. This was simply four flat pieces of wood lashed together at the corners with wet sinew. As the sinew dried, it held the corners firmly together. In stringing this type of loom, she wrapped the thread around and across the frame from top to bottom. Starting the beadwork near the top of the frame, she worked downward. When she reached the lower end, she gently slid the beadwork over the top.

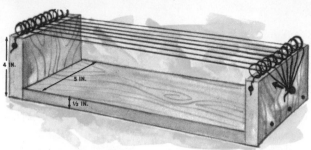

MAKING A LOOM

Use a piece of wood 5 inches wide by ½ inch thick for bottom. Length will depend on how long a piece of beadwork you wish to make. For a belt it should be at least 30 inches long. Screw two upright pieces to board. Across top of each fasten a piece of thin coil spring. Nail one end of coil to one end of upright. Pull a little of the tension out of coil, and fasten other end. Insert small nail or screw into outer side of each upright, and start thread up from one of them. Pass thread through left end of coil. Draw it across loom and down around nail on other upright. Take it back through coils, and continue back and forth until you have strung needed number of strands.

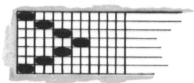

MAKING YOUR DESIGN

Copy your design on graph paper. Since beads are oblong, draw them 2 squares long and 1 wide. Color design with crayons, and make beadwork from it.

WEAVING YOUR DESIGN

Fasten thread to left of outer loom string. Pick up needed amount of beads with bead needle, and pass them under loom strings. Then put needle back through the beads on top of loom strings. To make your design, change from color to color as you continue.

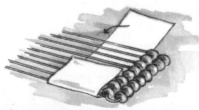

FINISHING YOUR DESIGN

When work is done, paste a strip of gummed tape around loom strings at each end to hold the beadwork in place.

▶ MAKING YOUR OWN BEADWORK

Belts for sports slacks or summer dresses can be made on a loom. Coin purses of skin, made with the overlay stitch, make nice gifts. And you can make attractive covers for books with the lazy-stitch method.

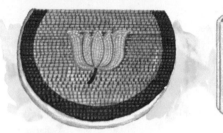

COIN PURSE

First draw an outline of the coin purse. Then draw design in the outline, and trace onto the skin. If center design is floral, bead outline first. Finally, add straight background.

BOOK COVER

Make paper pattern to fit the book. Trace this onto leather (split cowhide is good). Draw design on front of pattern and trace. Use lazy stitch.

If for any reason you need to remove the needle from your work to correct a mistake, don't try to push it through. Hold the thread, and pull the needle out backward.

To avoid knots along the beadwork when you have to start a new thread, put the thread through four or five beads of the row just finished. When it is brought under the loom strings and the next row is added, the thread will stay in place.

After the work is all done, carefully cut off the loose ends that show where the new thread was started. This will give a more finished appearance to your work.

ROBERT HOFSINDE (GRAY-WOLF)
Author and illustrator, *Indian Beadwork*

INDIAN MUSIC
OF NORTH AMERICA

The music of the American Indians consists mostly of songs and dances. The Indians have songs for games, children, love, work, and social dancing. But most of their music is associated with some kind of religious activity. Even love songs were originally an appeal to a guardian spirit for help in love.

▶ RELIGIOUS CEREMONIES

Among the Arapaho, Dakota, and other Plains Indians, music is used as a special part of the religion, the vision quest. Young men are supposed to have visions in which guardian spirits come to them, give them advice, and teach them songs. The guardian spirits may be animals, persons, or plants. For example, a young man may have a vision of a bird. The bird sings some songs to him, gives him advice, and then leaves. After the vision the young man wakes up and returns to his village. On the way he practices the new songs he has heard in his dream so that he can sing them for his friends.

Before 1900 the Plains Indians performed the ghost dance. It was supposed to drive away the hated white men and help the Indians get back their land and buffalo. It consisted mainly of singing and dancing. Although the Indians do not do the ghost dance anymore, they still sing the songs.

Ghost dance songs are different from other songs of the Plains Indians. They do not go very high or very low, and they repeat each phrase of melody before going on to the next. The older songs of the Plains Indians start very high and work their way down to a low, long, drawn-out tone. These songs are accompanied by a drum played loudly and slowly.

Another religious dance of the Plains Indians is the sun dance. The Indians dance around a pole in the summer heat, singing and praying for good hunting. The Arapaho and Dakota Indians sing some of their most impressive songs during this dance.

Music is also used in ceremonies to heal the sick. One example is the famous Yeibichai, or night chant, of the Navajo Indians—a ceremony lasting 9 nights. In addition to prayers it includes dances and songs sung by men with falsetto, or artificially high, voices.

Another example of healing by music comes from Yuma Indians of the southwestern United States. People who are feeling disturbed go to a hut away from their settlement for a few weeks. Here they make up songs. They think that the songs come to them in dreams or from the god that created the world. When they return, they feel cured.

▶ CHARACTERISTICS OF INDIAN SONGS

Although they have no harmony and few melody-making instruments, the Indians do use intricate melodies. In the eastern United States the Shawnee and the Creek tribes have songs in which a short bit of melody is sung alternately by a leader and a group. This kind of singing is called responsorial.

In many tribes, especially those of the Plains Indians, the singers put a great deal of tension on their vocal chords. The result is a kind of frenzied, intense tone. In some of the Pueblo tribes, singing in a low, growling voice is preferred. Elsewhere, singing in a high voice is heard.

Many songs of the Plains Indians are made up of two parts. In the first part the singer starts high and gradually works his way down the scale, singing only meaningless syllables, such as "hey-hey" or "ho-ho." Then he starts high again, singing the real words of the song. He ends on low tones, again with meaningless syllables.

A typical song of the Arapaho Indians has words like these: "Man, look up here, I am the bird," and "Young man, it is good that you are going on a war party; when you become a chief, you will be famous."

▶ TRIBAL MUSICIANS

Most members of a tribe participate in the musical life of the tribe. But there are usually no professional musicians. Often the people important in the religious ceremonies—the priests, shamans, or witch doctors—are the leaders of the musical life. As in the vision quest of the Plains Indians, many young men make up songs.

Most members of a tribe can sing and know many songs, but not so many can play instruments. A good singer in one tribe may not be considered good in another tribe. Some tribes think the quality of the voice is most important. Others think it is the loudness.

The ghost dance was once performed by the Plains Indians.

In the sun dance the Indians prayed for good hunting.

The Yeibichai was performed to heal the sick.

▶VALUABLE TREASURES

Many Indian tribes think of their songs as treasured possessions. They believe that a song belongs to a person. The owner of a song can give it away, sell it, or pass it on to his children. The Indians of the northwest coast buy and sell songs for large sums. They believe that music is something of the spirit and that a song has something to do with a person's soul. So to give a song away, or even to let someone hear it, is to give away part of one's soul.

BRUNO NETTL
Author, *Music in Primitive Culture*

INDIAN OCEAN. See OCEANS AND SEAS.

INDIANS OF NORTH AMERICA

North America was the home of the Indians long before Europeans came to the New World. Many centuries before the arrival of Columbus, Indians hunted, fished, and planted crops in the eastern forests. They brought the bison to earth with bows and arrows on the Great Plains. They fished for salmon in the rivers of British Columbia and gathered rye seeds in the Great Basin and acorns in California. They farmed the land in Arizona and southern Mexico. When Columbus arrived, Indians held all the territory within the great triangle formed by Panama, Alaska, and Labrador. They were masters of the North American continent.

▶ **INDIAN BEGINNINGS**

It was not always so. There was a time, more than 30,000 years ago, when Indians did not live in North America at all. No one did. The continent was then a virgin wilderness—much different from what it is today.

It was wetter and colder. Today's deserts of Utah and Nevada, for example, were covered with freshwater lakes. Lush grasses grew on

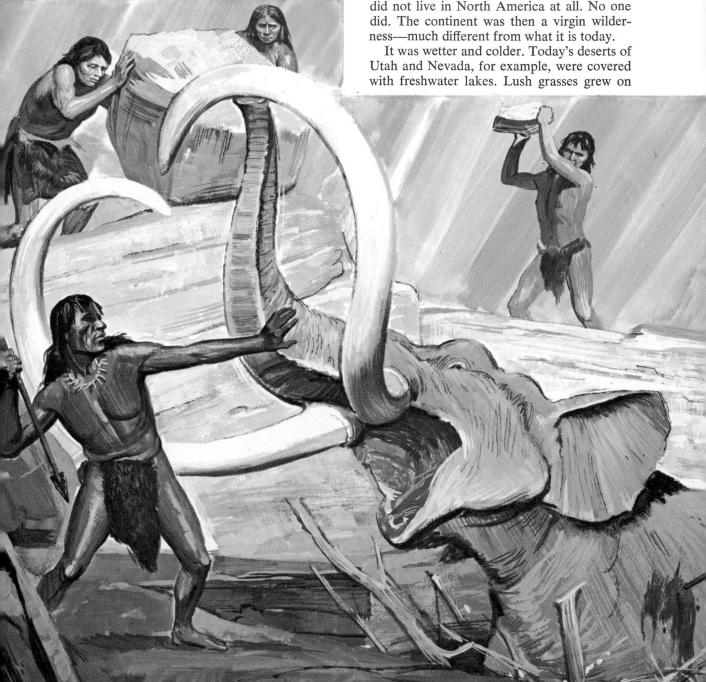

the southern Great Plains. Vast areas north of the Missouri and Ohio rivers were locked in by thick sheets of moving ice—glaciers.

The form of the continent was also different. Because much ocean water was frozen in glaciers, the sea level was lower than it is today. Land now under the ocean stood high above the water. In the far northwest, Asia and North America, separated by Bering Strait today, were tied together by a land bridge. Animals from North America could walk across the land bridge to Asia. Animals from Asia could cross to North America.

The grass-eating animals—the woolly mammoths and bison—were among the first to leave Asia. They moved slowly toward the land bridge into Alaska. The browsing and flesh-eating animals soon followed. So did the hunters, in search of their food supply.

Armed only with spears, stone spear points, darts, and scrapers, the hunters tracked the animals across the land bridge into Alaska. They trapped and speared the animals, cut the meat in slices, and dried it in the sun. Sometimes they cooked the meat over open fires. Sometimes they ate it raw. When hunting was good, they made camp and stayed until every bit of food was eaten. When hunting was bad, they kept to the trail. They and their descendants walked across northern Alaska into Canada and then south along the Mackenzie

River. They followed the animals south along the eastern edge of the Rocky Mountains. Twenty-five or thirty thousand years ago hunting peoples were already making camp on the great grasslands of North America.

▶ THE EARLY WAYS OF LIFE

Not all of the hunters stayed in the grassland. Some crossed the Rocky Mountains and entered the Great Basin. Others moved farther west to California. Many ceased to be hunters. They became fishermen and gatherers of wild seeds. And there were those, of course, who continued to hunt. Hunters traveled eastward, crossed what may have been an ancient Mississippi River, and built shelters in the eastern forests.

The migrations took thousands of years. The new ways of life developed slowly. On the Great Plains, in the Great Basin, and in southern California three distinct ways of life evolved. Each was flourishing 10,000 years ago.

The Old Bison Hunters. The hunters who stayed on the grassland—the Great Plains—continued to hunt woolly mammoths and bison. They moved from place to place following the animals. They continued to use stone points, darts, and scrapers. But they gave their points a new shape. They designed them beautifully, grooved them in the center, and made the edges razor-sharp. Archeologists call them Folsom points, after a site in New Mexico where many of them were found.

Some of the Old Bison Hunters moved into the eastern forests. Others set up their camps as far south as the Gulf of Mexico. Everywhere they lived by hunting and eating animals.

More than 1,500 years ago the Old Basketmakers wove Indian designs in use today.

The Old Basketmakers. Meanwhile, in the Great Basin, still a cool and wet land, the people had become fishermen as well as hunters. They fished in lakes and streams. Nets were used for the catches. They made mats and fine baskets from reeds that grew along the lakesides. They made fiber sandals and buried their dead in pelican skins.

From their homes in caves the Old Basketmakers watched the movement of camels, wild horses, and ground sloths. But they did little to disturb the animals. Unlike the Old Bison Hunters, they based their way of life upon the use of plants and the resources of the lakes.

The Old Millers. In southern California the people were gatherers of wild seeds. They lived largely by gathering acorns. The acorns were shelled and then crushed or pounded on rocks or milling stones. Bread was made from the crushed acorns. Other seeds, nuts, roots, and berries were also gathered and eaten.

The Old Millers lived in circular huts of earth. Many huts were partially underground. Five to twenty such huts made up a village. All the villages were located on hilltops or terraces near acorn groves.

▶ THE CENTURIES PASS

Thousands of years passed. The glaciers that covered the area north of the Missouri and Ohio rivers melted. In the Great Basin the lake waters evaporated and the land grew drier. The North American landscape began to look much as it does today.

Responding to the changes in the environment, the Indians spread out in all directions. They occupied much of North America. Some continued to earn their livelihood by hunting or gathering wild seeds. Some became fishermen. Others took part in one of man's greatest discoveries—the planting of seeds. They learned to plant the seeds of maize, or Indian corn, and became North America's first farmers.

It is as hunters, gatherers, fishermen, and farmers that we shall meet the Indians of history.

▶ THE HUNTERS

The Hunters lived in two vast areas of the continent—the Great Plains and the Canadian north. The Plains Indians—the Crow, Comanche, Blackfoot, Sioux, Assiniboin, Arapaho, Kiowa, Pawnee, and others—were hunters on the great American grassland. Much of their way of life was centered around the bison. The Chipewyan, Beaver, Yellow Knife, Dog-Rib, Montagnais, and Naskapi were hunters of the Canadian forests. One of their prime targets was the caribou.

The Bison Area

The Bison Area stretched from Saskatchewan to Texas and from the central Missouri River to the Rocky Mountains. It was a level land. Only near the few eastward-flowing rivers and in the foothills of the Rockies did hilly ground appear. Winters were cold and

ARCTIC OCEAN

SEAL

SEAL

PACIFIC OCEAN

SALMON

Yukon River

Eskimo

Hare

Mackenzie River

SEAL

HUDSON BAY

Eskimo SEAL

SALMON

Haida

CARIBOU

CARIBOU

Columbia River

Chinook

Blackfoot

Assiniboln

Missouri River

St. Lawrence River

Algonkin

Micmac

Nez Percé

CAMAS

Chippewa

WILD RICE

Menomini

Paiute

Cheyenne

Shoshoni

Sioux

Huron

Iroquois

Pomo

Pawnee

ACORN

PINON

BISON

NORTHERN MAIZE

Lenni-Lenape

Ohio River

Hopi

Mississippi River

Cherokee

Navajo

Creek

Zuni

SOUTHWESTERN

Apache

SOUTHEASTERN MAIZE

ATLANTIC OCEAN

MAIZE

Choctaw

MEXICAN
MAIZE

Rio Grande

Seminole

Coahuiltec

MESQUITE

GULF OF MEXICO

MEXICAN
MAIZE

Aztec

Maya

CARIBBEAN SEA

**FOOD AREAS OF
THE INDIANS
OF NORTH AMERICA**

Assiniboin braves stampeding bison into a log stockade.

snowdrifts deep. Summers were hot. Above all, the Bison Area was a natural grassland.

In summer the magic of rain and sun brought the grass to full bloom. It was then that the bison began to congregate in herds. It was then, too, that Bison Area peoples began to collect in individual tribes. The Crow, fresh from spring hunting, moved into a large camp circle. The Blackfoot did the same. The Assiniboin, Sioux, Kiowa, and others, eager to prepare for the rich summer hunt, also assembled in their individual tribes.

The Assiniboin planned well. It was their custom in the early 18th century to build log stockades. Wide entrances were left open in the walls. Lines of willows packed in bundles led away from the entrances. In late summer or early autumn a hunter dressed in a bison skin moved carefully into the herd. He stampeded the bison between the lines of willows into the stockade. Assiniboin arrows then brought the bison to earth. Other Bison Area tribes stampeded the bison over cliffs or set fire to the lush grass. The bison, stopped at the fire line, were easy targets for the hunters.

While the men did the hunting, it was the women who skinned the animals and prepared the meat for eating. Bison meat and fat, and berries were pounded into a pulp. The result was pemmican, the chief food of all the tribes in the Bison Area. It could be stored in raw-hide bags (parfleches) for many months.

Blackfoot Hunters. Success in hunting was important to the Blackfoot. Bison were often captured by stampeding them into large corrals made of logs, brush, and earth. Sometimes the "surround" was the chief hunting method. Blackfoot on horseback rode around and

around a herd, throwing the bison into utter confusion. Arrow or lance brought swift death to the terrified animals. Like the Assiniboin, the Blackfoot hunter sometimes hid under a buffalo skin and stalked the animals with bow and arrow.

Tipi and Travois. The women assembled and disassembled the tipis (tepees), or conical skin tents. They set up and took apart the travois, the litters of the Bison Area.

Tipis were made by tying several poles together and covering them carefully with bison skins. Twenty or more skins might be used to make a tipi. During travel two tipi poles were placed on the ground and hitched behind dogs. A bison skin or net tied between poles was a travois. It served to carry a family's belongings. Tipi and travois were excellent devices for people on the move.

The Coming of the Horse. Shortly before the middle of the 18th century, horses were introduced to the northern tribes. They came by way of the Indians west of the Rocky Mountains. The Blackfoot had horses before 1750. The Assiniboin were using horses as pack-animals in 1754. By 1766 Assiniboin warriors were riding in battle. The horse became important to all Bison Area tribes.

With horses the tribes could range over wider areas. Because horses could pull greater loads than dogs, larger tipis and travois were made. Horses helped to change hunting methods. Mounted hunters could ride swiftly around herds. The bison were easy prey.

The coming of the horse was not a complete blessing. The need for more and more horses grew rapidly. A Bison Area tribe that was horse-poor was poor indeed. Tribes often took the warpath to get horses. The Blackfoot fought the Sioux, Crow, Cree, and others for horses. The Assiniboin often went to the Mandan and Hidatsa villages on the upper Missouri River to trade for horses. When trading was impossible, warriors earned their "coups" (successful blows against the enemy) by stealing horses from the Blackfoot.

The Cycle of Life. Bison Area life was not always moving from place to place, hunting, stealing horses, or counting coups. There was time for birth, time to grow up, time for marriage, and time for death.

Bison Area babies were well cared for. Soon after birth a feast was held, and the baby was given a name. In the 19th century, babies spent much time in cradleboards. They were nursed until age 3 or 4. They were coddled by parents and grandparents alike.

When they grew older, young girls learned to sew. Their favorite garment was a T-shaped dress. They learned to make moccasins, leggings, and breechclouts. They made bison-skin robes to use in winter. They decorated clothing with porcupine quills, bison hair, or the teeth of animals.

Young boys worked less and played more. They ran races, played dice games, threw darts at rolling hoops, and learned to use bows, arrows, and lances.

Shortly before adulthood—age 12 or 13—a girl was secluded in a small tipi. She stayed there for 4 days. She ate little, did much work, and was taught what adulthood meant by an old woman of the tribe. A young man was taught from childhood that he must obtain a vision. All his success in life would depend upon having one. He must go off by himself and fast and thirst for 4 days. He must ask the gods for their help. Young men of the Crow were known to cut off finger joints to gain the pity of the gods and obtain a vision. For with his vision the young man might become a great chieftain or hunter. He might strike many coups for his people.

Marriage came soon after adulthood. Most were made by "buying." The young man would offer his services to the young woman's family for a year, sometimes two. In this way he would buy his wife. In many tribes it was necessary for the man to live with the woman's band or tribe. The Blackfoot insisted that the newlyweds go to the man's home. The Crow did not care.

At death the body was most often placed in a shallow grave, or put on a platform of poles across the forks of a tree. A long period of mourning followed.

Sioux

The Sioux were typical of the Bison Area tribes. When first seen by Europeans in 1640, the Sioux lived near the headwaters of the Mississippi River. They were hunters and fishermen. They grew fields of fine maize too. Around 1670—and for many years thereafter—their Chippewa neighbors, armed with French guns, attacked the Sioux villages. The Sioux fought back with bows and arrows. Sioux bands began to leave the upper Mississippi. By 1750 a number of bands had crossed the Missouri River. In 1765 the Sioux were in sight of the Black Hills of the Dakotas.

The Sioux who remained in Minnesota were called the Santee. Those who held the hunting grounds west of Minnesota and east of the Missouri River were known as the Yankton. It was the Teton Sioux who lived in the wide stretch of country between the Missouri and the Powder River of Wyoming and Montana. They became the prime Siouan bison hunters and warriors of the plains.

The bison-skin tipi, the cradleboard, and the pipe were common to the Blackfoot.

A Sioux village. The women sew and scrape the bison skins; the brave and his squaw return with meat on a travois; boys play shinny (hockey) or learn to decorate the tipis.

The Teton Sioux. The Teton country was a rolling grassland cut by a number of eastward-flowing streams. Elm, ash, and cottonwood trees grew along the stream banks. Wild plums, Jerusalem artichokes, strawberries, wild beans, chokecherries, and buds of the wild rose were found in favored places nearby. Wild turnips grew on the high prairie. Elk and antelope, or pronghorn, roamed the hills. Deer were plentiful. On the lush prairie grass the bison roamed in great numbers.

The slow-moving, poor-sighted bison were no match for the hunters. They fell by the hundreds to Teton arrows and bullets. In the summer camp the women scraped the bison skins clean, cut the meat in slices, and hung it on poles to dry. The Teton feasted on every part of the bison except the horns, hooves, and hair. And like the other Bison Area peoples they prepared pemmican.

They also built the tipi, used the travois, and moved from place to place in pursuit of the bison. When time allowed, the women made new skin clothing—shirts, robes, and moccasins. They repaired worn tipi skins, arrow quivers, and parfleches. And they decorated their work with paint or porcupine-quill embroidery. The children—and adults, too—played many games. They ran races and held archery contests. They swam in the rivers. In winter the boys enjoyed spinning tops on the ice. The men did the hunting and fighting. Their greatest joy was to collect blows—to count coups—against an enemy.

Teton bands swept south to fight the Pawnee. They moved north against the Arikara and west to the land of the Crow. Their chief object was horses.

At one time the Teton had obtained wild horses in the Platte and Arkansas river valleys. When settlers moving westward cut off that source, the Teton turned more and more against the Crow. Teton warriors raided Crow encampments and stole horses. The Crow struck back; they, too, collected coups.

The Coming of the White Man. Crow coups were not nearly so devastating as the blows of the white man. Western travelers moving over the Oregon Trail in the late 1840's and early 1850's passed directly through Teton country. They brought with them diseases the Teton had never known, particularly smallpox and measles. The Teton died like flies. The Brule Teton group, which numbered 2,500 in 1833, was reduced to only 750 by 1853.

The white man also brought the fur trade, the fort, the whiskey bottle, farm tools, and treaties. None of these helped the Teton. Indians took to the warpath—not to collect coups but to kill the white man.

Custer's Last Stand. In 1868 the Teton agreed to live on a reservation. It was to include all of South Dakota west of the Missouri River. The United States promised that the Black Hills, sacred to the Teton, would never be settled by white men. Unfortunately gold was discovered in the Black Hills in 1874. Gold seekers came to the area in large numbers. As a result, the movements of the Teton were restricted. They were not permitted to leave the reservation. To make certain that there would be no further trouble,

Lieutenant Colonel George A. Custer and the Seventh Cavalry were sent to the area.

Crazy Horse and Sitting Bull, Teton chiefs, led the Sioux and the Northern Cheyenne in the Battle of the Little Bighorn—Custer's Last Stand. Every man in the Seventh Cavalry was killed. The date was June 25, 1876.

In spite of victory, life was grim for the Teton. Old ways were no more. They were expected to farm reservation lands. "Women's work," they said. Where were the bison of old? Where could a warrior now count coups? What could he promise his children?

The Ghost Dance. The Teton, therefore, were ripe for the Ghost Dance. Wovoka, a Paiute shaman, believed that in a trance he had had a revelation from the gods. The Indians would get back all the land they had lost. They would be reunited with the dead. The old ways would return. The Indians must prepare for the great day by practicing the songs and dances given them by Wovoka.

The Ghost Dance was eagerly picked up by the Teton. They danced at the Pine Ridge and Rosebud reservations. It was December, 1890. White officials tried to stop the dancing. The Indians resisted. Sitting Bull was killed. Fearing the worst, many Teton left the reservations. One group surrendered. But they were butchered by soldiers at Wounded Knee, South Dakota, on December 29, 1890.

The spirit of the Teton—in fact, of all of the Sioux and of the Indians of the Bison Area in general—was completely broken.

The Sioux of the Present Day. More than 75 years after the massacre at Wounded Knee, the Sioux live on. Their homes are on reservation lands. About 400 live in Minnesota, 3,500 in North Dakota, 1,500 in Montana, and over 27,000 in South Dakota.

The Caribou Area

The Indians of the Caribou Area were forest dwellers. They lived among the tall trees of the Canadian north. Their land was extremely cold in winter and cool in summer. Snow lay on the ground for much of the year. It was a wet land. Fast-moving rivers and large lakes marked the landscape. It was a land rich in wildlife. Moose, elk, bear, and woodland caribou roamed the forests. Beaver and porcupines were plentiful. Musk oxen and Barren Ground caribou lived on the nearby tundra. The lakes bustled with trout, whitefish, and waterfowl.

The chief prize of the area was the woodland caribou, a big animal of 200 to 500 pounds. It was at home from Great Slave Lake to Newfoundland. It fed on the tender twigs of the forest. Its large hooves let it move easily through bogs and over soft snow. The hunters pursued it with vigor in all seasons.

Unlike the bison and the caribou of the Barren Grounds, the woodland caribou did not gather in herds. They often traveled in small groups. In summer they sometimes traveled alone.

Hunting the Woodland Caribou. The Kutchin

The Ghost Dance was performed to bring back the bison and drive away the white man.

built pounds (enclosures) of saplings and earth to catch the caribou in winter. Cleverly placed hedges and snares within the pounds trapped the caribou. In summer a favorite practice was to approach the caribou in rivers or lakes. They were speared from fast-moving canoes. When many caribou were about, the hunters, armed with bows and arrows, hid in shallow pits. The caribou were easily killed.

The Dog-Rib, Chipewyan, and Yellow Knife followed similar practices. But many of their bands did much of their hunting on the Barren Grounds in summer. There they pursued the Barren Ground caribou and the musk ox. The Slave did not build pounds. In early spring, wearing snowshoes, they ran the caribou down and snared them.

The Work of the Women. The women worked very hard in the Caribou Area. They helped to build the caribou-skin tents (the Sekani used spruce bark), made the clothing (shirt, leggings, moccasins, breechclout, robe, cap, and mittens), and prepared the pemmican. They carried heavy loads on their backs in summer and hauled toboggans over the snow in winter. They cared for the children.

Birth, Adulthood, Marriage, and Death. Strong babies were well provided for. The sick and the weak were often killed. Cradleboards were unknown, and the babies were carried on their mothers' backs.

Several of the customs known in the Bison Area were practiced in the Caribou Area. A number of the tribes secluded the girls before adulthood. The Sekani had a guardian spirit. The Chipewyan separated boys and girls at age 8 or 9. Polygamy was common, as was the custom of marrying sisters. Wives were often fought over in wrestling contests.

The dead were buried on scaffolds or platforms. The aged and infirm were left to die. Men mourned by cutting their arms and legs. Women mourned by cutting off their hair or severing finger joints. The Slave held a memorial feast one year after a death.

Religion. Little that can be called religion was known in the Caribou Area. There were no gods and no prayers. Some of the tribes had a vague notion of a guardian spirit, probably borrowed from the Bison Area.

The Chipewyan believed, however, that the dead took a trip in a stone boat. The boat traveled downriver to a beautiful island that abounded in caribou, moose, fish, and waterfowl. Only the good reached it. The evil were drowned when the stone boat sank.

Tribes of the Caribou Area. The Algonkin and the Micmac Indians were typical of the Caribou Area tribes.

Algonkin

The Algonkin of Canada, like the Montagnais, Cree, Ojibway (Chippewa), Malecite, and Micmac, spoke the Algonkian tongue. So did many Indian tribes who lived in the area between Newfoundland and North Carolina and as far west as the Rocky Mountains. While their languages were similar, the ways of life of the various Algonkian tribes were often quite different. In New England they were farmers; the Ojibway were gatherers of wild rice; the Montagnais and Naskapi were fishermen and hunters of the caribou, moose, and bear. The Algonkin of Canada lived north of the St. Lawrence River. They, too, were fishermen as well as hunters.

The Algonkin Country. Algonkin country was beautiful. White pines, silver maples, and yellow birches came down to the water's edge. Deer, elk, bear, and moose roamed the forests. The rivers teemed with fish. Berries, fruits, roots, and nuts grew wild. The short summers were warm and pleasant. The cold winters found the rivers frozen and the land packed hard with snow.

Food. Winter was the season of big-game hunting. In spring the Algonkin speared fish. In summer they used clubs to kill ducks, geese, herons, and cranes. In the fall, eels in large numbers were taken from the rivers. While men did the hunting and fishing, women and children scoured the forests for wild strawberries and blueberries, hazelnuts, wild apples, grapes, roots, and a variety of tubers.

Fish, meat, fruits, and berries were dried and stored in birch-bark containers. These were placed in pits lined with bark or under large rocks, safe from prowling animals. Hunger was sometimes known among the Algonkin, but it was not common.

The Campsite. The Algonkin campsite stood on high ground near a river or lake. The women gathered saplings in the forest, placed them upright in the ground, and bent them over. These were tied at the top. The pole framework was then covered with skin,

The Micmac Indians used pitch to waterproof their birch-bark canoes.

matting, or bark. This was the typical wigwam—the Algonkin family's winter home. Jesuit missionaries reported that it could be built in an hour. In summer the wigwams were built larger to allow more air to circulate.

Algonkin Bands. Algonkin preferred to wander over the country in small bands. They packed their belongings in large birch-bark containers. These were carried on their backs with the aid of a tumpline, a strap placed across the forehead and drawn tightly around the packs. Each band was made up of several families. The leader was often a fine hunter and fisherman, respected for his wisdom.

Gods and Spirits. All the Algonkin had the same gods. All felt the presence of the manito—the great spirit. All believed that the rocks, trees, rivers, fish, and animals were alive and had souls. Sacrifices were made in honor of fish and animals, lest they leave the Algonkin country. In bad times the medicine man often called upon the spirits to be kind and gentle to his people. He also used medicinal herbs and salves to cure the sick.

Unfortunately, the white man's diseases took a great toll of the Algonkin. Indian women married French fur traders, trappers, and farmers, further reducing Algonkin numbers. The tribe nearly disappeared into the greater Canadian population. Only about 2,000 Algonkin live today—on reserves in western Quebec and eastern Ontario.

Micmac

The Micmac Indians lived in Nova Scotia, northern New Brunswick, and Prince Edward Island. They may have been the first Indian people seen by white men in America. The Norsemen may have seen them in A.D. 1000. Certainly John Cabot saw them on his voyage to America in 1497. Because of their location near the Grand Banks off Newfoundland they were visited often by fishermen from Spain, Portugal, France, and England. Early in the 17th century, Jesuit missionaries from France began their stay in the Micmac country. They studied and learned much about the land and the people. And they described both in a series of documents called the *Jesuit Relations*.

The Micmac Country. The Micmac country was a land of bitter winters, cool summers, a rich and varied animal life, and an ever present forest. Spruce, balsam, tamarack, pine, hemlock, and birch trees grew everywhere. Caribou, moose, and porcupines roamed the forest. The rivers were crowded with fish, and the long coastline furnished an abundant supply of waterfowl and shellfish.

During the winter months Micmac hunters tracked the caribou and moose. They brought swift death to these animals with bow and arrow or spear. They set traps for porcupines and beaver. They killed bear and otter.

In the spring the salmon returned to the rivers of the Micmac country from the sea. The Jesuits reported the streams so full that you couldn't put your hands into the water without touching fish.

The quest for food did not cease in summer. Micmac hunters used clubs to kill ducks and geese. They took eels from the rivers. While the men were out with club and spear, the women and children searched the forest for wild berries, roots, and tubers.

In the autumn there was less concern about food. Only when summer fishing and gathering were poor did the Micmac return to the forest to hunt small game.

The Villages. Micmac villages were often located on river banks in the forest. Micmac wigwams, like those of the Algonkin, served well even in the coldest weather.

In the village there was much activity. Men worked hard to build birch-bark canoes. They made large wooden troughs in which to boil their food. They made tomahawks and knives of stone, spears of moose bone, and cradleboards of wood. Women sewed clothing and did fine work in porcupine-quill embroidery. There was time to dance, to obtain a guardian spirit, to marry, and to bury the dead.

The Micmac Today. Many Micmac adopted Christianity. They also adopted French tools and weapons. With muzzle-loading guns, for example, the Micmac raided the Beothuk Indians of Newfoundland early in the 18th century and destroyed that unfortunate people. In 1746 one third of the Micmac of Nova Scotia died of typhus. Through the French and Indian Wars the Micmac stuck to their French friends. They ambushed English parties on the road to Halifax.

Today over 4,000 Micmac live on small reserves in eastern Canada.

▶ **THE GATHERERS**

The Gatherers lived in five widely spread areas. A distinct plant food was gathered in each. The Paiute and Shoshone, for example, gathered piñon nuts in the Great Basin. Yokut and Pomo were acorn gatherers in California. The Nez Percé and their neighbors gathered camas in northeastern Oregon and Idaho. In the far south (northeastern Mexico) the Coahuiltec gathered pods of mesquite. Near the shores of the Great Lakes the Chippewa and Menomini gathered wild rice. Piñon, Acorn, Camas, Mesquite, and Wild Rice areas are shown on the map.

The Piñon Area

Piñon Area peoples lived in the Great Basin—the land between the Rockies and the Sierra Nevada. It was a harsh land of mountains and plateaus. Summers were unbearably hot; winters were cold. It was very dry. Rivers that left the mountains dried up in the basins. No large animals roamed the basin floors. Only rabbits, gophers, rats, and squir-

rels squirmed through the sagebrush. The air was filled with grasshoppers and crickets.

Up on the mountainsides, however, there were patches of grass holding rye and porcupine seeds. Willows and junipers grew at higher levels. Mountain goats and sheep grazed on the upper slopes, where pine trees—piñon—and their pine nuts were found.

The Seasonal Food Quest. Piñon Area bands could not afford to be particular. They hunted rabbits on the valley floors in winter and brought death by arrows to mountain goats and sheep. They scoured the hills for seeds, roots, bulbs, and berries in the late spring. In midsummer they battered grasshoppers to earth with clubs. Not until late autumn did they climb the slopes in quest of pine nuts.

The Paiute used poles to knock piñon cones from the trees. When their poles did not reach the upper branches, they climbed the trees. The cones were placed in large burden baskets and carried back to the village.

The Storage of Food. Piñon Area peoples could not eat all they gathered. Berries were pounded into paste, made into cakes, and stored in grass-lined pits. A flour was later made from the cakes. The chaff was removed from porcupine and rye seeds, which were then ground up, mixed with flour, and stored.

All the food in camp was stored in the ground before the pine-nut harvest so that the animals could not get at it. The pine nuts were crushed and stored in skin-lined pits. With all their food stored and safe, the Piñon Area bands were ready for the long winter.

The Settlements. Long winters were spent in small encampments. The Paiute home was the wickiup. A central fire pit was dug in the ground. Juniper and willow poles were set in the ground around the fire pit. The poles were bent over, tied with strips of bark, and covered with bark and grass. The wickiup stayed warm all winter. But Paiute hunters had to wear rabbit-skin blankets outdoors.

In the heat of summer when Piñon Area bands were on the move they built simple shelters from tree branches. The Southern Paiute built open-sided structures, which they covered with matting. It was so hot in summer that the men wore only a breechclout, moccasins, and leggings. The women wore fiber aprons. Children often went naked.

From Birth to Death. Before a baby was

The Northern Paiute covered their wickiups with reed matting, made fire with a twirling stick, and used rabbit skins for robes.

born in the Piñon Area, the father did all of the chores in the wickiup. But he was not permitted to hunt or to gather seeds. The newborn was washed and placed in a cradleboard. There the baby spent the first years of life.

Rituals and ceremonies were not as elaborate as they were in the hunting areas. A girl reaching adulthood simply walked down to a nearby stream and bathed. She repeated the bath every few days until after the pinenut harvest. She was not allowed to eat meat through the bathing period.

A young man reaching adulthood was required to kill a rabbit and eat the meat. He would cut the rabbit meat into a coil, from which he formed a loop. He jumped through the loop with a bow in his hand. No other demands were made upon him.

After reaching adulthood, young men and young women married. There was no marriage ceremony. The couple simply agreed to marry. They went to the girl's band to live, but soon moved to the boy's band.

At death an antelope skin was placed over the dead body. The body was placed in a crevice in a nearby mountain. The dead person's wickiup was burned. If a husband died, wife and sons showed they were mourning by cutting their hair.

Paiute

The Paiute were typical of the Piñon Area tribes. Paiute was the name given to many Indian bands in the Great Basin. The Southern Paiute lived in the desert of southwestern Utah, eastern California, northeastern Arizona, and southern Nevada. The Northern Paiute lived in southeastern Oregon and the mountain valleys of western Nevada and eastern California.

Southern Paiute. The region of the Southern Paiute was particularly harsh. The view from a mesa top or valley floor was bleak and grim. Only insects and mesquite were abundant. The Southern Paiute, therefore, were forced to wander from place to place in search of food.

The women and children pulled pine cones from the tall trees. They burned some to loosen the nuts; they stored others in brushlined pits. They gathered mesquite and wild beans. On the valley slopes they collected porcupine and wild rye grass seeds. In the lower valleys they found the seeds of bunch grass. They extracted bulbs and roots from the ground with digging sticks.

The men were the hunters. Rabbits were caught in long nets near watering places. They were skinned and dried. Sometimes the meat was ground into meal between rough stones. Traps were set for squirrels. Southern Paiute men also hunted caterpillars, grasshoppers, and crickets. All were considered delicacies.

Because the Southern Paiute moved constantly, they built temporary dwellings. A lean-to against the side of a hill or poles placed in the ground with a matted roof served as home. Sometimes large clumps of sagebrush served as shelter from sun or snow.

Northern Paiute. The Northern Paiute region was richer by far. There were streams and lakes. There were swans, geese, ducks, and pelicans. There were antelope and deer. But none of these were abundant. The Northern Paiute, too, were primarily gatherers.

The women gathered a wide variety of seeds, herbs, nuts, and berries. Chokeberries were pounded into a paste and made into small cakes. In late summer various seeds mixed with chokeberry flour were made into a gruel. Pine nuts were a favorite. A tea was made from chokeberry or wild rose stems.

Poisoned arrows served the men on the hunt. But deer and antelope both were taken at night by use of deadfalls. A prize catch was the mountain goat. Venison was eaten fresh or was dried and stored. The hides were tanned and used as clothing.

Birds were picked of their feathers, gutted, and hung in pairs on poles to dry. The sage hen was a great favorite.

Because they could depend on a regular food supply, the Northern Paiute lived in semipermanent dwellings. In winter they built the wickiup. It was made on a frame of juniper or willow poles lashed together at the top. The frame was covered with strips of bark or with dried brush or matting made from reeds or grass. In summer they used a lean-to.

The old ways of Paiute life are gone today. But the Paiute themselves survive. About 4,000 live on reservations in the Great Basin.

The Acorn Area

The Acorn Area was the land west of the Sierra Nevada mountains. It included the Central Valley of California, the Coast Ranges, and the low country near the sea. The Central Valley was almost surrounded by mountains. Much of it was level. Short streams fed the Sacramento and San Joaquin rivers. But the Acorn Area was very dry.

Animal life was plentiful. Many kinds of fish were found in the rivers and the sea. The valley and nearby lands abounded in seeds, nuts, and wild plants. The most important tree was the oak, provider of the acorn.

The Acorn. Acorns were gathered, cracked open, and pounded into meal. The meal was put into large baskets. To remove tannic acid, the Indians poured water over the acorn meal. They continued to pour until the tannic acid was gone. Only then was the acorn meal ready to be cooked.

Other Foods and Food Storage. Indians of the Acorn Area did not live on acorns alone. The Pomo gathered wild oats, berries, roots, and pine nuts. They built dams and made nets, spears, and basket traps for river and lake fishing. They captured waterfowl with nets and slings. They hunted the deer, rabbit, and squirrel. And like their Piñon Area neighbors, they knew how to preserve and store food.

Winter and Summer Dwellings. The winter dwellings were unlike anything we have yet seen. Poles were placed in the ground, and the tops bound together. The whole surface was thatched with tule (reeds or rushes). Several families might live in one hut.

Large dance houses and sweat houses with conical roofs, partly underground, were also found in the winter villages.

When traveling in the hot summer, the Acorn Area people would build a simple brush shelter or sleep under the stars.

The Pomo Basket. In winter, Pomo women made baskets. They used many techniques and made many varieties. They used feathers and beads as elaborate decorations. Pomo baskets made fine gifts. They were used in tribal ceremonies. Experts claim that Pomo baskets were the finest made in North America.

Birth and Adulthood. A newborn Acorn Area baby was placed in a basket cradle very much like a little chair. The baby's feet were allowed to hang free. Mothers were especially proud of their cradles—and of their babies.

Before adulthood the children were free to romp about the camp. They played the hoop-and-pole game and dice games and spun acorn tops. Girls learned to make baskets. They helped their parents gather seeds and nuts. They learned to make rabbit robes and feather blankets. They made aprons from shredded bark. The boys learned to hunt and fish.

In some tribes girls were secluded just before adulthood. They were forced to scratch and scar their backs with sharp sticks. A ceremony and dance followed. Most boys were initiated into adulthood by drinking a concoction of weeds and herbs. This produced visions and dreams. Acorn Area peoples believed that the Jimson weed helped them to see things that ordinarily could not be seen.

Marriage and Death. Couples intending marriage merely exchanged gifts. In some of the tribes brides were bought. Shells served as money. A bride felt particularly proud when many shells were offered for her.

The dead were either buried or cremated.

The Maidu and Yokut burned their dead, the dead person's house, and the dead person's possessions. They mourned all the dead in an annual ceremony.

The Camas Area

The Camas Area was a gently rolling plateau cut by deep canyons. High hills and mountains rose on the fringes. It was a comparatively dry land. At high elevations, however, rainfall was abundant. The Salmon and Clearwater rivers crossed the area. The Snake River, in its deep canyon, moved its way north to join the Columbia. All teemed with salmon. The hills supported a rich pine forest. Deer, elk, bear, and mountain sheep were plentiful. And beginning in the spring, the mountain meadows were aflame with the cowish, bitterroot, and camas.

The Camas. The camas is an edible bulb. It looks much like the hyacinth. It was gathered on the uplands in late summer. The women used long digging sticks to pry the bulbs from the earth. The bulbs were cleaned and placed on beds of grass over a fire pit. They were steamed overnight and then dried in the sun. Dried camas was a staple food.

Other Important Foods. Cowish roots, bitterroots, and berries were gathered and eaten in season. Deer, elk, and mountain sheep provided meat for feasts. Salmon was probably the most important food of all.

Salmon moved up Camas Area rivers in the spring. Nez Percé fishermen were ready for them. They speared, netted, and trapped the salmon by the hundreds. Nez Percé women cleaned them, cut them into slices, and hung them on drying frames. Dried salmon, like dried camas, was a staple food of the area.

The Villages. Villages were often placed near riverbanks where fishing was good. The dwellings were partly underground. Posts were set into the excavations to support an A-shaped roof covered with cattail mats or brush. Houses grew as families prospered. A number of families could live in one house. Special sweathouses for the men and isolation huts for the women were built. Temporary dwellings were built when the women and children went to the gathering grounds.

Camas Area Tribes and Horses. Horses were known among the Umatilla of Oregon in 1739. They had probably been purchased from the Shoshone. By the middle of the 18th century, Camas Area peoples were riding horses and even sending hunting parties east to the Great Plains. The Kutenai and Flathead were selling horses to the Blackfoot.

But it was the Nez Percé who became the horse breeders. The valleys of the Nez Percé country offered a protected environment for horses and fine year-round grazing.

The Life Cycle. Babies were born in an isolated hut in the Camas Area. They were swaddled in buckskin before they were placed on cradleboards. Mothers carried them on their backs on trips to the camas fields.

Girls grew up quickly. They learned the secrets of the wild plants. They learned how to prepare and dry the salmon. They learned to make aprons of cedar fiber and rabbit-skin robes, moccasins, and caps. Boys learned to hunt and fish. They joined the men in ball juggling, dice games, and walking on stilts.

Just before adulthood the girls went to live in an isolated hut. They gathered wood and water. The young men sought help from the spirits. The youths made cuts on their bodies. They dived into icy rivers. They hoped to become fine hunters or medicine men.

Couples married soon after reaching adulthood and went to live with the husband's people. A man might take several wives during his lifetime.

Camas Area peoples were not afraid to die, but they did fear the dead. The dead person's house was destroyed and his name never mentioned. The body was placed in a crevice in the hills or cremated.

Nez Percé

The Nez Percé were typical of the Camas Area tribes. The Nez Percé homeland was the plateau country of western Idaho, northeastern Oregon, and southeastern Washington. It was the land cut by the Snake, Salmon, and Clearwater rivers. It was a rich land. The hillsides grew lush with cowish, bitterroot, and blue camas. Thickets of haws and chokecherries could be found among the fir and pine trees. The rivers teemed with salmon and waterfowl. Antelope roamed over patches of fine grass, and elk, deer, and mountain sheep were everywhere.

Sweathouses. Because the Nez Percé believed that their bodies were purified by sweat bathing, their villages all contained sweathouses for the young men. Water was poured over hot stones. Steam filled the sweathouse. Sweating from every pore, the young boys raced from the house and plunged into the ice-cold river. This not only cleansed the body but also was good sport.

Cowish, Salmon, and Camas. In the early spring the Nez Percé left their villages for the cowish-covered hillsides. They dug the roots. Some roots were steamed and eaten immediately. Others were cooked in biscuit form and preserved. During the salmon run in late spring and early summer, the men were busy with nets, spears, and traps. The women cut the salmon into slices, hung them on drying racks, and then beat them into pulp. Salmon pemmican was a staple food.

In late summer and early autumn the women moved to the camas grounds. Temporary dwellings were built, fire pits were dug, and camas bulbs gathered. Like salmon, camas was a Nez Percé staple.

The Coming of the Horse. The Nez Percé acquired horses before the middle of the 18th century. They probably bought or stole them from their southern neighbors, the Shoshone. They sold inferior horses to neighboring tribes and imported the finest stock for themselves from New Mexico and Chihuahua (Mexico). When the explorers Lewis and Clark came upon them in 1805, the Nez Percé had large and magnificent herds. They were already breeding brown-and-white and black-and-white spotted horses—the famous Appaloosas.

Horse breeding produced many changes in Nez Percé life. The Appaloosas were excellent for trading. They were sold to the Crow in exchange for porcupine quills, embroidery, parfleches, bison skins, and tobacco, and to the Wasco-Wishram for *hiqua*—shells that served as a form of money in the Salmon Area.

Missionaries, Settlers, Miners, and the Reservation System. Changes were brought by missionaries, settlers, gold seekers, and the reservation system. In 1836 Henry H. Spalding started a mission at Lapwai. A home and school were built. The Spaldings (husband and wife) learned Shahaptian, the language of the Nez Percé, and devised a Shahaptian alphabet. The Nez Percé began to read and write in their own language. Some learned English. Spalding introduced the Nez Percé to hoe agriculture. The Indians began to raise potatoes and wheat and learned to care for sheep, chickens, and pigs. Spalding gained respect from the tribe by healing the sick. The Spaldings remained in the Nez Percé country until 1847.

Meanwhile, thousands of settlers were beginning to move to Oregon over the Oregon Trail. The Nez Percé often supplied the wagon trains with fresh horses, meat, salmon, and camas. Before long, settlers moved directly into the Nez Percé country. Fearful that war would break out, the United States Government proposed that the Indians be settled on a reservation. A treaty defining the Nez Percé reservation was signed in 1855.

When gold was discovered on the reservation lands, miners asked the government to change the treaty. A new treaty (1863) provided for a much smaller reservation. Land in the Salmon, Snake, Wallowa, and Grande Ronde valleys was taken from the Nez Percé.

The Nez Percé were dismayed. White settlers began a slow trickle into the Grande Ronde Valley. They pushed into the Wallowa. Government efforts to keep the peace were spurned by the Indians. A few angry Nez Percé fell upon the settlers and miners. The battle was on.

The War of 1877. Because the Nez Percé were under great pressure from the army, they decided to abandon their lands in Oregon and Idaho. It was a difficult decision to make. They started west over the Lolo Trail. But General O. O. Howard and his army command followed close behind.

The Nez Percé were led by Looking Glass, their chief. Chief Joseph commanded the rear guard. In the early skirmishes the Nez Percé were quite successful. They inflicted many casualties upon the enemy. The Nez Percé crossed Targhee Pass into Yellowstone National Park. Determined now to escape to Canada, they quickened their pace. But the army would not give up their pursuit. Colonel Nelson A. Miles caught the tired Nez Percé at the Bear Paw Mountains, about 40 miles from Canada and freedom.

Looking Glass and other Nez Percé chiefs had been killed during the trek. It was left for Chief Joseph to surrender. He is reported to

A Nez Percé camp. Chief Joseph and Looking Glass (on horseback) make plans during the flight of the Nez Percé to Canada to escape the white man.

have said, "Hear me, my chiefs, I am tired; my heart is sick and sad. . . . I will fight no more. . . ."

The Nez Percé were sent to Indian Territory (Oklahoma) and later to the Colville Reservation in Washington. Chief Joseph died there in 1904. Over 1,500 Nez Percé live on the Lapwai Reservation in Idaho.

The Mesquite Area

The Mesquite Area of northeastern Mexico, like the Piñon Area, was made up of mountains and basins. It was very hot and dry. The few streams that left the mountains evaporated. They never reached the sea. Animal life was scarce. Cactus, yucca, and creosote bush grew in the basins. Lower mountain slopes were covered with mesquite, and pine and fir trees were found on the upper slopes.

Mesquite and Other Foods. Mesquite is a tree that bears pods filled with seeds. Coahuiltec bands gathered the pods, ground the seeds in mortars, and boiled them. Hungry Indians sometimes ate the seeds raw.

When faced with famine or starvation—a frequent problem—the Mesquite Area tribes would eat almost anything. They ate rats and insects. They ate the fruit, seeds, and leaves of the cactus. Several bands ate the mescal bean, and they all drank a fermented liquid made from dried mesquite and water.

In Lower California, also considered a part of the Mesquite Area, the foods were little better. Fish, perhaps, provided the Indians of Lower California with a richer diet.

The Early Spanish Records. The Spanish explorers were surprised to find Mesquite Area peoples living so poorly. Early accounts told that the Coahuiltec roamed widely, seeking food. They told that the Indians did not live in houses and wore no clothing. They had no blankets, no cradles. Water was so scarce that newborn babies were washed with herbs.

The early Spanish stories were no doubt exaggerated. Many Coahuiltec bands did build crude domed huts. Some slept in rock shelters in summer. Some wore pieces of cloth. But the rest was quite true. The Coahuiltec were poor people living in a poor land.

When the Spaniards moved into northeastern Mexico to mine silver, the Coahuiltec fell upon them. They took scalps, tortured the Spanish captives, and cut up the bodies of the dead. To record each victim, they cut a notch on their own arms.

The Franciscan Missions. In 1677 a Franciscan mission was set up at Nadadores. The Indians were taught to become farmers. Before the 17th century had passed, other missions had been built. Early in the 18th century, Coahuiltec bands began to abandon their roaming for a new life at the missions.

The Wild Rice Area

The Wild Rice Area was very different. It was an area of much flowing water, many lakes (including Lake Superior and portions of lakes Michigan and Huron), and many ponds. It was very cold in winter and warm in summer. Much snow fell during the winter season. Spruce, hemlock, birch, and sugar maple trees grew right down to the edge of the water. Moose, white-tailed deer, wolves, and foxes lived in the forest. Beaver built small dams in the streams. The lake waters teemed with whitefish, pickerel, and pike. The ponds were covered with bulrushes and wild rice.

Wild Rice. In autumn the Menomini slipped their birch-bark canoes into the ponds. As the man of the family poled the canoe along, his wife used a long stick to pull bunches of wild rice over the top of the canoe. With another stick she knocked off the wild rice grains. When the canoe was filled, it was poled to shore.

On shore the wild rice was hulled, parched, and threshed. It was washed, put in birch-bark bags, and stored in deep pits. Wild rice was the chief food of the Menomini and an important food for the other tribes of the Wild Rice Area.

The Rest of the Year. In the autumn, too, the women gathered roots, bark, and bulrushes. The men hunted the beaver and the otter. In winter, hunters on snowshoes hunted the white-tailed deer.

April and May were the months to tap the sugar maples. The men cut holes in the trees. Dishes were placed under the holes to collect the sap. It was poured into large vats and then put into vessels. The sap was boiled. As it thickened, it was poured into birch-bark containers (makuks) to harden and be stored. Small amounts poured into molds became sugar cakes, a favorite candy of the children.

In summer, makuks were filled with wild berries, and the nets with fish.

Wigwams and Villages. The Indians of the Wild Rice Area lived in wigwams, which were made by putting saplings in the ground in an oval, bending them over, and tying them with bark. Other saplings were added to make a strong frame, which was covered with bulrush mats. In very cold winter, rows of mats were added, and the roofs were covered with birch bark. Several families might live in one wigwam.

Wigwams were not the only buildings in a Wild Rice Area village. Visitors were likely to see sweat lodges, weaving houses, and, in a Chippewa village, the meeting place of the Midewiwin, or Grand Medicine Society.

Wild Rice Area villages were very busy places. The women made deerskin shirts, robes, moccasins, and leggings. They made the makuk and wove bulrush mats. They strung beads and made earrings. Men made wooden bowls, spoons, and the famous calumet, or peace pipe. They made paddles, traps, snowshoes, and the birch-bark canoe. The children amused themselves at dice, the hoop-and-pole game, and spinning tops.

From Cradle to Grave. After birth the Wild Rice Area baby was wrapped in moss and strapped to a cradleboard. A "namer" chosen by the parents gave the child a name.

Prior to adulthood a young woman was secluded in a small wigwam for 4 days and nights. If possible, she would fast. She would touch her body only with a scratching stick. When the ordeal was over, a feast was given in her honor by the Grand Medicine Society. Young men were expected to fast. They hoped in that way to get a vision.

Youngsters were expected to marry soon after reaching adulthood. If a young man was serious about a young woman, he showed his courage, strength, and skill by killing a deer. The dead animal was brought to the girl's wigwam. It was a gift for her parents. The couple usually went to live in the boy's village.

After death the body was cleaned and the face painted. Then the body was set in a shallow grave. The feet were pointed toward the west—the direction in which the spirit of the dead body would move. A dead man's personal calumet and hide bag were buried with him. In a Chippewa village the members of the Grand Medicine Society would dance around the grave. The grave was then covered with bark and earth, and a period of mourning followed.

Chippewa

The Chippewa were typical of the Wild Rice Area tribes. The Chippewa—or Ojibway, as they are often called—were Indians of the eastern forests. They originally lived near the Atlantic Ocean. But when sickness and death struck their village, they began to move west. They settled for a time along the St. Lawrence River near Montreal. Later they explored the shores and waters of Lake Huron and built a large village at Sault Ste. Marie. Unfortunately scholars have not been able to date the early Chippewa migrations or the origin of their settlements. When the French explorer Nicolet visited Sault Ste. Marie in 1634 and again in 1639, he may well have smoked the calumet, or peace pipe, with the

Chippewa braves used bark to build wigwams and canoes. The brave in the canoe on the left sounds a moose call; the couple on the right harvest wild rice.

Chippewa. Spurred on by the fur trade, Chippewa bands continued to move west. In the beginning of the 18th century, Chippewa warriors drove the Fox Indians from northern Wisconsin. They attacked the powerful Sioux. Shortly after 1736 they gained control of the area west of Lake Superior. With the Ottawa and Potawatomi—whom they had joined in a loose confederacy called the Council of the Three Fires—they held the huge area on both sides of lakes Huron and Superior and west into North Dakota.

Hunting. Hunting was an all-year occupation of the men, but it was particularly important in winter. Chippewa hunters told tales of tracking the moose or deer on snowshoes until the animals fell to the ground exhausted. Meanwhile, in the large dome-shaped wigwams covered with birch bark and bulrushes, the women repaired the torn clothing, cared for the children, chopped the firewood, and told long stories into the night.

Clans. The Chippewa were divided into numerous bands, each of which held hunting, fishing, and gathering rights to a particular territory. A band was made up of between 100 and 300 people. Each had a leader, who was often a war chief. The Chippewa also had a clan system. Many clans might be represented in a single Chippewa band. Bear, Marten, Wolf, Loon, Crane, and Eagle clans were the most frequently encountered. If the father was a Crane, all the children were Cranes. Descent was traced through the father. The mother was a member of another clan, for members of the same clan were never permitted to marry.

Clan and band leaders were held in high esteem, and warriors were paid much honor. Able hunters and fishermen were known everywhere in the forest. But the Chippewa held particular reverence for the medicine man.

The Medicine Man was the healer of the sick. He knew the cures for the major illnesses. He rubbed roots, herbs, or bark into open wounds and cured his patients. But the medicine man was more than a healer. He consulted the gods on the causes of illness. He was able to withstand great pain himself. He would foretell the future. Because he was believed to be on good terms with the gods, the Chippewa thought that he could drive away evil spirits or permit them to flourish. They honored the medicine man, but they feared him too.

Medicine men and medicine women were all members of the secret Grand Medicine Society, or Midewiwin. A young man entering the society was taught the moral code of the Chippewa and the names and uses of a few herbs. He was given the Mide bag, in which the herbs were stored. As he advanced in the society, he learned more about herbs, roots, and vegetable poisons. All the instructions of the Midewiwin were written on birch-bark rolls, which were shown to a young man when he was initiated into the Midewiwin. The society's annual celebration was a highlight in Chippewa social life.

While the Midewiwin celebration was taking place, a young lad might be having a vision. In his dream he was visited, perhaps, by the manito—the supernatural being who watched over the Chippewa. His parents had been waiting some time for this event. They would make the boy fast through several meals. For they knew he was having a vision—the goal of every Chippewa child. The dream might help him predict his future.

While many of their old customs have long since disappeared, the Chippewa themselves yet remain. They can be found on reservation lands in Michigan, Wisconsin, Minnesota, Montana, Saskatchewan, Manitoba, Ontario, and Quebec. They number well over 40,000.

▶ THE FISHERMEN

The Pacific Northwest Coast between Alaska and northern California was the home of the fishermen. The northern tribes—Tlingit, Tsimshian, Haida, Kwakiutl, and others—fished the nearby streams for salmon. The Nootka sent their canoes into the ocean to hunt sea mammals. The southern tribes—the Chehalis, Wasco-Wishram, Klamath, and Yurok—were poor relatives of the northern tribes. But they, too, were salmon fishermen. Both groups lived in the Salmon Area.

The Salmon Area

On the Pacific coast of British Columbia the mountains rose almost directly from the sea. There were many islands offshore. The coastal plain was narrow. Farther south, in Washington and Oregon, the land between ocean and mountains was somewhat wider. Both the coastal areas and neighboring mountains were wet. Heavy rains gave rise to swift-flowing streams and fine forests of hemlock, spruce, fir, and cedar. The forests abounded in deer, elk, and mountain goats. The whale, seal, sea otter, and porpoise were found in the ocean. The all-important salmon swam in the rivers.

The Salmon. After 2 to 3 years of feeding in the ocean the salmon returned to the river of their birth. They fought their way upstream. Instinct led them to the spawning grounds.

The tribes of British Columbia used hooks and lines, spears, nets, traps, and dams to catch the salmon. Men were the fishermen. A favorite method was to anchor two canoes in the river and tie a long net between them. The salmon could not swim past the net.

The southern tribes often built scaffolds out over the rivers. They used dip nets to catch fish, and clubs and spears to stun them.

The women cut off the heads, tails, and fins.

They pounded the meat between stones. They mixed candlefish oil, berries, and salmon together to make salmon pemmican, the staple in the diet of the Salmon Area.

The Village and the Gable-Roofed House. Salmon Area villages were located along streams or overlooking the sea. The typical home was a rectangular gable-roofed house made of spruce and cedar. Spruce provided a sturdy framework. Cedar served for the planks. Roof planking was easily removed and carried to temporary houses during the salmon run. A number of families lived in a single gable-roofed house.

The Arts and Crafts. Unlike the hunters and gatherers, who were ever occupied with seeking food, the fishermen had much time to spend on other things. They devoted considerable time to arts and crafts.

They were excellent woodworkers. They made fine seagoing canoes, storage boxes and dishes, nets and baskets, masks and rattles. They made totem poles—some of them 60 feet high—and carved them to illustrate legends or tell the stories of their families. The Chilkat, using the wool of the mountain goat, made exceptionally fine blankets.

Clothing. Great care went into the making of clothing, although little clothing was actually worn. The men went naked in summer. In winter they wore sea otter skin robes. Ponchos were worn in wet weather. So were hats. The men wore ear and nose pendants.

Women wore bark aprons or bark garments that fell from the shoulders to the ankles. They wore nose rings and earrings.

Tsimshian, Haida, and Tlingit women had slits made in their lower lips. A piece of wood (a labret) was put into the slit. This was a mark of beauty.

Wealth and the Potlatch. Salmon Area peoples were deeply conscious of wealth. It mattered much whether one was a chief, a noble, a commoner, or a slave. The number of blankets, baskets, boxes, canoes, and skins and the amount of fish pemmican a man owned were important.

Wealth could be shown by giving property away at festivals. Each chief tried to outdo the other chief by giving away more and more. This custom was called a potlatch. After each potlatch the giver took a new name and was thought more of by his people. The desire

What does "potlatch" mean?

"Potlatch" is a Chinook Indian word that originally meant "to give." The Indians on the northwest coast of North America used the word to describe some of their ceremonies and feasts. Sometimes a potlatch was an auction to see who could pay the highest price for an item. The Indian who paid the most was covered with glory. The high price proved his power and wealth.

A potlatch was usually a lavish celebration for a wedding or the birth of a son. The host gave many gifts to the guests. Sometimes the host destroyed his own possessions to impress the visitors. The visitors were then obliged to return the hospitality with an even more elaborate affair. These celebrations proved that the host was an important man. His name would forever be linked with his deeds.

The Kwakiutl Indians of the Canadian coast were said to live in order to show off. Their potlatches were more elaborate than those of other Indian tribes. One powerful Kwakiutl chief sent invitations for a potlatch to tribes up and down the northwest coast. To impress his guests, the host overturned tables heaped with fish, berries, and apples, throwing them into a blazing fire. He

wasted barrelfuls of valuable fish oil by pouring it over the flames. Then he snapped his fingers and said, "Hah, I care only that much for food and oil! I have plenty to spare."

Now it was the turn of a visiting chief to show what he could do. He attempted to smother the flames with a huge sheet of copper worth 8,000 blankets. The host, in turn, had his men drag in five canoes. These were hacked to pieces and thrown into the smoldering flames. Each canoe, the host assured the guests, was worth 5,000 blankets. But the rival chief had come prepared. He ordered his men to heap 400 blankets on the fire. The host then hacked up additional canoes to rekindle the dying blaze. But even that did not satisfy him. He finally tore down a section of his house and threw it into the flames. The guest chief could not rival this deed. He left hoping to rebuild his fortune and entertain his host with a bigger and better potlatch.

The fortunes of the host were gone, and his house was ruined. But now he had the title of House Burner to add to other boastful names. His tribe was proud of him, and he was convinced his descendants would sing his praises.

A Haida village. Totem poles, storage boxes, and canoes show skill in wood carving. An Indian (*right*) lifts a boiling stone from the fire. The red-hot stone will be dropped into a watertight basket to cook food.

for wealth and the potlatch were unique to the Indians of the Salmon Area.

The Cycle of Life. A baby was born in a cubicle of the gable-roofed house. Slaves cared for both mother and child, and a feast was held in the baby's honor. The baby spent much time on a beautifully carved cradleboard. Two boards were pressed against the baby's head. The head would be pressed out of shape. But Salmon Area people considered the new head shape a mark of beauty.

Ceremonies for entering adulthood were not elaborate. A girl stayed in the house for 5 days. Dances were held in her honor. On the 5th night she presented gifts to her family. The boys had to seek visions.

Before a marriage took place, a grand feast was held. Many gifts were given away in the girl's name at a potlatch.

The dead were buried in canoes or wooden boxes. These were placed in trees or caves. Gifts were placed with the bodies. The dead person's name was not spoken for a year.

Haida

The Haida were typical of the Salmon Area tribes. Little is known about the Haida Indian past. Tradition says that the oldest Haida villages stood on the eastern shores of the Queen Charlotte Islands (British Columbia). The Haida may have moved to the islands from the Canadian mainland.

The Haida were fishermen and hunters of sea animals. Fishing for salmon and halibut and hunting the sea otter kept Haida men busy during late spring and summer. Traps, weirs, and nets were used to catch salmon. Halibut were taken with hook and line. Men in canoes shot the sea otter with arrows.

The ever present food supply permitted the Haida many luxuries. They were able to build permanent homes and villages. They could devote time to various forms of art. They developed a social system based upon class and wealth. Their strength enabled them to make frequent raids upon their neighbors.

Haida villages were set on rocky ledges near a river or facing the sea. The houses were large, rectangular, gable-roofed dwellings made of cedar planks. Several families lived in each house. The entrance was often an opening in the totem pole in front of the house.

Plank houses, canoes, totem poles, masks, rattles, storage boxes, and dishes were all evidences of Haida ability to work with wood. These objects were skillfully carved and painted. Haida totem poles traced the history of each family. Raven, eagle, beaver, whale, and thunderbird were common symbols.

When Europeans arrived in the 17th and 18th centuries, they introduced potatoes and metal tools. Potatoes as well as sea otter skins became important trade items. Sharp tools allowed the Haida to do especially fine carving. The introduction of money made it possible to accumulate more wealth of a different sort. But the Europeans also introduced diseases. Smallpox reduced the Haida population from over 8,000 in 1800 to 800 in 1885. But the Haida still live in the Queen Charlotte Islands, and the population is growing. In 1962 it stood at more than 1,000.

▶ THE FARMERS

The Farmers lived in four distinct areas of the continent: the Northern Maize, Southeastern Maize, Southwestern Maize, and Mexican Maize areas. All are shown on the map. In each, maize, or Indian corn, was planted, harvested, and prepared as a food. Its importance varied, however, from area to area. The Iroquois and Lenni-Lenape of the Northern Maize Area, for example, did much hunting, gathering, and fishing. They ate meat, fish, berries, fruits, nuts, and seeds in addition to maize. To the Zuni and Hopi of the Southwestern Maize Area, on the other hand, maize was the most important food.

The four farming areas and their peoples differed in many ways. They were also alike in many ways.

The Northern Maize Area

The Northern Maize Area extended from southern New England and Maryland to the Lower Missouri River. It was a land of seacoast, mountains, plateaus, and level lowlands. It was a wet land marked by numerous rivers and lakes. Trees covered most of the area. Deer, elk, and bear roamed among them. Varieties of wild berries, fruits, nuts, and seeds seemed to grow everywhere. Rivers, lakes, and seacoast teemed with fish. And the

Indians had learned that the soils were good enough to produce fine crops of maize.

Maize. Maize was grown originally in the southern part of the Mexican Maize Area. The idea of planting maize seeds moved north. Maize was grown in New Mexico in 4000 B.C. The idea spread to all farming areas.

In the Northern Maize Area, clearing the fields was the work of men. Women were the farmers. They heaped soil into small mounds set 2 to 3 feet apart. They dropped a half-dozen maize seeds into each mound. Bean and squash seeds were also planted.

There was little rest for the women through the summer. They watched the crops closely. When the mounds were on the verge of collapse because of rain or winds, they rebuilt them. They kept the maize rows free from weeds and chased squirrels, ground hogs, and skunks from the fields. At last, when the crops were ripe, the women harvested them.

Maize for winter use was stored in large rail cribs covered with bark. Beans were boiled, dried, and stored. Squash was cut into strips, dried, and put in large bark containers.

Hunting, Fishing, and Gathering. Northern Maize Area peoples were capable hunters, fishermen, and gatherers, as well as farmers.

Favorite targets were the deer and bear. Traps were used to hunt the fox, the skunk,

Totem poles and community house in Alaska.

SEA SERPENT TOTEM

BEAR UP MOUNTAIN TOTEM

the squirrel, and the porcupine. Some hunters caught wild geese, pigeons, and wild turkeys.

Meat was cut into strips and hung in the sun to dry. Sometimes the meat was eaten raw. It was often boiled with maize and beans.

Spears, clubs, fishhooks, lines, nets, and sinkers were all used by the fishermen. Shad, yellow perch, and trout were favorite catches. At the seashore the Lenni-Lenape gathered shellfish. Shellfish were not sought for food alone. Shell was used to make ornaments, utensils, and tools, as well as pottery and wampum, or shell beads.

Fruits, berries, herbs, nuts, and roots were all gathered. Berries and fruits were dried and stored. Nuts were eaten raw. Roots, herbs, and bulbs were baked in shallow pits.

The Villages and Dwellings. The villages were placed on high ground near rivers, lakes, or bays. The typical home was the wigwam, similar to the one built in the Wild Rice Area except that the cover was made of bark. The Iroquois of central New York built "long-houses"—rectangular dwellings made of a framework of logs also covered with bark. The

Pottery made by Indians of the American southwest about A.D. 1100.

roof was triangular or rounded and covered with bark strips. Eight to ten families lived in a longhouse. Stockades surrounding the villages kept the Iroquois safe.

In the villages much work was done. The women made breechclouts, moccasins, leggings, skin robes, and skirts. They made baskets and pots. The men spent time making arrowheads, knives, drills, and mortars of stone; dugouts; and canoes of bark. Iroquois men made masks from wood and cornhusks. The children played many games and watched the warriors play lacrosse.

The League of the Iroquois. The tribes that we have met thus far did not form leagues or confederacies. They did not fight together as a unit against common enemies. They did not attempt to unite to achieve peace. But the Iroquois—made up of the Mohawk, Oneida, Onondaga, Cayuga, and Seneca Indians— founded such a league in the 16th century. Legend has it that it was founded by the heroes Deganawidah and Hiawatha. The Tuscarora, who had migrated from North Carolina, joined in 1722. From then on the league was known as the Six Nations.

The league met each summer in the Onondaga country. Each of the tribes sent representatives. None could go to war unless the league gave its consent. But the league gave its consent often. Powerful Iroquois war parties inspired hatred and fear among the white settlers and other Indian tribes from the Atlantic Ocean to the Mississippi Valley.

Birth, Adulthood, Marriage, and Death. Immediately after birth a baby was washed. He was then tied to a cradleboard, which was used until he could walk. No real name was given him at birth. Instead he was called by a nickname that appealed to his parents.

Before reaching adulthood, girls and boys were put to severe tests. A girl was secluded in a wigwam. She stayed for 1 week. Only her mother or old women of her tribe were allowed to visit her. She could not talk to anyone. She could eat only vegetables.

A boy had to go for days without food and water. He was forced to swallow bad-tasting herbs and roots. He was deliberately put to shame by his elders. He wandered in the forest. There he sought a vision and often discovered his guardian spirit.

In a Lenni-Lenape village, girls who were

ready to marry wore strings of wampum around their necks. Marriages were often arranged by the parents. Small gifts were exchanged. The couple went to the young man's or young woman's village to live.

After death the body was cleaned and painted. It was dressed in the owner's best clothes. His favorite weapons, tools, and pipes were buried with him. Relatives of the dead went into mourning. They blackened their faces. Each year a feast in the dead man's honor was held near his grave.

Tribes of the Northern Maize Area. The Huron, the Lenni-Lenape, and the Iroquois were typical of the Northern Maize Area tribes.

Huron

When Jacques Cartier made his voyage up the St. Lawrence River in 1534, he passed many Huron Indian villages. Sixty-nine years later Samuel de Champlain reported those villages deserted. The Huron, pushed out of the St. Lawrence Valley by their enemies, the Iroquois, had moved west and joined other Huron bands south of Georgian Bay.

The Huron built new villages in the forest between Lake Simcoe, Georgian Bay, and Lake Huron. White pine and hemlock, elm, ash, blue beech, white cedar, spruce, and silver maple surrounded the Huron villages. During the winter, because of heavy snow, Huron traveled between villages on snowshoes and hauled goods on toboggans. In the summer, hunters drove deer into pounds and killed them with bow and arrow; and they fished with hook and line, spear, and net.

Farming. But the Huron relied chiefly upon farming for their food. After the men had cleared the trees, the women prepared the fields. They leveled the earth with wooden hoes. They used digging sticks to make holes in the soil. Into each they carefully placed ten seed grains of corn (maize). Through the summer the women cared for the crops. Corn was the chief crop, but squash, beans, sunflowers, and tobacco were grown too.

The fields were located near the villages. Only when the firewood was gone or when the soil no longer produced a good crop did the Hurons move to new homes. This might happen every 10 years.

Huron Villages. A Huron village was made up of from 20 to 30 longhouses surrounded by a circular palisade, or wall. Each house might have from 6 to 20 families living on opposite sides of a long hall.

Much time in the village was given to feasting. There were singing feasts, thanksgiving feasts, and feasts for getting better when sick. A singing feast in preparation for going to war was a favorite. The best known feast, however, was the Feast of the Dead, held once every 10 or 12 years. All the Huron who had died since the last feast were taken from their graves and buried with robes, pots, ornaments, tools, and weapons in one huge pit. The Huron danced and feasted.

But the best days for the Huron passed. The French brought smallpox to the villages. In 1648 and 1649 the Iroquois attacked again. The Huron fled in all directions. Some took refuge with the Potawatomi; others went to Oklahoma. Some were absorbed by the Iroquois; some went to live on the reservation at Lorette, near Quebec. Huron numbers today are small.

Lenni-Lenape

Lenni-Lenape, meaning "real men" or "native genuine men," is the name these Indians gave to themselves. The English settlers called them the Delaware after the river.

The Lenni-Lenape built their settlements on both sides of the Delaware River and in nearby lands reaching to the Atlantic Ocean. The land was lush. Trees were everywhere. The forest teemed with deer, elk, bear, and birds. Plums, blackberries, grapes, and persimmons grew wild. Walnuts and chestnuts were to be had for the picking. River and sea gave up rich fish life. The soils produced fine crops of corn, squash, and beans. But the Lenni-Lenape were primarily hunters.

Hunting, Fishing, and Farming. When a young man reached age 15, he was permitted to join a hunting party. With his bow of hickory and his arrow of reed tipped with stone, he was ready to make his kill. Elk and bear were the prime targets.

Fishing and the gathering of shellfish were also important. The Lenni-Lenape caught fish with hook and line, with a spear or harpoon, or with large nets. To reach the sea, the Lenni-Lenape built trails through the forest. The Minisink Path, for example, started from near Minisink Island in the Delaware River

The Lenni-Lenape were hunters, fishermen, and farmers.

and threaded its way across New Jersey to the Atlantic coast. Temporary dwellings were set up near the ocean. Much of the meat of the shellfish was carried home. The shells were used for making pottery and ornaments.

The Lenni-Lenape were also farmers. The women planted corn, squash, and beans. Storage cribs were built to store the harvests. The Lenni-Lenape rarely went hungry.

Every Lenni-Lenape village was dominated by the Big House, the extra-large wigwam that stood in a clearing overlooking the river. The Big House was the meeting place. Many religious ceremonies were held there. Wigwams were scattered nearby through the forest. There the women made pots, wooden bowls, and birch-bark containers; the men made stone and clay pipes, birch-bark canoes, drums and rattles, tomahawks, and war clubs.

The old Lenni-Lenape way of life was interrupted by the coming of the Dutch, the Swedes, and the English to the New World. As European population increased, bands of Lenni-Lenape began to move west. Many moved to Ohio and Indiana. In 1744 David Brainerd, a preacher, went among the Lenni-Lenape who remained in New Jersey. He founded one church at Crosswicks, and another at Cranbury. In 1758 Brotherton, the first Indian reservation in the United States, was established in southern New Jersey. But it was not successful.

After the French and Indian War some Lenni-Lenape bands moved to Kansas, to Oklahoma, and to Texas. On July 4, 1866, the Lenni-Lenape chiefs signed a treaty with the United States and moved to Indian Territory in Oklahoma.

Few pure Lenni-Lenape are left today. About 400 are on the reservation in Oklahoma. A few live in southern Ontario, Canada.

Iroquois

On July 30, 1609, the French explorer Champlain came upon a war party of 200 Mohawk Indians on the lake that bears his name. In the battle that followed, two Mohawk chiefs were shot dead and Champlain had made bitter enemies for France. The French learned, to their sorrow, that the Mohawk had many friends—the Oneida, Onondaga, Cayuga, and Seneca, all members of the powerful League of the Iroquois.

The heart of the Iroquois country was the lake region of central New York and the Mohawk Valley. It was a land of water, forest, and fine soil. Fish filled the waters. Beaver built their dams in streams. Ducks swam on the lakes and deer roamed the forests. Beneath the trees wild berries grew. Overhead, flocks of pigeons crossed the sky. The Iroquois were hunters, fishermen, gatherers. But they relied chiefly upon tilling the soil for their food.

The women were the Iroquois farmers. They owned the fields and passed them on to their daughters. The men cleared a patch of earth, and the women planted the seeds. They planted corn in long rows. Between the rows they planted beans and squash. They tended the crops during the long summer and harvested them in the autumn. Squashes were stored in underground pits lined with bark and covered with earth. Corn and beans were often stored in bark chests within the longhouse. Tobacco, a revered crop, was grown in separate plots and received special care.

Iroquois village. Women in front of longhouses prepare cornmeal.

The longhouse, the home of the Iroquois, was often up to 100 feet long. Four or five families lived on each side of a hallway that ran the length of the house. There were no windows. Smoke escaped through smoke holes in the ceiling.

Between 20 and 50 longhouses, plus one large council house, made up an Iroquois village. Villages were usually located near lakes or streams. They were abandoned only when timber gave out, when game was exhausted, or when the soil no longer yielded a good crop. Palisades (walls) of pointed poles often surrounded the villages for defense.

The Iroquois devoted much time to war, festivals, play, and work in secret societies. Men who had especially powerful dreams became medicine men and could become members of the False Face Society. Wearing a mask, the medicine man entered the longhouse of a sick person. He danced around the sick person, sprinkling tobacco on his face and asking the spirits to help cure the illness.

But the Iroquois are probably best known for the creation of the League. The Iroquois tribes had fought each other many times in the 15th and early 16th centuries. The League was formed to keep peace among themselves. Mohawk, Oneida, Onondaga, Cayuga, and Seneca banded together about 1570. Together they fought the French and waged war on other Indian tribes. Iroquois war parties raided north to the St. Lawrence River, south to the borders of Tennessee, and west to Lake Michigan. But the League could not withstand the American Revolution. Individual tribes took different sides. The League of the Iroquois grew weak.

But many Iroquois still remain—on reservations in New York, Ontario, and Quebec.

The Southeastern Maize Area

The Southeastern Maize Area reached from northern Virginia to southern Texas. Except for the Appalachian hill country the land was level and low. It was also wet. Many rivers flowed from the hills to the sea. The Mississippi River crossed the area. Numerous bays, ponds, creeks, and inlets dotted the landscape. Summers were hot and humid and winters mild.

Much of the area was covered with trees. Berries, fruits, and herbs grew wild. Deer, bear, otter, raccoon, and beaver were plentiful. The rivers teemed with fish. And the Cherokee, Choctaw, Chickasaw, and Creek all planted maize in the fine southern soil.

Maize and the Public Granary of the Creek. The women were the farmers. They used digging sticks to make many holes in the soil. These were filled with a dozen or more maize seeds and covered over. Squash, melons, and beans were often planted in separate fields.

During the hot summer the women did much weeding. They kept the animals out of the fields. From the tops of scaffolds old women and children waved their arms in the air to keep birds from attacking the crops.

All of the tribes stored maize. The Creek even maintained a public granary. In this way they assured themselves of a food supply when crops were poor. It helped them during war emergencies. It also helped the Creek towns to feed travelers at public expense.

Hunting and Fishing. Southeastern Area Indians hunted the deer for its meat and the bear for its fat. Their chief weapon was the bow and arrow. They hunted smaller game and birds with a blowgun.

Many of the usual methods were used in catching fish. One method was unique. The Indians pounded chestnuts, herbs, and roots in a mortar and scattered the mixture over a pond. The men stirred the water with long poles. The concoction was a poison. The fish were stunned. They would float to the top of the pond, where they were quickly gathered.

Clothing. The men of the Southeastern Maize Area wore breechclouts and ankle-high moccasins in summer. In winter they added leggings and buckskin shirts. Robes of feathers were worn by chiefs on special occasions. The women wore fiber skirts in summer and skin shawls in winter. The children went naked.

By the middle of the 18th century the women were wearing calico—red and blue cloth—wrapped around their waists and dangling to the knee. This cloth had been introduced by the English and French settlers and traded to the Indians for furs.

From Birth to Death. The baby was born in an isolated hut. Soon after birth the baby was named. A girl retained her name throughout her lifetime. A boy's name could be changed whenever he won war honors.

Mothers had a natural affection for their children and never spanked them. A naughty youngster might be punished by having his legs and thighs scratched with a pin or a needle.

Before reaching adulthood, girls were taught to make baskets and pots and to handle stone hoes. Boys were prepared to be warriors, for it was by getting a scalp that a young man rose in prestige. He received a new name after his first war party and was permitted to paint and tattoo his body.

Marriages were usually arranged by maternal relatives of the couple without consulting the young people. After a simple ceremony— the breaking of an ear of maize—the couple went to live with the young woman's people.

If possible, the dead were buried under their dwellings. The dwellings were then abandoned. A warrior was buried with his favorite weapons, ornaments, and pipe. All of the peoples had elaborate mourning ceremonies.

Creek

The Creek were typical of the Southeastern Maize Area tribes.

The Creek Indians once lived in the rich lowland valleys of Alabama and Georgia. They hunted deer, bear, otter, and raccoon, and planted corn, beans, and pumpkins.

Religion was important to the Creek. They believed in the spirits of streams, rocks, and trees. They imagined that dwarfs, giants, and goblins controlled their lives. Many taboos were connected with eating and drinking. For example, the Creek did not eat the flesh of clumsy animals because they believed the eater would take on the animal's qualities.

Creek Towns and Dwellings. Creek towns were beehives of activity. Leaders met daily in the public square to discuss war, plan religious ceremonies, or merely talk among themselves. Boys played ball or practiced with bow and arrow. Men hollowed out blowguns, wove fishing nets, and made canoes, digging sticks, and stone hoes. Women made clay pots, wove baskets, fashioned shirts, leggings, and moccasins, and prepared food.

The Creek were organized into about 50 clans. Every Creek child was a member of his mother's clan. If father belonged to the Turkey clan and mother to the Bear clan, all the children were Bears. Creek were not permit-

Creek men play lacrosse in the chunkey yard while women tend the crops.

ted to marry persons in the same clan. Turkey never married Turkey. Bear never married Bear.

Each town was built around a public square. The square was made up of four buildings facing the cardinal points of the compass. Near the southwest corner of the square stood the chunkey yard, where the Creek played lacrosse. At the northwest corner was the hothouse, where the winter dances were held.

The dwellings were not arranged in a pattern around the square. They were scattered in the forest. A chief might have a four-room dwelling patterned after the public square. But most of the Creek lived in rectangular frame houses. Some were plastered smooth with red clay. Many were covered with roofs of cypress bark. As late as 1777 almost 20,000 Creek lived in about 50 separate towns on the Chattahoochee, Flint, Coosa, and Tallapoosa rivers.

The Creek Confederacy. The Creek towns, like the Iroquois tribes, were organized in a league called the Creek Confederacy. Representatives from all the towns met once each year. They listened to complaints, talked of war and peace, and planned for the future.

The Coming of the White Man. The Spanish explorer Hernando de Soto was the first European to travel in the Creek country. He was followed by traders, missionaries, soldiers, and settlers. In the 1700's French and English fur traders bought thousands of deer, otter, and beaver skins from the Creek in exchange for guns, needles, knives, cloth, and brandy.

The Creek adopted many European customs. They dressed in red and blue cotton cloth. They began to use the gun as well as the blowgun and bow and arrow. Creek maidens married French soldiers. This led to the breakdown of the rigid clan system.

As white settlers moved into the Creek country, the Indians were driven from the land. During the years 1813 and 1814, the Red Stick, a Creek people, revolted against the United States. This was the famous Creek War, in which General Andrew Jackson played an important role. Defeated, the Red Stick and other Creek had to give up much of their land in Georgia and Alabama.

But the final blow came between 1836 and 1840, when the Creek were forced to move to Indian Territory (Oklahoma). During the march to Oklahoma and in the early years there, about half the Creek died. A once proud people was almost destroyed.

Today about 13,000 Creek live in northeastern Oklahoma.

The Southwestern Maize Area

The Southwestern Maize Area stretched from the Gulf of California to central Texas. It was a plateau land. But there were mountains and basins in the far southwest, high mountains through the center, and much lower land in the east. Everywhere it was hot and dry. The Gila, Colorado, and Rio Grande rivers, however, did maintain their flow across the area.

Cottonwood trees and willows grew near the rivers. But only cactus, sagebrush, and yucca grew in much of the low country. On the plateau walls juniper and piñon appeared. There was no real forest, and there were few animals. The Indians existed by taking advantage of the fine soil and available water.

Maize. The men of the Southwestern Maize Area planted fields where summer waters tumbled from the plateaus, or in the muds carried in the overflow of the rivers. The men were the farmers. They planted maize, beans, and pumpkins. The seeds were planted deep. The farmers took special care to allow much space between the plantings, for the crops might die for lack of water. During the heat of late summer the men tended the crops carefully. In September and October an entire family harvested their crops.

Much of the maize was ground to meal on milling stones. Hopi, Zuni, and Rio Grande Pueblo women made a batter of maize meal and water and grilled it over hot stones in wafer form. This was called piki. Most of the maize was eaten in the piki form. In many of the other tribes of the area maize meal was boiled and eaten in the form of mush.

The plants of the fields were not the only foods eaten. The women searched the land for seeds, nuts, and fruits. The men hunted deer, rabbits, and wild sheep.

The Dwellings. In the far southwest the Pima built a semi-subterranean pit house. It was dome-shaped, thatched with brush, and covered with earth. The Hopi, on the plateau, made a home of rock, wood, clay, earth, and water. Rock was the foundation for the walls.

A Hopi pueblo. Indians weave blankets and make pottery and kachina dolls.

Wood was used for the roof. Clay, earth, and water were used to plaster the face of the building. Many of the homes had two and sometimes three or four stories. A number of homes made up the pueblo, or settlement.

The Zuni and Rio Grande pueblos were similar, but little rock was used. The warlike Apache lived in the wickiup. The Navajo built the hogan of logs and earth.

The Influence of the Spaniards. The Spaniards arrived in the Southwestern Maize Area in the 16th century. They introduced Spanish and Catholicism to the Indians. They brought horses, sheep, cattle, wheat, and citrus fruits. They used the Spanish colonial loom for weaving cloth. But the influence of these new ideas was not very great. The Indians continued to live as they had before.

Arts, Crafts, and Clothing. The Pima and Papago were weavers. They used yucca, bear grass, and devil's-claw to make mats, bags, and baskets. They wore deerskin wraparounds, rabbit robes, and yucca sandals.

The Hopi wove cloth and blankets. They made kachina dolls representing supernatural beings. Later they became fine potters. The men wore breechclouts, cotton aprons, moccasins, and rabbit-skin robes. The women wore cotton garments that were passed under the left arm and over the right shoulder.

The Navajo and Apache wore little clothing. The men wore only breechclouts and leggings; the women wore short tunics. The Navajo have only recently become excellent weavers, workers in turquoise, and silversmiths.

The Life Cycle. Among the Hopi the new baby was washed with yucca suds. He was given a number of names. A few days after a birth in any Southwestern Maize Area tribe the mother and the paternal grandmother took the baby to the edge of the plateau and presented the newborn to the sun.

At about age 8, young boys were initiated into clubs or societies. There they learned particular dances, songs, and prayers that would help their people.

Ordeals and ceremonies on reaching adulthood were almost unknown in the area. Only Papago girls had an elaborate ceremony. They were secluded in a hut for 4 days, after which dances were held in their honor. Papago boys went to seek visions.

Young Hopi men and women arranged their own marriages. The young woman's mother began the proceedings by giving the young man's mother a tray of cornmeal. The bride's wedding clothes were prepared by the bridegroom or the men of his family. A man took only one wife.

At death the men were wrapped in robes and buried near the plateau. Children who died and had not yet been initiated into clubs were buried in crevices in the rocks and covered with stones.

Tribes of the Southwestern Maize Area. The Hopi, the Zuni, the Navajo, and the Apache were typical Southwestern Maize Area tribes.

Hopi

A Hopi myth says that the Hopi Indians had their beginnings deep inside the earth. By climbing a giant cane and moving through a great reed, they reached the earth's surface.

The Hopi Indians speak a Shoshonean dialect. Their ancestors were probably the

Kayenta, the cliff dwellers of northern Arizona who flourished from about 1050 to 1300. When the Kayenta disappeared, many Indian bands settled in their territory. Today they are called Hopi—"the peaceful ones."

The Hopi country of northeastern Arizona is a hot, dry plateau. Buttes and mesas dot the landscape. Summer temperatures often reach well over 100 degrees Fahrenheit. Winter brings much snow. Little more than 10 inches of rain falls in a year. Sagebrush, yucca, greasewood, and cactus grow in the low country. On the high mesas juniper and piñon pine appear, but there is no real forest. Some deer, wildcats, and coyotes manage to exist, but there is little game to hunt.

The Hopi Indians lived by learning to use available water for farming. They were floodwater farmers. They placed their fields in valleys where summer rainwater tumbled from mesa tops, or on slopes where natural springs provided water.

The Hopi man was the farmer. His crops were corn, beans, squash, pumpkins, and cotton. In early March he cleared his fields. Then he built windbreaks of brush and stone for protection from drifting sands. He dug ditches to conserve water and prevent damage from summer floods. In September and October he harvested the crops.

The Hopi had a clan system in which descent was traced through the mother. The women owned the fields, and all children were members of the mother's clan. When a couple married, they moved to the wife's mother's house. The wife cared for the children, prepared the food, and carried the water. She collected seeds and herbs. She made baskets. One of her most important contributions was helping to build the Hopi settlement—the pueblo.

In the heat of summer the Hopi sang, danced, and prayed. They prayed to Massauwu, ruler of the earth, and to the kachinas, supernatural beings representing the spirits of their ancestors. Kachina dolls were found in all the pueblos. Perhaps they could bring rain. Perhaps they could keep the Spaniards out of Hopi country.

But the Spaniards came and tried to establish missions. In 1680 the Hopi revolted. They moved most of their pueblos to the mesa tops. There they established the villages of Hotevilla, Walpi, and others.

Because they were remote, because they clung to their old lifeway, the Hopi survived. Several thousand still live on the mesa tops of northeastern Arizona.

Zuni

No one knows when the Zuni arrived in western New Mexico. They probably came in from the north and settled in the well-watered Zuni Valley. Later they were joined by people from the Yuma-Pima country to the west and then by people from other tribes.

The Zuni were farmers. Their fields were planted where gulches opened into the valley. Across the gulches they built earthen dams to hold rainwater in check. The rainwater sank slowly into the soil. There was enough water in most years to grow maize, beans, and pumpkins. During times of drought the Zuni priests were called upon to bring rain to Shi'wona, as the Zuni called their land.

The men worked the farms. They used wooden digging sticks and wooden hoes. They harvested the maize and spread the ears of corn on pueblo roofs to dry. They stored the ears in the back rooms of the lower stories.

Zuni women prepared the food in dome-

Zuni village about 1880. The women bake bread in an outdoor oven. A man drills a piece of turquoise with a pump drill.

Navajo village in Monument Valley, Arizona. The hogan at left is cut away to show a medicine man watching sand painting. Women at right spin and card wool and weave a rug.

shaped ovens. They made yucca-fiber clothing and fine pots and baskets. The women cared for the children and helped to build the pueblos. Young girls learned to do all the things their mothers did. Young boys, on the other hand, joined secret fraternities. They met in ceremonial rooms, or kivas. There they learned about religion and the Zuni world.

The Zuni World. The Zuni arranged the world in seven parts. There were north, south, east, and west; and the upper world, lower world, and midmost, or center, world. Each part had a number. Each had a color. The midmost was especially blessed, for it contained the colors of all the rest.

Zuni life was influenced by the seven directions. Each clan belonged to one of seven divisions corresponding to the directions. Each division played a specific role at Zuni ceremonials, dances, and tribal meetings. Chief Zuni priests always came from the north. The *pekwin* from the upper world determined the calendar by watching the rising and setting of the sun. They chose the days of the ceremonials. From the lower world came the priests representing the war gods who were associated with thunder. It was they who were called upon to bring rain in time of drought.

The pattern of the seven divisions and the power of the clans helped to make Zuni life rigid and orderly. Every Zuni knew his place within it. And the Zuni wanted it that way.

The Coming of the Spaniards. In 1539 a Franciscan missionary, Fray Marcos de Niza, saw Hawikuh, one of seven Zuni pueblos. In a report to his superiors De Niza called the seven villages the Kingdom of Cibola and praised them to the sky. He described them as well-populated centers rich in gold and jewels. The report excited the Spaniards in Mexico. In 1540 Francisco Vásquez de Coronado made his memorable trip to the "Seven Cities of Cibola"—the Zuni pueblos. He defeated the Zuni, but he found no gold, no jewels.

The Zuni Today. Drought, Spanish conquistadores and missionaries, the coming of American settlers, and the reservation system have not dampened the spirit of the Zuni, who number about 4,200 today. They live in one pueblo, but it is still divided, as of old, into seven divisions. Many of the old ceremonials are still performed. In mid-December they conduct the Shalako ceremony. The masked gods (some on stilts), the costumed dancers, the sacred clowns, and the healers march from house to house blessing the new Zuni homes.

Navajo

The Navajo can be traced back to a distant homeland in northwestern Canada. For unknown reasons they left the Canadian forests and moved south. Many bands followed the eastern flank of the Rocky Mountains. Some traveled through the Great Basin. Others are known to have moved over the Great Plains. They survived by hunting the deer, antelope, and bison. They ate birds and lizards and gathered wild edible plants. Everywhere they built homes by arranging three forked poles in the ground and covering them with brush, bark, or earth. This was the hogan of the Navajo. In the heat of summer they built a simple lean-to of tree branches. The men wore breechclouts and sandals. The women wore skirts. They made coiled baskets and crude pots. Their way of life was not elaborate. Constant movement and the need to obtain food allowed little time for the development of arts, crafts, religious ritual, or a complex social organization.

These were developed later by contact with the Pueblo peoples and the Spaniards. From the Pueblo the Navajo learned the art of weaving. They borrowed several Pueblo religious ceremonials. They borrowed the idea of healing the sick by sand painting. And they also learned the art of farming. Soon Navajo fields were producing corn and pumpkins. The small bands were organized into clans in which descent was traced through the mother.

Meanwhile, the Spaniards had made their first invasions of the Southwest. Coronado's expedition in 1540 and those that followed it were important to the Navajo. From the Spaniards the Navajo learned to raise sheep and goats as well as to ride and care for horses. Sheep and goats grazed on the fields too poor for farming. Horses permitted the Navajo to move about easily. They were able to raid the southern Pueblo as well as the white settlements.

When the United States obtained the New Mexico and Arizona territory in 1848, the Navajo came under the protection of the United States Government. In 1863 Kit Carson was commissioned by the government to capture the Navajo and move them to Fort Sumner on the Pecos River in New Mexico. Navajo fields were burned and livestock systematically destroyed. The Navajo surrendered by the thousands. Twelve thousand Navajo were forced to walk nearly 200 miles to Fort Sumner. The suffering was unbearable. Only 8,000 were alive in 1865.

The Navajo Indian Reservation was established in 1868. Traders, missionaries, teachers, and other government employees came into contact with the Navajo. The traders brought coffee, sugar, and flour. Velveteen cloth, still used in Navajo clothing, was introduced. The missionaries attempted to make Christianity attractive to the Navajo, but old beliefs were too strong. The government established day schools and boarding schools. Unfortunately, not all the children went to school. Many attended only for a year or two. Very few went to high school, fewer still to college. The school situation has not been helped by the rapid growth of population.

In 1872 there were about 9,000 Navajo. In 1900 the figure was about 20,000. In 1930 it was over 40,000. Today the Navajo population is well over 75,000. They are the largest Indian tribe in the United States. The land cannot support so large a population. The Navajo still pasture their flocks of sheep and goats. They still raise corn and pumpkins and have added squashes, beans, fruits, and melons. They weave rugs, work in silver, sell piñon nuts, and work as wage laborers. Coal and oil discovered on the reservation have increased their income and helped to lighten the Navajo burden. But the struggle is still grim.

Apache

The Apache Indians of the American Southwest probably came from the Mackenzie River valley of northern Canada. Around the 12th century they began to move south into the United States. By the 19th century fierce, independent Apache bands roamed the land in New Mexico and Arizona.

The Apache were hunters, farmers, seed gatherers, and raiders who had to know their land well to stay alive. They knew every feature of the rugged mountains and barren

Apache work under a summer shelter. Dome-shaped wickiups stand in the background.

Apache beadwork. Left: Bags. Right: Necklace and flower ornament.

plains. They could hunt animals and find wild plants for food.

Apache women built crude irrigation ditches and planted corn, squashes, and beans. But crops were scanty, and hunters had to comb the countryside for deer, gophers, wild turkeys, and lizards. The women, carrying baskets and seed beaters, gathered mescal, mesquite beans, giant cactus fruit, and acorns—all important Apache foods.

The nutritious mescal, or century plant, grew everywhere in the Apache country. The pulp was roasted in pits over heated stones. Layers of wet grass were placed between layers of mescal, and earth was heaped on the layers. After roasting, mescal could be stored for several months.

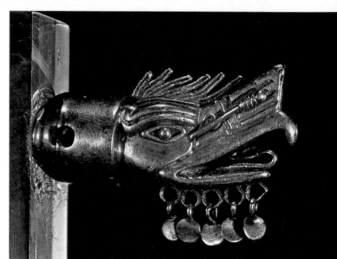

Gold Aztec ornament.

Temples to the Aztec gods stood in the heart of Tenochtitlán (Mexico City) early in the 16th century.

Apache loved raiding and warfare, and boys were trained almost from infancy to use bows and arrows and the lance. They walked for miles without food or water. They learned to hunt, stand guard, keep silent, and send and read smoke signals. By 15 years of age they were ready for the warpath.

Young girls were trained by their mothers to do household chores, plant garden crops, and gather food. They married early and brought their husbands home to live. Tribal custom prohibited an Apache warrior from talking to or seeing his mother-in-law. But he was duty-bound to protect his wife's family forever. Divorce was rare. The newlyweds' wickiup (winter home) was a framework of poles bent together at the top and covered with brush, bark, earth, or canvas. It was set up near the mother-in-law's wickiup, but faced the opposite way. An Apache settlement was usually made up of five or six wickiups. Several settlements formed a band; many bands formed the tribe. To the Apache warrior the tribe was never as important as his local band.

In the 1870's, attacks by Apache bands terrorized the settlers of Arizona and New Mexico. The establishment of reservations in 1871 did not bring peace. Renegade bands under such leaders as Cochise and Geronimo kept the frontier aflame. When the Apache finally surrendered to General Nelson A. Miles in 1886, Geronimo and many other Apache were taken prisoner. In 1909 Geronimo died at Fort Sill, Oklahoma.

Today over 6,000 Apache live on reservations in Oklahoma, New Mexico, and Arizona.

The Mexican Maize Area

The Mexican Maize Area extended south from the Gulf of California to Guatemala and Honduras. As in other farming areas, life was based largely upon the cultivation of maize. But unlike Indians in other areas, the Indians here developed a true civilization.

They developed hieroglyphic writing and bark paper. They learned much about astronomy and developed a calendar. They waged wars to get victims for human sacrifices. They built fine dwellings, palaces, and temples. Nowhere in North America was life so complicated. Nowhere was it so rich.

Tribes of the Mexican Maize Area. The Aztecs

Aztec calendar stone, 13 feet across, records the history of the world.

and the Maya are typical of the Mexican Maize Area tribes.

Aztecs

The Aztec Indians came from the north into central Mexico about A.D. 1250. Other Indian tribes had lived in central Mexico for many centuries. They had built cities there and set up governments. But one invader followed another, and the cities fell into ruins. By the time the Aztecs arrived, few of the old tribes remained.

The Aztecs were a warlike people who made many enemies among their neighbors. After several moves they settled in the Valley of Mexico on islands in Lake Texcoco. The lake was located on a high plateau between two mountain ranges. In the distance were towering, snowcapped volcanoes. Wild game and fish were plentiful, but as the Aztec population grew, the need for food increased.

There was not enough space to farm on the islands in Lake Texcoco. Farmland had to be built in the lake itself. The Aztecs collected mud from the shore and packed it onto rafts. The rafts were made of reeds and twigs, tightly woven to keep the mud from falling out. Then the Aztecs floated the rafts out into the shallow lake and sank them, one on top of

KACHINA DOLL

TOMAHAWK

CALUMET

ARTIFACTS OF NORTH AMERICAN INDIANS

CRADLEBOARD

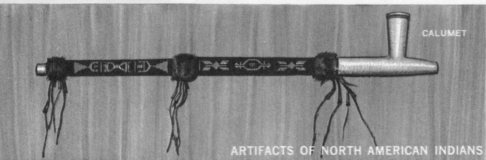

WORDS USED BY AND ABOUT NORTH AMERICAN INDIANS

Calumet—Long-stemmed pipe used by many Indian tribes of North America. It was often called a peace pipe and was smoked during ceremonies uniting hostile Indian tribes or nations.

Camas—Plant resembling the hyacinth. Its root was eaten by Indian tribes of the Camas Area.

Caribou—Animals of the deer family that were hunted by Indians of the Caribou Area. The meat was used for food, the hide for clothing and shelter, and the antlers for ornamental carving.

Chunkey yard—Special area in southeastern Indian towns that was set aside for playing games. A favorite game in Creek towns was a form of lacrosse.

Coups—Blows struck against enemies. Among the Indians of the Bison Area the bravest warriors were those who earned the most coups. The word "coup" comes from a French-Canadian word meaning "blow."

Cradleboard—Device on which an Indian baby was strapped and then tied to the mother's back. Cradleboards were often made of basketry or wood. Some were beautifully carved and decorated.

Dugout—Canoe or boat made by hollowing out a log, usually by burning.

Hogan—Navajo Indian home most often made of poles and covered with brush, bark, or earth. It was usually an eight-sided structure with a domed roof.

Kachina doll—Cottonwood figurine carved by Hopi Indians. It represented a supernatural being.

Kivas—Centers for religious ceremonies in Pueblo Indian villages. They were built partly underground with an entrance through a hole in the roof.

Labret—Wooden, stone, bone, or shell ornament worn through a hole pierced in the lip. Labrets were commonly worn among tribes along the Texas coast and the west coast of Florida. They were regarded by many tribes as a mark of high birth.

Lacrosse—French-Canadian name given to the favorite ball game of eastern Indian tribes from Hudson Bay to the Gulf of Mexico. The teams used a single stuffed deerskin ball and two rackets.

Lean-to—Rough shed with inclined roof. It was built against posts or trees and used by Indians as a temporary shelter.

Longhouses—Long wooden buildings having rounded roofs covered with bark. They were used by the Iroquois and Huron Indians. Several families lived together in one longhouse.

Maize—Indian corn.

Migration—Large-scale movement of tribes and their belongings from place to place.

Mission—Christian center established in Indian territory. Priests from the missions converted Indians to Christianity, educated them, and taught them farming.

Moccasin—Shoe of soft animal skin often dyed and decorated with beads.

Parfleche—Skin container (bag or box) of varying size made of rawhide skin. The skin was dried and the animal hair scraped off. Parfleches were used in the Bison Area to carry ornaments, food, clothing, or other possessions.

Pemmican—Mixture of dried ground meat, melted fat, and dried berries. It remained edible for a long time. Pemmican was eaten mainly in the northern parts of North America. It was a staple food of the Bison Area.

Piki—Type of food patty made from ground maize mixed with water and grilled over hot coals. It was a favorite food of the Southwestern Maize Area.

Pueblos—Indian settlements in the southwestern part of the United States. The buildings were made of stone and adobe.

Reservations—Specific areas of land on which Indian tribes were settled by treaty, Congressional act, or Executive order of the United States Government. There are about 250 separate areas of land in the United States designated as reservations.

Shaman—Indian medicine man, who cured disease by calling on spiritual powers.

196

the other. Finally great heaps of earth appeared above the water. On these floating gardens, or chinampas, they raised crops.

The Aztecs became fine painters, sculptors, and craftsmen. They learned to weave, make pottery, and embroider with beads and feathers. They were skilled stonecutters, silversmiths, and leatherworkers.

In 1325 the Aztecs began to build a city on one of the islands. They called the city Tenochtitlán. Today it is called Mexico City. Here the Aztec civilization grew and flourished. At first Tenochtitlán was a crude village of reed-and-mud huts, but by the early 16th century it had become a magnificent city. Government buildings and palaces were built of cut stone coated with white plaster. Ordinary homes, called adobes, were built of red-clay bricks. In the poorer sections of town the houses had roofs thatched with green palm leaves. Flowers bloomed in the gardens; fruits and vegetables filled the markets. The island was connected to the shore by several roads, or causeways. Pyramidlike temples to the Aztec gods stood in the heart of the city.

Religion and Customs. Religion was the strongest force in Aztec life. Each year thousands of human beings were sacrificed to Aztec gods. The chief god was Huitzilopochtli, the god of the sun and war. Once a year priests sacrificed the bravest warrior among the Aztecs' prisoners. With great ceremony the warrior was led to a sacrificial stone on top of a high temple. His heart was torn out and offered to the god.

The Aztecs waged war on neighboring tribes to get prisoners for sacrifice. The defeated tribes had to pay tribute to the Aztecs every year. Tribute included everything from farm produce and precious stones to feathers of the quetzal bird.

Another source of Aztec wealth was the active trade between Tenochtitlán and distant communities. Cargo was carried in canoes or by slaves. There were no pack-animals or wheeled vehicles before the Spaniards arrived. For money the Aztecs used cacao beans.

The chief weapons of the Aztec warriors were spears tipped with obsidian (volcanic glass) and wooden swords with jagged obsidian edges. The Aztecs also used bows and arrows, slings, and clubs. They wore armor of quilted cotton and carried painted shields.

Aztec children learned strict rules of conduct from their parents. At the age of 15, boys were sent to a school called the *telpuchcalli,* or "house of youth." They were taught good citizenship and the arts of warfare. Very bright youngsters attended the *calmecac,* a special school where they trained to become leaders in religion and government. Girls learned household duties, and some trained to become priestesses to the Aztec gods.

When Hernando Cortes and his Spanish soldiers began their conquest of Mexico in 1519, the Aztec civilization had reached its peak. Heavy fighting took place during the next 2 years, and Montezuma II, the Aztec leader, was killed. The once great Aztec Empire fell to the Spaniards. Today descendants of the original Aztecs continue to live in villages throughout Mexico.

Maya

Maya-speaking people have lived in Guatemala and southern Mexico for about 3,000 years. They were originally gatherers, hunters,

Stelae—Carved tablets used as calendars or records of events. They were common among the Maya.

Sweathouse—Type of bathhouse. It varied in structure from tribe to tribe. Water was usually sprinkled on hot stones placed inside the sweathouse. The steam given off heated the enclosure, causing the men inside to perspire. Evil spirits were sometimes thought to be cleansed out of the body in this way.

Taboo—Restriction placed by a medicine man against certain actions in Indian life.

Tattoo—Mark or picture scratched on the face or body by a needle dipped in colored dyes.

Tipi (tepee)—Cone-shaped Indian dwelling made of poles covered with animal skins. It was used mainly by Indians of the Bison Area and by some tribes farther northwest.

Toboggan—Sled used by Algonkian Indians of the northeast. Toboggans were made of thin, narrow boards 10 to 12 feet long, bent and tied at the end and covered with rawhide. They were used for hauling loads over snow and ice.

Tomahawk—Lightweight stone ax lashed to a wooden handle. It was using as a weapon or tool by the Indians.

Travois—Kind of sled drawn by a horse or a dog. It was usually made of two tipi poles covered with bison skin. At one end the poles were fastened to the animal; at the other they dragged on the ground.

Vision—Dream believed to be sent from the gods. It was thought to bring magical powers to the young Indian boy who fasted alone, awaiting his vision. Visions were also thought to foretell the future.

Wampum—Name given to strings of shell beads made by Indians in coastal areas. It was used for gifts, for decoration, or as a form of money in trade. Wampum was usually fashioned by women who developed great skill at using the beads to make beautiful patterns.

Wickiup—Dwelling used by Indians of the Piñon Area. It was made of brush-fiber matting.

Wigwam—Dwelling common in eastern North America. It was made of saplings covered with bark or rushes and having a rounded or conical shape.

and fishermen. At an early date (archeologists do not know it exactly) neighboring tribes introduced the Maya to farming. Fine fields of maize, beans, and squashes began to dot the land between the mountains of Guatemala and Yucatán.

Maya farmers felled and burned the trees. They turned the soil over with wooden digging sticks. When Chac, the rain god, delivered his life-giving water, the Maya planted their seeds. Then they waited patiently for Yum Kaax, god of maize, to bring forth the crop.

The Maya prospered as farmers. They devised a system of hieroglyphic writing and developed a calendar. They used local clays to make pots and began to build elaborate tombs, temples, and vaults of stone.

The Classic Period (A.D. 325–975). In the hot, wet, forested areas of Petén (region of northern Guatemala) Maya civilization flourished. The priesthood grew powerful. The Maya were orderly and content. Maya laborers worked hard to build religious or ceremonial centers at Tikal and Uaxactun. The architects watched closely as the courts and plazas were laid out. They urged caution in building the high-stepped pyramids and the steep stairways leading to the temples. They supervised work on the "palaces"—probably rooms for storing religious garments—and on the causeways that linked the ceremonial centers together. Sculptors and painters worked on the stelae, or dated monuments, that were set up in front of the pyramids and palaces.

The stelae were built to record the passage of time. Information on the moon, the planet Venus, the gods, and Maya rituals was also recorded. The stelae tell us about the advances made by the Maya in astronomy and mathematics.

The building of ceremonial centers spread rapidly. By the 8th century many could be found in Yucatán (Oxkintok), Chiapas (Palenque), and Honduras (Copan).

Ceremonial centers were not cities. They were places where the priests conducted their many activities; where the Maya worshiped; where market days were held; and where much of the recreation, including ball playing, took place. The Maya did not live in the ceremonial centers. Their thatch-roofed houses and fields were some distance away.

The Collapse. Maya sculptors, painters, potters, and lapidaries (stonecutters) were doing some of their best work when the ceremonial centers began to collapse in the 9th century. No one knows the reason or reasons for the collapse. Many explanations have, however, been offered: failure of the farming system, a change in climate, volcanic activity, invasion by enemies, ceremonial center fighting ceremonial center, the revolt of the lower classes against the priests.

Whatever the explanation, new stelae ceased to be built in the ceremonial centers. Copan added no dated monuments after A.D. 800, Oxkintok none after 849, Tikal none after 869. Many of the ceremonial centers were abandoned; others continued to serve for long periods. In Petén, however, the green jungle gradually covered the pyramids and temples.

The Toltec Invasion (A.D. 975–1200). In the 10th century, Toltec warriors from Tula moved southeast into Veracruz. They fanned out in two groups. One group moved into the Guatemala highlands, the other into Yucatán. The peaceful Maya were no match for the northern warriors. They were quickly beaten. In Yucatán the conquerors established themselves at Chichén Itzá, which had earlier been a Maya ceremonial center.

The Toltecs introduced much that was new to Chichén Itzá. They brought new ideas of government, new gods and culture heroes, and a new architecture to the conquered center. They often depicted Quetzalcoatl (Kukulcan in Maya), the feathered serpent, and Tlalchitonatiuh, god of the warriors, on Chichén Itzá's buildings. They introduced strong military orders whose leaders replaced Maya priests in positions of power. They adorned the buildings with jaguar, puma, and eagle sculptures—symbols of the warrior orders. They practiced human sacrifice and the use of the *tzompantli,* the rack where the skulls of the dead were hung.

But the Maya were not completely crushed. They accepted many of the changes; they resisted others. The farmers, for example, continued to call to Chac for rain. They paid little attention to Tlaloc, the Toltec rain god. And Maya was retained as the language of the people. Much of Maya life remained as before. But the Toltecs ruled.

The conquerors had also settled at

The stone pyramid in the background is a Maya religious center. At the left is a Maya noble; at the right are a farmer and his wife.

Mayapan (987) and Uxmal (1007) to strengthen their hold on Yucatán. Chichén Itzá joined her sister centers in a triple alliance. It lasted for nearly 200 years. Unfortunately fighting broke out among the leading families of the three centers. Chichén Itzá was crushed (1194), and Mayapan became the leading center in Yucatán.

The Mayapan Period and the Spanish Conquest (A.D. 1200–1546). The leaders at Mayapan held the country by forcing the head chiefs of the centers to live in Mayapan. They were really hostages. Mayapan was not a ceremonial center. It was a walled city that at its height contained more than 3,500 buildings and a population of over 15,000. It was a city of rough stone covered with stucco. The arts did not flourish there as they had at Chichén Itzá, despite fine work done in metal and turquoise. Temples were few. Mayapan, dominated by the military, thrived on warfare.

But the military tyranny could not last. The Maya rose in revolt. In 1441 Mayapan was sacked and left desolate. Warfare continued to plague Yucatán and the Guatemala highlands. The arts fell into virtual decay. No pyramids were built. Thatched huts were used in place of stone temples. The Maya no longer played their ball game. They ceased to repair their roads and causeways.

Demoralized and disunited, the Maya met the Spaniards. Spanish armies swept through Yucatán and Guatemala. They later conquered Petén. The conquest was swift and final.

But 400 years after the Spanish conquest Maya farmers still till the soil in Yucatán, Petén, and the Guatemala highlands.

▶THE IMPACT OF EUROPEANS AND AMERICANS UPON THE INDIANS

The conquest of the Aztecs and the Mexican Maize Area left southern North America in Spanish hands. Military expeditions and missionaries soon pushed into the Mesquite, Southwestern Maize, Acorn, and Piñon areas. In the 18th century, forts and missions were built in Lower and Upper California. At the missions the Indians were taught the Catholic religion, the Spanish language, and much about the Spanish way of life. It was hoped they would become stock raisers, carpenters, and farmers. But the Indians responded very slowly to Spanish training.

In the Northern and Southeastern Maize areas the impact of the European settlers was more devastating. The Indians were often forced to leave their old homes. The Lenni-Lenape, for example, began to move west soon after the planting of the English settlements. Smallpox and tuberculosis, introduced by the Europeans, cut their numbers sharply. They began to drink liquor. Even the establishment of the first Indian reservation in the United States—Brotherton (New Jersey) in 1758—did not save them. By 1802 few of the Lenni-Lenape lived in their old homes. They continued to move west. Some went to Canada. Many were finally removed to Indian Territory (Oklahoma) in 1867.

The Creek were violently uprooted. Between 1836 and 1841 the United States Government forced them to move to Indian Territory—up to 600 miles away. Nearly half the tribe died on the long and tragic journey, called the "trail of tears."

The gloom in the tipis of the Bison Area

Adobe pueblo at Taos, New Mexico.

was equally great. Assiniboin numbers fell from 10,000 in 1835 to 6,000 after the smallpox epidemic of 1836. They numbered less than 4,000 in 1900. The Blackfoot were staggered by smallpox and measles. Worst of all, the bison were disappearing through wanton killing. The Blackfoot went on their last successful hunt in 1879. By 1884 the bison herds had vanished.

There was much suffering and much change in all of the Indian areas. Between 1500 and 1900 the Indian population of the area that is now the United States declined from close to 1,000,000 to 300,000. The decline was even greater in Mexico. And for those who remained, the agony was great. Many were forced to take land in new and strange places. They were introduced to new tools, implements, and techniques. They were forced to abandon their old ways of life.

United States Government Action

Many of the tribes were resettled on reservations in the west. The land belonged to the United States Government but was reserved tax-free for the Indians. The federal government provided the tribes with rations, tools, and equipment. Boarding and day schools were set up. In many cases responsible agents were sent to administer the reservations.

But the change from a free life to the restricted life of the reservations brought the Indians near despair. They did not change easily.

In 1887 the General Allotment Act (Dawes Act) was passed. Heads of Indian families were permitted to buy a quarter-section (160 acres) of land. It was expected that the Indians would jump at the chance to farm acres of their own. Many land purchases were made, but results were disappointing. Most of the Indians did not make happy farmers.

In 1934 the Indian Reorganization Act was passed. It ended the allotment system. It permitted the tribes to organize themselves politically so they could enjoy self-government under the protection of the United States. The act provided money for scholarship loans, made provisions easier for Indians to enter the Civil Service, and allowed the tribes to engage in business.

In 1953 Congress passed a resolution calling for a policy of "termination" in Indian affairs. Termination meant freeing tribes from federal supervision and control. The Menomini of the old Wild Rice Area were one of the tribes that were terminated. They were expected to move slowly but surely toward self-government and self-support. A county in Wisconsin (Menominee) was carved out of their old reservation land. They took control of local mill operations. They worked hard. But the going was difficult.

In 1961, following meetings at the University of Chicago, a Declaration of Indian Purpose was published. It called for an end to the termination policy, and emphasized instead the government's responsibilities toward Indian peoples. It called for reviewing the conditions that produced Indian poverty. It asked that each Indian community and its problems be treated separately. It called for the expansion of health services, for better housing, for improvements in Indian education.

A Growing Public Concern

The 1960's was a time of growing concern about poverty and minority rights in the United States. Reports on the plight of the American Indian continued to be made. One major report pointed out that the economic position of the Indians was worse than that of any other American minority group. Most Indian communities were barely getting by. Some of the nation's worst slums were to be found on Indian reservations. Unemployment was high. Indians had inadequate sanitary facilities and water supplies, substandard housing, and food deficiencies.

Meanwhile Indians were moving in greater numbers to the nation's cities. New York, Chicago, Detroit, Minneapolis, Houston, Denver, and Los Angeles could all boast growing Indian populations. Many Indians moved into poverty rows. It was hard for them to find jobs. It was hard—almost impossible—to compete with the white man in the white man's world. Many Indians returned to the reservation. But if the reservation had been broken up there was no place to go. The gap between Indian American and white American was growing wider.

A Message From the President. The government gave up the termination policy and sought to help the Indians through its various antipoverty programs. In 1968 President Lyndon B. Johnson, in his Message from the President of the United States, spelled out the Indians' plight.

Fifty thousand Indian families lived in unsanitary, dilapidated dwellings—many in huts, shanties, even abandoned automobiles.

The unemployment rate among Indians was nearly 40 percent, more than 10 times the national average.

Fifty percent of Indian school children, double the national average, were dropping out of school before completing high school.

Indian literacy rates were among the lowest in the nation; the rates of sickness and poverty among the highest.

Thousands of Indians who had migrated to the cities found themselves untrained for jobs and unprepared for urban life.

Some modern Indian houses in the Southwest are still built of traditional adobe brick.

The average age of death of an American Indian was 44 years; for all other Americans it was 65.

President Johnson pleaded for the following goals:

A standard of living for the Indians equal to that of the country as a whole.

Freedom of choice: An opportunity to remain in their homelands, if they chose, without surrendering their dignity; an opportunity to move to the towns and cities of America, if they chose, equipped with the skills to live in equality and dignity.

Full participation in the life of modern America, with a full share of economic power and social justice.

Hope for the Future

As other American minority groups have become increasingly militant in their own behalf, so have the Indians. On November 9, 1969, a group of young Indians landed on Alcatraz Island in San Francisco Bay. They had captured Alcatraz, the site of an abandoned federal prison. Poverty, ill health, and the depressing conditions on the reservations as well as their own failure in college had spurred these young Indians to act. Authorities forced them to leave Alcatraz, but they returned in greater numbers. They claimed Alcatraz as Indian territory and proposed to build on it an Indian cultural center. Their action drew widespread publicity. It also drew sympathy and support from many Americans across the country.

So did the events at Wounded Knee. For many years the Oglala Sioux on the Pine Ridge Reservation in South Dakota had complained of their poverty, poor housing, inadequate water supply, and poor health care. They had complained about the corruption and inefficiency of the BIA (Bureau of Indian Affairs) and the failure of the reservation's economic programs. There were those who complained about the chairman of the tribal council, who was believed to be in league with the BIA. In December, 1972, therefore, a Civil Rights Organization was formed on the reservation. The wrongs of the past were to be made right. Members of AIM (American Indian Movement) were called in to help.

On February 27, 1973, a car caravan made up largely of Oglala raiders left Pine Ridge. At Wounded Knee the raiders piled out of their cars and quickly occupied the Roman Catholic Church. They raided the trading post and store and collected guns, ammunition, food, and supplies. They took eleven "hostages."

The national government responded quickly. Federal marshalls and FBI agents were called in to protect life and property. Representatives from the Department of Justice were sent in to negotiate with the Indians.

Lines for battle and for negotiation were drawn. The Indians dug in and fought from bunkers. So did the government forces. For 70 days the "battle" raged. Sometimes nothing happened. Occasionally there were bursts of gunfire from both sides. Two Indians were killed, one agent was paralyzed, and at least nine other persons were injured.

A disarmament pact was finally announced on May 6. All weapons were to be surrendered and nonresidents were to leave Wounded Knee by May 9. The battle was over.

But Wounded Knee was a shambles. The trading post was destroyed, the museum vandalized, and individual homes ransacked. The bridge on the road to nearby Porcupine was destroyed. Dead cattle and dogs could be seen scattered over the landscape. The Catholic Church was pockmarked with bullet holes. There were those who vowed that they would never again live in the village.

Alcatraz and Wounded Knee are both perhaps symbols of our times. They show the deep frustrations of the long neglected and long oppressed American Indians. They may also contain the seeds for new beginnings and new hopes. For both have made the American people more aware of the Indians' problems.

Meanwhile the Indians have been working hard in their own interests. They are building new communities, establishing new industries, and erecting new schools. They are developing motels and other recreational schemes on the reservations. There is a growing Pan-Indian movement. Indians have become active in writing and publishing. Some tribes have benefitted through settlement of their land or other claims against the government. They are using the funds for their own development. Perhaps a new day has already dawned for the American Indians.

DANIEL JACOBSON
Michigan State University

INDIANS OF SOUTH AMERICA

The Spanish and Portuguese explorers of the 16th century found the entire continent of South America occupied by brown-skinned people. The explorers called them all Indians. But it was clear that many societies (tribes or groups), speaking many languages, lived in South America. Some lived in independent bands of a few dozen people. They collected wild plants, hunted, fished, and used simple tools. At the other extreme was the great Inca Empire, which was larger than Spain and had more people. It had cities and roads, a government and taxes, irrigated farms, and a wide variety of manufactures.

Some of these Indian societies were destroyed completely within a few years of the European conquest. Others were conquered. Their wealth in gold and silver was taken from them. Their religion was replaced by Christianity. Their native rulers were replaced by Europeans, who used Indian labor to work the mines or plantations. Some of the conquered Indians have survived. Some have kept their language and their native way of life. A few groups resisted the conquerors. They survive as independent cultures to the present day. They live in deserts, tropical forests, or the cold lands of the Far South. Such places were hardly worth conquering.

In these lands the surviving independent Indians make only a poor living. They show little evidence of the great Indian civilization that once existed on the continent. But the reports written by early European explorers and conquerors describe the native life before it was changed. The ruins of cities and graveyards that modern archeologists are discovering also tell about the early Indian cultures of South America.

The ancient Indian societies of South America can be grouped into four levels of civilization. From the most complex to the simplest they are:

(1) Central Andean civilization.
(2) Circum-Caribbean tribes.
(3) Tropical forest and southern Andean tribes.
(4) Marginal tribes.

Each type except the first contained many separate groups, which often fought with one another. But their basic ways of living were quite similar.

CENTRAL ANDEAN CIVILIZATION

The coast of Peru is probably the driest place in the world. But little streams come down from the Andes across it and make possible irrigated farming. The great mountain system of the Andes contains many high, cool valleys. Those in the north receive enough rain to permit farming. From Bolivia southward, farming is largely restricted to irrigated oases. In these mountains and in the valleys of the desert coast the most advanced Indian civilizations in South America developed. At the time of the Spanish conquest in 1532 the great Inca Empire governed the whole region from Ecuador to central Chile, but this empire was only a little more than 100 years old. It had just conquered a series of smaller civilized states, each of which had a long history.

We know most about the ancient history of the coastal valleys because the climate is so dry that all kinds of goods are preserved in abandoned cities and graveyards. In addition to pottery and metal ornaments, there are embroidered cotton and wool textiles used to wrap mummies. There are pots of beans, maize, and other crops that are thousands of years old. The pottery of the Mochica period, about the beginning of the Christian Era, is beautifully modeled. Sometimes the pottery is modeled into faces of people or gods; often into the forms of animals or various crop plants, such as corn or squash. Such jars were buried in noblemen's graves and tell us something of prehistoric life. The ancient Indian cities on the desert were built largely of adobe bricks, but those in the highland were of cut stone and make imposing ruins. In Cuzco, the capital of the Inca Empire, most modern buildings are built on stone foundations laid by prehistoric Indians.

The Andean Indians farmed a great variety of crops. Maize, potatoes, squashes, and several kinds of beans are of importance to modern agriculture all over the world. They domesticated two large animals, distant relatives of the camel—the llama, used for meat and to carry burdens, and the alpaca, used for meat and wool. They also kept guinea pigs for food.

Ciboney

Arawak

CARIBBEAN SEA

Carib

Chibchan

NORTH

ATLANTIC

OCEAN

Chibchan

Arawak

Carib

Orinoco River

Arawakan
Tribes

Cariban
Tribes

Arawak

Rio Negro

River

Amazon

River

Tupian Tribes

Chimu

Quechua

Cuzco

Language

Arawakan and
Other Tribes

Madeira River

**MATO
GROSSO**

Tupian Tribes

Aymara

Ge
Tribes

Diaquita

CHACO

Paraguay River

Paraná River

Guaraní

**PACIFIC

OCEAN**

**SOUTH

ATLANTIC

OCEAN**

Araucanians

Paraná River

PAMPA

Puelche

PATAGONIA

Tehuelehe

Ona

Yoghans

INDIANS OF SOUTH AMERICA

Boundary of the Inca Empire

Marginal Tribes

Tropical Forest Tribes

Circum-Caribbean Tribes

Central Andean Civilization

(After Julian Steward)

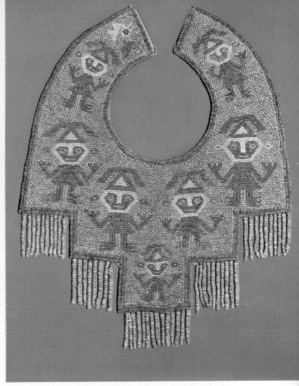

Examples of Chimu crafts found at Chan Chan, Peru. Left: Gold goblets. National Museum, Lima, Peru. Right: Beaded gorget (collar). Museum of Natural History, New York, N.Y.

Farming was in permanent fields, which were carefully irrigated in dry areas. The land was fertilized by llama manure in the highlands and by bird droppings (guano) in the coastal valleys. The guano was collected from the tiny offshore islands, where great numbers of seabirds roosted. Terraces were built in the mountains to reduce soil erosion and make fields on steep slopes. The crafts of pottery-making, weaving, and metalworking were highly developed. Axes made of bronze, an alloy of copper and tin, have been found that were sharper and harder than the iron tools the Spaniards had.

That 180 Spanish warriors could conquer the Inca Empire of many millions of people is still a wonder of history. They did so, however, and took the place of the native rulers and noblemen. The Indian commoners continued to work in the fields and mines for their new rulers, much as they had worked for their native ones. In the coastal areas the Indians died off or became mixed with the invaders and lost their own culture. In the highlands, however, Indians still form the bulk of the population. Racially, Ecuador, Peru, and Bolivia are chiefly Indian, and the Quechua language of the Inca Empire is still spoken

widely in all three countries. Aymara, the language of the people of the Bolivian plateau, who had been conquered by the Incas, similarly survives. The highland Indians of Peru have lost their native nobility, their cities, temples, and works of art. But the way of life for the ordinary Indian farmer or herdsman in the village is little different from what it was 500 years ago.

The Incas

In 1531 Francisco Pizarro first landed on the coast of what is now Ecuador. He entered an empire that extended nearly 3,000 miles along the western coast of South America. This was the great Inca Empire. With perhaps 16,000,000 people, it was larger than any kingdom in Europe at the time. It was well governed. Every citizen was employed. The royal storehouses contained grain, so that no one went hungry even if the crops failed in some province. There were good roads to all parts of the kingdom. Messengers carried news and delivered orders to every village.

These services were carried on despite the fact that the empire consisted of the driest desert and some of the most rugged mountains in the world. There had been no government

Detail of a handwoven tapestry shirt made by the Incas, 16th or 17th century. National Museum, Lima.

Above: Ear discs, Mochica style, early centuries A.D. Made of turquoise, gold, and shell, 4 inches in diameter, the pieces are in the Museum Rafael Larco Herrera, Lima. Right: Vessel (container) in the form of a llama, 29 inches high, in the coastal Tiahuanaco style. The figure is pre-Incan, but the date is unknown. Museum of Archaeology and Anthropology, Lima.

Chimu chopping knife. Collection of Miguel Mujica Gallo, Peru.

Poncho made of feathers by the Chimu. University Museum of Archaeology and Ethnology, Cambridge, England.

Mochica bird jar. Museum Rafael Larco Herrera, Lima.

Bird on a pedestal, copper, date unknown. Collection of Raymond Wielgus, Chicago, Illinois.

like it since the great days of the Roman Empire.

Early History. In the 11th or 12th century, the Incas were a small tribe that lived in an isolated valley of the Andes in southern Peru. They were a warlike people and became the ruling class of a great empire in the 15th century. They spoke an Indian language called Quechua, which became the official language of the Indian tribes they conquered. The ruler was called the Inca. The Inca Empire was named after him.

There was no writing in the Inca Empire. Therefore its history before the Spanish conquest comes from stories the Indians told to the Spaniards. We cannot be sure that they are true, and they do not agree in all details. According to these stories there were 13 Inca rulers. The first eight ruled from about 1200 to 1438. Until then the Inca tribe fought with its neighbors but did not expand more than 10 to 15 miles beyond its own little valley. After that, under Pachacuti and his son the Topa Inca, vast territories were conquered. Newly conquered tribes had to provide soldiers for fresh conquests. The children of their former rulers were held as hostages in Cuzco to ensure loyalty. By 1525 all the civilized tribes of the Andes and the coastal regions from the modern Colombian border to central Chile had been brought into the Inca Empire.

The many different peoples who were

Central Andean Indians. An Inca herdsman drives a pack of llamas through a village high in the Andes. In the foreground is an ancient effigy jar, showing a man playing reed pipes. In the background farmers till terraced mountain slopes.

conquered by the armies of the Incas had long histories of civilized life. For thousands of years they had been farmers. They had built stone terraces in the mountains to control soil erosion. They had irrigated the coastal deserts. A wonderful assortment of crop plants had been domesticated. These included potatoes, maize, several kinds of beans, cotton, peanuts, sweet potatoes, squashes, and tomatoes. Our supply of present-day foods owes much to these Indian crops. Llamas and alpacas were domesticated and herded in the mountains, yielding meat and wool. Fine cloth was woven of cotton and alpaca wool. Gold, silver, copper, and tin were mined and smelted. Copper and tin were alloyed to make excellent bronze tools and weapons. Great cities had been built in the irrigated coastal valleys. Fine pottery was made, and the jars were often modeled in the form of animals or plants, and sometimes portraits of individuals.

Before the rise of the Inca state a number of smaller empires or kingdoms, such as the Chimu on the northern coast of Peru, had been formed. They were all taken over by the Incas, and together with the smaller tribes and city-states, they were united into a single state.

Contributions of the Incas. The Incas accomplished little in the way of inventions. Their great achievement was in organizing and governing a vast land. They did this without any system of writing. Records were kept through use of the quipu, a series of knotted strings, some in color, tied to a main cord. The size, color, and position of the knots served as a memory aid for the quipu keeper in recalling important statistics and events. There were no wheeled vehicles, but roads and bridges were built throughout the empire over rugged, mountainous terrain. Special runners carried messages for the Incas. If revolt threatened, armies could be moved over these roads. These armies could be supplied from storehouses constructed along the roads and kept filled with provisions. Quechua, the language of the Incas, was spread throughout the empire. Even today it is spoken by millions of Indians in Ecuador, Peru, and Bolivia.

Daily Life. For the average citizen of the Inca Empire, life was both completely secure and controlled. He worked at farming or mining or some trade. If he was a farmer, one third of his produce supported his family, one third went to support officials and workers in other crafts, and one third was stored for emergencies such as crop failures or military needs. Labor not needed for farming was used to terrace new fields or to build irrigation systems, roads, cities, or temples. Government officials held their rank because of heredity. Often they were descendants of conquered rulers. A man born a commoner would work all his life and die a commoner. The emperor (called the Inca) was the absolute ruler of all. He was thought of as a god and was considered so noble that only his sisters were noble enough for him to marry. Important questions could be decided only by the Inca. He told the officials what to tell the common people. The people unquestioningly obeyed.

The End of the Empire. When Pizarro entered the empire with 180 soldiers, a contest was going on between Huascar and his half-brother Atahualpa over who would be the Inca (ruler). Atahualpa was winning the war. Pizarro captured him by treachery. In the meantime Huascar had been captured and killed. Pizarro then killed Atahualpa. Without a leader, the Inca Empire could not resist the brutal Spanish adventurers. The average Indian was used to doing what he was told. Now the Spanish conquerors gave the orders. Because the Spaniards wanted more men to work in the mines, farming was neglected, and many Indians died from overwork and lack of food. But many survived, and their descendants still form the majority of the population in the Andes of Ecuador, Peru, and Bolivia. They speak Quechua or Aymara in parts of Bolivia, and most of them farm as their ancestors did even long before the time of the Incas.

▶ **CIRCUM-CARIBBEAN TRIBES**

In the northern Andes, on the larger West Indian islands, and in Central America as far north as Honduras, the Indian groups were large and complex. Chieftains controlled many villages, with total populations in the tens of thousands. Fields were cultivated permanently wherever the soil was fertile. Gold, copper, and silver were mined and smelted and made into ornaments. Metal ornaments were traded in territories where there were no suitable ores. A few tribes with the same level of civilization also lived on the plains east of the central Andes.

We know very little about tribes who lived on the rim of the Caribbean. This region was the first to be conquered by the Spanish explorers. The early conquerors slaughtered the Indians or worked them to death, without regard for who would do the work in the future. When the Indians were gone, the Spaniards brought in Negro slaves from Africa.

To learn about the Indians, we must rely on the earliest records, written by fighters rather than scholars, and on archeology. But archeologists find little information in Indian remains. Since the Indians often buried gold ornaments with their chiefs, robbing Indian graves has been common for centuries in Colombia. Most gravesites are in total disorder. A few fugitive Indian groups survive in the mountains and forests, but they have lost much of their old culture.

The languages spoken in the Greater Antilles and much of Venezuela were of the Arawak family. Those in Colombia and Central America were largely Chibchan. There were many tribes in this vast area, and they were often at war with one another. In the West Indies, however, the Indians were quite peaceful. There seem to have been hereditary classes of rulers, noblemen, and commoners.

Rank was inherited through the mother's line. Rulers and noblemen must have been greatly respected, because gold offerings were buried with them in great pottery jars. Where warfare was important, a commoner might become a nobleman by capturing people to work for him or to be sacrificed in religious rites.

On the mainland, especially in western Colombia, war seems to have been especially vicious. Wars were fought to obtain captives to eat and for sacrifice. These practices may have come from the civilizations of central Mexico. The more vicious practices among the Indians of South America were often carried on by the more civilized Indian groups rather than the less civilized.

▶ TROPICAL FOREST TRIBES

Slash-and-burn agriculture was the main way of making a living for the tropical forest tribes. Trees were killed by cutting the bark all around. The dried leaves and branches were burned, and crops were planted with a digging stick between the tree stumps. The ashes served as fertilizer in what were usually poor soils. In a year or so the soil began to give out, and weeds became a problem. The garden was abandoned, and a new one cleared in the same fashion. Maize, which we know as

Caribbean tribe. The Arawak Indians, a peace-loving people, were expert swimmers, fishermen, and sailors.

Tropical Forest Tribe. A Carib Indian decorates a stool. A baby is secure in a "walker." A man rolls clay to make pottery. Two bowmen stalk fish on the riverbank while another Indian slashes and burns a patch of jungle to ready it for planting.

corn, root crops such as manioc and sweet potatoes, and squashes, beans, and some tropical fruit trees were cultivated.

The forest tribes hunted and fished for food. Fishing was very important along the coasts and larger rivers. Poisonous plants were chopped up and thrown into rivers to stupefy the fish so that they could be caught by hand. More violent poisons were applied to arrows and the darts used in blowguns. These poisonous darts were used both in hunting and in warfare. Often a poisonous plant substance has value as a medicine. Today scientists are discovering valuable drugs that have long been in use among the isolated tribes of the Amazon and Orinoco basins.

Most of the tropical forest tribes spoke languages that belong to one of four major language groups: Tupi, Carib, Arawak, or Araucanian. But there was no political organization beyond the individual tribe. The basic unit was the village, which usually consisted of 10 to 20 families related through their fathers. Marriage had to be with a woman from outside the village, so there would be some friendly relations with a few other villages. But no chief headed more than one village. Often the village consisted of one enormous house

built on a pole framework, with a thatched roof and woven mats for sides. It might be 100 feet long and be cut up into apartments. One family slept in each apartment.

Villages ranged in size from 100 to as many as 2,000 people. They were semipermanent. A house might last for 10 to 15 years, with several sets of nearby gardens being cultivated during that time. Pottery, basketry, and hunting and fishing equipment were made with a good deal of skill. Because the climate was hot, clothing was very limited. Many tribes painted their bodies decoratively and wore masks and headdresses for special ceremonies. The woven hammock, a wonderful bed in a hot, sticky climate, seems to have been invented by these people.

Because of their secure food supply, the tropical forest tribes could devote much time to games and ceremonies. They had a variety of musical instruments and drank *chicha* (a beer) and smoked tobacco on special occasions.

Most of the tropical forest tribes were warlike, and would fight their neighbors at any time. Two villages might speak the same language and even exchange wives, but they were always likely to attack one another in revenge for a similar attack some years before. Among the Tupi- and Carib-speaking tribes it was customary to take prisoners, who would be kept for months or years and then ceremonially killed and eaten. The word "cannibal" is a corruption of the word "Carib." Skulls and shrunken heads of enemies were kept as trophies. All these practices were designed to insult the members of an unfriendly village in revenge for a past insult. It is easy to see how this feuding prevented a government from being established for more than one village. Curiously, this brutal behavior was regarded as natural. A man captured in war would not attempt to escape, even though he knew he would be killed. His own village expected him to die bravely and not to come sneaking home.

Some tropical forest tribes survive today in the vast wilderness of the Amazon basin. But most were enslaved centuries ago to work on plantations in coastal Brazil or more recently to collect rubber.

The Guaraní of Paraguay, who speak a Tupian language, had a different history. Spanish Jesuits set up missions among them, forcing them to give up warfare and cannibalism. At the same time, the missionaries protected them from the Portuguese slave raiders. Most of the modern population of Paraguay is descended from these Indians and can still speak the Guaraní language. But the rest of their culture comes more from the missionaries than from native sources.

The Araucanians of south central Chile resisted conquest, and the many villages formed alliances in order to fight more effectively. Throughout the colonial period they maintained their independence. They learned from the Spaniards while they fought them. They learned to plant new crops and to use horses and modern weapons. When Chile became independent, the Araucanians became citizens. They were eventually given reservations and settled down as farmers. Today they tend to farm in village co-operatives rather than as individual landowners. This is a kind of survival of the Indian way of life, though they live and work in general like other Chilean countrymen.

▶ MARGINAL TRIBES

The poorest of the South American Indians were the marginal tribes. They usually lived in the most isolated, least attractive lands. They were least able to control their living conditions and had to exist on what nature offered. The struggle to get enough

Marginal Tribe. Indians of Tierra del Fuego wear guanaco skins as protection against the cold. In the lean-to one of the women weaves a basket. A baby is tied to a cradleboard. A bola lies beside the shelter. In background a lookout watches a band of strange Indians approach. In foreground a man practices with bow and arrow.

to eat took most of their time and energy. There was little opportunity to develop crafts and social activities. Two conditions probably led to the backwardness of these marginal peoples. Most of them lived in difficult country—the cold forests of southern Chile; the cold, dry lands of Patagonia; the tropical forests of the upper Amazon, where the soils are extremely poor; or the poor grasslands of the Mato Grosso of Brazil. The grasslands of the Pampa of Argentina and Uruguay are good for modern agriculture, but Indians using only digging sticks found the heavy turf impossible to cultivate. Also, they were far from the centers in which new ideas about farming, pottery-making, weaving, and working metals were being developed. Some lived at the ends of the continent. Others lived at the headwaters of rivers rather than along the lower streams, which served as lines of transportation.

A few of the marginal tribes of the Amazon basin and eastern Brazil did a little farming. But even they depended chiefly on hunting, fishing, and gathering wild plants for their food and other needs. Their farming was not very good. Food was always scarce. In the southern part of the continent there was no farming at all. Some groups had specialized hunting devices. *Bolas* consist of two or three stone balls attached to cords that are tied together. These could be thrown to entangle a large animal's legs. The Tehuelche and Puelche Indians of Patagonia and the Argentine Pampa used them to hunt guanaco and the ostrichlike rhea.

The marginal tribes were scattered over most of the continent and lived off different resources in their varied environments. They were organized into simple groups. The largest unit was the band, and it seldom had as many as 100 members. Though a number of bands in an area might speak the same language, each had its own chief and was completely independent of the others. The Yahgan, who lived on the cold, stormy coast of southernmost Chile, spent most of the year in separate family units. Each family had its dugout canoe and hunted for shellfish on its own stretch of rocky coast. If a big food supply, such as a stranded whale, became available, many families would come together to feed on it. For a few weeks there would be ceremonies to initiate young people into adulthood. Marriages would take place, and new families formed.

Because each band was so small, these marginal peoples could not resist attacks by larger and more advanced Indian groups. In the long pre-Columbian history of South America they had been driven into the least attractive lands, especially the places where farming was impossible or very difficult. They had been driven away from the major navigable rivers of the Amazon basin. Their thatched houses were built deep in the forests, at the headwaters of streams. They were ready to hide in the woods if some more powerful group approached. There was no time to build strong houses or to bother with clothing. Their tools were what they could carry away at a moment's notice. Their settlements were moved regularly, partly from fear of neighbors and partly to seek new hunting and fishing grounds.

From generations of fighting with their more advanced Indian neighbors, marginal tribes learned to be timid. This fear gave them some protection from the Spanish and Portuguese conquerors. Each band had to be caught separately. Often, when approached by an army, an Indian band would melt into the forest, shooting a few arrows from hiding to discourage pursuit. Usually the lands they occupied were hardly worth fighting for. As a result, many of these small bands survive in out-of-the-way places to the present day. They are of great interest to anthropologists, who feel that their simple way of life may tell us how mankind lived in the million years before farming was invented.

The Puelche are typical of the Indians of the Pampa. They have a special history. By 1580 a Spanish settlement at Buenos Aires had begun grazing horses and mules for sale to the mines of what has become Bolivia. The Puelche Indians hunted this livestock for food, but after a while they learned to ride the animals. On horseback these shy Indians became great and feared warriors just like the Comanche and Sioux of the North American plains. It was not until after 1880 that these bands of Indians on the Pampa were defeated. When their land came to be valuable for farming, their future was destroyed.

HOMER ASCHMANN
University of California (Riverside)

INDIAN WARS

In the dark woods around Jamestown, Virginia, wild war whoops shrilled on a March morning in 1622. Swooping down on the farms and tobacco plantations along the James River, Indian warriors slaughtered 422 men, women, and children. So began the long series of wars with the American Indians, which lasted for nearly 3 centuries. Despite the fierce resistance of the Indians, their final conquest by the white settlers was certain. They were a primitive people struggling against a powerful civilization.

In the East

Spaniards and Frenchmen had fought the Indians since the discovery of the New World by Columbus. The English had encountered them when the little settlement of Jamestown was founded in 1607. Jamestown survived only because Chief Powhatan did not choose to wipe out the newcomers. It was Powhatan's successor as chief who ordered the massacre of the planters at Jamestown. But the massacre came too late to break the foothold of the whites in Virginia.

The Pilgrims and other settlers were firmly established in New England on land that was at first freely given by the Indians. However, King Philip's War, which broke out in Massachusetts in 1675, ended friendly relations between the white settlers in New England and the Indians. Several thousand whites were killed and 12 towns burned before King Philip (as the Indian leader was called) fell and the uprising was crushed. And beyond the coast, where the white settlers were steadily thrusting westward toward the Mississippi, there was seldom peace.

There was conflict between England and France in Europe, Africa, and Asia. This conflict spread to their American colonies. Tribes fought on both sides in the long, bloody French and Indian Wars, which lasted from 1690 to 1763. Again New England settlements were raided and put to the torch. Indians herded many white captives to Canada for sale to the French. Those who could not make the dreadful marches were tomahawked. The British and their American colonists suffered such reverses as the defeat and death of British general Edward Braddock (1695–1755) on the Monongahela. But they finally won the war by capturing the French fortress of Louisburg on Cape Breton Island, Nova Scotia, and by capturing Quebec, the capital of French Canada. A dangerous uprising of western Indians ended when Chief Pontiac failed to take Detroit in his siege of 1763–64.

Westward Expansion

The Indians fought hard for their hunting grounds. But tribe after tribe lost them to an increasing flood of settlers by sale, treaty, cession, or outright seizure. Gold discoveries spurred the drive of white men. Huge herds of buffalo were killed by white men for hides and meat. This meant starvation for the western Plains Indians, whose whole civilization was based on the hunting of the buffalo. It was the task of the United States Army to carve a path through Indian country for the pioneers.

In the American Revolution (1775–83) the young United States faced the British, the Tories (colonists loyal to the British), and their Indian allies. Few tribes took the side of the American colonists. With his Mohawks and the Senecas an educated Iroquois chieftain, Joseph Brant, ambushed American militia marching to relieve Fort Stanwix in western New York in 1777. Nearly 200 of the American troops were killed, but the fort held out. The frontier was drenched in blood as Indians and Tories raided Pennsylvania and New York. General George Washington struck back.

In 1779 an expedition under General John Sullivan devastated the farms and villages of four hostile tribes of the Six Nations of the Iroquois, knocking them out of the war. Between 1779 and 1783 Colonel George Rogers Clark's little army won the Northwest Territory for the United States. They scored a remarkable series of victories over the British and their Indian allies. The British armed the Indians and paid them high bounties for all the American scalps they could bring in.

After the Revolution the Indians inflicted disastrous defeats on two American armies in Ohio. Little Turtle of the Miamis routed General Harmer in 1790, and the next year tribesmen smashed General Arthur St. Clair's force. This was the bloodiest battle of all the Indian Wars for the Americans. Of 1,400

American troops, 912 were killed or wounded. But an able general, "Mad Anthony" Wayne (1745–96) of Revolutionary fame, turned the tide. On August 20, 1794, his well-trained troops stormed the Indians' tree barricades in the battle of Fallen Timbers in northwest Ohio. Wayne's men won the battle.

In 1804 and 1805 two small military scouting parties went deep into Indian country. Meriwether Lewis and William Clark traveled from St. Louis to the Pacific coast. In 1807 Zebulon M. Pike (1779–1813) sighted the Colorado peak (Pikes Peak) named for him and returned by way of the Southwest and Mexico. These bold explorers blazed the way for coming conquest.

In 1811 one of the greatest Indian chiefs, Tecumseh of the Shawnees, was defeated. Tecumseh led a widespread, dangerous confederation of tribes. He was absent from his village in the future state of Indiana when General William Henry Harrison attacked. Harrison defeated Tecumseh's braves in the hard-fought battle of Tippecanoe. This victory helped make Harrison president of the United States with the slogan "Tippecanoe and Tyler [the vice-president] Too." The Indian Wars were stepping-stones to the presidency for two other generals, too, Andrew Jackson and Zachary Taylor. And Abraham Lincoln's brief but able service in the Black Hawk War helped him to attain the presidency. In the War of 1812, Tecumseh joined the British and fought gallantly until his death in the battle of the Thames in Canada in 1813.

After Andrew Jackson conquered the stubborn Creeks and defeated the British at New Orleans, he defeated the Seminoles in Florida in the First Seminole War. However, this defeat did not break the resistance of the Indians to their white rulers. The Second Seminole War broke out in 1835. It was a bitter conflict that lasted more than 7 years. Before the Seminole warriors, led by Chief Osceola, were finally beaten, both the Americans and the Indians suffered heavy casualties. The war cost the United States Government $19,000,000.

The Black Hawk, Sac, and Fox tribes were overwhelmed in the midwest. In the south, land- and gold-hungry whites forced the government to remove the civilized Cherokee from their homes. They were ordered to move to Indian Territory in Oklahoma. The Indians called the journey The Trail of Tears. While the Mexican War (1846–48) was in progress, soldiers besieged and took the fortresslike dwelling of the Pueblos in Taos, New Mexico. Next, the power of northwestern Indians was broken. Everywhere the tribes gave ground; they were outnumbered, seldom united, debauched by liquor sold to them by white men, and ravaged by smallpox.

Civil War

The outbreak of the Civil War (1861–65), dividing the nation, seemed to offer the Indians a great opportunity to win back much they had lost. The North and the South bid for the support of the Cherokee, Creeks, Seminoles, Choctaws, and Chickasaws. (These were southern tribes that owned Negro slaves.) Although the South made the Indians more promises of land and other rewards for their services than did the North, many southern Indians still wished to remain loyal to the Union. The issue of slavery was not as important to them as it was to white slave owners in the South. Their way of life would not be changed greatly if they lost the few slaves they held.

Indians did fight for the South in the battle

In 1838 the Cherokee began their journey into exile.

of Pea Ridge (1862). Two Indians became brigadier generals. Stand Watie (1806–71), a Cherokee, became a Southern brigadier general. A Sioux named Ely Samuel Parker gained the same rank in the United States Army. However, before the war ended the Santee Sioux, a western tribe, had massacred more than 800 whites in Minnesota. Despite the sympathy that individual Indians had for both North and South, the aim of the western tribes was to stop the white man from taking their land. Nor did the Civil War stop American attacks on the Indians. At Sand Creek in 1864 Colorado militia killed 300 Cheyenne men, women, and children who had tried to surrender.

The Far West

Combat raged on western prairie and desert and in the mountains. The Plains Indians fought on, though a chain of frontier forts closed in on them and the transcontinental railroad and telegraph lines cut through their hunting grounds. The United States Army never had more than 25,000 troops available for Indian fighting in the West. Since Indian country was so vast, these 25,000 men had to break up into many small groups in order to cover the area. These small groups were often outnumbered by attacking Indians.

Fort Kearny in Wyoming would not have survived a Sioux siege in 1867 if a courier, "Portugee" Phillips, had not made a heroic 236-mile ride through a terrific blizzard and brought help. On September 17, 1868, a little group of soldiers and scouts entrenched on Beecher Island, Colorado, and charged by massed Cheyennes was also narrowly rescued. In 1871 in present-day Oklahoma the famous General W. T. Sherman (1820–91) almost lost his scalp during a Kiowa uprising. In northeastern California the Modocs rose in 1873, took refuge in a natural fortress of volcanic rock called the Lava Beds, and repulsed all assaults. At a peace parley they treacherously shot and killed an American general and several members of his party. They were driven from their stronghold only by mortar fire.

In the southwest the Apache had long fought both the United States and Mexico. There was no more formidable foe than these fierce warriors. They had incredible endur-

ance in battle, and they treated prisoners brutally. Only after a series of tough campaigns in the years following the Civil War were they conquered. General George Crook, organizing packtrains for supply and using Apache scouts, thought he had subdued the Apache by 1875. However, they rose again in 1882 in protest against cheating by United States Government Indian agents. General Crook had to return. The Apache wars were over at last with the surrender of the Apache leader Geronimo in 1886.

Meanwhile the Army staged a three-pronged drive against the warlike Sioux, unrelenting enemy of the white man and of lesser tribes. A column under General Crook, with Shoshone and Crow Indian allies, clashed with the Sioux, led by the dashing Chief Crazy Horse. The two opposing forces met at the Rosebud River in Montana in 1876. The desperate day-long battle ended in a draw. Crook, forced to retreat and re-equip, was unable to combine in time with the other two columns for a roundup of the hostile Indians.

Custer's Last Stand

A second force, the 7th Cavalry, took the field. In command rode George Armstrong Custer, who had won fame as a young general in the Civil War but was now a lieutenant colonel because of the reduction in the size of the Army. Custer joined the third column of the force under generals Alfred Terry and John Gibbon and was ordered to march out and find the Indians' trail. If it led to the Little Bighorn Valley in Montana, he was not to follow it but to wait until reinforced.

There indeed the trail led when Custer found it. His scouts reported that 10,000 Indians had passed over the trail, headed for the Little Bighorn Valley. Disbelieving them, he prepared to attack, rashly risking all for the glory of a great victory. Furthermore, he separated the three battalions of his regiment for a three-part assault. He commanded one battalion, Major Marcus Reno another, and Captain Frederick Benteen the third.

On June 25, 1876, Major Reno and his battalion heard the rattle of rifle fire from Custer's direction. Galloping to the rescue, they were charged by masses of Sioux and Cheyennes. Reno's men reeled back, barely

Custer and his few remaining men making their gallant last stand against the Sioux.

managing to reach a bluff where, joined by Captain Benteen's men and the packtrain, they fought for their lives. Meanwhile Sitting Bull, top chief and medicine man of the Sioux, attacked Custer with his fighting chieftains and their warriors. The red tide flooded over the soldiers. Revolver blazing, Custer fell with two bullets through his body. Around him lay 211 dead.

The Last Battles

Relentlessly the Army harried the Indians with winter campaigns, catching them in their tepees or in snows that hampered their movement. The shivering warriors on their thin ponies were unable to cope with the better-equipped and -supplied troops. The strength of the Sioux, Cheyennes, Apache, and other tribes was steadily whittled down. The Army, disregarding its own heavy losses, forged on and conquered the Bannocks and Paiutes in Idaho and the Utes of Colorado.

The Nez Percé Indians had long been friends of the white man. However, when in 1877 the government, prompted by gold-hunters and settlers, tried to move them from the remnant of their land in northeastern Oregon, they took to the warpath. Chief Thunder-on-the-Mountain, called Joseph by the whites, led them expertly. With only 300 warriors, encumbered by women and children, he fought off troops that finally numbered 5,000 in the field. Column after column, aided by telegraph reports, attempted to cut off the retreating Nez Percé. In a 2,000-mile rear-guard action Joseph defeated them again and again. He was close to escaping across the Canadian border when he was cornered and forced to surrender.

In 1889 the Sioux were roused by the preaching of a medicine man who proclaimed that the Great Spirit was sending a messiah to redeem them from the white man's bondage. Day and night they staged wild ghost dances that worked them up to a fighting pitch. Sitting Bull urged them on, and his arrest was ordered to prevent an uprising. When an Indian-police lieutenant seized him, the old chief howled for rescue. As warriors shot down the lieutenant, two sergeants emptied their guns into Sitting Bull, killing him. Troops came up in time to save the hard-pressed police. Infantry, cavalry, and artillery hunted down rebellious bands and rounded them up for return to the reservations. But the ghost-dance madness was still on the Sioux. Captured warriors jerked hidden rifles from under their blankets and opened a murderous fusillade on the soldiers. The battle of Wounded Knee raged through the Sioux camp, and women and children were killed in the crossfire.

With the defeat of the Sioux on December 29, 1890, the Indian Wars were over except for a brief outbreak by the Chippewas in Minnesota in 1898. Indians, settled on reservations or merging into the nation's life, were granted American citizenship in 1924. Indians fought gallantly in both World Wars for the country that had conquered them.

FAIRFAX DOWNEY
Author, *Indian Wars
of the United States Army, 1776–1865*

INDOCHINA. See SOUTHEAST ASIA.

INDONESIA

Indonesia, formerly the Netherlands East Indies, is a republic in Southeast Asia. The country is made up of many thousands of islands, stretching along the equator between Australia and the Asia mainland. The word "Indonesia" means "islands of the Indies." Since 1950, after it won its independence from the Netherlands, the country has been known as the Republic of Indonesia.

▶ THE PEOPLE

Indonesia has a population of about 120,000,000. It consists mainly of Malay people who came to the islands from the mainland of Asia about 4,000 years ago. The more primitive people whom the Malays found upon arrival moved eastward into New Guinea and the islands of the western Pacific.

The majority of Indonesians have light-brown skin and straight black hair. They are rather short and slim. Of the foreign population, the Chinese, who number several millions, make up the largest group. There are also small groups of Arabs, Indians, and Eurasians.

More than 60 percent of the Indonesians live on the island of Java. In some of Java's fertile valleys population density is as high as 3,000 persons per square mile.

Language. Bahasa Indonesia was chosen as the national language of Indonesia in 1949, when the country became independent. It is closely related to Malay and is spoken in all the islands. Many other languages and dialects are spoken by the Indonesian people. Some of those spoken in Borneo are still little-known.

Education. A large portion of the population cannot read and write. This number, however, is steadily decreasing. Primary education is compulsory. Secondary and higher education are optional. Both secular and religious (Islamic) schools are supervised by the government. The three best-known institutions of higher learning are the University of Indonesia in Djakarta, the capital of the country, and the Gadjah Mada University and the State Institute of Islam, both in Jogjakarta. The number of universities is increasing so quickly that the government has established a Ministry of Higher Education and Science to supervise their function.

Religion. The major religion of Indonesia is Islam, and at least 90 percent of the people are Muslims. About 5 percent of the people are Christians. They live mainly in Sumatra, Java, Celebes, and the Moluccas. On the island of Bali, most of the inhabitants are Hindus. Also, many people in Indonesia still believe in spirits. The *adat,* or local custom, also plays an important part in the life of the people.

Bicycles and *betjaks* (pedicabs) crowd the streets in many Indonesian cities.

Way of Life. In the cities clothing in the western style is worn by Indonesian men. Native influence is seen only in the black velvet caps they wear on their heads. Indonesian women wear batik-patterned wraparound skirts, long-sleeved jackets, and scarves called *selendang* over their shoulders. The style of Indonesian houses varies from island to island and from rural regions to cities. In Java, for instance, most houses are one-story square-shaped structures with bamboo walls, while on Borneo the Dayak people build their homes on stilts.

A great majority of the Indonesians are farmers who till small plots of land. In large parts of the country rice is the main crop, but on the drier eastern islands maize (corn) or, in some cases, sago (a starch) is the staple crop. In addition to these crops, vegetables, fish eggs, chickens, and spices make up the daily diet.

Farm families are generally larger than city families. The entire family must work for their daily bread. Young girls help their mothers sew and thresh rice in the afternoons, after they have finished school and religious training. A boy of 8 will help his father weed and plow in the rice paddies. On Muslim religious holidays there are grand festivities, in which all the families of a community take part.

In the cities some people work in small local industries, where food is processed, leather tanned, and the famous batik cloth with color designs is woven and dyed. Many men are employed by the government. Their families get up very early every morning so that the men can get to the government offices by 7 A.M. The mother then goes to market, and the children go to school. At 2 P.M., when the workday is over, the entire family eats a big meal and then sleeps for a few hours. In the evening, after eating a smaller, informal meal, people usually get together with friends.

The Arts. As a result of foreign contact, art in Indonesia has flourished. Hindu and Buddhist influences are seen in the many temples, such as those on the island of Bali and the Borobudur in central Java. Drama is often in the form of puppet plays called *wayang,* in which puppets are used to enact stories from such ancient Hindu epic literature as the *Mahabharata* and *Ramayana.* The *wayang,* accompanied by music played on native instruments by a *gamelan* (orchestra), are very popular. Local dances based on legends also attract many spectators.

FACTS AND FIGURES

REPUBLIC OF INDONESIA is the official name of the country. Indonesia means "islands of the Indies."

CAPITAL: Djakarta.

LOCATION AND SIZE: Southeast Asia. **Latitude**—5° 54′ N to 11° S. **Longitude**—95° 01′ E to 141° 02′ E. **Area**—735,269 sq. mi. (including West New Guinea).

PHYSICAL FEATURES: Highest point—Mt. Djaja (formerly Carstensz) (16,400 ft.), highest island peak in the world. **Lowest point**—sea level. **Chief rivers**—Barito, Asahan, Kampar, Rokan, Indragiri, Hari, Musi, Solo, Brantas, and Kaptuas. **Chief mountain peaks**—Mt. Kinabalu (13,455 ft.), Mt. Kerinchi (12,467 ft.), Mt. Mahameru (12,060 ft.), and Mt. Rantemario (11,286 ft.).

POPULATION: 120,000,000 (estimate).

LANGUAGE: Bahasa Indonesia (official), regional languages and dialects.

RELIGION: Islam, Christianity, Hinduism, Buddhism, Confucianism, animism.

GOVERNMENT: Republic. **Head of government**—president. **International co-operation**—United Nations (withdrew, 1965; rejoined, 1966).

NATIONAL ANTHEM: *Indonesia Raya* ("Great Indonesia").

ECONOMY: Agricultural products—maize, sago, rice, sugar, sweet potatoes, yams, cassava, palm kernels and palm oil, soybeans, peanuts, copra, coffee, rubber, cocoa, tea, tobacco, spices (cloves, nutmeg, mace, pepper). **Industries and products**—handicrafts (wood carving, silversmithing); consumer goods (tires, shoes, cigarettes, textiles, glass, paper, matches); fishing; forest products (rattan, bamboo, teak, ebony, kapok, sandalwood, copal, cinchona); hides and skins; ship-building; food processing; sugar-refining; tin and petroleum refining; cementmaking; automobile and bicycle assembly works. **Chief minerals**—petroleum, tin, bauxite, iron ore, coal, manganese, gold, silver, salt, diamonds, asphalt, copper, nickel. **Chief exports**—rubber, petroleum, tin, tobacco, palm oil and kernels, copra, tea, coffee, spices, quinine, kapok. **Chief imports**—textiles, machinery and vehicles, iron and steel products, chemicals and pharmaceuticals, rice. **Monetary unit**—rupiah.

▶THE LAND

Indonesia has a total land area of some 735,000 square miles. The greatest distance from the northern tip of Sumatra to the eastern end of West Irian (West New Guinea) is about 3,500 miles.

The country is usually divided into several island groups. The four major islands (with Indonesian names in parentheses) are Java (Djawa), Sumatra (Sumatera), Borneo (Kalimantan), and Celebes (Sulawesi). As a group, these islands are known as the Greater Sunda Islands (Sunda Besar). To the east of Java lie the Lesser Sunda Islands (Nusa Tenggera), which consist of Bali, Lombok, Sumba, Sumbawa, Flores, Timor, and some others. Between Celebes and New Guinea are located the Moluccas (Maluku), which include Buru, Ceram, Ambon, Halmahera, the Aru Islands, Morotai, and many other small islands. The easternmost part of Indonesia is West Irian, which in 1963 was transferred to the republic by the Netherlands.

The vegetation—tropical hardwoods, evergreens, dense jungle, and abundant flowers—is pretty much the same throughout the region. The animal life of the western part, however, with elephants, tigers, and rhinoceroses, resembles that of Asia, while marsupials (kangaroos and opossums) like those found in Australia are more common in the eastern part.

The Greater Sunda Islands. With a population of 80,000,000 people, **Java** is the most highly populated and the most developed island in Indonesia. The island lies south of the equator. Java has an area of about 49,000 square miles. It stretches 650 miles from east to west, with a width that varies from 40 to 130 miles. A low coastal plain is found in the north, while inland there are volcanoes, mountain ranges, and plateaus. Some isolated plains are found in the south. Java's volcanic soil is fertile, and this has made it possible to grow many commercial crops, aside from such staples as rice and maize. The longest rivers in Java are the Solo and the Brantas. Other rivers are short, containing many rapids. In the Sunda Strait, which separates Java from Sumatra, is Krakatau (Krakatoa), noted for its terrible volcanic eruption of 1883.

Borneo is the third largest island in the world. It has an area of about 287,000 square miles, of which the greater part belongs to Indonesia. The northern coastal areas consist of Sabah and Sarawak, which are part of Malaysia. Indonesian Borneo has only some 4,000,000 people, who live mainly in the coastal regions. The population includes many Indonesians of Chinese ancestry, who combine Chinese and Indonesian traditions in their way of life. The interior of the island is rugged, with mountains, swamps, and dense rain forest and jungle. The people who live here, known as Dayaks, are members of primitive tribes who were once headhunters. Large quantities of rubber come from Borneo. Petroleum, diamonds, gold, and silver are also found here.

Sumatra, with about 16,000,000 people, covers an area of more than 163,000 square miles. Along the eastern coast are high swamps. The Bukit Barisan, mountains with many active volcanoes, stretch along the southwestern coast. Most of the rivers, including the Musi, Hari, Indragiri, and Kampar, begin in these mountains and flow eastward and northeastward. There are large rubber estates on Sumatra where the men work at tapping rubber trees. Palm oil, tobacco used for cigar wrappers, tea, and pepper are other leading agricultural products. The Indonesian government has encouraged many people to move from the crowded island of Java to Sumatra by giving away free land for small farms. Petroleum is found in central and eastern Sumatra, and there are large oil refineries on the island. Tin is mined on the nearby islands of Bangka and Belitung (Billiton).

Celebes consists of four peninsulas that branch out from a mountainous area in the center of the island and are separated by three gulfs: Bone, Tomini, and Tolo. Celebes covers an area of about 69,000 square miles and has a population of over 7,000,000 people, most of whom live on the southwestern peninsula. The island is bordered on the northeast by the Philippines, on the west by the Macassar Strait, and on the east by the Molucca Sea. Rice, maize, copra (dried coconut meat), and rattan (palm) are leading products. The Minahessa people of northern Celebes have Dutch names and practice the Lutheran religion. They are hardworking people, who take time off for fun only on Saturdays and on Sundays after church.

The Lesser Sunda Islands. To the east of Java stretches a chain of mountainous islands known as the Lesser Sunda Islands. Their total area is about 28,000 square miles. Bali, with an area of about 2,000 square miles, is the

A primary-school classroom in Indonesia.

World-famous batik cloth is woven and dyed in small local industries.

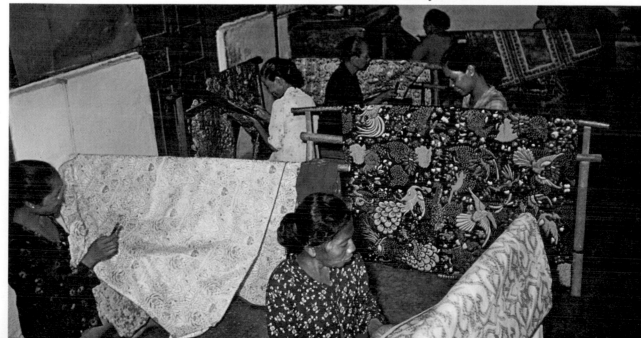

Above: A farmer plows his rice field with the help of water buffalo. Below: A street in Jogjakarta, a city on the island of Java.

best-known of the Lesser Sunda Islands. It is famous for its scenic beauty, temples, sculpture, and crafts. The temples date from the Hindu period, and Hindu customs and the Hindu religion are still widespread on the island. On the island of Bali girls at the age of 5 are taught to dance the intricate steps which tell old Hindu stories. By the age of 7 they start to take part in the village rituals.

Timor is the largest island of the group and is south of Flores, separated from it by the Savu Sea. The northeastern part of Timor belongs to Portugal. Indonesian Timor, the southwestern part of the island, covers some 5,700 square miles.

The Moluccas. The Moluccas, also known as the Spice Islands, lie between Celebes and New Guinea. They consist of hundreds of islands, with a total area of more than 33,000 square miles. Long before European traders arrived here, spices such as cloves, nutmeg, and mace had found their way from these islands to Indian and Chinese markets. The leading islands—Ternate, Tidore, Ambon, Halmahera, Ceram, Buru—later became a stronghold of Christianity. The major crop of the Moluccas is copra, while sago is a leading staple.

West Irian, with an area of about 160,000 square miles, is the Indonesian part of the second largest island in the world. About 400,000 rather primitive people, known as Papuans, live here. The lowlands are fever-ridden. In the interior, the peaks of the Djajawidjaja (or Snow) Mountains rise to great heights, with Mount Djaja (formerly Carstensz) rising to 16,400 feet. Not all of West Irian has been explored, but in the western part, known as the Bird's Head, a large supply of petroleum has been found.

Climate and Soil. In general the climate of Indonesia is tropical, with high temperatures, much rainfall, and a year-round growing season. Indonesia's location on and near the equator, and the monsoons, which are seasonal winds, determine its climate. From June to October is the season of the dry monsoon, while from November to March there is the wet monsoon. Because of the mountains, these seasons are often reversed on many islands. Year-round temperatures average about 80 degrees Fahrenheit in the lowlands. Only in the mountains can relief be found from the monotony and humidity. The western part of Indonesia receives more rain (over 200 inches in parts of Sumatra) than the eastern (less than 25 inches in parts of Celebes). Djakarta on Java receives about 70 inches per year.

Soils in general are not fertile, since high annual rainfall leaches out the soil's mineral content. Only in areas with volcanic soil, such as Java, and in the river valleys do soils produce a variety of crops in great amounts.

▶ INDUSTRIES AND PRODUCTS

Agriculture. Besides growing crops for local use, many Indonesians work on plantations where they raise mainly export products. Most of these plantations are on Java and Sumatra. Although production was higher before World War II, the country is still an important producer and exporter of rubber, copra, pepper, palm oil, kapok, and quinine. Because of the population increase, rice is now grown on several plantations and is imported from abroad to prevent famine.

Forestry. There are many products. from the tropical forest. Besides woods such as teak, sandal, and ebony, forests yield many resins, fibers, and fruits. The bark of the coastal mangrove is used for leather tanning, and that of the cinchona tree for the making of quinine. Bamboo is a plant having many uses, and rattan is made into wicker products, such as furniture.

Fishing. The nearness of sea and stream make it possible for the people to catch many fish. Also, the wet rice fields and flooded coastal areas are used as fish ponds. Fish are important as a daily food diet because religion often prohibits the eating of certain kinds of meat.

Mining. Many of the islands have valuable mineral deposits. Petroleum is found on Java, Sumatra, Borneo, and West Irian. Tin is mined on Bangka and Billiton. Diamonds, gold, and silver are found on Borneo and Sumatra. Coal, although not of a high grade, is also found on Sumatra.

Manufacturing. Just before World War II the country began to develop shipbuilding, cementmaking, and textile and paper production in many of the islands. People also engage in food processing, tire manufacturing, sugar-refining, the manufacture of chemicals, and glassmaking. Local craftsmanship is of high quality, especially in the field of textile design, wood carving, and silversmithing.

Trade. Indonesia's principal exports are agricultural and forest products, petroleum, copra, and tin ore. Imports consist of foodstuffs, machinery, textiles, iron and steel, and manufactured products.

Transportation and Communication. Although Indonesia is an island country, water transportation is not well developed. Distances and lack of shipping present serious problems. Java has the best roads and railroads. On the other islands, mountains and jungles interfere with land transportation, so most Indonesians walk or use buffalo carts. In the cities many people use bicycles or three-wheeled pedicabs called *betjaks*. Djakarta is served by many foreign airlines, while the Garuda Indonesian Airways supplies inter-island service and flies to cities in the Philippines and on the Asia mainland. Telephone, telegraph, and postal services are owned by the government.

Major Cities. Djakarta, the capital of Indonesia, lies near the northwestern coast of Java. It has a population of over 3,000,000. The city, which was founded in 1619, looks much like Amsterdam, with Dutch architecture, and many bridges crossing its canals. Other Javanese cities are Bandung, Surabaja, and Jogjakarta, the center of Javanese culture.

Bandjermasin is the largest city on Indonesian Borneo. Balikpapan, also on Borneo, is a petroleum center. Belawan and Padang are two important ports in Sumatra, while Palembang on the Musi River is a petroleum center.

Macassar is the largest city in Celebes, and Menado is a leading port. The largest town on Indonesian Timor is Kupang, a stepping-stone in air travel between Indonesia and Australia. Ambon on the island of the same name is the leading city of the Moluccas.

▶ GOVERNMENT

The Indonesian Constitution of 1945 instituted a presidential system of government in the republic. Another constitution, providing for a parliamentary form of government, was unsuccessfully attempted between 1949 and 1959, after which there was a return to the 1945 constitution.

The president is head of state, head of government, and commander in chief of the armed forces. He also has emergency powers to enact decrees that can serve as law. The Supreme Advisory Council is a body set up to advise the president. In theory the president is assisted by a first minister, who heads a cabinet appointed by and responsible to him. The president of Indonesia from 1949 to 1967 was Sukarno (1901–70).

The legislature is called the People's Consultative Assembly. The powers of the legislature have been restricted in recent years. In 1960 the President dissolved it and appointed a new body. This was done to set in action a policy of "Guided Democracy," under which all political parties are regulated by a set of principles formulated by the government. Since 1960 the legislature has been made up of delegates representing various social groups, as well as representatives of political parties.

There are three types of law in Indonesia. One follows the Dutch legal system. Islamic law applies to Muslims. *Adat,* or customary law, is applied mainly in local disputes. The Supreme Court is the highest judicial body in the country.

▶ **HISTORY**

Ancient History. Many scholars believe that the earliest civilization occurred on Java. Skull and bone remnants of a "Java Man," which were discovered in 1891, established that people lived there some 500,000 years ago.

The Hindu Era. Indian traders and priests from Asia began to settle in parts of Sumatra and Java around the 2nd century A.D. They later introduced both the Buddhist and Hindu religions and founded several kingdoms. The most important of these were Sriwidjaja, which flourished on Sumatra from the 7th to the 13th centuries, and Madjapahit, which was dominant on Java from the 13th to the 16th century. Islam was first introduced to the islands around the 12th century. It eventually replaced Hinduism as the major religion.

Coming of the Europeans. The Portuguese who captured Malacca in 1511 were the first Europeans to come to the islands. Dutch traders founded the Dutch East India Company in 1602. It lasted until 1798, when the Dutch Government took over its functions. Several other European countries, including the United Kingdom, France, and Spain, developed commercial interests on some of the islands. They were soon barred by the Dutch, who gradually established a full colony, called the Netherlands East Indies, in the region. From the 17th to the 19th century, the Dutch slowly spread their influence over the entire island group.

The Dutch Colonial Period. During the Napoleonic Wars the United Kingdom occupied Java and some of the other islands for several years. At that time the Dutch Government, which previously had been interested only in trade, began to establish political control. For a century after the Napoleonic Wars, the colony was strictly controlled both politically and economically from the Netherlands. In 1918, a limited voice in government was given to Indonesians when the Volksraad (People's Council) was formed.

The Road to Independence. During World War II initial Japanese military successes inspired Indonesian nationalists. The Japanese also encouraged a great amount of self-government after they occupied the Indonesian islands. On August 17, 1945, after Japan surrendered to the Allies, a revolutionary government was set up by Sukarno and Mohammad Hatta to resist Dutch reoccupation. The Dutch Government refused to recognize the newly proclaimed republic, and fighting broke out between the Dutch and Indonesian forces. Although the situation was brought before the United Nations, fighting continued for the next 3 years. Finally, on December 27, 1949, the Dutch Government granted Indonesia its independence. However, West New Guinea (now West Irian) remained a Dutch colony until the early 1960's, when it was transferred to Indonesia. West Irian officially became a part of the Indonesian republic in 1969.

In 1965 President Sukarno withdrew Indonesia from the United Nations. Later that year Indonesian Communists attempted a coup against the government. It was put down by the Army, and a new government, led by General Suharto (1921–   ), was formed. Sukarno was stripped of his power, although he retained the title of president until 1967. Indonesia returned to the United Nations in 1966. Suharto formally became president in 1968 and one year later began a development program designed to greatly improve Indonesia's economy by the mid-1970's.

ANTHONY SAS
Madison College (Virginia)

INDOOR ACTIVITIES
FOR RAINY DAYS

A rainy day can be dreary and dull, or it can be bright and filled with interesting activities. It's up to you.

If you just stand at the window, looking out at the rain, and ask in a sad voice, "What's there to do?" a rainy day will seem endless. But if you decide to explore some of the possibilities for rainy-day fun, either by yourself or with a few friends, the hours will fly by.

When you're looking for indoor activities, start with your books and games. There's something especially pleasant about curling up with a good book on a rainy day, or you can spend hours over board games like Chinese checkers, checkers, or chess. Card games are fun, and so are word games.

A rainy day is the ideal time, too, to take out games that have many small parts and pieces. With a whole day ahead of you, you can set up electric trains or work with your chemistry set. You can spread out jigsaw puzzles, all your dolls and their clothes, your coins, stamps, or any other collection you may be making.

If you enjoy art work, take out your materials and paint, draw, work with clay, or carve in soap. From clay, which is kept moist in a covered crock, you can make ashtrays or figures of people or animals.

You can make a paperweight by flattening out a small ball of clay, then cutting it with a cookie cutter. Clay hardens as it dries. When your models are dry, they can be painted with watercolors or poster paints.

▶ **WORKING WITH PAPER**

There are many interesting things to do with paper, crayons, and paste, too. You can use an old candy box to make a jewelry box or a box to hold nails and screws. Cut a piece of construction paper the same size as the lid of the box. Crayon any design you like on the paper, then paste it on the lid. Paste a number of small boxes without lids inside the bottom half of the candy box. These make the compartments for jewelry or nails. If you like, you can add legs by gluing four large wooden beads or small blocks to the bottom of the box.

A jewelry box can be made from a cardboard candy box.

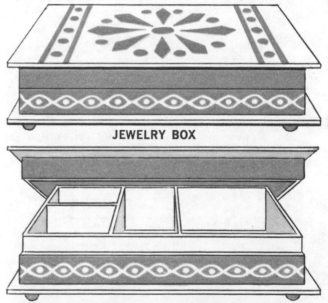

JEWELRY BOX

You and a friend may enjoy making silhouettes of each other. Tape a large piece of white paper to a wall at the height of your friend's head. Have him stand sideways about a foot from the paper. Then place a floor lamp so that it shines directly on the side of his face that is away from the wall. Pull down the shades and turn off all the other lights, and you'll see your friend's shadow very clearly on the paper. With a crayon, follow the outline of his shadow. Cut out this silhouette and mount it on black paper. Then your friend can cut out your silhouette.

Making your own gift-wrapping paper is another enjoyable activity for a rainy day. You can crayon designs on white paper, or you can try this: Take a small rolling pin and a long piece of string. Tie one end of the string around one handle of the rolling pin. Then wind the string around the rolling pin several

MAKING WRAPPING PAPER

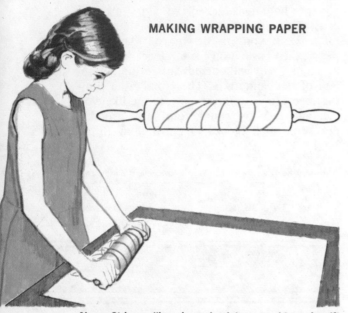

Above: String, rolling pin, and paint are used to make gift paper. Below: Mat of basket-woven paper strips.

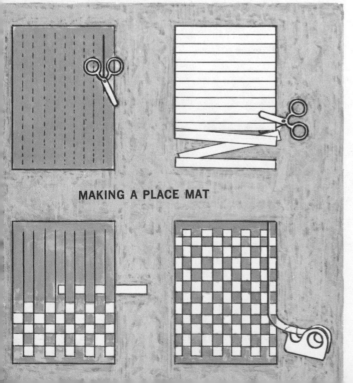

MAKING A PLACE MAT

times and tie it around the other handle. Pour some poster paint into a flat dish or bowl and dip the rolling pin into the paint so that the string is covered with paint. Roll the pin completely over a sheet of paper. You'll find that the string, covered with paint, makes an unusual allover design.

You can also weave a place mat, using two sheets of paper of different colors. On one sheet draw lines ½ inch apart down the length of the paper, leaving a margin of 1 inch all around. Now carefully cut along each of these lines, being sure to leave the margin. On the second sheet draw lines ½ inch apart across the width of the paper, leaving no margin. Cut along these lines so that you have a number of narrow strips of paper.

Then basket-weave these strips into the first sheet of paper. Slide one strip alternately over and under the slats of the first sheet. When you have woven all the way across, push this strip to the top of the first sheet, near the margin. Now start weaving with a second strip of paper, making sure you slide the second strip over the slat if you slid the first one under, and the second strip under if you slid the first one over. Continue in this way until the first sheet is filled with woven strips. You can fasten the strips on the back of the mat with cellophane tape.

▶CRAFTS

Making jewelry from shells or macaroni is another good pastime. If you have two small shells that are very much alike, they can be glued on earring backs to make a pair of earrings. One unusual shell or a group of small shells can be glued on a pin back to make a pin. (Hobby shops have earring and pin backs.)

You can paint uncooked macaroni different colors and make bracelets and necklaces of it. Use macaroni of any shape you like, as long as it's not too large. For a bracelet, string the pieces on elastic cording. Cut the elastic when the string of macaroni is long enough to go around your wrist, and knot the ends together. The bracelet will slide on and off easily. A necklace long enough to slip over your head can be strung on colorful yarn, which is then tied in a bow.

Macaroni can also be used to make a wreath to hold a table centerpiece. Cut out a wreath of cardboard about 1 foot across and 2 inches wide. Glue onto this as many different shapes of macaroni as you can find, so that the cardboard is completely covered. If you like, you can add a few acorns or holly berries. Then spray the wreath with gold paint.

Putting together boat, car, and airplane models is an absorbing activity for boys, and something about a rainy day seems to inspire girls to play dress-up in ladies' clothes, to make dolls' clothes, or to go into the kitchen and make cookies or fudge, or pull taffy.

▶HORSE REINS

A rainy day is a good time to learn to knit, crochet, or make horse reins. Horse reins are made on a wooden spool. You can buy a spool for horse reins, or you can make one very easily. Take a large empty wooden spool. Hammer four short nails with very small heads into one end. Place them at even distances from one another. If you want to make thicker horse reins, use six nails.

Take a ball of yarn and drop the end of it down through the hole in the spool. Take the piece of wool leading up out of the hole and loop it around each of the four nails in order,

as if you were writing small script *e*'s. When you've finished your fourth loop, carry the wool from the center out and around the outside of the first nail. With a thin knitting needle or a large safety pin, pick up the wool you have already looped over the nail and pass it over the wool you're holding and over and off the nail toward the center of the spool.

Continue around and around the spool, keeping the wool outside each nail, picking up the bottom thread and passing it over the thread you're holding and over and off the nail each time.

The finished horse reins, which look like a knitted rope, come out through the hole in the spool. When you have 2 or 3 yards and want to stop, break off the wool about 1 foot from the spool. Draw this short piece of wool through the loop of wool around one of the nails and make a loose knot. Do this with the other three loops of wool in turn. Then your knitting won't unravel.

If you place your long piece of knitting on a table and carefully wind it into a flat circle, you can sew it together with an overcast stitch to make a doll's rug or table mat.

Making horse reins requires only an empty wooden spool, four nails, and some yarn.

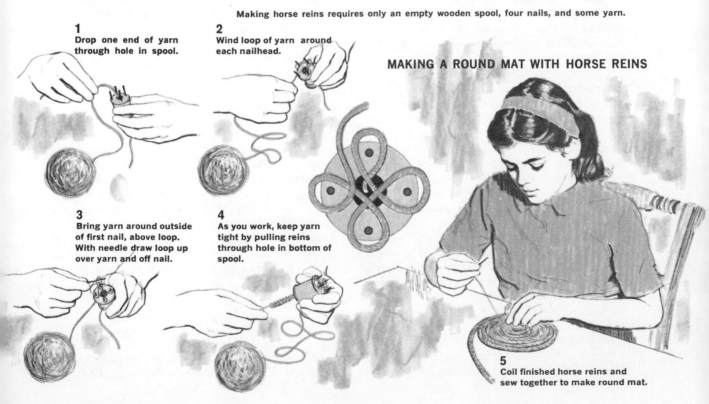

1 Drop one end of yarn through hole in spool.

2 Wind loop of yarn around each nailhead.

MAKING A ROUND MAT WITH HORSE REINS

3 Bring yarn around outside of first nail, above loop. With needle draw loop up over yarn and off nail.

4 As you work, keep yarn tight by pulling reins through hole in bottom of spool.

5 Coil finished horse reins and sew together to make round mat.

GROUP GAMES

In addition to all these activities, there are many group games you can play with your friends if several of them have come to spend the afternoon at your house. These games are good to remember for your next party, too.

To play Hot Potato, everyone sits in a circle on the floor. One person (who is not playing) puts on a record, and a potato or balloon is passed from person to person as long as the music plays. When the music suddenly stops, the person who has the potato or balloon in his hand is out. The game continues in this way until one person is left.

Musical Chairs is a game played in much the same way. Chairs are placed in a circle or a row with a chair for all but one player. The players walk around the chairs while music plays; when the music stops, everyone tries to sit down. The child without a chair is out.

Indian Chief starts with everyone seated in a circle. One person is "it." He leaves the room, and while he is out, a leader, or Indian Chief, is chosen. When the person who is "it" comes back, the Indian Chief starts an activity, like clapping his hands, which the other players quickly imitate. The leader then changes the activity. He may hit the floor or rub his ears. Everyone immediately imitates him. The person who is "it" must guess which person is the Indian Chief.

In a similar game all players stand in a circle, holding hands. The one who is "it" stands in the center. One person starts the game by squeezing the hand of the person next to him. This is repeated around the circle. The one who is "it" must catch a player just as he is squeezing the hand of the next person. Then "it" and the player he has caught exchange places.

In Beast, Bird, or Fish the players sit in a circle with a leader in the center. The leader calls on each player in turn to name a beast, bird, or fish before a count of 10. The player must remember all the creatures mentioned, because none may be used twice. The player who stays in the game longest changes places with the leader.

GUESSING GAMES

You and your friends may also enjoy playing guessing games, such as Coffeepot or Twenty Questions. In Coffeepot the person who is "it" leaves the room while the other players decide on a secret word. It must be a verb, or word showing action, such as *run, eat,* or *swim.* When "it" comes back he tries to guess the word by asking questions using "coffeepot" in place of the word. He may ask, "Do you coffeepot in any special room?" or "Do children coffeepot?" If you like, you may limit the number of questions he may ask each person.

Twenty Questions is also called Animal, Vegetable, or Mineral. One person selects an object and writes what it is on a slip of paper. He tells to which of these three groups it belongs. Then the other players try to guess the object by asking a total of 20 questions that can be answered by "Yes" or "No." If no one has the right answer by the time 20 questions have been asked, "it" wins.

SEARCHING GAMES

The simplest searching game is one in which one person leaves the room while another hides a small object that has been agreed upon beforehand. When "it" comes back he hunts for it, and the other person indicates that he is near it by clapping loudly or saying, "You're warm." When "it" moves away from the object, the other person claps softly or says, "You're getting cold."

For another searching game you need at least four players, so that you can have two teams. One team leaves the room while the second team hides an object that has already been decided upon. It must be hidden so that nothing needs to be touched or moved to discover it. The first team comes in and looks for it. As each person discovers it he quickly sits down without saying that he has found the object. Then the team that hid the object has its turn to search for an object that the other team hides. To add interest to the game, the teams may be timed to determine which one is the winner.

Reviewed by VIRGINIA MUSSELMAN
Director, Program Services
National Recreational Association

See also AIRPLANE MODELS; AUTOMOBILE MODELS; CARD GAMES; CHECKERS; CHESS; CLAY MODELING; DOLLS; DRESSMAKING; GIFT WRAPPING; LEATHERCRAFT; ORIGAMI; PARTIES; RAILROADS, MODEL; SOAP SCULPTURE; WEAVING; WORD GAMES.

In a vocational high school, students learn the fundamentals of construction by building a house to scale.

INDUSTRIAL ARTS

Boys and girls learn about the tools, materials, and processes of modern industry through industrial arts education.

Training in the industrial arts is often begun in elementary schools, where students are introduced to such crafts as pottery-making and leatherworking. In junior high school, students learn woodworking, metalworking, mechanical drawing, printing, and electronics. In senior high school, young people may elect to take courses in communications, transportation, construction, manufacturing, and mechanics. Many of those who decide to make a career in industry go on to college to learn the technology of materials and the structure of corporations.

▶ THE HISTORY OF INDUSTRIAL ARTS EDUCATION

Before the day of the power-driven machine and the great factory, many of the small but necessary industries of everyday life were carried on in the home. Parents taught their children to split logs, to weave cloth at the loom, and in some cultures, to make pottery. Through these tasks children learned about wood, fabric, and clay.

The industrial age began around 1830, when factories started to manufacture many essential products. As society became more mechanized, education in the trades and crafts switched from the home to the school. Around the turn of the century, shops were installed in schools and students were taught to use tools. Today schools are equipped to teach students about almost every aspect of modern technology and the processes of industry.

▶ THE VALUE OF INDUSTRIAL ARTS EDUCATION

In industrial arts classrooms young people learn to use tools, to understand how mechanical devices work, and to follow plans or diagrams. But the main purpose of industrial education is to introduce students to the complicated technology that shapes so much of modern life.

Classes in the industrial arts teach how a

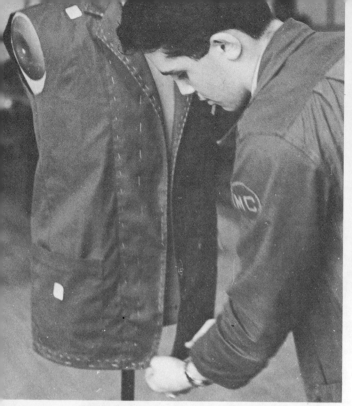

Above: A student in a fashion class makes an adjustment on a jacket. Below: School workshops provide modern equipment for teaching woodworking techniques.

A student and teacher examine a machine part.

product is made. If most products can be bought in stores, why should students learn how to make them? This question can be answered in a number of ways. First, it is helpful to know how a product is made in order to measure its limitations and capabilities. Our ancestors before the industrial age knew how to weave fabric and build furniture. Therefore they knew good fabric from bad, and they knew the kind of wood that was best for a certain purpose. It is very important that we, as consumers, learn the difference between a product of high quality and one that is poorly made.

Another reason for learning to make products is the increasing need for people to use tools in their own homes. Carpenters, tailors, and metalsmiths are growing scarce in the modern age. Their work is in great demand, and their fees are high. Anyone who has learned to handle tools can feel the satisfaction of accomplishment and, incidentally, save a great deal of money by making useful things, such as bookcases, at home. An understanding of how a household appliance works enables the consumer to buy the best brand and, if necessary, to repair it himself.

Just as physical education builds bodies, training in the industrial arts builds manual dexterity. In the shops a student may find that he has the ability to work with wood or metal, and he may choose to make a career using this talent. But students who will be doctors, engineers, and architects need industrial training too; for the shop is the first place where we learn to work from exact diagrams.

Reviewed by KENNETH DAWSON
Executive Secretary
American Industrial Arts Association, Inc.

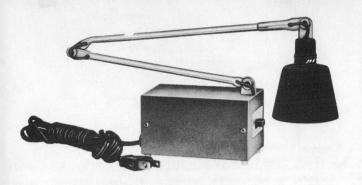

INDUSTRIAL DESIGN

Every man-made object has a design. Throughout history, people have learned that the shape of an object has much to do with its usefulness. As new materials were discovered, and as men learned to work more skillfully with their hands, designs slowly changed. Tools, weapons, utensils, and other everyday objects became easier to use.

When men made their objects by hand, design took a long time to develop. But with the increasing use of machines during the 17th century, changes took place more rapidly. By the 1830's machines of all kinds were being widely used. Products were no longer made by hand one by one; instead they could be manufactured by the hundreds or thousands. Many people could afford things that only the rich had been able to buy before.

Early machine-made products were copies of handmade objects. But the machines were too crude to reproduce many of the beautiful characteristics of a craftsman's product. As a result, many of the early manufactured goods were ugly. The man who operated the machine could not change the design of the object. If a product needed a new shape, someone else had to design it. Then parts had to be built for a machine that would make the new product.

Today these changes are made by people called **industrial designers**—special planners and stylists for mass-produced or machine-made goods. The designs of almost all the manufactured objects that we use—buses, bicycles, boats, toasters, telephones, and pencils —have been thought out by industrial designers.

▶ WHAT DETERMINES DESIGN?

Many things affect the design of objects. Among these are ways of living, the materials

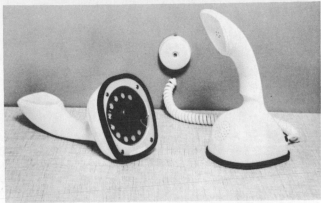

Above left: Small, compact lamp designed by the Tensor Corporation. Above: One-piece telephones, called Ericofons, designed by L. M. Ericsson, Stockholm.

Above: Small 8-pound television set. Sony Corporation of America. Below: Molded plastic and aluminum armchair designed by E. Saarinen, manufactured by Knoll Associates. Museum of Modern Art, New York.

Long-range Boeing 707–320B Intercontinental jetliner.

available for making objects, and the current ideas about design.

A well-designed product suits the age in which it is created. A silver coffeepot carefully made by hand in 18th-century England is characteristic of that gracious age. These coffeepots needed frequent cleaning, but the people who owned them had many servants. It took a long time to make the pot, but in those days the labor of craftsmen was cheap. Today labor is expensive and servants are scarce. A coffeepot of stainless steel suits the 20th century better. It can be made quickly and inexpensively, and it is easy to keep clean. Today's practical stainless steel, aluminum, or Pyrex glass coffeepots have simple, handsome designs.

The life of the upper classes in the 18th century was very formal. Chairs were made by hand with great care. Their value as useful objects was less important than how they looked. Life in the 20th century is more casual. Machine-made in simple designs, 20th-century chairs are planned as much for use as for decoration. They must be comfortable to sit on as well as good-looking.

Science and New Materials

Science makes possible the use of new materials and new methods of producing objects. For example, some 20th-century chairs are made of steel and plastic, materials undreamed of in the 18th century.

As new materials develop, one invention often leads to others. For example, steel was developed by engineers in the 19th century. Because of its strength it became a useful building material. With steel construction, buildings could have a great many stories. But no one could be expected to walk up 8, 10, or 30 flights of stairs. Therefore, to make tall buildings usable, the elevator was developed. By providing much-needed space in a world crowded with people, tall buildings have solved a great problem of the city and have completely changed our way of life.

The Principles of Design

Ideas of what is good design change with the times. By the beginning of this century much of the world had felt the effects of industrial progress. This industrial age, in which almost everything we use is machine-made, has developed its own rules and principles for design. One of these principles states that the design of a product must contribute to its use, or function. Equally important, the materials used must be suitable for the product. A third rule reminds industrial designers to consider the method of production. The taste and skill of the designer guides his use of these principles.

Functionalism. Functionalism in design means that the shape of an object must come from its use. A drinking glass must be shaped so it can contain liquids, stand on a table, and be held comfortably and securely. A car must operate properly in every possible mechanical

way—but it should also be comfortable and easy to drive. Designers also must find out what people want their cars to look like and what colors they prefer. The theory of functionalism was summed up by Louis Sullivan (1856–1924), an American architect. He said: "Form follows function." For example, an airplane must be shaped a certain way or it will not rise or move or float in air. A center of the modern style of functionalism was the Bauhaus, an art school in Germany. Founded in 1919, the Bauhaus helped spread modern design principles all over the world.

Use of Materials. The designer must be familiar with the possibilities of all the materials he can use. For example, because plastic does not break as easily as china, it is a good material for everyday dishes. But plastic melts or burns when it is heated, so it does not make a satisfactory frying pan. Different products require materials of different weights and strengths.

Methods of Production. The designer must also consider the technical problems of making the product. He must make sure that a machine is available or can be made that will produce the article correctly. Generally he must understand machine production and work closely with engineers.

▶ **HOW A DESIGNER WORKS**

When a designer is hired by the manufacturer, he is told about the product that must be designed or redesigned. He then gathers information about the purpose of the product and how and where it will be used. He studies the needs and tastes of the buyers—consumers—to find out what they like and why. He also studies all the similar products made by competing companies. This gives the designer a clue to differences that can be found for a new product or package design. Next he carefully looks at the equipment available in the manufacturer's factory. He talks to the engineers about materials and construction.

When he has gathered all this information, the designer makes sketches of the product. He shows these sketches to the manufacturer. Many changes may be made before the product is finished, and several designs are usually considered. Then **mock-ups** (full-sized models) are made out of clay, plaster, or cardboard. Sometimes sample products are placed in a store, and consumers' reactions are studied. The product is also tested to make sure it handles easily and operates well. If possible, a good designer will use the product himself to see if it performs the way he wants it to. When the manufacturer decides the design is good, a final model is made.

Large design organizations have a staff of specialists—draftsmen, illustrators, engineers, market researchers, and modelmakers—working under the direction of the industrial designer. Some industrial design firms offer many specialized services as well as a "total design" service: designing everything connected with a business from the buildings to the letter paper. Industrial design firms often serve as consultants or advisors to companies that have design departments. These consultants often bring in fresh ideas while working with the company's design staff.

▶ **INDUSTRIAL DESIGN SINCE THE BAUHAUS**

In the late 1920's and early 1930's nearly every mass-produced appliance was redesigned. The pioneers of American industrial design, Raymond F. Loewy (1893–   ), Henry Dreyfuss (1904–   ), and Walter Dorwin Teague (1883–1960), convinced manufacturers that good-looking products sell better than ugly ones. During this exciting period Loewy redesigned the Coldspot refrigerator for Sears Roebuck, Dreyfuss restyled the telephone, and Teague changed the appearance of the Eastman Kodak camera.

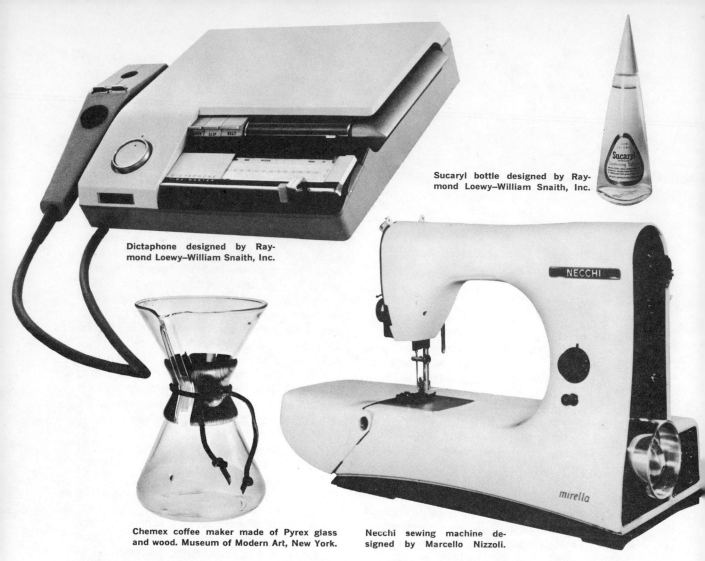

Dictaphone designed by Raymond Loewy—William Snaith, Inc.

Sucaryl bottle designed by Raymond Loewy—William Snaith, Inc.

Chemex coffee maker made of Pyrex glass and wood. Museum of Modern Art, New York.

Necchi sewing machine designed by Marcello Nizzoli.

Norman Bel Geddes (1893–1958) was among the first to use streamlining. **Streamlining** describes the shape of the bodies of birds and fishes. This shape is characterized by long, curving lines that allow air or water to flow easily past the object. There are no sharp angles and few straight lines. Streamlining is well suited to transportation units designed for speed, such as airplanes, boats, trains, and cars. But streamlining soon became a fad. It was applied to all kinds of objects that did not need to be streamlined, such as toasters and teapots. This kind of useless change went against the principle of functionalism. In general, however, industrial designers have improved objects so that they are more efficient and better looking.

Today industrial designers are very active in planning whole shopping centers. They also design buildings and exhibitions for world trade fairs. These buildings must be well designed to accommodate the large crowds who come to see the exhibits inside. Several revolutionary designs for the future have been developed at trade fairs. Many designers worked on the buildings and exhibitions of the fairs of the 1960's and 1970's. Among them was Buckminster Fuller (1895–   ), an engineer whose ideas have made him a leader in industrial design. His geodesic domes, huge structures that combine strength, mobility, and economy, are examples of how industrial design tries to meet the needs of the future.

Reviewed by RAYMOND LOEWY
Raymond Loewy—William Snaith, Inc.

See also BAUHAUS; COMMERCIAL ART; DECORATIVE ARTS; DESIGN AND COLOR; MANUFACTURING; MASS PRODUCTION.

INDUSTRIAL REVOLUTION

The Industrial Revolution began the modern world. It began the world we live in today and our way of life in that world.

It is called a revolution because the changes it made were so great. They were also sudden, although the preparation for these changes took many years. It is called industrial because it had to do with manufacture. "Manufacture" means the making of every kind of useful article, from cotton cloth to brass pins.

The changes in the way these things were made changed the entire life of the people. They completely changed the habits of the workers—the men and women who produced the goods. They brought down prices, so that people were able to buy things they could not buy before. They made some men rich, but they reduced the earning power of others. They gave work to many who had been unemployed. At the same time they took jobs away from many skilled workers.

The changes brought about by the Industrial Revolution at first caused tragedies. The principal change was the sudden introduction of machines powered by waterwheels or steam engines. This meant that manufacture had to be done in hot, crowded factories. It could no longer be done in comfortable homes—with spinning wheels, for example, or hand looms. Furthermore, the machines in the factories could be operated by completely unskilled labor. Children as young as 6 years old were set to work and kept at it for more than 12 hours a day.

These and a number of other bad practices were common for many years. Then the law caught up with factory owners, and the tragic conditions were done away with. This is the way with all revolutions. Very sudden changes always cause trouble until people get used to new ways. Reformers (those who wish to improve conditions) also must have time to bring order into new kinds of life.

▶ WHERE WAS IT, AND WHY WAS IT THERE?

The Industrial Revolution began in England in the middle of the 18th century. This was about the time the English throne passed from George II (1683–1760) to George III (1738–1820). It was in full swing at the time of the American Declaration of Independence in 1776.

It is true that there had been more and better manufacture on the continent of Europe than in England. In fact, the English had imported most of the manufactured goods they used. They had bought tools of Swedish steel, silk from Italy, Venetian glass, and French and Spanish wine. From the East they imported Indian muslin and tea, Chinese porcelain, and coffee and spices from the islands of what is now Indonesia.

In many parts of the world, too, certain kinds of machinery, such as that in flour mills, were powered by waterwheels in the rivers or by windmills. But most of the manufacture was done by hand, usually in guilds, each dedicated to a certain kind of craft. There were many guilds during the Middle Ages. But their development was too slow to be called a revolution.

In England farming and shipping had been the main occupations. Shipping had been particularly profitable during the 16th century. It was then the custom for the masters of English ships to attack and rob Spanish vessels coming from the Americas laden with gold. This gold had built up world trade, and many wealthy Englishmen were ready for new commercial ventures.

On the other hand, farming had become less important. The small farms had been taken into large landholdings by what was called the **enclosure system**. A great many farm workers were thrown out of their jobs. So there was much unemployed labor that could be put to work when the Industrial Revolution came.

Economists and political thinkers were concerned with the condition the country was in. They thought it would be a fine thing if England could devote herself to manufacturing and get her food and raw materials from her colonies abroad.

▶ COTTAGE INDUSTRIES

Meanwhile, there was one industry that had grown up in England and was becoming increasingly prosperous. This was the spinning of cotton fiber into thread, by repeated twisting together of the fibers, and the weaving of cotton cloth. Because the spinners and weavers worked in their own homes, the making of

One person could operate from 8 to 80 spindles at a time with the spinning jenny.

cotton cloth was known as a **cottage industry**.

In some cottages there were spinning wheels; in others, hand looms. The spinning was done by women; the weaving, by men. Agents would collect the thread as it was spun. They would take it to the weavers, who would put it on the loom and weave it into cloth. The agents would then collect the cloth and take it to market. Generally the hand spinning was slower than the hand weaving. This meant that the weavers were idle much of the time.

The life of the workers in the cottage industries was a pleasant one, at least in comparison with what followed. The boss was the father of a family and generally a kind person. The cottage was in the country, with plenty of fresh air. Probably there was a kitchen garden, a pig pen, and a cow barn.

The workers' hours were their own. But when spinning fell far behind the weaving, there was more pressure, and the spinners had to work harder. The girls at the spinning wheels were called "spinsters." They were kept so busy that they had no time to marry. That was how the word "spinster" came to mean "old maid."

▶ **THE WEAVERS FORGE AHEAD**

The start of the great change we call the Industrial Revolution came with improvements in weaving looms. The loom has two elements, or parts: the **warp** and the **weft** (or woof). The warp runs lengthwise on the loom and consists of two sets of threads. These sets are separated, and the weft is passed through them. Then they are closed, locking the thread of the weft in place, and the sets are again separated, but in the opposite direction. The instrument that carries the weft through is called the **shuttle**.

This operation was done entirely by hand. It was a slow operation until 1733, when an Englishman named John Kay (1704–?) patented the "flying shuttle." This was a hollow wooden object pointed at each end and containing the weft thread wound on a **bobbin**. The bobbin could be shot across the warp by a spring every time the warp threads were separated.

▶ **THE ACCIDENT OF JENNY HARGREAVES**

The invention of the flying shuttle meant that the spinsters had a harder time than ever trying to keep the weavers supplied with enough yarn. One day in 1764, so the story goes, a clever Englishman named James Hargreaves (?–1778) sat watching his daughter at her spinning wheel. As she stood up to rest from her work, the wheel accidentally tipped over and lay on its side. Hargreaves watched the wheel and spindle still turning. Like a flash, an idea came to him.

Many spindles might be set up in a row, all turning *vertically* (upright) instead of *horizontally* (on a level), as they had done on the girl's wheel. Then they could be belted together and all turn at once. Half a dozen or more threads could be spun at the same time.

James Hargreaves was a real inventor. He lost no time in constructing a spinning machine in which eight spindles could be turned at once. He tried it. It worked. Remembering the accident that had given him the idea, he named his new invention the "jenny," after his daughter. This machine has been called the **spinning jenny** ever since. Today it is a great power-operated machine that spins hundreds of threads at once.

The first spinning jennies, of course, were operated by hand. But they spun so fast that now the spinners were way ahead of the weavers. Working their hand looms, the weavers could not keep up with the tremendous supply of thread or yarn that came to them. Then in 1784 the Reverend Edmund Cartwright (1743–1823) built the first mechanical loom. This helped to even things up between spinners and weavers. Still, everything was done by hand in the comfortable little houses of the cottage industry. But the wave of invention had started to roll.

New things were being done all over England. Canals were being dug, new mining machinery was being installed, and sawmills were operating. There were even railroads, although the cars on them were drawn by horses. Everywhere there was a new interest in scientific discoveries.

▶ THE FIRST "PRIME MOVERS"

In this atmosphere of change, it was understandable that inventors should think up machines for applying power to both spinning and weaving. But where was that power to come from? Manpower and animal power had done most of the work of the world for thousands of years. They were not enough. There had to be ways of harnessing the forces of nature—the **prime movers**—to machinery so as to make it run without human effort.

Hundreds of threads are woven into fabrics on modern power-driven knitting machines.

The first useful steam engine was invented in the early 1700's by Thomas Newcomen. Engines of this type were used to pump water from the coal mines of England and America.

Waterpower

As we have seen, this had already been done with water in the rivers. In the swift streams of the European continent, waterwheels had been made to turn many sorts of mills for wood and iron work. In England water-powered gristmills, or flour mills, were common. Why not hitch a waterwheel to the new spinning and weaving inventions?

The task of doing this was undertaken by one of the greatest organizers in history. Richard Arkwright (1732–92) was not so much an inventor himself as a combiner of other men's inventions. Arkwright has been rightly called the "father of the factory system." He began by putting the English textile industry—the making of cloth—into factories that were run by water power.

Before Arkwright there was nothing that could really be called a factory. A **factory** is a place where workers and machinery are all together under one roof. Factories speeded up manufacture to an astonishing degree. They have since changed the world both scientifically and socially.

Coal and Iron

England had two great resources that made important contributions to the Industrial Revolution. This, indeed, was one of the reasons why the revolution took place there. These resources were coal and iron, deep down in the earth in the north of England.

For many thousands of years iron had been found in many places: swamps, lakes, and underground. It was dug up and separated from its rocky ore and various impurities. Then it was melted down to be made into tools, weapons, utensils, axles, and so on.

It had been melted—"smelted" is the technical term—by charcoal made from wood. This was easy to do in lands where there were large forests. But in England what wood there was had to go into shipbuilding. There was so little left that in the 1600's the production of iron was severely limited. That meant that the English had to import most of the iron products they used, such as cannons and ammunition.

Meanwhile, it was discovered that coal—which had been regarded as black stone—

would burn and produce great heat. This is not surprising, for coal is really wood that has been compressed, or squeezed together, for millions of years in the earth.

At the turn of the century, around 1700, an English inventor named Abraham Darby (1677–1717) began experimenting with coal as a means of smelting iron. By removing some of the gases and impurities from coal, he created a substance called coke, which burned even hotter than coal itself. When Darby found that coke could smelt iron as well as charcoal could, he opened the door to a new world of power.

Tremendous activity in the coal mines began, and all the coal near the surface was dug out. But when the miners went deeper, they ran into trouble. There is heavy rainfall in England, and deep down the mines were flooded with water. The miners worked bravely at the pumps, but the faster they pumped the water out, the faster it flowed in.

Steam

Inventors came thick and fast in the 18th century. Thomas Newcomen (1663–1729) was not the first boy to be fascinated by boiling water and by the steam that came with such force from the spout of the kettle. Men had watched this happen for centuries, and once in a while someone had done something about it.

A Greek scientist named Hero of Alexandria had made a little steam turbine in the 3rd century A.D. or earlier. But there was nothing, then, for the little engine to do. There was such an immense quantity of slave labor to do all the work that the idea of a labor-saving device was laughed at. So Hero's invention was regarded as just an amusing toy.

Centuries later others had made engines of a sort. An Italian, Giovanni Branca (1571–1640), an Englishman, Edward Somerset (1601–67), and a Frenchman, Denis Papin (1647–1712?), had all tried their hand, but without much success.

Another type of steam engine was the steam locomotive. English inventor George Stephenson's "Locomotion No. 1" made its first passenger run in 1827.

As a boy Newcomen dreamed of doing something about it. When he grew to manhood, he was able to make an engine that really worked. It was not a steam engine as we know it. It was an "atmospheric" engine that depended for its action on a vacuum created by condensing steam.

Newcomen's engine consisted of an upright cylinder with a piston at the top of it. Steam was shot into the bottom of the cylinder below the piston. This drove out the air, leaving only steam in the cylinder. A jet of cold water was then shot into the steam, condensing it into water. When the water was drawn off, a vacuum remained. Atmospheric pressure on the top of the piston forced it down into the vacuum, or, as we sometimes say, the vacuum "sucked" the piston down. When the piston reached the bottom of the cylinder, weights attached to a crossbar pulled it back.

This was the first useful engine. It was clumsy and slow and used an immense amount of coal. Still, it replaced manpower in the coal mines and pumped the water out so that the miners could go deeper than they had before. But it was costly, using almost as much coal as it helped to mine.

The reason Newcomen is hailed as one of the great inventors of history is that he started the practical use of steam power. Scotsman James Watt (1736–1819), who some 70 years later designed his efficient double-acting engine, depended on Newcomen for his idea.

The Water-Powered Mills

While this was going on in the English coal country, Richard Arkwright was busy assembling the various spinning inventions in one place, close to a river. He harnessed them by means of shafts and belts to a waterwheel, which was turned by the river's swift current. As soon as this factory got started, it began spinning its immense quantity of yarn.

Wealthy men who wanted to invest their money built other factories all over the Midlands of England, wherever there was a swift stream. Immediately there was an enormous demand for labor to work the machines. There was also a large supply. These were the people who had been forced off the farms by the enclosure system and those who had been forced by the new factory system to give up their home spinning.

The owners of the new factories, however, wanted to get the cheapest labor possible, in order to increase their profits. They found that tending the machines took so little strength and skill that even children of 6 were able to do it. Whole families were put to work. They worked in hot, often dark rooms, and they were forced to work 15 or 16 hours on end. There were no labor unions to protect the workers. There was much disease and many deaths, especially among the children.

America's Contribution

In 1775 the Revolutionary War began. Not until the end of the war did the English colonies along the Atlantic seaboard of North America become independent states. The war lasted about 8 years before the states, which then called themselves "united," emerged victorious.

Meanwhile, the English mills continued to spin, and the English had to import raw cotton from all over the world. This cotton was known as "long staple" cotton. Before it could be spun, it had to be separated from its little black seeds. This was not a difficult operation. It was done by "roller gins," which rolled the slippery seeds out. Even so, there was less and less raw cotton for the hungry mills.

In America a different kind of cotton grew

Women and children worked hard and long in crowded mills of the early 1800's.

wild. This was "short staple" cotton, with sticky green seeds, which were separated from the fiber with great difficulty. It took a whole day for one person to clean one pound of cotton. This was so slow that the southern landowners where the cotton grew did not bother to harvest it in any great quantity.

This was the situation in the 1790's, when a bright young man from New England came to Savannah, Georgia. There he invented a machine that launched an enormous new supply of cotton into the world. The man was Eli Whitney (1765–1825), and his machine was called the **cotton gin**. In it, toothed wheels drew the cotton through slots that held the seeds as the cotton passed through. One machine could clean 100 pounds of cotton in a day.

Instantly the southern landowners planted fields of cotton all over the South, beginning what was called the Cotton Kingdom. England became the principal market for this new cotton, and the Arkwright mills had as much as they could use.

Steam Changes the Factory Geography

By this time James Watt had perfected a steam engine very different from Newcomen's. He was assisted by a scientist named Joseph Black (1728–99) and a businessman named Matthew Boulton (1728–1809). Watt's engine did not depend on a vacuum. Its piston moved by the pressure of steam upon it, first in one direction, then in the other. That was why it was called "double-acting." Also, the condensing was done not in the cylinder but in a separate condenser. The Watt engine introduced some new scientific principles. It was far more efficient than Newcomen's because it used much less fuel per horsepower.

As soon as the engines made by Boulton and Watt were tried in the textile factories, it was obvious that they were far better than the waterwheels. No longer did the mills have to be built close to a stream or river. They could operate anywhere. They were set up, then, in the cities rather than in rural districts. In the cities the labor supply was more plentiful. The workers could live at home and go every day to the mill. They did not have to be housed in dormitories, as they had been when they had to work far from home.

By this time the textile factories were much larger. Here, too, there were power looms. Everything from the raw cotton to the finished cloth could be made in one place. This worked a great hardship on the cottage weavers, who were now crowded into dark, hot factory rooms.

Working Conditions Become Harder

With the introduction of steam, the work became harder for the workers. The textile factories became hotter and damper than ever. The hours were just as long. Women and children were still employed to tend the machines. The poorly paid workers lived around the factories in crowded, dirty, and unsanitary districts of a town or city.

By the end of the 18th century reformers in England had already begun to expose the bad conditions in the industrial towns. Bills (drafts of suggested laws) were being introduced in the Parliament to limit the hours and to forbid the employment of very young children.

When the 19th century dawned, the writers took a hand. Authors like Thomas Carlyle (1795–1881), Charles Dickens (1812–70), and George Eliot (1819–80) wrote books about the sufferings of the factory workers. These accounts were so moving that the whole English public became aroused. Some employers, such as Robert Peel (1788–1850), Robert Owen (1771–1858), and John Fielden (1784–1849), tried to improve conditions in the factories they owned. But this was difficult to do.

The factory system had laid such a hold on English industrialists that one employer could not raise wages or shorten hours unless all employers did. Competition was fierce. If a kind industrialist put through expensive reforms, it increased the prices of his cloth or yarn. He would be undersold and put out of business by a greedy man who did not try to improve conditions. But when the law stepped in, all employers were forced to change their ways.

▶ OTHER INDUSTRIES

The Industrial Revolution affected many other kinds of manufacture besides textiles. For the making of machines, tools, and engines, huge ironworks became necessary, and these used new methods. When the railways came, rolling mills for iron and steel rails did a large business. Pottery became an important English industry. The potteries that had long been owned by the Wedgwood family introduced new variety into tableware. As more and more machines, too, were invented, there were shops for everything from nails to the rigging of ships. But all of

these industries came more or less under the factory system. Not very much of the domestic, cottage, or small-shop industry was left.

▶ SOCIAL EFFECTS

It is easy to see how the Industrial Revolution changed more than the geography of England. It changed the living habits and economic conditions of almost all the English people as well. Families everywhere moved to the cities to get employment. Country villages were deserted. The cities grew by leaps and bounds. Now that waterpower was no longer necessary, towns grew up far from rivers. Under the new industrial ownership men grew enormously rich in a short time. When labor was paid almost starvation wages, there was an immense gap between the rich and the poor.

The nation was no longer self-supporting in food as agriculture became less important. More and more food, raw cotton, bar iron, flax, and other raw materials were imported. All the time the British Empire grew in size and activity.

After Britain lost the American colonies, it tried to keep the United States agricultural and to prevent it from becoming industrial. Parliament made laws that did not allow English machines to be sold to Americans. Laws even forbade English inventors and artisans to migrate to the new American states.

▶ THE INDUSTRIAL REVOLUTION IN AMERICA

The Industrial Revolution took a long time to cross the Atlantic. Americans were too busy exploring and settling the West to devote much time to invention and the making of machines. American women were still using the old-fashioned spinning wheel long after yarn was being spun by machines in England.

The factory system came to America from England. It was first introduced by an English textile worker named Samuel Slater (1768–1835). He realized that a fortune could be made by the person who introduced cotton manufacture to Americans. Slater disguised himself to avoid being caught under the new English laws. In 1789 he arrived in New York with all the knowledge of English textile machinery in his head. Sam Slater had a remarkable memory. When he got to Pawtucket, Rhode Island, he was able to build a whole factory of machines that could spin as fast and as well as those assembled by Arkwright in England.

But Slater was a kind man. He was determined from the start that there should never be such horrible conditions in his Rhode Island mills as were common in England even then (1791).

For a long time the only power used for manufacture in the United States was waterpower. This was because steam engines, when they were built in America, were used entirely for transportation. Transportation was the great American need. The country was so large that to explore and settle it quickly, steamboats and railroads were urgently needed. Thus it was not until about the time of the American Civil War (the 1860's) that steam-operated factories became common.

The first American industrial revolution did not produce the suffering and abuses of the English one. This was because there was endless opportunity for everyone in the new, unsettled country. Also, for almost a century farming was the occupation most Americans favored. This was true especially in the rich soil of the West.

In the last quarter of the 19th century the United States became thoroughly industrialized. It soon came to lead the world in machine manufacture. At the close of the century labor still suffered from the eagerness of employers to make money even at the expense of their employees. In later years conditions improved. Labor unions were formed to look out for the interests of the workers. American industrialists also made many changes that would benefit their employees.

It is interesting to realize that the growth of the factory system and machine production in the United States started from conditions exactly the opposite of those which had existed a century earlier in England. In England many thousands were unemployed, so they could be brought into the new factory system. But in the United States there was a labor shortage because everyone wanted to be a farmer in the West. The farmers had to be supplied with manufactured goods—cloth, tools, firearms, utensils, shoes, pottery, paper.

This meant that the factories in the East had to have as many automatic machines as possible. These were machines that could turn out goods by mass production. In other words, they could produce the greatest quantity of goods with the least possible human labor.

▶ IN OTHER COUNTRIES

Two Englishmen, William Cockerill (1759–1832) and his son John (1790–1840), brought the Industrial Revolution to Belgium when they set up machine shops at Liège. Belgium's industrialization centered about the textile, iron, and coal industries.

France had become an industrial power by 1848, but most other countries lagged far behind. The middle class of these countries did not have the power, opportunity, or wealth to industrialize. Between 1871 and 1914 Germany changed from a chiefly agricultural nation to an industrial one. Japan began to industrialize toward the end of the 19th century, and by the 1920's it was a full-fledged industrial power. Industrialization did not begin in the Soviet Union until the 1930's, and in India and China it did not begin until after World War II.

▶ LATER REVOLUTIONS

Several historians have written about second and third industrial revolutions. The second is generally believed to have come with the use of electricity in industry, transportation, and communication. The third may be said to have arrived with the internal-combustion engine (in which power is produced by the explosion of a mixture of air and fuel). The automobile and the airplane have certainly changed the geography of the world. The gasoline engine has replaced the steam engine in almost every kind of transportation, construction, and manufacturing.

Whether a fourth revolution will come with the application of nuclear power, it is too soon to say. These technical advances have created almost unbelievable revolutionary changes. Somehow sociologists, economists, and educators must help society live with these changes and keep our world free and peaceful.

ROGER BURLINGAME
Author, *March of the Iron Men*

See also CHILD LABOR; INVENTIONS; MASS PRODUCTION; WHITNEY, ELI.

Automobile manufacture is one of the largest mass-production industries.

INDUSTRY

Nearly all the things we eat, wear, and use every day are produced by industry. A food-processing company produces and sells frozen peas, canned corn, or other foods. A meat-packing company sells frankfurters, steaks, and ham. Companies that make the same kinds of products or perform the same kinds of services can be grouped into industries. All the meat-packing companies make up the meat-packing industry. Other companies make up the food-processing industry, the automobile industry, and so forth.

Not all industries are processing or manufacturing industries. Some companies mine coal; others operate supermarkets. Other companies perform services, such as providing electric power. Transportation of freight and passengers by trucks, buses, trains, planes, and ships is another important service industry. Banks, which lend money for the growth of business, are a well-known service industry.

Each industry has its own special kind of job to do. To get its job done, an industry often must have the help of other industries. The automobile industry, for instance, has to get steel, rubber, electrical equipment, and other materials from many other industries. The food-processing industry depends on agriculture to supply the food that it prepares.

Materials for automobiles and food from the farms must be taken to factories where the products are made. This is the job of the transportation industry—the railroads, truck and ship lines, and air freight carriers. After the automobiles are made and the foods are prepared and packaged, the transportation industry has the job of getting the products to the stores.

Almost all products go through many stages before they get to us. The efforts of a number of industries are involved. For instance, this book you are holding started out as a tree. The lumber industry cut down the tree and shipped it to a pulp mill. The tree was processed into wood pulp, which was mixed with chemicals and put through a paper-making machine. The paper went to the printers, who printed the pages with words and pictures provided by the book publishers. After printing, the pages were folded and bound in covers in a book bindery. Finally, the finished book was ready for sale.

An Age of Plenty

Compared to the past, we are living in an age of plenty. There are more industries making more products and doing more things for consumers than ever before. All of the companies in the industries are competing against one another to make a better product or provide a better service for their customers. Each automobile manufacturer tries to produce the best automobile he can so that more customers will buy his product. Every company within an industry competes against the other companies, trying to get more customers to buy its product. Industries also compete with each other. The trucking industry and the railroad industry, for instance, compete for the business of hauling freight. Airline freight carriers also are in this contest now.

The Effect of Machinery

Most of the giant network of industry is based on machinery. Machines now do most of the heavy digging, lifting, hauling, cutting, shaping, and assembling. In recent years machines have been taking on even more work—in automated factories.

Because machines do so much of the work now, workers have more free time. This has given rise to new industries that help people use their leisure time pleasantly. Boating, bowling, golfing, and other sports are favorite pastimes. Whole industries have grown up to produce the equipment and provide the facilities for these sports. Television is another large industry that helps fill leisure time. Many actors, writers, cameramen, and technicians are employed to produce programs for people to watch when their work is done.

Machines have brought about great changes in industry. The machines are only the instruments, however. The scientific discoveries and new methods and ideas are worked out by men. People still have to do much of the work in industry. They may tend machines, do research in a laboratory, type letters in an office, manage a factory, or do one of hundreds of other jobs, each of which is connected in some way with producing goods or services.

A Company's Income and Expenses

In order to pay people for their work, a company must make money. It does this by selling its products or services. Besides paying its employees for their services, a company has to pay for the buildings, machinery, and materials it uses. It also has to pay for the heat, light, and water it uses, just as a homeowner does.

To make his products, an automobile manufacturer must buy many things. He needs steel plates for the body of the car, axles, wheels, brakes, gears, spark plugs, batteries, tires, glass, paint, windshield wipers, and hundreds of other parts and materials. The manufacturer usually buys many of these things from other companies that specialize in making them. In this way he performs the service of bringing together many different kinds of goods and combining them into a new product. A large automobile manufacturer might set up his own factories to make some of the parts. A company has many expenses other than salaries and materials. In order to let the public know about its products, the company must advertise. Advertising can cost a lot of money, especially if the company sponsors an expensive television show or runs advertisements in a great many magazines and newspapers.

There are also the costs of storing goods in warehouses, insurance, research for new products, shipping, and interest on borrowed money. A company borrows money to buy supplies, to replace worn-out equipment, or to expand the manufacturing plant. All these expenses must be paid for with the money the company makes on its products. In other words, a company's income must be at least equal to its outgo of money.

To make money, a company has to put the right price on its products and sell enough of them. If the price is too low, the company will not make enough money. If the price is too high, customers will not buy the product.

Profits and Dividends

A company needs to do more than just make enough money to pay its bills. It should make more money than it spends. The extra money is called profit. The owners of a company go into business to make a profit.

With its profits a company does many

things. Some companies are owned by stockholders, the people who have put money into the company. The stockholders get some of the profits. They are paid according to the amount of money they have invested in the company. The money a stockholder receives is called a dividend.

▶ CHANGE AND DEVELOPMENT

One of the exciting things about industry is that it does not stand still. As the population increases, there are more customers, and more products have to be made. As people get more money, they want to buy more things and newer kinds of things.

Research workers and inventors are constantly developing new and better products. The horse and buggy was replaced by the automobile. The goose-quill pen gave way to the steel-nib pen, which in turn was replaced by the fountain pen and the ballpoint pen. Old-fashioned hand-cranked phonographs were replaced by electric-powered high-fidelity record players. Inside the record player—and in radios and television sets, too—transistors have largely taken the place of vacuum tubes.

Old industries change through discoveries in scientific fields such as electronics and chemistry. Transistor radios and television sets were not part of the electrical industry 50 years ago, because they had not yet been invented. The textile industry used to make fabrics only from natural fibers such as wool, cotton, and silk. Now the industry also makes great quantities of cloth from synthetic, chemically produced fibers, such as nylon and Dacron.

Competition between companies also keeps industry moving. If one company is making a good radio or electric shaver, this company's competitors will try to make a better one. This means that new ideas and new products are continually being developed.

Before Modern Industry

Today the pace of industrial life is swift. In the past, however, there was very slow progress in overcoming poverty and in producing greater amounts of goods and services. Until about two centuries ago, men had only crude hand tools, beasts of burden, and their own strength with which to provide for their lives.

The work load was lightened a little by the use of windmills and waterwheels to turn millstones and other types of machinery. Most people lived on farms. The farmer's family wove the cloth for their own clothes, and made their own leather boots, soap, and tallow candles. They carted wheat and corn to a gristmill, where waterwheels turned the grinding stones. The grain was ground up into flour and meal. The owner of the mill usually took payment for his services by keeping part of the flour and meal. The supply of money was small. Most farmers ate what they grew. They had little left over to sell. When the farmers took part of their produce to town, they usually traded the farm produce for things made by town craftsmen.

The craftsmen often had workshops in their homes. Most trades were family occupations, the son following his father in the craft. Craftsmen made shoes, hats, furniture, saddles, and other things to order. The blacksmith shaped plows and horseshoes at his forge. Here and there were foundries for casting and forging ironware. The workday in town was about as long as it was on the farm—sunup to sundown. Output per worker was not very high, because almost all the work was done by hand.

The Industrial Revolution

The invention of the steam engine in the 18th century caused great changes. The steam engine offered a ready source of dependable power. Windmills could run only when there was wind. Waterwheels creaked to a stop when streams dried up in summer or froze in winter. But the steam engine kept running as long as there was water to fill its boiler and fuel to burn under it. The steam engine could drive machines to make goods that had had to be made by hand before. Factories began to spring up, and the Industrial Revolution was under way.

By the mid-1800's many changes had been made. On the farm, sturdy steel plows had taken the place of iron ones. Farmers were enthusiastically using the newly invented horse-drawn machines for planting, cultivating, and harvesting. Not only was a day's work easier, but each worker produced more. Steam engines were being used to power the spinning and weaving machines in textile mills, and other kinds of factory machinery. Steamboats and railroad locomotives transported products over long distances with greater speed and ease than horse-drawn wagons.

Inventions and Discoveries

The growth of industry was aided by many inventions and discoveries. The steelmaking process of Henry Bessemer (1813–98) produced cheaper and stronger steel. Charles Goodyear (1800–60) developed an improved, vulcanized rubber. A chemistry professor at Yale University, Benjamin Silliman (1779–1864), investigated petroleum and found that it could be refined into useful lamp fuels and lubricants. Then Edwin L. Drake (1819–80) drilled an oil well in Pennsylvania and showed the way to large-scale production of petroleum.

These were important events, because steel, rubber, and oil are the basic materials of most industrial production today.

As industries grew up everywhere, quicker communications were needed. The invention of the typewriter, telegraph, and telephone helped solve this problem. For lighting, kerosene lamps had replaced candles and whale oil lamps. Gaslights were used in the large cities. In the late 1800's Joseph Swan (1828–1914) in England and Thomas A. Edison (1847–1931) in the United States developed practical electric lights.

▶ ELECTRICITY

Electric power became practical when the generator was perfected in 1870. Until then the only source of electric power was batteries, which were very expensive. The first large-scale use of electricity was for street lighting. Then it was found that electricity could turn motors and run machinery, as well as furnish light. More and more power stations were built, and electric power became readily available. The aluminum industry, which needs large amounts of electric power to refine its ore, expanded greatly. The increased supply of aluminum was used in making pots, pans, and other items. Electric home appliances, such as toasters and irons, began to be produced. Electric vacuum cleaners helped take the drudgery out of cleaning house.

As more houses were wired for electricity and more factories used electric power, larger power stations had to be built. This caused a growth in the electrical industry itself because more heavy electrical equipment had to be built. It also caused expansion of the iron and steel industries, which made the metal for the electrical machinery. Steelmaking requires huge amounts of coal, so the coal-mining industry also grew. The machine-tool industry grew because it makes the special machines that cut and shape metal parts for other machinery.

The Internal-Combustion Engine

While factories and homes were changing over to electricity in the early 1900's, another source of power was coming into use—the internal-combustion engine. The development of this engine greatly helped the growth of the automobile industry. This industry became the largest customer for steel, machine tools, gasoline, and rubber.

Horse-drawn vehicles were replaced by cars and trucks on the highways and by tractors on the farms. This mechanization made it possible to farm more land with fewer workers than before. Small, family-worked farms were bought up and combined into huge farms that produced enormous quantities of crops. Agriculture changed from a small-scale family operation to a big industry.

Machinery and power helped all industries grow and produce more. More food and goods were available to more people. The standard of living of the people—the amount and variety of things they could afford—was raised because of industrial growth.

▶ INDUSTRY AND LIVING STANDARDS

To see what a difference industry makes in a country's standard of living, we have only to look at countries without industry. In these so-called underdeveloped countries the people often are living on the same level as they were centuries ago. The farms do not produce much, so there is a constant shortage of food. There are not enough clothes or houses because these things are still produced by old methods. Most of the people in underdeveloped countries do not have the things they need for a fairly comfortable life. They certainly do not have the luxuries that people in industrialized countries usually enjoy.

Mining, an important industry all over the world, supplies raw materials needed for manufacturing.

To attain a good standard of living, a country must know how to use its natural resources wisely, whether these are water or coal for power, iron and other minerals, forests, soil for farming, or grazing land. Its human resources—its people—must also be developed and used wisely. The people who are to run the industries must have education in technology and business management. The people who are to work in the industries must learn how to run machines and keep them in good working order. Building industry in a country is not easy, but it is worth the trouble, because eventually the people reap the rewards of the hard work.

▶ SOME LEADING INDUSTRIES

Agriculture is the most valuable industry of all. It supplies grain, vegetables, fruit, milk, eggs, cotton, meat, wool, and leather. It also furnishes many of the raw materials for other industries. The food-processing industry turns agricultural products into flour, sugar, canned goods, preserves, frozen foods, soft drinks, baked goods, oils, and dairy products. Some agricultural crops yield chemicals that are used by the chemical industry.

Forestry supplies wood for houses and furniture, wood pulp for paper, cellulose for rayon, and veneer for plywood. Formerly lumbermen cut down trees recklessly, with no thought of what would happen when the trees were all gone. This kind of forestry was like mining, because the resources that were used

were not replaced. But modern lumber companies raise trees like a farm crop, according to the latest scientific methods.

Mining supplies iron, copper, aluminum, and many other metals that are vital for modern industry. Coal, the world's most important fuel, also comes from mines.

The **transportation industry** moves raw materials to the factories and finished goods to the stores. Railroads are still the largest carriers of freight. In recent years, however, the trucking industry has taken a lot of the railroads' business. The railroads and trucking lines compete against one another for business, but sometimes they also co-operate. There are now "piggy-back" trains, which carry truck trailers on flatcars from one shipping point to another. The trailers are then taken off and driven to their destinations. Water transportation is another important way of moving industrial goods. Steamships sail through coastal waters and rivers and across oceans. Barges offer cheap transportation of materials along rivers and canals. Tanker ships carry oil to markets thousands of miles from the oil wells. Overland pipelines are now also widely used for this purpose, as well as for carrying natural gas.

The **automobile industry** produces millions of new cars every year. To do this, it buys tremendous quantities of supplies from other industries. These industries employ many thousands of people. Many more thousands find work in the automobile service industry —gasoline filling stations, repair shops, and garages.

From the frequent mention of **steel** in the story of industry, it is easy to guess that steel is the most essential metal. Giant steel companies mine iron ore, smelt it for pig iron, refine the iron for steel, and roll the steel into rough shape. The steel is sent to manufacturers who turn it into everything from automobile bodies to barbed wire to washing machines. Steel is used to make so many products that it would be impossible to list all of them. Although steel is our most important material, it does have competitors for some jobs. Aluminum, for instance, is often used for making railroad cars. Plastic is a major material for making piping. Concrete is an important construction material.

The **rubber industry** produces materials for

water hose, tennis shoes, machine belts, and cushion stuffing. Most rubber, however, goes into the manufacture of automobile tires. Some large tire makers make almost everything that goes into their tires, the rubber as well as the fabric linings. These large companies may even have their own retail stores, where their tires are sold.

At one time rubber had to be obtained from rubber trees in the tropics. Now most rubber is made synthetically. For many uses, plastics have taken the place of rubber. Because of this, many rubber manufacturers are now in the plastic business as well.

The products of the **chemical industry** are valuable for many kinds of manufacturing. Industrial chemicals such as sulfuric acid, sodium carbonate, ammonia, and alcohol are widely used by other industries. Dyes, medicines, and perfumes are obtained by the chemical refining of coal tar. Plastics and synthetic materials are some of the newer products of the industry. These products are the result of chemical research. No other industry carries on as much research as the chemical industry. New products and methods are constantly being looked for and tested in laboratories.

The **petroleum industry** feeds oil and gas to millions of hungry automobile and airplane engines, as well as to many industrial machines. It also supplies many chemicals to the chemical industry for processing and produces fuel oil and natural gas for heating homes. Oil and gas burners have largely replaced the old coal furnace, which will soon become a museum piece. Diesel oil, another product of the petroleum industry, is the fuel for diesel engines in railroad locomotives, construction machinery, trucks, and buses—and even a few cars. The petroleum industry, in turn, purchases millions of dollars' worth of equipment for drilling, refining, storing, and transporting its products.

The **electrical industry** produces electric power to run factory machinery and home appliances and to provide lighting. A ready supply of cheap electric power is the first step toward industrialization in any country. This is why underdeveloped nations almost always first construct generating plants when they start building their industries. If water is available, dams with hydroelectric power plants can be built. The falling or running water is used to turn turbines in electric generators. When water power is lacking, coal, oil, or gas can be burned to produce steam to turn the turbines.

Modern industry uses vast quantities of oil to keep its transportation system going. Oil barges such as this one carry the oil to freighters.

The large telephone communications network requires constant service. Telephone repairmen are kept busy fixing and replacing poles and lines.

The power that turns the generator turbines is the biggest expense in the production of electricity. Hydroelectric power is the cheapest electricity at present. The future may see greater use of atomic reactors to produce power. First, however, the cost of operating the reactors must be brought down to a practical level. Atomic energy engineers think that this can be done. Some day plutonium, a radioactive element produced in nuclear reactors, may be the cheapest fuel for making electricity.

▶ SELLING INDUSTRY'S PRODUCTS

Many of the products made by industry are purchased by customers in **retail stores**. The small corner grocery, the large supermarket, the filling station, the shoe store, and many other establishments are retail stores. In spite of the growth of the population, the number of retail stores is decreasing. This is because bigger stores that sell many kinds of products are replacing smaller specialized stores. Large supermarkets are taking the place of small groceries. And besides selling food, the supermarkets now also sell household utensils, phonograph records, books, and cosmetics. Large drugstores sell everything from chocolate sodas to magazines to hardware. With huge stores like these selling such a variety of products, fewer stores are needed.

The trend toward larger stores has been accompanied by a trend toward more self-service in stores. It is easier to let the customers walk along the rows of merchandise and select what they want. And fewer clerks have to be hired to wait on the customers.

Advertising is now an important part of retail selling. Through advertising, manufacturers try to make customers want their products before they go into the stores. Advertising also lets customers know that products they might want are available.

Industry in the Early 20th Century

Industry was well established in many countries when this century began, but its growth in recent years has been tremendous.

Since the 1930's more and more highways have been constructed to carry automobiles and trucks. Combined with the network of railroads, the highways made long-distance transportation much easier. Manufacturers were able to do business all over the nation instead of only locally. With many people all over the country eager to buy products and with many people employed and able to buy, companies expanded their operations. As the population grew, more and more customers were available, and industry expanded still more.

Ease of transportation gave a company more choice about where to locate its factories. The company could settle wherever it thought best—near the source of raw materials, near the source of labor supply, or near the best market areas. Many large companies set up branch factories in several places around the country. The spread of industry to many parts of the country helped some small cities and towns become prosperous. When an industry moved into a locality, it brought new opportunities for jobs to the local inhabitants. More farm workers came to the towns to get jobs, as they had been doing since industry began to grow. By this time farming was mechanized, and fewer hands were needed on the farms.

As factories installed faster-working machines, fewer workers were needed. Some jobs became unnecessary. This meant that some people lost their jobs, but other events have balanced this out to some extent. Machines that could work faster turned out more products in a shorter time. This meant that the cost of a product could be lowered. Lower prices usually meant that more people could afford to buy things, and thus there was more and more demand for products. To keep up with the demand, a factory might have to hire some extra workers. The workers whose jobs were done away with sometimes found other jobs in new industries.

Industry at Present

Some of today's large industries did not exist 50 years ago. Television, aviation, electronics, and air conditioning are a few of the new industries. Television was a child of modern electronics research. As late as the 1940's there were few television sets available. Pictures were small and fuzzy. There were

Assembly-line production methods are now used in factories throughout the world.

The transportation industry's facilities are used by millions of passengers yearly.

Many underdeveloped countries, such as India, are now building modern industries.

taken the place of natural rubber for most uses. Plastics are widely used for many modern products, such as shower curtains, squeeze bottles, and chair coverings. The source of most of these synthetic materials is petroleum. In petroleum, chemists have also found substances that are used in glue, printing inks, automobile and house paints, refrigerator enamels, brake linings, and detergents. It is clear that research pays off in making possible new and better products. That is why so many companies today spend so much money for research. A company does not wait for a new invention to be brought in by someone. It hires a staff of research workers to look for new products and techniques.

Scientific and technical research are not the only kinds of "homework" that a company does. It also hires people to find out what the public wants in a product and how big a market there is for its products. This is called consumer and market research.

A company wants the best people it can get to work for it, so it looks for these people. Some companies send scouts to colleges to select and hire the best members of graduating classes. A good education is needed for most jobs in industry today. The time is past when most industrial workers were unskilled. Many industrial operations are now performed by machines or by electronic devices. More and more, the factory worker must know how to operate these machines and devices. To avoid accidents and delays, he must know something about how these things work. Therefore many more workers have to receive special training than had to in the past. Office jobs have increased as industry has grown. Many typists, filing clerks, and accountants are needed to help keep the records of modern industry. All kinds of trained people are needed to perform many varied tasks in industry. Besides the ones mentioned, engineers, scientists, managers, and financial experts are among the basic industrial workers. There are also places in industry for doctors, lawyers, teachers, artists, writers, librarians, and psychologists.

Running a modern company is a challenging job. Many kinds of tough questions come up. How can the company compete with other companies in the same business, including foreign companies that might sell the products cheaper? How should the company deal with

fewer programs for the viewer to choose from than there are today.

The Wright brothers made the first successful airplane flight in 1903. Their plane was a frail construction of wood and cloth. The pilot had to lie on his stomach in the open. Today there are large fleets of jet-powered airliners to fly passengers anywhere in the world.

Air conditioners used to be an almost unheard-of luxury. Now they are standard equipment in many new houses and apartments.

Synthetic materials are also newcomers to industry. Nylon, a man-made fiber, proved to be popular material for stockings and soon took the place of silk. Synthetic rubber has labor unions? Should the company start manufacturing a new product or a different type of product? Should it produce its own raw materials or buy them from someone else? Should it stay where it is or should it move elsewhere? The managers of the company must also decide whether prices should be raised or lowered, how to get money for expanding the business, and whether the design of a product should be changed. These are only a few of the questions that face company managers.

▶ TRADE ASSOCIATIONS

Each company has its own problems, but sometimes the whole industry faces some particular problem. For example, a strike in the steel industry may cause trouble for the automobile industry. Without steel, the automobile manufacturers cannot make cars.

An industry-wide problem can be tackled by the trade association of the industry involved. All the companies in the industry belong to the association because they know that co-operation can be helpful to all of them. The association may urge the government to pass legislation to help the industry. It may advertise its products to help the industry compete with a rival industry. Glass-bottle manufacturers, for instance, may advertise the superiority of their products over plastic bottles. The association may also set up standards of manufacturing, agree on a code of good business practices, or inform member companies of the latest developments in the industry.

Production Controls

Another job of the trade association is to gather information on what quantities of the industry's products are being made and how many are being sold. These figures help the companies to plan their production. When too many products are being made, the supply is greater than the demand. The companies will have to hold off production for a while. Workers may have to be laid off, and hired when production picks up again.

Under the **free enterprise system** of economy a company is free to try to make a profit in the way it thinks best. The only restriction is that the company's actions must not injure the economy of the nation as a whole. So, as long as a company is "minding its own business" and is operating legally, no one can tell it what it should do or how to do it.

Government Regulation

In countries that have free enterprise, industry is not controlled by many government regulations. Except during wartime or national emergencies, the government usually leaves industry to run itself. Sometimes, however, a government may try to avoid the over-production of certain kinds of goods, such as farm crops. If too much wheat is produced, for example, the price of wheat will fall, and the farmers will not get as much money for their wheat crops. The government therefore sets limits on how much of certain crops may be grown each year. Limits are also set on the amounts that oil wells are allowed to produce. Such limits help to conserve natural resources.

Other government regulations are also in effect to serve the public. Meat is inspected by health authorities to protect the consumers. Safety regulations in mines are enforced to protect the miners. The fees that gas and electric companies charge their customers have to be approved by government agencies. There are also laws governing the labeling of fabrics used in clothing, the sale of stocks and bonds, and the licensing of radio stations.

Other laws apply to all businesses. Some of these laws deal with child labor, minimum wages, unemployment insurance, and old-age pensions. To protect the free-enterprise system and encourage competition, there are laws that prevent unfair methods of competition and that forbid one company from monopolizing all the business in an industry.

In most societies a person is allowed to do what he wants as long as he respects the rights of others. The same is true of companies in industry. The final test of any company is whether it does right by its employees, its customers, its investors, and the public as a whole.

ALFRED LIEF
Author, *The Firestone Story*

See also INDUSTRIAL REVOLUTION; INVENTIONS; TRANSPORTATION; articles on individual industries, such as IRON AND STEEL.

INERTIA. See MOTION, NEWTON'S LAWS OF.
INFECTION. See DISEASES.

INFLATION AND DEFLATION

Inflation and deflation are periods of rising and falling prices. Inflation is a rise in prices. Deflation is a fall in prices.

Families, businesses, and government groups are all buyers. The things they buy are called goods and services. During an inflation people spend money faster than goods are being made. It is a period when too many dollars are chasing too few goods. During a deflation people have less money to spend, and so they do not buy goods and services fast enough to use up those available. They spend so slowly that prices drop and there are fewer jobs available.

During an inflation a dollar buys less; a deflation makes it buy more. Of course, a dollar is always worth 100 cents, but if the price of a milk shake increases from 25 cents to 50 cents, a dollar will buy only two milk shakes instead of four.

▶ WHAT CAUSES AN INFLATION?

Even if we knew all the causes of inflations, we might not be able to keep them from happening. Sometimes government spending is blamed for starting an inflation. Sometimes businesses and labor unions are blamed. Even family spending is blamed. Often inflations are really caused by wars.

We know that the economy is working best when everyone who needs a job has one, and when many goods and services are being produced. We know that a slight upward shift in prices sometimes helps the economy to grow. But what happens if small rises in prices continue?

First, a steady rise in prices cuts back the amount that a dollar will buy. When people realize that their money is steadily losing value, they hurry to buy before costs get any higher. Then businessmen think that there is a growing demand for their products. For this reason the businessmen put money into new products, machinery, and factories.

With new businesses growing up, there is a greater demand for workers. Because of this people get bigger incomes. They spend their extra money. These buyers may even borrow money to spend on goods before they get still more expensive. The businessmen see that the goods they are producing are selling well. They also may borrow money to expand their businesses.

▶ WHAT CAUSES A DEFLATION?

A deflation may start when some businessmen discover that their goods aren't selling anymore. They had expected a bigger market. Soon they are not making enough money to pay back money they had borrowed from their banks. They have to close down their factories. When this happens the workers in these factories are out of jobs—with no money to live on and no money to pay debts. Other businesses also are failing, and jobs are hard to get. A **depression** is the period when many businesses are no longer active and many people are out of work.

Inflation affects everyone—a price rise in one field easily spreads to another.

WHO BENEFITS FROM INFLATION?

Some people benefit during a period of inflation. Others suffer. The people who have debts benefit from inflation because the real value of their debts gets smaller. (The number of dollars of debt remains the same, but each dollar is worth less.) It is easier to pay back the debt during inflation because it is easier to earn dollars. Businessmen and real estate and stock buyers benefit temporarily because they can sell their goods at much higher prices than they otherwise could. There are also many more people who want to buy.

The people who suffer during an inflation are the savers, creditors (the people who have loaned money), people on pensions, and those who earn a fixed salary. Suppose a man borrows $100 from his neighbor. Prices double before he pays back the loan a year later. The man who borrowed the money gains $50 of buying power at the expense of his creditor-neighbor. There was a "galloping" inflation in Germany from 1920 to 1923. Prices rose a trillion times and completely wiped out Germany's savers and creditors.

WHO BENEFITS FROM DEFLATION?

Deflation is just the opposite of inflation. The people who benefit from deflation are in a situation just opposite that of the people who benefit from inflation. During deflations, creditors, savers, and people on fixed incomes get greater value for their money. Businessmen and investors in real estate and stocks lose money. Many people also lose their jobs.

Nobody in either an inflation or a deflation benefits for long. Inflations may bring on deflations, and deflations, after a while, may bring on depressions. Depressions spread like a disease from person to person over a whole country. They also spread from one country to another.

HOW CAN GOVERNMENTS CONTROL INFLATION AND DEFLATION?

Before a government tries to control an inflation, it tries to understand what is causing the inflation. If the wrong controls are used, they may do just the opposite of what they are intended to do. There are many different controls that may be used. The most important are monetary policy and fiscal policy.

Monetary policy is a government's deci-sions about the total amount of money being used. By using the powers of a central—or government—bank, a country tries to keep the total supply of money equal to the value of the goods and services being produced. The central bank is effective because it can pretty much control the total supply of money. There is always a flow of money back and forth between ordinary banks and the central bank. If most of the money in the central bank should suddenly not be available to ordinary banks, the flow of money all over the country is also changed. In the United States the central bank is called the Federal Reserve System.

Fiscal policy is the budgeting policy of the government—that is, the way the government spends its money. The government can spend more than it takes in, or it can spend less. During inflations the government may try to spend less than it receives in taxes. When it does this the total amount of money being spent in the country goes down. During deflations the government may spend more than it receives in taxes. With more money being spent, business becomes livelier.

In a free enterprise system like that of the United States the government can help to manage the economy. But it does not manage it in the same way that the United States manages the post office. In most of the economy much power is left with individuals and businesses.

We know that the government is sometimes able to control an economy to reduce economic ups and downs. But how much control should a government use? Too many controls would take away from businesses, workers, and families the right to make spending decisions.

At present, many different governments are trying out many different ways to control the money in their countries. Gradually these governments are learning how to control their economies and so prevent the extreme inflations and deflations of the past.

CARL H. MADDEN
Director, Economic Research Department
United States Chamber of Commerce

See also BANKS AND BANKING; DEPRESSIONS AND RECESSIONS.

INFLUENZA. See DISEASES.

INFRARED RAYS. See LIGHT.

INITIAL TEACHING ALPHABET

Pitman's Initial Teaching Alphabet is an experimental alphabet used to teach reading in some British and American schools. The name of the new alphabet is often shortened to "i/t/a."

The i/t/a has 44 characters, 24 of them the same as the letters we use. Fourteen are digraphs—that is, two familiar letters joined together to make a single sound. Here is the digraph for the long E sound found in "key" and "keep":

The remaining six i/t/a characters are new.

Sir James Pitman, a former member of the British Parliament, developed the new alphabet. (His grandfather, Sir Isaac Pitman, invented shorthand.) At first Sir James called the new alphabet the Augmented Roman Alphabet. By augmenting, or adding to, the established Roman alphabet, Sir James hoped to help beginning readers.

To read English, one must know the 26 letters of the traditional Roman alphabet. While learning the letters is easy for most students, confusion often arises when they begin trying to match letters to sounds. The English language has about 40 basic sounds, but to represent these sounds, the 26 letters must be combined in more than 2,000 ways. For instance, the I sound is common to the following words, but note the different spellings involved: *find, buy, sigh, island, fly, aye, die.*

The i/t/a attempts to lighten the burden of the beginning reader. The new alphabet gives him only 44 visual symbols to learn—the lower case and capital forms that make up i/t/a. These represent the 40-odd sound units that one speaks and hears. For example, the many ways of spelling the first sound in "island" are reduced to this single digraph:

The student then reads "ieland" and "flie" instead of "island" and "fly." With the new alphabet a sound and its spelling remain the same instead of changing from word to word. So it is with other letters and digraphs, all designed to make reading easier to learn.

Students using the i/t/a medium read only books and other reading materials printed in the new alphabet. In the first or early second grades, as soon as they can read third-reader i/t/a material, they switch from the i/t/a to the traditional reading alphabet. According to people experimenting with the i/t/a, this change appears to cause no trouble.

Reviewed by ALBERT J. MAZURKIEWICZ
Director, Reading and Study Clinic
Lehigh University

i/t/a used by permission Initial Teaching Alphabet Publications, Inc., N.Y.

INK

Ink is the material used to record the words of history. Most inks are used for writing or printing. There are also inks for drawing, marking, and copying. There are even invisible inks for secret messages. For different uses, some inks must be very thin, and other inks must be thick. Some drawing inks are actually pastes.

Ink has a long history in many parts of the world. With ink, knowledge has been preserved and passed from one generation to another. People far apart from one another have been able to communicate easily. The words on this page have been made possible by a quick-drying ink. Written and printed documents, magazines, books, and newspapers all depend on ink.

▶ **WRITING INKS**

Writing ink is used with steel pens and in fountain pens and ball-point pens. The color of writing ink must be very strong because the writing line is thin. Inks used in steel pens can be made by old methods of inkmaking developed in the Middle Ages. Fountain pen and ball-point pen inks must have special materials added to them to keep them flowing.

Fountain Pen Ink. The ink for a fountain pen should flow freely and make a smooth, varnishlike line on paper. This ink is made so that it will not dry up or thicken as it runs down to the point.

The ink most commonly used for fountain pens is a permanent blue-black ink. Permanent blue-black ink at first looks light on paper. As it stands it becomes darker and will not wash off in water. It is a good ink to use on important papers.

Most blue-black inks are made of an iron salt, water, a small amount of an organic acid, and tannin from nutgalls. Nutgalls are lumpy growths found on tree trunks after insects have laid their eggs under the bark. Small amounts of dye may be added to this ink to make it blacker.

Since permanent blue-black ink stains clothing, rugs, and other fabrics if it is spilled, washable inks for fountain pens are also made. These inks are good for general household or school use.

Both permanent and washable types of fountain pen inks are also made in many different colors. Blue, green, and red are among the most popular colored inks. Chemical dyes give these inks their colors.

There are some fountain pens that make instant ink. Just as water added to instant coffee powder makes liquid coffee, so water taken into a pen supplied with dry ink makes instant ink.

Ball-Point Pen Ink. Because the ink in a ball-point pen is transferred from the inside holder to paper by a rotating ball, the ink must flow more slowly than other inks. So ball-point pen ink must be thicker.

The average ball-point pen makes a line only half as thick as the line left by an ordinary fountain pen. Because the line is so thin, the color of the ink must be brighter than the color in other writing inks.

Since the ink of ball-point pens is supplied in a separate cartridge, one pen can be used with many different cartridges. Some pens are sold with three or more cartridges of different colors.

▶ **PRINTING INKS**

Printing inks vary with the type of job they are used for. But all printing inks contain pigments or dyes and a carrying liquid that spreads the color out. Printing inks also contain a varnish to fix the color to the paper. Printing ink is very similar to paint.

Most printing inks are used on paper. Newspapers, for example, use great amounts of ink. One New York City newspaper uses over 200,000 pounds of ink for its Sunday edition. One pound of ink covers 100,000 square inches of surface.

A small amount of printing ink is made especially for printing on surfaces other than paper. Metal cans require a special ink. Plastic bags require another specially mixed printing ink.

▶ **OTHER TYPES OF INK**

Invisible inks, also called sympathetic inks, cannot be seen until they are heated or have a chemical added to them to bring out color. They are made with the salts of metals. They may also be made with milk or lemon juice, which turn brown when heated.

During the American Revolution, John Jay, later the first Chief Justice of the

United States, wrote to his brother in London using an invisible ink. His brother also wrote back in invisible ink to tell of things happening in England that might affect the Americans.

Another type of ink is **rubber-stamp ink**. It stays moist on the inking pad but dries almost instantly when it touches paper.

There are also **copying inks** such as the ink found on carbon paper. There are special inks for typewriter ribbons. Closely related to these are the inks used in mimeographing and other duplicating machines.

And there are **marking inks** for many different jobs. Some are specially made for wood, some for metals, and others for cloth. Marking inks for cloth make a clear line without spreading out and becoming fuzzy. They must stay legible even after many washings. Felt-tipped marking-ink bottles make a bright, clear line on many different surfaces. They are used as much for decorative inking as for marking.

Recording inks are much like writing inks with glycerol added to keep them from evaporating. These are used in machines that make records, such as seismographs (earthquake detectors).

One of the oldest inks still in use is **India ink**, a heavy, black ink used in drawing and lettering. This ink is made by mixing lampblack with a gum to give the ink body and keep it from spreading too easily, and then adding water. Lampblack is a dull-black soot made by burning oils, waxes, resins, or other fuels without enough air for them to burn completely. The soot is then collected on a hard smooth surface.

▶ THE HISTORY OF INK

The oldest of all inks are the Egyptian writing inks. Mummies in some of the earliest tombs were found wrapped in linen marked with an ink made of iron oxide. Early hieroglyphics were written with inks made of soot, water, and vegetable gums.

What is now called India ink was actually first made in China in 2000 B.C. It was mistakenly called India ink years ago, and the name has stuck. According to Chinese tradition, a man named Tien-Tchen first made the ink from the soot of tung oil (oil from the seeds of the tung tree) and gum arabic or

---

AN INVISIBLE INK

Carefully squeeze the juice out of a large onion. Add a little water to it. This is your ink. When you have written your message and the ink has dried, hold the paper over a steady flame. The letters will show. Be careful not to hold the paper too close to the flame, or it will catch fire!

---

glue. India ink is very difficult to wash away. In central Asia there have been found pages printed with this ink that have lain under water so long they have turned to rock. The printing was still legible.

By the 1st century A.D., the Romans were making a variety of inks, using soot, lampblack, and sepia. Sepia is the black fluid thrown off by the cuttlefish when it is frightened. Sepia ink dries dark brown on paper.

Medieval monks invented a kind of ink much like our present blue-black ink. They used crushed galls, usually oak galls, mixed with an iron salt. Iron salts called copperas or green vitriol were also used in the Middle Ages to make ink.

In the 16th and 17th centuries, making ink was a task of the housewife. (This was done in those families that used ink, for not everybody could read and write.) In early America women kept inkmaking recipes along with their cooking recipes.

The development of Johann Gutenberg's press in the 15th century brought a need for printing ink. At first printers used the ordinary water-based writing inks. But these flowed too freely and would not stay on the type. Very soon the printers learned that inks mixed in boiled linseed oil worked much better. This type of ink became the standard printer's ink and remained so for over 400 years.

In recent years the boiled linseed oil has been replaced by materials made from petroleum, glycerin, and many other liquids that dry faster and reproduce colors better. Now there are inks suitable for every kind of printing or writing job. It would be difficult to imagine our world without them.

Reviewed by WILLIAM G. BEYER
The Parker Pen Company

See also PENS AND PENCILS; PRINTING.

INOCULATION. See VACCINATION AND INOCULATION.

INQUISITION

"Inquisition" means "inquiry" or "investigation." It has been used, mainly in the Roman Catholic Church, as the name for an organization set up to defend the Christian religion against those who might attack it. The Inquisition was also intended to prevent people from being led away from the teachings of the Church. Before anyone could be declared guilty of spreading ideas harmful to the Christian faith, it was necessary to find out if the ideas really were harmful and why people were spreading them about. Such an investigation was the first task of the Inquisition. The persons best qualified to conduct it were Catholic theologians. These were persons, usually members of certain monastic orders, who knew a great deal about the Bible and Christian doctrine, or teaching.

The Papal Inquisition

During the 12th century many people in the Church thought that persons whose ideas differed from those held by the Church must be wicked and ought to be punished. Such persons were called heretics. A **heretic** is someone who chooses what he wants to believe in Christian doctrine and refuses the rest. In 1232 Emperor Frederick II of the Holy Roman Empire decided that every heretic in his kingdom should be punished—even killed. The next year Pope Gregory IX declared that it was the business of the Church, not of the Emperor, to decide who was a heretic. He set up an organization known as the Papal Inquisition to look into each case.

Many of the inquisitors were good men, but it must be remembered that they shared two alarming ideas that were common at the time. The first was that people whose ideas about religion did not agree with those of the Church should be forced to change them. The second was that one acceptable way of doing this was by torture (because it was also used in ordinary trials of the time). Sometimes a person who would not change his mind was put to death by order of the king or ruler. The inquisitors believed their work was necessary to prevent ideas that were considered dangerous from spreading, wrecking religion and perhaps much of civilized law and order.

The Spanish Inquisition

The second organization, quite distinct from the Papal Inquisition, was the Spanish Inquisition. It was particularly active in Spain during the late 15th century. Thousands of Moors and Jews were expelled from the country, and their property was taken over by the state. King Ferdinand V's idea was that anyone in his Catholic kingdom who spoke against the Catholic faith was corrupting the people and was a criminal. The Inquisition became as much an instrument of the state as of the Church. Some dangerous people were punished by the Inquisition, but many innocent people were ill-treated and killed, sometimes not for saying anything wrong, but for saying things in new and unusual ways. Christians now agree that even if it is right to defend the Christian religion, it is certainly wrong to do so by using the extreme measures of the Spanish Inquisition.

The Holy Roman and Universal Inquisition

The third organization came into being during a period when the old Papal Inquisition was barely functioning and the Spanish Inquisition was a separate institution altogether. It occurred after improvements in the printing press made possible the spreading of ideas through books more quickly than ever before. In 1542 Pope Paul III set up the Holy Roman and Universal Inquisition. This was a committee in Rome whose main task was to warn people about teachings or writings that were against the Christian faith. Occasionally persons accused of spreading heretical doctrines were summoned to Rome and cross-examined. If they refused to change, they might be put in prison.

As time passed, the committee's duty was limited almost entirely to ensuring that Catholic writers and teachers did not spread ideas contrary to the doctrines of the Church. In 1908 its name was changed to Congregation of the Holy Office, as its activities had become so unlike those of the Inquisition. In 1965, Pope Paul VI changed the name to Congregation for the Doctrine of the Faith. He also removed the Congregation's right to act in secret and ordered that accused persons be permitted to defend themselves.

SEBASTIAN BULLOUGH, O.P.
Cambridge University

INSECTICIDES

Many insects are helpful to man, but some are harmful. Some insects hurt crops and farm animals, and some carry diseases. Others are household pests. To control these harmful insects we use poisons called insecticides.

Insecticides are often used on a large scale. Low-flying airplanes and helicopters dust fields, forests, and swamps with insecticides, covering wide areas in a short time. Large power-driven sprays protect orchards. Insecticides in the form of gas, called fumigants, are used to kill insects in an enclosed space, such as a grain warehouse, ship, or airplane.

In our homes we use spray guns and aerosol bombs to kill household pests. Aerosol bombs contain particles of insecticide mixed with gas. The insecticide and gas are held in a can under pressure. When a valve is pressed, the pressure is released and some of the mixture is shot into the air. In small gardens, dusts and liquid insecticides are put on plants with applicators and hand sprays.

▶ SOME POISONS THAT KILL INSECTS

There are two groups of insecticides. The older group is made up of poisons that come from minerals and plants. Many insect-killers contain the mineral arsenic. Three important insecticides that come from plants are nicotine, made from the tobacco plant; rotenone, made from certain tropical plants; and pyrethrum, made from dried chrysanthemum flowers.

The newer group of insecticides is made up of poisons that chemists have learned to make in the laboratory. These are man-made, or synthetic, insecticides. The first and most famous of these is DDT (dichloro-diphenyl-trichloro-ethane).

Insecticides work in different ways. One kind acts as a stomach poison. When a chewing insect eats a leaf coated with a poison of this kind, it dies. Insecticides containing arsenic or a substance called fluorine are examples of stomach poisons.

Another kind of insecticide acts as a contact poison. It affects the insect's nervous system and kills it. Sucking insects that are not hurt by stomach poisons can be killed by contact poisons such as DDT, nicotine, pyrethrum, parathion, and chlordane.

Although insecticides are helpful to man, they can also be dangerous. In nature certain insects are the natural enemies of other insects. In this way insects themselves help keep down the insect population. Some insecticides are so powerful that when a large area is dusted with them again and again, all the insect life in the area is killed. Harmful insects are destroyed, but their natural enemies are destroyed, too. When this happens, we say that the balance of nature is upset. Insecticides, such as DDT, which have long-lasting effects, can harm birds, fish, and possibly human beings.

Sometimes insects become used to an insecticide, and it no longer kills them. Then the insects may come back into an area in greater numbers than ever, because their natural enemies have already been killed off. Use an insecticide only when you are sure that it is needed.

▶ SAFETY MEASURES

Some of these dangers can be avoided by careful use of insecticides. This means controlling the amounts and the kinds that are used. It also means spraying limited areas or spraying only certain trees or plants in an area. Using natural methods of insect control along with insecticides is important, too, where practical. These methods include a plan for the planting of crops.

Insecticides used in the home also have their dangers. A number of them are harmful to human beings if their fumes are breathed in or if they touch the skin. Some contain poisons like arsenic. These should not be used if there are young children or pets in the household. Ant traps containing thallium should not be used where babies or pets can reach them. It is extremely important to read and follow the directions and warnings that come with any insecticide. It is also important for anyone who uses an insecticide to understand its purpose and properties. People interested in this subject can find many publications to guide them. Most city or county health departments will be able to supply helpful literature.

Reviewed by HAROLD R. LEWIS
Director of Information
United States Department of Agriculture

See also CONSERVATION; ENVIRONMENT; HOUSEHOLD PESTS; INSECTS; VECTORS.

INSECTIVORES

Moles, shrews, hedgehogs, and their relatives form a group of mammals known as insectivores. "Insectivores" means "insect-eaters," but these mammals eat other small animals as well as insects. Insectivores are among the most numerous mammals in the world. And they inhabit every continent except Australia. Yet many people have never seen one. Most insectivores venture out only at night. A number of them spend nearly their entire lives underground. Some may live in your backyard without your ever seeing them. Perhaps a velvety mole makes tunnels under the sod as he searches for earthworms. During the night a tiny shrew may scurry through the grass hunting for food—a beetle, moth, or mouse.

Moles and shrews are the only insectivores that live in North America. They also live in Europe and Asia. Shrews are found in Africa as well. A number of other strange and little-known insectivores live in the Old World too.

▶ MOLES, UNDERGROUND ENGINEERS

Moles have tubby, short-legged bodies that are covered with velvety fur. No matter which way it is pushed, the fur offers no resistance to the soil. A mole's front limbs are very broad and armed with strong, blunt claws. These serve as shovels for tunneling through the soil. Moles dig with a swimming motion, pushing the dirt underneath their bodies and behind them. In fairly loose soil one mole can dig a shallow tunnel 100 yards long in a single day.

When the loose dirt piles up behind it, the mole digs a shaft up to the surface. Then it pushes out the dirt in a mound, or molehill. Gardeners do not like these molehills. But moles repay some of the damage by eating many insect pests. Moles have hearty appetites and sometimes eat close to their own weight in food every day.

Because they spend most of their lives underground, moles do not need to see very well. Their eyes are very small and, in some species, are entirely covered with skin. But their sense of touch is very keen. So is their sense of smell, which helps them find the earthworms and insects that they eat.

Moles usually have two sets of tunnels—deep ones and shallow ones. The deep tunnels are 1 to 2 feet below the surface. They serve as underground highways to and from the nest. They also connect with the network of shallow tunnels that moles make just under the sod in searching for food.

Young moles—usually 2 to 5 but sometimes as many as 8 in a litter—are born in the spring, 4 to 6 weeks after their parents have mated. They are born in a nest of grass or other vegetation. The nest is usually in a deep, underground chamber.

Different Kinds of Moles

The common garden mole of eastern North America measures about 7 inches long when fully grown. It has grayish or brownish fur. The slightly larger Townsend's mole lives in the Pacific coastal area. It has beautiful fur that is almost black.

The strangest-looking of all the American moles is the star-nosed mole. It has 22 fleshy "fingers" flaring out from the tip of its nose. These help the mole to locate its prey. The star-nosed mole usually lives near marshes or ponds and gathers much of its food in the water. Both sexes have fat, scaly tails.

Many other kinds of moles live in other parts of the world.

A mole can dig a shallow tunnel 100 yards long in one day.

Star-nosed mole cannot see but feels his way with the "fingers" of his sensitive nose. Note digger's claws.

▶ SHREWS, TINY AND FEROCIOUS

The smallest mammal in North America is the pygmy shrew of Alaska, Canada, and some of the northern and eastern states. Not counting its inch-long tail, it has a body little more than 2 inches long. It weighs less than a dime. A number of other shrews are almost as small.

Tiny though they are, shrews have huge appetites. Meat-eaters, they prey on all sorts of insects and other small animals. Some of a shrew's victims are much larger than it is. A shrew may eat food equal to its own body weight in 3 hours. Sometimes shrews eat twice as much as their own body weight in a day. If they lack food for even a few hours, they may die of starvation.

Shrews are very active, and they burn up their body fuel at an unbelievable rate. The common shrew is reported to breathe at the rate of 800 times a minute—and even faster when excited. Its heart beats at about the same rate. Living at a fast pace, shrews mature rapidly. They begin to shift for themselves when they are about a month old. They rarely live more than a year or so.

Many different kinds of shrews live in North America, Europe, Asia, and Africa; one is found in northern South America.

Almost all shrews have long, pointed snouts, tiny eyes, and very small outer ears. They seldom burrow underground but travel in mouse runways or through the grass. Their grass nests are hidden under logs or other shelter. Most shrews breed two or three times each year, and have many young at a time. They need to bear large families, for shrews have many enemies. Hawks, owls, weasels, foxes, and other larger predators kill many of them.

Many shrews have poison in the glands that produce saliva. Biting a mouse, the shrew paralyzes its victim with this poison; like cobra venom, it affects the victim's breathing. Within a few minutes the mouse usually dies. No other mammal has a poisonous bite like this.

The American water shrew has hind toes equipped with long stiff hairs. These act as webs and help it in swimming. This little animal can even skitter across the surface of the water for a short distance. The hairs on its toes hold tiny globules of air, which help to keep it on the surface.

▶ HEDGEHOGS, LIKE SPINY PINCUSHIONS

Many people make the mistake of thinking that porcupines are the same as hedgehogs. Both of them, it is true, have spines. But porcupines are rodents, or gnawing mammals. The true hedgehogs are insectivores. A number of different species of hedgehogs live in the Old World.

About 7 to 10 inches long, the European hedgehog has a plump body, short legs, and a long, pointed nose. Its tail is only about an inch long. Its face, legs, and undersides are covered with fur. Its back and sides have an armor of stiff spines. When threatened, the hedgehog rolls up into a ball, presenting a bristling surface from any angle. If you are careful, though, you can pick up a hedgehog without hurting yourself. The spines protect it from enemies, but they will not penetrate your skin like the needle-sharp quills of a porcupine.

Hedgehogs live in burrows, which are often dug in a bank or under a stump. Here litters of 5 to 7 young hedgehogs are born once or twice a year. Hedgehogs usually sleep in their burrows during the day. Coming out at night, they feed on insects, snails, and other small animals, as well as eggs, fruit, and vegetable matter. When cold weather comes, hedgehogs hibernate for a while in their snug underground nests.

Hedgehogs.

Common shrew.

Short-tailed shrew.

▶ MANY OTHER INSECTIVORES

Moles, shrews, and hedgehogs are the best-known insectivores. But there are many other kinds as well: solenodons, tenrecs, potamogale, golden moles, and elephant shrews. All of these, except for the solenodons, are natives of Africa or Madagascar.

Solenodons live in Cuba and Haiti, and are now very rare. Looking something like large rats, they have long, slender snouts, long claws, and almost naked tails.

Their close relatives, the tenrecs, are found only on Madagascar. Ranging from mouse-size to about 18 inches long, they also live in underground burrows. Some of them, called spiny tenrecs, are partly covered with spines. Another species, the marsh tenrec, has soft fur and webbed hind feet for swimming.

The potamogale, or otter shrew, has a streamlined body and a long, flat-sided tail, which it uses as a scull for swimming. With tiny eyes and ears that are mere flaps, it looks something like a miniature otter. It inhabits streams in equatorial Africa.

Among the strangest of the insectivores are the golden moles, which are found only in southern Africa. Their eyes are covered with skin, and they have no outside ears, for they live practically their entire lives underground. From 5 to 9 inches long, they get their name from the appearance of their fur.

By far the prettiest of all the insectivores are the little elephant shrews. They look something like tiny kangaroos and have large eyes and ears and very long snouts. Active during the day, they leap about, using their long tails as balancers. Most of them are the size of large mice or small rats.

ROBERT M. McCLUNG
Author, science books for children

INSECTS

Insects are the largest single group of animals in the world. About 700,000 different kinds of insects are known, and more are being discovered every year.

Insects are found almost everywhere on earth. Some live deep in underground caves, and some on the tops of the world's highest mountains. There are insects that live on the surface of the ocean, far from land. Some live in dry deserts. Some live in hot springs whose water temperature is 120 degrees Fahrenheit.

Many different insects have been found in cold, barren Antarctica. One insect is able to live in vinegar. The young of another insect live in salty lakes. Insects can live in a great many different kinds of places. This is one of the reasons they have remained on earth for over 300,000,000 years.

Most insects are very small. Only a few kinds grow to more than 1 or 2 inches. Some are so tiny that they can hardly be seen. But the largest ones are bigger than some mice.

The small size of insects makes it possible for them to escape their enemies by crawling into cracks or other hiding places. And because they are so small, they need very little food and water to live. Thus their small size is a very great advantage.

▶ WHAT IS AN INSECT?

All adult insects have six legs, three on each side of their bodies. This is the one sure way to tell an insect. Each insect's body has three main parts—a **head**, a **thorax**, and an **abdomen**. Insects also have one pair of feelers, or antennae, at the front of the head. Most insects have one or two pairs of wings.

Look carefully at a spider and count its legs. There are eight of them. Its body has two parts instead of three. A spider, therefore, is not an insect. The close relative of the spider, the scorpion, also has eight legs. It is not an insect either. Neither are the many-legged centipede and millipede.

MAIN EXTERNAL BODY PARTS OF AN INSECT

ANTENNA
HEAD
EYES
LEG
WING
THORAX
LEG
LEG
ABDOMEN

Although very different looking, these animals are all insects. Each has six legs; a body divided into three main parts; two large compound eyes, one on either side of the head; two pairs of wings; and a pair of feelers (antennae) on its head.

Grasshopper.

Leaf bug.

Ground beetle.

Peacock butterfly.

▶ THE INSECT'S OUTSIDE APPEARANCE

If you can do so, catch a grasshopper and examine it. The grasshopper is a typical insect. See if you can find the three sections of the body.

The antennae at the front of the head are easy to see. Although the head is small, you should be able to see the eyes. You will have to look closely to see the mouth unless the grasshopper is chewing.

The thorax is next to the head. The wings and the three pairs of legs are attached to it. There are powerful muscles in the thorax, which you cannot see without cutting the insect open. These muscles control the movements of the legs and wings.

The hind portion of the insect's body is the abdomen. It is the biggest part of the body. The abdomen is in sections, or segments, that look like rings attached together at the rims. This makes the insect's body flexible—that is, it can bend and twist easily.

The mating and egg-laying organs are at the tip of the abdomen. Some insects also have another set of feelers, called **cerci**, at the end of the abdomen. Silverfish and many water insects have large cerci.

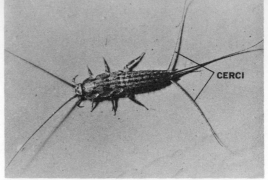

Some insects, like the silverfish, have an extra set of feelers, called cerci, at the end of their bodies.

The Outside Skeleton

A tough outer coat covers the grasshopper's body. Most insects have such a coat. This is the insect's skeleton. It is like a shell enclosing the insect. It covers the soft parts of the body and supports them. Did you ever see an insect collection? What you saw were the outside skeletons of the insects with the wings attached.

Most insects have tiny hairs, or spines, growing out from the skeleton. Such hairs are often also found on the legs, the antennae, and the mouthparts. The skeleton is firm but lightweight, and so does not hamper the insect's flight.

The skeleton is made of a waterproof

Although they appear at first glance to resemble insects, these animals are quite different. All have two-part bodies. The number of legs ranges from eight on the spider to hundreds on some millipedes. None has the large compound eyes of an insect. Upper left: Garden spider lacks antennae of an insect and has eight legs. Upper right: House centipede has a pair of legs on almost all of its body segments. Lower left: Millipede has two pairs of legs on most body segments. Lower right: A scorpion, like a spider, has eight legs. Its body ends with a sharp poison stinger.

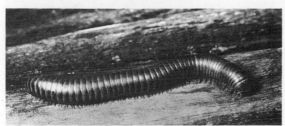

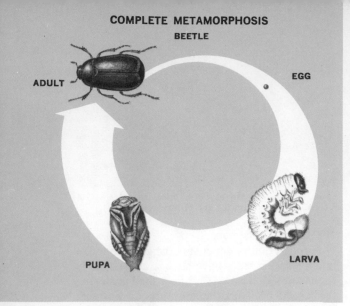

COMPLETE METAMORPHOSIS
BEETLE

ADULT

EGG

PUPA

LARVA

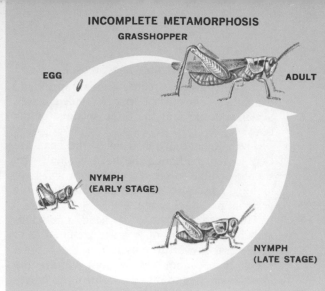

INCOMPLETE METAMORPHOSIS
GRASSHOPPER

EGG

ADULT

NYMPH
(EARLY STAGE)

NYMPH
(LATE STAGE)

substance. This is a great help to the insect because it prevents water from soaking into its body. It also keeps the body from drying out. This outside skeleton, therefore, makes it possible for insects to live through long periods of wet or dry weather.

The hard outer shell protects the insect in other ways as well. It helps keep out germs. The shell acts as a shock absorber and as a shield against too much heat or cold. It also protects the insect from some of its enemies.

▶ HOW INSECTS DEVELOP

Most insects hatch from tiny eggs. Insect eggs are of many shapes. Some are long and oval; others are round like a ball. They often show beautiful surface markings and color patterns when seen through a magnifying glass.

Some insects lay only one egg at a time. Others, like termites, lay 10,000 or more in a day. They may lay this large number of eggs several times each year. Certain insects deposit large clusters of eggs in a protective case. The praying mantis and the cockroach are such insects.

Most insects go through several distinct forms as they grow from egg to adult. This method of growth is called metamorphosis. The word "metamorphosis" means "change in shape."

The Insect Larva

The young that hatch out of most insect eggs are called **larvae** (singular: larva). They look like worms and are sometimes incorrectly called worms. The "worm" in an apple or a tomato is really a larva.

You have probably seen caterpillars. They are the larvae of moths and butterflies. You may find it hard to think of a crawling caterpillar as the young of a butterfly. It does not look at all like the adult. The same thing is true of most insects. Their larvae sometimes have more than three pairs of legs. They have no wings. And their mouths and other body parts are quite different from those of the adult.

As soon as a larva hatches out of the egg, it begins to eat. It eats constantly, biting and chewing its food with powerful jaws. Its appetite never seems to be satisfied. It grows very rapidly, but its outer skin does not grow with it. Instead, the larva molts, or sheds its skin when it becomes too tight. Each time a new and bigger skin grows in place of the old one.

The Pupa

When a larva is full-grown, it stops eating. It attaches itself to a leaf, the bark of a tree, or some other suitable place, and goes through a resting stage. This is called the pupal stage or **pupa**. A moth larva spins a **cocoon** around itself before becoming a pupa. A butterfly develops a shiny covering through which you can often see the body parts. The butterfly pupa is called a **chrysalis**. Other larvae develop a hard coat, or pupal case, as protection.

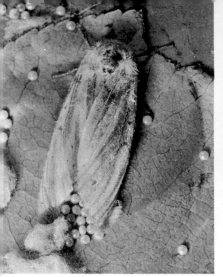

Left: Gypsy moth covers eggs with scales from its own body. Center: Spittlebug produces a mass of bubbles to cover its eggs. Right: Newly hatched praying mantises scramble from egg cases.

The Adult

An insect may remain in the pupal stage for several weeks. Many kinds remain in this stage all winter. Meanwhile great changes take place within the insect's body. The parts of the body develop and fit it for life as an **adult**. When these changes are complete, the pupal case splits and the adult insect crawls forth. In a few hours its body dries out. If it is a winged insect, it is ready for flight.

Butterflies, moths, bees, ants, wasps, and beetles all develop in this way. All go through the egg, larval, pupal, and adult stages. Scientists say these insects go through a **complete metamorphosis**. But many insects skip some of these stages. Those that do are said to go through an **incomplete**, or **gradual**, **metamorphosis**.

Incomplete Metamorphosis

Grasshoppers, crickets, cicadas, and dragonflies are among the insects that go through an incomplete metamorphosis. When the young hatches from the egg, it looks like the adult except that it is smaller and has no wings. It is called a **nymph**.

Larva of the swallowtail butterfly spins chrysalis about itself. Larva lacks the compound eyes and wings of the adult.

As the nymph grows, it molts when its skin becomes too tight. Tiny wings appear, which grow larger with each molt. With the last molt the wings become full size, and the insect is now an adult. Some insects with incomplete metamorphosis never develop wings. Lice and some crickets are examples of these.

How Long Do Insects Live?

There is no average length of life for adult insects as a group. The life of one kind of

Left: Cecropia moth larva spins its silken cocoon on a twig. Center: Chrysalis of monarch butterfly hangs by a thread from a leaf. Right: Pupa of common housefly.

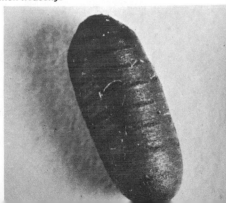

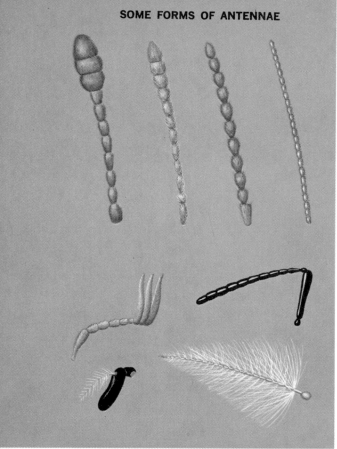

Insects feel, smell, and taste with their antennae. For some insects, antennae also serve as ears.

insect may be very short. Mayflies, for example, live for less than a day. During that time they do not eat. They mate, lay their eggs, and die. Most adult moths and butterflies live for only a few days or weeks.

Some insects live for one summer; some live for several years. Probably the insect with the longest life is the queen of one kind of termite that lives in the tropics. Some scientists think

this queen termite may live for as long as 50 years.

▶ THE INSECT'S SENSES

Insects have special organs for sensing the world around them, just as you have. The parts of an insect that receive sensation are called **receptors**. Insects' receptors are very different from our sense organs. For example, insects' "ears" are not found on their heads. Insects have no nostrils for smelling, yet their sense of smell is much stronger than that of a human being.

The Antennae

The antennae are remarkable sensation receptors. There are many different sizes and shapes of antennae among insects. All insect antennae are jointed, but some look like little knobs on the head of the insect. Others, such as those of the grasshopper, look like tiny strings of beads. The antennae of many moths are like waving feathers; butterfly antennae have clubbed tips.

Watch an insect as its antennae wave about in the air or feel the surface on which it is standing. The insect can feel, smell, and taste with its antennae. Some insects, such as the male mosquito, can hear with them. Insects use their antennae to feel whether a surface is wet or dry, smooth or rough, hot or cold. They also use them to sense the outside temperature and the humidity. Bloodsucking insects can sense the difference in temperature between an animal's body and the surrounding air with their antennae. This is how these insects find their victims.

The antennae contain most of the insect's smell receptors. Thousands of tiny cells on the

Insects see with three simple eyes on top of head (*left*) and two compound eyes, made up of many tiny lenses (*center*). Complete image of object—such as flower (*right*)—is formed in brain, which combines separate images sent to it from lenses.

antennae receive odors that inform the insect of a food supply. For example, flies smell the odors given off by decaying plants and animals. Cabbage butterflies smell the odor given off by cabbage leaves. Ants find their way to a source of food supply by scent trails left by other ants in their colony.

Smell helps insects find the right kind of plant or animal on which to lay their eggs. It also helps them spot a natural enemy. The antennae of male insects can detect the scent of a female of the same kind, sometimes at a distance of more than a mile. In some insects the feet, mouthparts, and hairs on the skeleton are also sensitive to smell.

How an Insect Sees

Adult insects have **compound eyes**, made of many individual lenses called facets. You can see these if you examine a grasshopper's eye with a magnifying glass. The eyes of some insects have as few as nine facets each; the housefly's have 4,000; some dragonflies' eyes have 28,000.

Scientists have found a way of taking photographs through the lenses of the insect's compound eye. These photographs picture what an insect probably sees. They show that each facet sees a separate image of only a part of the object. Nerves going from each facet carry these separate images to the brain, where they are combined into one complete image. The more facets there are in the eye, the sharper is the complete image. But all insects are nearsighted. They cannot see an object clearly if it is farther than 2 or 3 feet away.

Each insect has two compound eyes. In most insects the eyes are on the sides of the head. This position of the eyes makes it possible for these insects to see in most directions. They are particularly able to detect moving objects.

Insects can see some colors. Plant-eating insects are especially sensitive to green. Butterflies that gather nectar from red and yellow flowers are more sensitive to these colors. Some insects, such as the honeybee, are able to see certain colors that the human eye cannot see. But the honeybee cannot see some colors that we can. Red looks like black to the honeybee.

Most adult insects have another set of eyes.

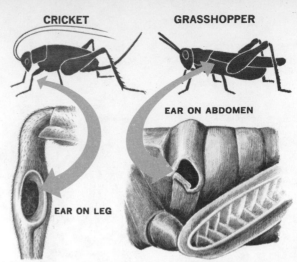

CRICKET   GRASSHOPPER

EAR ON ABDOMEN

EAR ON LEG

Ears never are found on an insect's head—they are usually on its legs or abdomen.

These are three simple eyes, each with one lens. They are called **ocelli**. The ocelli are set in the form of a triangle at the top of the head. Scientists think these simple eyes do not actually see an image, but can only detect motion. The ocelli probably make an insect's compound eyes more sensitive to light.

Taste and Feel

Tiny hairs on the mouthparts and the antennae contain most of the insect's taste receptors. Many insects taste with their feet as well—these insects can taste food by walking on it.

The hairs on the insect's skeleton, feet, and antennae are very sensitive feelers. Many insects have hairs on their abdomen that are also feel receptors. The receptors on the abdomen can sense vibrations in the earth when an insect is on the ground. They sense air currents when the insect is in flight.

Some insects have feel receptors on their wings. The receptors can sense that a solid object is approaching by the way air is displaced as the object moves. This is how a fly can sense that you are trying to swat it and why it darts away.

The Insect's Ears

Some insects locate the opposite sex for mating by means of sound. The organs for hearing, or "ears," are never found on an insect's head. The head is too small to contain organs of hearing.

Ears are found on different parts of the body in many different insects. For example, a grasshopper's ears are on the sides of the

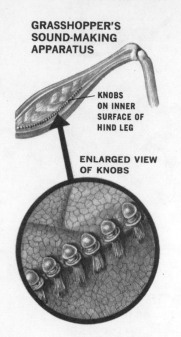

GRASSHOPPER'S SOUND-MAKING APPARATUS

KNOBS ON INNER SURFACE OF HIND LEG

ENLARGED VIEW OF KNOBS

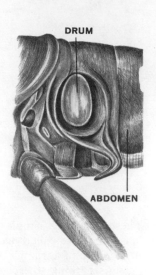

CICADA'S SOUND-MAKING APPARATUS

DRUM

ABDOMEN

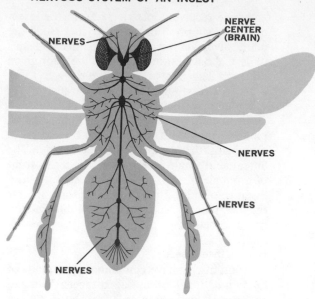

NERVOUS SYSTEM OF AN INSECT

NERVES

NERVE CENTER (BRAIN)

NERVES

NERVES

NERVES

abdomen, underneath the wings. The ears are small, round disks that pick up sound vibrations and send them to nerves inside the body. Some moths also have this type of ear. There are simple ears near the tips of the antennae of many other insects. In many insects some of the hairs on the body are also sensitive to sound.

Some butterflies and moths are deaf. But other insects, such as the katydid, can hear sounds that the human ear cannot.

▶ HOW INSECTS MAKE SOUNDS

Insects make sounds that carry messages to other insects of the same kind. The ears of each kind of insect can pick out the sound intended for it. The sounds are usually mating calls made by the male to attract the female. But with mosquitoes the female makes the sound to attract the male. Sometimes males make sounds to drive off rival males or to frighten away enemies.

A beekeeper can tell by the way the bees buzz whether they are angry or contented. Some ants, also, make sounds, probably as danger warnings to other ants in the colony.

Insects do not have voices, as we do. Most insect calls, or "songs," are made by the rubbing of one part of the insect's body against another. The katydid is a good example of an insect that "sings" in this way. This insect's sound-making apparatus is located on the two front wings. A series of notches, called

the **file**, is on the left wing. A part of the right wing is hardened to form a **scraper**.

When ready to sing, the katydid raises its front wings and moves them rapidly in and out. This causes the scraper to saw back and forth across the file, something like the way a violin bow scrapes across the strings. The sounds produced by the katydid's wings are carried through the air to the ears of any female katydid that may be nearby.

Some grasshoppers have little knobs on the inner surface of their hind legs. The insect makes sounds by rubbing these hard knobs against the hard edge of the front wings.

Cicadas have a different way of making sounds. Their songs are made with drums. The drum is in the abdomen of the male. Muscles attached to the drumhead pull it in and then let it snap back. This is done very quickly—sometimes as fast as 480 times a second. The shrill buzzing song of cicadas fills the air on a summer evening and can be heard a long way.

▶ THE INSECT'S NERVOUS SYSTEM

An insect has nerves and a brain to switch sensations it receives into action. But an insect's actions are automatic.

For example, an insect cannot think, "Danger is approaching; I must fly away." Instead it feels a certain kind of air current on its body. Feel receptors send the sensation to nerve centers. The nerve centers automatically cause certain muscles to contract. This contraction makes the wings move, and the insect flies away.

A large nerve center in the head is the insect's brain. The more intelligent the insect is, the larger the brain. A honeybee, for example, has a larger brain than a beetle of the same size. Nerve branches go from the brain to the eyes and the antennae. When an insect smells suitable food with its antennae, nerves from the receptors send the message to the brain. The brain in turn sends a message through nerves to the legs or wings, and the insect moves toward the food.

▶ WHAT INSECTS EAT

Insects eat many different kinds of material. Wood, paintbrushes, pepper, vinegar, wine-bottle corks, wool, paper, flour, mushrooms, bits of meat, and decayed matter are only a few of them. Some bore into plants and suck their juice. Some bite off pieces of leaves and can strip a plant bare. Bees and most butterflies and moths sip nectar from flowers and eat pollen, without harming the plant.

Many insects hunt other insects for food. The little orange and black ladybird beetle is one of these. It eats tremendous numbers of aphids, which it finds on plants. The praying mantis is another. Almost any insect is food for the mantis. Often, after mating, the female even eats the male. And as the young hatch out of the case, some of them devour the others. But the praying mantis is harmless to man. In fact, it is useful because it destroys many garden pests.

You may have seen dragonflies darting about over ponds, catching small gnats and mosquitoes. The giant waterbugs, which may be up to 4 inches long, kill tadpoles, minnows, and small frogs, as well as other insects, for food. Hunting wasps capture insects of various kinds and store them in their nests. These serve as food for the wasps' larvae.

There are insects, such as the female mosquito, that pierce the skin of other animals and suck drops of their blood for food. There are others, such as the cattle grub, that live inside another animal's body. A number of insects lay their eggs right on the body of other

Ladybird beetle, or "ladybug," eating aphids.

A dragonfly chases a gnat.

Cocoons of braconid wasp cover body of moth larva.

A female praying mantis eats its mate.

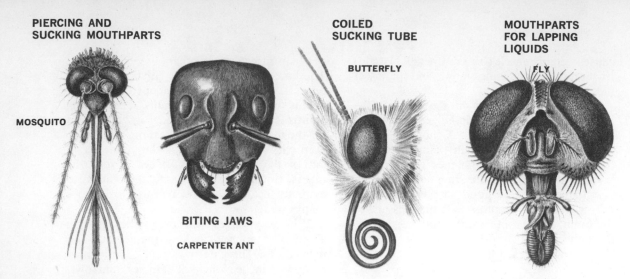

PIERCING AND
SUCKING MOUTHPARTS

MOSQUITO

BITING JAWS

CARPENTER ANT

COILED
SUCKING TUBE

BUTTERFLY

MOUTHPARTS
FOR LAPPING
LIQUIDS

FLY

An insect's mouthparts are suited to its diet.

insects. When the eggs hatch, the larvae start eating the insect.

Some insects, like the cockroach, eat almost anything. But most insects will eat only one kind of food. The caterpillar of the monarch butterfly, for example, eats only milkweed leaves. It will starve to death if it cannot get these leaves. The caterpillar of a cabbage butterfly eats the leaves of plants in the cabbage family. It will also eat nasturtium leaves, because these contain an oil like that in the leaves of the cabbage family.

Termites are destructive wood-eaters. They get into damp wood through the ground. As they eat they bore tunnels inside the wood. They cannot live in daylight, so they never bore through to the surface. They may leave the inside of a wooden fence post hollow, while the outside seems firm. Often there is only one way of knowing that termites have attacked a post. This is when it collapses.

How Insects Are Able To Get Their Food

The feeding habits of an insect depend upon its mouthparts. Insects that have powerful jaws bite and chew their food. Grasshoppers, beetles, cockroaches, and ants are examples of such insects. The mouthparts of some insects are developed into a hollow tube like a soda straw. These insects suck plant juices. Butterflies and moths have very long sucking tubes. When not in use the tubes are coiled beneath the insect's head.

Many insects have different mouthparts at different stages in their lives. For example, the caterpillar of the monarch butterfly has biting

and chewing jaws, with which it eats milkweed leaves. During the pupal stage the mouthparts change to the sucking tube of the adult.

The hollow tubes of bloodsucking insects are like sharp, hollow needles. When a bloodsucking insect bites, saliva from glands in the mouthparts is injected under the victim's skin. The saliva prevents blood from clotting at the puncture until the insect has finished its meal. A chemical in the saliva causes the sting and the swelling of a mosquito bite.

Some kinds of flies and mosquitoes carry disease germs in their saliva. When these insects bite, they inject the disease germs into a person's body. Malaria and yellow fever are spread in this way.

The fact that the larva seldom eats the same food as the adult is a great help in insect survival. The adult does not eat the larva's food supply. The larva does not have to compete with the adult for food.

Digesting the Food

An insect's body cannot use food as it is eaten. The food must first be changed in order for the body to be able to absorb and use it. The process by which this is done is called digestion. Insects, like most animals, have a special digestive system for this purpose.

The insect's digestive system is a hollow tube that goes from the mouth to an opening in the tip of the abdomen. Near the head of the tube are little saclike projections; these are the salivary glands. The glands pour saliva into the mouth. Saliva contains a chemical that starts to digest the food.

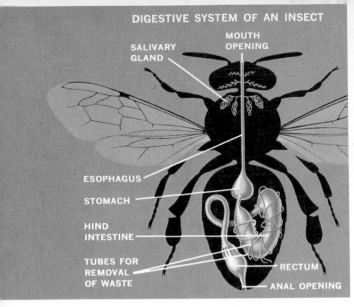

SALIVARY GLAND

MOUTH OPENING

ESOPHAGUS

STOMACH

HIND INTESTINE

TUBES FOR REMOVAL OF WASTE

RECTUM

ANAL OPENING

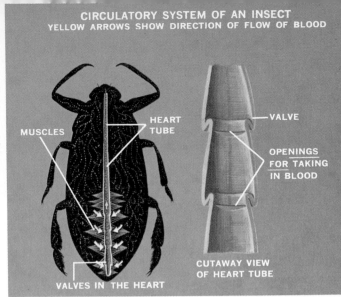

MUSCLES

HEART TUBE

VALVE

OPENINGS FOR TAKING IN BLOOD

VALVES IN THE HEART

CUTAWAY VIEW OF HEART TUBE

The tube is widened out in several places to form digestive organs. One of these is the stomach. A number of glands pour digestive juices into the stomach. This is where most of the food is digested.

The last part of the digestive tube is called the hind intestine. Digested food passes from the stomach into the hind intestine. The food is absorbed into the blood through the intestine wall.

Slender tubes are attached to the hind intestine. These tubes remove waste material from the blood and empty it into the hind intestine. From there the waste is carried out of the insect's body along with other wastes from the digestive system.

▶ THE INSECT'S BLOOD SYSTEM

An insect's blood is not red like ours. Our blood contains a red chemical, hemoglobin, that carries oxygen throughout the body. The

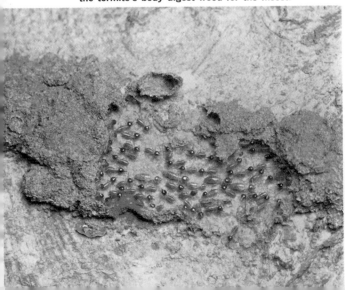

Termites eating through a tree trunk. Tiny animals inside the termite's body digest wood for the insect.

oxygen-hemoglobin combination gives our blood its bright-red color. An insect's blood does not carry oxygen; therefore it does not need hemoglobin. Its blood is usually clear instead of red. Sometimes it is a yellowish or greenish color.

The insect's heart is part of a long tube running along the top of the body, right under the skin. The tube opens just under the brain. There are tiny openings with valves along this tubelike heart. Blood is sucked into the heart through these openings. The heart contracts and forces blood to flow toward the head.

In the head the blood pours out over the brain and then flows backward through the body. As it flows backward it bathes the body organs, muscles, and nervous system. It brings them digested food and takes away waste material.

You can see an insect's heart in some living specimens. If you look carefully at a cutworm, a mosquito larva, or some caterpillars, you can see the tubelike heart along the back. Watch it beat. You may be able to notice that the heart beats faster when the insect is warm than when it is cold.

▶ HOW AN INSECT BREATHES

Like all animals, insects must breathe. They need oxygen from the air to burn digested food. When the food burns, it gives the body energy. A waste product of this burning is a gas called carbon dioxide. The body breathes out the carbon dioxide together with the parts of the breathed-in air it did not use.

You breathe in and out through your mouth

Lacy, delicate wings of the dragonfly show thickenings, called veins, which help stiffen wings.

Crane fly has knobbed stalks—called halteres—in place of hind wings.

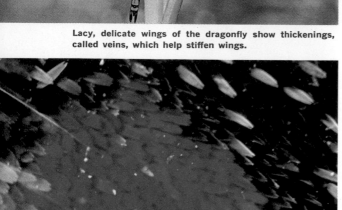

Wings of butterflies and moths are covered with many tiny scales, which give these insects their colors.

FOREWINGS

Beetles have hardened forewings that can fold over hind wings and body for protection.

and the two nostrils in your nose. Insects have about 10 pairs of "nostrils" along the thorax and abdomen. Each segment of the insect's body has a pair of nostrils. They are little holes called **spiracles**. If you look at a grasshopper through a magnifying glass, you can easily see the spiracles along the side of the abdomen.

Most insects breathe through their spira-

Most insects breathe through spiracles—tiny openings on each segment of the insect's body.

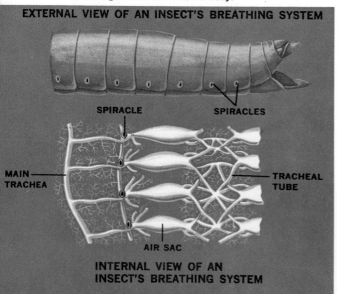

EXTERNAL VIEW OF AN INSECT'S BREATHING SYSTEM

SPIRACLE SPIRACLES

MAIN TRACHEA

TRACHEAL TUBE

AIR SAC

INTERNAL VIEW OF AN INSECT'S BREATHING SYSTEM

cles, but there are some exceptions. The water scorpion has a long breathing tube attached to the tip of its abdomen. It pushes the tip of this tube up through the surface of the water to get air. Many insects that live in water have gills instead of spiracles for breathing. The gills are special organs for taking in air that is dissolved in the water.

▶ INSECT FLIGHT

Insects were probably the first animals to fly. They developed wings many millions of years before there were birds or bats. The ability to fly has helped insects to survive. If conditions for life were not favorable, the insects could fly off to a different place.

Insect wings are very thin, like cellophane. They have many ribs, called veins. The veins help stiffen the wings. While all insect wings are alike in this way, they may be very different in other ways. The wings of butterflies and moths are covered with scales, which may be brightly colored. The forewings of beetles are hardened and shell-like. They fit like shields over the folded hind wings and protect them.

Some insects, such as flies and mosquitoes, have only one pair of wings. The hind wings have developed into stumps that help the insect balance itself when flying. Insects such as fleas, lice, bedbugs, and silverfish have no wings. Cockroaches have wings but do not often use them to fly. Among the ants the workers never have wings. Only the males and the queens have wings, at mating time. After the ants mate, the wings drop off and the insect remains wingless.

The wings of many insects move at great speeds. The wings of the housefly beat about 345 times a second. The wings of butterflies move much more slowly. They move only about 12 times a second.

Insects fly at different speeds. The housefly's speed is about 5 miles an hour. The butterfly's speed is about 12 miles an hour. Hawkmoths have been clocked flying at 30 miles an hour, and some scientists say that dragonflies can fly even faster than that. These are average "cruising" speeds of the insects. They can fly faster if they are escaping from an enemy.

▶ HOW INSECTS MOVE

Watch a fly as it walks. At each step it moves three legs forward at almost the same time. These are the front and hind legs on one side and the middle leg on the other. At the next step the other three legs move. In this way the insect is always resting solidly on three legs as it moves forward.

The insect's leg ends in a pair of claws with a pad in between. In walking, the claws hook onto objects and help pull the insect along. This makes it possible for an insect to run very quickly. The pads between the claws have many tiny hairs with a sticky substance on them. They grip a smooth surface, such as a pane of glass, so that an insect can walk on it.

The legs of some insects are fitted for special purposes. For example, the hind legs of grasshoppers are long and have powerful muscles for jumping. This enables the grasshoppers to escape their enemies. The hind legs of some water beetles are very long and are set with stiff bristles. These legs work like oars in propelling the insect through the water. If you watch one of them swimming, you can see that it swims with a jerky motion, like a man rowing a boat.

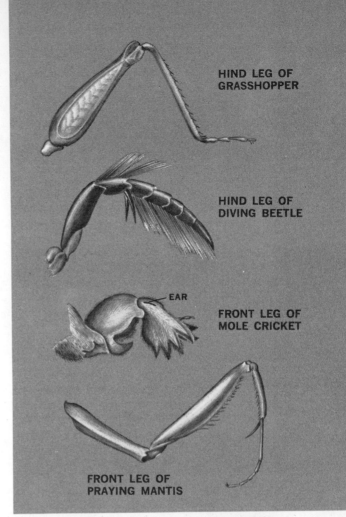

HIND LEG OF GRASSHOPPER

HIND LEG OF DIVING BEETLE

EAR

FRONT LEG OF MOLE CRICKET

FRONT LEG OF PRAYING MANTIS

Insects have jointed legs, covered by a hard outer skeleton, which protects muscles and tissues inside.

An insect's legs, like the rest of its body, have skeletons on the outside. Muscles that control the leg movements are inside the skeleton. This protects the muscles and helps them work more efficiently.

▶ INSECT STRENGTH

Have you ever seen ants carrying sticks or pebbles? A scientist once saw an ant lifting a stone out of its nest entrance. He took both the ant and the stone back to his laboratory and weighed them. He found that the stone weighed 52 times as much as the ant. If a man of average weight were as strong as the ant is for its weight, he would be able to lift nearly 4 tons.

Other insects are even stronger than the ant. A bee can pick up things 300 times its own weight. Beetles are probably the strongest

An ant can lift 52 times its own weight. If a man could do the same, he could lift a 4-ton weight.

If a man could jump as high and as far as a flea can for its size, he could easily clear these tall buildings.

living things in relation to their size. If you had as much strength for your size as a beetle has for its size, you could easily lift almost 10,000 pounds.

Considering their size, insects are remarkably strong. One reason for their strength is the thickness of their muscles. The strength of a muscle depends on its thickness, not on its length. Another reason for the strength of insects is that they have more muscles than many animals. Man has about 800 muscles. A grasshopper has about 900, and some caterpillars have about 4,000. The muscles of insects also work better because of the way they are attached to the outside skeleton.

The strength of an animal does not depend entirely on its size. An animal may be 10 times larger than an insect, but it does not have 10 times the strength. This is because the ability of animals to lift things does not increase at the same rate as their size. The long muscle of a large animal, if it is no thicker than an insect's, is no stronger.

Some insects are able to jump great distances. Grasshoppers can jump 20 times the length of their bodies. At that rate a man would be able to jump one third the length of a football field. Fleas are probably the champion jumpers among insects. A tiny flea can make a jump 8 inches high and can go a distance of 13 inches. If a man could do as well, he could jump over a tall building.

The chief reason insects are such good jumpers is that they are so small. Large animals are heavier for their size than smaller animals are for theirs. For example, a 6-foot man may be about five times as long as the largest insect, which is about 15 inches long. But the man weighs hundreds of times more than the insect does. The insect can jump better because it carries less weight on its body for its size.

Considering the muscles, body structure, and weight of insects, scientists have come to this conclusion: If insects were to grow as large as humans, they would be little, if any, stronger.

▶ HOW INSECTS PROTECT THEMSELVES

Insects have many natural enemies. They are captured and eaten by birds, bats, moles, frogs, and other animals. They also prey on each other. Yet in spite of their enemies, insects remain the most abundant of all animals. Most insects lay a great many eggs at one time. Often the young that hatch from these eggs become adults in a few weeks and are able to lay eggs in turn. Their ability to reproduce rapidly in such large numbers is one reason they are so numerous.

Protection by Disguise

Insects protect themselves from their enemies in many ways. One of these is by disguising themselves so that they blend into their surroundings. This is called **camouflage**. Many caterpillars and walkingstick insects are camouflaged to look like twigs. Many insects are colored and marked with different patterns that make them look like the background upon which they rest. They may look like tree bark, leaves, or soil.

Some harmless insects look ferocious and thus frighten off their enemies. For example,

Caterpillar of royal walnut moth has spines and frightening appearance, which are thought to discourage enemies from attacking it.

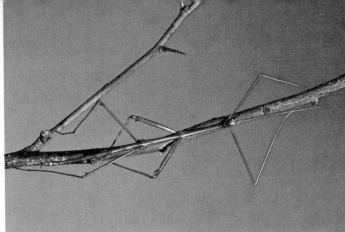

A walkingstick's shape is good protection. The insect is almost impossible to see when it is lying motionless on a twig.

This moth is almost invisible against a tree trunk. Its colors blend in with the bark and keep the moth well hidden from would-be attackers.

Larva of swallowtail butterfly may frighten enemies with huge false eye spots on its head. Real eyes are on underside of head and are quite small.

the hickory horned devil is a large caterpillar with vicious-looking spines. It scares its enemies away by its appearance.

Insect Mimicry

Some moths and butterflies fool their enemies by looking like an insect that is bad-tasting or has a poisonous sting. This is called **mimicry**. For example, the viceroy butterfly looks almost like the monarch butterfly, which has a bad taste to animals that try to eat it. These animals leave both butterflies alone after having tasted a few monarch butterflies.

Another insect that protects itself by mimicry is the hornet fly. It has markings like those of a hornet but has no stinger. Insects, toads, and other small animals whose mouths have been stung by hornets do not try to eat hornets again. Neither do they try to catch the hornet fly.

Viceroy butterfly (left) is rarely attacked. Its colors are much like those of the monarch butterfly (right), which has an unpleasant taste to insect eaters.

LARVAE AND ADULTS OF SOME COMMON INSECTS

Mosquito larvae breathe through tube at end of body.

Adult mosquito can be a carrier of many serious diseases.

Bluebottle fly larvae hatch from eggs in less than 24 hours.

Adult bluebottle fly scavenges for food in decayed matter.

Ladybird beetle larva feeds on insects harmful to plants.

Adult ladybird beetle develops from larva in 2 to 4 weeks.

Protection by Chemical Warfare

Many insects defend themselves by "chemical warfare." If you have ever been stung by a bee, you know how effective this kind of protection is. Poison stings are used by many bees, wasps, hornets, and some ants. Some caterpillars protect themselves in the same way.

Many stinging insects are brightly colored. This is how such an insect warns its enemies that it is poisonous and to stay away.

Some insects give off a bad-smelling chemical to drive enemies away. Stink bugs are such insects. Perhaps the most unusual kind of chemical warfare is that used by the bombardier beetle. When disturbed, this beetle ejects

Dobsonfly larva (hellgrammite) is prized as fish bait.

Adult Dobsonfly lacks the gills of its larva.

Gypsy moth larva feed on over 500 kinds of plants.

Adult gypsy moth is one of the most common insects.

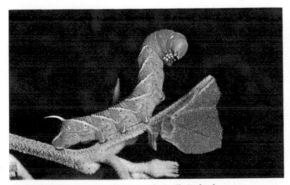
Sphinx moth larva curls over when disturbed.

Adult sphinx moth feeds while hovering over plants.

a puff of gas from the rear of its body. The gas has an irritating effect on the enemy.

▶ INSECT SHELTERS

Most adult insects live by themselves in crevices, in soil, under rocks, or under loose bark. They are called solitary insects. Certain insects live together in colonies. These are called social insects. Ants, termites, most bees, hornets, and some wasps are social insects.

Shelters of Social Insects

Social insects build elaborate homes to shelter the colony. Bees build honeycombs and beehives. Hornets and wasps build paper nests. They make the paper by chewing bits of

Nest of bald-faced hornets hangs from trees or tall shrubs. It is made of paper material.

Interior of bald-faced hornets' nest shows floors and cells in which eggs are laid.

The leaf roller wraps itself in a leaf every morning. It comes out at night to search for food.

Female organ-pipe wasp builds a nest of tubes. Each tube contains an egg and a spider—food for the larva.

Gall, or swelling, on oak tree is cut in half, showing insect inside that causes the unusual growth.

Female potter wasps lay eggs inside jar-shaped nest, then make a top to seal the jar.

Eastern tent caterpillars live in tents spun from silk that they secrete.

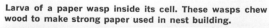

Larva of a paper wasp inside its cell. These wasps chew wood to make strong paper used in nest building.

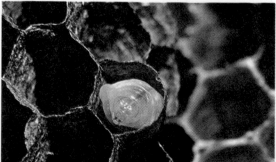

rotten wood and stems of plants. The material is mixed with saliva and becomes a pulpy mass. When it dries, the pulp stiffens into a gray, paperlike material.

Most ants build nests in the ground. The nests are honeycombed with tunnels. The activities of the colony are conducted in the tunnels. Termites nest in darkness. Their nests are made of chewed-up wood. Some termites that live in tropical regions build tall mounds in which the colony lives.

Shelters of Solitary Insects

Only a few solitary insects build shelters. One of these is the leaf roller, a type of cricket. Each morning it rolls a leaf around itself. It seals the ends with silk thread from glands in its mouth. At night it breaks out of its shelter to hunt for food.

Some females build shelters for their eggs. Most common of these are the solitary bees and wasps. One kind of wasp digs a small tunnel in the ground. She stocks the tunnel with food for the larva that will hatch from the egg. She does this by paralyzing a caterpillar with her sting and dragging the still-alive insect into the hole. Then she lays an egg in the "nursery" and seals the opening.

Solitary wasps called mud daubers build mud nests, in which they lay their eggs. They lay in a stock of paralyzed spiders as food for the young and then deposit their eggs in the nest. The potter wasp builds a jar-shaped nest of mud on a twig. Another, the organ-pipe wasp, builds a nest in the shape of long tubes cemented together like an organ pipe. Each tube is a cell in which she lays an egg.

Shelters Built by Larvae

Some adult insects do not build nests for their young but make it possible for the larvae to build shelters. Certain wasps, aphids, and flies pierce leaves or stems of plants and lay eggs inside the plant tissue. When the larvae emerge, they cause that part of the plant to swell—that is, they produce a **gall**.

Galls are of many different shapes and sizes. Some have only one larva in them, and some have many. The soft plant tissue inside the gall supplies food for the larva, and the hard outside covering gives the insect shelter. You can find galls on many plants. Cut one open and look for an insect inside.

The larvae of some insects build shelters without any help from the adults. You may have seen the gray "tents" of tent caterpillars fastened in the forks of tree branches. The tent caterpillars build the tent from silk that they secrete.

Caddis-fly larvae also build shelters. Caddis flies are a group of insects that live near the shores of ponds and streams. The eggs are laid in the water. The larvae that hatch out are called caddisworms. The "worm" builds a case around itself of small pebbles or sticks, glued together or bound with silk. It moves by pushing the front part of its body and its legs out of its case and pulling the rest of its "house" along with it.

Protection for the Pupa

When it is in the pupal, or resting, stage, an insect is helpless. It needs complete protection. Cocoons spun by moth caterpillars give the pupae this protection. The cocoons are made of silk spun out from the salivary glands.

Cocoons are usually white, gray, or brown. They are easy to find in the winter, when trees are bare. You can see some kinds hanging down from the branches, like tiny dull Christmas-tree decorations. If you try to tear one open, you will see why a cocoon is such a fine shelter for the pupa. The cocoon is so tough it will not tear easily.

Other insect larvae do not spin cocoons. Instead they develop a hard coat that serves as a shelter for the pupa.

▶THE IMPORTANCE OF INSECTS

Many insects are very useful to man. Honeybees give us honey and wax. Silk comes from the cocoon built by the silkworm, the larva of a moth. Shellac is made from a substance given off by the lac insect.

Insects carry pollen from flower to flower as they flit about to gather nectar. This transfer of pollen helps plants produce fruit and seeds. Insects also serve as food for many birds.

But insects are man's chief competitors for shelter, clothing, and food. Termites eat the wood of homes; carpet beetles eat carpets; and the larvae of clothes moths eat holes in woolen clothing. The cotton-boll weevil destroys cotton crops. These are only some of the destructive insects. Even more important, insects do

Flowers are dusted with an insecticide (insect killer).

insects.) For many years scientists have also been fighting harmful insects with other insects. The scientists have done this by bringing in natural enemies of insect pests.

Insects are being studied for two main reasons. Scientists want to find ways to encourage the spread of useful insects and new ways to control insect pests. To destroy the pest without harming useful insects is one of the chief aims of scientists. They study an insect in all its life stages, to find when it is easiest to destroy the insect. They have found that some are easier to attack as larvae and some as adults.

Spraying insects with insect-disease viruses or germs is being studied. In one experiment low-flying planes sprayed viruses on areas infested with tent caterpillars. After being sprayed once a year for 2 years, tent caterpillars in those areas were wiped out.

Each time scientists discover a disease that affects an insect, they look for a way to spread that disease. One of these ways is to catch some of the insects in traps, infect them with the disease, and release them. The insects then spread the disease to others.

Modern entomologists—scientists who study insects—think that probably the best way to wipe out insect pests is to prevent the females from laying eggs. If no eggs are laid, in a few years that particular insect may be wiped out.

To do this, research in methods of making insects sterile is being carried out. (Sterile means unable to reproduce.) The insects are treated with chemicals or are exposed to

tremendous damage to food crops. A swarm of locusts can eat a field bare in a few hours. The larvae of certain moths spoil apples, pears, and other fruits.

Some insects spread disease germs. The germs of encephalitis, or sleeping sickness, as well as those of yellow fever and malaria, are carried by insects. Flies live on filth and carry germs on their feet and antennae.

▶ CONTROLLING HARMFUL INSECTS

Man fights a constant battle against harmful insects. He does this in a number of ways.

One of these is by the use of insecticide sprays. (An insecticide is a chemical that kills

INSECT CLASSIFICATION: ORDERS OF SOME COMMON INSECTS

ORDER	MEANING OF NAME	ORDER INCLUDES	DISTINCTIVE CHARACTERISTIC OF ADULTS
Ephemeroptera	"Living for a day"	Mayflies	Brief life-span Chewing mouthparts
Hemiptera	"Half wings"	True bugs (water bugs, squash bugs)	Partly leathery, partly clear wings Piercing and sucking mouthparts
Hymenoptera	"Membrane wings"	Bees, ants, wasps	Thin, filmy wings Chewing and sucking mouthparts
Coleoptera	"Sheath wings"	Beetles	Shieldlike front wings Chewing mouthparts
Odonata	"Toothed"	Dragonflies, damselflies	Mouth with beak resembling tooth Chewing mouthparts
Diptera	"Two wings"	Flies, gnats, mosquitoes	One pair of wings Piercing and sucking mouthparts
Orthoptera	"Straight wings"	Grasshoppers, roaches, crickets	Straight-edged wings (when present) Chewing mouthparts
Lepidoptera	"Scale wings"	Butterflies, moths	Scale-covered wings Sucking mouthparts
Homoptera	"Similar wings"	Aphids, cicadas	Filmy wings of similar size Sucking mouthparts

Mayfly (Ephemeroptera)

Grasshopper (Orthoptera)

Dragonfly (Odonata)

Butterfly (Lepidoptera)

Greenbottle fly (Diptera)

Cicada (Homoptera)

Beetle (Coleoptera)

Leaf-legged bug (Hemiptera)

Black carpenter ant (Hymenoptera)

radiation. Mosquitoes, flies, aphids, beetles, boll weevils, and cockroaches are some of the insects being sterilized experimentally.

Scientists are also studying certain special chemical sprays for plants. These chemicals are harmless to the plants and to other animals. But they cause insects that eat them to become sterile.

Baiting Traps for Males

It is often difficult to trap large numbers of insects in order to sterilize them. Entomologists have therefore experimented and found a way to trap the males.

Entomologists know that the females of many kinds of insects give off a scent to attract the male. The scent-producing chemicals of females are extracted and used to bait insect traps. Chemists have been able to make some scents artificially in the laboratory.

Males are attracted by the scent and flock to the traps in great numbers. Some kinds of male insects caught in this way are killed outright. Scientists have found it more effective to control other kinds by giving the males a disease or by sterilizing them. Then the males are released. Those infected with disease spread it to others. The sterile males mate with females, but the eggs never hatch out.

Entomologists hope that the experiments they have been conducting will lead to control of insect pests.

Ross E. Hutchins
State Plant Board of Mississippi

See also Ants; Butterflies and Moths; Insects and Animals Harmful to Man.

Coral snake.

Timber rattlesnake.

Black widow spider.

Blowfly.

Yellow jacket.

INSECTS AND ANIMALS HARMFUL TO MAN

In nature there are many insects and animals that are helpful and friendly to man. But there are also insects and animals that may sting and bite and insects that carry diseases that people catch.

Some insects and animals are harmful at all times and should be avoided. Black widow spiders are in this group. Other insects and animals are dangerous only under certain conditions. Rabbits, for example, are usually the gentlest of creatures. It is only when they are infected with a disease that can be passed on to human beings that they become dangerous to handle.

It is a good idea to know about some of the insects and animals that can be harmful to man if you go on outings in the woods, if you go hunting, or if you have pets.

▶ INSECT BITES AND STINGS

Most insect bites and stings hurt for a time but are not serious. If you are bitten by a bee, a stinger is usually left in the skin. It should be removed with a pair of tweezers. There is an old belief that putting mud on a sting or bite will help cure it. But it is unwise to put mud on any kind of insect bite. A bite makes a break in the skin, and this should be kept as clean as possible.

Yellow jackets, a kind of wasp, can sting painfully. They often nest around deserted buildings. It is best to avoid stirring up a nest of yellow jackets, since they are especially ready to sting. Putting ice on a bee, wasp, or hornet sting or any other insect bite may relieve the pain.

Some people are allergic to the poison in a

bee or wasp sting. If they are stung, they should see a doctor right away so that they can be given medicine to prevent an allergic reaction.

Some kinds of mosquitoes carry germs that cause disease. A bite by a disease-carrying mosquito can be serious. But your chances of catching a serious disease through a mosquito bite are slight.

The mosquitoes that carry the virus of yellow fever, for example, are being wiped out of many tropical areas in which they were once found. There is also a vaccine to protect people who plan to visit an area where the virus of yellow fever is known to exist. Malaria is also carried by a mosquito, the *Anopheles* mosquito. Drugs to cure malaria and insecticides to control mosquitoes have wiped out malaria in many places. But this is still a serious problem in some tropical areas. In such places mosquito-proof tents and well-screened houses are necessary.

At times mosquitoes carry germs that cause brain diseases, including sleeping sickness. The main kinds of sleeping sickness found in the United States are Saint Louis encephalitis and equine encephalitis. Both of these are diseases of animals carried to man by mosquitoes in this way: a mosquito bites an animal that is infected with sleeping sickness; then the mosquito bites a person. The germs of sleeping sickness are passed on to the person through the mosquito bite. Sometimes in warm weather a number of cases break out in one area. But sleeping sickness is a rare disease.

Dengue is another disease carried by mosquitoes. It is also called breakbone fever because when you have it, your bones ache so that you think they will break. Dengue usually runs its course in a few weeks, and the people who have it recover.

Typhus is a disease carried by the body louse. It is a serious danger whenever people must live in crowded conditions. Throughout history there have been outbreaks of typhus in times of war. But during World War II the insecticide DDT killed body lice and kept typhus under control. Antibiotics help cure typhus. Today there is also a vaccine to prevent the disease.

Flies play a part in the spread of a number of diseases, including cholera, dysentery, poliomyelitis, hepatitis, and typhoid fever. These diseases, like all those that are spread or carried by insects, are less apt to occur if an area is kept free of dirt and filth and if insecticides are used to prevent insects from breeding.

▶**ARACHNID BITES AND STINGS**

Arachnids, or members of the spider family, sting and bite like insects. Although they are often called insects, arachnids have eight legs, while insects have only six. Ticks, mites, spiders, and scorpions are in this group.

Ticks are flat, brown creatures that wait for victims at the tip of branches or tall grass. Brushed off onto your skin, they bury their heads in it to draw blood. If you try to pull a tick off, its head may be left under the skin. The best way to remove a tick is to cover it with a little oil. Then it cannot breathe and will come off easily.

Some ticks carry Colorado tick fever, which is common in the western part of the United States but is not a serious disease. Other ticks may carry **Rocky Mountain spotted fever**, which is a painful and dangerous disease.

Mosquito.

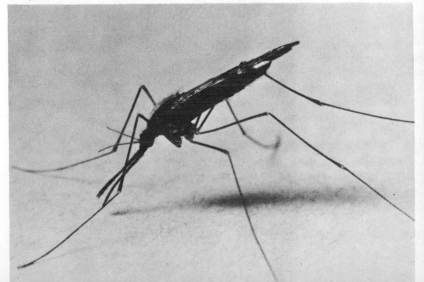

Body louse.

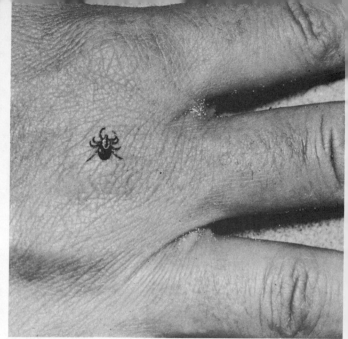

Female scorpion and young.

Dog tick.

Many people are vaccinated against it in areas that are infested with the ticks that carry it.

Chiggers, or red bugs, which are the larvae of mites, also attach themselves to the skin. They cause itching that can last several days. But they do not bury themselves under the skin, as many people believe. Chiggers are often found in the southern part of the United States in areas where there are tall grasses. They can be annoying to dogs and other animals as well as to people. Putting an insect repellent on your outer clothing helps keep them off.

Most of the spiders you will see in your lifetime are harmless. But the black widow is dangerous. It may be found from southern California to Chile, usually in damp, sheltered spots. The male almost never bites. The female black widow has a shiny, black body about half an inch long. On the underside of the body there are red markings in the shape of an hourglass.

The poison of the black widow spider causes stiffening of the muscles of the abdomen and great pain. Anyone who is bitten by a black widow should see a doctor at once for treatment. Many victims of the black widow spider die. Patients who survive recover slowly as the body gradually destroys the poison.

The scorpion is often found in cool, damp places. The stinger is at the end of its tail. Most scorpions are not dangerous. But two kinds in the southwestern part of the United States are harmful, especially to very small children. These scorpions are less dangerous to grown-up people because an adult's body is larger and can throw off the effects of the poison more easily.

Tarantulas are the biggest of all spiders. They have hairy bodies that are sometimes 3 inches long. But tarantulas are not usually harmful to man.

▶ **SNAKEBITES**

There are many non-poisonous snakes in North America. Some of these are the grass snake, garter snake, and bull snake. If you know that the snake that bit you is not poisonous, you need not be alarmed. Just treat the bite as you would any other wound. Keep it clean and bandaged if necessary.

There are only two groups of poisonous snakes in North America: the coral snakes of the South and the pit vipers, which include copperheads, cottonmouths, or water moccasins, and rattlesnakes. The pit vipers are found scattered across the North American continent. Copperheads are found mainly in the eastern section. Cottonmouths, or water moccasins, are found on the Atlantic Coast as far north as Virginia. They are found as far west as eastern Texas. In the Mississippi Valley water moccasins live as far north as southern Illinois. Rattlesnakes are found mostly in the Southwest, but some are found in almost every state.

Most coral snakes have bands of red, yellow, and black. The pit vipers have a deep pit, or hollow, on each side of the head. The rattlesnake, one of the pit vipers, can be recognized by the rattling sound it makes with its tail.

When a snake bites a person, it injects venom, or poison, through the fangs in its jaw. If a snake has bitten an animal recently, it may have very little venom left to inject. Then the bite is not as severe as one in which the snake's full supply of venom is injected. The venom of the coral snake acts on the nervous system. It affects breathing especially. The venom of the pit viper affects the blood.

If you live in an area where there are poisonous snakes, you have probably been warned many times to watch where you step and sit and where you put your hands when you climb. It is a good idea to wear gloves and to keep your legs well protected when you go hiking. Most bites are on the lower part of the leg. It is also a good idea, when you are walking through tall grass, to carry a stick or strong branch and place it ahead of you at each step. Often this warns a snake that someone is coming, and it will disappear.

The best first-aid measure in the case of snakebite is to have the person who has been bitten sit or lie very still. This is to try to slow down the spread of snake venom through the body. If you have some ice with you, apply it to the bite. By slowing down the circulation, ice helps confine the venom to the area near the bite. If the bite is on an arm or a leg, tie a handkerchief firmly in a band above the bite.

The most important thing of all is to get a doctor as quickly as possible. The only way the action of snake venom in the body can be stopped is by the injection of a special medicine, called an antivenin. If you are with someone who is bitten by a poisonous snake, run as fast as you can for help.

▶ STINGRAYS AND JELLYFISH

Certain creatures in the ocean can sting painfully. One of these is the stingray, a flat, diamond-shaped fish. When you go swimming off the coast of California or along the southern Atlantic Coast, you may accidentally step on a stingray. It has a long tail with a number of sharp spines. It protects itself by injecting

venom through the spines in this tail. If any part of this stinging equipment is left in the skin, it should be removed. The wound should be washed with cold salt water, then bathed in hot water for an hour.

A jellyfish is a sea animal with a body that is like jelly. It has long tentacles, or arms, that

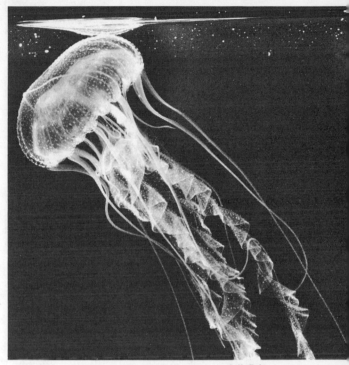

Jellyfish.

Stingray.

Pigeon.

can sting. Cloths soaked in alcohol may relieve the pain of a jellyfish sting.

▶ DISEASES FROM ANIMALS

A number of animals that are usually mild and harmless can be harmful to man under some conditions. If an animal is infected with a certain disease, it may pass on this disease to human beings.

Birds, for example, can pass on a disease called ornithosis, or psittacosis, which is like pneumonia. Parrots, parakeets, lovebirds, canaries, pigeons, and poultry can all be infected with it. The disease is passed on to people when they clean the cages or breathe in the dust from the feathers of sick birds.

There is an antibiotic to cure ornithosis, but it is best to try to avoid the disease by avoiding infected birds. It is not always possible to do this because you cannot always tell when a bird is infected. Not all birds with ornithosis act sick. Still, it is certainly the safest plan to stay away from a pigeon in the park if it looks sick. If you should notice that a pet bird seems sick, report it to an adult in your family.

Another illness that can be passed on by a family pet is cat scratch fever. This is not a serious disease, but it is common. It starts with a cat scratch. In 2 or 3 weeks a fever develops, and the lymph nodes, which are like glands, become swollen. Cat scratch fever runs its course and disappears by itself.

Sometimes it is hard for the doctor to tell when a person has cat scratch fever. Many other diseases cause fever and sore lymph nodes. There is a skin test that helps the doctor decide when a person has cat scratch fever, and not a more serious illness.

One of the most dangerous diseases man can catch from animals is **rabies**. Most cases of rabies are passed on to man by dogs. But other warm-blooded animals—skunks, foxes, cats, wolves, bears, and bats—can pass on rabies as well.

Rat.

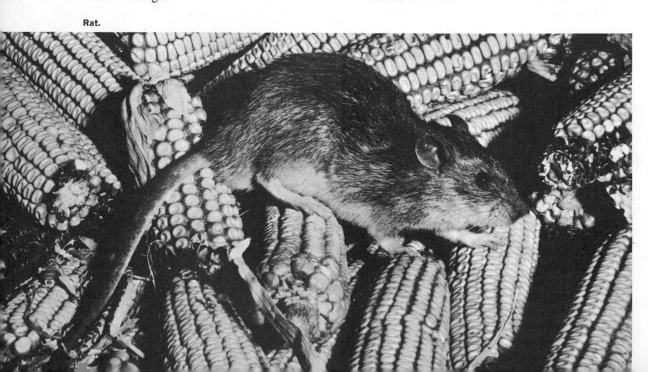

The disease is caused by a tiny organism called a virus. The rabies virus is in the saliva of an infected, or rabid, animal. When the animal bites a person, the disease is passed on. It can only be passed on through a break in the skin. But even the lick of an infected animal is dangerous if there is already a cut on the skin through which the virus can enter the body.

Rabies attacks the nervous system. You may have heard the other name for rabies: hydrophobia. In Greek this means "fear of water." The name was given to the disease because people with rabies become unable to swallow and may even have convulsions at the sight of water.

Rabies has been feared throughout history. There is still no cure for it, but today there is a vaccine to prevent it, so the disease is kept well under control. In areas where people live, dogs are vaccinated against rabies and stray dogs are taken off the streets.

If you should ever be bitten by a dog, the most important thing to do is to report it to your family immediately. There are certain steps they will want to take. A dog bite, for example, should be washed right away with soap and water, then cared for by a doctor. Every effort should be made to find a dog that has bitten a person. If the dog has been vaccinated against rabies, no special treatment is necessary. But the dog must be carefully watched by a veterinarian for a week. If the dog shows any signs of rabies during that week, the person who has been bitten should be given anti-rabies vaccine.

When a person is bitten by a wild animal, by an unknown dog, or by a dog that is tested and found to have rabies, anti-rabies vaccine is given. The vaccine makes it possible for the body to fight off the rabies virus. Even after a person has been bitten by an animal with rabies, the vaccine can prevent the disease. This is because rabies develops slowly. It takes an average of 50 to 60 days for the disease to develop in a person who has been bitten by a rabid animal. The vaccine can take effect in a much shorter time. Often the vaccine is given once a day for 14 days. This means that in 14 days the body can build up its defenses against rabies.

But anti-rabies vaccine is given only when it is absolutely necessary. This is because it must be given in a long series of injections and because it can cause serious reactions.

Tularemia, a disease that causes a fever and other signs of severe infection, is passed on to man mainly by wild rabbits. Muskrats and beavers can also give people tularemia. Butchers, hunters, and people who work with animals in laboratories often become infected. There are drugs to cure the disease, but it is important to try to avoid it. The germ that causes tularemia can enter the body even through unbroken skin. If you go hunting and handle wild rabbits, especially if you skin the dead animal, be sure to wear rubber gloves.

Anthrax is a disease of goats, cattle, sheep, and horses. Farmers who work with infected animals sometimes develop anthrax. People who work in factories and handle the wool and hair of infected animals may also develop it. But anthrax in man is rare. Great efforts are made to prevent the disease by vaccinating animals, and factory workers wear rubber gloves and aprons to protect themselves from anthrax.

At one time the most dreaded disease caused by animals was **bubonic**, or black, **plague** (also called black death). Epidemics of plague killed thousands of people during the Middle Ages. Plague is a disease of rats and other rodents, like ground squirrels, prairie dogs, and wild mice. It can be caused by the bite of an infected rat or it can be carried to man by certain fleas. Modern methods of controlling rats and fleas have made the disease very rare on the North American continent, but it still occurs in several countries in the Far East.

Anyone who has ever had a pet knows how much pleasure and enjoyment animals give man. If you have ever had a garden, you know how helpful certain insects can be. Often they destroy other insects that are harmful to trees and plants. But it is wise, too, to understand that animals and insects can sometimes be harmful to man. It does not mean that you must be afraid of animals and insects. But if you understand that certain dangers can exist, you may be able to take certain simple steps to avoid being hurt.

Reviewed by FREDERIC T. JUNG, M.D.
Northwestern Medical School

See also DISEASES; FIRST AID; HOUSEHOLD PESTS; PUBLIC HEALTH; VECTORS.

INSTALLMENT BUYING

Today a family can buy almost anything from a bicycle to an airplane trip on the installment plan. Even swimming pools, pets, and clothing are sold by the method of paying part of the price down and signing a contract to pay so much every month. Installment plans and loans increasingly are used to finance college expenses too.

The installment plan makes it possible for people to use goods now and pay later out of income, rather than wait until they have saved up the entire price. About 60 per cent of all families use installment plans for at least some purchases.

Installment plans are no longer used primarily by low-income families. Federal Reserve Board surveys have found that the larger number of installment-plan buyers are what are usually called middle-income families—those who have incomes of $5,000 to $10,000 a year.

This arrangement for using goods while you pay for them instead of waiting to save the money can be useful in the case of really necessary purchases. A mother who has no washing machine might have to spend a large amount of money every week in a commercial laundry while she is saving money to buy her own machine. Or a man who has no car to get to work might have to wait a long time to save the $2,000 or more that a new car costs. Nor can children graduating from high school wait to go to college while a family saves up the money needed for tuition and board fees.

But installment buying costs more than buying the same goods for cash. In fact, the cost is higher than many people realize. When you buy on the installment plan, you are really "hiring money." You must pay a fee for the use of this money, just as you do when you get a cash loan from the bank. This fee is called the **finance charge**.

▶ FINANCE CHARGES

The finance charge for the purchase of a new car on the installment plan usually is the equivalent of a true annual interest rate of 12 to 15 per cent. For used cars, the finance charge usually amounts to 15 to 30 per cent, depending on the age of the car. For household appliances and furniture, finance charges are usually the equivalent of true interest rates of 18 to 22 per cent a year.

So while the installment plan can be a useful tool, it also can add extra expense to a family's living costs. If a family makes installment buying a habit or uses the installment plan unnecessarily, in the long run it will not be able to buy as many goods as if it paid cash. The reason is that part of its income then must go to pay finance charges.

For example, many young families pledge as much as one fourth of their income for installment payments, and sometimes even more. A family that owes installment debts of $1,500 typically pays an additional $180 to $270 a year in finance charges. Or a family that buys a car for $3,000 and pays $500 down and the balance in 36 monthly payments will find that the car finally costs approximately $3,500 with the finance charge.

▶ OVERBUYING ON THE INSTALLMENT PLAN

Even more serious problems may result if the family finds that it has bought too much on installments and cannot keep up with the payments. In that case the installment contract permits the finance company to repossess (take back) the goods. Not only does the buyer then lose all the money he has paid so far, but he even may owe an additional sum for repossession fees.

When it is necessary or desirable to buy on installments, a family can keep the costs to a minimum by following these policies:

(1) Pay down as much as you can, not the least the seller will permit.

(2) Make the monthly payments as large as you safely can.

(3) Compare both the cash prices of the merchandise and the finance charges among different sellers.

(4) Borrow from the lowest-cost source, not necessarily from the most convenient.

The fact is that the amount of finance charge a family pays is affected not only by the amount owed but by how long the family takes to pay the debt. If you pay a $2,500 debt on a car in 30 months instead of 36, the finance charge will be about $375 instead of $450. If you can pay in 24 monthly installments, the finance charge drops to about $300.

Surveys have shown that families today

sometimes buy on installments even when they have savings they can use to pay for the purchase. Since installment finance charges are much higher then the interest rates usually paid on savings accounts or government bonds, these families pay more for purchases than if they used their own savings. Government and university surveys have found that some families tend to buy on installments even when they have the cash, chiefly because they usually do not understand how much they pay in finance charges.

Different lenders and sellers state their finance charges in different ways. In order to compare the fees charged, an alert buyer needs to know how to translate the stated rate into the true annual interest rate.

▶ TRUE INTEREST RATES

Some lenders and sellers state finance charges as a percentage of the declining balance of a debt. For example, when a loan company states that it charges 2 per cent a month on the declining balance of a debt, the true annual interest rate is 24 per cent. When a store or finance company charges 1½ per cent a month, the true rate is 18 per cent a year.

Thus when the credit charge is stated as a percentage of the declining balance, you multiply the monthly rate by 12 to find the true annual interest rate.

When a bank or finance company charges a rate of so many dollars a year on a loan that you repay monthly, the true annual interest rate is approximately double the stated rate. The lender makes the charge on the original amount, not just on the remaining or declining balance each month. But you pay back part of the loan each month. So during the life of the loan, you really owe an average of about half the original amount. For example, a bank or finance company may charge you $6 for $100 to be repaid in 12 monthly installments. Since you are paying back $8.33 each month, you really owe an average of approximately $50 during the period of the loan, so the $6 fee is a true annual interest rate of about 12 per cent a year on your average debt of $50.

Thus when a finance charge is figured on the full amount of the debt that you repay monthly, the true annual interest rate is approximately double the stated rate.

INSTALLMENT PLANS, LOANS, AND COSTS

Installment Plans and Loans	Typical Stated Rate	Approximate True Annual Interest Rate
Bank personal loans	$4–$7 a month per $100	8–14%
Car finance charges (new car)	$6—$7.50 per $100	12–15%
Car finance charges (used car)*	$9–$18 per $100	18–36%
Credit union loans	⅔–1% a month	8–12%
Education loans (college loan funds)	1–5%	1–5%
Education loans (commercial lenders)	3–5%	6–10%
Small loan companies	1½–3½% a month	18–42%
Store revolving charge account	1½% a month	18%

* Variation due to age of car as well as variations in finance company charges.

Of all the widely used installment plans and loans, only mortgages and life-insurance loans are usually stated with true annual interest rates. A 6-per cent mortgage actually is a true rate of 6 per cent a year.

Another occasional exception is the personal loan offered by some Canadian banks. A number of banks in Canada do state their installment-loan charges as true annual interest rates and charge interest only on the remaining balance each month. Others follow the practices of banks and finance companies in the United States. The finance charge is calculated on the original amount of the debt.

Sometimes a family can plan its purchases to take advantage of short-term charge accounts that require no finance charge. Most stores allow families who have past records of prompt payment to "charge" purchases for 30 days, and sometimes for as long as 60 days, with no additional fee. Then if the family does not pay within the "free" period, the store will usually charge 1½ per cent a month on the remaining balance (the equivalent of a true annual interest rate of 18 per cent a year).

Generally finance charges are highest on very small debts and on goods that have limited resale value if repossessed. Finance charges on used cars often are twice as much as those on new cars, and at times more.

SIDNEY MARGOLIUS
Author, *The Consumer's Guide to Better Buying*

INSTINCT. See PSYCHOLOGY.

INSTRUMENTS, MUSICAL. See MUSICAL INSTRUMENTS.

INSULATION AND INSULATING MATERIALS

There are three kinds of insulation: heat, electrical, and sound. Heat insulation slows down the flow of heat from one place to another. Electrical insulation prevents electricity from escaping as it travels through a wire. Sound insulation helps cut down noise in offices, factories, and other buildings.

▶ HEAT INSULATION

Heat insulation has many uses. It keeps a house comfortable in winter by keeping the heat in and preventing drafts. It saves money on heating bills. Not as much fuel is needed to heat a well insulated house as is needed to heat a poorly insulated house. Insulation also keeps a house cool in summer by keeping the heat out.

Hot pipes and tanks need insulation to keep them from losing heat. Insulation is also needed on hot pipes to prevent people from being burned by them. The insulation brings hot surfaces down to 140 degrees Fahrenheit or lower.

Insulation is used in refrigerators and cold-storage rooms, and on air-conditioning pipes and ducts. Not only does the insulation serve to keep the heat out of these cold spaces, but it helps prevent "sweating." Sweating, or condensation, occurs when drops of moisture form out of the air that touches cold surfaces. Moisture that drips off pipes running between floors can harm ceilings.

Because insulation is usually kept out of sight, most people do not realize how important it is. Almost every house has some insulation in the ceiling or in the attic roof. In well-made houses it is also put into the walls when the house is built. A refrigerator has insulation between its inside and outside walls. Refrigerated freight cars and trucks are also insulated.

Natural Insulation

Snow, fur, feathers, and wool are all good natural insulators. These are used by animals and people to keep their bodies warm. Cork and straw are good natural insulators to use in buildings.

Huskies, the Eskimo dogs, burrow into snowdrifts to sleep. Grainy, loosely packed snow has plenty of air spaces trapped between snow crystals. It holds in the heat of a dog's body. When snow covers the roof of a house, it also works to keep heat inside.

A polar bear prowls in an area with bitterly cold winds and sleeps on a bed of ice. But he is not cold, because his fur keeps him well insulated. Animals with good coats of fur can live in very cold areas. People learned long ago that animal furs would help to keep them warm. People also wear wool to stay warm. Feathers keep birds warm.

For thousands of years straw has been used in many parts of the world as a roofing material. When a house has a heavy thatched roof and thick clay and straw walls, it is well insulated. The more straw there is in the clay, the better is its insulating ability. It is the air trapped in the hollow stems of the grass or straw that actually does the insulating.

For many years people have used cork to insulate their homes. The many small air-filled cells in cork make it an especially good insulator. Spanish peasants sometimes used cork bark to line the stone walls of their houses.

Manufactured Insulation

There are two main types of manufactured insulation. The one most often used is **mass insulation**. Mass insulation works by preventing the movement of heat. The materials used for mass insulation conduct heat poorly themselves and are filled with tiny closed-in spaces of air or gas, which also are poor conductors. Examples of these materials are rock wool, slag wool, glass fibers, cellulose fibers, and chemically foamed products. The thicker these are, the better they insulate.

The most common form of manufactured mass insulation is a copy of a natural material found on the Hawaiian Islands. When volcanoes on these islands erupted, they threw molten rock violently into the air. As the molten rock fell it sometimes cooled in the form of threads, or fibers. The Polynesians called the fibers Pele's hair, after their mountain goddess Pele.

Now similar rock fibers, called rock wool, are manufactured by dropping molten rock onto a whirling wheel. The wheel tosses droplets of the molten rock into a current of air, which cools them into thin fibers. Fiber glass is a similar product. It is made by forcing molten glass through tiny holes called spinnerets into a cooling current of air.

Mass insulation is manufactured in many forms. Loose-fill types and blanket types of insulation are most commonly used. With the loose-fill types, the loose insulating material is poured or blown into the space in a double wall. The blanket types of insulation come in sheets of material, which are nailed into wall spaces. Boards or slabs of insulating materials are also used.

Reflective insulation is the other main type of manufactured insulation. The shiny surface of reflective insulation sends back heat that is shining on it from a heat source. The heat may be the sun, a flame, or simply the facing wall. Aluminum foil is the most common form of reflective insulation. The foil is usually attached to strong paper to make it sturdy. Other shiny metal surfaces and even light-colored paints also reflect heat. An attic under a white roof is cooler than one under a black roof, because the white roof reflects most of the heat shining down on it, while the black roof absorbs it.

Reflective insulation works best when it is in layers. There should be about an inch of air space between each layer. Air trapped between the layers provides additional insulation.

Recent Developments

Insulation foam is a fairly new insulation material. To make insulation foam, air or gas is blown into molten glass or plastic. The bubbles of glass or plastic do not absorb water, so this is a highly water-resistant type of insulation. Glass foam is used for insulating underground chilled-water piping. It is also used to insulate cold tanks and for hot tanks up to about 400 degrees Fahrenheit. Foamed plastics are important in the insulation of refrigerated storage rooms and piping.

Calcium silicate, mineral wool, fiber glass, and asbestos are some of the new insulating materials. Other new kinds of insulation are continually being developed as more needs

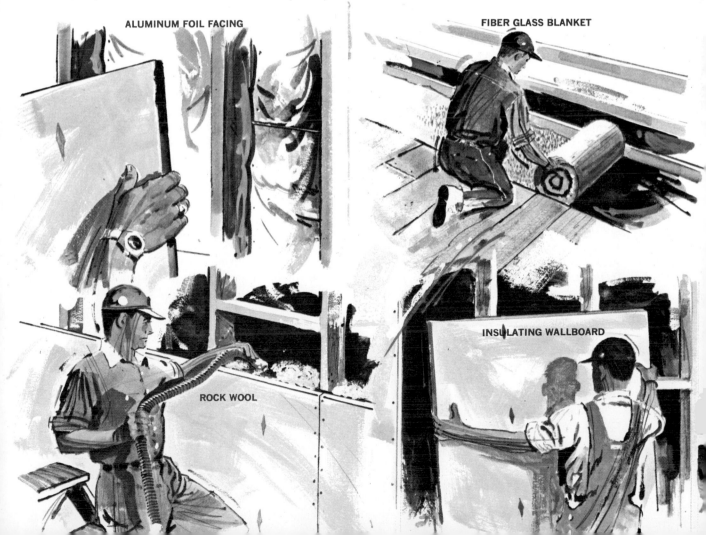

ALUMINUM FOIL FACING

FIBER GLASS BLANKET

ROCK WOOL

INSULATING WALLBOARD

arise. Rocket nose cones, for example, need excellent insulation. The friction of the air when the rocket re-enters the atmosphere creates extremely high temperatures. Without this insulation the rocket might become so hot that it would be vaporized.

▶ELECTRICAL INSULATION

Electrical insulation is used to prevent the flow of electricity. It keeps current from escaping from its conductors.

There are no perfect electrical insulators. Even the best insulators will conduct a little electricity. Since electric current can make a wire hot, an electrical insulator must be a fairly good heat insulator to be used safely. In addition, good electrical insulators do not absorb water. Ordinary water conducts electricity, so wet materials are not good insulators.

Rigid Insulation

Rigid insulation is used to support wires and to space them apart. Switches, transformers, circuit breakers, spark plugs, and similar electrical equipment all need rigid insulators. Glass, ceramic (including porcelain), and plastic are the most common of the rigid insulators. They are cheap and not much affected by water. They may be exposed to weather on electric power and telephone poles and not lose their value as insulators.

Some electrical apparatus that use a large number of wires, like switchboards, have their wires spread over a panelboard. Panelboards are made almost entirely of man-made plastics that conduct electricity poorly.

Flexible Insulation

Most forms of wire are insulated with plastic. Rubber-covered wires used to be the most common, and many are still used. When many wires have to be laid over the same path, they are often bound together into a cable. Each wire in a cable is first covered by a spiral layer of paper. Over this is a fabric braid that has been soaked with water- and fire-resistant materials. On top is a layer of wax.

The type of insulation required for an ordinary cord is determined by the amount of electrical current needed by the appliance it serves. The three main types of wire cord are lamp cord, heater cord, and cord for large appliances.

Lamp Cord. Rubber or plastic insulation is used for electric lamps, clocks, radios, coffee percolators, and other similar appliances.

Heater Cord. For irons, toasters, and portable household heaters, a heavier wire insulation is necessary because these appliances use more current than lamps, clocks, and radios. Cotton is wrapped around the wire to keep the layer of rubber from sticking to it. Asbestos is wrapped over the rubber to protect it in case the wire touches the hot appliance. On top of all these materials is a layer of cotton or rayon.

Cord for Large Appliances. A heavy cord is needed for vacuum cleaners, dishwashers, washers and dryers, and electric machine tools. The conducting wires are wrapped in two or more separate bunches. First there is a cotton wrapping and then the rubber or plastic insulation. Jute, a plant fiber, may be twisted with the conductors. All of this is held together by a fabric braid. The outside of the wire cord is tough rubber or plastic.

▶SOUND INSULATION

Some people live in apartment houses where they can hear their neighbors' radios, quarrels, and even ordinary conversations. Most people would rather live in a building that is insulated to keep sound from passing through its floors and partitions.

To soundproof a building, the floors and walls must be specially constructed. The heavier the walls are, the less sound passes through them. Double, or hollow, walls also help to prevent the passage of sound. Double walls pass on the least sound when there are few points of connection, such as nails and beams, between them. It is the closed-in air space between the walls that provides the sound insulation.

On ceilings, insulation board effectively deadens sounds. Blanket insulation (a continuous piece of insulation) between double floors also helps.

If an apartment is furnished with many soft surfaces, some sound is absorbed by them. Draperies, rugs, and upholstered furniture all absorb sound. Thus there is considerable sound absorption in most living rooms.

JOHN M. BARNHART
National Insulation Manufacturers Association
See also AIR CONDITIONING; HEATING.

Insurance policies of almost every kind are handled by famed Lloyd's of London.

INSURANCE

No matter how careful a person is, there are many losses beyond his control. There is no way to tell what may happen to any one person tomorrow, next month, or next year. Insurance is a system for protecting people from these losses.

Insurance companies can protect people because they follow a rule known as the law of large numbers. When a large number of people face the same danger during the same period of time, the chances are that some will suffer a loss, but most will not. From past experience it is possible to figure out how often the same loss will happen in the same group.

Insurance companies charge a fee called a **premium** to the person who wants insurance. The companies use the money to pay insurance benefits and to cover expenses, but a large part of the premium is put in reserve until the policyholder needs it. These assets are usually invested by the insurance company, and the money earned helps to keep down the cost of the insurance.

When a person becomes insured, he takes out a **policy**. A policy is a statement that tells the buyer exactly what kind of insurance he has, what sort of losses it covers, and how much the company will pay on losses. When a policyholder suffers a loss, he fills out a report called a **claim**. The insurance company checks the claim to see if a real loss has occurred and whether it is covered under the policy. If the claim is correct, the insurance company pays all or part of the loss, as called for in the policy.

▶HOW INSURANCE WORKS

There are many different kinds of insurance policies. But they fall into three basic groups: property and casualty insurance, life insurance, and health insurance.

Property and Casualty Insurance

Property insurance can pay all or part of the cost if a person suffers a loss or damage to his house, car, furniture, clothing, office building, or almost any other kind of property. The damage may be caused by fire, robbery, wind, a car wreck, or many other misfortunes.

Suppose Mr. Smith owns a $10,000 frame house in a medium-size city. A fire could burn it down tonight, tomorrow, next month, or next year. It might never happen, but Mr. Smith does not know. To protect himself, Mr. Smith buys fire insurance. If his house does not catch fire, he will never collect on his policy. But the money that he has paid to the insurance company is a small fraction of the cost of replacing his house, clothes, furniture, and other possessions should a fire take place.

When Mr. Smith buys fire insurance, he is sharing the risk with the owners of many other homes. If more houses catch fire than the company expected, the company may have to pay claims amounting to much more than the money it received. The company would then have to draw upon the reserves it put aside for this possibility.

Casualty insurance is sometimes called liability insurance. "Liability" means the responsibility of paying for the damage caused by an accident or injury. When two automobiles collide, the driver of one car is usually at fault. That car's owner then is liable for the damage done to the other car and for any injuries to people in the car. If a guest slips on a highly polished floor and breaks his arm, the owner of the house may be liable and, if so, must pay for the injury. Liability is based on whether or not the driver of the car or owner of the house was negligent—that is, careless.

An important change that has been proposed for automobile insurance is "no-fault" liability coverage. Under "no-fault" coverage, a person who has been hurt or whose car has been damaged in an accident receives certain payments for medical costs and other expenses, no matter who is responsible for the accident. The purpose of this change is to eliminate the need to prove negligence in automobile accident cases and to provide faster payments to everyone entitled to them.

Life Insurance

No one knows when he will die. Life insurance is one way to make sure a man's family will have enough money to carry on after his death. The wages that will no longer be brought home must be replaced. The family must have money to cover funeral costs and repay debts.

Life insurance premiums are based on the length of time the insurance company expects the policyholder to live. A young person in good health pays a small premium because he is expected to make yearly payments for a long time.

There are several different kinds of life insurance. Suppose Mr. Smith, who is 30 years old, buys a $10,000 permanent life insurance policy on a **whole-life** basis. That means he can keep the policy in force as long as he lives. When he dies, the insurance company will pay his family $10,000. Mr. Smith might have been able to save this amount or more in a savings bank, but if he died unexpectedly at 34, he probably would not have had time or enough money to save $10,000.

If at any time Mr. Smith decides to give up his policy, the company will pay him the policy's **cash value**. The cash value is part of the amount Mr. Smith has paid into the policy. When he takes the policy out, he is told what its cash value will be at any time. Some policies are designed to build up values more quickly than other policies.

Mr. Smith can also borrow against the cash value without giving up his policy. But he has to pay interest on the loan because the money comes from the company's assets. If he should die, the amount of the loan is subtracted from the insurance money. It is a good idea to borrow like this only in an emergency and to repay the loan as quickly as possible.

There are also policies that meet special needs for short-term life insurance protection. A man with a growing family usually needs most of his income to provide for his children and wife. He may not always be able to afford enough permanent life insurance to protect his family if he should die. Often he takes out a special policy, such as:

A **family income** policy, which combines permanent life insurance and some extra, temporary life insurance during the years that the children are growing up. If the father dies before his children are grown, his wife will receive monthly payments as well as the face value of the insurance policy at some prearranged date. If the policyholder dies after his children are grown, his wife receives only the face value. The premiums are higher when the policy is first taken out. As the children grow older and are better able to take care of themselves the extra insurance becomes less.

Term insurance is the name for temporary insurance. It can be bought with permanent insurance or by itself. Term insurance is taken out for a certain period of time and promises a certain sum to a beneficiary if the policyholder dies within a given period. If he lives, the policy expires. Since term insurance is temporary, it builds up no cash value. Many term policies, however, can be renewed until a person reaches the age of 65. But the premium goes up each time the person renews the policy. Term insurance can cover many emergencies. For instance, a person may have gone deeply into debt and wants to be sure the debt is paid if he should suddenly die. Term insurance is good temporary protection until he has paid off the debt.

Other types of policies cover several different insurance needs. Under the **family plan** policy, a man can insure himself, his wife, and all their children, including additional children soon after they are born.

Group life insurance includes a large number of people under the same policy. People usually get this insurance at the place where they work. The premiums for the employee are very low mainly because this is term, or temporary, insurance. The employer may pay part or all of the insurance cost.

Life insurance companies also sell **annuity** contracts. An annuity gives its owner a certain amount of money every month after he retires or after he has reached a certain age. Annuities can be paid for either by a series of installments or in one lump sum.

Health Insurance

The main purpose of health insurance is to help pay expenses for illnesses and injuries. The same policy may include several types of health insurance or it may cover just one.

Hospital insurance helps pay a person's hospital bill. His policy may cover part or all of the cost of his room, meals, laboratory tests, operating room, nurses, medicines, and other expenses in the hospital.

Surgical insurance pays part or all of a doctor's fee for an operation. Insurance companies usually list set amounts that they will pay for different kinds of operations.

Regular medical insurance helps pay a doctor's fee for treating a person for care other than surgery.

Major medical insurance is designed for very long or very expensive illnesses. Unlike regular medical insurance, it continues to cover medical fees for a very long period of time. The person who takes out this insurance pays all expenses up to a certain amount, such as $250 or $500. The insurance company may then pay as much as 80 percent of all the rest until a maximum limit—as much as $10,000 or more—is reached. Without major medical insurance, a person might have to use his life's savings or borrow large sums of money to cover his medical bills.

Loss of income insurance pays money every week to someone who is not able to work for a long time because of sickness or injury.

Accident insurance provides special payments if a person is injured or killed. If he is permanently crippled in an accident, he may receive a large amount of money all at once. Or it may be spread out in smaller payments for a number of years or for the rest of his life. Some policies cover only certain kinds of accidents, such as an airplane crash.

Medicare is an insurance program conducted by the U. S. Government. It helps pay medical expenses for nearly everyone aged 65 or older. Medicare has a basic plan for hospital expenses and an optional plan for doctors' fees and similar expenses. The program is part of the Social Security system.

▶HISTORY OF INSURANCE

From the earliest times people have tried to protect themselves from loss. The Bible tells that in ancient times Joseph taught the Egyptians to put aside part of their crops in good years. Then they would not go hungry in poor years.

The ancient Greeks organized a life insurance system. Some temples collected money every month from their members. If the member paid his dues faithfully, he was given a good burial. The Romans and later the medieval guilds followed the same system. The guilds used the money to take care of losses from fire and robbery, too.

The first insurance company was chartered in Flanders in 1310 to protect cargoes. But insurance did not really begin until about the 17th century, when ship owners, navigators, and merchants in London began to share the risk of losing a ship at sea. These men met at Lloyd's coffeehouse. The owner of the coffeehouse, Edward Lloyd, attracted his customers by gathering all the latest shipping news for them. Sailors looking for berths, merchants trying to ship cargoes, and ship captains waiting to sail came to Lloyd's to arrange business. A man who wanted to insure his ship or goods put a list on a table. Any person could insure a part of the cargo by putting his name under the articles he was willing to cover. That is how underwriters got their name. Soon insurance was handled by special men who did nothing else.

Lloyd's eventually changed from a coffee-house to one of the largest insurance organizations in the world. It is not a true insurance company. It is a group of underwriters who are willing to take on any legitimate risk. Although they still mainly insure ships, Lloyd's is also famous for insuring, say, a pianist's fingers, or a tennis match against bad weather.

Insurance companies began to be organized around 1700. These companies took on life, fire, and casualty insurance as well as marine (sea) insurance. Fire insurance was especially popular. But after a big fire many companies went bankrupt because they could not meet so many claims.

Since insurance companies could not foresee the future, they never knew how many claims they would have to pay each year. Edmund Halley (1656–1742), the discoverer of Halley's comet, was the first to work out scientific tables of average life expectancies. By studying the tables, insurance men could find out how many men out of 100 were likely to die at 45, how many at 55, and so on. Halley's work helped the companies plan policies and premium costs that would balance out the expected claims.

Insurance, however, was still a gamble for everyone. Even if there was enough money to meet the claims, insurance practices were still primitive. For instance, a man taking out life insurance in the early 1800's could usually buy only term insurance and had to pay higher and higher premiums as he got older. Not only that—if he failed to meet a payment, he lost all the money that he had put into the policy. In England many old men found that their premiums were so high that their only choice was to sell their policy to the highest bidder. They were paid very little for these policies, and their families were left with no money when they died.

An American, Elizur Wright (1804–85), was shocked by this practice. When he returned to the United States, he devoted his life to insurance reform. He put several bills through the Massachusetts legislature. These bills required the companies to keep enough reserves to cover the policies. Today if a man cannot keep up his insurance, part of the money he has paid is returned to him in the form of cash values that have built up. Or he can borrow against the cash values and still keep the rest of his insurance in force.

Many other insurance reforms took place over the years. Today insurance in the United States is controlled by state laws. These laws cover licensing of agents and brokers, types of policies, business methods, taxation of companies, and many other areas of insurance.

A special body of trained men administers these laws. The head of this body is generally called the insurance commissioner. He belongs to the National Association of Insurance Commissioners. The commissioners represent each state, and together they make sure that insurance regulation is basically the same throughout the country. The companies also work together to make sure that insurance practices are fair and financially sound.

Some countries do not have different laws for different sections of the country. They regulate insurance mainly through an agency in the central government. This bureau makes regulations and reviews insurance practices.

▶ INSURANCE COMPANIES TODAY

Insurance companies are set up in two ways. They can be either stock or mutual companies. A **stock** company is owned by stockholders, who may share part of any profit the company may make. A **mutual** company is called a nonprofit organization and is owned by its policyholders. Usually a person taking out a policy with a mutual company pays a higher premium than he would with a policy from a stock company. At the end of the year the mutual company adds the earnings from its investments and the premiums it receives. It then subtracts the claims it pays out, the reserves it must set aside for future benefit payments, and the expense of operating the company. Usually there is money left over. It is refunded to policyholders in the form of dividends. Because dividends can vary from year to year, there is no way to tell ahead of time whether insurance will cost less with a stock or a mutual company.

Insurance companies may specialize in one kind of insurance, such as life insurance, or they may sell all kinds. Some fraternal and religious organizations also issue insurance policies.

People buy policies from an insurance company's local agent. The agent is considered an independent businessman who is paid a commission on each policy he sells. A few companies employ their own local representatives, who are paid a regular salary not based on sales. Policies can also be bought through an independent insurance broker who may deal with several companies.

Insurance companies are divided into groups of specialists. Besides selling policies to people, there are many other kinds of jobs in insurance companies.

Actuaries. An actuary is a mathematics expert. He figures out how much the premiums must be and how much reserves the company should have. He calculates the earnings on investments and dividends that can be paid. Actuaries work with tables of figures that give the average length of time people live (for life insurance), how many car accidents take place in 1 year (for automobile insurance), and similar information. These tables are called **actuarial tables**. With these figures plus the amount of incoming premiums and the expected earnings from investments, actuaries calculate the insurance company's probable expenses and earnings for 1 year.

Underwriters. When a person applies for insurance, an underwriter decides whether the company can afford to take the risk of issuing him a policy. A **life** or **health** underwriter bases his answer on a person's age, health, and the kind of work he does. Some jobs are so dangerous that even a young person in good health must pay a high premium.

A **property** or **casualty** underwriter looks into the possibility of an accident's happening. For instance, a person who has had several automobile accidents may have difficulty getting automobile insurance. In any case, the person would have to pay a higher premium because an accident seems more likely to happen to him than to the average driver.

Claims Adjusters. Settling claims is a harder job in property and casualty insurance than in life insurance. Unless a person dies a short time after taking out a life insurance policy, there are not many questions the insurance company asks about his death. But in property and casualty insurance, a man called the claims adjuster must know many things. If a ring is lost, he must find out what its true value is. If rain destroys ceilings and rugs, he checks into the exact amount of damage. The claims adjuster makes sure that his company is not paying more than the policy allows for or replacing a loss that was not covered by the policy.

Lawyers. An insurance company needs lawyers for many reasons. The insurance companies themselves must follow certain regulations about where they invest their money and how much reserves they must keep. Their lawyers need to make sure they are following these regulations. Lawyers also check new policies to see if they meet the laws of the different states. Lastly, if there is a question about a claim made by a policyholder, the lawyers may help to investigate the facts.

Accountants and Auditors. An insurance company takes in and pays out large amounts of money every day. Keeping track of the money is a major job. Accountants handle reports, tax returns, commissions, and salaries. In general, auditors check the business accounts of the insurance company to see that everything is in order.

▶**INSURANCE INVESTMENTS**

Insurance companies obtain part of their income through investing their funds. They lend money to build new homes, factories, shipping centers, and office buildings. Insurance funds were used by the airlines to replace propeller planes with jets. Insurance companies also put money in federal, state, and local government bonds. These bonds help build schools, highways, libraries, and parks.

BLAKE T. NEWTON, JR.
President, Institute of Life Insurance

INSURANCE, UNEMPLOYMENT. See UNEMPLOYMENT AND UNEMPLOYMENT INSURANCE.

INTELLIGENCE TESTS. See TESTS AND TEST TAKING.

INTER-AMERICAN HIGHWAY. See PAN AMERICAN HIGHWAY.

INTEREST. See PERCENT AND INTEREST.

INTERIOR DECORATING

It is natural for people to love their homes. From the earliest times men have decorated the places where they live to make them as beautiful as possible. Interior decoration is therefore one of the oldest of the arts. It is also an important one, for the rooms you live in affect your life. The best interior decoration makes people feel comfortable and happy. The furnishings of a room are not just for show; furniture should please the people who use it and suit the way they live. Simple rooms are usually the best. If curtains, rugs, and furniture get in the way of day-to-day activities, the decoration is not successful.

▶ THE HISTORY OF INTERIOR DECORATION

The earliest interior decoration came from the desire for comfort, convenience, and beauty. The interior decoration we know—with furniture, carpets, and curtains—began about the time Columbus discovered America. There is a beautiful palace in Mantua, Italy, where the suite of Isabella d'Este (1474–1539), the Marchioness of Mantua, can still be seen. She had rooms designed that were small enough to be comfortable and private. They were more cozy than the great stony halls of the palace. Palaces were built in those days to impress people with the wealth and power of the owner. They were not well suited to human needs.

It is interesting to think about the reasons for certain furnishings. Curtains, for instance, were not hung just to look pretty, but to control light and ventilation (the movement of air).

The way that people live affects the type of furniture they use. Early American furniture, for example, was very sturdy and plain. The first settlers were too busy farming, clearing the wilderness, and fighting the Indians to make anything but necessary and useful objects. As life became easier, frontier furniture became more graceful, for the pioneers had more time to spend on making furniture.

Many things continue to affect styles of decoration: world's fairs, travel to other countries, scientific discoveries, and changes in architecture and building methods. Indeed, one great interior designer may start a completely new school of thought.

▶ HOW TO PLAN YOUR OWN ROOM

The first rule of all good decoration is to consider the needs of the person who will occupy the room or the family that will live in the house. When planning a room for yourself, you should first decide what your own needs and interests are. Do you have many hobbies and collections? Do you do your homework in your room? Do you lie on your bed in the daytime to talk on the telephone or to read? The answers to such questions affect the decoration you ought to have.

For instance, if you like to lie on your bed in the daytime, you should choose a foam rubber mattress that will last a long time and won't sag. An attractive but sturdy bedspread fitted with bolsters—long, firm cushions—would make your bed into a sofa for daytime use. There should be one chair in which you can read comfortably and another for company. If you like to display snapshots and souvenirs, you will need a bulletin board. If you study in your room or make model ships, for example, one wide table could serve both as a desk for homework and as a hobby board. If you work with paints, glue, or other things that are likely to spill, a vinyl floor that can be washed would probably be better than a carpet. Shelves are useful for books, storage, and collections. Wall shelves are helpful in small rooms. A place for each thing you use makes it easier to keep a room in order and to find things without a search.

When you have learned as much as you can by studying yourself, study the room. What shape, how long, how wide, how high is it? (Accurate measurements are important in dealing with any room.) How many windows and doors does it have, and how are they placed? The location of windows is important in choosing curtains and arranging furniture. You must decide what is the easiest way to get into, out of, or through the room. This is called a traffic pattern, and it also affects the placing of furniture. How much furniture do you need, what kind, and where would it be best to place it with regard to the traffic pattern and light of the room? A floor plan of the room will help you choose and arrange furniture in relation to traffic patterns and light. If you cut out pieces of paper to represent furniture, you can experiment by arranging and rearranging the paper pieces.

► COLOR SCHEMES

Color is very important. The color of a room can have a bad or good effect on your habits and personality. Trying to decide how different colors make you feel is an interesting game.

The colors you choose for your room should be becoming to you. Strong primary colors and clear, fresh color schemes are suitable for most young people.

The location of a room also affects the choice of colors. Cool colors—pale blue, blue-green, pale gray—are not good in a north or east room. They are best in the usually sunny rooms on the south or west sides of a house. Yellow, orange, gold, or any of the hot colors make a room look warmer.

Color can be used for optical illusion to make a room look larger or smaller. Light colors make rooms look larger. Dark colors make rooms look smaller. A light-colored ceiling makes a low ceiling look higher. If a room has an odd shape, its color scheme should be simple. Too many colors in a small room will make it look more crowded.

A color scheme is either a set of blending and harmonizing colors or one of contrasting colors. Colors that blend are restful. But a contrasting color often works well as a bright accent on a chair seat or a sofa cushion. A color scheme can also be a combination of several shades of one color.

► FLOORS, WALLS, AND LIGHTING

Bare wood floors, especially if they are stained a dark walnut color and waxed, are attractive but apt to be noisy. Vinyl, rubber tile, cork, and other tile floorings are quiet, good-looking, and easy to keep. Wall-to-wall carpets make a small room look larger. But these carpets show wear, since they cannot be turned around. Small, or "area," rugs can soften the look of bare floors. They can also be used to add color to a room.

Above: Good decorating requires careful use of different patterns. In a room with solid-colored walls, rug, and sofa, printed draperies and a striped chair provide tasteful contrasts. Below: Not everyone would want to live in a room with a checkered sofa, striped chairs, and draperies, rug, and wallpaper of different prints. Decorating a room with such extreme mixtures is very difficult, but many people like the challenge.

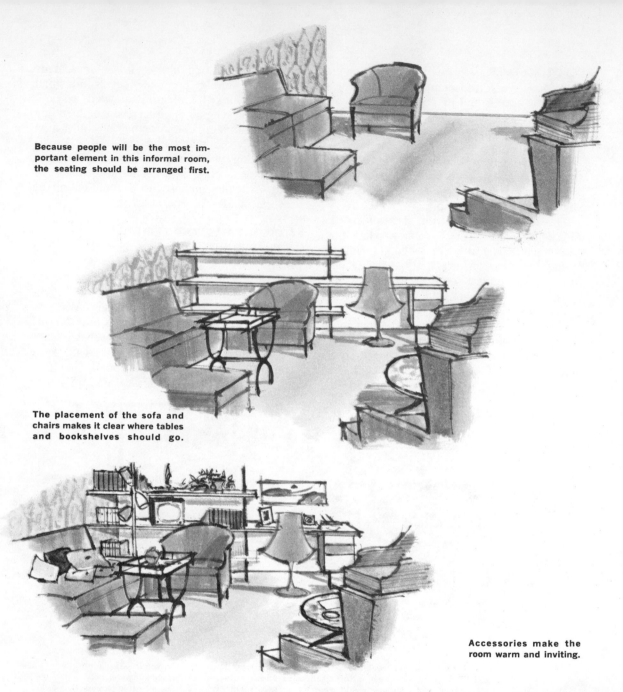

Because people will be the most important element in this informal room, the seating should be arranged first.

The placement of the sofa and chairs makes it clear where tables and bookshelves should go.

Accessories make the room warm and inviting.

One of the easiest ways to improve a drab room is to paint or paper it in attractive colors. Wood paneling is one wall treatment that requires little care. A popular new way to cover walls is with fabric. Sometimes the ceiling is made into a canopy, like a tent. Tent rooms are warm and fun to live in; and the fabric deadens noise. The military quality of tent rooms pleases boys.

A room should have overhead light and pools of light from lamps for special activities.

Lamps should be chosen by how well they provide light—not by the color or fancy nature of the base. Try out a lamp to see if you can read by it comfortably. For reading in bed, it is best to use a wall lamp that sends the light over your shoulder and focuses on the open book.

▶ FURNITURE AND ACCESSORIES

The many uses of a room must be considered when choosing furniture. The furniture

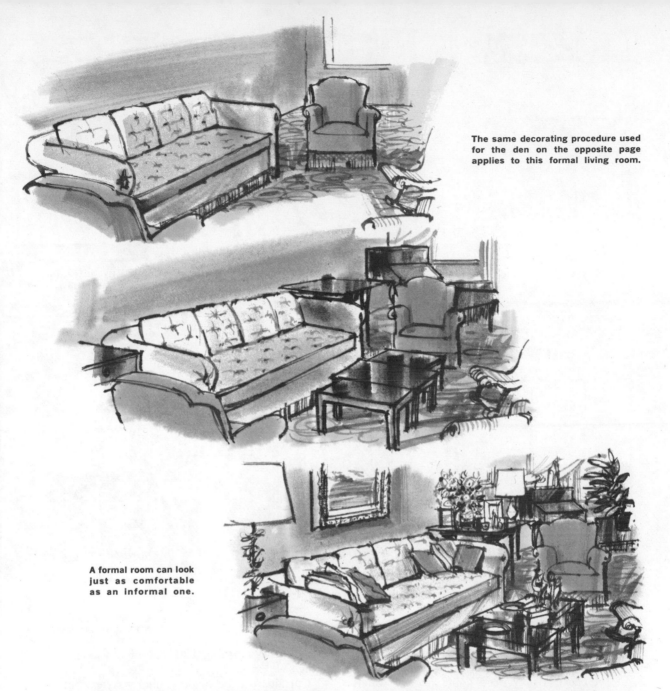

A formal room can look just as comfortable as an informal one.

of a living room, for example, must suit the purposes of the room: entertainment, relaxation, and family gathering.

To find out what sort of furniture appeals to you, study different historical periods. Many styles of furniture can be seen in model rooms in department and furniture stores or in museums. Furniture should be chosen for its sturdiness, good lines, and proportions. If you buy simple, well-designed furniture you can use it all your life.

Accessories are those extra ornaments in a room: pictures, maps, mirrors, boxes, bottles, vases, and personal treasures. Accessories give style to a room, just as jewelry and hats do to a woman's costume. They are the little things that especially appeal to you. If you make airplane models as a hobby, you may want to mount your best one and put it on your desk. If you draw or do needlepoint, some of your work might be framed and hung on the walls. Seashells or rocks make interest-

**CAFE
CURTAINS**

TRAVERSE DRAPERIES

**OVERLAPPING
CURTAINS**

**DRAPERIES WITH
SWAG VALANCE**

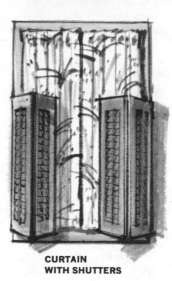

**CURTAIN
WITH SHUTTERS**

**STATIONARY DRAPERIES
WITH AUSTRIAN SHADE**

WINDOW TREATMENTS

ing displays. Girls often like to display a doll collection. Plants add to the looks of a room. But because they need light, air, and water, you must be willing to take care of them. A room can be brightened with colorful sofa pillows, floor cushions, or books.

▶WINDOW CURTAINS

The basic reason for curtains is the proper control of light and air. Rooms must get enough fresh air. Curtains that prevent air from coming into the house do not serve their purpose. Curtains that can be pulled together will make a room cozier at night and will shut out the early morning light that might waken a light sleeper.

Curtains can be made in many styles, but they should never be skimpy. It is not wise to use fragile or flimsy fabrics in rooms that are used a great deal and need constantly moving air. Floor-length curtains look good in most rooms, but short café curtains or sturdy roll blinds are good-looking in rooms that are used a great deal.

▶ANTIQUES

Many present-day homes have pieces of old furniture or accessories that are called antiques. "Antique" means "very old"; the accepted definition of an antique is something made before 1830. Most things before then were handmade, and good antiques show skilled craftsmanship and tasteful design. Some people collect antiques as a hobby. Antiques tell us about the ideas and habits of people in other times and places.

However, there is a difference between fine antiques and things that are just old or old-fashioned. Some old things were ugly when they were first made, and time has not made them better-looking. It is not sensible to admire an ugly old shaving mug just because it is old or to expect someone to sit in an antique chair if it is uncomfortable. Houses are to be lived in, not just looked at.

▶ INTERIOR DESIGNERS

Interior designers or decorators are professional people who, through education and training, are qualified to plan the interiors of rooms. They have studied interior architecture, the use of space, color, and design, styles of furniture and fabrics, and all the subjects that deal with interior design.

When an interior designer is commissioned, he shops for everything that goes into a house, from furniture to doorknobs. He submits his findings to the person who has hired him. He plans color schemes, furniture arrangements, storage space, and lighting effects. Sometimes he will correct architectural defects inside the room by new construction.

In planning an entire house, the first considerations are the facilities that make the home comfortable and workable—heating, air-conditioning, plumbing, lighting, and ease of housekeeping. Privacy for every person and every age group is of great importance in a home, since people need to have places to be by themselves. Thoughtful home planning enables people to live more peacefully together. The basic rules for decorating are the same for any interior. In addition to homes, interior designers plan the inside decoration of hotels, restaurants, stores, factories, office buildings, hospitals, ships, airplanes, and automobiles.

WILLIAM PAHLMANN
Fellow, American Institute of Interior Designers

See also ANTIQUES AND ANTIQUE COLLECTING; DESIGN AND COLOR; FURNITURE DESIGN; HOMES; TAPESTRY; TEXTILES.

INTERJECTION. See PARTS OF SPEECH.

INTERNAL-COMBUSTION ENGINES

An internal-combustion engine changes the heat energy of burning fuel into power and motion. This power can be harnessed to turn the wheels of an automobile or truck, the propeller of an airplane, the shaft of a generator, and many other machines.

"Internal combustion" means that the fuel is burned inside the engine, where it does its work. Gasoline engines, diesel engines, and gas turbines are all internal-combustion engines. The steam engine is an external-combustion engine ("external" means "outside"), because its fuel is burned in a separate firebox, away from its moving parts. The burning fuel heats water to make steam, which does the work in the engine. When fuel is burned in an internal-combustion engine, it produces great quantities of rapidly expanding gases. These expanding gases drive a piston or a rotor directly.

Internal-combustion engines are divided into two basic classes. These are reciprocating engines, in which the work is done by a piston moving back and forth in a cylinder, and rotary engines, in which the work is done by a turning rotor. Gasoline and diesel engines are reciprocating engines. Gas turbines and the Wankel engine are rotary engines.

The internal-combustion engine began to come into wide use about 70 years ago. Since that time it has almost completely replaced the steam engine. The internal-combustion engine is more efficient than the steam engine in most uses. It delivers more power for the amount of energy put into it than the steam engine does. The internal-combustion engine also takes up much less room than a steam engine.

Internal-combustion engines are now one of the world's most used sources of power. They are used in automobiles, ships, and airplanes. They are found on the farm in tractors, reapers, and other farm vehicles.

They are used to power chain saws, derricks, cranes, air compressors, and lawnmowers. Almost everywhere you look there is an internal-combustion engine at work.

▶ **HOW THE GASOLINE ENGINE WORKS**

How does a gasoline engine turn the heat energy from burning fuel into power and motion? The basic principle is actually rather simple, although the engine, with all its parts and equipment, may seem very complicated.

Fuel is burned in a **cylinder**, which is a chamber closed at one end. As the gases burn, they expand and press outward in all directions. They cannot escape through the sides or the closed end of the cylinder. But at the other end of the cylinder is a movable stopper, or **piston**, which slides back and forth. The pressure of the expanding gases drives the piston down with great force. If it were not prevented somehow, the piston would shoot out of the cylinder like a bullet from a gun. But the piston is kept from doing this by being connected to a **crankshaft**. As the piston travels down, it turns the crankshaft, just as a boy pressing down on the pedals of a bicycle turns the pedals. In this way the straight-line motion of the piston is converted into rotary, or turning, motion. The turning crankshaft brings the piston back up in the cylinder again. A strong metal rod called the **connecting rod** links the piston to the crankshaft.

Early designers ran up against the problem of keeping the expanding gases from leaking past the piston and wasting power. The obvious answer would seem to be to make the piston fit very tightly in the cylinder. Unfortunately, if this were done the piston would soon expand as it became heated by the burning fuel. Then it would get stuck and not run at all. The problem was solved by the use of **piston rings**. These are thin, springy metal rings that fit in grooves around the piston and project a short distance. The rings press tightly against the cylinder walls and keep gas from leaking past. At the same time, the piston fits freely in the cylinder.

The Four-Stroke Cycle

Gasoline engines do not produce power on every stroke of the piston. Most are so designed that only one stroke out of every four produces power. The other three strokes get the engine ready for the next power stroke. Let us follow a simple one-cylinder gasoline engine through its cycle of operations.

On the first stroke the piston moves downward, sucking in a mixture of fuel and air through a small hole in the top of the cylinder called an **intake port**. This stroke is called the **intake stroke**. A valve in the intake port, called

FOUR-STROKE CYCLE IN A GASOLINE ENGINE

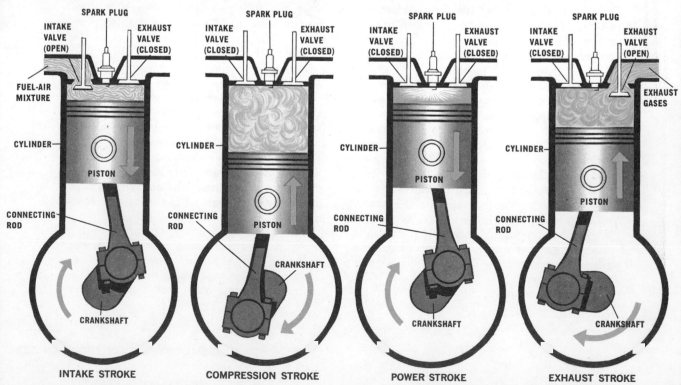

INTAKE STROKE   COMPRESSION STROKE   POWER STROKE   EXHAUST STROKE

the **intake valve**, opens up to let in the fuel-air mixture and closes again at the end of the stroke.

The second stroke is called the **compression stroke**. The piston moves up toward the top of the cylinder. Since the intake valve is now closed, the fuel-air mixture cannot escape, and the rising piston squeezes it into a much smaller volume. The more tightly the piston compresses the fuel-air mixture, the faster it will burn and the more power it will produce. The amount that the piston compresses the fuel-air mixture is called the **compression ratio**. Most automobile engines have a compression ratio of about 8:1. That is, the fuel-air mixture at the beginning of the compression stroke takes up about eight times as much space as it does at the end of the stroke.

When the piston reaches the top of the compression stroke, an electric spark ignites (sets fire to) the fuel-air mixture. The mixture burns with almost explosive violence, although it does not actually explode. The gases produced by this rapid burning of the fuel expand with great force—about 60 to 70 times that of normal atmospheric pressure—and drive the piston down, in the **power stroke**.

The last stroke in the cycle is the **exhaust stroke**. When the piston begins to rise again after the power stroke, an exhaust valve in the top of the cylinder opens. The rising piston pushes the burned gases out. When the piston reaches the top of its stroke, the exhaust valve closes and the engine is ready to begin a new power cycle. This cycle is repeated as often as several thousand times a minute.

Why More Than One Cylinder? As anyone who has ever run a gasoline-powered lawnmower knows, a one-cylinder engine gives a very jerky operation and vibrates a great deal. The reason for the vibration is that only one stroke out of every four is a power stroke. The larger the engine, the worse the vibration. Engine designers learned that they could get around this problem by using a number of smaller cylinders instead of one large cylinder. With a number of cylinders attached to the same crankshaft, at least one cylinder is always giving a power stroke. The engine produces a steady flow of power rather than a jerky, interrupted flow.

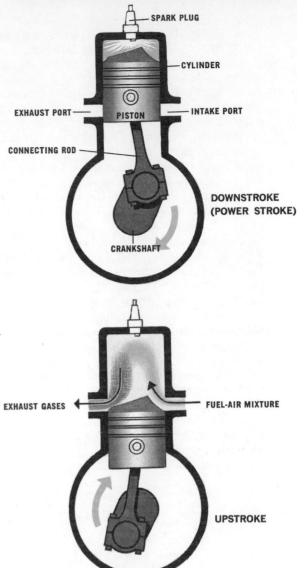

SPARK PLUG

CYLINDER

EXHAUST PORT

PISTON

INTAKE PORT

CONNECTING ROD

DOWNSTROKE (POWER STROKE)

CRANKSHAFT

EXHAUST GASES

FUEL-AIR MIXTURE

UPSTROKE

The Two-Stroke Cycle

An engine that works on a two-stroke cycle produces power on every downstroke of the piston, or every second stroke. It does this by combining three operations—exhaust, intake, and compression—into one stroke.

The two-stroke engine has no intake or exhaust valves. Instead, it has open ports in the sides of the cylinder. The piston covers and uncovers these ports as it rides up and down.

The fuel-air mixture is compressed before it enters the cylinder. This is sometimes done by leading the mixture into the crankcase and letting the piston compress it as it travels down during the power stroke. Other engines use a blower to compress the mixture.

As the piston reaches the bottom of the stroke, it uncovers the intake and exhaust ports. The fuel-air mixture sweeps in through the intake port as the burned gases go out the exhaust port. In theory, the incoming fuel-air mixture sweeps the exhaust out of the cylinder. A ridge across the top of the piston deflects the fuel-air mixture toward the top of the cylinder to keep it from mixing with the waste gases of the exhaust. But in practice the fuel-air mixture always mixes with the exhaust to some extent. Sometimes some of the fuel-air mixture passes out the exhaust port along with the burned gases. This wastes fuel. Sometimes part of the burned gas remains in the cylinder. This means that the fuel-air mixture does not burn as well as it should.

In theory, a two-stroke engine should give twice as much power as a four-stroke engine of the same size. In actual use, it does not work quite this well. But the two-stroke principle permits smaller, lighter engines to be used. A two-stroke engine uses more fuel than a four-stroke engine. Because of this, two-stroke engines are chiefly used where small size and light weight are important, as in outboard motors for boats and in some lawnmowers. Since these small engines do not use much fuel anyway, the greater fuel consumption does not matter.

▶PARTS OF THE GASOLINE ENGINE

The cylinder block and head, piston, connecting rod, and crankshaft are the basic parts of the engine. But there are many other parts without which the engine will not run, as motorists who do not take proper care of their cars often find out.

One of the most important parts is the **carburetor**, which mixes the fuel with air so that it will burn properly. If this were not done, the fuel would burn too slowly to create a push on the piston. The carburetor first breaks up the liquid fuel into a fine mist of tiny droplets by means of a high-speed jet of air. On their way to the cylinder the tiny droplets of gasoline turn to a vapor. This mixture of gasoline vapor and air burns with great rapidity and therefore expands with great force.

An engine needs a richer mixture (one that contains more gasoline) when it is just starting than it does when it has warmed up. This is taken care of by a valve in the carburetor called the **choke**, which controls the proportions of gasoline and air in the fuel-air mixture. Another valve called the **throttle** controls the speed of the engine by regulating the

CROSS SECTION OF A GASOLINE ENGINE

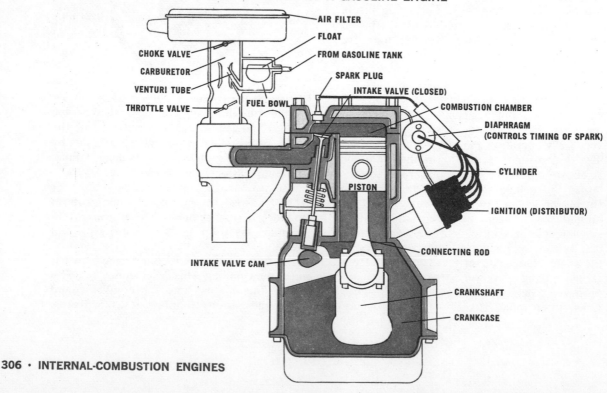

AIR FILTER
FLOAT
CHOKE VALVE
FROM GASOLINE TANK
CARBURETOR
SPARK PLUG
VENTURI TUBE
INTAKE VALVE (CLOSED)
THROTTLE VALVE
FUEL BOWL
COMBUSTION CHAMBER
DIAPHRAGM (CONTROLS TIMING OF SPARK)
PISTON
CYLINDER
IGNITION (DISTRIBUTOR)
INTAKE VALVE CAM
CONNECTING ROD
CRANKSHAFT
CRANKCASE

amount of fuel-air mixture that can leave the carburetor.

Lubricating System. The engine must be kept lubricated so that its moving parts will slide smoothly over each other. Without lubrication the moving parts would soon become overheated and jam. Also, they would wear out very quickly. An oil pump forces oil from the crankcase through tiny openings in the cylinder block, the crankshaft, and the connecting rods, so that the oil reaches every moving part. The crankcase serves as a central oil reservoir. Most engines have an oil filter to strain dust and grit out of the oil.

Cooling System. It takes more than lubrication to keep the engine from becoming overheated. There must be some way of getting rid of the unused heat from the burning fuel. In small reciprocating engines this can be done by simply covering the cylinder block and cylinder head with metal fins that give off heat to the air. But this is usually not practical for big automobile or truck engines. These engines usually have a liquid cooling system. A water pump circulates water through passages in the cylinder block. The water takes up heat from the engine and gives it up to the air as the water passes through the radiator. The radiator is basically a set of thin-walled metal tubes through which heat can easily pass. These tubes are covered with metal fins to increase the area that gives off heat to the air. A fan driven by the engine pulls air through the radiator.

Exhaust System. The poisonous gases made by the burning fuel must be led away after they have done their work of driving the piston. A chamber called the exhaust manifold collects the burned gases from each cylinder. From the manifold the gases pass through an exhaust pipe and out into the air at a safe distance from the person who is operating the engine. Since an internal-combustion engine is very noisy, a silencer called a muffler is usually added to the exhaust pipe. The muffler is a hollow, thin-walled chamber several times larger than the exhaust pipe. Inside the muffler are baffles—parts that slow down the exhaust gases and thus cut down the volume of noise.

Actually, the engine could run perfectly well without an exhaust system. But it would be neither safe nor pleasant for the operator.

CROSS SECTION OF A FOUR-STROKE DIESEL ENGINE

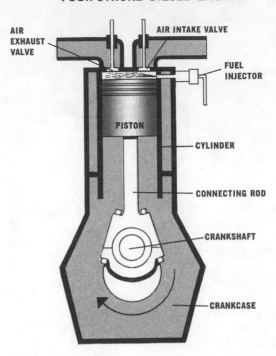

AIR EXHAUST VALVE

AIR INTAKE VALVE

FUEL INJECTOR

PISTON

CYLINDER

CONNECTING ROD

CRANKSHAFT

CRANKCASE

▶ DIESEL ENGINES

The diesel engine, named after its inventor, Rudolf Diesel (1858–1913), works very much like the gasoline engine. The main difference is that the diesel engine needs no spark plugs, coils, or distributor. In the diesel engine the fuel to be burned (usually oil) is ignited directly by the heat of the air that is compressed in the cylinder.

When air is compressed rapidly, as in pumping up a bicycle tire, it becomes hot. The more the air is compressed, the hotter it becomes. The diesel engine compresses the air in its cylinders so tightly that the air becomes red-hot. When the piston reaches the top of the compression stroke, fuel is sprayed into the cylinder through a nozzle called an **injector**. When the fine spray of fuel hits the red-hot air, it burns immediately.

The diesel engine runs on cheaper fuel than the gasoline engine. It is also more efficient—the diesel engine can make use of as much as 40 percent of the energy in its fuel. The best gasoline engine can make use of only about 30 percent of this energy.

On the other hand, diesel engines must be built much more strongly than gasoline engines. This makes them bulky and heavy. As a result, diesel engines are chiefly used where size and weight are no objection, as in ships,

CROSS SECTION OF A GAS TURBINE

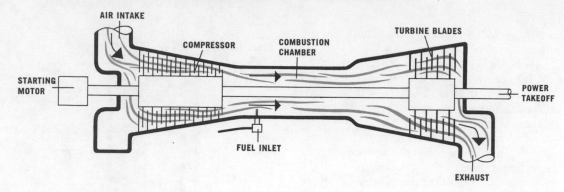

electric power plants, locomotives, and heavy-duty trucks and tractors.

GAS TURBINES

One of the newest types of internal-combustion engine is the gas turbine. This engine has no cylinders and no pistons. The fuel-air mixture is burned in a combustion chamber. The hot gases from the combustion chamber flow with great force through a turbine rotor, which they turn at very high speeds. The shaft of the turbine rotor can be connected to machinery, such as an electric generator.

The jet airplane engine is a type of gas turbine. However, the forward thrust that drives the plane comes from the exhaust gases. The turbine is used to turn an air compressor that supplies air to burn the fuel. In some jet engines the turbine also turns a propeller or a fan.

The gas turbine may one day be used to power cars and trucks. It has already been used experimentally. It runs much more smoothly than the piston engine and has fewer moving parts to wear out or get out of order. However, it is more expensive to make than the piston engine and consumes more fuel.

HISTORY

As far back as the 17th century, scientists were interested in the idea of an internal-

OPERATION OF THE WANKEL ENGINE

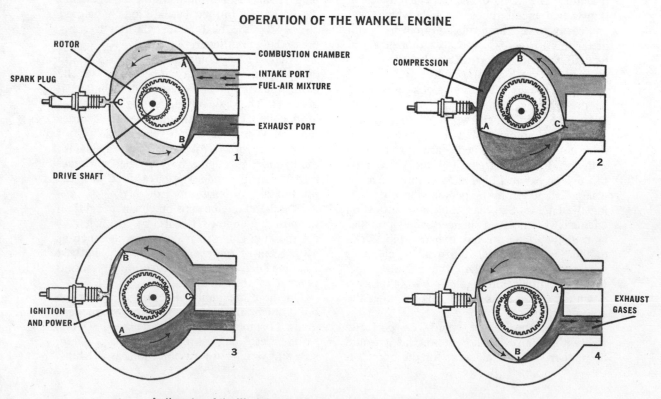

As the rotor of the Wankel engine turns, it passes through all four stages of the power cycle. The process is repeated as each side of the rotor comes into position.

combustion engine. However, the first practical internal-combustion engine was not built until 1859. This engine was the invention of a French engineer, Étienne Lenoir (1822–1900). Lenoir's engine ran on street-lighting gas, which was ignited by an electric spark. The Lenoir engine operated very smoothly. But it was not very powerful, because the fuel-air mixture was not compressed and so did not burn fast enough. Also, it used up enormous amounts of fuel. Still, several hundred Lenoir engines were sold for use in factories.

The next step forward was the four-stroke cycle, including compression of the fuel-air mixture, patented in 1862 by another Frenchman, Alphonse Beau de Rochas (1815–91). However, Beau de Rochas only patented the idea and never built an engine.

The first four-stroke engine was built in 1878 by Nikolaus A. Otto (1832–91). It is generally accepted that Otto never heard of Beau de Rochas' ideas and invented the engine by himself. The four-stroke power cycle was named the Otto cycle in his honor. Many inventors after Otto added improvements to the internal-combustion engine.

In 1954 a German engineer named Felix Wankel patented a new type of rotary engine. Instead of a piston, the Wankel engine has a three-sided rotor sweeping around inside an oval combustion chamber. The Wankel engine has many of the advantages of a gas turbine, but it is simpler and cheaper to manufacture.

Reviewed by FORD MOTOR COMPANY
Technical and Product Information Division

See also AUTOMOBILES; DIESEL ENGINES; ENGINES; JET PROPULSION.

INTERNATIONAL DATE LINE

The international date line is an irregular north-south line that runs along or close to the 180th meridian. It extends from the North Pole to the South Pole. This line separates the regions of earliest and latest standard time on the earth's surface. On the western side of the line the time is always 24 hours, or 1 full day, later than on the eastern side. For example, when it is 6 P.M. Friday (see chart) on the western side of the line, it is 6 P.M. Thursday on the eastern side. Let us see why.

Beginning at the prime meridian (0 degrees longitude), which runs through the site of the original Greenwich Observatory in England, the earth is divided into 24 standard time zones. Each time zone is 15 degrees longitude in width. The earth rotates eastward at the rate of 15 degrees longitude an hour. Therefore the standard time in each zone is 1 hour later than in the zone to the west and 1 hour earlier than in the zone to the east.

Suppose it is 6 A.M. Friday at the prime

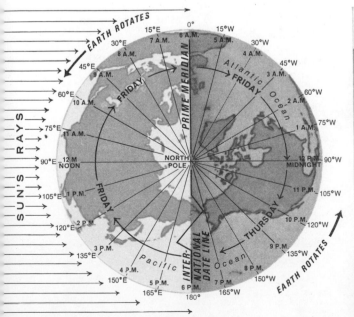

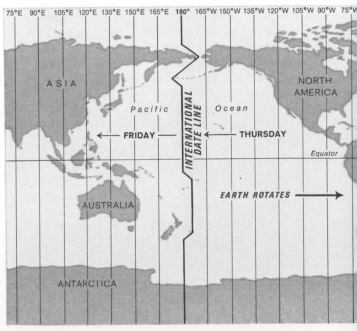

meridian. What time is it in the standard time zones of the later half of the world (from the prime meridian east to the 180th meridian)? Each eastward zone is 1 hour later than the preceding zone. Therefore this half of the world shows all hours from 6 A.M. Friday to 6 P.M. Friday. The latest time, 6 P.M. Friday, is found at the 180th meridian.

What time is it at the same moment in the earlier half of the world, west of the prime meridian? Each westward zone is 1 hour earlier than the preceding one. Therefore this half of the world shows all hours from 6 A.M. Friday at the prime meridian to 6 P.M. Thursday at the 180th meridian. This means that on opposite sides of the 180th meridian the time differs by 24 hours, or a full day. Here are the latest and earliest times on the earth. And since the western side of the 180th meridian's zone always has the latest time on the earth, this is where each new date begins.

Why did the nations of the world select the 180th meridian for the dividing line between the earth's earliest and latest hours? The answer is that they wanted to avoid all possibility of having two different dates in nearby villages or towns. The 180th meridian runs largely through ocean rather than land. Furthermore, by swerving away from the 180th meridian at a few places, the line avoids land entirely. This zigzag dividing line is the international date line.

In the North Pacific the international date line swerves away from the 180th meridian to pass between Siberia and Alaska. It swerves again at the Aleutian Islands. In the South Pacific the international date line leaves the 180th meridian north of the Fiji islands and returns to it south of New Zealand.

When ships and planes cross the international date line, they must change the date on their calendars to correspond with the area they are moving into. Ships going westward (from San Francisco to Tokyo, for example) advance the date, as from Thursday to Friday. Ships going eastward set the date back, as from Friday to Thursday. In a westward crossing this may mean the complete omission of a calendar day. In an eastward crossing a calendar day may be repeated.

SAMUEL NAMOWITZ
Author, *Earth Science*

INTERNATIONAL GEOPHYSICAL YEAR

From July 1, 1957, to December 31, 1958, thousands of scientists from more than 65 nations worked together studying our planet, the earth. Never before had so many scientists worked together on a single investigation. It was called the International Geophysical Year (IGY). "International" meant that many nations took part. "Geophysical" meant that the scientists were studying the physical things of the earth—the land, oceans, and air. The IGY lasted 18 months. But it was called a year because all the studies were planned as part of one big program.

▶ THE BEGINNING

The IGY had its beginning many years ago, in 1872. At that time Lieutenant Karl Weyprecht (1838–81) of Austria led a scientific expedition to the regions around the North Pole.

The Weyprecht expedition spent 2 years in the Arctic, studying weather and the earth's magnetism. But there was so much to do that the small expedition could hardly make a start on it. What was really needed, Weyprecht felt, was many scientists working together. There should be scientists in the Arctic and in other parts of the world all making their studies at the same time. And he wanted special times set aside for these studies.

Polar Years 1 and 2

Karl Weyprecht died in 1881, but his ideas were not forgotten. In 1882 and 1883—and again 50 years later, in 1932 and 1933—scientists of many nations did carry out Weyprecht's plans. Each of these special periods of scientific research at the poles was known as an International Polar Year (IPY).

The scientists taking part in IPY-1 and IPY-2 made observations on weather and the earth's magnetism. They studied ocean currents, glaciers, and auroras—the lights in the atmosphere above both polar regions.

(Northern lights, or aurora borealis, is the name given to the auroras seen in the Northern Hemisphere. The south polar lights are called aurora australis.) Studies were also made of the ionosphere, the layer of the atmosphere that conducts electricity.

During IPY-1 most observations were made in the Arctic regions. There were only two stations in the Antarctic. But many more observations were made in the Antarctic in IPY-2. Both Polar Years resulted in much new knowledge about the earth.

A New Idea: IGY

The two Polar Years showed scientists how useful it was to make observations in many places at the same time. They could thus see how what happened on one side of the earth was related to what happened on the other side. Scientists therefore began thinking about a third Polar Year, to be held in 1982 and 1983.

In the spring of 1950 an American scientist, James A. Van Allen, invited some scientists to his home to meet a visiting English scientist, Sydney Chapman. During the evening one of the Americans, Lloyd Berkner, suggested that the next Polar Year be held in 1957 and 1958. Berkner had good reasons for advancing the date. The most important one had to do with the sun.

The earth depends on the sun for all its energy. And whatever takes place on the sun affects the earth in some way.

The sun's bright surface usually shows some darker regions known as sunspots, and it seethes with geyserlike jets of hot gas. There are periods, however, when the gases on the sun are very active. During these periods of peak activity many more sunspots appear. They are accompanied by unusually bright eruptions of gas.

The gases on the sun are most active about every 11 years. As Berkner knew, the next period of peak activity would be in 1957 and 1958. That was one reason for his suggestion.

Another important reason was that great improvements had been made in scientific equipment since IPY-2. During World War II many advances had been made in radio and radar. These and other electronic instruments could be used in scientific research.

Also, during World War II the governments of the world had learned to move large amounts of men and equipment rapidly to all parts of the globe. Scientific expeditions could make use of these techniques, too.

Berkner and the other scientists decided that the whole earth—not just the polar regions—could now be studied at one time. Thus, they gave their project a new name— Geophysical Year. The next problem was to make it international.

Five Years of Planning

For many years scientists of the world have joined together in international organizations known as scientific unions. The aim of the scientific unions is to let scientists from all nations meet regularly. At the meetings they share their knowledge and plan scientific studies. All the separate unions—there is one for each branch of science—are joined in a central council named the International Council of Scientific Unions. This is usually called ICSU.

It was to ICSU that Berkner, Chapman, and Van Allen sent their idea of an IGY. The idea was welcomed. And in 1951 the ICSU and the separate unions began more than 5 years of hard work to plan what was needed.

▶ THE PLAN OF THE IGY

The IGY was based on a huge plan. Observation stations were set up all over the world—from the North Pole to the South Pole. In the Antarctic alone scientists of 12 different nations set up more than 50 stations.

Every nation whose scientists took part in the IGY agreed to send their data (the results of their measurements) to World Data Centers. This meant that all could share the facts discovered.

World Days

Some measurements were carried out every day at hundreds of observation stations. Other kinds of measurements could be made only now and then. It was important that these should all be made at the same time. So the scientists planned to make them only on special days. These were called Regular World Days. Yet even this was not enough.

Scientists studying the weather wanted some groups of days on which special weather observations could be made all over the world.

They picked six groups of 10 days in the IGY when they would do this.

▶ THE SUN AND THE IGY

During the IGY a constant watch was kept on the sun. This was possible because there were observers all over the world. When it was night in one hemisphere, the sun could be studied in the other. The only thing that could stop solar (sun) observations was bad weather. As a result, scientists were able to observe the sun for an average of 21 hours each day of the IGY.

Some of the solar observations were made by taking photographs of the sun through telescopes. Another method used was to split the sun's light into its various colors, just as you may have done with a prism. The various colors were then analyzed with an instrument called a spectroscope. This enabled scientists to study the elements in the sun and also measure its temperature.

The Sun and Our Earth's Magnetism

For nearly 400 years scientists have known that the earth acts like a huge magnet. But

Studies of the earth's magnetic field are made with a magnetometer.

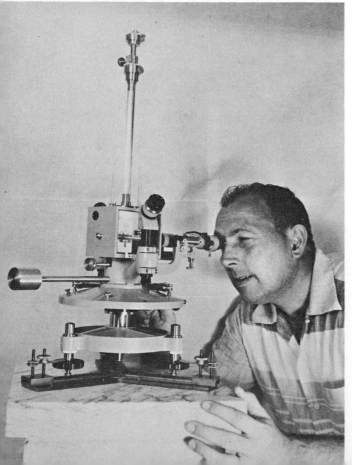

why it does so has always been a mystery. Plans for the IGY called for a special study of the earth's magnetism and its relationship to the sun.

The magnetism can be detected and measured at the surface of the earth, deep within the earth, in the sea, and high up in the air. The total reach of the earth's magnetism is known as its magnetic field. The field stretches from pole to pole, surrounding the earth in the curved shape of a shell.

A complete study of the earth's magnetic field calls for observations made from submarines, mines, balloons, and rockets. The scientists of the IGY were able to make such observations at the same time. And they could compare their measurements of the earth's magnetism with the observations that other scientists were making of activity on the sun.

Solar Flares

Scientists of the IGY were very careful to keep a watch out for solar flares. Flares are great explosions of hot, extremely bright gas from the sun's surface. Flares always occur near sunspots. Since the IGY was planned for a time when the number of sunspots would be greatest, scientists expected a lot of flares. They were not disappointed.

When a flare occurs on the sun, it is seen on the earth about 8½ minutes later. That is the amount of time light takes to travel across the 93,000,000 miles between the sun and earth. The flare also sends out other kinds of high-speed radiation. This radiation is in the form of ultraviolet rays and X rays. It travels almost as fast as light. When this radiation reaches the earth, the magnetic field around our planet is changed for a short time, and there is also a shortwave radio fade-out.

A flare also sends out showers of atomic particles. One kind, called protons, travels at very high speeds, reaching the earth about an hour after leaving the sun. The chief effect of these particles is to increase the number of cosmic rays bombarding the earth.

The second kind of atomic shower travels more slowly. This shower is made up of ions, which are atoms that carry an electrical charge, and electrons, which are atomic particles. This shower takes 20 to 40 hours to reach the earth. When the shower is big

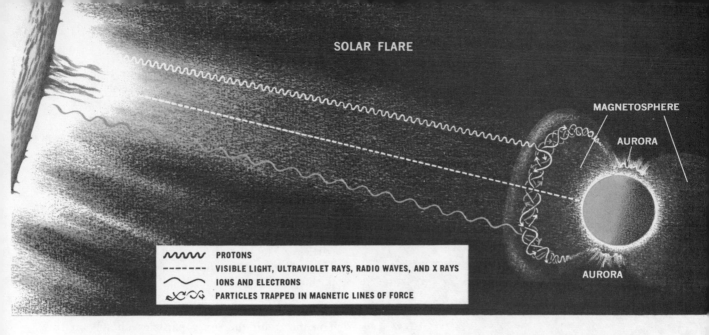

SOLAR FLARE

MAGNETOSPHERE

AURORA

AURORA

∿∿∿ PROTONS
- - - - - VISIBLE LIGHT, ULTRAVIOLET RAYS, RADIO WAVES, AND X RAYS
~~~ IONS AND ELECTRONS
∾∿∾ PARTICLES TRAPPED IN MAGNETIC LINES OF FORCE

enough, its arrival triggers a magnetic storm, for it affects the earth's magnetic field and the ionosphere. Brilliant auroras light the night skies. Long-distance radio and telephone communication may be disrupted for hours. During the IGY one such storm occurred about 28 hours after a gigantic flare.

World Warning Agency

Once a flare was sighted, IGY scientists had at least 20 hours to get ready for the slower atomic shower. Of course, they had to be warned that a flare had been seen. And so the World Warning Agency was set up at a United States Army post in Virginia.

Whenever a flare was expected or had been sighted, "alert" messages were sent to observers all over the world. If it seemed likely that the magnetic storms would go on for a long time, a Special World Interval was declared.

Solar Prominences

Next to flares the most spectacular events on the sun are solar prominences. These are huge, glowing clouds of gas that rise to heights of 50,000 miles and more. They look like giant flames above the sun's surface. Solar prominences do not seem to have much effect on the earth. Probably this is because they are less violent than flares. Their gases rarely escape the sun's gravity and never smash into the earth's upper atmosphere.

Scientists filmed the prominences with a

movie camera fitted to a special telescope. The telescope blocks out the bright central disk of the sun. And so the prominences appear as a moving fringe of flame.

Radiation Belts and Auroras

During the IGY much research was done by means of rockets and satellites. Rockets

The World Warning Agency used a globe model of the sun. Whenever a solar flare occurred on the sun, it was plotted on the globe (white spots). Lines were used to show exact location of flares.

Rockets carried aloft satellites that detected the radiation belts around the earth.

were shot into the upper atmosphere to take samples of the air. Some rockets were equipped with electronic devices that recorded conditions in the atmosphere. When the rockets fell back to earth, they brought their information with them. Satellites in orbits that pass through a large part of the earth's magnetic field can record information at many points.

Both rockets and satellites showed IGY scientists that the earth's magnetic field traps two layers of electrically charged atomic particles. The layers are called radiation belts. Their discovery was one of the great accomplishments of IGY.

When a solar flare shoots out atomic particles, some are trapped in the radiation belts. Together with the other particles already in the belts, these race back and forth between the earth's magnetic poles. They set up new and stronger electrical activity within the belts. Near the poles many particles escape into the atmosphere. The escaped particles produce an electrical charge in the air. The auroras result.

IGY thus showed what scientists had long suspected—solar flares, magnetic storms, and auroras are closely connected.

From their many observations scientists discovered much about auroras that had not

The radio telescope at Jodrell Bank, England. The dish of the telescope is aimed into space and can "hear" radio signals from orbiting satellites.

An aurora is an atmospheric effect produced by solar flares.

been known before. For instance, they discovered that auroras occur at both poles at the same time. They also found that the auroras at both poles last for the same length of time and behave in the same way. However, the auroras at the South Pole spread out more than those at the North Pole.

▶ PROBING THE EARTH

We live on the thin covering of the earth—its crust. Under the land the crust may be 20 to 22 miles thick. Under the seas it is about 3 miles thick. What lies beneath the crust? What is the center of the earth like? Answers to questions such as these are important to any study of the earth as a planet. They would also help scientists understand why the earth acts like a huge magnet.

Yet the center of the earth is nearly 4,000 miles underground, far too deep for scientists to reach. To date they have been able to drill only a short distance into the crust. And so they have had to rely on other methods to find out what lies beneath the crust. One way is to study earthquake shock waves.

Information from Earthquakes

Earthquakes set off two main kinds of shock waves. One kind may travel as far as 1,800 miles into the earth. The other travels all the way through the core and comes out on the opposite side of the earth. Each kind travels at its own rate of speed. The speed and direction of shock waves change slightly as the waves pass through materials of different densities.

Scientists use an instrument called a seismograph to study earthquake waves. Through study of the waves they have been able to find out a great deal about the kind of rock through which the waves have traveled.

For many years before the IGY, scientists

had used seismographs for studying earth-quake waves. But the IGY provided a wonderful opportunity for them to make more studies than ever before. And these studies gave strength to their theories about the interior of our earth.

Man-Made Earthquakes

Scientists also made their own shock waves by setting off underground explosions. This is called seismic shooting. Although the shock waves are small compared with those of real earthquakes, they can be recorded on seismographs. Some of the man-made waves travel along the crust. Others go down to the rocks deep below the crust and bounce back again. By comparing these waves IGY scientists were able to make detailed studies of the thickness of the crust and of the rocks of

which it is made. They were also able to get more information about the earth's mantle—the region beneath the crust.

Studying volcanic eruptions also helps in this work. Volcanoes throw out gas, steam, and hot molten rock. By examining this material, which comes from below the surface of the earth, scientists can obtain still more information.

▶ THE EARTH'S ATMOSPHERE

The atmosphere—the vast ocean of air surrounding the earth—received careful study during the IGY.

IGY and Weather Studies

Meteorologists, whose job it is to study the weather, hoped to learn more about how our weather is produced. During the IGY they

Meteorologists launch a balloon from the deck of an icebreaker. Balloons are often used to study the upper parts of the earth's atmosphere.

observed the weather in many ways. One was to send up balloons carrying measuring instruments. The instruments radioed information back to earth.

Meteorologists made a special study of the ozone layer of the air. This is a part of the atmosphere between 12 and 22 or more miles up. In this layer ultraviolet rays from the sun cause a large amount of ozone to be formed. (Ozone is a type of oxygen in which three atoms of oxygen are grouped together. Ordinary oxygen has only two.)

The ozone layer is very important to us. Because of it a dangerous amount of ultraviolet radiation is prevented from reaching the earth's surface. Balloons, aircraft, and rockets were used in making observations of the ozone layer.

Meteorologists also kept a careful check on thunderstorms. They did this by listening in to the radio crackles that thunderstorms cause. They sent up rockets to find out how much the air around the thunderstorms is electrified. Rockets also sent back information about chemical changes in the air caused by thunderstorms. This helped meteorologists find out more about the way thunderclouds are formed.

Air Movements

Knowledge about air movements plays an important part in making long-range weather forecasts. IGY meteorologists were stationed on land and on weather ships. By using balloons, and by other methods, they could easily study air currents in the lower atmosphere.

To discover how air moves at higher altitudes, they used rockets. Some of these research rockets carried small bombs that were shot out and exploded in the upper air. By timing the flash of the explosion and the bang, scientists were able to trace the movement of air, because light travels much faster than sound.

Above 50 miles a different method was used. To trace air movements at that altitude, a cloud of sodium vapor was shot out of rockets just after sunset. Since it was high in the sky, the cloud of sodium vapor was lighted up by sunlight. Meteorologists studied the cloud's direction of motion. They timed how quickly it was blown apart by the winds.

Meteorologists use special instruments to study the ozone layer of the air.

Layers of Electrified Air

Rocket, satellite, and radio studies were also made of the electrically charged layers of air. These electrified layers are called the ionosphere because they contain ions—atoms that are electrically charged.

Radio waves for long-distance communication travel in straight lines. They cannot follow the curve of the earth. The ionosphere makes long-distance communication possible, because it acts as a mirror. Radio waves beamed from one point are reflected back to another by the ionosphere.

When flares occur on the sun, the ionosphere is affected and no longer acts as a mirror—it absorbs radio signals instead of reflecting them. This is known as radio fade-out.

Scientists used rocket observations to measure the electrification of the ionosphere. They also used artificial satellites with orbits that dipped in and out of the ionosphere. Information from these satellites made it possible to compare the ionosphere with conditions in space. Scientists expected such knowledge to help in planning for space travel. In particular, they hoped to learn how to set up better radio communication from satellites.

▶ THE OCEANS OF THE EARTH

Almost three quarters of the earth is covered by water. And so the IGY was of course planned to include studies of the oceans. For one thing, scientists wanted to find out how

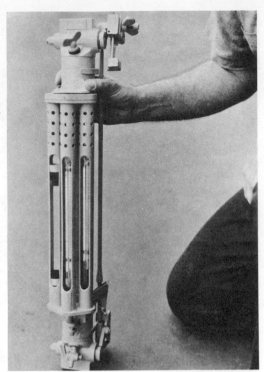

Above: A Nansen bottle with the cover removed, showing the tubes inside. The Nansen bottle is allowed to sink in the ocean to collect water samples. It is constructed so that it may be held at any depth in the water while samples are being collected. Left: Preparing to launch a Nansen bottle from a ship.

Below: A neutral-buoyancy float being launched from a ship. The float is adjusted to sink to a certain depth and is used to trace ocean currents.

salty the oceans are and whether this saltiness changes. They also wanted to know how the water circulates in the oceans and to add to their knowledge of the tides.

The saltiness of the oceans was measured by electrical probes. This was possible because the saltier the water is, the more readily it conducts electricity. Therefore saltiness can be determined by an instrument that measures how much electricity is conducted in ocean water. During the IGY such measurements were made all over the world.

The sun and the moon cause tides by pulling the oceans, with the result that water heaps up. But the coastlines of continents are uneven. And so they cause a tidal drag on the water. This in turn affects the level of the tide.

During the IGY tide gauges were set up at hundreds of observing stations. The tide gauges were simply measuring sticks like long rulers, fixed on the shore. As the high and low tides came, their levels could easily be measured against the gauges. In this way scientists discovered many facts about tidal drag.

To study ocean currents, scientists used an instrument called the neutral buoyancy float. The float is a long, narrow package of batteries and weights. Scientists can make it float at whatever depth they wish. At the bottom of the float there is a signaling device that sends out sound waves. As the float moves with the flow of the current, it sends out sound waves. By picking up these signals, scientists aboard ships can trace ocean currents at different depths.

More than 70 ships were used for this work during the IGY, and a number of important finds were made. For instance, several new currents were discovered. Among these were the counter-currents—ocean currents flowing beneath known currents and in the opposite direction. The discovery of these deep-flowing currents has helped scientists to understand how ocean waters circulate, carrying warm water from the tropics toward the poles and cold water from the poles toward the tropics.

▶ THE SHAPE OF THE EARTH

More than 2,000 years ago ancient scientists discovered that the earth was round. Modern scientists have long known that the earth is not exactly round. But they have not known its shape as accurately as they would like. IGY scientists undertook to study the shape of the earth.

Armed with many new tools, including artificial satellites, IGY scientists were able to draw a much better picture of the earth. They proved that the earth bulges slightly at the equator. And they discovered that there is a small bulge at the North Pole as well.

New instruments enabled IGY scientists to make accurate measurements on the face of the earth. For the first time latitude and longitude could be measured almost exactly, with a possible error of only 5 feet. Because of this the exact location of towns and cities could be obtained.

Such exact information about the location of places provided another tool for studying the earth. In recent years many scientists have come to believe that all the earth's land once formed a single continent. Millions of years ago, they think, one landmass split into several

continents. These continents drifted into their present positions and are still slowly drifting. By measuring the exact location of certain spots on each continent every year, scientists may finally be able to tell whether the continents are indeed moving.

▶ THE ANTARCTIC

During the IGY some scientists lived in Antarctica, the world's coldest continent. About 6,000,000 square miles in size, Antarctica is always covered with ice and snow.

The scientists in Antarctica observed the auroras, the weather, the upper air, and the earth's magnetism. They also made studies of the huge continent itself and of the seas around it.

One group studied the Antarctic's ice cover and the rock surface beneath it by seismic shooting. Scientists dug deep pits straight down into the ice, to study the ice layers. They

Scientists in Antarctica set off explosions to learn about the ice cover and the rock structures beneath it.

also used special drills that reached more than 1,000 feet down into the ice. The drills brought up cores of ice, which the scientists examined. In this way they were able to learn about ice and snow laid down in Antarctica many years ago.

▶ AFTER THE IGY

The IGY was a great scientific success. It brought scientists new knowledge about our planet. In fact, scientists found the IGY so useful that much of the work is still going on. Studies of glaciers and of the ice in the Antarctic are continuing. Scientists are still making measurements of earthquake waves on land and sea. Rockets are still being sent into the upper atmosphere. Measurements of the earth's magnetism are being continued as well.

Since the end of the IGY, rockets and artificial satellites have been very much improved. They have been used to probe the radiation belts around the earth. Some of them are taking pictures of the sun by the X rays that it sometimes sends out. There are communications satellites and weather satel-lites like Tiros. Scientists have sent instrument-carrying rockets to the moon and to the earth's neighbor planets.

The Year of the Quiet Sun

The IGY was planned for a time when there would be the greatest number of sunspots on the sun. Soon after the IGY ended, scientists began planning a second watch on the sun. This one was scheduled for a time when the sun would have the smallest number of sunspots—January 1, 1964, to December 31, 1965. It was named the International Quiet Sun Year (IQSY).

That such a plan was agreed to so soon shows how useful the IGY was. And we should remember one more important fact. The IGY showed the world how scientists of every nation can work peacefully together.

COLIN A. RONAN
Fellow of the Royal Astronomical Society

See also ATMOSPHERE; EARTH, OUR HOME PLANET; EARTH AND ITS SUN; EARTHQUAKES; GEOLOGY AND GEOPHYSICS; ICE; ICE AGES; OCEANOGRAPHY; RADIATION BELTS; VOLCANOES; WEATHER AND CLIMATE; WINDS AND WEATHER.

INTERNATIONAL LANGUAGES. See UNIVERSAL LANGUAGES.

INTERNATIONAL LAW

National law has long been an effective method of keeping peace and justice among citizens of a nation. Many people interested in international relations have wished that the system of law among nations (called international law) were as effective as this system of law within a nation (called national law). Interest in international law began with the discovery of the Americas, regions of Africa, and the islands of the Far East. The competition of the European countries for these lands stimulated the first writings on international law. The earliest of these legal writers was the Spanish scholar Francisco de Vitoria. In the 16th century he wrote *De jure belli* ("The Law of War") in Latin. The Dutch author Hugo Grotius also wrote in Latin *De jure belli et pacis* (*The Law of War and Peace*) in 1625. Grotius is called the father of international law.

International law developed slowly through the periods of war and peace during the more than 300 years that followed. Many modern textbooks still divide the subject as Grotius did, into two parts: international law of war and international law of peace.

▶ INTERNATIONAL LAW OF WAR

The international law of war developed from a general tendency to regulate the conduct of war. For example, captured soldiers were not killed or enslaved unless they had tortured, enslaved, or murdered innocent civilians. Gradually the customs of war set a pattern for the conduct of armies and soldiers. This pattern applied to the relations of armies to civilian (nonmilitary) populations. The rights of peaceful neutrals—those who had no part in the war—were also assured. Today, for example, a series of international conventions (treaties) agree on how prisoners of war should be treated. These treaties were negotiated at Geneva, Switzerland, and The Hague in the Netherlands between 1864 and 1949.

The Hague Convention of 1907 stated laws of land and naval warfare. However, there is still no general agreement on the most important of all warfare in this atomic age—aerial warfare.

▶ INTERNATIONAL LAW OF PEACE

International law for time of peace has developed much further. It states the principles of conduct that countries follow in subjects of common interest for which they are no longer ready to go to war. Individual cases have often been settled on the basis of these written or unwritten principles. Cases are also settled by diplomatic agreement, by treaties, or by international bodies that hear both sides of a dispute and then work out a solution. Finally, some cases are decided by the Court of International Justice.

The treaties that marked the end of World War I and World War II advanced the organization of international law. Most notable is the International Court of Justice, commonly called the World Court. This was set up in 1921 at The Hague and was associated with the League of Nations. The World Court later was made a part of the United Nations. The United States and all the other nations of the world (virtually all of whom are members of the United Nations) now accept the authority of the World Court.

In the Western Hemisphere the United States and most countries of Latin America have worked out a regional organization of peace and international law. They are pledged to try to avoid the use of force in the settlement of disputes between nations. In 1948 they put together some of their Pan-American peace treaties in a charter for the Organization of American States (OAS). The OAS has its own system of American international law. Its main idea is the doctrine of nonintervention. This means that no nation can interfere in the internal or external affairs of another nation. But these inter-American treaties do not necessarily bind members in their relations with non-American countries or with Canada. The American republics are also members of the United Nations and parties to the International Court of Justice.

The nuclear test-ban treaty of 1963 is among the most advanced of all the multi-lateral (many-sided) treaties in time of peace. The treaty outlaws nuclear tests underwater, in the air, or in outer space. The treaty on the nonproliferation of nuclear weapons of 1968, which prohibits non-nuclear states from acquiring nuclear arms, is another step in the development of a system of international law.

Another important agreement which further develops those principles is the treaty of 1967 dealing with outer space. This treaty attempts to insure peaceful development of outer space and to prevent the establishment of weapons stations in outer space for purposes of war.

In April, 1972, a treaty outlawing the development, production, and stockpiling of bacteriological (germ warfare) weapons was signed by some 80 nations. Among them were three of the major powers: the United States, the Soviet Union, and Great Britain.

▶ LEGAL SOURCES OF INTERNATIONAL LAW

What are the legal sources that contribute to the development of international law? The International Court of Justice defines them in this order:

(1) Treaties, particularly when nations before the court are parties to them;
(2) International custom;
(3) General principles of law as recognized by civilized nations;
(4) Judicial decisions of international or even national courts;
(5) The teachings of the most qualified international relations experts of the different nations.

International law has progressed in its definition of principles and even in applying them. But when a great power or group of powers decides to ignore international law, there is nothing to prevent its violation except the use of force by the nations who might want to defend it. That is why the United Nations Charter did not prevent the Korean War in 1950. But United Nations armed forces did successfully defend the Republic of Korea against the North Korean aggressor.

International law rarely applies to the individuals of the world; it concerns only nations. But even if international law were never again broken by any country, its validity and fate would remain uncertain.

SAMUEL FLAGG BEMIS
Yale University

INTERNATIONAL RELATIONS

International relations is the study of how the nations of the world get along with each other. Differences of color, religion, and nationality sometimes complicate international relations. The objective of international relations is a world in which people will live together in peace as free and independent men and women. It may be many years before this ideal comes to pass. History has shown that nations often find it difficult to remain at peace when they fear that their national interests are threatened in some way by another power or group of powers.

▶ BALANCE OF POWER

Countries wish to protect their interests, welfare, and independence. An important way of gaining protection is the **alliance**. (An alliance is a formal agreement between two or more states to support one another in a common policy toward another state or states.) Members of an alliance are called **allies**. Nations form alliances with other nations with whom they share a common interest or a common enemy. If one state becomes too powerful, weight is added to the other side of the scale to balance it. Usually this weight is provided by an alliance of states. This is called keeping the **balance of power.**

After World War II two great power centers developed. These are the United States and the Soviet Union. The United States is trying to hold the balance of power against the world revolutionary forces of the Soviet Union. Population, natural resources, location, communication and transportation networks, and industrial development all contribute to national power. A state may increase its national power by building up its armed forces and making military or trade alliances with other states. The United States, for instance, is allied with other nations in a number of defense pacts. These include the North Atlantic Treaty Organization (NATO), 1949, the Southeast Asia Treaty Organization (SEATO), 1954, and the Central Treaty Organization (CENTO), 1959. (Consult the articles NORTH ATLANTIC TREATY ORGANIZATION in Volume N and SOUTHEAST ASIA TREATY ORGANIZATION in Volume S.)

The Charter of the United Nations provides for separate regional organizations among its member nations. Among these are the Organization of American States (OAS), comprising 21 nations of the Western Hemisphere, and the Commonwealth of Nations, comprising independent nations developed in the 20th century out of the British Empire. The Communist countries of Eastern Europe are allied under the Warsaw Pact. The French Community of certain former French colonies, the Arab League, and a federation of independent African nations, founded in 1963, are other regional organizations.

▶ FOREIGN POLICY

The course that a nation pursues in international affairs is determined by its **foreign policy**. This is a statement of the role a nation will play in the balance of power. Foreign policy seeks to protect national security (physical, political, and economic) and to advance the national interest. It is influenced by the power available to achieve these goals as well as by the interests and power of other nations. National history, traditions, and public opinion may also influence foreign policy.

Neutrality. Some nations try to avoid taking an active part in international affairs. If they refuse to aid either side in a conflict, they are following a policy of neutrality. If they refrain from alliances with any power in peacetime, they are following a policy of isolation. Isolation from Europe was the principal foreign policy followed by the United States throughout the 19th century. It was established by President George Washington in his Farewell Address (1796). The United States was able to pursue this policy because of its distance from Europe.

Status Quo. As a foreign policy, status quo (Latin for "existing state of affairs") means that a nation wishes to preserve unchanged its power and the power of other nations. The Monroe Doctrine, proclaimed by President James Monroe in 1823, was such a policy. It stated that the nations of Europe are not to disturb the status quo or to interfere in the affairs of any American nation. The article MONROE DOCTRINE in Volume M gives more detailed information.

Imperialism. The policy of increasing national power and position in world affairs at the expense of other nations or peoples is called imperialism. This is the dominion of one power over another nation or people against their freely expressed will. It may be based upon a desire to increase national security by extending boundaries or obtaining seaports or to acquire colonies as markets or sources of raw materials, or for any of a number of other reasons. Imperialism is the policy that often leads to war. Nazi Germany under Adolf Hitler was pursuing a policy of imperialism when it attacked Poland in 1939. The Soviet Union's encouragement and control of socialist governments (as in Cuba and East Europe) is considered by some political scientists to be imperialistic.

Foreign policy is determined by the head of state. In the United States the president has sole responsibility for the foreign policy. He is advised by the Secretary of State and the Department of State as well as by the National Security Council and other special bodies. In Great Britain the prime minister, together with the Secretary of State for Foreign Affairs, decides upon the foreign policy with the assistance of the Foreign Office. In democracies, such as these, the nation's foreign policy must be approved by a majority of the people through the election of their governments.

Diplomacy

Diplomacy and war are the two ways of carrying out foreign policy. Diplomacy is the art and practice of achieving national goals by peaceful means. The established means of diplomacy are a country's diplomatic corps and office of foreign affairs (such as the Foreign Office or Department of State). For more information see the article on FOREIGN SERVICE in Volume F.

International Conferences. Conferences among nations may be held for the purpose of regulating trade, making disarmament agreements, arranging peace treaties, or settling international issues. They are usually attended by ministers of the office of foreign affairs or their representatives. If the conferences are held between the heads of state themselves, they are called **summit conferences**. An agreement between two nations is called a **bilateral** (two-sided) agreement; one between several nations is called a **multilateral** (many-sided) agreement.

What was the Iron Curtain?

In 1946 Prime Minister Winston Churchill of Great Britain said an imaginary barrier stretched across Eastern Europe from the Baltic Sea to the Adriatic Sea. It separated the Communist nations in Eastern Europe, under the control of the Soviet Union, from the nations of the West. Churchill called this invisible screen the Iron Curtain.

What was the Bamboo Curtain?

Mainland China sealed itself off from the Western world in much the same way in 1949. The term "Bamboo Curtain" was used to describe the imaginary barrier that prevents communication and contact between Communist Asia and the West. It takes its name from bamboo, a woody plant grown in Asia.

China's long period of isolation seemed to have ended in 1971 when the government invited an American Ping-Pong team to enter their country to play against the Chinese team. Soon afterward President Nixon was invited to visit China in 1971–2. This began a new phase in postwar international relations. The Chinese Government seemed interested in making itself a third major world power with the United States and the Soviet Union.

▶ WAR

When diplomacy fails, war may become a means of carrying out a foreign policy. A nation usually does not go to war if it can achieve its goal by diplomacy or by a show of force. And it will go to war only if it thinks it can win. When attacked, a nation will go to war to defend itself.

Nations took shape in Western Europe as kingdoms on the fringes of the North Atlantic Ocean. They were Portugal, Spain, France, and England, and later Holland and the Scandinavian kingdoms. The rise of these maritime nations coincided with the age of geographical discoveries overseas. The new nations soon established colonial dominion over the recently discovered continents and their peoples in North and South America, Africa, Asia (long since known, but now reached by sea), and eventually in Australia, New Zealand, and the islands of the Pacific Ocean.

Behind the Atlantic nations lay the ancient nation-states of Central Europe and the Mediterranean region. Behind them stretched the great, slowly growing land empire of Russia, and in the Far East the ancient empires and civilizations of China and Japan.

Through the centuries the maritime powers warred with each other for control of the seas, for expansion of their empires, and for colonial monopolies of commerce and trade. These were called colonial wars. The new national powers were also warring on the continent of Europe. One would try to establish its mastery over another by getting hold of the kingship through royal marriages and territorial conquest. These efforts at take-over were called dynastic wars. They were sometimes connected with the colonial wars. Several times one king or emperor almost gained control of all Europe—Charles V of the Holy Roman Empire in the 16th century, Louis XIV of France in the early 18th century, and Napoleon Bonaparte of France in the early 19th century. During the 20th century there have been two great world wars for supreme world power.

It has been said that throughout modern history there have been as many years of warfare as of peace. Even in time of peace there has been continual diplomatic disagreement. Rarely has there passed a year in which an international or civil war has not been going on somewhere in the world. Modern science and industry have created the most destructive armaments man has ever known. Of these the nuclear bomb is the most powerful. Airplanes and missiles can deliver it anywhere in the world in a matter of hours or minutes, destroying whole cities. War is no longer limited to the soldier on foot. It now involves the entire land and all the people of a warring nation. It is total war.

International Organizations

In 1815 the Congress of Vienna ended the wars being waged in Europe by Napoleon I of France. At the Congress, Russia, Austria, Prussia, and Great Britain had joined together against Napoleon in the Quadruple Alliance. Later the first three countries formed what became known as the Holy Alliance. Fifteen years later the Holy Alliance was no longer functioning, but the great European powers

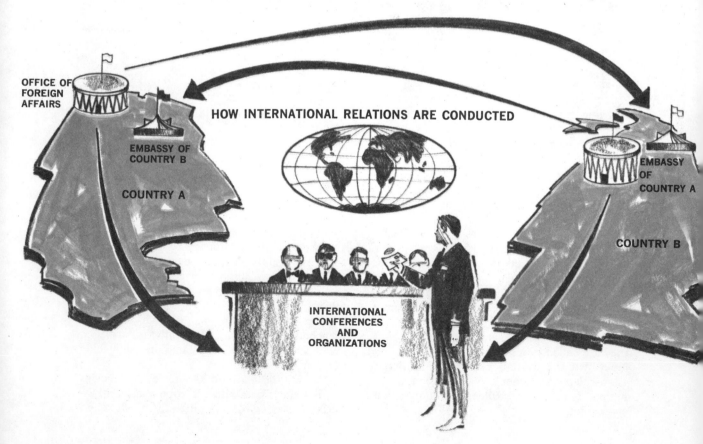

HOW INTERNATIONAL RELATIONS ARE CONDUCTED

OFFICE OF FOREIGN AFFAIRS

EMBASSY OF COUNTRY B

COUNTRY A

EMBASSY OF COUNTRY A

COUNTRY B

INTERNATIONAL CONFERENCES AND ORGANIZATIONS

continued to consult with each other. This so-called Concert of Europe succeeded in preventing the outbreak of any world war for almost 100 years (until the start of World War I in 1914).

For many years philosophers and statesmen sought some kind of international umpire to develop an international organization that would settle disputes among nations, just as disputes between neighbors in private life are settled by courts of law. Not until 1899 was there an international meeting for that purpose: the First Hague Conference of the great European powers and Japan. It set up a Permanent Court of Arbitration. To it nations could voluntarily submit their disputes if both parties agreed to do so. The Second Hague Conference (1907) agreed on certain rules of international law, including the regulation of warfare on land and sea.

Meanwhile, many people were urging some sort of world league to enforce peace among nations. At the end of World War I a treaty of peace with Germany was drawn up by the allied powers at Versailles, near Paris. The Treaty of Versailles (1919) provided for a League of Nations and a Permanent Court of International Justice. Most nations (the United States was an exception) accepted both the League and the World Court. This story is told in the article LEAGUE OF NATIONS in Volume L.

In the Kellogg-Briand Pact (1928) the United States and most other nations agreed to settle their disputes by peaceful means and to outlaw war as an instrument of national policy. Hitler broke all these treaties when he invaded Poland in 1939 and started World War II. After the war the nations of the world joined in another international organization set up in 1945 under the Charter of the United Nations.

▶ THE COLD WAR

From the end of World War II in 1945 until the early 1970's, a state of political tension called the Cold War existed between the Communist and non-Communist nations of the world. The term Cold War was first used in a speech given by the American statesman Bernard Baruch in 1947. The Cold War began with the expansion of Soviet influence and control over the Eastern European countries after World War II. Eventually Europe divided into the West, or non-Communist bloc of nations, led by the United States, and the East, or Communist bloc, dominated by the Soviet Union.

In the late 1940's President Harry S Truman announced that the United States national interest required that assistance be given to countries threatened by the Communist bloc, as in the case of Turkey and Greece. The Truman Doctrine was part of the postwar United States policy of **containment**, which aimed at containing Communism, or preventing its spread. To support this policy, the United States introduced the Marshall Plan in 1948. The Marshall Plan, later called the European Recovery Program (ERP), aided economic recovery in Europe.

The first incident in the Cold War was the Soviet blockade of the overland routes to Berlin from the West in June, 1948. Located 110 miles within the Soviet military zone of East Germany, the city was divided into four zones—British, French, American, and Russian. Until the blockade was lifted, almost a year later, the Western powers used the **Berlin airlift** to fly in supplies for their zones. The second major incident was the attack in 1950 by North Korea, supported by Communist China, on the Republic of Korea, supported by the United Nations.

Other Cold War actions such as the Vietnam War took place over the years. The Cold War also became an arms race as the nations on both sides increased their armed power.

▶ SIGNS OF A THAW

A thawing of the Cold War began in the 1960's during the Kennedy and Johnson administrations and continued into the early 1970's. In 1972 the Soviet Union and the United States signed a strategic arms limitation agreement (SALT) and several scientific and cultural exchange pacts. At the same time, diplomatic channels were opened between the United States and China. China's emergence as a great power in the 1970's marked the start of a new balance of power in the world.

SAMUEL FLAGG BEMIS
Yale University

See also IMPERIALISM; INTERNATIONAL LAW; ORGANIZATION OF AMERICAN STATES; PEACE MOVEMENTS; TREATIES; UNITED NATIONS.

INTERNATIONAL TRADE

International trade is buying and selling between nations. When countries trade with one another, their people have more products to use. The people put their energies into making what they can make well and cheaply. Then they exchange these products with other countries for products they need.

▶ WHY NATIONS TRADE WITH EACH OTHER

Nations trade with each other for many reasons. First of all, they trade because there is a difference in natural resources in different parts of the world. The plants that can be grown are different. The mineral resources in the ground are different also.

For example, Canada has nickel mines but is too cold to grow oranges. The United States has only a few small nickel mines but produces large crops of oranges. So the United States buys nickel from Canada, and Canada buys oranges from the United States. (We say that the United States **exports** oranges and **imports** nickel. Canada exports the nickel and imports the oranges.)

The second reason nations trade with one another is that it pays to specialize. One country may have people with special skills, or it may have more capital (factories, machines, tools) to work with. With these advantages, there are some goods that one country may be able to produce more cheaply than another country.

For example, the United States has factories, machines, and tools for manufacturing jet planes. Belgium has women who are skilled at making lace. So the United States sells jet planes to Belgium. Belgium sells lace to the United States. If the Belgians built factories and trained engineers for the few jets they need, those jets would be very expensive. If the United States began to train women to make lace, that, too, would be expensive. By trading, both countries get a good product for less than it would cost if made at home.

It pays a country to specialize even if it can produce everything more cheaply than another country. Within each country there are some things that are produced more efficiently than other things are. This is called **comparative advantage**.

For an example of how comparative advantage works, we can take the case of the best teacher in town, who is also the best carpenter in town. He will, of course, work as a teacher and leave the carpentry to the carpenter. How can he give up the important job of being a teacher? The children of the town benefit when he remains a teacher. The carpenter is also better off when the teacher gives up the carpentry. If the teacher did the carpentry the carpenter would not have a job.

Japanese goods are loaded for export to New York.

When a country specializes, it can make some goods that are of better quality than goods made elsewhere. Wedgwood china made in England, carpets woven in Iran, and wine produced in France are all examples of these special goods.

Specialization makes the best use of a country's productive resources—its natural resources, the skill of the workers, and the factories and tools. By doing so, the world's total quantity of goods is made larger.

▶ WHO DOES THE TRADING?

Most of the trade in the world is between industrial nations that have high living standards. These are the United States, Canada, Japan, Australia, and the countries of Western Europe. In recent years the United States has been first in the world in the amount of foreign trade. West Germany has been second, Britain third, France fourth, and Canada fifth.

There are two reasons why these countries do most of the world trade. First, in these countries people have enough money to buy foreign goods. Most of the people of Asia, Africa, and Latin America are poor. Their per capita income is small. (**Per capita** income is the income of all the people in a country added together and divided by the total number of people in the country.) For instance, the per capita income of Indonesia is low. The yearly cost of American goods sold to Indonesia averages $1.76 per person. The per capita income of Canada is high. The average yearly cost of American goods sold to Canada is $406 per person.

The second reason that most international trade is among the richer countries is that these countries have done more specialization. And the more specialization there is in a country, the more trade there can be.

Countries Trading in Primary Products

Many countries get a large part of their national income from selling one or two primary products. Primary products are the raw materials from which manufactured goods are made. They may be farm products—wool, cotton, beef, or wheat. Or they may come from beneath the surface of the earth—copper, iron, coal, or crude oil. They may come from forests—wood or natural rubber.

For example, 63 percent of Colombia's trading comes from selling coffee. Copper brings in 76 percent of Chile's earnings. Ghana depends heavily on cocoa exports. Malaysia depends on tin and rubber, and Venezuela depends on oil.

These countries have "all their eggs in one basket." If anything happens to the sales of their primary products, they are in trouble. If a country depends on the sale of coffee, and the price of coffee goes down, then the total earnings of that country go down. Such countries will not be able to count on stable economies until they have more products to trade.

The People Who Do the Trading

Trading in most countries is done by businesses. There are some countries in which the governments may do the trading. For example, the United States government buys minerals from other countries in order to have the minerals on hand in case of national emergency.

In Communist countries business is controlled by government, and it does the buying and selling. For example, if someone from another country wants to buy furs from the Union of Soviet Socialist Republics, he buys them through a Soviet government agency.

▶ THE PROBLEMS OF INTERNATIONAL TRADE

International trade has many more problems than there are in domestic trade. Money differences between nations create difficulties. Language differences often cause misunderstandings. Different customs cause confusion and disagreements. Tariffs and other trade barriers may be set up by the government of each country where goods cross national boundaries.

Problems of Money

Within one country everyone uses the same money. The rupee is used in India, the mark in Germany, the dollar in the United States, and the franc in France. But when a Frenchman wants to buy American goods, his French francs must be changed into American dollars. So he must know the **rate of exchange**—that is, how many dollars he will get for his francs. The rate of exchange changes constantly. This makes it difficult for businessmen to figure costs ahead of time. (The process of settling accounts between people in different countries is called **foreign exchange**.)

Some countries have the same name for their money. Canada and the United States both use dollars. France, Belgium, and Switzerland all use francs. But the moneys are not worth the same, although it is possible that they might be. In 1964 the American dollar could be exchanged for $1.07 in Canadian money; the Swiss franc was equal to about 1⅛ French francs.

Wages also make problems for international trade when they are so high that they make the final product more expensive than it would be if made in another country. For instance, workers in a wealthy country are often higher paid than workers in a poor country. The workers in the wealthy country, then, want trade barriers to protect them from the competition of lower paid foreign workers.

"Dumping" causes other problems in international trade. If a big country like the United States decides to charge less when it is selling, or pay more when it is buying, it upsets the buying and selling of smaller countries. For example, if the United States should "flood the market" by selling huge quantities of cotton at very low prices, growers in other countries would find it difficult to sell cotton at the usual prices.

Problems of Customs, Units of Measurement, and Language

People in different nations differ in language, custom, and tastes. For example, the British drive their cars on the left side of the road. The French drive on the right. It is safer for the British to use cars with right-hand drive and for the French to use cars with left-hand drive. If an automobile manufacturer wants to sell cars to the British, he will sell more cars if he makes them with right-hand drive. If the manufacturer wants to sell to the French, he will sell more cars if he makes them with left-hand drive.

Units of measurement differ. Some countries use inches, feet, pounds, and tons for measuring and weighing. Other countries use metric measurements. Even units with the same name may be different. The imperial gallon, used in Great Britain and Canada, is one seventh larger than the United States gallon.

If a German publisher wants to sell a book to Americans, he has to have it translated into English. If Swiss games are going to be sold in Spain, the instructions should be translated into Spanish.

Language may also present the very obvious problem of making it difficult for the traders to understand one another. A businessman who deals with other countries seldom can learn all the languages that may be necessary.

Tariffs and Other Trade Barriers

Governments sometimes set up barriers to international trade. One of these is the **import duty**. It is a tax on foreign goods that makes them more expensive for people to buy. All of one country's import duties are known as that country's **tariff**. Some countries also charge a duty on goods that are exported.

Another kind of trade barrier is called a **quota**. A quota limits the number of goods that can be brought into a country in one year.

If international trade benefits both the buyers and sellers, why do countries put blocks, or barriers, in the way of trade?

One reason is that countries want to help their own industries grow. Countries also want to set up new industries so that they will not have to depend on another country for important needs. If cheaper goods are allowed to come in from another country, the home country may set a tariff on the foreign goods. If the tariff makes the foreign goods very expensive, everyone is likely to buy the home-produced goods instead of the foreign goods.

A second reason for trade barriers is that in most countries there are some goods that are not produced as efficiently as they are produced in another country, even after the industries are well established. If trade were free, the more efficient producers would push the less efficient producers out of business. But in many countries tariffs are set up to protect these less efficient producers.

Why do buyers, who would benefit from cheaper goods, not complain about tariffs? Buyers are not organized. Producers are. In addition, buyers often think more of their jobs in industry than of the cost of buying.

Many countries also set up trade barriers for political reasons. Important war materials are not allowed to go to a country that might someday use them against the country that made them.

▶ **LOWERING TRADE BARRIERS**

Trade barriers have been used for a long time. But since World War II there have been strong efforts to lower them. People all over the world are learning that more international trade benefits everyone.

Reciprocal Trade Agreement Act. The United States has been one of the leaders in moving toward freer trade. It passed the Reciprocal Trade Agreement Act in 1934. It has broadened the original agreement many times since then. The word "reciprocate" means mutual giving and taking. In this agreement the United States promises to lower its tariff on another country's goods if the other country agrees to lower its tariff on American goods. The president of the United States was given the power to make the agreements. Under this act the United States has made agreements with such countries as Canada, the United Kingdom, and France. Trade barriers have gradually been lowered.

General Agreement on Tariffs and Trade. In 1947 the General Agreement on Tariffs and Trade (GATT) was signed. The signers were a group of 23 of the leading trading nations of the world. Among them were the United States, Canada, and many of the nations of Western Europe.

The signers of GATT continuously confer about getting rid of trade barriers. Since 1947, trade barriers have been made much lower. In 1970 there were 76 members in GATT.

The GATT countries try to agree to certain rules of the game that they will all follow in their international trading. One of these rules is that the tariff will be the same for all countries. That is, the goods from one country will have the same tariff as the goods from every other country. For example, in a GATT country such as Switzerland a sweater from Hong Kong will have the same tariff as a sweater from Scotland.

Trade Expansion Act. In 1962 the United States passed the Trade Expansion Act. Under it the United States Congress gave the president great new powers to cut the Ameri-

A Coca-Cola truck makes a delivery in Istanbul, Turkey.

can tariff when he was dealing with other countries. It was the first time the president was given the power to get rid of an import duty altogether instead of just lowering it.

The European Economic Community. The European Economic Community, sometimes called the EEC or the Common Market, was set up by the Treaty of Rome in 1957. The original six members were France, Italy, West Germany, Belgium, the Netherlands, and Luxembourg. Three new members, Great Britain, Ireland, and Denmark, joined in the 1970's. Other European nations are expected to join in the future.

The aim of the EEC is to create a united Western Europe in which goods flow freely and trade barriers are eliminated among the Common Market nations. Besides agreements among members, the EEC has trade agreements with a number of European and African states. These agreements provide for the exchange of goods among the EEC nations and the nonmember states without regard to tariffs or other trade barriers.

▶ **BALANCE OF PAYMENTS**

The **balance of payments** is a country's record of all the buying and selling it does with other countries. It is the difference between all of the country's exports and all of its imports.

Individual buyers do not have to worry

about the balance of trade. If a storekeeper in Chicago buys perfumes from Paris, he arranges the payment through his bank. The Chicago shopkeeper's bank charges him the dollar equivalent of the price of the French perfume plus a charge for this service. Then the Chicago bank instructs a bank in Paris to pay the French perfume manufacturer in francs.

But how are banks around the world able to change francs for dollars and dollars for francs?

They are able to do this because international trade is carried on through banks in which official records are kept of all the exchanges. Sales of goods to a foreign country must be matched by an equal amount of goods and gifts (foreign aid, food, and the like). If the imports and exports do not stay equal, they must be paid for with gold or must be owed.

Reviewed by MOE L. FRANKEL
Director, Joint Council on Economic Education
See also TARIFF; TRADE AND COMMERCE.

What is a free port?

Many nations have ports where ships from other countries can unload goods for trade, storage, processing, or transfer to another ship. Merchants who send their goods to the port of a foreign country usually pay a tariff, or tax, on their goods as soon as they are unloaded from the ship. However, some countries have free ports, and others, like the United States, have foreign-trade zones. A free port may be an entire port city where foreign merchants may unload their goods without paying a tariff. In most instances it is a section of a port. As long as the goods remain in the free-port area, or foreign-trade zone, they cannot be taxed.

Nations have tariffs to protect their own merchants and manufacturers from foreign competition. If a foreign merchant must pay a tax on his goods, he must charge more for them. In this way a country encourages its people to buy less expensive goods made at home, instead of more expensive imported products. However, it is important for every modern nation to engage in foreign trade. A country sets up a free port to encourage foreign merchants to trade, and to increase its own trade.

How a free port operates. The right to unload goods without paying a tariff is very important to merchants in foreign trade. A European merchant, for instance, may send a large ship to a United States port with some goods he intends to sell in the United States, and other things he wishes to sell in a South American country. The trader expects to pay a tariff on the goods he is going to sell in the United States. However, he may want to transfer the goods he is going to sell in South America to a smaller ship. In a free port, or a United States foreign-trade zone, this transfer can be made without paying a tariff. In a regular port, the merchant would probably have to pay a tariff on any goods that left his ship.

The laws governing free ports in some nations vary from port to port. In many free ports goods may be moved from one ship to another or to a plane. Many free ports have warehouses where foreign merchants may store goods for various periods of time without paying tariffs. In some free ports the foreign merchants may display their products for customers. There are even factories in some free ports and in the United States foreign-trade zones where foreign raw materials may be made into manufactured products.

Free ports give many advantages to the people of the port city in which they are located. Since they make trading easier, more ships come to free ports. More jobs are available for dock workers.

History. The free-port idea originated in ancient times in the Middle East. Miletus, Sidon, Tyre, and other cities were free ports under the Persian Empire in 500 B.C. In the Middle Ages some Western European cities gave special privileges to traders. But the real growth of free ports in Europe began in the 16th century. Because of improvements in ships and navigation, European nations began trading a great deal with each other and the rest of the world. They also began to pass laws to protect their merchants at home from foreign competition. Although the tariff barriers helped countries in some ways, they also made free trade difficult. Leghorn, Italy, was opened as a free port in 1547. The Italian port of Genoa was made a free port in 1595. Other European free ports, or ports with free zones, which also are still in operation, were opened later in Hamburg, Stockholm, Bremen, Trieste, Copenhagen, and Antwerp. There are now more than 100 free ports around the world.

The United States Congress passed the Foreign Trade Zones Act in 1934, permitting foreign-trade zones in the United States. New York City set up the first such zone on Staten Island in 1937. Since then zones have been established in New Orleans, San Francisco, Seattle, Toledo, and Mayaguez, Puerto Rico. Two special zones for manufacturing have been established in San Francisco and in Penuelas, Puerto Rico.

United States foreign-trade zones are administered by the Foreign Trade Zones Board, located at the Bureau of International Commerce, United States Department of Commerce, Washington, D.C.

Reviewed by EUGENE M. BRADERMAN
Director, Bureau of International Commerce

INTERSTATE COMMERCE

In the United States people and products are free to cross from one state into another without restrictions or payment of customs. This has not always been the case. Between the time of the Declaration of Independence (1776) and the time when the United States Constitution was adopted (1787), states considered themselves independent of each other and of the central government. There were many restrictions on trade among the states.

Under the Articles of Confederation (1781) states were almost like separate countries banded together for mutual aid and defense. Different kinds of money and different tax systems were used. States levied tariffs (import taxes) at their borders on incoming goods that could compete with the state's own products. These border obstacles tended to strangle trade.

Many people saw that the country might not survive unless trade improved. The federal government under the Articles of Confederation had no power to regulate commerce between states and therefore could do nothing to improve the situation. The only interstate commerce that the national government could control was the postal service. That power had been created before the Revolution and continued under the Articles of Confederation.

A major aim of the United States Constitution was to end trade restrictions and to encourage a free flow of trade across state lines. To achieve this aim, the Constitution gave Congress the authority to regulate interstate commerce.

Once the Constitution was ratified, states removed their border restrictions. For about the next 100 years Congress did not need to use its power to regulate commerce to any great degree. As border barriers dissolved, the new country began to expand as quickly as the means of transportation permitted.

How Transportation Affected Interstate Commerce

In the 18th century roads were often little more than animal paths or Indian trails that traders had widened for packhorses or coaches. The mountains west of the colonies were almost as much of a trade barrier as the Atlantic Ocean. By the end of the 18th century, western roads began to appear. Daniel Boone and other frontiersmen opened the Wilderness Road through the Cumberland Gap into Kentucky. The route through New York's Mohawk valley also carried traders west.

At this time coastal ships and riverboats were the major freight carriers. Where there were no waterways, wagons struggled over rocky paths and rutted, swampy roads. The country needed better transportation if interstate commerce was to prosper. In 1811 the federal government began building the Cumberland, or National, Road. At first the road went from Cumberland, Maryland, to Wheeling, on the Ohio River, where riverboats could carry freight farther. After many years the road was built through to Vandalia, Illinois.

Overland wagons carried products over these roads. However, the wagons were not able to carry heavy and bulky loads. For almost 50 years people thought that canalboats would solve the inland transportation problem. The Erie Canal, from the Hudson River to Lake Erie, was the most important of the great freight-carrying arteries. Then the "iron horse" was introduced in the 1830's. Soon railroads replaced the slow-moving mule- or horse-drawn canalboats and the overland wagons. Railroads grew from about 20 miles in 1830 to 19,000 miles in 1860.

The Growth of Railroads

As railroads grew longer, more of them ran across state lines. Railroads, at first local in character, now linked the Atlantic to the Pacific. The driving of a golden spike at Promontory, Utah, in 1869 celebrated the completion of the first transcontinental rail line.

Soon railroads crisscrossed the whole continent. Rail freight and passenger service gave great advantages to every town that the rail lines reached. These towns grew and prospered, and so did the railroads. Railroad power to help or hinder commerce was immense. Some railroad companies used their power selfishly. Companies were free to charge any rate they wished and to change rates without notice. There were no laws requiring fair and reasonable rates. Railroads could fix rates to favor some and hurt others.

During the 1860's and 1870's state governments found that they did not have enough power to keep railroads from acting unfairly. Farmers, shippers, and communities appealed to Congress for help. They asked for federal regulation of railroads involved in interstate commerce.

In 1887 Congress passed the **Act to Regulate Commerce**, now called the **Interstate Commerce Act**. Any railroad participating in interstate commerce is subject to control under this law. The Interstate Commerce Commission is the agency created by Congress to administer the law. Though it is called an **independent regulatory agency** (because it regulates an industry), it carries out laws passed by Congress with funds appropriated by Congress.

Members of the commission are appointed for 7-year terms by the president of the United States with the consent of the Senate. Anyone who feels that a decision of the ICC is unfair may appeal the decision to the federal courts. At first the commission had five members. It has grown until today it has 11 members. The commission's **jurisdiction** (matters under its control) has also grown. In addition to railroads, it regulates trucks and buses. It also regulates barges on inland rivers and waterways, coastal ships, oil pipelines, freight forwarders, and express companies.

Other Independent Regulatory Agencies

Though the ICC was the oldest and first agency of its kind, it was by no means the last. Congress has created many similar agencies to regulate other kinds of interstate commerce. The **Civil Aeronautics Board** regulates air fares. It also encourages civil aviation. The **Federal Power Commission** is responsible for regulating all companies that send natural gas and electric power across state lines. The **Federal Communications Commission** regulates telephone and telegraph companies and radio and television broadcasting. Regulatory agencies also include the **Federal Trade Commission** (advertising and marketing practices), **Securities and Exchange Commission** (stocks and stock exchanges), **Federal Maritime Commission** (ocean shipping), and the **Atomic Energy Commission** (the uses of nuclear energy).

In addition to the independent agencies, there are regulatory agencies connected with the executive branch of the government. Some of these promote or protect interstate commerce: the United States Army Corps of Engineers (developing and maintaining waterways); the Department of Transportation, which has under its jurisdiction the Federal Aviation Administration, the Federal Highway Administration, and the Federal Railroad Administration; and the Department of Commerce, with its Maritime Administration.

States also work together to keep the arteries of commerce free and open across their borders. By 1939 many states had joined in an effort to remove interstate trade blocks. Sometimes states form agreements (interstate compacts) to work together for this purpose. These agreements must have the approval of Congress. For instance, the Port of New York Authority is an agency formed by New Jersey and New York. It helps the flow of commerce through the port that the two states share.

Congress also uses its constitutional interstate trade authority to pass laws that keep people from shipping dangerous or illegal goods across state lines. Illegal drugs, gambling devices, and switchblade knives are some of the things that may not be shipped. There are laws that regulate the wages paid to workers by a business engaged in interstate commerce.

Generally the laws of competition set the patterns of interstate commerce. In case of arguments between shippers and railroads or other carriers, the federal government acts as a referee.

The ICC requires carriers to let everyone know their rates. Carriers must file lists of rates that the public can examine. If a new rate seems unfair, objectors can protest before the rate goes into effect. The ICC can block new rates and investigate to see if rates are reasonable.

A healthy system of interstate commerce needs both free trade and modern transportation. Today the United States is covered by a vast network of rail lines, highways, airways, pipelines, rivers, and waterways. Federal regulatory agencies protect the public interest in a free flow of trade.

Reviewed by GEORGE M. STAFFORD
Chairman, Interstate Commerce Commission

INVENTIONS

Popular stories and movies have helped spread the idea that invention is a simple matter. A man has a sudden inspiration while strolling in the woods or working at his job, and at once fame and fortune are his. Nothing could be further from the truth. Many inventions have been the result of flashes of inspiration. But these inspirations may come only after an inventor has been at work on a problem for a long time. And after the inspiration a great deal more work must be done to turn the idea into a working reality.

The person popularly recognized as the inventor of a machine or process is usually not the first one to have had the idea. The process of invention goes through many stages. First, some new knowledge makes possible the idea of doing or building something. Second, someone has such an idea and proposes it, but cannot put it into practice. Third, more knowledge is acquired, often from the experience of people trying to make the idea work. Finally, someone succeeds, and he becomes known as the inventor.

The process of invention does not stop when the first successful model is built and tested. Other inventors continue to make improvements on the original idea. A modern single-wing jet airliner with kitchens and lavatories and comfortable seats in an air-conditioned cabin is a far cry from the Wright brothers' original biplane, in which the pilot lay on his stomach out in the open air.

Sometimes one invention leads to another. The invention of the steam engine led to the invention of many machine tools needed to make metal parts. The development of the gasoline engine led to the invention of better motor fuels.

An automobile is a combination of hundreds of inventions. Every part of it, from the engine and the transmission to the nuts and bolts, had to be invented. The same holds true for a jet plane, a television set, or an electronic computer. Such devices represent the work of many inventors.

Who Is the Actual Inventor?

It is often difficult to decide who really deserves the credit for inventing a new device or a new method for making things.

Often two men may have been working separately on the same invention at the same time. One might have been quicker to patent the invention. Who should get the credit? Sometimes an inventor fails to make a business success of his invention. Years later another man does succeed with the same invention. Which of these men is the true inventor? Sometimes a well-known inventor takes credit for an invention that is really the work of his assistants. For these reasons historians often prefer not to single out any one person as the inventor of a device or process.

▶ MANY INVENTORS MET FAILURE

Many inventors have failed because the technical knowledge of their time was not enough to allow them to carry out their ideas.

The English inventor Thomas Savery (1650?–1715), who pioneered in the development of the steam engine, could never get enough steam pressure to make his engine work as well as he wished. Why? Because the temperature needed to produce high-pressure steam melted the solder at the joints of the steam pipes.

A number of men invented electric light bulbs years before Edison did, but their efforts failed because they had no good material for the filament (the tiny wire that glows and makes light when the electric current passes through it). One English inventor produced a successful light bulb before Edison but failed to patent it in time.

▶ THE INCANDESCENT LIGHT

The case of the incandescent light, or electric light bulb, is a good example of the stages in the development of an invention.

Why has no one invented a perpetual-motion machine?

For hundreds of years people have been fascinated by the idea of a perpetual-motion machine—one that would keep going forever once it was set in motion, without any outside source of power. Many men have tried to design such a machine, but without success. These men failed to reckon with one of the basic laws of physics: that a machine can never deliver more energy than is fed into it. Some energy is always used up by the friction of moving parts. This would stop any "perpetual-motion" machine sooner or later.

Toward the end of the 18th century many people became interested in electricity and began conducting experiments. However, they had no way of producing a steady stream, or current, of electricity. Then, in 1800, an Italian scientist named Alessandro Volta (1745–1827) invented the electric battery. With the battery an electric current could be obtained.

A few years later, in 1808, the famous British scientist Sir Humphry Davy used electricity to make light. Using a battery, Davy made electricity jump between two carbon rods, or electrodes. The electricity leaping across the gap made a continuous spark, or arc, which glowed brilliantly. Scientists began using the new arc lamp for laboratory experiments, but the best batteries of that day could not keep such a lamp going for very long. There was no source of electric current good or inexpensive enough to make the arc lamp practical for lighting purposes.

The invention of the electric generator was another important step in making electric lighting possible. It is also one of the early examples of an invention based on scientific research. The electric generator is based on a discovery made about 1831 by Michael Faraday. This discovery was that when a wire is moved near a magnet, electricity moves in the wire. During the years that followed, many men from many different countries helped to develop this idea into the electric generator. By the middle of the century steam-powered generators were being used to run arc lamps in lighthouses. In 1870 Zénobe Théophile Gramme (1826–1901), a Belgian engineer and inventor, developed the first really practical generator. With this source of current, arc lamps came into wide use for lighting city streets. The arc lamp gave a very bright light, but it was not suitable for indoor use. For one thing, it was very noisy. For another, it was dangerous. Furthermore, such lights produced serious eyestrain.

But many engineers and scientists had been working for years on another idea—an idea that was the basis of the electric light bulb. They were experimenting with the use of a fine wire, or filament, heated white-hot by an electric current as a source of light. In 1845 an American named J. W. Starr (1822?–47) patented an electric lamp that used a piece of metal or carbon in a vacuum. Other inventors tried to make lamps of this kind. In 1860 an English chemist and inventor, Joseph Swan (1828–1914), made such a lamp. It used a strip of carbon in a bulb from which much of the air had been pumped out. The carbon burned up very quickly, however, because Swan was unable to get a good enough vacuum. It was not until the German chemist Hermann Sprengel (1834–1906) invented the mercury air pump in 1865 that a good enough vacuum was possible. Swan then built better lamps.

After 1865 all the discoveries and inventions necessary to make an incandescent light bulb were known. The fact had been discovered that an electrically heated filament could give light. The carbon filament had been invented. The need for a vacuum had been realized, and men had invented the means to produce it. Lamps were being made in both England and the United States. In 1879 Thomas Edison made a practical incandescent lamp. He patented it in both Britain and the United States.

Credit for inventing the incandescent lamp is usually given to Edison, but his invention was partially the result of many earlier inventions and the work of many other people.

Edison's invention of 1879 was not the last step in the development of the electric light bulb. Other inventors contributed their ideas and their work to its improvement. One of the most important of these improvements was the use of tungsten instead of carbon for the filament. Tungsten is a metal with a very high melting point. A filament of tungsten glows more brightly than one of carbon, and it lasts much longer. But tungsten filaments had to wait until an American scientist named William B. Coolidge (1873–   ) discovered a way of treating tungsten metal so that it could be formed into wires. (In its natural state, tungsten is too brittle to be shaped.)

Another important improvement was to fill the light bulb with an inert gas. (An inert gas is one that does not react chemically with other substances, even at very high temperatures.) The gas helped make light bulbs last longer by keeping the white-hot filament from evaporating away. This improvement was the work of Irving Langmuir, an American scientist.

A third important improvement was to frost the inside of the bulb. Frosting reduces glare and causes the light to spread more evenly. Improvements of the light bulb are still being made.

▶ INVENTIONS IN THE PRODUCTION OF ENERGY

Today great amounts of energy are available for doing man's work. This was not always so. During much of man's history his only source of energy was his own muscles. Many early inventions were devices for helping man to make better use of his muscular energy. These simple devices help men to do things that otherwise would be difficult or impossible. For example, a person can use a stick as a lever to pry up a rock that is too heavy for him to lift with his bare hands. The inclined plane, or sloping ramp, is another such invention. A person can raise a heavy object by sliding it up an inclined plane, even though he could not possibly lift it straight up by hand. The Egyptians used inclined planes to raise the great stone blocks of the pyramids into position.

The bow and arrow is older than the inclined plane. By releasing the arrow, a man could deliver the stored-up energy from his arm muscles quickly and sharply at a single point some distance away.

When man learned to tame animals such as cattle and horses, he was able to use their muscle power for carrying loads. Later, the invention of harnesses, enabling animals to pull loads, made animal power much more useful. A horse or an ox can pull a much heavier load along the ground than it can carry on its back. With the harness, animals could also be used to turn primitive water scoops and mills that ground grain into flour.

At first loads were dragged along the ground on simple sledges. About 3000 B.C. wheels were added to the sledge to make the cart or wagon. The wheel made it possible for animals to pull loads with less effort. Thousands of years later, around the 2nd century B.C., the invention of the nailed horseshoe gave the horse a better grip on the ground and so increased his pulling power. The type of horseshoe that is used today dates from about the 9th century A.D. The invention of the horse collar about the 10th century enabled the horse to pull a heavy load without being choked by the harness. These two seemingly minor inventions made the horse more useful as a work animal. The horse replaced the slow-moving ox in many tasks. Land transportation and plowing were speeded up.

Another advance was made when man learned to make use of the energy of natural forces such as running water, wind, and burning fuel. The invention of the waterwheel about 2,000 years ago gave man the first source of energy that did not depend on muscle power. Animals get tired and must rest, just as human beings do. But a waterwheel keeps on running as long as there is water to turn it. The waterwheel was probably first used in the Roman Empire.

By the 4th century the waterwheel was in widespread use from Ireland to China. During the Middle Ages many different kinds of machinery that could be driven by waterpower were invented.

The windmill, another source of nonmuscular energy, was invented in Persia perhaps 1,300 years ago. By the 10th century Persians were using windmills to pump water and grind flour. When the windmill became known in Europe, it came into wide use, especially in broad, flat areas like eastern England, the Low Countries, and northern Germany. In these areas there are few swift-flowing streams to turn waterwheels, but there is nearly always some wind.

With the great amounts of energy made available by the windmill and the waterwheel, man could accomplish greater physical tasks than ever before. Pumps run by wind or waterpower drained swamps and marshes,

---

What president of the United States was also an inventor?

Thomas Jefferson, third president of the United States, invented a number of ingenious devices. He invented a clock that told the day of the week as well as the time of day, a dumbwaiter to bring food from the basement kitchen to the first-floor dining room of his home at Monticello; a four-sided music stand that held the sheet music for four players at once; an odometer (a device for measuring the distance traveled by a wheeled vehicle); a swivel chair; a device that he called the polygraph, which made exact duplicates of letters as they were being written; and an improved plow. Most of Jefferson's inventions were simply designed for his own amusement, but the plow was important in the development of scientific farming.

lifted water out of mines, irrigated fields, and supplied cities with water.

The invention of the steam engine brought a new source of energy—the energy of burning fuel. During the 17th and 18th centuries a number of engineers and inventors, of whom James Watt is the most famous, contributed ideas for the steam engine. Each of these men improved on the work of those who had gone before. By 1800 steam engines were in general use. Although waterwheels and windmills—and, for that matter, muscle power—are still used, the invention of the steam engine made it possible to have large quantities of power wherever it was needed. This power was available whether or not the wind blew or water flowed.

Once a steady power supply was available, hundreds of new factories were built, and for the first time machines began to replace muscle power on a really large scale.

A steam engine uses the heat energy of burning fuel to boil water and turn it into steam. The force of the steam pushes a piston that is in a cylinder, and the piston, in turn, drives the machinery.

During the 19th century the internal-combustion engine was developed. This engine is more efficient—that is, it wastes far less energy—than the steam engine. The expanding gases produced by the burning fuel move the piston. The automobile engine is an example of an internal-combustion engine. During the past 100 years the internal-combustion engine has steadily replaced the steam engine for many uses. Steam locomotives have been almost entirely replaced with diesel and electric locomotives.

The electric motor was invented during the 1830's. A number of men in different countries took part in its development. But the electric motor could not be put to practical use until a good source of electrical energy became available. For years batteries were the only source of electricity. But batteries were heavy, clumsy, and expensive. In 1870 the electric generator was perfected. Together the electric generator and motor gave man a new way of transmitting power from one place to another. Before the invention of the electric motor and generator, factories were usually built close to sources of energy, such as coalfields or waterfalls. Otherwise coal or other fuel had to be brought to the factories. This was inconvenient and expensive. Today only the electric generator plant has to be near the source of energy. The factory may be many miles away. Centrally produced electric power has made it possible for industry to spread out.

The electric generator in itself is not a new source of energy. It must be driven by another power producer, such as a steam engine, a water turbine, or an internal-combustion engine. Burning fuel or running water is still the original source of energy. But electrical energy is easier to transmit, to control, and to use. The electric generator and electric motor were among the first inventions based on scientific study.

Another invention resulting from scientific work is the nuclear reactor. The nuclear reactor provided a new source of energy: nuclear energy. Even though man has only begun to develop the many uses for nuclear energy, nuclear-powered electric generators are already in use.

▶ **INVENTIONS IN TRANSPORTATION**

Land Transportation. The earliest forms of transportation used muscle power. At first this was only by walking and carrying. The litter, or barrow (a device like a hospital stretcher), is a prehistoric invention. By 5000 B.C. sleds were being used to ease the moving of heavy objects. About the same time, man domesticated animals and used them to carry and pull heavy loads.

The next advance in land transportation was the invention of the wheel about 3500 B.C. Wheeled vehicles could be pulled by men or animals.

The wheel was the last major development in land transportation for thousands of years. Wheeled vehicles were improved by inventions like spoked wheels for lightness and springs for a smoother ride. But, basically, land transportation was almost the same in George Washington's time as it had been in the time of the Babylonian Empire, thousands of years before. Then, in the 19th and 20th centuries the steam engine and later the internal-combustion engine were used to drive wheeled vehicles. The development of these two inventions made possible locomotives, automobiles, trucks, and buses.

Water Transportation. The boat is another invention that developed very slowly. The first "boat" was probably a floating log used as an aid in swimming. The next step was tying a number of logs together to make a raft. Rafts were also made from other materials that floated well, such as bundles of reeds and inflated animal skins. Rafts could carry heavy loads, but their shape made them slow and hard to maneuver. The change from a raft to a true boat came long before history was recorded, when someone thought of hollowing out a log. Like many basic inventions this idea was a simple one. But it made a great difference. The hollow log floated better than a solid log and carried a bigger load.

Rafts and boats had to be propelled, however. Men could let the current carry them downstream. Traveling upstream, they could tow their craft from the shore, or if the water was not too deep, push them with poles. With the invention of the paddle, another very old device, men could handle boats or rafts even in water too deep for poles. Oars were developed from paddles. Sails, too, were invented before the beginning of written history.

Over the centuries boat design was improved by additional inventions. One of these inventions was building boats with planks instead of hollowing them out of great single logs; another improvement was the keel, which gave strength and stiffness to the hull, or body, of a boat. By the time of the Phoenicians (about 1200 B.C.), whose ships traded all around the Mediterranean Sea, boat design had become standardized into two types. These were the broad-beamed merchant ship, usually driven by a sail, and the long, slim galley, or warship, propelled by a large crew of oarsmen. The merchant ship was slow but more seaworthy, and it could carry large cargoes. The galley moved swiftly, but it had little room for cargo and was not designed to ride out storms at sea. These two basic designs hardly changed for hundreds of years.

In the late Middle Ages a number of inventions revolutionized water travel and made possible worldwide voyages of exploration. One was the sternpost rudder, which greatly increased control over the steering of a ship. Before the invention of the rudder a ship was steered by a large oar attached to its side. This gave rather poor control. It was hard to steer a boat except in the general direction that the wind was blowing. The sternpost rudder made it possible to steer a ship in almost any direction except directly into the wind.

Another important invention was the tun, a wooden cask for water. With a supply of fresh water stored in tuns, a ship could make long voyages far from land. Previously, ships had had to put in to shore every few days to replenish their water supply. So important was the tun that a ship's carrying capacity came to be measured in "tunnage," meaning the amount of space in the ship. Today the word is spelled "tonnage," but in shipping terms the ton is still a unit of space rather than a measure of weight.

Late in the 18th century, when steam engines were becoming better-known, several inventors applied steam power to the driving of boats. Practical designs were worked out in the early 19th century, and steamboats were soon in widespread use. Although at first steamboats were slower than sailboats, they were completely independent of winds and currents. As a result, by the end of the 19th century steamboats had replaced sailboats for most purposes. Steam engines in turn were replaced by the more efficient internal-combustion engines. Today nuclear energy is used to drive some naval vessels and some cargo ships.

Air Transportation. For thousands of years men have dreamed of traveling through the air. Designs for flying machines go back to the 15th century. One famous inventor who designed a flying machine was Leonardo da Vinci. However, none of the early flying machines worked, because of their inventors' lack of knowledge of the laws of flight. In 1783 the first successful flight was made in a lighter-than-air craft—the balloon—in France. Steady improvements led to the invention of the airship. However, airships have not been successful, because their gas-bags are easily damaged.

The first successful airplane was invented in 1903 by the Wright brothers, Wilbur and Orville. But many earlier inventions went into the making of the first airplane. One of the most important of these was the glider, a motorless heavier-than-air craft that depended on air currents in order to stay up for any length of time. A leading inventor of gliders was the German engineer Otto Lilienthal (1848–96).

The invention of the airplane had to wait until a suitable source of power was available. Steam engines were too heavy, as were battery-driven electric motors. The internal-combustion engine finally made the airplane possible. The internal-combustion engine was the first engine that was both light enough and strong enough to power an airplane.

Airplanes have changed a great deal since the Wright brothers launched their airplane at Kitty Hawk in 1903. Today more and more airplanes have jet engines instead of propellers.

The helicopter, perfected in 1939 by the Russian-American engineer Igor Sikorsky (1889–   ), uses many of the same principles as the airplane. The basic difference is that the helicopter's rotor is a wing that moves, while the airplane's wing does not move.

A very old invention, the rocket, has become important in the 20th century as a possible means of travel. Already rockets have been used to carry astronauts into orbit around the earth and to cushion the force of their return. Rockets have also been sent to the moon and to the planets. Robert H. Goddard, an American engineer, was a pioneer in the development of modern rockets. He patented 214 inventions dealing with rockets. Every rocket today uses some of Goddard's many ideas.

▶ **INVENTIONS OF COMMUNICATION**

Man first communicated by means of gestures and grunts. But gradually he developed language, which helped him to express his ideas more clearly. In early times he also used pictures to communicate ideas. A writing system was not developed for thousands of years. Even so, writing is a very ancient invention. The earliest writing we know of is about 5,500 years old. Writing made knowledge more permanent. Knowledge no longer had to be passed down from generation to generation by word of mouth. The knowledge stored in the millions of books in modern libraries is available to us because of the invention of writing.

Early writing was done on all sorts of materials. Rock, bone, ivory, clay tablets, animal hides, and wood were all used. The writing was carved, scratched, or painted on these materials. Thousands of years before the Christian era the Egyptians invented papyrus, a new material on which to write. Papyrus is a paperlike material made from the stems of the papyrus plant. The Egyptians also invented the book. They pasted sheets of papyrus edge-to-edge to form one long sheet. This long sheet was then rolled up into a scroll, for ease of storage. These scrolls were the first books. The book as we know it today, with one page on top of another, was invented about 2,000 years ago.

Papyrus was used for hundreds of years in many countries. Another writing material, parchment, was invented about 2,000 years ago. Parchment, a thin-scraped piece of sheepskin, was stronger and lasted longer than papyrus. Also, mistakes on parchment could be erased more easily.

Paper was a Chinese invention. It reached Europe by the 12th century A.D. Paper was made from such plant fibers as linen and cotton. Then, in the 19th century paper made from wood pulp was invented. Wood-pulp paper is much cheaper than other kinds. But it

SOME SIGNIFICANT INVENTIONS

INVENTION	INVENTOR	DATE	PLACE
Adding machine	Blaise Pascal	1642	France
Air brake (for trains)	George Westinghouse	1869	United States
Air conditioning	Willis H. Carrier	1902	United States
Airplane	Orville and Wilbur Wright	1903	United States
Air pump	Otto von Guericke	1654	Germany
Aqualung (scuba)	Jacques Yves Cousteau; Émile Gagnan	1943	France
Arc lamp	Humphry Davy	1808	England

INVENTION	INVENTOR	DATE	PLACE
Automobile	Nicolas Cugnot (first self-propelled vehicle—crashed on trial run)	1769	France
	Richard Trevithick (first successful steam-powered road vehicle)	1801	England
	Siegfried Marcus (self-propelled carriage with liquid-fuel internal-combustion engine)	1865	Austria
	Karl Benz (first practical gasoline-powered automobile)	1885	Germany
Balloon	Jacques Étienne Montgolfier Joseph Michel Montgolfier	1783	France
Barometer	Evangelista Torricelli	1643	Italy
Battery, electric	Alessandro Volta	1800	Italy

INVENTION	INVENTOR	DATE	PLACE
Bessemer process (first low-cost, large-scale method for producing steel)	Henry Bessemer	1855	England
	William Kelly	1851 (not patented until 1857)	United States
Bicycle	K. MacMillan	1840	Scotland
Canning of food	Nicolas F. Appert	1804	France
Cannon	Unknown	About 1300	Probably Western Europe
Cash register	J. Ritty	1879	United States

INVENTION	INVENTOR	DATE	PLACE
Celluloid	J. W. Hyatt	1870	United States
Clock:			
Mechanical clock	Uncertain (sometimes credited to Henry de Vick of Württemberg, Germany, about 1360)	14th century	Europe

Pendulum clock	Christian Huygens	1656	Netherlands
Marine chronometer (first really accurate timepiece)	John Harrison	1735	England

Computer, electronic digital	J. P. Eckert; U. W. Mauchly	1946	United States
Cotton gin	Eli Whitney	1793	United States
Cyclotron (first atom-smashing device)	Ernest O. Lawrence	1931	United States
Dictaphone	C. S. Tainter	1885	United States
Diesel engine	Rudolf Diesel	1898 (principle patented 1892)	Germany

Diving suit	William H. James	1825	England
Earth scraper, self-powered	Robert G. Le Tourneau	1923	United States
Electric motor	Michael Faraday (demonstrated basic principle— the electric motor is the work of many inventors)	1821	England
Electromagnet	Joseph Henry	1828	United States
Elevator	Elisha G. Otis	1853	United States
Escalator	Jesse Reno	1891	United States
Ether (anesthetic)	W. T. G. Morton and J. C. Warren	1846	United States

INVENTION	INVENTOR	DATE	PLACE
Force pump	Ctesibius	3rd century B.C.	Egypt
Generator, electric	Michael Faraday (discovered basic principle)	1831	England
	Zénobe T. Gramme (first really practical generator)	1870	France
Gyrocompass	E. A. Sperry	1911 (patent issued 1915)	United States
Gyroscope	Jean B. L. Foucault	1852	France
Hall-Héroult process (for producing aluminum)	Charles M. Hall	1886	United States
	Paul Héroult (working independently)	1886	France

INVENTION	INVENTOR	DATE	PLACE
Harvester	Charles and William Marsh	1858	United States
Helicopter	Igor Sikorsky	1939	United States
Incandescent lamp	Thomas A. Edison	1879	United States
Internal-combustion engine	Jean J. E. Lenoir	1860	France
Jet engine	Frank Whittle	1936	England

INVENTION	INVENTOR	DATE	PLACE
Linotype machine (first successful device for setting type mechanically)	Ottmar Mergenthaler	1884	United States
Lock, pin-tumbler cylinder	Linus Yale, Jr.	1865	United States
Magnetic compass	Unknown	About 12th century	Possibly China
Magnetic recorder (wire recorder)	Valdemar Poulsen	1898	Denmark
Mechanical refrigeration	Jacob Perkins	1834	England

INVENTION	INVENTOR	DATE	PLACE
Microscope	Uncertain (Zacharias Janssen is known to have built an early microscope; Anton van Leeuwenhoek was first to use microscope for scientific observations)	About 1590	Netherlands

INVENTION	INVENTOR	DATE	PLACE
Motion-picture camera	E. J. Marey	1888	France
Motion-picture projector	Thomas A. Edison	1888	United States
Nuclear reactor	Enrico Fermi and others	1942	United States
Nylon	Wallace H. Carothers	1936 (patented 1937)	United States
Paper	Tsai Lun, a Chinese court official	1st century A.D.	China
Papermaking machine	Nicolas L. Robert	1798	France
Phonograph	Thomas A. Edison	1877	United States
Photography	Joseph Nicéphore Niépce	1826	France
Pneumatic drill	S. Ingersoll	1871	United States
Pneumatic tire	R. W. Thompson	1845	United States
Portland cement (the kind of cement used in modern construction)	Joseph Aspdin	1824	England
Power loom (for weaving cloth)	Edmund Cartwright	1786	England
Printing with movable type	Usually credited to Johann Gutenberg; sometimes credited to Laurens Coster of the Netherlands	About 1440 About same time	Germany
Quick-freezing of food	Clarence Birdseye	1924	United States

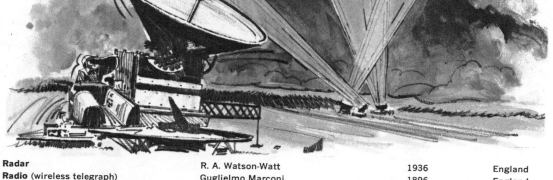

Radar	R. A. Watson-Watt	1936	England
Radio (wireless telegraph)	Guglielmo Marconi	1896	England
Reaper	Cyrus McCormick	1834	United States
Revolver	Samuel Colt	1835 (patented 1836)	United States

Rocket, liquid-fuel	Robert Goddard	1926	United States
Rotary printing press	Richard M. Hoe	1847 (press actually built in 1846)	United States

Safety match	Gustaf Erik Pasch	1844	Sweden
Safety pin	Walter Hunt	1849	United States

INVENTION	INVENTOR	DATE	PLACE
Sewing machine	Barthelemey Thimonnier	1830	France
	Elias Howe	1845 (patented 1846)	United States
Spinning jenny	James Hargreaves	1764	England

Steamboat	Claude F. D. Jouffroy d'Abbans (first boat propelled by steam)	1783	France
	John Fitch (first steamboat capable of sustained operation)	1787	United States
	Robert Fulton (first commercially successful steamboat)	1807	United States
Steam engine, reciprocating (working with back-and-forth motion of a piston in a cylinder)	Thomas Newcomen (first steam-powered engine)	1712	England
	James Watt (separate condenser, double-acting rotary engine)	1769 1782	Scotland England
Steam hammer (used in making heavy metal forgings)	James Nasmyth	1839 (patented 1842)	England

Steam locomotive	Richard Trevithick	1804	England
Steam shovel	William S. Otis	1838	United States
Steam turbine	Charles A. Parsons	1884	England

Submarine	David Bushnell (first boat to move underwater—hand-powered)	1776	United States
	J. P. Holland (first power-driven submarine)	1887	United States

INVENTION	INVENTOR	DATE	PLACE
Tabulator (punch-card machine)	Herman Hollerith	1890	United States
Telegraph	Samuel F. B. Morse (other men had invented telegraphs earlier, but Morse's worked better)	1837	United States

INVENTION	INVENTOR	DATE	PLACE
Telephone	Alexander Graham Bell	1876	United States
Telescope	Unknown (an early telescope maker was Zacharias Janssen, of the Netherlands, who made a telescope in 1604)	Late 16th century	probably Italy or Netherlands

INVENTION	INVENTOR	DATE	PLACE
Television	Vladimir K. Zworykin	1923	United States
Thermometer	Unknown (one of the earliest inventors of a thermometer, however, was Galileo Galilei)	1593	Italy
Threshing machine	Alexander Meikle	1786	Scotland
Transistor	John Bardeen; Walter H. Brattain; William Shockley	1948	United States

INVENTION	INVENTOR	DATE	PLACE
Typewriter	Christopher L. Sholes; Carlos S. Glidden; Samuel W. Soulé	1868	United States
Vacuum tube (used in radio, television, and many other electronic devices)	John A. Fleming (the diode)	1904	England
	Lee De Forest (the triode)	1907	United States
Vulcanization of rubber	Charles S. Goodyear	1839	United States

INVENTION	INVENTOR	DATE	PLACE
Washing machine	J. T. King	1851	United States
Water screw (for raising water)	Archimedes	3rd century B.C.	Greece

INVENTION	INVENTOR	DATE	PLACE
Waterwheel	Unknown	1st century B.C.	Roman Empire
Windmill	Unknown	About 7th century A.D.	Persia
X-ray tube	Wilhelm Konrad Roentgen	1895	Germany
Zipper	W. L. Judson	1896	United States

NOTE: Whenever possible, date given is that of the patent. In some cases, however, the invention was completed several years before the patent was issued. In other cases, the idea was patented before the inventor had a working model. Dates before 1700 are in many cases approximations, since records are not reliable.

does not last as long because of chemical changes that take place in the paper as it ages. In fact, documents from 500 years ago are often in better condition than those written 20 years ago.

When books had to be written out by hand, word by word, it took a very long time to make one. Because of this, books were very expensive. With the invention of the printing press and movable type in the 15th century, books became much cheaper. More and more books were printed, and more and more people were able to buy them. One of the first men to print books was the German printer Johann Gutenberg. Many improvements have been made in the printing press. In the 19th century another invention cut the cost of printing even more by eliminating the slow process of setting type by hand. This invention was the Linotype, a machine that set type for printing presses. It was invented in 1884 by the German-American inventor Ottmar Mergenthaler (1854–99).

Even with the invention of writing and printing, communication was slow. In ancient times signal fires were sometimes used to communicate simple ideas quickly. If an army were attacking a city, a watchman on a far-off hill could see it coming and light a fire to warn the people in the city. In the 18th century chains of towers were built, and messages were sent by signal from one tower to the next.

Speedier methods of communication grew out of discoveries about electricity that were made during the 18th century. One was that electricity will move along a wire. Another

was that electricity moves very quickly. A third was the invention of the Leyden jar, in which electricity can be stored. These discoveries led people to think about the possibility of sending messages along wires by electricity. If a Leyden jar was connected to one end of a long wire, that fact would be known very quickly at the other end. In 1837 the British inventors William F. Cooke (1806–79) and Charles Wheatstone (1802–75) designed an electric telegraph. The next year a 13-mile telegraph line was built between two English railway stations. In that same year an American painter, Samuel F. B. Morse, invented a better type of telegraph. He also invented a code system of dots and dashes that is called Morse code.

After the invention of the telegraph many inventors tried to find a way to send spoken words, instead of just a coded message, through a wire. Several successful telephones were invented. In 1876 the Scottish-American inventor Alexander Graham Bell was the first to patent the telephone.

Wireless telegraphy was another invention that became possible because of earlier scientific work. After many years of research by many inventors the Italian electrical engineer Guglielmo Marconi invented the wireless telegraph, which he patented in 1896.

In 1904 the British scientist Sir John Ambrose Fleming (1849–1945) invented the vacuum tube. With improvements made by the American scientist Lee De Forest (1873–1961), the vacuum tube proved to be of great importance for controlling and amplifying electrical signals in wireless telegraphy. It also made the development of radio possible. Marconi's wireless could only send beeps; radio could send voice or music. Radio broadcasts began in the early 1920's. Within a few years many inventors had begun work on the development of television and radar. Thus, the vacuum tube led to the growth of a new branch of engineering: electronics.

▶ SCIENTIFIC INSTRUMENTS

The instruments with which man observes and measures the world around him make up another important group of inventions. Modern scientific instruments have enabled man to make very accurate measurements and to observe things previously unknown. Yet some of the most important instruments have been very simple. Many date back thousands of years. The invention of the measuring rod made it possible to measure length in standard units. This was important because measurements based on the human body, such as length of the foot or of the pace, varied from person to person. A field 50 paces long by 100 paces wide, for example, would be much bigger if it were paced out by a man with long legs than if it were paced out by a man with short legs. When land had to be divided up, when irrigation systems had to be laid out, or when huge temples and palaces had to be built, exact measurements were useful.

Scales, another ancient invention of great importance, helped trade by allowing people to measure weight. Later, scales became useful in scientific work.

Man learned early to measure time, as well as distance. Primitive man told the time of day by the sun's shadow. Early civilizations used this idea for the sundial. By 1500 B.C. water clocks and hourglasses were also in use. In the 14th century A.D. mechanical clocks were invented in Europe. The pendulum clock was invented in the 17th century. The pendulum made clocks more accurate than they had ever been before. In the 18th century a British instrument maker, John Harrison (1693–1776), invented the marine chronometer. The marine chronometer was the most accurate clock that had yet been made. It was the first clock accurate enough to enable ships' captains to know the time in their homeland when they were far out at sea. This was essential in helping to find the ship's position.

A number of very important scientific instruments were invented in the 17th century. Most of these instruments contained parts or used ideas that had been known for a long time. The invention of the new instruments consisted of putting these parts together or applying these ideas in a new way. For example, eyeglasses had been invented by the 13th century. Early in the 17th century some unknown inventor—probably in the Netherlands—invented the telescope. The first telescopes were simply two lenses in a tube. They were not very important. In 1609 the Italian scientist Galileo Galilei invented the astronomical telescope. Galileo's important invention was the idea of using the telescope to look at the stars, sun, and planets. With it he discovered mountains on the moon, the satellites of Jupiter, the phases of Venus, sunspots, and many new stars.

The microscope was invented by using one of Galileo's instruments to look closely at small objects. It was first used to study bees and has been particularly important in biology.

Two other important scientific instruments that were invented in the 17th century are the thermometer and the barometer. Both were developed slowly, in a number of stages. For this reason it is not possible to say that a particular person invented either the thermometer or the barometer. These instruments led to the scientific concepts of temperature and atmospheric pressure. Both are important in meteorology, the science of weather.

Today many thousands of instruments, from the simple ruler to giant nuclear accelerators, or "atom smashers," are used in science and engineering.

▶ OTHER INVENTIONS

Many inventions throughout the centuries have had to do with food, clothing, or shelter —man's basic needs. The idea of salting or drying foods to preserve them was a very early invention. So was the idea of preserving food by keeping it cold. In the early 19th century the French chef Nicolas Appert (1750–1841) invented canning, a major advance in food preservation. The development of refrigeration equipment by the American inventor John Gorrie (1803–55) made it easier to keep food cold. Clarence Birdseye (1886–

What is a patent?

A patent is an official document by which an inventor can control the right to use his invention. When an invention is patented, no one may make, use, or sell it without the permission of the patent's owner. Generally patents are granted only to the inventor himself. Should an inventor die before he is able to patent his invention, his heirs may patent it.

Once the patent is granted, it is a piece of property. It may be bought, sold, or inherited just like money, a building, or a piece of land. Often an inventor will sell his patent rights to a manufacturer. The inventor may also license his rights—that is, he may allow a company to manufacture or sell his invention in return for a share of the profits. The share of the profits received by the inventor is called the **royalty**. Unless the inventor has a patent, anyone can copy the invention and sell it without paying the inventor a cent.

In order to qualify for a patent, an invention must be original and must not be obvious. That is, it must be something that no one has ever invented before, and it cannot be an idea so simple it would occur to everyone at once. Many different types of inventions may be patented. It is possible to patent not only a new machine or device but also an improvement on another invention, a new process or method of doing something, or a new chemical, such as a plastic.

Patents are granted by the patent office of a government. The United States Patent Office is a part of the Department of Commerce. A patent is only good for a limited time. In the United States a patent is good for 17 years. In Great Britain it is good for 16 years. It is possible for an owner to lose a British patent if he does not make use of the invention.

Patents are good only in the country where they are granted. An American patent, for example, is not good in France. However, most countries have agreements with one another making it possible for an inventor in one country to apply for patents in other countries.

When an inventor in the United States wishes to patent an invention, he first files an application with the United States Patent Office. The application must describe the invention in detail and, if possible, include a diagram or drawing of the invention. Enough information must be included so that an expert could use the application to make or use the invention. To protect the inventor, this description is kept secret until the patent is granted. At one time it was necessary to include a model with the application. So many applications are received every year, however, that it is no longer practical to require a model.

When the Patent Office receives the application, a search is made to make sure that the invention is a new one. If it is, the patent is granted and is given a number. The manufacturer of a patented product usually prints the word "patent" and the patent number on either the product or the package it comes in. This is to warn other manufacturers that the product is protected by a patent. If a patent has been applied for but has not yet been granted, the manufacturer may print "patent applied for" or "patent pending."

There are many legal problems connected with obtaining a patent. For example, the application must be very carefully worded. If there is any confusion or misunderstanding, the patent might not be granted or the inventor might not be fully protected. Therefore, when an inventor applies for a patent, he usually hires a **patent lawyer** to take care of all legal matters. A patent lawyer is a lawyer who is an expert in the laws regarding patents. Patent lawyers also argue cases in which a patent owner claims that someone has infringed on his patent—that is, that someone is making, using, or selling the invention without the patent owner's permission.

Some of the earliest patents were granted by the Republic of Venice (now part of Italy) in the 15th century. In England the first patents were issued during the reign of Queen Elizabeth I (1533–1603). When the English colonists went to America, they took with them the idea of patents, and the colonial governments granted patents.

1956), also an American, invented still another method of preserving foods: quick-freezing.

Clothing is another very ancient invention, so old that we cannot say when it was first used. The earliest clothing was probably made from animal skins. But later (about 10,000 years ago), weaving was invented. Weaving is basically no more than interlacing fibers to form a fabric. Yet this simple idea made cloth possible.

Clothing today is more comfortable and more attractive than it was in primitive times. The invention of dyeing and of many different kinds and colors of dyes has helped make clothing more attractive. In the 20th century artificial fibers, such as nylon, rayon, and Orlon, have made clothing easier to take care of and more comfortable. The practical sewing machine invented by an American, Elias Howe, made clothing easier to manufacture and therefore less expensive. Many small inventions help to hold clothing together. Some are quite old, such as the safety pin, which was invented about 3,000 years ago. Others are 20th-century inventions, such as the zipper.

Early man took shelter in caves from storms and cold. Then he began to build shelters from the weather. When men started to live in villages and towns, larger and more permanent structures were built. Those involved many new inventions. The earliest builders used rocks and dead trees, but even in prehistoric times man had begun to shape the building materials to suit his desires. Tools were invented for cutting down trees and making planks from them. Other tools were invented for cutting and shaping stone. At first these tools were themselves wood or stone. Later, metal tools were invented. The Egyptian pyramids show us how long ago man learned to build massive structures. The Great Pyramid of Cheops at Giza, Egypt, was built over 4,000 years ago. It is still one of the largest structures in the world. Some of the stone blocks in this pyramid weigh over 50 tons. There are Egyptian obelisks that weigh hundreds of tons. To cut such large pieces of stone, shape them, and move them into position required the invention of many tools and means of handling stone.

Today the construction of any building, from a small shack to a large office building, requires the use of many, many different inventions. Many different tools are used, such as hammers, saws, drills, planes, and pulleys. The construction of large buildings requires the use of cranes and power shovels run by gasoline or diesel engines. Many of the materials used in buildings are ancient inventions, while others were invented quite recently. Bricks have been used since prehistoric times. Concrete was an invention of the Romans. Iron and steel were not used for building until the 19th century. The 20th century brought the use of reinforced concrete, aluminum, plastics, and many other building materials.

▶ SCIENCE AND INVENTION

Inventions have been important to scientists in many ways. New instruments have helped scientific work. But inventions have served science in many indirect ways as well, for many centuries. The invention of the wood block in the 15th century made it possible to print many copies of a drawing. This was important in the sciences of botany and zoology. The invention of printing with movable type, also in the 15th century, helped make all kinds of knowledge more widely available—including scientific knowledge. The invention of artificial lighting made it possible for scientists, as well as other people, to work after dark. Thus, almost every invention has helped scientists in some way.

Scientists are interested in understanding the natural world. Engineers and inventors are concerned with controlling the natural world. Today these two interests overlap. However, such was not always the case. Until about 200 years ago science was not important in engineering. Since the late 18th century a new branch of engineering has developed: applied science. Applied science uses scientific knowledge to help in controlling natural phenomena. Much of our modern scientific knowledge has been very useful to inventors. Knowledge from the science of chemistry is used today in the making of better steel. Knowledge from biology is used in medicine. Knowledge from physics is used in aircraft design. Inventors have available today all of the present knowledge of science.

▶ INVENTIONS TODAY

Millions of inventions are in use today. Some date from prehistoric times; others are quite recent. Every year there are thousands more. These new inventions in turn will lead to other inventions and improvements.

Many of today's inventions are the work of groups of men. These teams of inventors and engineers, working in well-equipped laboratories, are developing complicated new inventions, such as supersonic aircraft and spaceships. Each of these involves thousands of earlier inventions.

However, the invention of something new involves ideas. People have ideas. Many inventions are still being made by individuals working alone. The pace of invention has been speeded up, but though many conditions have changed, the basic process of invention is the same as ever.

DUANE H. D. ROLLER
The University of Oklahoma

See also PATENTS; SCIENCE, HISTORY OF; SCIENCE AND SOCIETY; TECHNOLOGY.

IODINE AND OTHER HALOGENS

Iodine, bromine, chlorine, fluorine, and astatine are the members of a family of chemical elements called the halogens. The halogens are very active chemically. They react with metals to form a type of compound called a salt. In fact, the word "halogen" means "salt maker."

Iodine. Iodine is a gray-black solid with a metallic appearance. It is very important in several forms as a disinfectant (germ killer). Tincture of iodine—iodine dissolved in alcohol—is used to disinfect cuts and scratches. Higher animals need a certain amount of iodine in their food every day in order to keep healthy. Lack of iodine in a person's food will cause his thyroid gland to work improperly. Seafoods contain iodine.

Iodine compounds are very useful in industry. Like compounds of bromine and chlorine, iodine compounds are sensitive to light and are used in photography.

The most important source of iodine is Chile saltpeter, a mineral that is found in great quantities in Chile. Another source is oil brine deposits—underground bodies of salt water found near petroleum deposits. A small amount of iodine is obtained from the sea. Seaweed, which absorbs iodine from seawater, is collected and burned. Then iodine is removed from the ashes.

Bromine. Bromine is a reddish-brown liquid. It causes burns if it touches the skin. When it evaporates, it forms a poisonous gas that irritates the eyes and nose. In medicine, bromine compounds are used as sedatives (drugs that calm the nerves). The chemical industry uses bromine and bromine compounds to prepare other important chemicals. Bromine compounds are used also in photography and in hair-waving lotions.

Bromine is obtained from seawater and from underground brine deposits. Close to 15,000 tons of seawater are needed to obtain 1 ton of bromine.

Chlorine. Chlorine is a greenish-yellow gas. It is poisonous and, like bromine, irritates the eyes and nose. However, to kill germs, it is added in small amounts to drinking water and to the water in swimming pools. Laundry bleaches are usually chlorine compounds. Chlorine bleach is often used to disinfect floors and walls. As bleaches, chlorine compounds are used to whiten cloth and paper. Like bromine compounds, they are very important in photography and for making other chemicals. A common chlorine compound is ordinary table salt. Table salt is sodium chloride, a compound of chlorine and the metal sodium.

Chlorine is obtained from sodium chloride by **electrolysis**; that is, by passing an electric current through sodium chloride solution. Most sodium chloride comes from salt lakes, underground brine deposits, or salt mines.

Fluorine. Fluorine is a pale yellow gas. It is the lightest and most active halogen. In fact, fluorine is the most active nonmetal element; it will form compounds with almost any other element.

The most important use of pure fluorine is in nuclear-energy work. It is used to separate uranium into its different types (isotopes). Although pure fluorine has very few uses, its compounds are very important. Fluorine compounds in water and toothpaste help to prevent cavities in teeth.

An important use of fluorine compounds was discovered in ancient times. Certain minerals, called fluxes, were added to melted ores or glass to make them flow more easily. In modern times scientists have found that these fluxes contain fluorine compounds. These compounds are still very important in glass and metal industries.

Fluorocarbons are another important group of fluorine compounds. These compounds of carbon and fluorine are used as lubricants and for making stain-resistant cloth.

In general, fluorine compounds are made from compounds found in minerals such as fluorspar and cryolite. Pure fluorine, when it is needed, is made by electrolysis of hydrofluoric acid, a fluorine compound.

Astatine. Astatine is the only halogen that is of no commercial importance. It is a very rare element; there is less than one ounce in all the earth's crust. When it is needed for scientific studies, it is usually made in the laboratory by means of an atomic reaction. Astatine is radioactive.

JOHN PRICE
Chemical Week

See also ELEMENTS.

IONOSPHERE. See ATMOSPHERE.

IONS AND IONIZATION

An ion is an atom or group of atoms that carries an electric charge.

All atoms are made up of smaller particles, called subatomic particles. Some of these smaller particles carry an electric charge at all times, but the charges are not always apparent. The reason is that there are two different kinds of charges: positive and negative. The two sometimes balance each other inside the atom. This causes the atom to behave as though it carried no charge at all.

At the center of every atom is a **nucleus**, containing one or more particles called **protons**. Each of these protons has a positive charge. Surrounding the nucleus are particles called **electrons**. Each of these has a negative charge.

An ordinary atom has exactly as many protons as electrons. This means that it has exactly as many positive charges as negative charges. All the charges balance, and the atom is **electrically neutral**.

Suppose you upset the balance by removing some of the particles. You will then produce an electric charge and form an ion. This process is **ionization**.

The particles removed are usually electrons. Protons are heavy particles in the nucleus. It is difficult to do anything to them. Electrons, however, are light particles, and some are bound rather lightly to the rest of the atom. They are easy to remove.

In fact, some electrons in atoms of metals are so easily removed that under certain conditions they can be made to flow through the metal. We describe this as an electric current flowing through the metal. An electric current in metal is actually the flowing of loose electrons.

It is possible to cause atoms to give up electrons by bombarding the atoms with energy in the form of light or heat. If an element can be made to give off electrons when it is struck by light, those moving electrons will make up an electric current wherever they go. We can construct a **photoelectric cell** (or an "electric eye") out of such elements.

A photoelectric cell is sometimes used to open and shut doors automatically. Light shining on the cell causes it to give off electrons. The electrons make up an electric current that causes the door to stay shut. As you approach the door, your body interrupts the beam of light. As a result, the electric current stops. The door opens in time for you to pass through.

Atoms will also release electrons if heated strongly enough. In a radio tube a metal wire is heated so that electrons are given off. The movement of these electrons can be strictly controlled because they carry negative charges. This means they can be attracted to any object that carries a positive charge. (Opposite charges attract each other.) It also means that they can be pushed away by any object that carries a negative charge. (Similar charges repel each other.)

By controlling the flow of electrons in this fashion, we can make electric currents start and stop. We can direct them, strengthen weak currents, and so on. Instruments that make use of such controlled electron flows are **electronic**. Radio and television sets are common examples of electronic devices.

▶ **POSITIVE IONS**

Once electrons leave an atom, the remaining electrically charged particles no longer balance. There are not enough electrons left to cancel the charge of every proton. If one

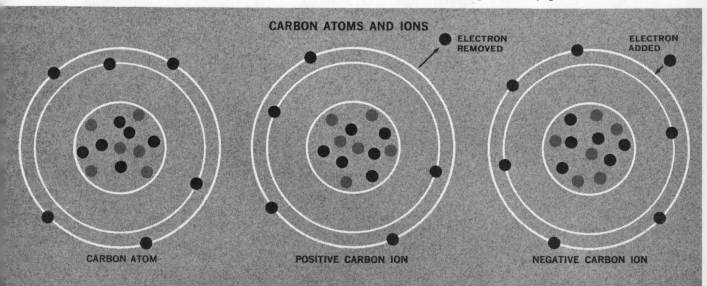

CARBON ATOMS AND IONS

ELECTRON REMOVED

ELECTRON ADDED

CARBON ATOM   POSITIVE CARBON ION   NEGATIVE CARBON ION

FUEL CELL—IONS IN ACTION

A fuel cell is a device that uses ions to make electricity. The cell is made up of two electrodes separated by an **electrolyte** — a substance that serves as a medium for the movement of the ions. The electrodes, made of metal or carbon, are porous—that is, substances can pass through them. In one type of fuel cell the chemical substances used are hydrogen and oxygen. Hydrogen gas is pumped into a chamber next to one electrode, and oxygen gas is pumped into another chamber next to the other electrode.

As it passes into its electrode the hydrogen gives up electrons and hydrogen ions are formed. The hydrogen ions flow through the electrode and into the electrolyte. The electrons lost by the hydrogen pass into an external wire connected to the electrode. The constant flow of the electrons through the wire is an electric current that can be tapped and used to provide electric power.

The electrons return to the fuel cell through another external wire. As the electrons enter the oxygen electrode they are picked up by the oxygen, and oxygen ions are formed. The oxygen ions pass through the electrode into the electrolyte. The

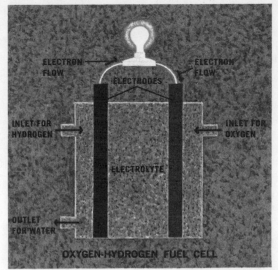

OXYGEN-HYDROGEN FUEL CELL

oxygen ions and the hydrogen ions combine with the electrolyte, forming water and more electrolyte.

Fuel cells are used as a source of electric power on long space flights. These cells were first used in space flight in the Gemini 5 capsule, launched by the United States on August 21, 1965.

---

electron is gone, one proton is left unbalanced; if two electrons are gone, two protons are left unbalanced, and so on. The atom as a whole is now a **positive ion** because it carries a positive electric charge.

Since these positive ions are electrically charged, they can be controlled by other electric charges. Scientists think that some day spaceships may be powered by such ions.

For that purpose, the metal cesium may be used. Cesium atoms lose electrons more easily than any other variety of atom does. And so cesium ions are more easily formed than any other. Cesium ions can be made to travel very quickly. Fast-moving cesium ions can be hurled out through tubes at the rear of a spaceship. Each ion will give the ship a tiny "kick" forward. Little by little the ship will go faster and faster. Such an **ion-drive** may provide greater speed than any form of ordinary rocket could.

▶PLASMA AND FUSION

If a quantity of matter is heated more and more strongly, it first turns gaseous. Then its atoms start losing electrons. More and more atoms lose electrons until, at quite high temperatures, all the atoms have lost at least one electron. The gas then consists of charged particles only—negatively charged electrons and positively charged ions. Matter made up of gas containing balanced quantities of charged particles is called **plasma**. The sun and all the stars are made up of plasma.

In some cases temperatures are extremely high—in the millions of degrees. Then all the electrons are stripped off the atoms, and bare nuclei are left behind.

In ordinary atoms the nuclei are hidden behind clouds of electrons and cannot approach each other. In very hot plasma the bare nuclei can approach and collide. Colliding nuclei can exchange particles or can join together to form a new and larger nucleus. This joining together is called **nuclear fusion**.

The nuclear fusion of small nuclei releases a great deal of energy. The center of the sun is at a temperature of some 10,000,000 degrees Centigrade. There the nuclei of four hydrogen atoms can fuse to form a helium atom nucleus. This is the chief type of fusion reaction that occurs. The energy produced radiates outward and bathes earth with heat and light.

On earth, scientists have learned to produce very hot plasmas by means of an exploding atomic bomb. If these hot plasmas contain certain kinds of hydrogen atoms, the nuclei of these atoms will undergo fusion. Then far

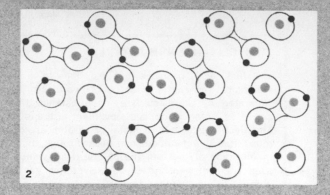

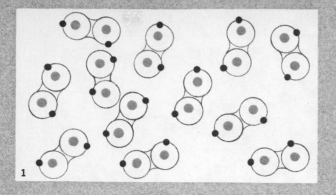

CHANGING A GAS INTO A PLASMA

(1) Molecules of the gas hydrogen at room temperature. Each molecule is made up of 2 atoms of hydrogen. The molecules are constantly in motion. They bounce off each other and off walls of container. (2) Hydrogen is heated, using electrical energy as a source. Molecules move and vibrate with greater force and speed. Some

of the hydrogen molecules stretch and break apart. (3) With an even greater amount of electrical energy applied, all hydrogen molecules split apart into atoms. Some atoms ionize, forming protons and free electrons. (4) At even higher temperatures all atoms have ionized, and a plasma forms.

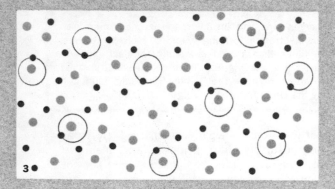

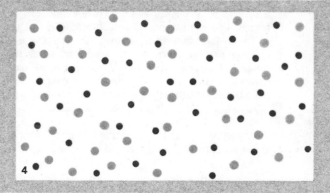

more energy is liberated than in an ordinary atomic bomb. The result is a **hydrogen bomb**.

Scientists are trying to find out how to form very hot plasmas without using an atomic bomb. If they can form such hot plasmas in small quantities, they can start nuclear fusion going in a quiet way. Instead of reacting all at once, the nuclei will fuse and produce energy a little at a time. This energy can then be put to a thousand peaceful uses.

Stream of plasma shoots from the nozzle of a plasma torch. The torch can provide temperatures of from 600 to 60,000 degrees Fahrenheit.

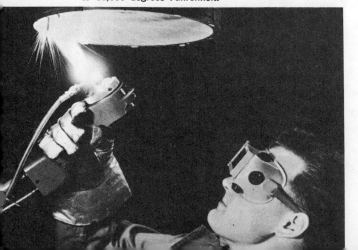

▶ THE RADIATION BELTS

Ionization can take place not only through heat but also through the bombardment of atoms by tiny charged particles.

The sun, for instance, is so hot that it sprays electrons out into space. Positively charged ions are also shot out.

As some of these charged particles near the earth they are trapped in our planet's magnetic field. The particles then shuttle back and forth in regions called the radiation belts.

When these particles or energetic X rays and ultraviolet rays from the sun approach the atoms in the upper reaches of our atmosphere, there may be a collision. Then electrons are knocked out of the atom, leaving behind a positively charged ion. The upper region of the atmosphere, 50 miles and more above the earth's surface, is therefore rich in electrons and ions. It is called the **ionosphere**. (Radio waves bounce back from the charged particles in the ionosphere. That is what makes it possible for men to communicate by radio over long distances.)

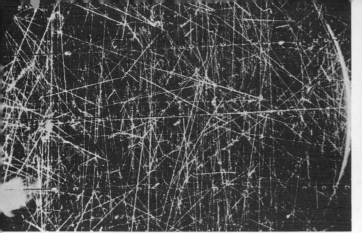

Paths of atomic particles in cloud chamber.

Paths of particles in bubble chamber.

The particles of the radiation belts come nearest the atmosphere in the polar regions. For that reason, more ionization takes place in the upper atmosphere there than anywhere else on earth. Each bit of ionization releases a tiny spark of light. The result is that the polar skies usually glow at night with beautiful colored lights. These are the **northern lights** (aurora borealis) in the Arctic and the **southern lights** (aurora australis) in the Antarctic.

Occasionally the sun throws up huge spouts of flaming matter (solar flares) and blasts unusually large quantities of subatomic particles into space. Auroras then become particularly bright and can be seen in many parts of the world. Such "storms" also affect communications. When the ionosphere is upset by a flood of particles, radio waves begin bouncing back in odd ways and radio contact may fade out.

Some of the bare atomic nuclei that collide with the earth's atmosphere are very energetic indeed. Many of these may come from the sun, but some also seem to come from far out in space. Scientists are not quite certain how they are formed. These very energetic bare atomic nuclei are called **cosmic rays**.

▶ DETECTING RADIOACTIVITY

On earth there are continuous sprays of subatomic particles from radioactive atoms, such as those of uranium, thorium, and radium. These release negatively charged electrons (**beta particles**) and positively charged bare helium nuclei (**alpha particles**). When these strike the atoms of the atmosphere, they knock electrons off the atoms and form ions.

These ions can carry an electric current,

and this characteristic is used to detect radioactivity. A **Geiger counter**, for instance, contains a gas that can almost carry a current (but not quite). If a subatomic particle from some radioactive atom enters, it collides with an atom, forming an ion. The ion is pulled along by the electric charges in the instrument. It collides with several other atoms and produces more ions. Each ion produces still more until—in a tiny fraction of a second—the gas contains enough ions to carry a sizable electric current. The current sweeps through the gas and produces a clicking sound or lights up a dial. In this way, counters can be used to prospect for uranium.

Water vapor forms droplets about charged ions more easily than it does about ordinary, uncharged atoms or molecules. Imagine a chamber filled with water vapor that is on the point of settling out as a dew. If a charged particle flashes through that chamber, it forms a line of ions and a water droplet settles about each ion.

In such a **cloud chamber** the path taken by the particle is outlined by a trail of water. Scientists can tell from the path so outlined what kind of a charge the particle has. They can tell how heavy it is, how long it exists before breaking down, what happens if it hits another particle, and so on.

A chamber can also be filled with a liquid that is on the point of boiling. If a particle flashes through the liquid, it forms a line of ions about which a little boiling does take place. Such a device is called a **bubble chamber** because the path of a particle is outlined by a trail of tiny bubbles.

Scientists have learned much about subatomic particles from their studies of ions in cloud chambers and bubble chambers.

Ions are also formed as the result of chemical reactions.

Consider the sodium atom, for instance. Its electrons are arranged in three shells. The outermost shell contains only one electron. This electron, far from the positively charged nucleus, is held very weakly. It can be driven away from the atom very easily.

The chlorine atom has electrons distributed in three shells, too. But the third shell contains seven electrons. Now that shell is most stable when it contains eight electrons. So the chlorine atom has a tendency to pick up one electron.

Now suppose a sodium atom collides with a chlorine atom. The sodium atom gives up an electron, and the chlorine atom accepts it. The sodium atom, with one electron missing, carries a positive charge; it is a sodium ion. The chlorine atom has one electron extra and thus carries a negative charge; it is a chloride ion. (The names of negative ions are usually slightly different from the name of the ele-

ment; here "chloride" is used instead of "chlorine.")

The chemical symbol for the sodium atom is Na. To show that the sodium ion carries a positive charge, we write the symbol for the ion Na^+. The chemical symbol for the chlorine atom is Cl and for the chloride ion it is Cl^-.

It is possible for an atom to lose more than one electron or to gain more than one in the course of collisions. Then it becomes a doubly or triply charged ion. The calcium atom can easily lose two electrons; so the calcium ion is Ca^{++}. The aluminum atom loses three electrons; so the aluminum ion is Al^{+++}. The sulfur atom, on the other hand, can gain two electrons; so the sulfide ion is $S^=$.

All chemical reactions seem to involve a shift of electrons in one way or another. Sometimes the shift isn't complete. Then two atoms may share several electrons, neither giving them up completely. Two nitrogen atoms will share six electrons, for instance. They will then cling together, forming a nitrogen molecule, but not forming actual ions. This is a very stable arrangement, and one nitrogen molecule will attract other nitrogen molecules only very feebly. For that reason, nitrogen molecules move along independently, without clinging together, and form a gas.

Sometimes a chemical reaction involves a complete shift of electrons, so ions are formed. Each ion attracts any oppositely charged ion in its vicinity. For instance, sodium ions (Na^+) will attract all the chloride ions (Cl^-) and vice versa. All the ions will stick closely together, and a solid will be formed. Thus, sodium and chlorine will form the solid sodium chloride, which is the chemical name of common table salt.

Sometimes a number of atoms will stick together through the sharing of electrons. And yet some of the atoms will also lose or gain electrons. For instance, a nitrogen atom can share electrons with four different hydrogen atoms. But one of the hydrogen atoms will also lose an electron in the process. Therefore the whole group of atoms will carry a single positive charge. The symbol for the group will be NH_4^+. This is called the ammonium ion because its formula resembles that of the gas ammonia.

Another example is one in which a sulfur

HOW TO CLEAN SILVER BY ELECTROLYSIS

You can put ions to work cleaning tarnished silverware. The black tarnish that often coats silverware is caused by sulfur ions. You can remove the sulfur ions (tarnish) easily without having to polish the silver. You need salt, baking soda, aluminum foil, and an enamel pan. Do not use an aluminum pan because it will be blackened by the sulfur ions. An enamel pan will not.

Cover the bottom of the pan on the inside with aluminum foil. Measure 1 quart of water into the pan. Dissolve 1 tablespoonful of baking soda and 1 teaspoonful of salt in the water. (You may need more than 1 quart of solution. Just remember to add a tablespoonful of baking soda and a teaspoonful of salt to each quart of water.)

Bring the solution to a boil, and carefully place the silverware in the pan. Make sure that each piece of silverware touches the aluminum foil and that each piece is completely covered by the solution. Boil the solution for about 5 minutes (longer if the silver is badly tarnished). Allow the solution to cool, then remove the silverware, rinse in hot water, and dry with a soft cloth. The silver is now clean of tarnish.

When dissolved in water, salt and baking soda make an ion-carrying solution. The sulfur ions flow from the silver to the aluminum. A process in which ions flow from one material to another through an ion-carrying solution is called electrolysis.

Cleaning silver by electrolysis is quick and easy. Also, none of the silver is worn away as it would be if it were polished with silver polish.

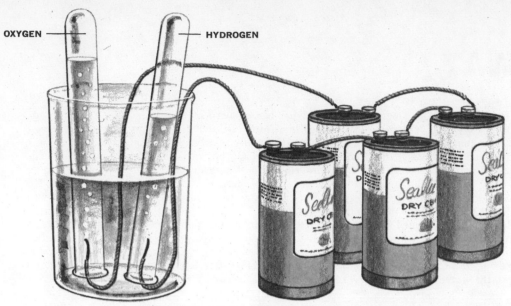

OXYGEN — HYDROGEN —

Water is separated into hydrogen and oxygen. Each molecule of water is made up of two hydrogen atoms and one atom of oxygen; thus, twice as much hydrogen forms as oxygen.

atom shares electrons with four different oxygen atoms. But here two of the oxygen atoms pick up an electron apiece from other atoms in the vicinity. The formula is $SO_4^=$, and this is the sulfate ion.

Large molecules, made up of thousands of atoms, may have numerous little combinations of atoms that can lose or gain electrons. The protein molecules of living tissue have electric charges here and there on the molecule. Indeed, every different kind of protein molecule has its own pattern of charges. This is one reason why different protein molecules can behave in so many different ways.

▶ ELECTROCHEMISTRY

When a substance made of ions (such as sodium chloride) is dissolved in water, the ions separate and move about freely. If oppositely charged strips of metal (electrodes) are placed in the solution, the positive ions all travel toward the negative electrode (cathode); they are therefore called cations. The negative ions all travel toward the positive electrode (anode); they are therefore anions. This method of separation of ions is called **electrolysis**.

When ions travel to the two electrodes, they are carrying charges with them. We say that an electric current is passing through the solution. For this reason, substances like sodium chloride are said to be electrolytes. A substance like sugar has molecules made up of

atoms that share electrons and do not form ions. It may dissolve, but it carries no electric current. Sugar is a nonelectrolyte.

If the proper chemicals are combined in the proper way, a reaction produces ion concentrations that can be drawn off as a flow of electricity. Such chemical combinations are called **chemical cells**, **electric cells**, or **batteries**. When the chemical reaction has produced all the ions it can, the battery is used up. Some types of batteries, however, can be charged. Electricity is put into them, and the chemical reaction is made to go backward. After that has been done, the battery (a storage battery, in this case) can produce electricity again.

When ions reach the electrodes to which they are attracted, they either lose their additional electrons or gain the electrons they are lacking. Thus they become ordinary atoms again. If the ions are formed from metal atoms, they become metal again on the electrodes, sometimes forming a hard smooth layer. This is called **electroplating**.

Indeed, much can be done in chemistry by controlling ions through an electric current. And so a very important branch of the science has grown up under the name **electrochemistry**.

ISAAC ASIMOV
Boston University School of Medicine

See also ATOMS; BATTERIES; CHEMISTRY; ELEMENTS; GEIGER COUNTER; NUCLEAR ENERGY.

IOWA

He was a bit under medium height—a wiry, black-haired man with the look of a born adventurer. The Fox Indians of Iowa called him Little Night. This man was Julien Dubuque—first permanent settler of Iowa and founder of the city that bears his name.

Dubuque was born in the Canadian province of Quebec in 1762. As a young man, well-educated and polished in manner, he traveled into Wisconsin country to seek his fortune. There he learned that the Fox Indians had valuable lead mines west of the Mississippi. He gained their friendship, and they gave him permission to work the mines. The agreement was signed at Kettle Chief's village on Catfish Creek in 1788.

Because Spain owned the territory at that time, Dubuque obtained legal right to the land from Spain in 1796. Courteously he named his holdings the Mines of Spain. He built a settlement and carried on a thriving trade in pig lead and furs. When he died in 1810 the Indians buried him with all the honors of a great chief. Today a limestone tower at Dubuque marks the grave of the Indians' Little Night—the Miner of the Mines of Spain.

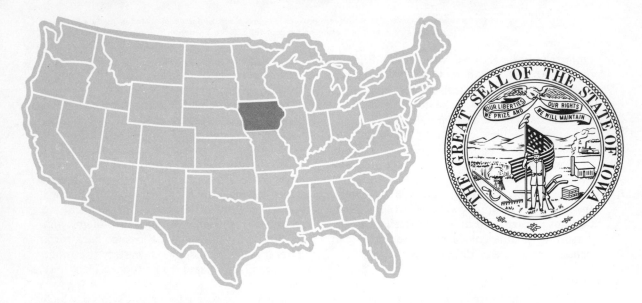

Iowa has many nicknames. It has been called the Food Market of the World. It has been described as the state "where factory and farm share prosperity."

As a visitor crosses the state in summer, he soon understands what such descriptions and nicknames mean. Huge areas are planted in crops, especially corn, oats, and soybeans. When the weather is good, the farmers are in the fields doing work with many kinds of machines. Beef cattle and some dairy herds graze in the pastures. Hogs and cattle are in the feedlots being fattened for market.

For good reason Iowa is known as the land where the tall corn grows. It is also a land of towns and cities, well spaced through the rolling farmlands. The visitor in Iowa will notice the many factories, large and small, in the towns and cities. He may also notice that there is a relationship between many of the factories and the farms. Some factories process farm products. For example, there are meat-packing plants and mills that turn grains into breakfast cereals or livestock feeds. Other factories make the machines and equipment used on the farms.

It is easy to see that factories and farms share prosperity in Iowa. But not all of the industries and activities of the state are related to agriculture. Years ago factories at Muscatine began to manufacture pearl buttons from the shells of freshwater clams. Fort Madison became known as the home of the Sheaffer pen. Recently Iowa's factories have been making a variety of products.

Iowa also makes important contributions to the nation in education and research. The university at Ames has long been known for its programs in agriculture. The famous agricultural scientist George Washington Carver studied at Ames and taught there before going to Tuskegee Institute in Alabama in 1896. Today the university at Ames is known also for its engineering programs and for atomic research. The much discussed Van Allen radiation belt that surrounds the earth is named for its discoverer, James A. Van Allen, a physicist at the University of Iowa.

Iowa's official nickname is the Hawkeye State. This name was suggested by a Fort Madison newspaper editor in the 1830's. He chose it to honor an Indian chief. It is also said that Iowa's nickname comes from the name of the pioneer scout and woodsman in *The Last of the Mohicans*. This novel by James Fenimore Cooper was published in 1826—20 years before Iowa became a state.

Whatever the origin of its nickname, Iowa still contains many reminders of its first people, the Indians. There are many Indian names, such as Keokuk, Tama, Sioux City. The first explorers of what is now Iowa were the French. They, too, left many names on the land—Dubuque, Des Moines, Le Claire.

STATE FLAG.

STATE TREE: Oak.

STATE BIRD: Eastern goldfinch.

STATE FLOWER: Wild rose.

IOWA

CAPITAL: Des Moines.

STATEHOOD: December 28, 1846; the 29th state.

SIZE: 56,290 sq. mi.; rank, 25th.

POPULATION: 2,825,041 (1970 census); rank, 25th.

ORIGIN OF NAME: From a Dakota Indian word; the name had many different spellings until it became Ioway and then Iowa.

ABBREVIATION: Ia.

NICKNAME: Hawkeye State.

STATE SONG: "The Song of Iowa," by Major S. H. M. Byers, to the tune "O Tannenbaum."

STATE MOTTO: "Our liberties we prize and our rights we will maintain."

STATE SEAL: In the foreground a citizen soldier, representing defense, supports the national flag. A liberty cap is on top of the flagpole. At one side of the soldier are farm implements, a sheaf of wheat, and a wheat field. All these represent agriculture. The pile of pig lead and the smelting factory at the other side stand for the early mining industry of the state. In the far background a steamboat, the *Iowa*, sails upon the Mississippi. It represents commerce. The eagle at the top of the seal holds in its beak a streamer on which the state motto is printed.

STATE FLAG: The flag bears the tricolor of France (vertical stripes of blue, white, and red) because French explorers were the first to enter Iowa. The white also stands for the white unwritten pages of Iowa's history. In the center of the white stripe a flying eagle carries in its beak a blue streamer with the state motto. The word "Iowa" appears in red letters below the streamer.

Through the years people from many countries have helped to develop Iowa. In turn, they have shared in its prosperity.

▶ THE LAND

Iowa is one of a group of states sometimes known as the West North Central States. It is centrally located, west of the Mississippi and in the northern half of the nation.

Landforms

The land surface of Iowa has been formed by glaciers, rivers, rain, and wind. The last three—rivers, rain, and wind—are still changing the surface of the state. The glaciers left their marks thousands of years ago. Iowa is a good place in which to study the effects of glaciers. Within the state there is evidence of each of the last continental ice sheets that covered large parts of the Middle West.

How Glaciers Helped Form the Land. A million years ago all of Iowa was covered by a continental glacier named the Nebraskan. When the ice melted, it left a jumble of clay, sand, gravel, and boulders. Material of this kind left by glaciers is called till. In northeast Iowa the ice was thin, and it left only patches of till. The patches were in a hilly area where the bedrock is chiefly limestone or sandstone.

In time seeds that were blown by the wind or dropped by birds took root in the soil. Gradually all of Iowa was covered with vegetation. Thousands of years later another glacier, the Kansan, moved south from

Canada. It covered all of Iowa except the northeast corner. After a long time the ice melted. It left clay, sand, gravel, and boulders on top of the till left by the Nebraskan glacier. And again vegetation took root. Again trees and grass covered the land.

Then another glacier, the Illinoian, slowly moved southward and westward from Canada. It approached Iowa from the east. When the glacier reached the Mississippi River, it pushed the river westward. For a while the river flowed in a channel along the western margin of the ice. When the glacier melted, it dropped all the material that it had carried with it. After a time the Mississippi returned to its old channel. In southeastern Iowa it is possible to dig a deep hole and find three different glacial deposits. Of course, the Illinoian deposit is on top of the other two.

The last glacier, the Wisconsin, covered only the northern part of Iowa. This glacier moved south, then melted back, and then moved south again. At each stage it left slightly different deposits. Recent scientific studies show that the last ice sheet melted about 10,000 years ago.

The times between the ice sheets are called interglacial periods. During these periods and for the last 10,000 years, the land surface has been changed by rivers, rain, and wind.

The Present Land Surface. All of Iowa is included in a large natural region of the United States known as the Central Lowland. The state itself may be divided into two main

A riverboat passing through a lock on the Mississippi River at Dubuque.

sections—Young Glacial Plains in the north and Older Till Plains in the south.

Most of the northern part of Iowa is called Young Glacial Plains. This is the area that was covered by the last glacier. Wind, rivers, and rain have had only about 10,000 years to wear the land away. This may seem to be a long time. But it is really not long for nature's forces to work. The land in this part of Iowa is somewhat level and poorly drained. Swamps, lakes, and creeks were common when the early settlers arrived. Now much of the swampy land has been drained. It makes very good land for crops.

The rest of the state is made up of areas called Older Till Plains. Southern Iowa is hilly. The rivers have had time to form good

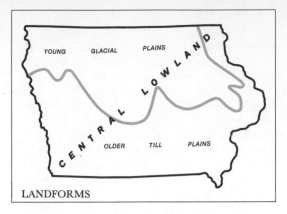

LANDFORMS

channels and to drain the land. There are few swamps. The valleys make fertile croplands, and the hill slopes are used for pasture. In western Iowa high bluffs, somewhat like sand dunes, rise from the floodplains along the Missouri River. These bluffs are made up of very fine earth material deposited by the wind.

There are also high bluffs in northeastern Iowa along the Mississippi River. These bluffs are made of beds of limestone and sandstone. The valleys are narrow, and the sides of the valleys are quite steep. Because of the steep hills and valleys, this section is frequently called the Switzerland of Iowa.

Rivers and Lakes

Iowa lies between two great rivers—the Mississippi on the east and the Missouri on the west. The Big Sioux River also forms part of the western boundary. The rivers within Iowa are separated by a low divide in the western part of the state. Tributaries of the Mississippi flow in a southeasterly direction from this divide. Tributaries of the Missouri flow southwestward.

The largest rivers are the ones that flow into the Mississippi. Waterfalls are located along some of these rivers. Early settlers used the waterfalls as a source of power to grind grain or make lumber. Many of Iowa's larger cities began as small mill communities.

Most of the natural lakes are located in the northwestern part of the state. These lakes were formed by glacial deposits that blocked drainage from the glaciers. Throughout the state there are numerous other lakes, both natural and man-made. The lakes are not large, but they are busy places during the summer months for resort owners and people who enjoy water sports.

THE LAND

LOCATION: Latitude—40° 23′ N to 43° 30′ N. **Longitude**—90° 08′ W to 96° 38′ W.

Minnesota to the north, Wisconsin and Illinois to the east, Missouri to the south, Nebraska and South Dakota to the west.

ELEVATION: Highest—Ocheyedan Mound in Osceola County on the northern boundary, 1,675 ft. **Lowest**—In the southeast corner where the Des Moines River flows into the Mississippi, about 480 ft.

LANDFORMS: The Central Lowland, made up of Young Glacial Plains and Older Till Plains.

SURFACE WATERS: Major rivers—Wapsipinicon, Iowa, and Des Moines flowing southeasterly into the Mississippi; Floyd, Little Sioux, and Nishnabotna flowing southwesterly into the Missouri. **Largest man-made lake**—Coralville Reservoir. **Largest natural lakes**—Spirit, West Okoboji, East Okoboji, and Clear.

CLIMATE: Temperature—January average, 17°–19° F. in the north, 20°–22° in the central area, 23°–25° in the south. July average, 73°–78° throughout the state. **Precipitation**—Yearly average varies from 26 in. in the northwest to 36 in. in the southeast. Yearly average snowfall, 30 in. **Growing season**—Averages about 140 days in the northwest and 170 days in the southeast.

Climate

Iowa has four rather distinct seasons. But during some years the winter season may come early, cutting the autumn short. Sometimes winter may last into April, and summer arrives after a short spring.

The average annual precipitation (rain and melted snow) varies from 26 to 36 inches. Most of it comes during the summer months in the form of rain from thunderstorms. Usually the rainfall is dependable. Severe summer droughts are rare. During the winter, storms move across the state from west to east. These storms often bring snow. The average yearly snowfall is about 30 inches.

The months of June, July, and August have an average temperature of more than 70 degrees Fahrenheit. Daytime temperatures sometimes go above 100 degrees, especially during July. January is the coldest month, with an average temperature of 21 degrees throughout the state. Below-zero temperatures are common. Generally there is no frost between early May and early October. The growing season is about 5 months long.

Each season brings delightful weather as well as some disagreeable days. Blizzards do not happen often. But when a blizzard strikes, the roads are blocked, and schools are closed. Heavy winter snowfalls may mean flooded rivers in the spring. Spring also is the season for tornadoes. During the summer high temperatures and high humidity may come at the same time. The result is sultry weather, day and night, when only corn does well.

Natural Resources

Iowa's most important natural resource is soil. Other resources include minerals and an abundance of water.

Soils. Prairie soil is the kind of soil most widespread through the state. It developed on top of materials dropped by the glaciers. The native grasses that covered Iowa in early days also helped to make the soil rich. This prairie grass was tall. It easily reached the top of the settlers' wagon wheels. In some low, wet places the grass stood 7 to 8 feet high. Each year the grass died. Then it decayed to form humus, which made the soil rich.

Forests once grew along the rivers. Where forests grew, the soil is low in humus. It is more acid than is the prairie soil. Loess—a fine earth material deposited mainly by the wind—helped to form the soil in western Iowa. This soil is yellowish brown in color. Loess was also deposited over much of southern Iowa.

Forests. About 20 percent of Iowa once had native oak, hickory, ash, and other trees. Most of the original forests were cut down long ago. Today only about 5 percent of the state is in woodlands. There are several small state forests and a state forest nursery. The nursery makes scientific studies of forestry. It also helps in the work of reforestation. Most of the forest areas have public shooting grounds and nature trails besides a small lumber industry. The more important trees used for lumber are oak, elm, cottonwood, and maple.

Minerals. The lead deposits in the Dubuque area were important in early days. But there has been no production of lead in Iowa for many years. Today the major minerals are coal, gypsum, clay, limestone, and sand and gravel. Nearly all of southern Iowa contains beds of low-grade soft coal. Sand and gravel deposits, left by the last glacier, are numerous in the northern half of the state.

Gypsum is a mineral used in the making of wallboard, fertilizers, and other products. The best-known gypsum deposits are in the Fort Dodge area. A slab of Fort Dodge gypsum was used to make the "Cardiff giant," a famous hoax of the late 1800's. Pranksters had a statue of a man about 10 feet tall carved from the gypsum. The statue was specially prepared to make it look very old. Then it was secretly buried near Cardiff, New York, where it was "discovered" in 1869. It created great excitement. Newspapers and magazines everywhere carried stories about it, calling it a prehistoric man. It was widely displayed. Finally, in the early 1900's, it was exposed as a fake.

Wildlife. The many lakes and streams are well stocked with fish, but fishing in Iowa is mainly recreational rather than commercial. There are more than 150 state-owned public hunting areas. Game animals and birds in these areas include ring-necked pheasants, deer, and wild ducks and geese.

▶ THE PEOPLE AND THEIR WORK

Many of Iowa's earliest settlers came by water. People from Kentucky and Tennessee traveled down the Ohio River, then up the Mississippi. Settlers from the northeastern part of the nation came by way of the Great Lakes to Chicago. Then they took boats down the Illinois River to the Mississippi or traveled overland in ox-drawn wagons. Dubuque and Burlington were the earliest centers of population.

European immigrants settled in Iowa in small groups. It was customary for them to write home, describing life on the American frontier. Gradually relatives and friends were added to the national groups in Iowa. Over the years more immigrants came to Iowa from Germany than from any other country. The Amana colonies near Iowa City are perhaps the best known of the many German settlements. People from Holland settled at Pella and Orange City. Norwegians came to Decorah. Bohemian (Czechoslovakian) settlements grew up at Cedar Rapids, Spillville, and other places. A British community was formed at Le Mars. Dubuque attracted many persons from Ireland. In most of these communities the people still keep some of the customs of the home country.

As settlers arrived, the Indians of Iowa were forced to sell their lands and move westward. Some of those who left Iowa did not like their new homes. They longed to return to the prairie and wooded valleys they had left behind. In the 1850's they began to come back to the Iowa River valley in Tama County. These Mesquakie Indians, as they are called, now number more than 1,000. The place where they live is a settlement, not a

POPULATION

TOTAL: 2,825,041 (1970 census). **Density**—50 persons to each square mile, unevenly distributed.

GROWTH SINCE 1840

Year	Population	Year	Population
1840	43,112	1920	2,404,021
1850	192,214	1940	2,538,268
1870	1,194,020	1960	2,757,537
1900	2,231,853	1970	2,825,041

Gain Between 1960 and 1970—2.4 percent.

CITIES: Population of the largest cities in Iowa, based on the 1970 census.

Des Moines	201,404	Council Bluffs	60,348
Cedar Rapids	110,642	Iowa City	46,850
Davenport	98,469	Ames	39,505
Sioux City	85,925	Clinton	34,719
Waterloo	75,533	Burlington	32,366
Dubuque	62,309	Mason City	30,491

reservation. The land is owned by all of them, but farming areas are assigned to individuals for lifetime use.

Where the People Live

In 1970 the population of Iowa was fairly evenly divided between urban and rural. About 57 percent of the people lived in what the Bureau of the Census defined as urban areas. The rest lived on farms or in places with fewer than 2,500 people. The eastern part of Iowa had more people than the west.

Industries and Products

Iowa is known as a major agricultural state. It also ranks high in manufacturing.

Agriculture. Productive soil is a chief reason for Iowa's importance agriculturally in the nation and the world. About one fourth of all

Rich farmlands make Iowa a leading corn-producing state.

Above: Rotary tillers are among Iowa's manufactured products. Below: Stockyards at Sioux City, one of the nation's leading livestock markets.

the Grade I agricultural land in the United States is in Iowa. Few areas of the state are too hilly or too swampy for agriculture, and nearly 95 percent of the total land area is in farms.

Northeastern Iowa is often included as part of the dairy region of the United States, centered mainly in Wisconsin. It is a hilly area, and the land is better suited to hay and pasture than to corn or other grains. Although this is the most important dairy area, the farmers usually earn more from the sale of livestock than from dairy products.

The north central part of the state is known as the cash-grain area. Here grains are grown to be sold for cash. This area was the part of the state covered by the last two stages of the Wisconsin glacier. The natural drainage is poor, and drainage ditches have been built in many places to bring more land under cultivation. The gently rolling land is well suited to the use of heavy machinery. Only a limited amount of the land is used for hay and pasture. Corn, soybeans, and oats are the most important crops. Many farmers also raise hogs and cattle.

Most of the rest of Iowa's agriculture may be classified as a crop-and-livestock combination. The river floodplains are used mainly for grain crops. The hilly slopes are used for pasture. But many of the slopes become good croplands when the right conservation methods are used. The sale of livestock is the main source of income. Many feeder cattle and lambs are shipped into north central Iowa from the West. Here they are fattened on grain from Iowa farms.

Manufacturing. The processing of food and related products is the leading kind of manufacturing in Iowa. More than one half of the persons who work in this kind of manufacturing are employed in meat-processing plants. These plants prepare beef, pork, and lamb for markets throughout the nation. Products made from grains include flour, breakfast cereals, and animal feeds. Usually the animal feeds are sold near the cities where they are manufactured.

Machinery, especially farm machinery, is the second most important kind of manufactured product. Nearly every kind of farm machinery and equipment is made somewhere in the state. The tractor plant at Waterloo is one of the largest of its kind in the world.

Factories in Iowa also turn out a surprising variety of products not related to agriculture. Some began as inventions of Iowans or as small local industries. Nationally known products that had their beginning in Iowa include writing pens and various home appliances, such as washing machines and refrigerators. Recently a number of out-of-state companies have built factories in Iowa. These include manufacturers of chemicals, rubber products, and airplane parts.

Mining. Limestone is the most valuable stone quarried in Iowa. Sand and gravel rank second. Much of the limestone and sand and gravel go into the making of concrete for highways, sidewalks, and buildings. The poorer grades of limestone are powdered and used as fertilizer.

Iowa is one of the nation's leading producers of gypsum, which is used in making building materials and fertilizers. Most of the coal mined in the state is used for heating and in the steam power plants that produce electricity. South central Iowa is the state's principal coal-producing region.

Transportation and Communication

Barges on the Mississippi River carry much freight to and from Iowa. The Missouri River also has some barge traffic.

Railroads began to be built across Iowa in the 1850's. The railroad mileage increased for many years until no town in Iowa was more than 12 miles from a railroad. Today there are more than 8,000 miles of track.

Iowa ranks high among the states in the number of miles of concrete paved roads.

WHAT IOWA PRODUCES

AGRICULTURAL PRODUCTS: Cattle and calves, hogs, corn, soybeans, milk, eggs.

MANUFACTURED GOODS: Processed foods, principally meat products, grain-mill products, and dairy products; machinery, principally farm equipment and construction machinery; electrical equipment and supplies; chemicals and allied products; printing and publishing material; fabricated metal products; rubber and plastics products; primary metal products.

MINERALS: Cement, limestone, sand and gravel, gypsum, bituminous coal, clays.

Several major highways cross the state from east to west and from north to south. The interstate highway system is being extended each year.

Approximately 100 cities and towns have air service. The airport at Des Moines is the largest in the state.

The first newspaper in Iowa was the *Du Buque Visitor,* published in Dubuque in 1836–37. The Burlington *Hawk-Eye* is the oldest paper in continuous publication. It began as the *Territorial Gazette and Burlington Advertiser* in 1837. Today there are approximately 350 weekly newspapers and about 40 dailies. The Des Moines *Register and Tribune* is Iowa's largest newspaper. There are more than 75 AM radio stations, spread evenly through the state. A dozen cities have both FM stations and television stations.

▶ **EDUCATION**

Visitors in Iowa will notice the many educational institutions as well as the farms and factories. Prosperity has helped Iowa build good schools within reach of all the people.

Schools and Colleges

Iowa's first school was opened in Lee County in 1830. The building was provided by Dr. Isaac Galland. It was a small structure made of clapboards and heated by a fireplace. A replica of the building, made of logs, is in Galland School State Park near Montrose.

By the time Iowa became a territory in 1838, there were more than 40 schools. All these were private institutions. But a law passed in 1840 prepared the way for the establishment of free schools. The present system of public education is based on a state law of 1858. Today Iowa has more than 5,500 public and private schools. These include three state institutions of higher learning, more than 20 private 4-year colleges and universities, and numerous junior colleges.

The State University of Iowa at Iowa City (now called the University of Iowa) was established by an act of the first General Assembly in 1847. Opened in 1855, it now has many graduate and professional divisions. It is known especially for its medical center. Iowa State University of Science and Technology at Ames was established by law in 1858. When it

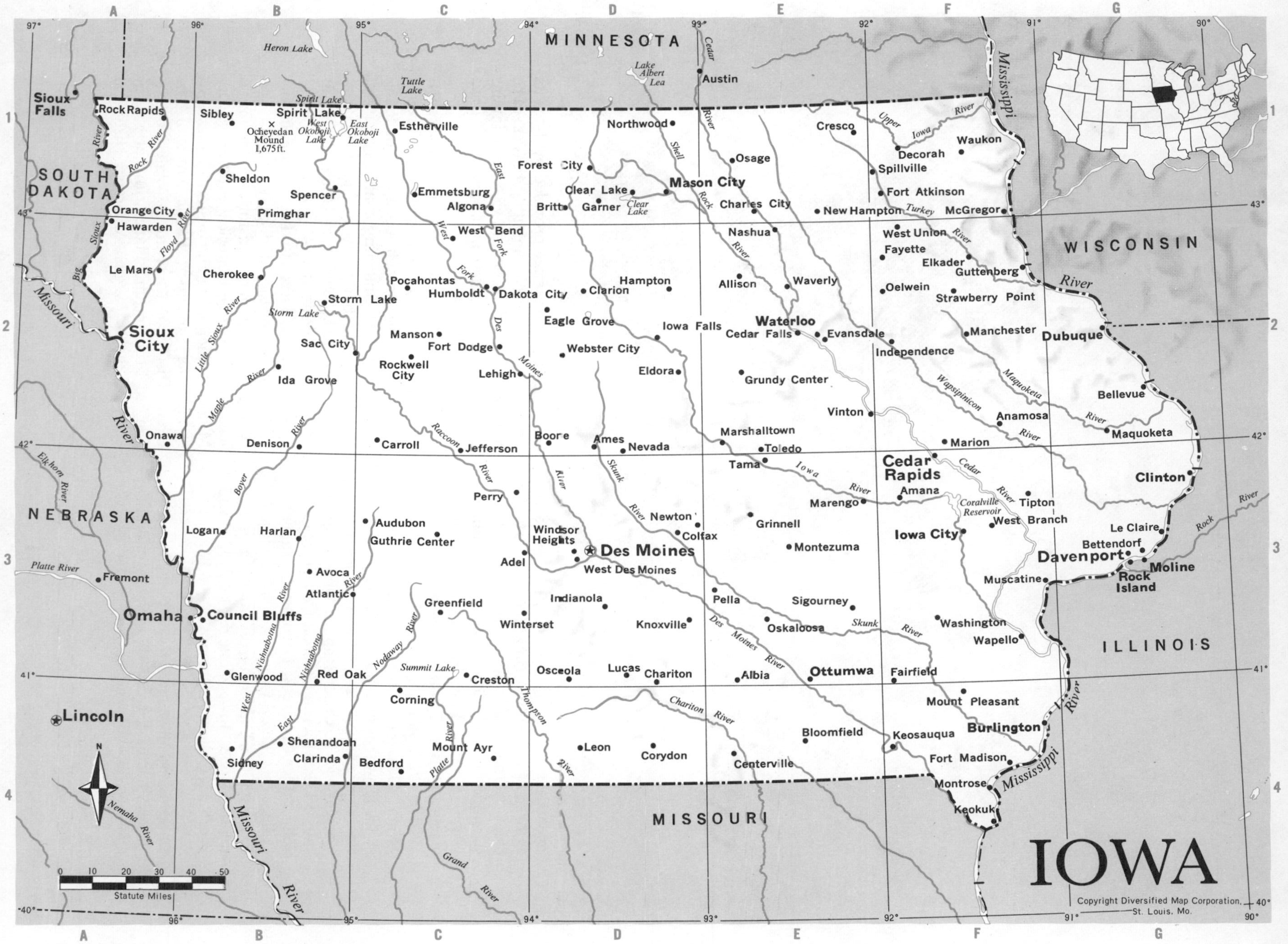

IOWA
Copyright Diversified Map Corporation, St. Louis, Mo.
MINNESOTA
WISCONSIN
ILLINOIS
MISSOURI
NEBRASKA
SOUTH DAKOTA
Sioux Falls
Rock Rapids
Sibley
Spirit Lake
Ocheyedan Mound 1,675 ft.
West Okoboji Lake
East Okoboji Lake
Estherville
Heron Lake
Tuttle Lake
Lake Albert Lea
Austin
Northwood
Cresco
Decorah
Waukon
Spillville
Fort Atkinson
McGregor
New Hampton
Osage
Mason City
Clear Lake
Forest City
Britt
Garner
Charles City
Nashua
West Union
Fayette
Elkader
Guttenberg
Strawberry Point
Oelwein
Waverly
Allison
Hampton
Clarion
Dakota City
Humboldt
Pocahontas
Emmetsburg
Algona
West Bend
Spencer
Primghar
Sheldon
Orange City
Hawarden
Le Mars
Cherokee
Storm Lake
Sac City
Ida Grove
Manson
Fort Dodge
Rockwell City
Lehigh
Eagle Grove
Webster City
Iowa Falls
Eldora
Waterloo
Cedar Falls
Evansdale
Independence
Manchester
Dubuque
Bellevue
Maquoketa
Anamosa
Grundy Center
Vinton
Marion
Cedar Rapids
Amana
Clinton
Tipton
West Branch
Coralville Reservoir
Iowa City
Le Claire
Bettendorf
Davenport
Rock Island
Moline
Muscatine
Washington
Wapello
Sioux City
Onawa
Denison
Carroll
Jefferson
Boone
Ames
Nevada
Marshalltown
Toledo
Tama
Marengo
Grinnell
Newton
Colfax
Montezuma
Perry
Audubon
Guthrie Center
Harlan
Logan
Windsor Heights
Des Moines
West Des Moines
Adel
Avoca
Atlantic
Fremont
Omaha
Council Bluffs
Greenfield
Winterset
Indianola
Knoxville
Pella
Oskaloosa
Sigourney
Glenwood
Red Oak
Summit Lake
Creston
Osceola
Lucas
Chariton
Albia
Ottumwa
Fairfield
Mount Pleasant
Burlington
Lincoln
Corning
Shenandoah
Clarinda
Sidney
Bedford
Mount Ayr
Leon
Corydon
Centerville
Bloomfield
Keosauqua
Fort Madison
Montrose
Keokuk
Mississippi River
Missouri River
Big Sioux River
Rock River
Floyd River
Little Sioux River
Maple River
Boyer River
West Nishnabotna River
East Nishnabotna River
Nodaway River
Platte River
Grand River
Thompson River
Chariton River
Des Moines River
East Fork
West Fork
Raccoon River
Skunk River
Iowa River
Cedar River
Shell Rock River
Wapsipinicon River
Maquoketa River
Turkey River
Upper Iowa River
Elkhorn River
Nemaha River
Statute Miles
0 10 20 30 40 50
97° 96° 95° 94° 93° 92° 91° 90°
43° 42° 41° 40°
A B C D E F G
1 2 3 4

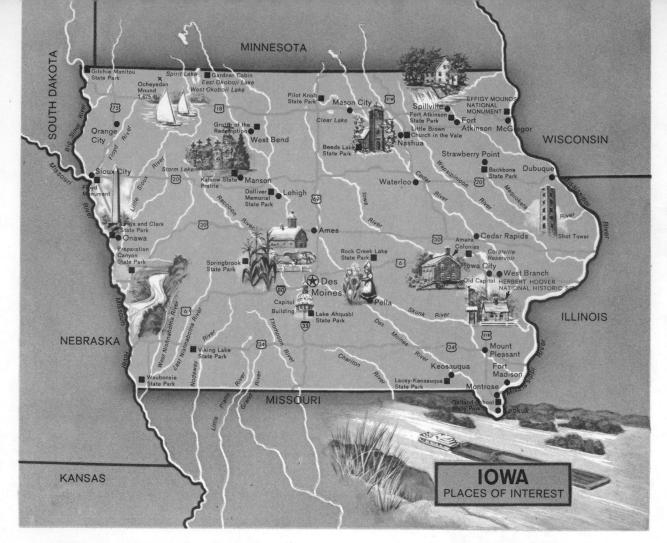

IOWA
PLACES OF INTEREST

opened in 1868, it was called Iowa State College of Agriculture and Mechanic Arts. Its chief purpose at that time was to teach scientific farming. The University of Northern Iowa at Cedar Falls was established as a teacher-training institution in 1876.

Iowa Wesleyan College, a private college at Mount Pleasant, is the oldest college in the state. It was established in the early 1840's. Other private colleges and universities include Coe College at Cedar Rapids, Drake University at Des Moines, Grinnell College at Grinnell, Luther College at Decorah, Morningside College at Sioux City, Parsons College at Fairfield, the University of Dubuque at Dubuque, Upper Iowa College at Fayette, and Wartburg College at Waverly.

Libraries and Museums

Iowa has more than 400 municipal libraries and several independent county library sys-

tems. A traveling service provided by the state helps to develop community libraries. The State Historical Society at Iowa City maintains a library that specializes in the history of Iowa and the Middle West.

Iowans take special pride in the Herbert Hoover Library-Museum, which was opened in 1962 at West Branch, birthplace of President Hoover. The building contains many of his papers and books. A special exhibit includes the desk, chairs, and flags from his office in the White House.

Almost every large city has a museum that is known for historical displays or fine-arts collections. The major historical museum is located in the State Historical Building at Des Moines. Other important historical museums include the Davenport Public Museum, the Grout Historical Museum at Waterloo, the Sanford Museum and Planetarium at Cherokee, and the Norwegian-American Historical

Museum at Decorah. The Des Moines Art Center has important collections of painting and sculpture, as does the Davenport Municipal Art Gallery.

▶ PLACES OF INTEREST

Reminders of Iowa's past are preserved in the many historical monuments and museums throughout the state. The beauty of the land is conserved in parks and forests. Other places of interest range from quaint villages to atomic laboratories.

Historic Places

Iowa has two national areas and numerous other places associated with notable persons or events.

Effigy Mounds National Monument near McGregor contains important examples of mounds built by Indians nearly 1,000 years ago. They are called effigy mounds because they are effigies (images or representations) of animals or people. Some of the mounds are shaped like birds, bears, or foxes. A museum on the grounds exhibits relics from the mounds.

Herbert Hoover National Historic Site in West Branch includes the grave of President Hoover, the restored cottage in which he was born, a replica of his father's blacksmith shop, and the Herbert Hoover Library-Museum.

The Amana colonies are a group of small communities near Iowa City. They were founded by members of a German religious sect who came to Iowa in the 1850's and bought thousands of acres of land. The people wore plain, dark clothes and followed strict religious teachings. They became known both for farm products and for handicrafts. For many years the Amanas were a communal center—a place where all the people worked and ate together and everything was owned by the community. But since 1932 the Amana industries have been organized on a free-enterprise basis. Products manufactured there include refrigerators and freezers, furniture, and woolen goods. A house in one of the villages has been restored as a museum.

Floyd Monument at Sioux City is a memorial to Sergeant Charles Floyd, a member of the Lewis and Clark expedition. He died in August, 1804, while the party was traveling near Sioux City on the Missouri River. The monument, a granite shaft 100 feet high, stands on the bluff where Sergeant Floyd's body was buried.

Gardner Cabin near Spirit Lake was the site of an Indian uprising in 1857 known as the Spirit Lake massacre. The victims were members of the Gardner family and other settlers. The story of the massacre has been told in the novel *Spirit Lake* by MacKinlay Kantor.

The Grotto of the Redemption at West Bend was started in 1912. It is built of rocks, fossils, shells, and other materials said to be from every state in the Union and every country in the world.

The Little Brown Church in the Vale is located near Nashua. It gained fame through the popular hymn "The Little Brown Church in the Vale," or "The Church in the Wildwood." Thousands of tourists visit this small church each year, and many wedding ceremonies are performed there.

Old Capitol, on the campus of the University of Iowa at Iowa City, was the last capitol of the territory of Iowa and the first capitol of the state. The building now serves as a university administrative center.

Shot Tower in Dubuque is a stone tower built in 1855 for the making of lead shot. Molten lead was dropped through a screen at the top of the tower. The lead pellets cooled as they fell. They became solid when they dropped into water at the bottom of the tower.

Spillville, a town in northeast Iowa, is known as the place where the Czech composer Antonín Dvořák spent the summer of 1893. Rooms in the building where he stayed have

The Old Capitol, now an administration building at the University of Iowa, Iowa City.

been preserved with many mementos of his visit. In the same building there is an unusual collection of hand-carved musical clocks. The clocks were made by the Bily brothers, natives of Czechoslovakia who lived on a farm near Spillville.

State Parks

Some time ago Iowa made plans for a state park, with a natural or man-made lake, within 25 miles of every family. This goal has almost been reached. Today there are more than 90 state park areas. The following are among those noted for a particular feature.

Backbone State Park is located in northeastern Iowa near Strawberry Point. It contains rugged limestone bluffs and a lake formed by a dam across the Maquoketa River. Richmond Springs, one of Iowa's largest springs, feeds a state trout and bass hatchery in the park.

Dolliver Memorial State Park, northwest of Lehigh, is one of several large parks located on the Des Moines River. The park is known for deep ravines, wooded hills, and Indian mounds.

Fort Atkinson State Park is located at the town of Fort Atkinson in northeastern Iowa. It preserves a historic fort that was built by the federal government in 1840.

Gitchie Manitou State Park in the northwestern corner of the state contains stands of the native grasses that once covered most of Iowa.

Kalsow State Prairie near Manson preserves an example of the original native Iowa prairie.

Lacey-Keosauqua State Park is at Keosauqua in the southeast. It covers a large wooded area in the great horseshoe bend of the Des Moines River. One of the historic sites in the park is Ely's Ford, a river crossing used by the Mormons on their trek westward through Iowa in 1846. The park is named for Major John F. Lacey, who is known for his work in establishing Iowa's state parks as well as some of the national parks.

Lewis and Clark State Park near Onawa includes the site where the Lewis and Clark expedition camped in 1804. A popular feature of the park is Blue Lake, which was formed by a change in the course of the Missouri River.

Pilot Knob State Park in northern Iowa takes its name from Pilot Knob, one of the highest elevations in the state. In pioneer days the knob was a landmark that guided travelers. A small spring-fed lake, named Dead Man's Lake, is a special feature of the park.

Preparation Canyon State Park provides a spectacular view of the rolling bluffs and the floodplains of the Missouri River. The Mormons stopped at this site on their westward trip. Here they established a temporary village, which they named Preparation.

Annual Events

Iowa's best-known yearly events are farm fairs and livestock shows. The Iowa State Fair is one of the largest agricultural fairs in the world. It gained special fame when it was used as the background of a novel, *State Fair,* by the Iowa-born writer Phil Stong.

May—Tulip festivals, Pella and Orange City.
June—North Iowa band festival, Mason City.
August—Iowa State Fair, Des Moines; Mesquakie Indian powwow, Tama; Iowa championship rodeo, Sidney; annual hobo convention, Britt.
September—Old Threshers' Reunion, Mount Pleasant.
October—National Dairy Cattle Congress, Waterloo.

▶CITIES

Most of the largest cities are in the eastern part of the state. The exceptions are Des Moines in central Iowa and Sioux City and Council Bluffs on the western border.

Des Moines

The capital and largest city of the state is located on the Des Moines River. A fort built in 1843 was the forerunner of the present city. By 1851 there were 500 settlers in the area. In 1857 the capital was moved from Iowa City to Des Moines.

The capitol stands on a hill overlooking much of the city. Nearby are state and federal office buildings. Besides being the center of government, Des Moines is the industrial, financial, and social center of Iowa. It is

COUNTIES

known especially as a convention city and as the home of large insurance firms and publishing companies.

Cedar Rapids

Iowa's second largest city is located on the Cedar River in the east central part of the state. It was named for the swift rapids in the river. The first cabin was built close to the rapids in 1838.

Cedar Rapids, home of Coe College, is an important industrial center surrounded by a rich farming area. Its many manufactured products include oat cereals, corn products, machinery, and radio transmitters and receivers.

Sioux City

Sioux City is western Iowa's largest city, and it reminds one more of the West than docs any other city in the state. It is one of the largest livestock markets in the nation. Cattle from western ranches are sold in Sioux City, fattened on nearby farms, and returned to the city's meat-packing plants.

Sioux City is notable for its fine parks and places of scenic and historical interest. It is also a center for highways, railroads, and air routes. Barge traffic on the Missouri River also reaches the city.

▶ GOVERNMENT

The government of Iowa is based on a constitution adopted in 1857. The governor is the head of the executive branch of the state government. He is elected for a 2-year term, and there is no limit to the consecutive terms he may serve.

The Iowa legislature is called the General Assembly. It meets in regular session every year. Members of the House of Representatives are elected for 2-year terms. Members of the Senate are elected for 4 years.

The highest state court in Iowa is called the Supreme Court. It is made up of nine

justices. The major trial courts are called district courts. Justices and district judges are appointed by the governor initially, then run for re-election on their records.

▶ FAMOUS PEOPLE

Iowa has produced many leaders in public affairs, including Herbert Hoover, the first president of the United States born west of the Mississippi River. The state also claims a long list of writers and artists.

Robert Lucas (1781–1853), first governor of the territory of Iowa, was born at Shepherdstown, Virginia (now West Virginia). While serving in the War of 1812, he kept a journal that was published as *The Robert Lucas Journal of the War of 1812*. In 1838 President Martin Van Buren appointed him governor and superintendent of Indian affairs for the territory of Iowa. In his later years he worked in the interest of public education and railroad projects in Iowa. His house at Iowa City, named Plum Grove, has been restored and preserved as a historical monument.

Herbert Clark Hoover (1874–1964), 31st president of the United States, was born at West Branch. His father died in 1880. When his mother died 3 years later, he went to Oregon to live with relatives. The story of his life is included in Volume H.

Henry Agard Wallace (1888–1965) was born in Adair County. He was secretary of agriculture (1933–40) and vice-president of the United States (1941–45) under President Franklin D. Roosevelt. He was also secretary of commerce (1945–46) under Presidents Roosevelt and Truman. His father, Henry C. Wallace (1866–1924), was secretary of agriculture (1921–24) under Presidents Harding and Coolidge. Both

Bridges span the Des Moines River, which flows through Des Moines, the capital city.

father and son are remembered also for their many contributions to agriculture and as publishers of nationally known farm journals.

Grant Wood (1892–1942) was a well-known painter of people and scenes in the Middle West. He was born at Anamosa. A biography of Grant Wood is included in Volume W.

Paul Hamilton Engle (1908–   ) is widely known as a poet, novelist, and teacher. He was born at Cedar Rapids. Some of his volumes of verse are *Worn Earth, Break the Heart's Anger, Corn,* and *West of Midnight.* In 1937 he became professor of English at the State University of Iowa.

Writers besides Paul Engle who were born in Iowa include Bess Streeter Aldrich (Cedar Falls), Susan Glaspell (Davenport), James Norman Hall (Colfax), Emerson Hough (Newton), MacKinlay Kantor (Webster City), Philip Duffield "Phil" Stong (Keosauqua), Ruth Suckow (Hawarden), and Carl Van Vechten (Cedar Rapids).

Other famous native-born Iowans are the Indian scout and showman William F. "Buffalo Bill" Cody (Scott County), labor leader John L. Lewis (Lucas), circus owner Charles Ringling (McGregor), and evangelist William A. "Billy" Sunday (Ames). Harry L. Hopkins, adviser to President Franklin D. Roosevelt, was born at Sioux City. Edwin T. Meredith, founder of the magazine *Successful Farming* and secretary of agriculture (1920–21) under President Woodrow Wilson, was born near Avoca. Biographies of Buffalo Bill and John L. Lewis are included in Volumes B and L.

▶ **HISTORY**

Several groups of Indians lived in Iowa in prehistoric times. They have left thousands of mounds and campsites throughout the area. The Indians who lived in Iowa during historic times are of two major groups—the Woodland and the Plains Indians. The Woodland Indians lived along the rivers. They included the Sauk, Fox, and Muscoutin tribes. The Plains Indians —the Ioway, Omaha, Winnebago, and other tribes—roamed the prairies in search of game. The two groups were often at war with each other.

Exploration

In 1673 the French explorers Marquette and Jolliet entered the Mississippi River near the present site of McGregor, Iowa. They had come downstream on the Wisconsin River. On seeing the bluffs in northeast Iowa, they described them as "a chain of very high mountains." They continued down the Mississippi to a point near the mouth of the Iowa River.

Robert Cavelier, Sieur de la Salle, reached the mouth of the Mississippi in 1682 and claimed the whole Mississippi Valley for France. He named it Louisiana in honor of Louis XIV, King of France. In 1762 France ceded the Louisiana country to Spain. Spain returned it to France in 1800, and France sold it to the United States in 1803.

Exploration of the Iowa country began immediately after the Louisiana Purchase. Members of the Lewis and Clark expedition explored along the Missouri River in 1804. The next year Zebulon Pike, an explorer and army officer, traveled up the Mississippi and recommended the sites of Burlington and McGregor for military posts. Stephen Kearny

---

IMPORTANT DATES

1673	Marquette and Jolliet, exploring the Mississippi for France, became the first Europeans to see Iowa.
1682	La Salle claimed the entire Mississippi Valley, including what is now Iowa, for France.
1796	Julien Dubuque received a grant of land in Iowa and became the first permanent settler.
1803	Iowa became part of the United States as a result of the Louisiana Purchase.
1804	Lewis and Clark expedition explored the Missouri River.
1805	Iowa included in Louisiana territory (in Missouri territory, 1812; in Michigan territory, 1834; in Wisconsin territory, 1836).
1808	First United States military post in Iowa established at Fort Madison.
1838	Territory of Iowa created on July 4; first territorial assembly met at Burlington.
1839	Iowa City founded as territorial capital.
1843	Second Fort Des Moines built on site of future city of Des Moines.
1846	December 28, Iowa became the 29th state.
1855	State University of Iowa (now University of Iowa) opened.
1857	State capital moved to Des Moines.
1867	First railroad completed across the state.
1913	Iowa's largest hydroelectric dam completed at Keokuk.
1952	Iowa became the first state to produce a $1,000,000,000 corn crop.
1962	Herbert Hoover Library-Museum opened at West Branch.
1968	Voters approved a constitutional amendment to have the General Assembly meet every year. Previously it met every other year.

was another army officer who took part in exploring expeditions on the western frontier. Kearny's record of an expedition in 1820 is the first description of Iowa's prairies, river valleys, and wildlife.

The first United States fort in Iowa was built at Fort Madison in 1808. It was burned in 1812. Kearny was in charge of the construction of the first Fort Des Moines at Montrose in 1834. Other military forts erected during Iowa's early history were Fort Atkinson, the second Fort Des Moines, and Fort Croghan (Council Bluffs).

Settlements

The first legal settlement in Iowa was made on land granted by Spain to Julien Dubuque in 1796. Two other grants were made while Spain owned the territory. In 1799 Louis Tesson was granted land in Lee County. He planted apple trees, and for this reason his grant was known as Tesson's Apple Orchard. In 1800 Basil Giard received a grant of more than 5,000 acres in Clayton County. Many trappers and soldiers took Indian wives and settled near the forts or on new land. In 1824 an area called Half-Breed Tract was set aside for them in southeastern Iowa.

At first the settlers located along the rivers. Here they found rich bottomland, water, and lumber for building and for firewood. The log cabins of the settlers were crude structures. Insects buzzed through them in the summer, and cold drafts invaded them in the winter. Livestock grazed on the prairie, but there were no fences, and someone always had to stand by to watch the animals.

As settlers moved in and took land, the Indians of Iowa were pushed westward. Gradually between 1824 and 1851 the Indians sold their lands and moved out of Iowa.

Territorial Changes

As a territory of the United States, Iowa was passed from hand to hand. In 1812 it was included in the Missouri territory. Missouri became a state in 1821, and for 13 years Iowa had no legally authorized civil government. In 1834 it became part of the territory of Michigan. Two years later the Iowa area was included in the territory of Wisconsin. Finally, in 1838, the territory of Iowa was formed.

Robert Lucas was named the first territorial governor, and the first legislature met in Burlington on November 12, 1838. Land surveys were made, land offices were opened, roads were built, and schools were started. Iowa City was founded as the capital in 1839. In 1846 Iowa became the 29th state.

Statehood and After

The land was productive, crops were good, and increasing amounts of farm products were sent east to market. The river towns of Keokuk, Burlington, Muscatine, and Davenport benefited from the flow of agricultural products from their ports. Inland towns also grew. They prospered further when energetic European immigrants settled in them. By 1850 the population of the state was almost 200,000. During the next 10 years the population more than tripled.

At the start of the Civil War, President Abraham Lincoln called for troops. The enlistments from Iowa far exceeded expectations. Nearly 80,000 men answered the call.

The state continued to grow after the Civil War. The first rail line across the state was completed in 1867. Good times and high prices alternated with depressions, such as those of 1873 and 1893. Farm organizations, especially the Grange, were formed to help the farmers. Industry grew in importance after 1880, and the farm-and-factory combination began to benefit the state.

During World War I more than 100,000 Iowans served in the armed forces. After the war, land prices continued to rise until the depression of the 1930's. About 265,000 Iowans served in the armed forces during World War II. The first Women's Army Corps (WAC) training camp in the nation was located at Fort Des Moines.

The Future

Iowa has continued to grow since the end of World War II. The value of agricultural products and manufactured goods has increased. New industries have come to the state. More important, school and college enrollments grow larger every year. Iowans long have considered well-trained young people to be the state's most valuable resource.

HERMAN L. NELSON
University of Northern Iowa

IRAN

Iran, or Persia, as it was once called, was one of the world's great empires. Its territory once stretched from India to the Mediterranean Sea. For centuries the Persian empire greatly influenced both Asian and European civilizations. Today Iran is no longer a vast empire, but it still is at the strategic crossroads of Asia and Europe. It is also one of the world's leading producers of petroleum.

▶ THE PEOPLE

Iran has a population of over 28,000,000. Most Iranians are descendants of people who originally came from the region near the Aral Sea in Central Asia. The most important of these were the Medes and the Persians, who settled in Iran after 2000 B.C. They later united under Cyrus the Great and established the first Persian empire. Other peoples who settled in Iran were the Parthians, Bactrians, Scythians, Kurds, and Lurs. Iran has small numbers of Armenians, Assyrians, and Jews.

Persian is the major language of Iran. It is written from right to left in the Arabic alphabet. The Persian language has changed very little in the past 1,000 years. Old texts can still be read by educated Iranians. A large number of Iranian people speak a Turkish dialect known as Azari. A variety of other languages and dialects are used by the different minority groups.

Free public school education is provided, but there is a shortage of teachers and classrooms. A Literacy Corps made up of army draftees who have been given teacher-training courses has helped to ease the teacher shortage, and the number of primary and high school students has doubled during the past 10 years. Iran's eight universities include the University of Teheran.

An ancient mosque in the city of Isfahan.

Islam, the faith of the Muslims, is the predominant religion in Iran. Nearly the entire population is Muslim. Other religious groups in Iran are the Armenian Orthodox, the Nestorian Christians, the Protestants, the Roman Catholics, the Jews, the Bahais, and the Zoroastrians.

Persian literature contains some of the world's finest writing. Iran's great era of classical literature took place between the 10th and the 16th centuries. Among the best Persian writers were Firdausi (940?–1020?), Saadi (1184–1291), and Jami (1414–1492). Omar Khayyàm (?–1123?) is best-known in the West for his poem *The Rubàiyat*. But he was more famous in Persia as an astronomer and mathematician than as a poet.

From early times Iranian artists have been particularly skilled at book illustration and in painting miniatures on ivory or bone. Iranian ceramics in the form of pottery and tile are noted for their design and their lovely colors, especially the blues and greens. A famous craft is the weaving of so-called Persian or

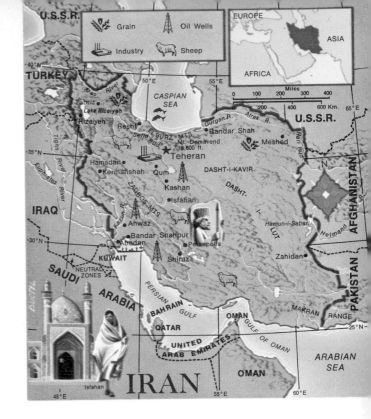

World-famous Persian rugs are washed after being woven.

Oriental rugs. Other crafts include making silverware, jewelry, and brass and copper bowls, trays, and plates, especially those with inlay and mosaic work.

Way of Life. The majority of Iranians are subsistence farmers. Until the 1950's, most were sharecroppers who rented land by paying a percentage of their crops to rich landlords. Due to recent land reform programs, a large number of farmers now own their own land.

There are several million nomadic and seminomadic people in Iran. Unlike the true nomads, the seminomadic people maintain permanent residence in villages to which they return each fall. These seminomads are often very poor people who spend a large part of their time raising enough food to live on. Besides their flocks of sheep and goats they usually have donkeys and horses for riding.

Because there is a lack of timber in Iran, village houses are made mostly of stone or of sun-dried brick. A brick or stone wall is usually built around the village to give the people protection and privacy.

In the larger cities houses and apartment buildings are made of fired brick or concrete. Along the coast in the south, houses are often made of reeds or wattle (narrow branches) covered with mud.

▶ THE LAND

Iran is located in southwestern Asia. Although no longer the vast empire it once was, Iran still has an area of about 636,000 square miles, which is about three times the size of France. The country is a high plateau circled by high and rugged mountains. The Zagros Mountains run along the western border of the country. In the north are the mountains of Azerbaijan and the Elburz

The Elburz Mountains, in northern Iran.

Nomads ride horses and donkeys as they move about the country with their flocks of sheep and goats.

Mountains, with Mount Demavend at 18,600 feet their highest peak. To the east are the eastern highlands, and to the south the Makran Range. In the center of the country is a great plateau covering 100,000 square miles. The elevation of the plateau ranges from 1,000 to as much as 6,000 feet. Water draining into the plateau from the surrounding mountains either sinks into the ground or forms temporary salt lakes.

The only lowlands are narrow plains located along the edges of the country—that is, along the Caspian Sea or the Persian Gulf, or separated from the interior of the country by high mountain ranges. The two most important plains are the Caspian and Khuzistan. The Caspian plain lies along the southern shore of the Caspian Sea. It is the most productive and most densely populated area. The Khuzistan plain is situated at the northern coast of the Persian Gulf.

Most rivers in Iran do not reach the sea. In the interior only temporary or seasonal streams can be found. These flow down the mountains and are absorbed by two vast deserts—Dasht-i-Kavir and Dasht-i-Lut. The permanent rivers are found mainly in the north and the southwest. They are sources of irrigation water and potential hydroelectric power. But only the lower 150 miles of the Karun River in the Khuzistan plain are deep enough and wide enough to be used by boats.

Climate. The climate of Iran is generally dry. Throughout much of the year the sky is clear. The country averages about 10 inches or less of precipitation each year. Almost all of it falls during the winter, and much of it is in the form of snow.

Winter is mild on the Caspian plain and warm in the south. In the rest of the country winter is cold, with January temperatures averaging near or below freezing. Summer is very hot except in the mountains. July temperatures average in the 80's in the north and in the 90's in the south.

Natural Resources. Petroleum is the major natural resource, and Iran ranks 5th among the world's producers. The Iranian Government receives over $1,000,000,000 a year in royalties from oil production. Most of the oil is produced in the foothills of the Zagros Mountains. There are several refineries. The largest is at Abadan.

Iran produces enough coal for its needs. Other minerals include rock, chromite, lead, iron ore, copper, manganese, and antimony.

Plant Life. The natural plant life of Iran is made up mostly of either steppe grasses (grass growing in semi-arid areas) or desert scrub. The Caspian forest on the wet, northern slope of the Elburz is the only important one in the country.

▶ **HOW THE PEOPLE EARN A LIVING**

Between 60 and 70 percent of the people earn their living directly from the land. They grow crops and breed livestock. The main food crops are wheat, barley, and some vegetables and fruits. Rice is important in areas where there is enough water, as in the Caspian plain. Cash crops include cotton,

---

FACTS AND FIGURES

IRAN is the official name of the country. It was called Persia until 1935.

CAPITAL: Teheran.

LOCATION AND SIZE: Southwest Asia. **Latitude**—25° N to 40° N. **Longitude**—44° E to 63° E. **Area**—636,294 sq. mi.

PHYSICAL FEATURES: Highest point—18,600 ft. **Lowest point**—Caspian Sea, 92 ft. below sea level. **Chief rivers**—Karun, Aras, Sefid Rud, Gurgan, and Atrek. **Chief mountain peaks**—Elburz Mts.: Mt. Demavend (18,600 ft.); Zagros Mts. (14,000–15,000 ft.). **Chief deserts**—Dasht-i-Kavir, Dasht-i-Lut.

POPULATION: 28,000,000 (estimate).

LANGUAGE: Farsi or New Persian, Turki, Armenian, Arabic.

RELIGION: Islam.

GOVERNMENT: Constitutional monarchy. **Head of state** —Shah. **International co-operation**—United Nations, Central Treaty Organization (CENTO).

NATIONAL ANTHEM: *Soroud-a Shahanshahi* ("Long Life to Our Shahanshah").

ECONOMY: Agricultural products—wheat, barley, sugar beets, rice, cotton, dates, grapes (raisins), apricots, tobacco, citrus fruits, vegetables, nuts, seeds, pulses. **Industries and products**—food processing (sugar, flour, fruit, tea), handicrafts (carpets), textiles (cotton, jute, silk), oil refining, fishing (caviar), manufacturing (building materials, glass, cigarettes), livestock products (dairy, hides and skins, wool). **Chief minerals**— oil, coal, lead ore, chromite, iron ore. Also some zinc, sulfur, copper, salt, gypsum, manganese, antimony. **Chief exports**—oil, fruits and nuts, cotton, carpets, wool, hides, leather, rice, mineral ores. **Chief imports**— vehicles, iron and steel, machinery and electrical equipment, sugar, chemicals, pharmaceuticals. **Monetary unit**—rial.

sugar beets, tobacco, tea, and dried fruits and nuts. About 30 to 40 percent of the people earn their living in manufacturing, in all types of services, and in extractive industries, which include mining, lumbering, and fishing.

The livelihood of the seminomadic tribes of the mountain areas is based mainly on sheep- and goat-herding. From these herds the Iranians get milk, meat, wool, and hides.

Transportation. Partly because of the high mountains and partly because of the heat, it is hard to build and maintain roads and railroads in Iran. Despite these obstacles, however, Iran has good railroads. The Trans-Iranian Railway, built in the 1930's, runs from Bandar Shahpur on the Persian Gulf across the Zagros and Elburz mountains to Bandar Shah on the Caspian Sea. Another railroad connects Tabriz in the northwest with Meshed in the northeast. A third line, running from Qum on the Trans-Iranian Railway to Kashan in north central Iran, will extend to Zahidan on the Pakistani border.

In recent years, Iran has done much to develop a good system of all-weather highways. The country does not, however, have good secondary roads. Although donkeys, camels, and animal-drawn carts are still widely used in the country, autos, trucks, and buses are growing in number. Iran has several very modern airports, and the country is well serviced by local and international airlines.

Major Cities. Teheran, the capital and largest city of Iran, is located at the base of the Elburz Mountains just southwest of Mount Demavend. It has a population of almost 3,000,000. Teheran is the political as well as the major commercial center of the country.

Tabriz is another large city, with a population of over 400,000. Located in a rich farming area near the Soviet and Turkish borders, it is the political and commercial center of northwestern Iran. Two other important Iranian cities are Meshed and Isfahan.

▶ GOVERNMENT

Iran has been a constitutional monarchy since 1906. The Shahanshah (King of Kings), or Shah, as he is usually called, is the hereditary monarch.

The law-making organ of the government is made up of two houses: a lower house, called the National Assembly, or Majlis, and an upper house, called the Senate. The Majlis has over 200 members, who are elected for 4-year terms. The Senate has 60 members. Half of them are elected and the other half are appointed by the Shah. Executive powers are exercised by a premier, who is appointed by the Shah and who is responsible to the Majlis. The premier is assisted by a cabinet, which he appoints.

▶ HISTORY

Early in its history Persia was a great empire. Under the rule of Cyrus the Great, Persia was the first country that succeeded in unifying all of what is known today as the Middle East. This great empire flourished between 550 B.C. and 331 B.C. and produced one of the world's first highly organized states. It had coinage, a civil service, a postal service, and a uniform language (Aramaic).

Another great Persian era—between 331 B.C. and 129 B.C.—was that of Alexander the Great and his successors. Still another well-known period of Persian history took place under the rule of the Parthians, from 129 B.C. to A.D. 224. The Sassanians conquered the Parthians in the 3rd century and ruled Persia for more than 400 years. In the 7th century A.D., Arab Muslims took control of Persia and brought an end to the Golden Age enjoyed under the Sassanians. The Arabs introduced the religion of Islam to the Persian people, who had formerly been Zoroastrians. From the 13th century until the 1400's, Iran suffered a series of invasions. First the Mongols under Genghis Khan and later the Tatars led by Tamerlane devastated the country and left a state of chaos in their wake.

Conditions improved in the early 1500's when Shah Ismail, the founder of the modern Persian nation, established the Safawid dynasty. This dynasty reached its peak under Shah Abbas, who ruled from 1587 to 1628. Isfahan, his capital, was built up into a city of unmatched beauty. Later, under Nadir Shah (ruled 1736–1747), Persia conquered Afghanistan and invaded India. When Nadir Shah died, the country plunged into civil war.

Finally, in 1795, the Qajar dynasty took control of the country. But Persia continued to grow weaker and weaker, and by the 19th century the country had been hurt not only by

Street scene in Teheran. The shop owner's name, Mithra, is written in Persian.

bad financial policies but also by the loss of large areas of territory in the north to Russia. In 1907 Russia and Great Britain created zones of influence in Persia—Russia in the north and Great Britain in the south—with a neutral area between the two. Later, during World War I, Persia was further weakened when it was used as a battleground by the great powers.

Then in the 1920's a strong leader named Riza Khan became Shah and founded the Pahlavi dynasty. He worked to modernize the country. In March, 1935, the name of Persia was officially changed to Iran.

Pressured by the Soviet Union and Great Britain, Riza Khan had begun to rely heavily on Germany as a neutralizing force in Iran. When he refused to expel German spies during World War II, the British and the Russians forced him to give up the throne. He was followed by his son Mohammed Reza, who assumed the throne in 1941. Shah Mohammed Reza made many sweeping social and economic reforms. In 1971, Iran officially celebrated the 2,500th anniversary of the founding of the Persian Empire.

JOHN R. RANDALL
Ohio State University

Reviewed by Permanent Mission of Iran
to the United Nations

IRAQ

Iraq was known as Mesopotamia, or land "between rivers," in ancient times. It occupied the area between the famed Tigris and Euphrates rivers. The region is believed to be one of the places where civilization began. Today Iraq is an oil-rich independent republic and a leading Arab country of the Middle East.

▶ **PEOPLE**

Iraq has a population of about 8,600,000. The people are known as Iraqis. The majority are Arabs whose forefathers migrated north from the Arabian Peninsula in the 7th century. The Arabs speak Arabic and are Muslims. The Kurds, a group in the northern mountains, are an Indo-Aryan people who originally came from Persia (modern Iran). The Kurds are also Muslims, but their language is Kurdish. In 1970, after a long struggle, the Kurds won the right to administer their own affairs within the Iraqi state.

A small percentage of the population is Christian. There is a small group known as Yezidis whose religion combines Islam and earlier forms of worship. There are also a few thousand Jews. Many thousands left Iraq after the founding of Israel in 1948.

Way of Life. Most Iraqis earn their living by farming or raising livestock. Farmers live in rural villages in permanent homes that are usually flat-roofed houses made of sun-dried mud brick. They rarely raise more than they need to live on. Most of them are sharecroppers, who pay the landowner for the use of the land or turn over to him a certain percentage of what they raise. Fruits and vegetables, along with milk and cereals, make up the diet of the farmers. Those who raise livestock are the nomads of the desert. They have no permanent homes, but live in tents that they can carry with them from place to place as they seek food for their animals. The leaders of the nomads are called sheikhs. Many of them are rich and powerful.

Traditional Iraqi dress for men is an ankle-length white shirt. Women wear long woolen cloaks, and Muslim women usually wear face veils. In the cities most people wear Western-style dress.

Education. The government is trying to bring education to all the people. Primary-school education is both free and compulsory. Since there is a shortage of teachers and buildings, however, many children are still

Kurds lead their livestock through the Zagros Mountains in northeastern Iraq.

unable to attend classes. It is estimated that nearly 1,000,000 students now attend primary schools. The percentage of Iraqis who can read and write is therefore increasing. A smaller number of students go on to secondary schools. There are three national universities and a number of technical schools and teacher-training schools.

Literature, Art, and Music. Because Iraq did not become an independent state until 1932, its literature, art, and music are still mainly a part of the much larger Arabic culture. Iraqi art and handicrafts are essentially Arabic. Miniatures painted on camel bone or ivory, mosaic inlay work, copper and brass utensils, and rugs and textiles are all produced in Iraq for the local market and the tourist trade.

One distinctive type of artistic work that is always associated with Iraq, however, is the silverware produced by the Mandeans, or Sabeans. The Mandeans are a small religious sect whose beliefs require that they live close to running water. The silverware they make is decorated with scenes or figures well known in Iraq: the Arch of Ctesiphon, the date palm, and the reed houses and boats of the Marsh Arabs. Iraq is also known for the embroidered rugs made in Samawa, south of Baghdad.

▶ **THE LAND**

Iraq is located in Southwest Asia at the head of the Persian Gulf. With an area of 167,925 square miles, the country is about the size of Sweden. Geographically Iraq is divided into four regions: the lower Tigris-Euphrates valley (ancient Babylonia); the upper Tigris-Euphrates valley (ancient Assyria); the mountains and hills of the northeast (inhabited by the Kurds); and the desert upland of the southwest and west.

The lower Tigris-Euphrates valley is a poorly drained plain that begins just north of Baghdad and reaches southward to the head of the Persian Gulf. There are several large, shallow lakes and a very large marsh area in the southern part of this region.

The upper Tigris-Euphrates valley is made up of several river valleys created by the Tigris River and its major tributaries. This region is higher and much more hilly than the lower Tigris-Euphrates valley.

The mountains of northeastern Iraq are a continuation of the Zagros Mountains of Iran.

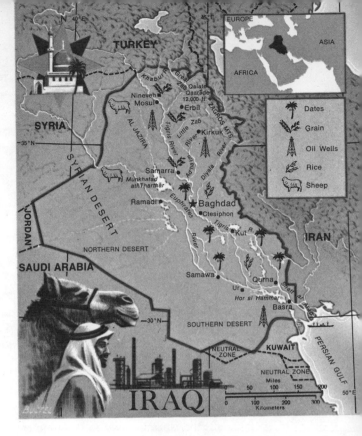

They are high and rugged, with peaks more than 10,000 feet above sea level. Oil fields are located in the foothills along the southeast side of the mountains.

The western desert upland is part of the much larger Syrian desert and is a rather level and featureless plain. The Euphrates River cuts through this desert in a deep and flat-floored but steep-sided valley. The surface of the desert is marked by many wadis (river beds that are dry except during the rainy season).

Rivers. Both the Tigris and Euphrates rivers rise in mountains in Turkey. The Euphrates is considerably longer than the Tigris and flows across eastern Syria before it reaches Iraq. Near Baghdad the two rivers come within 20 miles of one another, and near Qurna, in southern Iraq, they join to form the Shatt al Arab, which empties into the Persian Gulf. The Shatt al Arab marks part of the boundary between Iraq and Iran. Navigation rights on the river have sometimes been a cause of friction. The Euphrates is generally rather shallow. The Tigris is deeper and normally navigable as far upstream as Baghdad.

The water of the Tigris-Euphrates is the lifeblood of the country. Historically, how-

Goatskin raft on the Tigris River.

ever, the rivers have at times caused great destruction by flooding. Their waters rise regularly in the spring and early summer, flooding vast areas in the lower valley every year. Because the lower Tigris-Euphrates plain is so poorly drained, much potential cropland cannot be used. Almost half the land lies idle each year because of excessive salt in the soil—the result of lack of drainage. With the money earned from the sale of oil, Iraq has been developing the Tigris-Euphrates area in order to increase the amount of cropland and lessen the danger of floods. Since World War II the rivers have been brought under control by a system of dams, spillways, and storage reservoirs.

Animal and Plant Life. Iraq's only forests are in the mountains. But because of the indiscriminate cutting of trees these forests have been largely reduced to scrub growth of little value. Some reforestation has taken place since World War II. Steppe grass and desert scrub furnish food for livestock. The natural vegetation of Iraq consists mainly of wild oak, hawthorn, willow, and pine trees. Partridges, eagles, buzzards, and hawks make up the country's bird life. Ibex, bear, and hyenas roam northern Iraq. Gazelle and grouse can be found in the south, and fish are plentiful in the lower reaches of the Tigris-Euphrates.

Climate. Iraq receives little rainfall except in the high mountains of the northeast. The entire southwestern half of the country is tropical desert, receiving less than 10 inches of rain a year. The climate of the northeastern half of the country, excluding the mountains, is semi-arid, or steppe, with a rainfall of between 10 and 20 inches. The summers (May through October) are dry. Winter (November through April) is the season of rain, when winter-sown grains such as barley and wheat are grown in the steppe without irrigation. These crops are harvested in the spring or early summer. Crop production is possible in the desert only with irrigation. Summer crops in the steppe must also be irrigated.

Temperatures in the summer are very high. The average temperature in July, the hottest month, is in the high 80's to mid 90's. Nights are cooler, but still hot. In the winter the temperatures vary from about 45 degrees Fahrenheit in the north to about 55 degrees in the south. Winter days are usually warm and pleasant, but winter night temperatures are often close to freezing.

▶ **ECONOMY**

Natural Resources. With the exception of oil, Iraq is poor in mineral resources. But its vast oil deposits make Iraq one of the major oil producers of the Middle East. Oil is the main export and source of income. Iraq's oil is moved almost entirely by pipeline. There are pipelines running from the Kirkuk field in the north to ports on the Mediterranean Sea. One pipeline runs to Banias, Syria. Other lines carry oil from the large field near Basra in the south to the mid-sea loading base in the Persian Gulf.

Several dams have been planned to control flooding of the major tributaries of the Tigris. These dams may eventually be used as sources of hydroelectric power.

Industries and Products. The major food cereals of Iraq are barley and wheat. In the south, where irrigation water is abundant, rice is grown. The major crop grown for sale is dates, of which Iraq is the world's largest producer.

The most common livestock of Iraq are camels, sheep and goats, cattle in irrigated areas, and water buffalo along the rivers. Oxen, water buffalo, donkeys, and mules are

A copper bazaar in Baghdad.

used as draft animals. Since Islam prohibits the eating of pork and the Iraqi population is almost entirely Muslim, no hogs are raised. Livestock, except donkeys and mules, are also used for milk production and for skins and hides.

There is, as yet, very little modern manufacturing. Textiles are most important, followed by brickmaking. There is a great concentration of factory and craft production in Baghdad. The major exports of Iraq are oil, barley, dates, cotton, and animal hides. Iraq imports sugar, tea, textiles, timber, vehicles, machinery, modern domestic luxury items, and chemicals. Construction has become a leading industry in recent years.

Transportation and Communication. There are three main railroad lines in Iraq. One, with its terminus at Baghdad, is part of the original Berlin-to-Baghdad Railroad and gives Iraq direct rail connection with Europe. The line has now been extended to Basra, and this is considered the second line. The third line, beginning at Basra, runs through Baghdad to

---

FACTS AND FIGURES

REPUBLIC OF IRAQ is the official name of the country. Iraq means "cliff" in Arabic and is a reference to the Iraqi plateau extending into Syria. The ancient name of Iraq was Mesopotamia, meaning land "between rivers."

CAPITAL: Baghdad.

LOCATION AND SIZE: Southwest Asia. **Latitude**—29° 06' N to 37° 22' N. **Longitude**—38° 40' E to 48° 34' E. **Area**—167,925 sq. mi.

PHYSICAL FEATURES: Highest point—Qalate Qaarāde (12,000 ft.), in Zagros Mountains of Kurdistan. **Lowest point**—sea level. **Chief rivers**—Tigris, Great Zab, Little Zab, Diyala, Euphrates, Shatt al Arab.

POPULATION: 8,600,000 (estimate).

LANGUAGE: Arabic (official), Kurdish, Persian, Turkish.

RELIGION: Islam (official), Christianity, Judaism.

GOVERNMENT: Republic. **Head of government**—president. **International co-operation**—United Nations, Arab League.

NATIONAL ANTHEM: Al-Salam al-Jumhuriya ("Salute of the Republic").

ECONOMY: Agricultural products—barley, wheat, dates, rice, millet, maize, cotton, tobacco, livestock (cattle, water buffalo, sheep, goats, donkeys, horses, mules). **Industries and Products**—oil refining, date packing, leather tanning, handicrafts (rugs, silverware), bricks, woolen and cotton textiles, cigarettes. **Chief minerals**—oil. **Chief exports**—oil, barley, dates, raw cotton, raw wool, animal skins and hides. **Chief imports**—industrial machinery, vehicles and parts, iron and steel, tea, sugar, textiles and clothing, chemicals and pharmaceuticals, timber, domestic luxury items (refrigerators, washing machines, and vacuum cleaners), paper and cardboard. **Monetary unit**—Iraqi dinar.

Kirkuk and Erbil and connects the southern and northern parts of the country.

Since the end of World War II, money from the sale of oil has enabled Iraq to improve its road system. It now has all-weather highways connecting the important cities within the country, and international highways to Jordan and Syria on the west and Iran on the east. For traveling across the desert, some people still use camels, horses, and donkeys. But modern means of transportation are also used, of course.

There are international airports in Baghdad and Basra. A network of smaller airports spread out over all parts of the country serves local needs.

Points of Interest

The country has many places of historical interest. The ruins of Ur, in the southwestern part of the country, are a tourist attraction. The ziggurat (Babylonian temple tower) at Ur is believed to date back to about 2500 B.C.

South of Baghdad are the remains of the Arch of Ctesiphon, an imposing arched palace that dates back to about A.D. 225. In the Baghdad suburb of Kadhimain is the famous and beautiful Shia mosque (Muslim church). The mosque has two domes and four major minarets (towers), all covered with gold.

▶MAJOR CITIES

Baghdad, the capital and largest city of Iraq, has a population of over 1,745,000. The city is located on the Tigris River in the east central part of the country. Baghdad is the seat of government and also the most important commercial and manufacturing center of the country. For 500 years, between the 8th and 13th centuries, Baghdad was the center of Islamic art, learning, and trade. Today Baghdad is a modern city. Outdoor bazaars and narrow streets have been replaced by wide avenues lined with tall office buildings and air-conditioned hotels.

Mosul, with a population of about 243,000, is the major administrative and commercial city of the north. It is located on the west bank of the upper Tigris, across the river from the site of ancient Nineveh of Biblical fame. The city produces wool and artificial silk textiles. Leatherwork is also important.

Basra, with a population of approximately 313,000, is the trade and administrative center of the south. It is Iraq's only important port and handles most of the country's foreign trade. Basra is also the center of Iraq's date-growing region.

▶HISTORY AND GOVERNMENT

As an independent country Iraq dates back only to 1932, but as the area that the Greeks

Baghdad, the capital of Iraq.

called Mesopotamia, it has one of the longest histories of any country in the world. It shared the culture and history of the ancient states of Sumer and Akkad, Babylonia, Assyria, Greece under Alexander, Persia, Parthia, Rome, the Arab empire, and Ottoman Turkey. But only the last two can be said to have had any direct effect upon modern-day Iraq. As part of the Arab empire, its capital, Baghdad, was for a long time the center of learning of the Muslim world. Under the Turks the area underwent a slow decay for a period of 385 years. With the breakup of the Ottoman Empire after World War I, Iraq was created as a state and was mandated to Great Britain by the League of Nations.

Faisal I. Iraq, under its first king, Faisal I, became independent in 1932 and was made a member of the League of Nations. Faisal I was an outstanding leader and did much in a short time to improve the country's economy and develop its relations with other Arab states.

From its founding, following World War I, until 1958, Iraq was a constitutional monarchy headed by a hereditary king. Iraq had a written constitution that provided for a national legislature. But since the death of Faisal I in 1933, Iraq has suffered greatly from political instability. At various times the constitution was ignored or set aside.

The Revolutions. In July, 1958, the monarchy was overthrown, and the king, Faisal II, was assassinated. General Abdul Karim Kassim, who led the revolt, ruled Iraq as a military dictator. In February, 1963, a six-member military junta (council) overthrew Kassim and took control of the government. The new government was headed by President Abdul Salam Mohammed Arif. An attempt by Iraqi Communists to overthrow it failed.

In 1964 President Arif announced a provisional constitution modeled after that of the United Arab Republic (Egypt) and designed to prepare Iraq for a future union with that country. The constitution provided for a transition period of 3 years in which Arif was to continue in the office of president and the National Council of the Revolutionary Command was to maintain legislative power. At the end of that period a National Assembly would be elected to prepare a permanent constitution. Egypt and Iraq agreed to create

Gold-domed Kadhimain Mosque.

a joint military command and presidential council.

In 1966 President Arif was killed in a plane crash, and his brother, General Abdul Rahman Mohammed Arif, became president. In 1968 Arif was overthrown in a military coup and forced into exile. General Ahmed Hassan al-Bakr was named president.

JOHN R. RANDALL
Ohio State University

Reviewed by SALIM A. SALEEM
Counsellor, Permanent Mission of Iraq
to the United Nations

IRELAND

If you dislike extremes of temperature and take kindly to wind and rain, you will find Ireland a pleasant place. The rains have made the land so green that Ireland is often called the Emerald Isle.

Ireland is located in the Atlantic Ocean, west of the larger island of Great Britain. Ireland is divided into two sections, which are composed of 32 counties. The six northeastern counties of Northern Ireland are part of the United Kingdom of Great Britain and Northern Ireland. Northern Ireland has over 1,500,000. The remaining 26 counties, which have a population of 2,900,000, make up the republic of Ireland. The two countries have been ruled separately since 1921.

▶ THE PEOPLE

Most Irish people are descended from the Gaels, a branch of an ancient Celtic tribe. Norsemen, French Normans, Scots, and English also settled in Ireland. These peoples intermarried, and today there is no ethnic division among the Irish.

Language

English was not always the language of the Irish. For over 2,000 years the people spoke Irish, or Gaelic, one of the oldest languages in Europe. When the Irish Free State was established by a treaty in 1921, its leaders tried to make Gaelic the everyday language of the people in place of English. Irish-speaking teachers were trained to spread the language among the English-speaking population. But the results so far have not been satisfactory. Irish is spoken in a few rural areas, and it has become the language of some intellectual and cultured people. But English is still the language of the majority of the people.

O'Connell Street, Dublin's main street, is named for the Irish statesman Daniel O'Connell.

Education

Religious and moral training is a basic goal of Irish education. Education is compulsory and free for all children to the age of 14. Almost all primary education is run by religious groups and is supported by state funds. There are Catholic schools, Church of Ireland schools, Presbyterian and Methodist schools. All pupils follow the same curriculum. The teachers are paid by the state, but the management of the schools is mainly under local control.

Secondary schools are privately run but are subject to state inspection and receive some state funds. The majority of Catholic secondary schools are managed by religious orders. Abolition of fees and free transport from rural areas have helped to increase the attendance at secondary schools. Vocational schools are financed partly by the local authorities and partly by the state.

The government has established a small number of comprehensive schools. Pupils from secondary, vocational, and comprehensive schools sit for the same state examinations, the intermediate and leaving certificates.

There are four university colleges, as well as colleges of technology and teacher-training colleges. A Higher Education Authority has been set up by the government in an effort to unify the system. There are two university colleges in Dublin, Trinity College and University College. Other university colleges are located at Cork and Galway.

Religion

The Irish people are deeply religious. More than 90 percent of the inhabitants of the republic are Roman Catholic. As a result, laws on divorce and on censorship of films and literature are more restrictive than in most other countries in Europe. The Constitution of Ireland guarantees freedom of worship to all religions. The republic's small Protestant and Jewish populations are active in commercial and political life.

Cities

The principal cities of Ireland are seaports. The largest is Dublin, the capital, with a population of approximately 600,000 people. Dublin is located on the eastern coast of Ireland, at the mouth of the River Liffey.

IRELAND

It is the cultural, political, and business center of Ireland. It is the home of Trinity College, of the National Museum and the National Gallery of Ireland, and of the Abbey Theatre. Christ Church and Saint Patrick's are two beautiful Protestant cathedrals.

Other important Irish cities include Cork (population, 122,000), the second largest manufacturing city; Limerick, close to Shannon International Airport; Waterford, the home of beautiful glassware and crystal; and Galway, on the west coast. Among the best-known city festivals each year are the Dublin Theatre Festival, the Wexford Opera Festival, and the Cork International Film Festival.

Sports

The Irish are great sports lovers. Hunting and fishing have always been popular.

FACTS AND FIGURES

IRELAND is the official name of the country. It is called Éire in Gaelic.

CAPITAL: Dublin.

LOCATION AND SIZE: Island in Eastern North Atlantic Ocean. **Latitude**—51° 27′ N to 55° 23′ N. **Longitude**—5° 27′ W to 10° 29′ W. **Area**—27,136 sq. mi.

PHYSICAL FEATURES: Highest point—Carrantuohill (3,414 ft.). **Lowest point**—sea level. **Chief rivers**—Shannon, Boyne, Blackwater, Lee, Suir, Nore, Barrow, Liffey, Slaney. **Chief mountains**—Macgillycuddy's Reeks, Wicklow, Comeragh, Knockmealdown, Galty, and Benna Beola.

POPULATION: 2,900,000 (estimate).

LANGUAGE: Gaelic, or Irish; English.

RELIGION: Roman Catholic, Protestant.

GOVERNMENT: Republic. **Head of state**—president. **Head of government**—prime minister (*Taoiseach*). **International co-operation**—United Nations, Organization for Economic Co-operation and Development (OECD), Council of Europe, European Economic Community (EEC).

NATIONAL ANTHEM: *Amhran na bhFiann* ("The Soldier's Song").

ECONOMY: Agricultural products—livestock and livestock products, milk and other dairy products, wheat, barley, potatoes, turnips, sugar beets, oats. **Industries and products**—bread and biscuit baking, brewing, textile milling, whisky distilling, metal products, manufacture of paper and paper products, refining and manufacture of sugar and sugar products, tobacco processing, electrical machinery, and automobile assembly. **Chief minerals**—lead, iron, copper, barites, zinc, gypsum, marble, limestone, slate. **Chief exports**—live animals, foodstuffs, beverages, processed tobacco, textiles, manufactured goods. **Chief imports**—machinery and electrical goods, vehicles, iron and steel, coal, petroleum products, foodstuffs, tobacco, textiles, chemicals, dyes. **Monetary unit**—Irish pound.

Hockey, soccer, rugby, tennis, and golf are played all over Ireland. The most popular games are Gaelic football and hurling. The 32 counties of Ireland take part in national football and hurling contests. The all-Ireland championship finals attract huge crowds.

Irish horses have an outstanding reputation. They have won races all over the world, including the English Grand National Steeplechase. The Dublin Horse Show, held each summer, is an important sports event in which many nations compete. Horse trading is an activity at many local fairs.

The Arts

Dancing is a popular recreation. On Saturday and Sunday evenings thousands of young people attend dances and *céilis* held in ballrooms or halls or even in the open air. At a *céili* lively dances are performed to traditional Irish jigs and reels. Irish music is probably the country's greatest contribution to the arts. Some of the melodies are very ancient and rank with the most beautiful in the world.

But the other arts have not been neglected. Lovely gold ornaments of great antiquity can still be seen in the National Museum and are now reproduced in jewelry. The decoration of manuscripts reached a degree of skill that has seldom been equaled. The most famous example is the *Book of Kells,* which was written about A.D. 800 and is now in Trinity College, Dublin. Fine architecture can be seen in the large cities, especially in Dublin, with its magnificent 18th-century Georgian houses.

Literature and drama are fields in which Irish writers have won fame. Much fine poetry has been written in the Gaelic language. But the best-known writers wrote in English. The greatest poet of this century was William Butler Yeats (1865–1939). James Joyce's prose has influenced the English novel more than that of any other writer in recent years. The great names in drama from the 19th century on are those of Oscar Wilde (1854–1900), George Bernard Shaw (1856–1950), John Millington Synge (1871–1909), Sean O'Casey (1884–1964), and Samuel Beckett (1906–).

THE LAND

Ireland's area of 31,839 square miles makes it the second largest of the British Isles. Several small islands lie off Ireland's coast. The most important are the Aran Islands, which lie outside Galway Bay.

Ireland itself can be divided into two main physical regions: a large central lowland and a rim of hills, plateaus, and mountains. The fertile plain, or lowland, is covered with farms, pastureland, and peat bogs. The highest point in Ireland, Carrantuohill, rises 3,414 feet above sea level in the Macgillycuddy's Reeks range in the southwest.

Lakes and Rivers

Ireland has many lakes and rivers. North of Macgillycuddy's Reeks are the Lakes of Killarney, which are among the most beautiful in all Europe. The central plain is dotted with many lakes.

Lake Gougane Barra on the Cork-Kerry border, one of Ireland's loveliest spots.

The Lee River flows through Cork, Ireland's second largest city.

Turf is cut from peatbogs, dried, and used as fuel in many Irish homes.

The Shannon, which is the longest river in the British Isles, has been made navigable by a system of canals linking it with the Irish Sea at Dublin. Boating on the Shannon has become a major tourist attraction. The "sister" rivers of the Nore, Suir, and Barrow in the southeast are all great fishing rivers. The Blackwater, which is famous for its salmon, is one of the loveliest rivers in Europe. The Liffey is known as Dublin's river. The Boyne at Oldbridge near Drogheda is famous as the site of a great battle between James II and William III of England in 1690.

Climate

The weather in Ireland is a favorite topic of conversation because it changes so often. It rains for brief periods for over 200 days a year in some parts of Ireland. Even during the driest months it rains for short periods almost every other day. On the west coast the annual rainfall ranges from 40 inches to almost 100 inches in the mountains of Kerry and west Cork, while in the east it ranges from 30 to 40 inches.

Ireland's climate is greatly affected by the sea. Because it is exposed to the prevailing

Luttrellstown Castle near Dublin, one of Ireland's many castles.

westerly winds that cross the Gulf Stream, Ireland's climate is milder than that of other countries in the same latitude. Ireland's average annual temperature is 50 degrees Fahrenheit. The winters are usually mild, with average temperatures in the low 40's. Summers are pleasantly cool, with average temperatures in the high 50's.

Natural Resources

Many of Ireland's old lake basins are filled with peat bogs, which supply an almost unlimited amount of fuel in the form of turf, or peat. However, Ireland has to import coal and oil.

Although the country has few mineral resources, small quantities of iron, copper, barites, lead, zinc, and silver are found. Gypsum, marble, limestone, flagstone, and slate are also quarried.

▶ INDUSTRIES AND PRODUCTS

Agriculture. Ireland's most important crops are oats, potatoes, barley, wheat, turnips, and beets. The high rainfall and the freedom from extremes of temperature make Ireland one of the finest grass-producing areas in the world. As a result, the main rural occupation is the raising of cattle, sheep, pigs, and · horses. Cattle and cattle products account for about 50 percent of the total agricultural output and are the most important export.

Industry. The republic of Ireland has made great strides, particularly in recent years, in balancing an economy that had been largely agricultural. The harnessing of the Shannon River for electricity was the first great undertaking. It was followed by the development of a successful sugar-beet industry.

In recent years there has been considerable state investment in oil refining, shipbuilding, and the manufacture of fertilizers. During the 1960's about 50,000 new jobs were created in industry. Most of the new firms involved were started with the help of foreign capital.

The Shannon Free Airport Industrial Estate, which was begun in 1958, is now a large area of industry. British, German, American, Dutch, and Canadian companies have become interested in the low cost of labor and the duty-free facilities of the airport.

Raw materials can be brought into Shannon and the finished products shipped out without any duty being paid on them.

Tourism and travel have contributed large sums of money to Ireland's income. A recent estimate puts the value of the industry each year at close to $250,000,000.

Many Irish people have moved to the United States and Great Britain, seeking higher wages and greater choice of work. Although there has been a decline in emigration in recent years, there are more Irish-descended young men and young women living throughout the world today than there are in the republic itself.

Trade. Exports from the republic go mainly to the United Kingdom, and include food, beverages, farm animals, raw materials, clothing, and manufactured goods. The Anglo-Irish Trade Agreement (1965) has led to a great increase in imports from the United Kingdom.

Transportation and Communication. Córas Iompair Éireann (the Irish Transport System) takes charge of all rail and bus lines. There is also a well-developed system of roads —larger main roads lead to country ones that go through the towns and villages.

There are airports at Dublin, Shannon, and Cork. Irish Airlines fly to Europe and North America. At Shannon Airport, a gateway to Europe, people work around the clock in the duty-free shopping center. Tourists often stop there to buy cameras, perfume, clothing, and gifts from all over the world.

Dublin, Cork, and Limerick are the major seaports. At Whiddy Island near Bantry in the south, a new deep-sea port can berth the greatest oil tankers afloat.

Radio and television are under the control of the Radio and Television Authority, whose members are nominated by the government. Commercial firms sponsor programs and run advertisements on both television and radio. Five daily newspapers that circulate throughout the country are published in Dublin, and many other cities and towns have their own newspapers.

▶ GOVERNMENT

Ireland, which was proclaimed a republic in 1948, is a democratically governed country. All citizens over the age of 21 may vote. The Oireachtas, or National Parliament, is composed of Dáil Éireann (house of representatives), Seanad Éireann (senate), and the president. There have been two main parties in the Dáil almost since its beginning—Fianna Fáil and Fine Gael.

Dáil Éireann elects a *taoiseach,* or prime minister, who nominates the members of his cabinet. These ministers receive their seal of office from the president of Ireland, the titular head of state, who is elected for a 7-year term by the whole electorate.

▶ HISTORY

The early history of Ireland is clouded by myths and legends. It is now known that men lived there during the Stone Age and used objects of flint. About 350 B.C. the Gaelic Celts, a tall, reddish-blond-haired race, came from the region known as Gaul, or France. By the 2nd century B.C. they dominated the earlier inhabitants, developed an exact code of laws, and honored their poets as much as their kings. They were ruled by a High King at Tara, in County Meath.

In the 5th century, St. Patrick (389?–461?) came to Ireland and converted the people to Christianity. As a result, many monasteries were built and Irish monks brought the Christian faith and culture to Europe. Ireland became a center of learning and was known as the Island of Saints and Scholars. However, a series of petty kingships made strong government impossible. The country became the victim of foreign invaders.

The first invaders were sturdy Viking sailors from northern Europe. They founded many of the coastal cities of Ireland. Dublin, Cork, and Limerick owe their origin to these sea raiders, who first struck about the beginning of the 9th century. They remained in control of the cities for several centuries and married Irish women. However, the invaders did not have any power after the famous battle of Clontarf, near Dublin, won by the Irish king Brian Boru (926–1014) in 1014.

Kings of England had long been aware of the island to the west. In 1169, during the reign of Henry II (1133–89), an attacking force led by Norman barons came to Ireland. Henry himself came in 1171, and the Gaelic kings submitted to him. They were used to the loose authority of the Irish High King and were willing to transfer their allegiance.

But they were wrong. Gradually, year by year, the English rulers tightened their grip. Toward the end of the 13th century the first parliament of Ireland was formed. But it was made up almost entirely of English colonists. They spoke English and Norman French rather than Gaelic. In time, however, the English began to intermarry with the Irish and to adopt their customs.

In 1366 laws were passed to keep the English and the Irish apart. It became illegal for the English to intermarry with the Irish. After the Protestant Reformation in the 16th century the feelings of hatred developed into a religious war. Henry VIII (1491–1547) of England and his Protestant successors wanted the Catholics of Ireland to follow the Church of England. His daughter Queen Elizabeth I (1533–1603) took land in the southwest of Ireland and gave it to Englishmen. A part of it was given to Sir Walter Raleigh (1554?–1618), and he planted the first potato in Ireland.

The Irish resisted the English strongly on occasions. The great Hugh O'Neill (1540?–1616) rallied the Irish forces and won victories during a 9-year war. The battle of Kinsale in 1601, one of the decisive battles in the country's history, ended in defeat for the Irish. Oliver Cromwell (1599–1658), the Puritan leader of England, finally crushed the Irish resistance during the middle of the 17th century. He filled almost the entire country with British settlers and forced Catholic tenants holding land east of the Shannon River to move to the less fertile and rocky province of Connaught or to County Clare. Irish Catholics were allowed to keep only about a third of all the land in Ireland.

When a Catholic king, James II (1633–1701), came to power in England, the Irish felt new hope. But the Protestant English nobles were opposed to James's Catholicism and offered the throne to his son-in-law, the Protestant William III (Prince of Orange) (1650–1702). James came to Ireland. William followed and defeated him at the battle of the Boyne (River) in 1690.

As a result of the Catholics' opposition to William, the English Parliament passed the Penal Laws. By these laws Irish Catholics lost their legal and religious rights, and many were reduced to poverty.

The French and American revolutions seemed to herald a new dawn of freedom. But the rebellion of 1798, organized by Theobald Wolfe Tone (1763–98), a young Protestant lawyer, failed. In 1803 Robert Emmet (1778–1803) planned an outbreak, but that also failed.

An Act of Union was enforced through the influence of William Pitt the Younger (1759–1806), prime minister of Britain. By this act Ireland was to become part of the United Kingdom. Irish Catholics were promised seats in the British Parliament by Pitt, but King George III (1738–1820) refused to grant this right. Not until 1829 was the Penal Law repealed that denied Catholics representation in Parliament. This was brought about mainly through the efforts of Daniel O'Connell (1775–1847). He was a great figure who once more gave hope to the people. But he failed to get repeal of the Act of Union.

Further troubles beset Ireland. The famine of 1845–49, caused by a fungus that attacked the potato crop, wiped out the food supply for more than half the people. It reduced the population by 2,500,000. About 1,500,000 are believed to have died of disease and hunger, and the remainder emigrated to the United States and other countries.

Home Rule then became the popular demand, and a new leader rose to rally the people—Charles Stewart Parnell (1846–91), a Protestant landowner and defender of the small farmers. He led the Irish group in the House of Commons. However, he lost his following when he was involved in a divorce case, and Home Rule action was delayed.

When World War I broke out, Catholic and Protestant Irish joined the British Army and fought together. But many others joined the Irish Volunteers, formed in 1913 to defend the rights of the Irish people. In 1916 the Irish Volunteers joined forces with the Citizen Army, formed for the defense of the workers after the great Dublin strike in 1913. Led by Pádhraic Pearse (1879–1916) and James Connolly (1879–1916), they attempted to capture Dublin on Easter Monday, 1916. They proclaimed an Irish Republic and with about 1,000 men held parts of Dublin for about a week. But they had to surrender to the British, and 15 of their leaders were shot.

Although the rising was a military failure, the soldiers' heroism excited the people. They flocked to support the Sinn Fein (Ourselves Alone) party, which wanted political and cultural independence for all of Ireland. This party became active in the Irish Republican Army (I.R.A.), a development of the Irish Volunteers. A bitter war followed until 1921. Irish and British representatives then signed a treaty by which the 26 counties became largely self-governing. Ireland was made a free state in the British Commonwealth, but six of the nine counties of Ulster remained apart as Northern Ireland, a province of the United Kingdom. The treaty was accepted by a small majority of Dáil Éireann, and civil war followed between supporters and opponents of the treaty.

Eamon de Valera (1882–   ), who had been elected President of the Republic in 1918, led the opposition to the treaty. In 1923 there was peace once more. De Valera left the Sinn Fein party and formed his own republican party (Fianna Fáil). By 1932 his party was in control of the government. Under a new constitution, drawn up in 1937, the country was to be ruled by a president and a *taoiseach* (prime minister). In 1948 the republic of Ireland was set up, and Ireland left the Commonwealth.

Irish nationalists have always resented the partition of the country, and this resentment has often led to violence. In the early 1970's the activities of the Irish Republican Army led to guerrilla warfare in Northern Ireland. Hundreds of lives were lost. With a change of government in the Republic in 1973, prospects of settlement of the Northern problem seemed brighter.

Ireland belongs to the United Nations, the Organization for Economic Cooperation and Development (OECD), the Council of Europe, and the European Economic Community (EEC or the Common Market). Although the problem of partition remains, both areas of Ireland are striving to find a place in today's Europe.

THOMAS FITZGERALD
Department of Education, Dublin, Ireland
Reviewed by JOHN O'BRIEN
Consul General of Ireland

See also UNITED KINGDOM.

IRELAND, NORTHERN. See UNITED KINGDOM.

IRISH LITERATURE

Ireland is a small country with a long and proud history. Viking invasions from the 9th to the 11th centuries first disturbed its peaceful independence. There followed the Norman invasion, beginning in 1169, which led to the occupation of the country for many centuries by the English. In 1922, after years of struggle, hardship, and battle, most of Ireland gained independence. Six counties of Northern Ireland remained under British rule.

Early Irish Literature

Bards were poet-singers who made up and recited verses about heroes and their deeds. The earliest Irish literature was their stories, told long before any were ever written down. One of the bards' great heroes is Cuchulain, who lived in the ancient region of Ulster under King Conchobar. Cuchulain got his name, which means "the hound of Culann," because as a boy he slew the famous hound of Culann the smith. Cuchulain was known for his strength and daring, and there are many stories of his brave deeds. He finally died in battle, but not until he had tied himself to a stone pillar so that he could die standing up.

This story comes from a group of tales known as the Ulster Cycle. Another from the same cycle is about Deirdre. At birth a curse was put upon this beautiful girl. King Conchobar raised her especially to be his bride, but unhappily she fell in love with the noble warrior Naisi. Together with his brothers the couple escaped from the kingdom and Conchobar. He was angry about this, and had them followed and returned to him. The brothers were killed, and Deirdre took her own life. Many later writers have used this legend in plays and poetry.

The other famous collection of stories about old Irish heroes is known as the Fenian Cycle. These tales and poems record the exploits of a band of warriors led by Finn Mac Cool. He and his men were known as the Fianna. Anyone who wanted to join the tribe had to show great feats of strength. Other skills were required, too; there was even a test in poetry. Members of the Fianna swore to avenge themselves when trouble occurred and not to look for outside help. When Ireland was struggling for independence centuries later,

many men joined a secret organization called Sinn Fein—"ourselves alone." This organization goes back to the time of Finn Mac Cool. It had as its purpose the liberation and defense of Ireland.

Two legends from the Fenian Cycle have been retold many times. One is the story of the wanderings of Ossian, the son of Finn. The other is the sad story of Grania, a king's daughter who was betrothed to Finn Mac Cool. At their wedding feast at Tara, legendary seat of the kings of Ireland, Grania met and fell in love with Diarmuid the Brown, and great troubles followed. The story of Grania and Diarmuid is in many ways like the earlier legend of Deirdre and Naisi.

12th to 18th Centuries

Gaelic was the language of old Ireland. All the great sagas and romances of ancient days were preserved in that language. Gradually, with the Norman English rule over the land and people, the quality of Irish literature declined. Bards kept up some of the Gaelic tradition in their elaborate, stylized verse, but their influence was slight. Only a few works of interest to the modern reader survive from the troubled years of wars and conquest that stretch from the 12th to the 18th centuries. One notable exception is the 16th-century poem "My Dark Rosaleen." In it the poet identified Ireland with a dark and beautiful woman to whom he pledges his honor and the promise of her liberation. It is one of the earliest and most moving of the patriotic poems for which Irish writers in later years became known throughout the world. A 19th-century version of the poem contains these lines:

> 'Tis you shall have the golden throne,
> 'Tis you shall reign, and reign alone,
>   My Dark Rosaleen . . .

18th Century

Modern Irish literature has its beginning in the early 18th century. Although most of the people still spoke Irish (Gaelic), the English had taken over the country, and almost all of the literature is in English. Dublin, the capital of Ireland, was one of the liveliest cities in Europe at this time. There was a good deal of communication between it and London. Some noted Irish writers of this period, as in later

Villagers tie up Christy Mahon and plan to hang him for the murder of his father. Christy is the hero of Synge's *Playboy of the Western World*.

years, gained fame after leaving Ireland. Among these are the poet Oliver Goldsmith (1728–74), the dramatist Richard Brinsley Sheridan (1751–1816), and the essayist Richard Steele (1672–1729), all of whom lived in England. Jonathan Swift (1667–1745) is the greatest Irish writer of this century. Born and educated in Dublin, he lived in England for a time. He returned to Dublin, where he served as dean of St. Patrick's Cathedral. A proud, strong, witty, often angry man, he wrote many poems and political pamphlets, as well as the celebrated *Gulliver's Travels* (1726). He died insane in 1745 and is buried in St. Patrick's.

19th Century

After 1800, for almost 100 years Ireland's history is one of continuing struggle against foreign domination and problems at home. Poverty and disease were the conditions of the common man. The famine years 1846–48 caused many deaths and untold suffer-ing. Vast numbers emigrated to England and the United States.

Bad conditions do not generally produce good literature, but the work of Thomas Moore (1779–1852) proves an exception to this rule. His songs and poems were patriotic, sentimental, sometimes sad. Irishmen everywhere still sing them. Among the noblest are "Believe Me if All those Endearing Young Charms," "The Minstrel Boy," "The Meeting of the Waters," and "The Harp That Once Through Tara's Halls." He is Ireland's favorite songwriter. Other poets of this era, some of whom also translated older Irish poems and stories into English, were James Clarence Mangan (1803–49), Sir Samuel Ferguson (1810–86), and John Todhunter (1839–1916).

Irish Literary Renaissance and 20th Century

At the end of the 19th century a great revival of interest in the old Irish legends, myths, and stories took place. Many call this

Sean O'Casey's first plays were performed at the famous Abbey Theatre in Dublin.

movement the Irish Literary Renaissance because it revived for the first time in many centuries a tradition in prose and poetry. Standish James O'Grady (1846–1928) translated the heroic tale of Cuchulain and others into living, vital prose that excited the minds and imaginations of his readers. Ireland's ancient history awakened the interest of other writers. One, Douglas Hyde (1860–1949), was a co-founder of the Gaelic League, an organization formed to bring back Irish as a language. The league had a strong political influence, and when Ireland finally gained independence, Douglas Hyde became the country's first president.

Yeats. The most important outgrowth of the renaissance was the Irish Literary Theatre, founded in 1898 by Ireland's greatest poet, William Butler Yeats (1865–1939). A tall, proud, independent man, he worked hard to create drama and poetry that would equal or surpass the best of ancient Ireland. He wrote many plays, including *Cathleen ni Houlihan* (1902). This is a patriotic play about a peasant boy who leaves his fiancée and family,

on the eve of his wedding, to join the fight for his country's independence. Together with Lady Augusta Gregory (1852–1932), Yeats helped the Irish National Theatre become famous throughout the world as the Abbey Theatre. Yeats, however, is best known as a poet. He wrote many volumes of beautiful verse, for which he won the 1923 Nobel prize for literature. He was always active in public affairs in Ireland and had a very strong influence on the rebirth of Irish culture.

Synge. One of Yeats's early "discoveries" was the playwright John Millington Synge (1871–1909). They met in Paris, and Yeats encouraged Synge to return to Ireland and write about the common people there. Synge took the advice. The result is one of the finest modern plays in English, *The Playboy of the Western World* (1907). There was great controversy about the play when it was first produced, but it is now generally regarded as a classic. Synge's ability to catch the rhythm and the poetry of ordinary peasant speech sets his plays apart and gives them an almost poetic quality. Synge did not live to finish his last play, *Deirdre of the Sorrows,* published in 1910.

O'Casey. Another Irish playwright given his first chance at the Abbey Theatre was Sean O'Casey (1880–1964). He was born and raised in the slums of Dublin, where early disease and poverty permanently damaged his eyesight. He was past 40 when his first play, *The Shadow of a Gunman,* was produced in 1923. This was followed by his two finest and most popular plays, *Juno and the Paycock* (1924) and *The Plough and the Stars* (1926). O'Casey writes with great humor and passion about the ordinary people of an Irish tenement, but many of his themes and his characters are universal. His early plays have been called tragic comedies because they are both sad and funny. O'Casey's later plays are more abstract and symbolic and are not set in Dublin. They have not had the popular success of the earlier ones. For many years O'Casey lived in England, where he completed his remarkable six-volume autobiography.

Other Dramatists. The Abbey Theatre enjoyed a great reputation in England and America for many years. Many Irish men of letters wrote plays for the theater in the early years. Among them are George William Russell (1867–1935), who used the pen name AE; George Moore (1852–1933); Edward Martyn (1859–1923); Padraic Colum (1881–1972); and T. C. Murray (1873–1959). Later dramatists whose works were produced at the Abbey and who did much to keep its standards high were Lennox Robinson (1886–1958), who served also as manager and director; Denis Johnston (1901–); Paul Vincent Carroll (1900–68); and one of the liveliest of the younger generation, Brendan Behan (1923–64).

Joyce. Modern Ireland has produced one of the 20th century's greatest writers of prose, James Joyce (1882–1941). Although he wrote only a few books, he has had a strong influence in contemporary British and American fiction. He changed the traditional story-telling method by developing a technique called stream of consciousness. His most celebrated work, written in this style, is the huge novel *Ulysses* (1922). The story of Homer's famous Greek warrior is retold in a modern setting. All the action is seen through the minds of the three main characters—Stephen Dedalus, Leopold Bloom, and Molly Bloom. The scene is Dublin on June 16, 1904. Although Joyce had a very difficult time getting *Ulysses* published, it has since had a very strong effect on much modern writing.

Joyce grew up in Dublin, but he was very unhappy in the city and left it for Europe when he was a young man. Although Joyce was very bitter about Ireland and returned there only a few times, he continued to write about the Irish and his native city until he died. He is Ireland's best-known writer because he wrote about common people and common experiences in a very uncommon way.

O'Flaherty. Another novelist of a later era who has written powerful books about Ireland is Liam O'Flaherty (1896–). *The Informer* (1925) tells the story of a slow-witted man who turns traitor against his comrade during the Irish revolution. The poverty, hardship, despair, and suffering of the peasants during the great famines of the 19th century is the subject of his well-known novel *Famine* (1937).

Short Stories. In the last century the short story has become an important form of literature. Two of the ablest short-story writers of

James Joyce wrote one of the 20th century's most celebrated novels, *Ulysses*.

our times are Irishmen: Seán O'Faoláin (1900–) and Frank O'Connor (1903–66), whose real name was Michael O'Donovan. Although both have written novels, they are best known for their many, almost perfect stories of life in Ireland. They draw heavily on their experiences as boys growing up and as young men participating in Ireland's struggle for independence. They tell their stories with humor and deep feeling. Liam O'Flaherty, Kate O'Brien (1897–), Bryan McMahon (1909–), and James Plunkett (1920–) are other story writers of contemporary Ireland who deserve attention.

Ireland is small and, compared to other countries, so is the amount of literature that has been produced there. But no one should confuse size with quality. The best Irish literature is among the best in the Western world. Songs and stories and plays and poems are here in plenty, to fire the imagination, to awaken the spirit, to nourish the reader's mind and heart.

PHILIP DRISCOLL
Brandeis University

IRON AND STEEL

Iron and steel have a greater effect on our daily lives than any other metals. By itself, iron is used for only a few products, such as automobile engine blocks and water and sewer pipes. Iron is important, however, because it is the basic ingredient of steel, which is one of our most useful materials.

Steel and steel products are used almost all the time in daily life. About 60 percent of an automobile is made of steel. Underneath their shiny enamel surfaces, refrigerators, stoves, washers, and driers are almost all steel. Steel framework holds up skyscrapers and adds strength to houses. Each year the average person uses about 300 tin cans. These cans are made of steel, except for a very thin coating of tin or other materials. Steel goes into knives, forks, spoons, pots, pans, needles, paper clips, scissors, and bedsprings. The list of steel products could go on for hundreds of pages.

Steel is also important for manufacturing other materials. The nylon for a sweater or dress was originally produced in a steel vessel. The material was spun and woven into fabric by steel machines. The aluminum pots and pans in the kitchen were probably stamped out and shaped by machines of steel. The soap in the bathroom was made in giant steel cauldrons. Almost all the machinery and equipment used in industry is made of steel. Centuries from now, an archeologist digging up the remains of 20th-century civilization might call this the Age of Steel.

▶ WHAT IS STEEL?

Basically, steel is an alloy of iron and carbon. Other ingredients may be included to give the steel characteristics such as hardness or toughness. Thousands of different kinds of steel can be made.

Steels differ so much that it is hard to make a statement that holds true for every kind of steel. For example, most steels lose strength at very high temperatures, but the steels used in missiles and rockets retain their strength. Some steels become brittle and break at very low temperatures. Other steels remain strong at the same low temperatures. At normal temperatures there are steels that can be stretched, hammered, and drawn into complicated shapes. Other kinds of steel are so hard that they can be used to cut and shape other metals.

The kind of steel we usually see is a hard, silvery-gray metal. It has great strength in proportion to its weight. It can be easily bent into various shapes without breaking, and it keeps its strength after it has been shaped. This steel can be machined to a very small size for a tiny part in a wristwatch, or it can be made into a huge beam to support a skyscraper.

Besides all these advantages, steel is also one of the cheapest of metallic substances.

Many Kinds of Steel

About 20 different elements can be added to the iron and carbon alloy to produce various types of steel.

The most important element added is **manganese**. It helps to prevent the steel from being brittle and improves the strength, hardness, and ductility of the metal. Ductility is the ability of a metal to be stretched out or hammered thin without breaking.

Chromium is added to give the steel resistance to corrosion. This type of steel is known as stainless steel. Some stainless steels contain nickel as well as chromium. Stainless steels are often used for such things as surgical instruments, kitchen equipment, knives, forks, spoons, and skins for missiles.

Small quantities of tungsten and cobalt give steel added resistance to wear and abrasion. This kind of steel can be used to cut and form other metals.

Adding silicon produces a steel that has low electrical energy loss. This steel is used in electric transformers and in electric motors and generators.

Other elements, including molybdenum, titanium, tantalum, columbium, vanadium, and zirconium, also may be added to steel. These elements can be added to steel in various combinations and in different quantities. This is why so many different kinds of steel are possible.

▶ STEELMAKING

A steel mill might be compared to a gigantic kitchen. As in a kitchen, the raw materials are brought together, measured out carefully, and put into different vessels to be "cooked." The most important raw materials used in a steel

The tremendous heat of this electric furnace refines iron into steel.

mill are iron ore, coke (a fuel made by heating bituminous coal without air), and limestone.

Steelmaking really begins with a **blast furnace**. This is a tall, round structure, about 10 stories high. The base of the furnace is 30 feet or more in diameter. An inclined railway runs up the side to the top so that the furnace can be filled from above. Little cars shuttle up and down the railway, carrying iron ore, coke, and limestone and dumping them into the furnace in alternating layers.

Next to each blast furnace are tall towers. These are stoves to heat air that is blown into the furnace under pressure. The air, heated to about 1600 degrees Fahrenheit, burns the coke. The coke gives off intense heat and huge quantities of carbon monoxide gas. The gas combines with the oxygen in the iron ore and passes off as carbon dioxide, leaving molten iron metal that collects in the bottom of the blast furnace.

The limestone, which has melted in the intense heat, combines with the waste materials in the iron ore. It makes a fluid scum called slag, which floats on top of the iron.

A blast furnace operates day and night. Raw materials are fed into it as fast as they are needed. The furnace is shut down only for repairs or if the demand for iron decreases.

Every 4 or 5 hours the blast furnace is tapped. First the slag is removed through an outlet in the side of the furnace called the cinder notch. Then another hole called the taphole is opened, and the iron runs out, 100 to 300 tons at a time. The molten iron, often called hot metal by steelmakers, flows into heavy railroad tank cars. The cars take the hot metal away to steelmaking furnaces or to molds where the iron is poured and allowed to solidify for future use.

When cooled and solidified, iron is called **pig iron**. It was given this name because at one time the molten iron was allowed to run out into small sand molds surrounding the blast furnace. Old-time ironmakers thought that the molds looked like suckling pigs around their mother.

The amount of raw materials that go into a blast furnace is enormous. To make 1 ton of pig iron, about 1½ tons of iron ore are needed, plus ⅗ ton of coke and ⅓ ton of limestone. During a 24-hour period, a blast furnace may consume nearly 150 railroad carloads of solid raw materials. It also consumes about 4 tons of air for every ton of iron produced.

Steelmen are working to make the blast furnace more efficient by adding fuels that create extra heat. This makes the furnace produce metal faster. Such fuels include oil, natural gas, and pulverized coal.

The raw iron from the blast furnace must be purified to turn it into steel. This is done by several different processes.

The Bessemer Process

The Bessemer process is the oldest method for producing large quantities of steel. The method was invented a few years before the Civil War by two men working independently of one another—Henry Bessemer (1813–98), an English engineer, and William Kelly (1811–88), a Kentucky ironmaker. The Bessemer process produces steel by blowing air through molten iron at high pressure—22 to 28 pounds per square inch.

The molten iron is placed in a pear-shaped container called a Bessemer converter. Air is blown in from the bottom through hundreds of small holes called **tuyeres**. The oxygen in the air burns away most of the unwanted materials mixed with the iron. The flames burn away silicon, manganese, carbon, and other materials. Some of these materials are added later to make alloy steel. The reason for adding them after going to the trouble of removing them is that exact amounts of each element are wanted for the steel. The manganese, silicon, and carbon in pig iron are not usually present in the right amounts and proportions.

The drawback of the Bessemer process is that it does not efficiently remove some unwanted elements, such as nitrogen. This can make the steel brittle. As improved methods were developed, the Bessemer process gradually went out of use. It is no longer used in the United States, and it is used only to a limited extent in Europe.

The Open-Hearth Furnace

For many years most of the world's steel was produced in open-hearth furnaces. An open-hearth furnace is like a huge, shallow tank lined with heat-resistant bricks. Gas, oil, powdered coal, or tar may be used as fuel. The fuel is mixed with hot air in burners located at each end of the furnace. Flames sweep down from the burners and across the open hearth just above the materials to be melted. To start with, the furnace is fed with limestone and steel scrap. Molten iron is added later. The limestone melts and forms a slag that floats on top. It helps purify the metal by absorbing impurities. Various elements are added to the mixture to give the steel the qualities that are required.

Up to 12 hours may be needed to produce one **heat**, or furnace load, of steel. During this time, samples are taken from the furnace. The samples are sent to a laboratory for testing to make sure that the steel is of the right chemical composition.

To help speed up the process, oxygen is often blown into the furnace through pipes that are lowered through the roof. A heat of steel can be made in 4 to 6 hours by this method.

The Basic Oxygen Process

More steel is now produced by the basic oxygen process than by any other method. In this process the molten iron from the blast furnace is poured into a furnace that resembles a Bessemer converter, except that it has no holes in the bottom for an air blast. Instead, a long, water-cooled pipe called an oxygen lance is lowered through the mouth of the furnace until its end is just above the molten metal. Pure oxygen is blown through the pipe onto the metal. The oxygen combines with the impurities, which either form part of the slag or pass off as exhaust gases. (The exhaust gases are collected by a hood over the furnace and are cleaned before being released into the atmosphere.) In about 45 minutes the steel is ready. The furnace is tilted onto its side, and the molten metal is poured off.

The Electric Furnace

High-quality steel, such as stainless steel, is often made in electric furnaces. The electric furnaces most widely used are steel shells lined with heat-resistant brick. Large sticks of carbon, called electrodes, extend down from the roof of the furnace to within a few inches of the metal. When the power is turned on, the current jumps the gap between the electrodes and the metal, making an electric arc. The arc generates terrific heat and melts the metal. When the heat (batch of metal) is finished, the furnace is tilted to pour the steel into a ladle. Electric furnaces are also used to make ordinary carbon steel, especially at small steel plants where a blast furnace would be too costly. Electric furnaces can make steel completely out of scrap.

Molten steel pours from furnace into giant ladle. Slag overflows into smaller ladle.

Vacuum and Electroslag Remelting

Vacuum remelting is used to produce steels that are especially strong and dependable. A bar of alloy steel of the type needed is refined in a special sealed furnace connected to a vacuum pump. The bar is connected to an electric power supply and lowered inside the furnace until it strikes an arc against the bottom of the furnace. As the intense heat of the arc melts the bar, most of the impurities in the steel are vaporized and are drawn off by the vacuum. The purified steel is collected in the water-cooled bottom of the furnace.

The electroslag process is very similar, except that a blanket of slag over the molten steel is used instead of a vacuum.

Steels made by these processes are used for products that must withstand great stress, such as aircraft propeller and turbine shafts, rocket parts, and ball and roller bearings.

From the Furnaces to the Mill

After steel has been made in the furnaces, it is poured into large ladles. It is then usually poured into molds where it is allowed to harden into solid pieces of steel called **ingots**.

The molds in which ingots are made are usually of cast iron. They are stripped off after the steel is solid but while it is still red-hot. The ingot is carried to an underground furnace called a **soaking pit**. There it stays until its temperature is about 2200 degrees. The steel is now ready for the next step in the manufacturing process.

Rolling Mills

Most steel is rolled—that is, passed back and forth between giant rollers. Rolling forms the steel into shapes and sizes that are easier to use in manufacturing. Rolling also improves the steel by making it stronger and more workable. Some rollers are flat. Others are made with grooves to shape the steel.

To understand how the steel is improved, we must know something about the structure of metals. When a metal is melted, its atoms move about freely. After the metal cools and becomes solid again, the atoms line up into clusters called crystals. The crystals in turn form larger groups called grains. Before steel is rolled, its grains may be bunched together. Rolling makes the grains flatter and longer. Thus the steel becomes stronger and better able to stand being pulled, bent, and twisted when it is shaped.

The first rolling takes place in roughing mills, which are also called blooming or slabbing mills. From the roughing mill the steel

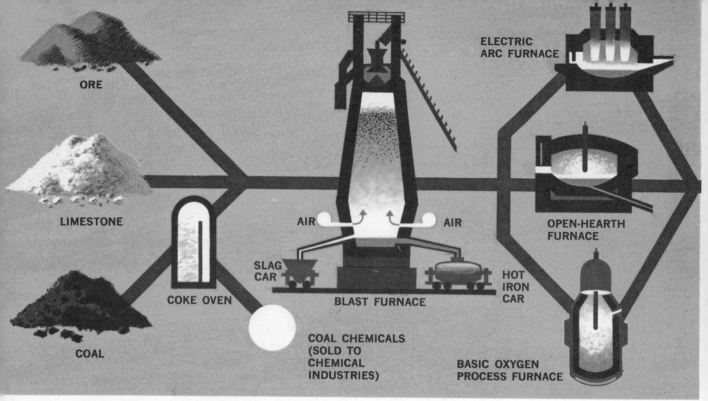

ELECTRIC ARC FURNACE

ORE

LIMESTONE

OPEN-HEARTH FURNACE

COKE OVEN

AIR AIR

SLAG CAR

HOT IRON CAR

BLAST FURNACE

COAL

COAL CHEMICALS (SOLD TO CHEMICAL INDUSTRIES)

BASIC OXYGEN PROCESS FURNACE

Diagram traces the steps in steelmaking from raw materials to finished products.

comes out in the form of blooms, billets, or slabs. Blooms and billets are squared pieces of steel. Slabs are wide, flat, rectangular pieces. All the pieces are about 8 to 12 feet long.

Finishing Mills

Blooms, billets, and slabs go to finishing mills to be rolled into shapes for different products. There are four main types of finishing mills.

Structural and **rail** mills roll the steel that goes into bridges, buildings, heavy machinery, railroad rails, and supporting towers for electric lines.

Modern construction uses many structural steel parts called **shapes**. They are rolled from blooms into several hundred different sizes and shapes for many kinds of building needs. Some of these steel pieces look like the capital letter I, and some are like a capital H. Others resemble T's and Z's. Another important structural shape is the channel, which is shaped like a shallow trough with a flat bottom. All these shapes have special uses in construction work. Millions of tons of structural steel shapes are in service in the frameworks of buildings and bridges. Skyscrapers could not be built without them.

Pipe and **tube** mills turn out steel for such products as furniture, bicycles, aircraft, boilers, and all kinds of pipe for carrying water, oil, and gas.

Plumbing and sewage pipes get little attention because they are usually hidden away from sight. They are very important steel products, however. There are two main types of steel pipe—welded pipe, which has a tight seam along its length, and seamless pipe, which has no seam.

Bar, **rod**, and **wire mills** turn out steel for bolts and nuts, reinforcing rods for concrete, staples, nails, piano strings, and pins and needles.

Bars are among the most widely used steel products. About 600 pounds of steel bars are needed to make an automobile. They are rolled from steel billets into many shapes—square, round, half-round, oval, hexagonal, octagonal, flat, and other special shapes. A modern bar mill can produce up to 85 tons of finished bars per hour. The bars are turned out at the rate of 3,000 feet per minute.

Like other steel products, bars are rolled while they are still hot. Some of them are sold with no further treatment. Others are cooled and polished to improve their surface finish.

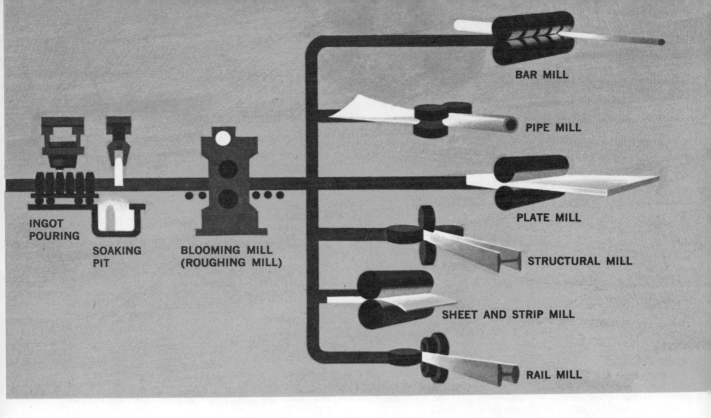

INGOT POURING

SOAKING PIT

BLOOMING MILL (ROUGHING MILL)

BAR MILL

PIPE MILL

PLATE MILL

STRUCTURAL MILL

SHEET AND STRIP MILL

RAIL MILL

This process is called **cold-drawing**. Bars are cold-drawn by being pulled through a shaping tool called a die. The die is slightly smaller in diameter than the bars. When the bar is pulled through the die, it is squeezed down to the size desired. The friction against the smooth walls of the die also polishes the surface of the steel.

Steel wire has more than 150,000 uses. Among the most common wire products are paper clips, coat hangers, fences, staples, nails, and springs. Wire is made by pulling hot-rolled steel rods through a series of dies. To begin with, the rods are sprayed with water to make them rust. The coating of rust helps the rods pass through the dies more easily. The rods are then dipped in lime and dried in ovens. The lime also helps lubricate the rods as they pass through the dies.

The rods are drawn through dies that have smaller and smaller holes. As they are pulled through each die the rods get thinner and longer, until they reach the size desired. The dies must be strong. They have to resist the friction as well as the force from the steel rods being pulled through the small holes. Dies are made of the hardest materials available—alloy steels, tungsten, carbide, or diamonds.

Steel for automobiles, household appliances, farm machinery, ships, tin cans, license plates, and many other products are made in sheet, strip, and plate mills.

Plates are the oldest steel products. They are used where thick, strong pieces of steel are needed. The main uses for plates are in ships, railroad locomotives and cars, oil tanks, water tanks, gas tanks, and floors for bridges and buildings. Plates are also among the most important commercial steel products. They account for 8 to 12 percent of all steel shipments each year.

Plates are rolled from slabs of steel. After rolling, the plates are leveled on another rolling machine, then carefully inspected.

Plates may be anywhere from ¼ inch to over 15 inches thick. Where thinner pieces are needed, sheet and strip steel are used. Sheet and strip steel are usually less than ⅛ inch thick. **Strip** steel is usually no wider than 12 inches. Anything wider is called **sheet** steel in the language of steelmakers.

About a third of all finished steel made in the United States is sheet and strip steel. The steel is used for automobiles, refrigerators, stoves, kitchen cabinets, furniture, and many other products. An automobile top is one wide

Steel is poured into molds to make ingots.

sheet of steel. Automobile body panels and fenders are also made from sheet steel. Strip steel is used for razor blades, garden tools, handsaws, and some automobile parts and home appliances.

Sheet and strip steel are made from heated slabs of steel. They are rolled out into long, thin ribbons of steel, which are coiled for easy handling. Sheet and strip steel are usually rolled in huge mills known as continuous rolling mills. These mills, which were developed during the 1920's, are one of the outstanding technical achievements of the steel industry. The mills work extremely fast. They allow cheap production of steel that is needed by many consumer goods industries.

A **continuous rolling mill** is a series of rolls, one above the other, housed in a building nearly ½ mile long. A slab of hot steel goes through the rolls, becoming thinner and thinner and moving faster all the time. At the end of the mill the steel may be traveling as fast as 3,000 feet a minute. Each bank of rollers is powered by several electric motors. Modern continuous mills are operated by remote control from air-conditioned enclosures high above the mill.

Some of the hot-rolled steel is sold in coils or in sheets. When the customer orders steel of better finish, however, the sheets or strips are cold-rolled.

Cold-rolling is done in mills that are similar to continuous rolling mills. The coils of hot-rolled steel are first cleaned by pickling (bathing) them in a weak acid solution. After being washed, dried, and oiled, the steel is ready for cold-rolling. When it is rolled to the desired thickness and surface finish, the steel is given a heat treatment. This helps to relieve stresses in the steel that were caused by the rolling. A final cold-rolling may be given to polish the surface of the steel. Some modern cold-rolling mills turn out steel at the rate of 7,000 feet per minute. This is faster than the speed limits on many automobile turnpikes!

Coated Steels

Many steels are manufactured with special coatings. Some coatings are put on to protect the steel against corrosion. Some are used to make the finish of the steel more attractive.

Perhaps the most important coated steel is tinplate. It is best known in the so-called tin can, used for packing foods and other products. A tin can is really about 99½ percent steel, with a light coating of tin. The tin protects against corrosion. Food packers in the United States and Canada use approximately 60,000,000,000 (billion) tin cans a year.

Tinplate is usually made by the electrolytic process. A coil of steel is passed through a chemical solution while an electric current passes through a piece of pure tin into the solution. The tin decomposes, and its atoms pass through the solution and are deposited on the steel. Less than ½ pound of tin is needed to coat 100 pounds of steel by this process. However, tin is expensive, so many cans are now coated with other substances.

Galvanized steel is another widely used coated steel. It is steel covered with a thin coating of zinc for protection against rust.

Galvanized steel is used in construction, especially for farm buildings and equipment where moisture is liable to be present. Garbage cans and the frames and underbodies of some automobiles are also made of this steel.

To make galvanized steel, an average of about 1½ ounces of zinc is applied to each square foot of steel. Because so much galvanized steel is used, the steel industry is one of the largest customers for zinc.

Some coatings make it impossible to tell that there is steel underneath the finish. **Porcelain enamel** is one of these coatings. It is being used more and more in construction, because it gives an attractive, corrosion-resistant finish to the exteriors of buildings. Porcelain-enameled steel is best-known, however, in household appliances. It provides attractive, easy-to-clean surfaces for refrigerators, stoves, dishwashers, and sinks. Porcelain-enamel coatings are made by baking the enamel onto the steel at very high temperatures.

One of the newest steels with a special finish is **vinyl-coated steel**. Vinyl plastic is baked onto the steel, giving it a tough protective covering. Unlike most other steels, vinyl-coated steel seems warm to the touch. It is available in many colors and textures. Some of its most common uses are for kitchen cabinets, wastebaskets, filing cabinets, office furniture, and lawn furniture. Like tinplate and galvanized steel, vinyl-coated steel can be shaped without damage to the coating.

Annealing

After steel has been rolled, it tends to become hard and brittle. This makes it unsuited for certain uses or for working the steel into various shapes. To correct this condition, steel is **annealed** after rolling.

Annealing rearranges the internal structure of the steel—that is, it changes the lineup of the metal atoms into new patterns. They stay this way when the steel cools. This relieves internal stresses so that the steel is more ductile and easier to form. Steel is annealed by heating it to a high temperature and then letting it cool slowly.

The heating and cooling may set up other stresses in the steel. To make sure that there are no stresses in the steel after annealing, the steel is tempered, or temper-rolled. This rolling smooths out irregularities in the groups of atoms in the steel, making it stronger and giving it a fine surface finish.

▶ THE RAW MATERIALS OF STEELMAKING

The most important material for steelmaking is iron. Iron does not usually occur in nature as a pure metal. Most of it is found combined with other elements in the form of iron ore.

In the United States the area around Lake Superior, which includes Michigan, Minnesota, and Wisconsin, is the chief source of iron ore. This region at one time supplied about 80 percent of the iron ore used in the United States and Canada. In recent years imports of iron ore from abroad have increased. This has led to a decrease in the Lake Superior production.

Lake Superior ores average about 51 percent iron. These high-grade ores are mostly near the surface of the earth. They can be mined simply by stripping away the covering layer of earth and scooping up the ore. The high-grade deposits have been running low. The past half century saw industrial production at an all-time high. The demands for steel in two world wars have also cut deeply into the ore supply.

The richest sources of iron are iron ores, such as magnetite, hematite, limonite, and siderite. **Magnetite** contains a higher percentage of iron than any of the other iron ores, sometimes as much as 72 percent. It is a black mineral in which 3 parts of iron are combined with 4 parts of oxygen. Sizable deposits of magnetite are found in the Adirondacks region of New York, in New Jersey, and in Pennsylvania. Magnetite is also found in Sweden, Norway, Russia, and Germany.

Hematite is the most common iron material now used as a commercial source of iron. It is a soft, sandy or earthy, red-colored ore. The best grades of hematite contain 70 percent iron. Hematite is found in the Lake Superior region, in Alabama, and in Newfoundland.

Limonite often occurs in combination with hematite. It is brown or yellow in color and is used for yellow ocher, the coloring ingredient in paints. Limonite is found in Alabama, Tennessee, England, and France.

Siderite is usually white or gray in color. It is found in Canada on the northern shore of Lake Superior, and in Spain, England, Wales, and Germany.

Mining the Ore

There are two main ways to mine iron ore—by open-pit mining and shaft mining. The open-pit method is used when the ore deposits are close to the surface of the earth. Power shovels dig away the covering earth, scoop out the ore, and load it into trucks or railroad cars. Most of the ore mined in open pits is high-grade ore. It usually contains about 52 percent iron.

The shaft method of mining is used when the ore is buried deep in the ground. Miners dig shafts and tunnels into the earth and bring up the ore. When the ore has been mined, it is inspected for impurities and graded according to its quality. High-grade ore is sent directly to the blast furnaces. Low-grade ore is processed to remove impurities.

Transporting the Ore

Most iron ore is loaded into railroad cars and hauled to docks, where specially designed ships pick it up. The ships take the ore to ports, where it is transferred into trucks or railroad cars. Unloading the ships is done quickly by enormous power scoops that dig out 20 tons of ore at a time. Unless it needs to be processed, the ore goes directly to blast furnaces to be smelted into pig iron.

Processing Low-Grade Ore

With the supply of high-grade iron ore running low, steelmakers have had to find other sources of iron. Some ores with low iron content can be processed to remove impurities and raise the percentage of iron in the ore. One of the most important low-grade ores processed in this way is **taconite**. This is a hard rock found in abundance in the Lake Superior region. In its natural state taconite contains only a little over 30 percent iron.

Large chunks of the rock are blasted out of the earth. Taconite rock is so hard that it wears out steel drills. Holes for explosive charges are burned into the rock with flame jets. The chunks of blasted taconite are taken to mills and ground up. Magnets are used to draw out the iron-bearing minerals from the ground-up rock. The waste rock is thrown away, and the powdered ore is dried and formed into pellets that contain about 60 percent iron. The pellets are then sent off to the blast furnace.

Processing taconite is this way is expensive, but as more steel is needed, more iron also has to be available. Taconite offers one of the best sources of low-grade iron ore.

Coke

Coke is the most important fuel used in ironmaking. It is a grayish-black substance that gives off intense heat when burned. Coke is composed mostly of carbon. It is made by heating bituminous coal in closed containers called coke ovens. Air is kept out of the ovens so that the coal does not burn but decomposes chemically instead. The coal gives off gases and tars that are collected and drawn off. What is then left of the coal is coke. The chemicals in the gases and tars are also valuable products. Fertilizers, dyes, plastics, explosives, drugs, and medicines are made from them.

Limestone

Limestone is used in blast furnaces and in steelmaking furnaces to help remove impurities. It acts as a cleaner—steelmen call it a flux—because it soaks up unwanted sulfur and phosphorus.

Limestone is one of the most common rocks. It is found in many parts of the world. It is composed mostly of the shells and skeletons of prehistoric sea organisms that lived in oceans once covering the land.

▶ IRON IN USE

Iron is one of the oldest metals known to man. It is believed that the ancient Egyptians

Ingots are lifted from the soaking pit by a giant crane.

were using iron about 6,000 years ago, following the Copper and Bronze Ages. Iron is still widely used by itself, although most iron produced nowadays goes into steel. The most important types of iron used now are cast iron and wrought iron.

Cast iron is an alloy of iron and carbon. It is produced by melting pig iron together with scrap iron. This mixture is then poured, or cast, into molds. The most common form of this iron, called gray cast iron, is brittle and lacks toughness and tensile strength—that is, it cannot stand heavy loads that tend to pull or bend it. Cast iron cannot be shaped by hammering or rolling, for it will break. If gray cast iron is given a heat treatment, however, it is made more malleable. This means that the iron can be more easily formed into shapes. Cast iron is most frequently used in automobile engine blocks and in cast-iron pipe.

Wrought iron is very low in carbon. It is made by heating cast iron in a refining furnace. The impurities in the cast iron combine with oxygen and pass off as gas or form a slag that is drawn off. Some of the impurities, however, remain in the iron. They give the iron a fiberlike internal structure. This iron is very easy to work. It can be formed into many shapes, is easy to weld, and has good resistance to corrosion. Wrought iron is most often used for making furniture, decorative ironwork, and pipes that have to be corrosion-resistant.

▶ **IRON AND STEEL IN HISTORY**

Iron has served men for thousands of years. This tough metal has always been identified with strength. The famous Duke of Wellington was called the "Iron Duke." Sailors used to speak of "wooden ships and iron men."

Steel, too, has been known almost since the beginnings of recorded history. When the troops of Alexander the Great marched into India in the 4th century B.C., they found steel in use. Steel went into the blades of the famed swords of Damascus and Toledo. Clock springs and other precision-made articles were made of steel. But all of this steel was made slowly and in small quantities, a few pounds at a time. Iron remained the backbone of the growing technology of the Western world until only a little over a century ago.

Iron was so important that as early as 1646 America's first successful ironworks was established at Saugus, Massachusetts. This ironworks, which has been rebuilt as a historical museum, is regarded as the real birthplace of America's steel industry.

At first, the little Colonial iron furnaces used mostly bog iron. This is a spongy type of iron ore that was deposited in swamps by the action of bacteria. Charcoal for the furnaces came from the forests that covered the countryside. Southern New Jersey was a leader in bog-iron production.

Iron kept its dominant place for 200 or more years after the Saugus works was founded. With the advance of the Industrial Revolution, iron formed the rails for newly invented railroad trains. It was also used to armor the sides of fighting ships. About the mid-19th century the new age of steel began with the invention of the Bessemer process (1856). The Bessemer process opened the way to the new age. It made steel available in large quantities at reasonable cost.

Abundant, cheap steel replaced iron for the railroads that spread across the nation. Steel was also used in barbed wire to fence in the Western plains, in tools and machinery for agriculture, in equipment for oil fields and chemical industries, and as the basic material for the tools and equipment of the country's mass production industries.

About the time the Bessemer process was proving itself, Bernard Lauth (1820–94), an Alsatian-born foreman in an American steel mill, developed a method for cold-rolling steel bars. The method was later adapted for cold-rolling sheet steel also, making possible the sweeping lines of modern automobiles and appliances. In 1865 the first steel rail was rolled. In only 4 years steel rails were being used to span the continent. During the following years the railroads crisscrossed America, finally extending to nearly 250,000 miles.

The first open-hearth furnace was used in Europe shortly after 1864. The first one in the United States was built in 1868. By 1908 the production of steel by open-hearth furnaces was greater than the output by the Bessemer process.

The first continuous rod mill was built in Worcester, Massachusetts, in 1869. The mill supplied long strands of wire for telegraph and telephone lines and for the cables that support suspension bridges. Nails made from steel wire were soon available at low cost to builders.

By 1879 the United States was turning out over 1,000,000 tons of steel a year. Within another decade the country achieved the position it still holds as the largest producer of steel in the world.

In 1885 the first steel beams were rolled. Two years later such beams were used in the construction of a Chicago office building, the forerunner of modern skyscrapers.

Seamless steel pipe was first produced in 1895, in Pennsylvania. Through the years this pipe has filled countless needs. One of its important uses is to pierce deep into the earth to draw out the oil that is so vital to the world's industry.

The electric furnace, the key to making fine alloy steels, appeared in 1906. The steels made by the electric furnace helped to build the machine tool industry. The machinery made by this industry made possible the mass production of many new products.

The steel industry took another big step forward in 1923 with the development of the continuous hot-strip mill. This mill made it possible to roll a steel slab quickly into strips or sheets of steel. The rapid, low-cost production of steel sheets and strips paved the way for the growth of the automobile industry and other consumer-goods industries. The later 1920's also saw the first commercial production of special-purpose steels that were stainless, rustless, and corrosion-resistant.

In the mid-1930's electrolytic tin-plating of sheet steel was developed. A few years later the process was improved so that a thin, uniform coating of tin could be applied to steel more quickly and easily. In the late 1950's this method was improved even more by the discovery of a way to reduce the amount of tin needed to cover the steel "tin can."

Since World War II the steel industry has made almost incredible advances. In the early 1950's continuous galvanizing was developed to produce galvanized steel with more even coatings of zinc. Mills to produce other types of coated steels also came into operation. In the late 1950's the basic oxygen process for steelmaking began to be widely used. Improvements of methods already used were also being made. Mills operated faster and with greater precision. At the beginning of the 1960's electronic computers started to take over the operation of many routine tasks, performing them with greater speed and accu-

Mighty rollers shape the red-hot steel into I-beams and other structural shapes.

racy. The steelworker was freed for jobs that required human judgment.

The steel industry is continually looking for new and better ways to make steel. One revolutionary technique that is now growing rapidly in importance is **strand casting**, or **continuous casting**. In this process molten steel is poured into a tall, open-bottom mold that cools the steel so rapidly it can be removed in one continuous piece, or strand. This does away with several complicated steps of steelmaking: pouring steel into ingot molds, heating the ingots in soaking pits, and passing them through a rolling mill to make blooms, slabs, and billets. Strands as long as 2 miles have been cast. The strand is cut into short lengths for processing.

Another process that holds promise is **direct reduction** of iron ore. In this process iron ore and coke are fed directly into a furnace that refines the ore into iron pellets. The pellets are so pure that they can be used directly in steelmaking furnaces.

The development of large, high-powered electric furnaces and of the strand-casting ma-

chine has resulted in the growth of a new type of steel mill, the mini-mill. The typical mini-mill is a small mill that makes steel by melting scrap in electric furnaces and pouring it into strand-casting machines. By this arrangement, the tremendous cost of blast furnaces, coke ovens, soaking pits, and large rolling mills is avoided.

The Importance of the Steel Industry

Steel is truly one of the basic industries. Besides the products it makes and helps other industries to make, the steel industry is an important customer for products and services of other industries. The steel industry of the United States, for example, buys about $6,000,000,000 worth of materials and services each year. It also invests more than $1,000,000,000 each year in new steel mills, in new machinery, and in improving the plants and equipment it already has.

Suppliers to the steel industry number in the tens of thousands. More than 90 percent of the suppliers are small companies. Just look at a shopping list for the steel industry. It needs about 5,400 pounds of raw materials, such as coal, iron ore, and limestone, for each ton of steel it produces. Huge amounts of materials such as chromium, nickel, and manganese are needed for alloy steels. Each year approximately 135,000,000 tons of steel ingots are turned out. Besides raw materials, the industry must purchase huge amounts of bricks, fuel oil, electric power, and machinery.

The steel industry is one of the largest employers in the world. Steel companies in the United States employ more than 500,000 men and women just in steelmaking activities. This means that more than 2,000,000 people receive their income directly from the steel industry. The wages, salaries, and benefits paid to steel industry employees amount to about $5,000,000,000 a year in the United States. It has been estimated that throughout the world, between 2,000,000 and 3,000,000 people work in steel industries.

Because the steel industry is such a large customer for products and services, it helps to create jobs in other industries. In the United States nearly 3,000,000 workers in other industries are employed to help fill steel's needs, or use steel in making other products.

A few of the industries that use more than 1,000,000 tons of steel a year are construction, railroads, automobile manufacturing, agriculture, oil and gas, household appliances, electrical equipment, and machinery and tool manufacturing. Rifles, artillery, trucks, tanks, airplanes, rockets, missiles, and many other military items are also made of steel.

It is easy to see why an enormous supply of steel must be available. Modern civilization as we know it could not exist without steel, the most useful and versatile of all metals.

W. C. BENZER
Metallurgical Engineer
American Iron and Steel Institute

See also ALLOYS; INDUSTRY; INVENTIONS; METALS AND METALLURGY; MINES AND MINING.

IROQUOIS INDIANS. See INDIANS OF NORTH AMERICA.

IRRIGATION

Irrigation is the artificial application of water to land in order to increase the growth and production of plants.

The principal countries practicing irrigation are China, India, the United States, the Soviet Union, and Pakistan. It is estimated that the total irrigated land in the world is about 400,000,000 acres. China leads all other countries, but the exact acreage receiving water is not known. In the United States about 37,000,000 acres are irrigated. About 90 percent of this irrigated acreage is in the 17 western states. The Bureau of Reclamation provides much of the irrigation.

Natural Irrigation

In ancient times irrigation was a natural process. The annual flooding of the Nile River spread a thin layer of silt (mud) across the land. At the same time the land received enough water so that crops could be grown. In ancient Sumeria and Mesopotamia the Tigris and Euphrates rivers rose in the highlands of Asia Minor. Meltwater from the mountain snows flooded the plains of these two great rivers. Irrigation developed in India and China in the same way. Each year the Indus, Ganges, and Hwang rivers overflowed and irrigated the lowlands.

Where irrigation was a natural process, the people sometimes built canals, reservoirs, and drainage ditches. Floodwaters could then be directed where needed or stored for future use. This was the earliest form of man-made irrigation.

Irrigation in Arid Lands

About one third of the world's land area is arid or semiarid. These dry areas are made up of deserts and steppe lands.

Deserts and semiarid lands cover large areas of the world. They are located on every continent. Because water is scarce in these places, only a small part of the land can be irrigated. With increased irrigation, more of the great steppe lands may someday be used for grazing or dry-land farming. Drought-resistant crops, such as millet, grain sorghum, barley, and wheat, may be grown there.

As the population of the world increases more dry lands must be made to grow food. In the United States and the Soviet Union thou-

Modern sprinklers are a most efficient method of irrigation. A self-propelled system waters a stand of alfalfa in the state of Washington.

sands of acres that have long been too dry for farming are now being irrigated. As new water resources are developed more dry land will be used for growing food.

Irrigation in Humid Lands

Irrigation is not restricted to the dry, or arid, areas in the world. Even where the rainfall is relatively heavy (60 inches or more each year) irrigation is necessary. This is true in the densely populated areas of India, East Pakistan, Burma, Southeast Asia, Indonesia, the Philippines, China, and Japan. Irrigation is necessary to raise rice, the principal food of most of the people. Rice fields must be covered with water at all times, until the rice crop is ready to harvest.

Types of Irrigation

In order to supply enough water for irrigation, costly dams and reservoirs are needed. Irrigation water may be so expensive that only good land can be irrigated profitably. Only such crops as vegetables and fruits can produce enough income to cover the costs.

In Egypt and in a few desert areas all of the water needs must be met by irrigation. **Supplemental irrigation** has become common in many areas of Europe and the eastern United States. In such places there is some rainfall, but not enough falls at the right time. By using aluminum and plastic pipes and sprinklers,

Rice is grown on terraces in Java. Water flows from one terrace to another to irrigate the fields.

water can be carried to places where it is needed most. The use of supplemental irrigation may save a valuable crop from serious damage by drought.

The kind of irrigation depends on the type of crops grown. Occasional flooding may be enough for hay, pasture, and the small grains. Furrow distribution (spreading water in ditches between rows) may be required for such crops as sugar beets and vegetables. In some cases underground pipes with overflow standpipes are used.

Problems of Irrigation

The irrigation of dry lands is often difficult and expensive. Fortunately much of the soil in arid and semiarid regions is naturally fertile. It needs only water to make it productive. But the land may need grading and leveling to permit the proper distribution of irrigation water. The soils must be friable (easily crumbled) so that water will soak through to the root zone. But the soil and underlying materials must not be so porous that the water is lost below the root zone.

Irrigation systems are costly and require continual upkeep. Reservoirs may fill up with mud and silt. The surrounding land (watershed) must be well covered with trees or grass to prevent soil erosion. If too much water is used for irrigation, the reserves are reduced, and fresh or sweet water is wasted. If too little water is used, the soil may become filled with alkaline salts and require over-irrigation to restore the land to productive use.

In spite of the many difficulties in developing and maintaining irrigation systems, more cropland will have to be brought under cultivation to meet the food requirements of a growing population. Supplemental irrigation is more and more important. Sprinkler irrigation has also been increasing where enough capital is available. The return from crops will justify the expansion of irrigation.

GUY-HAROLD SMITH
Ohio State University

IRVING, WASHINGTON (1783–1859)

One day in April, 1789, an elderly Scottish nurse and a small boy followed George Washington into a shop on New York's Broad Way. "Please, your Honor, here's a bairn that's named after ye!" said the nurse. Washington, just inaugurated as America's first president, placed his hand on the boy's head and blessed him. Scottish Lizzie was delighted. "Now he'll amount to something!" she is said to have declared.

Washington Irving did amount to something. He was the first American writer to achieve lasting popularity among Europeans. He was the first, too, to write a complete biography of the man for whom he was named, George Washington.

Washington Irving was born on April 3, 1783, in New York City. The American Revolution had just ended, and the new baby was named for its hero. Washington was the 11th child in the Irving family. His father was a merchant and a deacon in the Presbyterian Church—a pious and strict man.

Washington started school at the age of 4. He never took school seriously, however, even when he was older. He would rather read travel and adventure books and explore the town than study. He was good at writing, though, and he loved the theater. He used to steal out of the house in the evening to attend performances, returning home for family prayers and sneaking off again.

He did not wish to go to college, so he became an apprentice in a law office. Quite a handsome man-about-town, he went to the theater often and wrote about it and about New York society for his brother Peter's paper, the *Morning Chronicle*. He signed himself Jonathan Oldstyle. Visits to his married sisters in upper New York State, an excursion into the wilderness of Canada, and a trip to Europe in 1804 helped satisfy his urge to travel.

In 1806 Washington passed the bar examination, admitting him to the practice of law. Soon after, he joined his brother William and his friend Jim Paulding to begin a humor magazine called *Salmagundi*. It was received enthusiastically and lasted over a year. In 1809 Washington published *Diedrich Knick-*

erbocker's History of New York from the Beginning of the World to the End of the Dutch Dynasty, the first great book of comic literature written by an American. Its success made Irving well-known abroad. When he next went to Europe, Sir Walter Scott welcomed him at Abbotsford in Scotland. People everywhere were eager to meet Irving. From 1815 to 1832 he lived in England, Dresden, Paris, and Spain. During 1819 and 1820, while he was living in England, he published *The Sketch Book of Geoffrey Crayon, Gent.,* a collection of essays and stories. "Rip Van Winkle" and "The Legend of Sleepy Hollow" were among the stories. They were based on old German legends.

Irving joined the American embassy in Madrid to translate a Spanish life of Columbus. Instead he wrote his own, published in 1828. Part of his next book, *The Conquest of Granada* (1829), was written in Seville. He lived in the Alhambra Palace while working on *The Alhambra* (1832), but finished the book in London when he was appointed secretary of the London legation.

Irving resigned his London post and returned to America in 1832. He traveled down the Ohio and Mississippi rivers and through parts of the Midwest. *A Tour on the Prairies* (1835) describes his trip. Then he settled down at Sunnyside, near Tarrytown, New York, and began work on his long-planned life of Washington. He planned to write a history of the conquest of Mexico, too, but in 1838 he decided to leave that task to William H. Prescott. One or two of his nieces always lived with him at Sunnyside, for he had never married. A girl he had loved deeply, Matilda Hoffman, had died in 1809. He may have proposed to a woman much younger than he, Emily Foster, whom he had met in Dresden, but this is not known definitely.

In 1842 Irving accepted the post of United States minister to Spain. His understanding of the country and his reputation there enabled him to carry out many difficult diplomatic missions. But in 1845 he resigned. He still wished to finish the book about Washington. The work, in five volumes, was published between 1855 and 1857. On November 28, 1859, Washington Irving died.

Reviewed by REGINALD L. COOK
Middlebury College

▶ RIP VAN WINKLE

The following passage is taken from Irving's tale about Rip Van Winkle. Rip had been squirrel shooting in the Kaatskill Mountains.

As he was about to descend, he heard a voice from a distance, hallooing, "Rip Van Winkle! Rip Van Winkle!" He looked round, but could see nothing but a crow winging its solitary flight across the mountain. He thought his fancy must have deceived him, and turned again to descend, when he heard the same cry ring through the still evening air: "Rip Van Winkle! Rip Van Winkle!"—at the same time; Wolf bristled up his back, and giving a low growl, skulked to his master's side, looking fearfully down into the glen. Rip now felt a vague apprehension stealing over him; he looked anxiously in the same direction, and perceived a strange figure slowly toiling up the rocks, and bending under the weight of something he carried on his back. He was surprised to see any human being in this lonely and unfrequented place; but supposing it to be some one of the neighborhood in need of his assistance, he hastened down to yield it.

On nearer approach he was still more surprised at the singularity of the stranger's appearance. He was a short, square-built old fellow, with thick bushy hair, and a grizzled beard. His dress was of the antique Dutch fashion: a cloth jerkin strapped round the waist, several pair of breeches, the outer one of ample volume, decorated with rows of buttons down the sides, and bunches at the knees. He bore on his shoulder a stout keg, that seemed full of liquor, and made signs for Rip to approach and assist him with the load. Though rather shy and distrustful of this new acquaintance, Rip complied with his usual alacrity; and mutually relieving one another, they clambered up a narrow gully, apparently the dry bed of a mountain torrent. As they ascended, Rip every now and then heard long rolling peals like distant thunder, that seemed to issue out of a deep ravine, or rather cleft, between lofty rocks, toward which their rugged path conducted. He paused for a moment, but supposing it to be the muttering of one of those transient thunder-showers which often take place in mountain heights, he proceeded. Passing through the ravine, they came to a hollow, like a small amphitheatre, surrounded by perpendicular precipices, over the brinks of which impending trees shot their branches, so that you only caught glimpses of the azure sky and the bright evening cloud. During the whole time Rip and his companion had labored on in silence; for though the former marvelled greatly what could be the object of carrying a keg of

liquor up this wild mountain, yet there was something strange and incomprehensible about the unknown, that inspired awe and checked familiarity.

On entering the amphitheatre, new objects of wonder presented themselves. On a level spot in the centre was a company of odd-looking personages playing at ninepins. They were dressed in a quaint outlandish fashion; some wore short doublets, others jerkins, with long knives in their belts, and most of them had enormous breeches of similar style with that of the guide's. Their visages, too, were peculiar; one had a large beard, broad face, and small piggish eyes, the face of another seemed to consist entirely of nose, and was surmounted by a white sugar-loaf hat, set off with a little red cock's tail. They all had beards, of various shapes and colors. There was one who seemed to be the commander. He was a stout old gentleman, with a weather-beaten countenance; he wore a laced doublet, broad belt and hanger, high-crowned hat and feather, red stockings, and high-heeled shoes, with roses in them. The whole group reminded Rip of the figures in an old Flemish painting in the parlor of Dominie Van Shaick, the village parson, which had been brought over from Holland at the time of the settlement.

What seemed particularly odd to Rip was, that though these folks were evidently amusing themselves, yet they maintained the gravest faces, the most mysterious silence, and were, withal, the most melancholy party of pleasure he had ever witnessed. Nothing interrupted the stillness of the scene but the noise of the balls, which, whenever they were rolled, echoed along the mountains like rumbling peals of thunder.

As Rip and his companion approached them, they suddenly desisted from their play, and stared at him with such fixed, statue-like gaze, and such strange, uncouth, lack-lustre countenances, that his heart turned within him, and his knees smote together. His companion now emptied the contents of the keg into large flagons, and made signs to him to wait upon the company. He obeyed with fear and trembling; they quaffed the liquor in profound silence, and then returned to their game.

ISAAC

Isaac, son of Abraham, was the second of the patriarchs, or fathers, of the Jewish people. Isaac was born to Abraham and Sarah in their old age, when they had almost given up hope of having a son. In Hebrew the name Isaac (Yitzhak) means "he laughs" or "laughter."

The wonderful faith of Abraham and the great loyalty of Isaac were shown when God commanded Abraham to offer Isaac up as a sacrifice. Abraham tied Isaac to the altar and was about to place the knife to his throat when God's angel stopped him.

Shortly after Sarah died, Abraham sent his faithful servant Eliezer back to Ur, the land of Abraham's kindred in the north Arabian desert, to find a proper wife for Isaac. (This was an ancient custom.) Eliezer decided to choose the first young woman who would offer water to him and his thirsty camels. This was the test of kindness. He discovered Rebekah at the well in this way. He made arrangements with her father and brother and brought her back to Canaan, home of Abraham and Isaac. Soon afterward, Isaac and Rebekah were married.

Isaac and Rebekah had twin sons, Esau and Jacob. From birth they were different. Esau, the firstborn, grew up to be "a cunning hunter, a man of the field." Jacob was "a plain man, dwelling in tents." Isaac seemed to prefer Esau; Rebekah loved Jacob.

Esau, in a moment of hunger, sold his birthright to Jacob for a pot of lentils. The birthright brought honor as head of the family and a double share of the inheritance. Afterward Esau regretted his deed. When Jacob, with Rebekah's help, tricked Isaac into giving Jacob a blessing intended for Esau, Esau threatened to kill Jacob. Jacob, at Isaac's command, fled to Padanaram, his mother's former home, where he lived many years.

The Bible says Isaac "died, and was gathered unto his people, being old and full of days: and his sons Esau and Jacob buried him."

MORTIMER J. COHEN
Author, *Pathways Through the Bible*

ISABELLA. See FERDINAND AND ISABELLA.

ISAIAH

Isaiah was a prophet who lived in the southern kingdom of Judah in the 8th century B.C. He has been called the prophet-statesman. He was a great preacher who explained to the people what God wanted of them. He was also a fine poet. His work is in the Book of Isaiah in the Old Testament.

Isaiah was a native of Jerusalem, and he was sad to see the evil that he believed would bring the city to ruin. Isaiah may have been a member of the royal family, for he had great influence with the leaders of his country.

He was married to a woman whom he called the prophetess. They had two sons. He gave them strange names that expressed his beliefs about his country. One son's name was Mahershalalhashbaz, which in English means "Speed-booty-hasten-prey." By this name Isaiah threatened Judah that unless the country became more honest and just, it would soon become the prey of its terrible enemy, Assyria. His other son's name was Shearjashub, which means "A remnant shall return." It expressed Isaiah's belief that no matter what disaster might overtake Judah, its good part, though a mere remnant, or small piece, would survive. In this way Isaiah dramatically told his people that they must correct their evil ways or else be punished by God. At the same time he said that God would have mercy and not destroy them completely.

Isaiah lived during terrible times of war and the destruction of the northern kingdom of Israel. In that war-torn world he uttered an immortal call for peace:

He [God] shall judge between the nations,
And shall decide for many peoples;
And they shall beat their swords into plowshares,
And their spears into pruning hooks;
Nation shall not lift up sword against nation,
Neither shall they learn war any more.

Isaiah lived past the age of 60. We do not know the date or manner of his death. One belief is that he was put to death in a very cruel way in the reign of King Manasseh.

MORTIMER J. COHEN
Author, *Pathways Through the Bible*

ISLAM

Islam is the religion of over 465,000,000 people (the Arabic word "Islam" means "commitment, or dedication, to God"). It is very closely related to Judaism and Christianity. The followers of Islam try to live according to the rules for life set down by God and by the Arab prophet Mohammed. For this reason some people have called them Mohammedans. But they prefer to be called Muslims (sometimes spelled Moslems), which means "people who give themselves to God." This is because they worship only God, not Mohammed. Besides, they say that there were many Muslims before Mohammed, so they should not be named after him.

▶ HOW ISLAM BEGAN

Abraham is mentioned in the Old Testament as a man who gave himself to God and as the father of a people who believe in God. He had two sons, Ishmael and Isaac. Through Isaac, Abraham became the ancestor of the Hebrew people, and through Ishmael he became the ancestor of the Arabs.

Some Jews and Arabs tried to worship God and follow His laws, but others worshiped idols. Men called prophets were sent to warn them and tell them what God wanted. Yet when a prophet died, people forgot what he had said or twisted its meaning. Muslims believe that Jesus Christ was merely one of these prophets. They do not believe that he was God's son, and this is one reason they are not Christians.

Finally, Muslims say, God decided to send down a message whose meaning could not be twisted. It would tell men what they needed to know in order to be happy in this world and in the next. He chose a man named Mohammed, from the town of Mecca in Arabia, to be His prophet. He also sent the angel Gabriel to reveal the message, which later was written down verse by verse and chapter by chapter in a book called the **Koran**, or "recitation."

Mohammed's tribe did not like the message of the Koran. They were afraid it would make too many changes in their lives. At last Mohammed, with the people who believed in the Koran, had to leave Mecca. They moved in A.D. 622 to the oasis city of Medina, where they had friends. This "Year of the Emigra-tion," or **Hegira** (from the Arabic word *hijrah*), is the first year of the Muslim calendar. In Medina, Mohammed tried unsuccessfully to be accepted by the Jews.

▶ THE GROWTH OF ISLAM

The Muslims prospered in Medina, and many people joined them. The Meccans (the people of Mecca) sent armies to fight them, but the Muslims won every war. Finally, the Meccans became Muslims too.

Now, the tribes of Arabia had always fought each other. Mohammed could not stop this. But he did forbid his people to fight other Muslim tribes, because all Muslims were to be brothers. You can see what this meant for other tribes: if they wanted peace, they could have it by following Mohammed.

By the time he died, in 632, Mohammed was the ruler of almost all of Arabia. His friend abu-Bakr became the new leader of the Muslims and followed the same policies. In a short time Muslims had conquered Syria and Palestine, Iraq, Iran, and Egypt. A little later they conquered North Africa, Spain, and part of present-day Pakistan.

Many of the people in these countries were Christians and Jews. If they wanted to join Islam, the Muslims welcomed them as brothers. If they did not, they were allowed to follow their own religion as long as they promised to accept the Muslims as their rulers.

Of course, some people did not want to accept the Muslims as overlords, and so there were wars between Christians and Muslims. Charlemagne fought against the Muslims in Spain in the 8th century. Later, during the 11th, 12th, and 13th centuries, there were the Crusades. The Crusades were attempts by armies of Christians to win back the Holy Land—Palestine—from the Muslims. Despite these wars there were times when Christians and Muslims were able to live in peace and friendship. In the Middle Ages, Muslims had a great civilization, and Europe learned many useful things from Muslim doctors and teachers.

People of many races in many countries came to follow the religion of Mohammed. Muslim missionaries carried Islam to Indonesia and the Philippine Islands and deep into Africa. Muslim armies conquered India,

Turkey, and southern Europe, and many people in these countries joined Islam.

▶ MUSLIM LAW

Muslims try to live according to God's book, the Koran, and by the rules Mohammed taught them. Their wise men have made all this into laws, called the **Sharia**, or "God's Way."

Every Muslim should pray five times a day: at dawn, noon, afternoon, evening, and night. He prays facing Mecca. He is expected to give some of his money every year to help poor Muslims. Once in his lifetime, if he can, he must go to the holy city of Mecca on a pilgrimage. Once a year, if he is well, he fasts. For one whole month, from very early morning until the sun goes down, he does not eat or drink anything. This is very hard to do, but at night he is allowed to eat what he needs.

Most especially, he must never, never worship anything or anyone but God. He should not eat pork, drink wine or alcohol, or taste blood. He must not fight, except for Islam. He must not gamble. He must help orphans and be kind to strangers. He must never be mean or stingy, and he should treat other Muslims as his brothers.

He must respect women. For this reason girls and women used to be kept in the house, where they would be safe. When they went out, they wore veils to cover their faces. Today some wear the veil and some do not. So that every woman would have someone to take care of her, Mohammed allowed men to

The small stone building in the center of the courtyard of the Great Mosque in Mecca is the Kaaba. The Kaaba was built to enclose the Black Stone, which is Islam's most holy object. Muslims believe that the Black Stone was given to Abraham by God.

Muslims in Nigeria face toward Mecca while praying.

Muslims in prayer in a mosque at Rabat, Morocco.

Minarets appear at either side of this Pakistani mosque.

marry as many as four wives. Of course, not many wanted more than one wife, but if they did, they could marry more. However, they had to treat them equally.

On Friday at noon, Muslims go to the **mosque** (a Muslim temple) to pray. After praying, they hear a sermon. There is no priest or minister, only a leader who is called the **Imam**. The mosque is built so that when the people pray, they will face toward Mecca, and there is a pulpit for the preacher. There are no bells, but there is a tower called the **minaret**, from which five times a day a man (the **muezzin**) calls the people to pray, thus:

> God is greatest! God is greatest!
> I testify that there is no god but God!
> I testify that Mohammed is God's messenger!
> Come to prayer! Come to salvation!
> God is greatest! There is no god but God!

Before they pray, the people wash themselves. God is the greatest king of all, and no one should stand before Him with a dirty face. Some of the mosques are beautiful buildings with domes and fine decorations. But there are no pictures of any living thing in them. This is so the faithful will think only of God, the Muslims say.

▶ ISLAM TODAY

Today not all Muslims belong to the same sect, or group. There are different groups, just as there are among Christians. However, all of them agree on the basic ideas of the Muslim religion discussed here, and follow them. Some Muslim branches have sent missionaries to North America, and other Muslim people have gone there to live. Mosques are found in several large North American cities.

Because Arabic is the language of the Koran, Muslim prayers are usually in Arabic, just as Catholics have used Greek or Latin and Jews use Hebrew. Arab Muslims speak Arabic, but the Muslims of other lands speak the languages of these lands.

Muslim civilization stood still or went downhill in the 17th and 18th centuries, while Europe and America went forward rapidly. In the end, most of the Muslim countries were conquered by European countries. Because Muslims had been a great people, they naturally felt bitter about this.

Today most Muslim countries have won back their political independence. They are trying to build a new kind of life—one which will combine the best of the past and the best of the present. Of course this is not easy. But it is an exciting time for Muslims to be alive. The best of it is that there are completely new opportunities for Muslims and other peoples to live together in friendship.

JOHN A. WILLIAMS
McGill University

See also KORAN; MOHAMMED.

ISLAMIC ART AND ARCHITECTURE

Islam is the religious faith preached by the Arab prophet Mohammed (A.D. 570?–632). During the 500 years after his death, the followers of Mohammed—the Muslims—successfully invaded Persia, Turkey, India, Spain, and all of North Africa. Most of the defeated people accepted the religion of the conquerors. Believers were required to make at least one trip in their lifetime to Mecca, the holy Arabian city where Mohammed was born.

As they traveled Muslims saw the art and customs of neighboring lands. They were greatly influenced by the art of the powerful Byzantine (Eastern Christian) Empire. Gradually the Muslims developed a distinctive style, which included features of the art of the conquered lands and the places on the route to Mecca.

Islamic art was greatly affected by two religious restrictions. Mohammed himself disapproved of painting or carving pictures of people. He warned artists not to imitate God (Allah) by creating images of people. Religious art, therefore, consisted of ornamental designs. The second restriction affected the use of expensive materials. The artist learned to skillfully decorate objects of clay or wood until they looked as beautiful as gold and silver.

The tomb-mosque of Sultan Hasan, in Cairo (14th century).

▶ ARABESQUES

Because of these religious restrictions, **arabesque**—Arabian ornamentation—is the outstanding feature of Islamic art. An arabesque is a very complicated design. It can be geometric, with star shapes and straight-line patterns. It can be filled with circles and curving lines and ribbons that twist and turn and tie knots over each other. It can take the shape of vines, leaves, and flowers. An arabesque often combines many kinds of patterns. Sometimes the designs are made into the shape of an animal whose tail is made of leaves and whose back is covered with ribbons and bows instead of feathers or fur.

In addition to these forms, Arabic letters were part of Islamic ornament. The letters can be beautifully written in several kinds of script. **Kufic** is straight and geometric:

Naskhi is rounded, and many letters are joined together, as in English handwriting:

Nastaliq is slanted and delicate:

When looking at Islamic books, remember that the script is read from right to left. This is the opposite of the way English is read.

Beautiful writing (**calligraphy**) was considered the highest form of art by Muslims. They decorated the Koran, their holy book, with arabesques and calligraphy.

The Muslims greatly respected the knowledge contained in books, especially the Koran. They made book covers with a front and a

Above left: Persian ceramic tile in star shape (13th century). Metropolitan Museum of Art, New York. Above: Glass mosaic from the Dome of the Rock, Jerusalem (late 7th century). Left: A page from the Koran of Arghun Shah (14th century) of Egypt. National Library, Cairo. Below: Illustration from a 14th-century book called *Kalilah and Dimnah*. National Library, Paris.

The Mosque of the Sabers in Kairouan, Tunisia.

back and an added flap to cover and protect the page edges. These bindings were made of beautifully tooled leather, often with gold and bright colors added. The Koran of Arghun Shah (1368–88) is a good example of the lavish and intricate designs so typical of later Islamic **illumination** (manuscript decoration in colors and gold).

▶ MOSQUES

The first mosques were simple buildings made of palm trees and clay. Then in A.D. 661, 29 years after Mohammed's death, the city of Damascus in Syria became the capital of the Islamic world. To rival the splendor of Christian churches, the Muslims began to build large mosques of cut stone and brick.

Because they had no tradition of architecture, the Muslims began by copying the buildings of other civilizations. The oldest existing mosque, the Dome of the Rock in Jerusalem (A.D. 691), is partly modeled after a Christian church.

A new Muslim plan was used for the Great Mosque in Damascus (707–15). The mosque is entered through a rectangular court with covered arcades on three sides. In the court is a fountain for washing before prayer. The mosque (prayer room) itself is on the fourth side of the court. It is covered by gabled (triangular) roofs supported by columns that form three aisles. All Muslims face in the direction of Mecca when they pray. This direction is shown by a prayer niche in the end wall. Over the aisle leading to this niche is a dome. A tower, or **minaret,** is used to call the faithful to prayer. The mosque at Kairouan, Tunisia, has domes over each end of the aisle leading to the prayer niche. They are **squinch domes**, a special type favored in the Near East. A squinch is a beam or arch across the corner of a square opening that makes a base for a round dome. Often many layers of squinches are used in Muslim domes. These layers create decorative forms that look like honeycombs, scales, or stalactites (iciclelike shapes). Many domes have melon-shaped ridges on the outside.

In Persia a different type of mosque developed. It had four great halls around a central court. The main hall acted as the entrance to the court, and another led to the prayer area. These large rooms could be used for lecture halls, and schools were soon combined with mosques.

In some cases the mausoleum (tomb) of a ruler was combined with the mosque and school that he had built. The tomb-mosque of

Interior of the Great Mosque at Kairouan, Tunisia (8th century).

Sultan Hasan (1356–62) in Cairo, Egypt, is such a combination. It is laid out like a cross with four halls opening off a large square court.

Around 1400 the Tatar warrior Timur the Lame (also called Tamerlane) built a tomb-mosque in Samarkand. This building has a melon-shaped dome covered with brilliant blue and gold tiles. The tiles were made of glazed earthenware—pottery covered with a thin layer of glass. They were cut into various sizes and shapes and arranged in elaborate patterns like a jigsaw puzzle. The delicate Taj Mahal in Agra, India, was built (1630–53) by the ruler Shah Jahan as a tomb for his wife. The building is so famous that its very name calls up images of almost unreal splendor and beauty.

In the 16th and 17th centuries mosques became more complex with many domes and minarets. The Sultan Ahmed (Blue) Mosque in Istanbul, Turkey—sometimes called the City of Mosques—is a typical example.

Decoration of Mosques

Muslim artists got ideas from the decoration of Christian churches. They decorated their earliest mosques with **mosaics**—pictures made by pressing tiny bits of colored glass into wet cement. In the Dome of the Rock in Jerusalem classical Greek forms of the acanthus plant and Persian wing motifs are covered with jewels. The acanthus plants appear to grow through crowns, representing religious and royal power. Above the brilliant mosaics is an inscription in gold Arabic letters on a blue background. In the Great Mosque in Damascus there are glass mosaics showing houses and pavilions set in a landscape. They are similar in design to ancient Roman wall paintings.

Later mosques were decorated with arabesque designs like those used for the Koran. The area around the prayer niche was usually decorated in a special way with glass mosaics, carved stucco, or tiles. The borders of this decoration were inscribed with quotations from the Koran.

The pulpit sometimes was decorated, and often oriental rugs covered the mosque floors, since the worshiper removes his shoes at the door. Glass lamps that hung by long chains from the ceiling were decorated with arabesques and Arabic letters.

▶ PALACES

The early Muslim rulers—caliphs—were used to desert life; they did not like living in crowded cities. They built palaces in the desert where they could go to relax and hunt. The palaces looked like Roman fortresses, for they were built of stone and surrounded by walls with big towers. The throne rooms, prayer rooms, baths, and living quarters were decorated with murals and mosaics.

In the 8th century the capital of the Muslim world moved from Damascus, Syria, to Baghdad, Mesopotamia (now Iraq). The architecture of palaces changed. Domed palaces were built of brick covered with thick layers of stucco, and the interiors were decorated with stucco reliefs. In the Jawsaq Palace (A.D. 847–61) of Samarra, Mesopotamia, the stucco ornament was of three distinct styles. One type showed deeply carved vine forms, and another added patterns to the surface of the main design. The third style used more abstract patterns, as in the metalwork of Central Asian nomads. The combination of these three styles created a new style—the arabesque, typical of Muslim art all over the world.

Of later palaces, the Alhambra at Granada, Spain, built in the 14th century, is the best-known. Its many rooms are built around three open courts. The Court of the Myrtles features a long rectangular pool flanked by hedges. In the center of the inner Court of the Lions there is a fountain made of 12 lions. The lower part of the palace walls are decorated with colored tiles set in geometric patterns. Painted and gilded plaster designs cover the upper part of the walls. Arabic inscriptions in the midst of the ornament say that there is "no conqueror but Allah." The ceilings are sometimes made of painted beams and sometimes of multiple squinches.

▶ PAINTINGS AND MOSAICS

Some Islamic caliphs and princes ignored the religious restrictions when they decorated their palaces. While sculpture remained abstract with arabesques, there were many paintings and mosaics of figures. Good examples are the **frescoes**—paintings on wet plaster—of Qusayr Amra, an 8th-century palace in Jordan. The frescoes include hunting scenes, scientific diagrams of the stars, and illustrations of myths—stories of the gods. Some figures are shaded to make them appear three-dimensional. Others are flat and decorative and look like figures in Byzantine paintings.

The 9th-century Jawsaq Palace was decorated with paintings of dancing girls, hunting scenes, and other royal pastimes. Except for those on pottery, no more paintings of people are known until the early 13th century. Then the best examples were to be found in illustrated books.

Book illustrations were completely different from the earlier frescoes. Illustrators were greatly influenced by storytellers and puppet shows. The figures in the illustration were simple and often had the jointed stiffness of puppets. They were usually painted without shadows to look flat or two-dimensional. These qualities may be seen in a book of fables called *Kalilah and Dimnah,* after the two jackals who are the main characters.

A little later more realism of detail and surroundings is found in the illustrations in the *Maqamat of al-Hariri.* A **maqamat** is a collection of amusing stories. The *Maqamat of al-Hariri* is about a rogue who finally reforms. The artist, Yahya al-Wasiti, was a keen observer of life.

By the end of the 13th century, parts of the Islamic world, including Persia, had been overrun by the Mongols from the East. From this time on the influence of Chinese ink paintings, especially landscapes, can be seen in Islamic painting. The last of the great invaders from Central Asia was Timur the Lame (1336?–1405). He and his followers liked paintings of people. They ignored the leaders of their new religion. With the encouragement of the Timurid princes, painting flourished in Islamic countries as it never had before. Paintings of people, however, were still found mostly in nonreligious books.

The most famous Islamic painter was Bihzad. He illustrated scenes from Persian poetry and life. He combined the ornamental style of Persian illustration with direct observations of people and animals.

The Court of the Myrtles in the Alhambra, a palace built in the 14th century at Granada, Spain.

By the 16th century, painting had become very delicate, yet bold. The action-filled illustrations of early books were replaced by quiet, moody scenes. Yet most Islamic illustration remained essentially ornamental, uniting many elements into an intricate pattern.

▶ DECORATIVE OBJECTS

Bowls, pitchers, and lamps were decorated with arabesques of geometric and plant forms. Often when animal forms were used, patterns of holes were made in the object. The use of these holes was perhaps a way of avoiding religious disapproval.

In the 11th century a new class of wealthy merchants arose in the cities throughout the Islamic world. They traded ceramics—objects made of baked clay—leather goods, metalwork, and textiles as far as India and China in the east and Europe in the west. These merchants were not interested in royal power or entertainment. Their exclusive concern with the events of their own lives led to a new kind of art. Scenes of everyday and popular stories were realistically portrayed on all kinds of objects. These decorations later influenced the pictures in illustrated books.

Metalwork

Scenes with figures as well as arabesques were skillfully adapted to each particular object. The most delicate drawings were transformed into designs in any material. Gold, silver, and bronze were sometimes used, despite earlier restrictions. Artisans were able to do this intricate work because they had been trained in their craft since childhood. The quality of products was also determined by laws and inspections of work and materials. A fine example of the artisan's skill is a 12th-century inlaid bronze cauldron. The decoration is made of inlaid copper and silver in five bands—two with pictures of warriors and hunters and three with Arabic writing. The letters often end in bodies or heads of people or animals.

Ceramics

By the 9th century, Islamic potters had developed many different kinds of pottery. One of the most outstanding is their **lusterware**—pottery covered with shining metallic glaze. Luster glaze also covered the tiles and pottery mosaics used in decorating prayer niches and the outside of domes and minarets.

Rugs

Rugs were made for use in the mosques and the home. The design on prayer rugs, unrolled by the believer wherever he was, copied the arch of the prayer niche in the mosque. Nonreligious rugs were decorated with geometric patterns. Designs imitated gardens filled with arabesques of flowers and plants. Animal and hunting scenes were added to floral patterns. Chinese dragons were often placed next to Persian lions and gazelles. The carpets were made by knotting single strands of wool. Fine woolen carpets have over 100 knots to the square inch; and silk rugs sometimes have 800. The quality of these rugs is another example of the extraordinary skill of the Muslim craftsman.

▶ ISLAMIC ART AFTER THE CRUSADES

During the Middle Ages, Christians and Muslims fought wars known as the Crusades. The nations of Islam were united in religion and in their common wars against the Christian Europeans. Islamic art was also unified. From Spain to India, the art of the countries of Islam was almost identical.

By the 15th century there was less to unify the Islamic world. Many people in Islamic nations belonged to other religions. The Crusades were over, and Muslim countries sometimes fought against each other.

Artistic activity in the Islamic style has not stopped since the 16th century. Mosques are still being built; objects of metal, clay, and leather are still ornamented with arabesques; books are illuminated with miniatures; and rugs are still woven in the traditional way. However, as the Western world ascended to power, some artists in Persia, Turkey, Egypt, and other Islamic countries began to study in Europe and follow European styles, especially those of Italy and France. The present art in Islamic countries has an international character, although the scenes or subjects may relate to a single Islamic nation.

GULNAR K. BOSCH
Florida State University

See also DECORATIVE ARTS; ILLUMINATED MANUSCRIPTS; ORIENTAL ART AND ARCHITECTURE; SPAIN (Spanish Art and Architecture); TAPESTRY.

Amsterdam Island's volcanic crater is filled with seawater. The island, a French scientific research base in the Indian Ocean, has 35 inhabitants.

ISLANDS

An island is any body of land that is entirely surrounded by water. Islands range in size from tiny coral atolls to huge islands like Greenland (840,000 square miles). Australia is even larger than Greenland. But most geographers call Australia a continent rather than an island.

Continental Islands

Continental (or offshore) islands are close to a continent and were probably once connected to the mainland. Changes in the earth's crust may have forced the seabed to rise, forming offshore islands. Or a rise in sea level may have cut off a piece of land and formed an island. Some continental islands are really the tops of submerged mountain ranges.

Continental islands have the same geologic origin and structure as the nearby mainland. The bedrock is similar. Plants and animals are like those on the mainland. The British Isles are continental islands because they were once part of the European mainland.

Oceanic Islands

Most of the world's islands are oceanic. Oceanic islands were never connected to a continent. They are often located thousands of miles from the mainland. Oceanic islands can be classified as volcanic and coral islands.

Volcanic islands rose from the bottom of the sea by volcanic action. Lava eruptions formed volcanic cones that reached above sea level—often thousands of feet high. The Hawaiian Islands are the result of volcanic eruptions that began 3 miles below the surface of the ocean.

Coral islands are found in shallow tropical waters. They are the work of tiny sea animals called coral polyps. Many islands in the South Pacific are coral islands. How coral islands, reefs, and atolls are built is described in the article CORALS in Volume C.

Other Islands

Mont St. Michel, in France, is an example of a **tidal island**. It is really part of the mainland, but it becomes an island during high tide. **Floating islands** are found in rivers (such as the Nile) or along certain coasts (such as Southeast Asia's). They consist of thickly matted vegetation often mixed with soil.

Deposits of sediment (fine dirt mixed with other materials that are carried by water) sometimes connect offshore islands to the nearby land. Former islands then become peninsulas, or bodies of land almost surrounded by water. This has occurred in the Adriatic Sea along the coasts of Italy and Yugoslavia.

The Importance of Islands

Islands differ not only in size and in origin but also in importance and in the life found on

Above: Bahia Hona Bridge on Key West is part of the highway that links the Florida Keys (coral islands) with the Florida mainland. Left: Scientists investigate a glacier on Ellesmere Island, Canada. Below: Sea lions sun themselves on Santa Fe Island in Ecuador's Galápagos Islands.

them. An island may have economic or military significance or its history may be unusual. Some islands, like Java and Hong Kong, are heavily populated. Others, like most Arctic and Antarctic islands and the thousands of tiny coral atolls, have little or no human habitation.

Animal Life. Animals and birds were sometimes isolated on islands far from any mainland. Unusual animals and birds often developed there in ways not seen elsewhere. For example, the island continent of Australia is the home of marsupials (pouched animals), like the kangaroo. The koala is native only to Australia. The emu and the cassowary of Australia are large birds that have no power to fly. Giant lizards and tortoises inhabit the Galápagos Islands. Komodo lizards exist only on a few islands in Indonesia.

Powerful National States. In a few cases, islands have become powerful states and centers of empires. Great Britain was for many years the heart of a great empire. During World War I almost one fourth of the world's land area was under the rule of the British Empire. Japan, a country made up of four major islands, became a powerful empire after World War I. Though Japan lost much of its empire following World War II, it is today once more a busy, prosperous nation.

Islands Having International Political Significance. Throughout history certain islands, because of location off the shores of a political rival, have been the cause of international concern. Examples are Helgoland near Germany, the Channel Islands near France, Quemoy and the Pescadores near China, and Cuba near the United States.

Naval Bases and Refueling Stations. Islands have often served as bases for naval forces and as fuel and storage stations. Ships stop to refuel and pick up supplies at Malta and Cyprus in the Mediterranean Sea; at Mauritius in the Indian Ocean; and at Guam, Wake, and Unalaska in the Pacific Ocean. Most of these islands are also stops on air routes.

Centers of Commerce and Mining. Some islands are commercially important for ocean shipping. Ceylon, Java, Oahu, Zanzibar, and Madagascar are among the islands that are important centers of commerce.

Other islands are noted for their valuable minerals. Both Nauru and Ocean Island have large phosphate deposits. Petroleum has been found on Bahrain. New Caledonia is rich in minerals, especially nickel. Coal is mined on Cape Breton.

Island Cities. Large cities sometimes developed on islands. Venice, Hong Kong, and Singapore have locations that offered protection and security. The city of Paris grew up around the Île de la Cité, a fortified island in the Seine River.

Islands as Isolation Centers. Islands have often been used to isolate criminals or other persons considered dangerous to society. In times of widespread epidemics sick people have been quarantined on islands to protect the rest of the population. Devils Island and Fernando de Noronha have been used to harbor the sick or the criminally dangerous.

Islands as Tourist Centers. Many islands and island groups have become famous tourist centers. Capri, Majorca, Minorca, Bermuda, the West Indies, Bali, Tahiti, and Oahu are among the islands that attract visitors.

ANTHONY SAS
Madison College (Virginia)

▶ISLANDS AND ISLAND GROUPS

Admiralty Islands (Australia). This island group, part of the Bismarck Archipelago, is located in the southwest Pacific Ocean, 250 miles west of New Ireland. The islands are administered by Australia as a part of the Trust Territory of New Guinea. Manus is the major island in the group. A United States naval base important during World War II was located at Seeadler Harbour on Manus from 1944 to 1948. Copra (dried coconut meat) is the island's major product. Area, about 800 sq. mi.; pop., about 23,000.

Aland Islands (Finland). More than 6,000 islands make up this group, located between Finland and Sweden. The population is Swedish in origin. The people engage in agriculture, fishing, and cattle raising. These islands have strategic importance because control of them means control of the entrance to the Gulf of Bothnia and the Gulf of Finland. The Russians obtained control over the islands in 1809. After World War I Sweden and Finland

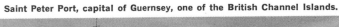
Saint Peter Port, capital of Guernsey, one of the British Channel Islands.

Above: Manhattan and Governors Island are part of New York City. Below: San Giorgio Maggiore, one of the islands on which the Italian city of Venice is built.

claimed the group, but the League of Nations awarded the islands to Finland in 1921. Fortification is prohibited by international agreement. Area, about 570 sq. mi.; pop., about 22,000.

Aleutian Islands (U.S.A.). This group of some 150 volcanic islands extends for about 1,200 miles southwest from the Alaska Peninsula, between the North Pacific and the Bering Sea. The islands were discovered by the explorers Vitus Bering and Aleksei Chirikov in 1741 and were once known as the Cather-ine Archipelago. In 1867 the United States bought the islands, along with Alaska, from Russia. There are four main groups: the Fox Islands, the Andreanof Islands, the Rat Islands, and the Near Islands. Unimak, one of the Fox Islands, is the largest of the Aleutians. The volcano Shishaldin (almost 10,000 feet) stands on Unimak. The Aleuts, who are related to the Eskimo, inhabit the islands. The climate is cool, wet, and foggy. Fishing and fur trading are the main occupations. During World War II the Aleutian Islands were invaded by the Japanese. Since the war the United States has set up permanent military bases on the islands. They are an important part of the air route to the Far East. Pop., about 8,000.

Alexander Archipelago (U.S.A.). This is a large group of about 1,100 mountainous islands off the southeastern coast of Alaska. These islands are heavily forested. The climate is mild, and rainfall heavy. The Danish navigator Vitus Bering and the Russian navigator Aleksei Chirikov discovered the islands in 1741. Sitka and Ketchikan are the most important communities.

Andaman Islands (India). This group, consisting of five large and many small islands, is located in the Bay of Bengal, southwest of Cape Negrais (Burma). The large islands are mountainous, with a heavy cover of tropical hardwood forests. From 1857 to 1945 the islands were used as a penal colony. Many displaced families, mostly from East Pakistan, have settled on the islands since 1953. The people are mainly engaged in agriculture, raising tea, copra, coffee, rubber, and rice. Lumber is exported. Area, about 2,500 sq. mi.; pop., about 55,000.

Anticosti Island (Canada) is an island located at the entrance to the St. Lawrence River. It is part of the province of Quebec. Most of the people make their living by lumbering. The island was discovered by Jacques Cartier in 1534. Area, about 3,100 sq. mi.; pop., about 550.

Antilles. This is a group of islands in the West Indies, bordering the Caribbean Sea. See CARIBBEAN SEA AND ISLANDS.

Ascension Island (Britain), a small island of volcanic origin, lies in the South Atlantic, some 700 miles northwest of St. Helena. It was discovered by the Portuguese in 1501. Britain gained possession in 1815. Ascension is a breeding ground for turtles. The island serves as a link in the underwater cable system that runs between England and South America. Area, about 34 sq. mi.; pop., about 1,300.

Azores (Portugal). The nine islands of this group are located 800 miles west of Portugal. The islands are of volcanic origin and are subject to earthquakes. The climate is mild. The main occupation is agriculture, and the islands produce such products as wine, pineapples,

oranges, and bananas. There is some cattle raising and fishing. On Santa Maria island there is an important refueling base for transoceanic air flights. In 1431 the Portuguese navigator Gonzalo Cabral claimed the islands for Portugal, and they have remained Portuguese ever since. During World War II the British used the islands as a naval base. The name of the group is derived from the Portuguese word *açôre,* which means "hawk." Area, about 890 sq. mi.; pop., about 320,000.

Baffin Island (Canada). This cold, rocky island is part of Canada's Northwest Territories. It is located in the Arctic Ocean and is the fifth largest island in the world. Though the island is large, the population is small. The people live along the coast in eight isolated settlements. Most of the inhabitants are Eskimo. Their main activities are hunting, whaling, and trapping. Baffin Island was first visited by the Englishman Martin Frobisher in 1576 in his search for the Northwest Passage. The island was named by the English navigator William Baffin, who explored parts of the island in 1616. Since then there have been many scientific explorations and experiments on the island. Area, about 190,000 sq. mi.; pop., about 2,500.

Balearic Islands (Spain). This group of four main islands and several lesser ones is located east of Spain. Most of the people live on the islands of Majorca (Mallorca) and Minorca (Menorca). These islands, whose history goes back thousands of years, were conquered many times and by many nations. They were ruled by the Phoenicians, Carthaginians, Romans, Vandals, and Moors. Today they form a province of Spain. The islands are mountainous but have a mild climate. Citrus fruits, olives, almonds, and wine are the leading products. Tourists visit the islands in increasing numbers. The island of Iviza is especially popular with artists. Area, about 1,940 sq. mi.; pop., about 440,000.

Borneo is the third largest island in the world. See BORNEO.

British Isles. See UNITED KINGDOM; IRELAND.

Canary Islands (Spain). This group contains seven major islands and is located some 70 miles off the northwestern coast of Africa. The islands are volcanic and subject to earthquakes. The climate is mild, and the soil fertile. The vegetation is abundant and the agricultural products are bananas, sugarcane, potatoes, citrus fruit, and tobacco. The economy is based on agriculture, fishing, cattle raising, tourism, and shipping. Las Palmas, on Grand Canary, is the largest city. The island of Tenerife contains the highest peak in the Canaries (12,200 feet) as well as the city of Santa Cruz. Grand Canary and Tenerife are both popular island resorts. The canary bird was first discovered in this region. Area, about 2,900 sq. mi.; pop., about 1,000,000.

Cape Breton Island (Canada) is part of the province of Nova Scotia. It has long, cold winters and warm summers. Storms and fog are frequent. The island became a French possession in 1712 but was conquered by England in 1758. Until 1820 it was a separate province, but in that year it was united with Nova Scotia. Cape Breton Island contains valuable coal and gypsum deposits. Fishing is important. The largest city is Sydney, which has a thriving steel industry. Area, about 4,000 sq. mi.; pop., about 170,000. Cape Breton Island is discussed in the article NOVA SCOTIA.

Cape Verde Islands (Portugal). This group of 10 large islands and five smaller ones lies off the African coast, west of Senegal. These volcanic islands are mountainous and the climate is tropical. They became a Portuguese possession in 1456. There was much intermarriage between the Africans and the Portuguese, and their descendants make up most of the population. The language, too, is a mixture of Portuguese and African tongues. The people raise a limited amount of coffee, fruit, corn, and beans. Fishing is the only other important industry. Area, about 1,560 sq. mi.; pop., about 250,000.

Capri (Italy) is located at the southeastern entrance to the Bay of Naples, in the Tyrrhenian Sea. The island has long been famous as a tourist resort and a producer of grapes, olives, figs, and lemons. It has a mild climate and many scenic attractions. The Blue Grotto, near the town of Anacapri, and the ruins of palaces built during the reigns of the Roman emperors Augustus and Tiberius attract many visitors. Area, about 4 sq. mi.; pop., about 11,000.

Caribbean Islands. See CARIBBEAN SEA AND ISLANDS.

Caroline Islands (U.S.A.). This is a group of about 963 small islands, part of the United States Trust Territory in the western Pacific. See PACIFIC OCEAN AND ISLANDS.

Channel Islands (Britain). This group consists of nine islands located just off the Normandy coast of France. The climate is mild, and the soil is fertile. Three of the islands—Guernsey, Jersey, Alderney—have become famous for their fine breeds of cattle. The early Romans explored these islands. In 1066 they became part of Britain under William the Conqueror. They have remained part of Britain ever since. However, the islands are self-governing and not bound by British laws unless the laws definitely name the islands. The islands were the only part of Great Britain to be occupied by German forces between 1940 and 1945. Area, about 75 sq. mi.; pop., about 117,000.

Comoro Islands (France). This group of four large islands and numerous small ones lies at the northern entrance to the Mozambique Channel. The islands are mountainous, of partly volcanic origin, and have a tropical climate. The people are mainly farmers and raise coffee, cacao, sisal, sugarcane, and rice. The islands have local independence and are represented in the French Assembly. Area, about 840 sq. mi.; pop., about 270,000.

Cook Islands (New Zealand). In 1901 these South Pacific islands were declared a part of New Zealand. They have internal self-government. See PACIFIC OCEAN AND ISLANDS.

Corfu, or Kerkyra, (Greece) is a mountainous island located west of Greece in the Ionian Sea. The climate is mild, with moist winters and dry summers. The island produces citrus fruits, olives, and wine. Tourism is an important source of income. The island was first colonized in 734 B.C. by Corinthians. Later it was plundered by Spartans and by Illyrian pirates. In 229 B.C. it came under Roman protection. Area, about 230 sq. mi.; pop., about 100,000.

Corsica (France) is located south of the Gulf of Genoa and north of the island of Sardinia. The climate is pleasant, with warm, dry summers and mild, rainy winters. Agriculture is the major occupation. The people raise citrus fruits, olives, grapes, and mulberries. Sheep and goats graze in the interior. The forests yield pine, oak, and cork. Fishing is carried on along the coast. Mining products include marble, asbestos, antimony, silver, and copper. The tourist industry is growing in importance. Corsica's history dates back to about 560 B.C., when Phoenicians settled there. Since then it has been conquered or ruled by Etruscans, Carthaginians, Romans, and Vandals; and by the Papal States, Genoa, France, and Britain. In 1796 Napoleon, who was born there in the town of Ajaccio, sent an expedition to establish permanent French control. Area, about 3,367 sq. mi.; pop., about 270,000.

Crete (Greece) is a mountainous island located in the Mediterranean Sea, about 60 miles southeast of Greece. The climate is mild, with warm, dry summers and rainy winters. Agriculture is the chief industry. Products include wine, olives, citrus fruits, and almonds. The people raise sheep and goats. Fishing and some mining (gypsum, copper, iron, limestone) are other important industries. Several ancient civilizations flourished on Crete. One of the greatest was the Minoan civilization, which lasted from about 3300 B.C. to about 1400 B.C. Great engineering works and architectural structures were built during this era, and many ancient relics have been discovered by archeologists. Since the days of the Minoans the island has been subject to many invaders: Romans, Byzantines, Venetians, and Turks. Greece obtained the island after the Balkan Wars (1912–1913). German paratroops invaded Crete in 1941 and occupied it until 1944. Area, about 3,240 sq. mi.; pop., about 485,000.

Cuba is an island republic in the West Indies. See CUBA.

Cyclades (Greece). This group of about 220 islands is located southeast of Greece, in the Aegean Sea. The name is derived from the Greek *kyklos* ("circle"), for the islands form a ring around the island of Delos. According to legend, Delos was raised from the sea by Poseidon and anchored there by Zeus. The climate is mild, with warm winters and hot dry summers. Area, about 1,000 sq. mi.; pop., about 130,000.

Cyprus is the third largest Mediterranean Island. See CYPRUS.

Dodecanese (Greece). This group consists of 14 large and several small islands, despite the fact that the Greek word *dodekanesos*

means "12 islands." They are located off the southwestern coast of Turkey, in the Aegean Sea. At different times in history these islands belonged to the Greeks, Romans, Venetians, and Turks. From 1912 to 1947 they belonged to Italy, despite treaties that had awarded them to Greece. The latter country finally gained control over the group in 1948. The climate is mild, but only two islands—Rhodes and Kos—have much fertile soil. Most of the population is engaged in agriculture (citrus fruits, cereals, grapes, tobacco, olives). Sponge fishing is important. Sheep and goats are raised. Area, about 1,030 sq. mi.; pop., about 120,000.

Easter Island (Chile). This small volcanic island in the South Pacific is inhabited mostly by Polynesians. People lived on this island before recorded history. Yet very little is known about them. The present-day inhabitants are unable to understand the prehistoric picture writing found there on wooden tablets. Neither do they know the origin of the island's many stone statues. Easter Island has a warm climate and fertile soil. The people raise tropical fruit, sugarcane, tobacco, and potatoes. There is also much fishing. The island was named on Easter Sunday, 1722, by the Dutch explorer Jakob Roggeveen. Spain claimed it in 1770, and it became a dependency of Chile in 1888. The island is now considered part of Chile's Valparaiso province. Area, about 50 sq. mi.; pop., about 1,000.

Elba (Italy) is located 7 miles off the western coast of Italy. The climate is mild, and agriculture is an important source of income, with such products as wines, mulberries, and olives. Iron ore has been mined there since ancient times, and there are important marble quarries. Elba was the first place of exile for Napoleon I, who arrived there on May 4, 1814, but escaped on February 26, 1815. Area, 86 sq. mi.; pop., about 30,000.

Ellesmere Island (Canada). This rugged, glaciated island is the largest and most easterly of the Queen Elizabeth Islands. It is part of the Arctic Archipelago of Canada's Northwest Territories. Cape Columbia on the northern coast of Ellesmere Island is within 7° of the North Pole and represents the northernmost point of North America. Although the remains of Eskimo settlements have been found on the east coast, there are today no permanent settlements on Ellesmere Island. Two weather stations are maintained, at Alert and on Eureka Sound. Royal Canadian Mounted Police posts have been located at Craig Harbor, Kane Basin, and Bache Peninsula, all on the east coast. The island was first explored by Sir E. A. Inglefield in 1852. He named his discovery in honor of the first Earl of Ellesmere.

Falkland Islands (Britain). The two large and numerous small islands of this group are located east of the Strait of Magellan, in the South Atlantic Ocean. Cold winds blow across the bleak, hilly moorlands. The inhabitants are mainly of British descent. They make their living raising sheep for wool, the chief export. British rule was established in 1833. The islands are claimed by Argentina, which calls them Islas Malvinas. Area, about 4,600 sq. mi.; pop., about 2,200.

Faroe Islands (Denmark). This group of 21 volcanic islands is located in the North Atlantic, between Iceland and the Shetland Islands. The islands are hilly, with stony soils. Some of them are uninhabited. Summers are cool and humid, with overcast skies. Winters are mild because of westerly winds and the Gulf Stream. Agriculture is limited, but horse and sheep raising are important activities. Other industries are fishing (cod, herring) and the gathering of eiderdown (from eider ducks). From the late 800's until 1380 Norway ruled the islands. Since then, with a few short interruptions, the group has belonged to Denmark. In 1948 the islands were granted self-government within the Danish commonwealth. Area, about 540 sq. mi.; pop., about 38,000.

Fiji. This island group is an independent state located in the southwestern Pacific Ocean. See FIJI.

Galápagos Islands (Ecuador). This is a group of islands in the Pacific Ocean, 650 miles west of Ecuador. See ECUADOR.

Gilbert and Ellice Islands (Britain). These islands are located in the central Pacific. See PACIFIC OCEAN AND ISLANDS.

Greenland is the world's largest island. It is located in the North Atlantic Ocean and is part of the Canadian Shield. See GREENLAND.

Hawaii is the 50th state of the United States. See HAWAII.

Hebrides (Britain). This group of more than 500 rocky and mountainous islands is located off the western coast of Scotland. The climate is rainy but mild, because of the Gulf Stream. The people speak Gaelic, as well as English. About 100 of the islands are inhabited. The people earn a living from farming (barley, oats), fishing, and gathering eiderdown. Tourism is important in the summer. The islands were invaded by Norsemen in the 800's, and Scandinavian influence is seen in the names of people and places. Area, about 3,000 sq. mi.; pop., about 80,000.

Helgoland (West Germany) is a tiny island (about one fourth of a square mile) strategically located in the German Bight. After having belonged to Denmark and Britain, it became a German possession in 1890. The island was heavily fortified by the Germans, but after World War I Germany was forced to destroy all coastal batteries and the naval port. Helgoland again became a German strongpoint during World War II, but the Allies destroyed the fortifications in 1947. At present the island is a leading resort area in the North Sea. Area, about ¼ sq. mi.; pop., about 1,500.

Hispaniola, located east of Cuba and west of Puerto Rico, is shared by Haiti and the Dominican Republic. See DOMINICAN REPUBLIC; HAITI.

Hong Kong island, the major island of the British colony Hong Kong, lies off the southern coast of China. See HONG KONG.

Indonesia is an island republic of Southeast Asia. See INDONESIA.

Ionian Islands (Greece). This group of seven large and many small islands is located in the Ionian Sea, west of Greece. The largest islands are Corfu (Kerkyra), Leukas, Zante, and Cephalonia. At different times in their history, the Ionian Islands belonged to the Romans, Sicilians, Normans, and Venetians; and to Naples, France, and Britain. They became part of Greece in 1864. The islands are mountainous. Winters are mild and moist, and summers warm and very dry. Citrus fruits, grapes, and olives are leading products. Shipping, trade, and fishing are also important in the economy. Area, about 900 sq. mi.; pop., about 250,000.

Above: Village on Akutan Island in the Aleutians off Alaska. Right: Santa Maria Island in Portugal's Azores. Below: Majorca in Spain's Balearic Islands is a popular tourist resort.

Above: Mykonos, one of the Greek Cyclades Islands. Below: Tourists arrive at the Italian island of Capri in the Bay of Naples.

Prehistoric stone heads on Chile's Easter Island in the South Pacific.

Corfu, a Greek island in the Ionian Sea.

Above: Norwegian fishing village in Lofoten Islands. Below: Porto da Cruz in Portugal's Madeira Islands.

Japan. Located in the Pacific Ocean, off the eastern coast of Asia, this island country is made up of four large islands and many smaller ones. The four main islands are Honshu, Kyushu, Shikoko, and Hokkaido. See JAPAN.

Java (Indonesia), the most heavily populated island of Indonesia, is located between Sumatra and Bali. See INDONESIA.

Kurile Islands (U.S.S.R.). This island group is located in the Pacific Ocean north of Japan. The islands contain 16 active volcanoes. The population is now mostly Russian. The original Ainu population died out while the islands were still under Japanese rule. Economic activities are based on the sea, and include fishing, whaling, sealing, and production of iodine. The Kuriles formally came under Japanese sovereignty in 1875 in agreement with Russia. After World War II the Soviet Union took over the islands. Japan claims the islands closest to Hokkaido.

Lofoten Islands (Norway). This group of six large and several smaller islands is located northwest of Norway. The islands are mountainous, and the coastline rugged. Farming is possible only in a few fertile valleys. The major industry is fishing (cod, herring). The Maelstrom, a strait famous for its whirlpool, is located here. During World War II, when the group was under German occupation, British Commando units made two daring raids on the islands. Area, about 500 sq. mi.; pop., about 60,000.

Madeira (Portugal). This group of mountainous islands consists of two large inhabited islands (Madeira Island and Porto Santo) and a number of small uninhabited ones. They are located off the northwestern coast of Africa. Madeira has a mild, subtropical climate, with winter rain. The fertile volcanic soil produces a variety of crops. Madeira is famous for its wine and embroidery. Tourism is an important source of income. The major city is Funchal, which has air and sea communications with South America, Africa, and Europe. The group has belonged to Portugal since 1418 but has been occupied by the British for short periods in its history to prevent the French from taking the islands. Area, about 305 sq. mi.; pop., about 270,000.

Maldives is an independent country southwest of Ceylon. See MALDIVES.

Magdalen Islands (Canada) lie southeast of Quebec in the Gulf of St. Lawrence. The group consists of nine major islands and several islets. Most of the islanders are of French origin. Their main occupations are fishing and sealing. Jacques Cartier discovered the islands in 1534. They became the property of Sir Isaac Coffin (1759–1839) in 1787 and were purchased by the Magdalen Island Company in 1903. Area, about 102 sq. mi.; pop., about 12,500.

Man, Isle of (Britain). This island is located in the Irish Sea. It is a popular summer resort. The island has many rocky coastal inlets and rolling highlands, and a low mountain range covers the center of the island. The climate is mild. Agriculture (oats, fruits, flowers, vegetables), sheep raising, fishing, and catering to tourists are the main occupations. The tailless, short-haired Manx cat is found on the island. Annual motorcycle and automobile races are held there. Britain acquired the island in 1765. It has home rule, with a governor appointed by the British crown. Area, about 220 sq. mi.; pop., about 50,000.

Marianas Islands (U.S.A.) are a group of islands located in the western Pacific. See PACIFIC OCEAN AND ISLANDS.

Marquesas Islands (France). This group of islands is located in the southeastern Pacific. See PACIFIC OCEAN AND ISLANDS.

Marshall Islands (U.S.A.) are a group of 34 coral atolls in the Pacific. See PACIFIC OCEAN AND ISLANDS.

Mauritius, located in the Indian Ocean, is a self-governing member of the Commonwealth. See MAURITIUS.

Melos, or Milo, (Greece) is a small mountainous island of the Cyclades group. It lies between Greece and Crete in the Aegean Sea. It is known for its obsidian, a volcanic glass used for making cutting tools, and for its archeological discoveries. A famous statue of Venus and antique jewelry were unearthed there in the 19th century. The island was settled by Dorians and Phoenicians. The Athenians captured it in 416 B.C., massacring or enslaving the population. Agriculture, mining, and fishing are important industries. Area, about 60 sq. mi.; pop., about 10,000.

Nauru, the smallest independent country in the world, is located in the central Pacific. See NAURU.

New Caledonia (France). This island is located in the southwest Pacific. See PACIFIC OCEAN AND ISLANDS.

Newfoundland is an island lying off the eastern coast of Canada. The province of Newfoundland comprises this island and the mainland area of Labrador. See NEWFOUNDLAND.

New Guinea is the second largest island of the world. It is located at the eastern end of the Indonesian archipelago, just north of Australia. See NEW GUINEA.

New Hebrides (France and Britain). This group of islands, administered by Britain and France as a condominium (joint control by two or more powers over a dependent territory), is in the southwest Pacific.

New Zealand, located in the South Pacific, is a self-governing member of the Commonwealth. See NEW ZEALAND.

Nicobar Islands (India). This group of 19 islands is located in the Bay of Bengal, to the south of the Andaman group. Only seven of the islands are inhabited. The population consists mainly of people of Malay origin, who make their living by fishing and trading in timber and copra. The climate and vegetation are tropical, and the islands are surrounded by coral reefs. Area, about 630 sq. mi.; pop., about 12,000.

Orkney Islands (Britain). The islands of this group (about 90) are located between northern Scotland and the Shetland Islands. The people are mainly of Scandinavian and Scottish descent. These low, rocky islands have a mild climate. Agriculture and fishing are major occupations, and tourism provides added income. Scapa Flow, the base of the British Grand Fleet in World War I, is an enclosed anchorage south of Pomona, the main island. Area, about 375 sq. mi.; pop., about 21,000.

Pacific Islands. See PACIFIC OCEAN AND ISLANDS.

Philippine Islands. These islands form an Asian republic located on an archipelago between Taiwan and Indonesia. See PHILIPPINES.

Pribilof Islands (U.S.A.). The four islands of this group are located in the Bering Sea, north of the Aleutians. Discovered by a Russian, Gerasim Pribilof, in 1786, the islands came into the possession of the United States when Alaska was purchased in 1867. There are two large islands in the group (St. Paul, St. George) and two smaller ones (Walrus, Otter). The islands are famous as the breeding grounds for millions of fur seals. In 1911 several countries signed an agreement to protect the seals from becoming extinct, and the United States was given charge of the herd. A limited number of skins are permitted to be taken each year. Pop., about 600.

Prince Edward Island is a province of Canada. See PRINCE EDWARD ISLAND.

Puerto Rico is a commonwealth of the United States. It is the easternmost and smallest island of the Greater Antilles, and is located some 1,000 miles southeast of Miami. See PUERTO RICO.

Rhodes (Greece) is an island located in the Aegean Sea, southwest of the Turkish mainland. Rhodes is mountainous and has a mild, humid climate. Agriculture (citrus fruits, wine, olives, tobacco, vegetables), sponge fishing, and commerce are the main occupations. In ancient times the island was the home of many poets, philosophers, and artists. The *Colossus of Rhodes*—a huge statue of Apollo (Helios)— was one of the seven wonders of the ancient world. In ancient times the island was controlled by the Phoenicians. Later it belonged in turn to the Roman Empire, Greece, and Genoa. In 1309 the Knights Hospitalers of St. John settled the island. In 1522 Rhodes was taken over by the Turks, who held it until 1912, when the Italians captured it. The island was finally given to Greece after World War II. Area, about 540 sq. mi.; pop., about 69,000.

Saint Helena (Britain) is historically famous as the place of final exile for Napoleon I. He lived there from 1815 until his death in 1821. The volcanic island lies 1,200 miles west of Angola and 700 miles southeast of Ascension Island in the South Atlantic. Saint Helena was annexed by the Portuguese in 1502. It was occupied by the Dutch in 1600. The British East India Company acquired it in 1651. In 1834 it passed to the British crown. Area, about 47 sq. mi.; pop., about 5,000.

St. Pierre and Miquelon (France) are two small, rocky islands located some 10 miles south of Newfoundland. The population is engaged mainly in fishing (cod) and fish processing. The islands were controlled in turn by France and England until 1814, when France gained final possession of them. In 1947 the islands became a self-governing overseas territory of France. Area, about 93 sq. mi.; pop., about 5,000.

Sakhalin (U.S.S.R.) is a long (about 600 miles in length) and narrow (average width 60 miles) island off the Siberian coast, in the Sea of Okhotsk. It is mountainous and has a damp and changeable climate. Leading activities are fishing, forestry, coal mining, and petroleum production. The Russians and Japanese disputed possession of the island for many years. In 1875 the Japanese agreed to Russian ownership, in exchange for the Kuriles. After the Russians were defeated by the Japanese in 1905, the latter occupied southern Sakhalin. This was relinquished to the Soviet Union after World War II. The Ainu, supposedly among the first inhabitants of Japan, still live in the southern part of the island. Area, about 30,000 sq. mi.

Salamis (Greece) is located in the Aegean Sea, just west of Athens. It became historically famous because of the great naval battle fought nearby between the Greeks and the Persians in 480 B.C. The island was also a temporary refuge for Athenians after they had been defeated at Thermopylae. The inhabitants make a living by farming in the few valleys and the coastal regions of this rugged island. Area, about 40 sq. mi.; pop., about 12,000.

Samoa is an island group in the South Pacific. See SAMOA.

Sardinia (Italy) is the second largest island in the Mediterranean Sea. It lies some 160 miles west of Italy and due south of Corsica. The coast has many gulfs and inlets, and the interior is mountainous, with lowlands in the southwestern part. The climate is mild, with rainy winters and dry summers. The main occupations are farming (olives, citrus fruits, tobacco, grapes, flax, cereals, herbs, almonds); raising sheep, horses, and goats; mining (lead, zinc, copper, iron, manganese); and fishing. This island also produces much cork. Area, about 9,200 sq. mi.; pop., about 1,500,000.

Scilly Islands (Britain). This group consists of 140 tiny islands and numerous reefs. It is located some 28 miles southwest of Land's End on the Cornwall coast. The climate is mild but windy and stormy. The inhabitants make a living by raising vegetables and flowers and by fishing. Another part of their income comes from tourism. Area, about 6 sq. mi.; pop., about 2,000.

Seychelles (Britain) is a group of some 100 islands and islets located in the western Indian Ocean. The population is made up largely of descendants of freed slaves from Africa. They live mainly on the islands of Mahé, Praslin, and La Digue. These islands were taken by the British from the French in 1794 and became a crown colony in 1903. The islands are mountainous and have a tropical climate. Important export products are copra, cinnamon, guano, and patchouli oil. The capital is Victoria on the island of Mahé. Area, about 145 sq. mi.; pop., about 50,000.

Shetland Islands (Britain). This group of some 100 rocky, hilly islands is located about 105 miles northeast of Scotland. Twenty-four of the islands are inhabited. Most of the people are of Scandinavian descent. They are engaged mainly in fishing and in raising cattle and Shetland ponies. Agriculture is not important, because the soil is poor and the climate bleak and damp. Some oats, barley, and potatoes are raised. Few trees grow there, because of the violent winds. Peat is used for fuel. Area, about 550 sq. mi.; pop., about 20,000.

Sicily (Italy) is the largest island in the Mediterranean Sea. Shaped in the form of a triangle, it lies just off the southwestern tip of Italy. It is separated from the Italian mainland by the Strait of Messina. The island is mountainous (highest point is the active volcano Mt. Etna: 10,705 feet) and is subject to earthquakes. It has a mild Mediterranean climate, with dry summers and rainy winters. The people live mainly along the coast. They are engaged in agriculture (citrus fruits, especially lemons and oranges; olives; grapes; vegetables; wheat), sheep and goat raising, fishing (tuna), some manufacturing, and petroleum drilling. Because of its location between Europe and Africa the island has been invaded and conquered many times in history. Greeks, Phoenicians, Romans, Carthaginians, Goths, Vandals, French, and Spanish followed each other in succession. Garibaldi, the Italian liberator, freed Sicily from Spanish rule in 1860, when the island became part of a united Italy. The latest conquest was made during World War II, when the Allies occupied it in 1943. They used Sicily as a springboard for the invasion of Italy. Sicily contains many ruins of temples built during Greek times. The capital is Palermo on the northwestern coast. Other cities are Messina, Catania, Syracuse, Trapani, and Taormina (a tourist center). Area, about 9,900 sq. mi.; pop., about 4,800,000.

Society Islands (France) consist of 14 volcanic and coral islands in the South Pacific. See PACIFIC OCEAN AND ISLANDS.

Sumatra (Indonesia) is the westernmost island of the Republic of Indonesia. See INDONESIA.

Svalbard Islands (Norway). Formerly known as Spitsbergen, this group of five large islands and many small ones is located north of Norway, within the Arctic Circle. The Gulf Stream has a moderating influence on the islands' Arctic climate. The islands are mountainous. The people make their living from coal, copper, and asbestos mining, and from fishing and reindeer raising. The islands were the major base for polar expeditions under Roald Amundsen, Richard E. Byrd, Lincoln Ellsworth, and Umberto Nobile. Area, about 24,000 sq. mi.; pop. about 3,000.

Taiwan is the island seat of the Chinese Nationalist Government and lies about 100 miles off the coast of the Chinese mainland, across the Taiwan Strait. See TAIWAN.

Tonga is an independent nation in the Pacific. See TONGA.

Tristan da Cunha Islands (Britain). This group, a dependency of Saint Helena, is located midway between Capetown and Buenos Aires. There is a meteorological and radio station on Tristan da Cunha, the only inhabited island. When a volcano erupted in 1961, the island was evacuated. Most of the people have since returned. They are dependent on fishing for a living. Area, about 40 sq. mi.; pop., about 285.

Tuamotu Islands (France). This group of about 80 atolls is located in the South Pacific. See PACIFIC OCEAN AND ISLANDS.

Wight, Isle of (Britain). This island is located south of Southampton, in the English Channel. It is separated from the English mainland by the Solent and Spithead gulfs. The island has a mild, pleasant climate and varied scenery, which makes it a popular resort for tourists. Cowes on the northern coast is noted for its yachting events. Area, about 147 sq. mi.; pop., about 95,000.

ANTHONY SAS
Madison College (Virginia)

ISOTOPES. See ATOMS.

ISRAEL

Thousands of years ago a people of shepherds and farmers lived in a small corner of the eastern Mediterranean between the Jordan River and the sea. These people were descended from the patriarchs Abraham, Isaac, and Jacob, of Biblical fame. This small nation called Israel was surrounded throughout its history by great empires—such as those of Egypt and Assyria, Babylon and Persia, Greece and Rome—which exceeded it in physical strength and in economic wealth. But small as it was, Israel made a deep impression on history. The religious, moral, and social ideas that it recorded in the Hebrew Bible became the source of Judaism, Christianity, and Islam. The Bible itself has been read and honored by more people than any other piece of literature.

When the nation of ancient Israel was finally conquered, the land of Israel passed under the rule of successive conquerors. Meanwhile the Jews, the people of Israel, lived in other nations, for the most part in conditions of persecution and degradation. But the people never forgot the land of Israel and always prayed and hoped for a return to its soil.

During World War II (1939–45) the Jewish people suffered its greatest tragedy. Six million Jews, including over 1,000,000 children, were murdered by the German Nazis—simply because they were Jews. The gates of nearly all countries remained closed to Jews fleeing from persecution.

In 1947 the United Nations voted in favor of the establishment of a Jewish state in the old Israeli homeland, then called **Palestine**. On May 14, 1948, the State of Israel was proclaimed by David Ben-Gurion in a ceremony in Tel Aviv. The new state was immediately recognized by the United States, the Soviet Union, and other governments.

▶**THE PEOPLE AND HOW THEY LIVE**

Israel has a population of about 3,000,000. The great majority of the people are Jews. There are several hundred thousand Muslims and smaller numbers of Christians and Druses. A little over half the Jews are immigrants who came to Israel after 1948 from Europe and America and from Asia and Africa. The rest of the Jewish population, about 45 percent, was born in Israel.

Languages. Most Israelis speak Hebrew,

English is taught in many schools.

the official language of Israel. Since there are immigrants from 70 lands in Israel, over 20 different languages are spoken by Israelis. Language courses are given by the government to teach Hebrew to the newcomers. It is largely due to the children, who are educated in Hebrew (except in the Arab communities), that Hebrew has become a common medium of communication.

Religion. The Proclamation of Independence of Israel states, "The State of Israel . . . will guarantee freedom of religion and conscience. . . . It will safeguard the Holy Places of all religions. . . ." The great majority of Israelis are of the Jewish faith. Saturday is the Jewish Sabbath and is the official day of rest. Jewish festivals are observed as official holidays. However, all people are free to worship according to their own customs and religion. All people are entitled to observe their own weekly day of rest and holy days.

Israel has thousands of synagogues. The Chief Rabbinate supervises the Rabbinical Courts, in which religious authority is vested. Jewish dietary laws are observed in all public institutions and government undertakings.

Most Arabs are Muslims. Their religious dignitaries are the Kadis of the Muslim Religious Courts. There are many mosques in Israel. Most of the Christian community, numbering over 75,000 people, are Arabs. Various Christian denominations are represented. There are several hundred churches and chapels. The country also has religious courts belonging to the Greek Orthodox, Greek Catholic, Latin, Maronite, and Armenian Gregorian denominations.

The Druses constitute an independent religious community, numbering over 35,000 people, in Israel. Their community is governed by their own religious courts in all matters concerning their faith.

Education. In the national budget education is second only to defense. The emphasis placed on education stems from the traditional Jewish attitude toward education and from the special needs of the very large immigrant population.

Since the establishment of Israel the population of the state has increased more than threefold, and the school population more than sixfold. There are about 825,000 students attending the various educational institu-

tions in Israel. Of the institutions of higher education, the most important and largest is the Hebrew University in Jerusalem. There is a total enrollment of about 45,000 students in the institutions of higher education.

Primary education (between the ages of 5 and 16) is free and compulsory. Most schools are co-educational and are supervised by the Ministry of Education and Culture. Secondary schools are run by municipal councils and public bodies under the supervision of the ministry.

Hebrew University in Jerusalem is one of Israel's five schools of higher learning.

The language of instruction is Hebrew in Jewish schools and Arabic in Arab schools. But Arabic or Hebrew is taught as a secondary subject where it is not the language of instruction.

Literature. The new generation of Hebrew writers express and describe contemporary Israel. The Bible, the Talmud, and outstanding works of rabbinic literature also enjoy a wide distribution. Encyclopedias of various types are popular. Ancient and modern classics have a wide readership. There is also a very large demand for books in foreign languages. On the average, over 2,000 books are published each year.

Interest in the Bible, the basis of the Jewish cultural heritage, continues unabated. The Bible is taught in schools and forms the basis of quizzes for adults and youths.

Israel's press is diversified both in political opinion and in language. There are more than 20 daily newspapers—over half in Hebrew and the rest in English, German, Arabic, Hungarian, French, Polish, Yiddish, Rumanian, and Bulgarian. Over 400 periodicals are published.

Sports. Football (soccer), basketball, swimming, gymnastics and calisthenics, hockey, tennis, rowing, handball, volleyball, boxing, wrestling, and fencing are the popular sports in Israel. All are conducted on an amateur basis.

On the national level, league and championship competitions are conducted every year. There are a number of sports organizations, with thousands of members.

On the international level, Israel participates in regional and world Olympic competitions. In addition, individual teams often play by invitation against foreign teams. Once every 4 years the Maccabiah Games for Jewish athletes are held in Israel.

Art. Israeli artists engage in all branches of the arts, including painting, drawing, and sculpture in various modern styles. There are art schools and artists' colonies, as well as museums, in the large cities. Arts and crafts are taught in schools and in post-secondary art schools.

Music and Dance. Music is taught in schools by specially qualified teachers. There are two colleges for music teachers, and thousands of students study at conservatories.

Music is composed in a variety of styles in Israel. Many Israeli composers' works have been successfully performed overseas. There are several orchestras, the best known of which is the Israel Philharmonic Orchestra. There are also a number of chamber ensembles and chamber-music groups.

An outdoor market in the ancient city of Nazareth.

Singing and folk dancing are also very popular. There are many choirs in the country. Every 3 or 4 years the Dahlia Folk Dance Festival takes place, with the participation of a large number of folk-dance troupes. The Israel National Opera presents a variety of works with the participation of local and guest artists. The annual Music Festival is held at Ein Gev, on the shores of Lake Kinneret (which is also known as Lake Tiberias or the Sea of Galilee). It attracts large numbers of local and foreign musicians.

Theater. Four major repertory companies and a number of smaller companies present serious drama. Theater is a popular form of entertainment, and it is estimated that well over 1,000,000 people attend theaters every season.

There are also many amateur groups, school drama circles, and companies performing for newcomers in Yiddish and English. Foreign artists and companies frequently perform and attract large audiences.

▶ THE LAND

Israel lies on the eastern seaboard of the Mediterranean, at the meeting point of Asia and Africa. Nearly half of its area of almost 8,000 square miles is desert, and 172 square miles are water.

In shape Israel is an irregular narrow strip 265 miles long, extending from the hills of Galilee in the north to the port of Eilat (Elath) on the Gulf of Aqaba in the south. It has common boundaries in the north with Lebanon and Syria, in the east with Jordan, and in the southwest with Egypt. On the west the coastal plain borders the Mediterranean for 120 miles.

North of the port city of Haifa the country broadens out into one of the most beautiful areas of Israel. Along the coast lies the Zebulun Valley. The Plain of Jezreel runs roughly east to west, and the hills of Galilee overlook the Hula valley and Lake Kinneret.

South of Haifa, past the city of Tel Aviv, and down to the Gaza Strip stretch the Plain of Sharon and the Judean Plains. The latter is a narrow strip leading up to the Judean hills and Jerusalem and down to the triangular-shaped Negev.

The Negev comprises about half of the country's area. In the north it is an extension of the coastal plain. In the east it is a long, irregular valley. In the center the Negev is a plateau, with hills extending westward halfway to Eilat.

The Jordan River valley extends from the northeastern corner of Israel, through Lake Kinneret (696 feet below sea level) and the

Children on a *kibbutz*, a settlement where the land is owned collectively by the entire community.

Vegetables are grown on *kibbutz* farms.

Kingdom of Jordan, to the Dead Sea (about 1,300 feet below sea level—the lowest point of the earth's surface). A chain of mountains lying west of the Jordan valley stretches 200 miles from Lebanon to the Sinai desert. The average height is 2,000 feet. In the Negev the high mountain ranges are multicolored, and many mountains have tremendous craters.

Israel has a Mediterranean climate—warm, sunny summers and cool, rainy winters. Hot, dry winds blow from the east in the beginning and end of summer. Snow occasionally falls in the hills in winter. The rainy season generally lasts from November to March, and spring and autumn are usually very short.

Biblical Israel was "a land of wheat and barley and vines and fig-trees and pomegranates, a land of olive oil and honey." Today many fruits are grown in Israel, citrus being the most important. Vegetables and the basic grains are grown. Industrial crops, such as tobacco, cotton, peanuts, bananas, and sugar beets, have been successfully introduced.

To the native pine and tamarisk trees have been added eucalyptus and acacia. Wild flowers abound in the country.

In the unpopulated areas wild boars, hyenas, jackals, lynx, otters, wildcats, mongooses, and spotted weasels roam. Occasional wolves and leopards appear in the Galilee region. About 400 species of birds are found in Israel, and Lake Kinneret is rich in fish.

Most of Israel's mineral resources are in the Negev. These include potash, bromine, magnesium, common salt, phosphates, copper, manganese, feldspar, glass sand, flint clay, ball clay, kaolin, bitumen, granite, marble, gypsum, petroleum, and natural gas. Iron ore has been discovered in Galilee.

▶ HOW THE PEOPLE EARN A LIVING

Half of Israel's working population is engaged in providing services of one sort or another, while the other half provides the food, mans the industries, and builds the homes, roads, and factories.

Industry. Israel turns out a variety of industrial products, ranging from foodstuffs to furniture, processed diamonds to newsprint, and chemicals to transport equipment.

The growth of industry has been rapid and planned. The main branches of industry are food processing, metal products, textiles, chemicals, petroleum products, clothing, wood products, minerals (nonmetallic), paper and printing, vehicles, diamonds, leather, rubber and plastics, electrical equipment, and mines and quarries.

Building. With the population tripling itself since independence, the building industry has been called upon to make great efforts to keep pace with the need for housing. During this period hundreds of thousands of permanent housing units have been erected, in addition to large numbers of schools, factories, offices and public buildings, roads, and harbors.

Agriculture. Three quarters of the population's food is locally grown. All the vegetables, most of the meat, the dairy products, fruits, and potatoes are locally produced. Industrial crops such as peanuts, sugar beets, and cotton are being expanded.

Agriculture is intensive. Soil conservation and reclamation and modern scientific methods of crop rotation and fertilization are widely practiced. The limited water resources are utilized to the maximum.

Almost all agriculture is organized on a co-operative or collective basis. There are the *kibbutzim*—collective settlements—and the *moshavim*—co-operative smallholders' settlements.

▶ MAJOR CITIES AND PLACES OF INTEREST

Jerusalem, the capital city of Israel, is situated 2,500 feet above sea level, in the Judean hills. It has a population of almost 300,000. It is one of the oldest continuously inhabited cities in the world. Its history is practically synonymous with that of the Jewish people. In about 1000 B.C. King David made it his capital. It has since remained the center of the religious and national aspirations of the Jews. The modern city, which includes the government buildings, the Hebrew University, and many holy places, was built during the last 100 years and lies to the west of the Old City.

Tel Aviv–Jaffa, with a population of about 400,000, is the largest city, with about one seventh of Israel's total population. Founded

---

FACTS AND FIGURES

STATE OF ISRAEL is the official name of the country.

CAPITAL: Jerusalem.

LOCATION AND SIZE: Southwest Asia. **Latitude**—29° 29′ N to 33° 17′ N. **Longitude**—34° 11′ E to 35° 26′ E. **Area**—7,992 sq. mi.

PHYSICAL FEATURES: Highest point—Mt. Meron (3,963 ft.). **Lowest point**—Dead Sea (about 1,300 ft. below sea level). **Chief rivers**—Jordan, Kishon, Yarkon. **Chief mountain peaks**—Mt. Ramon (3,395 ft.), Mt. Scopus (2,736 ft.), Mt. Tabor (1,929 ft.), Mt. Carmel (1,791 ft.).

POPULATION: 3,000,000 (estimate).

LANGUAGE: Hebrew and Arabic (official), English, French, Yiddish, and various other languages.

RELIGION: Judaism, Christianity, Islam.

GOVERNMENT: Republic. **Head of state**—president. **Head of government**—prime minister. **International co-operation**—United Nations.

NATIONAL ANTHEM: *Hatikvah* ("The Hope").

ECONOMY: Agricultural products—wheat, barley, citrus fruit (oranges, grapefruits, lemons), cotton, sugar beets, potatoes, peanuts, grapes, bananas, vegetables, livestock (cattle, sheep, goats, horses, donkeys, mules). **Industries and products**—food processing, textiles, shoes, clothing, electrical equipment, metal products, chemicals, construction, pharmaceuticals, glass and ceramics, paper and printing, plastics, precision instruments, fruit canning and processing, leather goods, polished diamonds, building materials, wood and tobacco products, handicrafts. **Chief minerals**—potash, bromine, magnesium, common salt, copper, phosphates, oil, iron. **Chief exports**—citrus fruit, polished diamonds, textiles, rubber tires, fruit juices. **Chief imports**—machinery, grain and flour, fuels, transport equipment, iron and steel products. **Monetary unit**—Israeli pound.

in 1909 as a suburb of Jaffa, which is more than 4,000 years old, Tel Aviv is today a modern metropolis, serving as the hub of Israel's commerce, light industry, culture, and entertainment.

Haifa, with a population of over 200,000, is Israel's main port and one of the most developed harbor centers in the Middle East. During the last 35 years it has developed into a center of heavy industry.

Israel is an archeologist's and sightseer's paradise. Archeological sites have been discovered throughout the length and breadth of the country. These include the Dead Sea area, where the Bar-Kochba letters were discovered; Tel Nagela, a fortified city of the Middle Bronze Age; Caesarea and Beit Shaan, where ruins of Roman theaters still stand; and Lake Kinneret in the lower Galilee region, where archeologists unearthed the skeleton of a Neanderthal man.

▶ GOVERNMENT

Israel is a parliamentary democracy. Supreme authority is vested in the Knesset, or parliament—the legislative chamber, with 120 members. Members of the Knesset are elected by universal suffrage for a period of 4 years. The powers and functions of the Knesset include electing the president, approving the annual budget, and keeping executive policy under survey, as well as enacting laws. The president is the formal head of state, elected by the Knesset for a 5-year term.

The executive branch of the government is composed of the Cabinet and the various ministries. The Cabinet is headed by a prime minister and includes a deputy prime minister and the heads of the several ministries.

The Cabinet is responsible to the Knesset and requires the confidence of that body to remain in office.

▶ HISTORY

The State of Israel dates only from 1948, but the link between the Jewish people and the "Land of Israel" dates back 4,000 years.

For some 2,000 years Canaan, as the country was then known, was under Jewish hegemony. The first Kingdom of Israel, ruled successively by Saul, David, and Solomon, was divided into the realms of Judah and Israel. Both of them fell victim to the Assyrian and Babylonian conquerors. The Second Commonwealth lasted for 4 centuries, until the Roman conquest of Judea crushed its independence. Political rule was exercised successively by the Romans, Arabs, Crusaders, Turks, and British until 1948, when Israel's sovereignty was again proclaimed.

The economic rebuilding of the land and the cultural and linguistic revival of the people in its ancient homeland began toward the end of the 19th century, under the banner of Zionism. Immigration grew, a Hebrew renaissance flowered, and the foundations for the rebirth of Israel's independence were laid.

In 1947 the Palestine question was brought before the United Nations. On November 29 the United Nations General Assembly approved the partition of Palestine into independent Jewish and Arab states. On May 15, 1948, a few hours after the proclamation of Israel's independence, armies of six Arab states invaded Israel. After 7 months of fighting they were repulsed, and armistice agreements were signed. Because of the unwillingness of the Arab states to accept the existence of the State of Israel, these agreements have never been replaced by peace treaties. In 1956 Egypt nationalized the Suez Canal and refused use of the canal to Israel. Aided by France and Great Britain, Israel invaded Egypt and occupied the Sinai Peninsula. The United Nations intervened, and in 1957 the invading nations withdrew.

In May, 1967, Egypt mobilized its troops near Israel's southern border and closed the Gulf of Aqaba, leaving Israel no convenient water route to East Africa and Asia. The following month, hostilities broke out between Israel and Egypt, Jordan, and Syria. The fighting lasted only a few days. The Arab forces were defeated. After the war Israel controlled the Sinai Peninsula, the Gaza Strip, the Golan Heights of Syria, and the west bank of the Jordan River, including the former Jordanian-controlled sector of Jerusalem.

On October 6, 1973, the Day of Atonement, the fourth Arab-Israeli war began with two simultaneous attacks—by Egyptian forces across the Suez Canal into Sinai, and by Syrian troops against the Israeli forces in the Golan Heights. The Arab armies held the advantage of surprise and initiative. The 1973 war was short, but bitter, hard-fought,

Haifa, Israel's main seaport.

Tel Aviv's beach on the Mediterranean Sea.

and immensely costly in lives and weapons. The Syrians, reinforced by Iraqi and Jordanian units, were at first successful in retaking the Golan Heights, but Israeli counterattacks drove them back toward Damascus. While the Egyptians held the ground they won in the Sinai during the first days of the war, the Israeli forces launched an attack westward across the canal. They established their forces on the west bank, encircling one of the Egyptian armies and cutting off its supply lines. After 16 days of fighting, a cease-fire resolution was adopted by the Security Council of the United Nations at the initiative of the United States and the Soviet Union. Peacekeeping forces of the United Nations were sent to supervise the cease-fire. For the first time the United Nations accepted the principle of "negotiations between the parties" as the means of establishing permanent peace. There seemed to be a concrete prospect that the negotiating era had begun.

ABBA EBAN
Minister for Foreign Affairs of Israel

ITALY

The boot-shaped peninsula of Italy was the center of the ancient Roman Empire. Today it is the home of the Republic of Italy. Nature and history have lavished so much on Italy that man-made monuments compete with the beauties of the seashore and the mountains to make the country a wonderland. For centuries some of the world's great painters, sculptors, artists, musicians, and thinkers have lived and worked in Italy.

In spite of their great cultural achievements, the people of the different regions of Italy have been united in one nation only since the second half of the 19th century. In 1861 they declared themselves citizens of a nation rather than members of individual states.

Two world wars in the 20th century damaged much of the land as well as the people. After World War II, Italians were living under a new form of government in a country that was in chaos. Food and jobs were scarce. People in agricultural southern Italy had to exist with few natural resources and ruined land. In the north fuel for heating homes and running factories was often unavailable.

With financial aid from the European Recovery Program the citizens began to rebuild their country, improve economic and living conditions, and develop industry. Although some sections of the country are still poor, Italy is rich in the traditions of its cultural and historical past. Paintings, works of sculpture, churches, and buildings abound in Italy. Each year thousands of visitors go to the country to be a part of it themselves.

▶ THE PEOPLE

Italy has a population of over 53,000,000. Most central and southern Italians are olive-skinned, dark-haired, and short, as are people in other Mediterranean countries. Because of the invasion of Germanic tribes from beyond the Alps, however, many of the people in northern Italy are tall and blond.

Education. Italians must attend school until they are 14 years old. Elementary education is free, and children go to 5 years of grade school, or *scuola elementare*. Yet until recently there were many people, especially in southern Italy, who could not read or write. In

The Leaning Tower of Pisa is the bell tower of the adjoining cathedral. The tower leans because the ground beneath it is settling.

recent years, however, illiteracy has decreased tremendously. Beyond grade school everybody now attends a unified junior high school, or *scuola media,* for 3 years before going on to a more specialized secondary school. Schools are run by the state, which sets a nationwide program for each of them. Secondary study at the upper level totals 5 years, after which one must pass a difficult state examination to obtain a diploma and be admitted to a university.

In all senior secondary schools students study such basic subjects as a foreign language (English, French, Spanish, or German), Latin, world history, Italian literature, geography, mathematics, chemistry, physics, and biology. Latin, ancient Greek, history, and philosophy are stressed in the classical *liceo,* or high school. Scientific subjects are emphasized in

the scientific *liceo,* and bookkeeping and geometry in the commercial technical institutes.

There are also industrial technical institutes for various types of technicians, nautical institutes for merchant sailors, and agrarian institutes for those interested in the land.

Other schools beyond the *scuola media* but at a lower level than the university include the *istituto magistrale* for future grade-school teachers, industrial vocational schools for mechanics, and commercial vocational schools for secretaries.

Students may also attend art schools, music schools, and private schools at all levels.

About 500,000 students are working toward the university degree (*laurea*), which requires from 4 to 6 years. This number increases annually, as more and more people are becoming lawyers, teachers, doctors, and engineers.

Religion. Except for a tiny sprinkling of Waldensian Protestants (a Christian sect dating from the Middle Ages) and a very small Jewish community, the majority of Italians are Roman Catholic. Catholicism is the official religion. The Holy See (seat of government) of the Roman Catholic Church is the Vatican City, which is a separate state within Rome. The church's pageantry, imagery, and ceremonial art have deeply affected the imagination of Italians at all levels. The results can be seen in the large number of great church-inspired monuments and paintings as well as in colorful local traditions.

Every village has its patron saint. An annual feast is celebrated everywhere by a procession parading the saint's covered statue of painted wood through town to the accompaniment of hymns, candles, and fireworks. Merry banquets and a country fair often go with the feast.

The patron saint of Naples, Saint Januarius (San Gennaro), is famous for the miracles attributed to him and the devotion he is given by all Neapolitans, even those living abroad. Saint John's Day (San Giovanni), June 24, is a widely observed festival. In several places peasants will tell you that if you rise with the sun on that day, you will see the beheaded saint's face lighting the sky.

Easter and Christmas are joyously observed. Chocolate eggs and cake doves, along with lamb or kid roast, are served at the Easter meal. Passion plays re-enacting the story of the last days of Jesus are performed by villagers in some communities. In northern Italy trees are decorated at Christmastime. The *presepio,* or manger, with its fancy figurines, can be seen in many Italian homes from December 24 through January 6, which is Epiphany. On that day children receive gifts just as Jesus was given gifts by the three Magi. Some of these *presepi* portray the scene of Jesus' birth, and large, magnificent *presepi* can be seen in churches throughout Italy.

▶ **CULTURAL AND SOCIAL LIFE**

The Italians are a gifted, lively, and sociable people, and they are proud of their contribution to the arts. Many museums, churches, statues, and palaces remind the world that for many centuries in the past the greatest painters, sculptors, and architects came from Italy, including Leonardo da Vinci (1452–1519), Michelangelo (1475–1564), Titian (1488?–1576), and Raphael (1483–1520).

But Italians are not content to live in the past, and they have contributed to contemporary art, too. Many painters and sculptors are working in Italy, and many come from abroad. Exhibitions of their work are usually held in Milan or Rome, and they attract visitors, fellow artists, and buyers.

In Venice's Public Gardens an exhibition of the selected works of painters and sculptors from all over the world takes place every 2 years, and is therefore called La Biennale di Venezia. Prizes are awarded to the best works. So many tourists flock to Venice in the *biennale* season (from June to October) that it often takes half an hour to walk a few hundred yards in town. An annual international film festival and an international festival of contemporary music vie with the *biennale* exhibition in drawing crowds to Venice.

Opera is an Italian creation. One of the most famous opera theaters in the world, called La Scala, is in Milan. It is not uncommon to hear people sing at work, and almost everybody, no matter how poor, knows by heart tunes or whole scores from favorite operas by Gioacchino Antonio Rossini (1792–1868), Giuseppe Verdi (1813–1901), and Giacomo Puccini (1858–1924). Italians everywhere closely follow the performances of operatic singers and passionately boo if they do not like them. Sacred music and chamber music have a following, while jazz finds favor with younger people. Singing is very popular, both as a profession and as a pastime. Folk song festivals are held each year at Piedigrotta in Naples in memory of the Madonna of Piedigrotta. A popular-song festival is held annually at San Remo.

Whether for singing or acting, the theater has a great place in Italian life. The National Academy of Dramatic Arts, founded in 1937, was the first modern school of acting in Italy. During intermission a theater's foyer is the scene of social gathering. Another favorite spot for leisurely conversation is the café, where between sips of espresso coffee or vermouth important business is often transacted.

The Galleria Vittorio Emanuele in Milan has many stores and cafés.

Since World War II, Italian movies have won worldwide fame.

Italy is also a land of dedicated craftsmen. Peasants' kitchens shine with copper pans and jugs. Earthenware has been in use for countless centuries. Furniture from Chiavari and Cantù; ceramics from Faenza; Florentine-wrought leather; enamelware from Gubbio; and lacework from Burano and glasswork from Murano, near Venice, bring timeless grace to many Italian homes.

▶CITIES

Italy has been called a nation of cities. Rome was the capital of the ancient Roman Empire. It is the capital of modern Italy and is the center of the Roman Catholic world. The city spreads over several low hills, and the Tiber River flows through the western part of it. Ruins of Roman temples, stadiums, and aqueducts stand side by side with Renaissance and Baroque churches and palaces. There are many world-famous architectural master-

The busy Piazza della Repubblica in downtown Rome.

The cathedral and the tower of the Palazzo della Signoria (city hall) dominate Florence's skyline.

pieces, such as St. Peter's Church, with its majestic square graced by fountains and enclosed by a huge colonnade.

Florence, a smaller city on the Arno River, is a jewel of beauty. Among its famous buildings are the Palazzo della Signoria, the present-day city hall; the Uffizi and the Pitti galleries, which house world-famous art collections; the Florence Cathedral with its dome by Brunelleschi and its campanile designed by Giotto; and the Baptistery with its famous bronze doors by Ghiberti. In November, 1966, heavy rains caused the Arno to overflow. This disastrous flood damaged many of Florence's art treasures and destroyed thousands of valuable books.

The city of Naples is a gateway to Italy. The gaiety and spirit of Neapolitans can be felt everywhere. This picturesque city is built beside a beautiful bay and is a great tourist center. Although many sections are poor, it is also an important seaport and commercial city.

Venice, built on water, has palaces like marble lacework and a maze of canals for avenues. It is built on more than 100 small islands joined by hundreds of bridges. People travel about the city in boats such as motorboats (*vaporetti*), ferryboats (*traghetti*), and gondolas. It is also famous for its beautiful Renaissance paintings, its churches, such as Saint Mark's, and the nearby Lido Beach.

Milan is the center of industry in Italy. In recent years many new factories have been built in and around the city, which is the financial and banking center of northern Italy. Turin is the home of the Fiat automobile factory. Genoa, another commercial city, is Italy's chief port. It is the birthplace of Christopher Columbus (1451?–1506). Today it is a center of the Italian shipping industry.

▶ EVERYDAY LIFE

In the industrial cities the average citizen's life is like that of most people living in the West today. They work during the day and spend the evening at home with their families or at some entertainment, such as the movies. Italian weekends are shorter than elsewhere, for Saturday morning is still spent in the office or factory. In most parts of Italy people come home for lunch and stay at work until evening.

Naples is built on the Bay of Naples. Mount Vesuvius rises in the background.

After work nearly everybody goes out for a daily walk in the smaller towns. In the evenings the Italian towns come to colorful life.

Since sports are popular, on Sundays cheering crowds fill the stadiums to root for their favorite soccer teams. Nearly everybody is a soccer fan, and boys learn to play the game when they are very young. Bicycle races and *bocce,* which resembles bowling, are other Italian passions.

Fun bursts out in the pre-Lenten carnival season. In Viareggio, with its parades of floats and masked balls, a spirit of gaiety prevails. In summer many well-to-do city families go to the seashore or to the mountainside to spend their vacations away from the city. In winter they crowd the ski resorts.

Food

One of the most enjoyable times of the Italian day is mealtime. Pastas—as noodles, spaghetti, macaroni, and ravioli are called in Italy—have become world-famous foods. Tomato sauce and Parmesan cheese added to thin slices of veal cooked in butter or olive oil is known as veal Parmigiana. Flat noodles, chopped meat, ricotta and mozzarella cheese, and tomato sauce are baked together to make lasagna. Spaghetti is served with various sauces, such as clam, tomato, meat, or simple butter. Spices and anchovies are added for flavor, especially in the southern region. In the north of Italy less garlic and oil are used in cooking than in the south.

In addition to pasta and the famous Italian pizza (round dough covered with cheese and tomatoes and baked), the people eat a lot of rice, fish, cheese, chicken, fresh vegetables, and fruit. Wine, which is abundant in Italy, is drunk at lunch and supper. Espresso coffee seals every meal with its strong aroma. Dessert is often fruit and cheese. On special occasions it may be Italian ice cream (*spumoni* or *tortoni*) or elaborate layer cake (*zuppa inglese*).

▶ THE LAND

Italy's mainland is a slender, boot-shaped peninsula slanting toward the center of the Mediterranean Sea. On a map the tip of the "boot" seems to be touching one corner of Sicily, the triangular island that is separated from the mainland by the narrow Strait of Messina. The island of Sardinia, which is also part of Italy, is northwest of Sicily. Including these two major islands and other smaller ones, the territory of Italy is a little smaller than that of the British Isles.

Italy shares land borders with four European nations: France on the west, Switzerland and Austria on the north, and Yugoslavia on the east. But the greater part of Italy's boundaries are seacoasts. The Adriatic Sea separates Italy from Yugoslavia and Albania. The Ionian Sea separates it from Greece. The Mediterranean Sea separates Italy from Africa on the south. The Tyrrhenian Sea separates it from the French island of Corsica; and the western Mediterranean, from Spain.

Italy is a country of mountains and hills. To the north the great range of the Alps protects the green Po valley like a fortress wall. The Alpine massif Mont Blanc (Monte Bianco), the Monte Rosa mountain group, and the Matterhorn (Monte Cervino), which are shared with France and Switzerland, rise to heights of from 14,700 to almost 15,800 feet above sea level. They are among the tallest in Europe.

The Po valley is Italy's largest plain. To the south of it begins another and less steep range, the Apennines. It runs all the way down to the tip of the boot, bypassing the heel. The latter is a region called Apulia and is all flatlands and plateaus. Smaller plains nestle here and there in the central part of the peninsula, near Rome and Naples. Vesuvius, the nearly 4,000-foot-high volcano, can be seen from Naples.

Sicily and Sardinia are mountainous, too. Sicily has the tallest active volcano in Europe, Mount Etna (10,705 feet high). North of Sicily other Italian mountains form little islands by themselves. Along with volcanic eruptions, southern Italy occasionally has violent earthquakes.

Rivers and Lakes

The Po River is Italy's main river. It springs from the Monte Viso in the Cottian Alps and crosses the northern plains eastward to flow into the Adriatic Sea. Along its 405-mile course it is enlarged by several tributary rivers.

Between the Alps and the Po some northern

tributaries swell into beautiful lakes, such as Lake Orta, Lago Maggiore, Lake Como, Lago d' Iseo, and Lago di Garda. They look like oblong sapphires set in green hills. Nothing else in Italy compares with this elaborate water system.

But the central part of the peninsula has the Arno River, winding 150 miles generally westward into the Tyrrhenian Sea; and the Tiber, flowing southwest for 251 miles. Between these two rivers appear a few round lakes, such as Trasimeno near Perugia.

Climate

The barrier of the Alps shelters the country from much northern cold. The sea and a favorable geographic position gives most of Italy a mild climate.

However, the length of the peninsula and its different land formations cause certain differences. The Po valley plains have damp, warm summers, fairly cold winters with snow, and much rainfall, especially in spring and fall. Southern Italy is drier and enjoys a lovely spring season. The heat can be intense there in summertime, although winter brings snow to the Apennine highlands. A city like Naples, located at about the same latitude as New York, can practically do without heating during the winter.

In the mild season Italy becomes a garden. Forests of fir trees, larches, chestnuts, and beeches cover parts of the Alpine slopes. Poplars line the wheat and rice fields of the northern plain. Oakwoods, chestnuts, and olive trees offer relief from the noonday sun in the Apennines. Here, however, careless tree-cutting has caused much damage, and Italian authorities have been working out plans to build up forests again. The umbrella-shaped pine trees of Rome, the smooth cypresses of Tuscany and Lago di Garda, and the bright oleanders (evergreen shrubs) of Lake Como and of the Tyrrhenian Riviera are among the typical decorations of the landscape. Thickly populated Italy has very little room left for any large-size wildlife. In the Gran Paradiso area of the western Alps and in the Gran Sasso d'Italia region of the Abruzzi Apennines, national parks have been made to protect certain animals from becoming extinct.

Natural Resources

Italy is poor in mineral resources. There are iron ore mines in the Val d'Aosta in the western Alps and on the island of Elba near the Tuscan shore of the Tyrrhenian Sea. However, their output is a very small part of the nation's need. A limited amount of coal is found in Sardinia. Oil, which recently was discovered in Italy, is being drilled in the Po valley, in the Abruzzi, and in Sicily. With it goes a vast supply of natural gas. Sulfur is mined in Sicily. Although tin and copper are not abundant, there are important deposits of iron pyrites, iron ore, bauxite, and mercury. The sea provides a steady supply of salt. Geyserlike activity in Tuscany near Larderello has been harnessed to generate power. Some of the world's most highly prized marble is obtained from the quarries in Carrara. A plentiful water supply in the north has made it possible to produce electric power for industrial, civic, and domestic use. The Terni waterfall in central Italy keeps towns lighted and factories going in the area.

The soil of the Po valley is the richest for tilling and cattle-breeding purposes. The

---

FACTS AND FIGURES

REPUBLIC OF ITALY is the official name of the country. Italy is called Repubblica Italiana in Italian.

CAPITAL: Rome.

LOCATION AND SIZE: Southern Europe. **Latitude**—36° 39′ N to 47° 06′ N. **Longitude**—6° 37′ E to 18° 31′ E. **Area**—116,303 sq. mi. (including Sicily and Sardinia).

PHYSICAL FEATURES: Highest point (entirely in Italy)—Gran Paradiso (13,323 ft.). **Lowest point**—Sea level. **Chief rivers**—Po, Tiber, Arno, Adige. **Chief mountains**—Alps, Apennines.

POPULATION: 53,200,000 (estimate).

LANGUAGE: Italian.

RELIGION: 99% Roman Catholic.

GOVERNMENT: Republic. **Head of state**—president. **Head of government**—premier. **International co-operation**—United Nations, North Atlantic Treaty Organization (NATO), European Economic Community (Common Market).

NATIONAL ANTHEM: "Hymn of Mameli," also known as *Fratelli d'Italia* ("Brothers of Italy").

ECONOMY: Agricultural products—wheat, sugar beets, potatoes, maize, tomatoes. **Industries and products**—tourism, textiles, wines, chemicals, automobiles, machinery. **Chief minerals**—iron pyrites, crude sulfur, iron ore, bauxite, oil (Sicily). **Chief exports**—fruits, vegetables, wines, automobiles, shoes, cheeses. **Chief imports**—coal and crude oil, metals, raw materials, machinery, fertilizer, wheat, coffee, meat, foodstuffs. **Monetary unit**—lira.

clayey and stony soil of the Apennines is less valuable for cultivation—except for the Terra di Lavoro plain near Naples and the recently irrigated Apulian flatlands, where olives, grapes, and other vegetables are grown. Tree-cutting in the south has made erosion a problem in many places. As a result, the timber supply is not large enough to meet national needs.

▶ INDUSTRIES AND PRODUCTS

Italy used to be primarily an agricultural country, but today only about 20 percent of the labor force are farmers.

The main problem of Italy's economy is the south, but it is the area undergoing a huge industrial expansion. The soil is too rugged, dry, and scanty to feed its large population. Agriculture and sheepherding are still the basis of economic life there. Many factories have moved to areas that were once poor. Oil drilling has also begun. Food processing and glove manufacturing are major industries near Naples. Fishing has been an important activity for centuries.

In 1950 the government established the Southern Italy Development Fund, or *Cassa per il Mezzogiorno,* which offered loans, reduced tax rates, and even gave sums of money to help companies that would move there. As a result, many have done so.

Vineyards cover many of Italy's hills and plains, north and south. The plains of the north supply plentiful amounts of wheat, maize, rice, and hay for cattle, and they are tilled with modern machinery. The silk industry is the pride of Lombardy, while wool and cotton mills dot all of the Po valley. Automobiles are produced in Turin and Milan; ships, in Genoa and Monfalcone; railroad cars, in Milan; and arms, in Brescia. The chemical industry is growing fast. Oil refineries have developed. Milan and Genoa are centers of world trade.

Italy's exports are very important to the economy, but Italy must still import more than it exports because it needs so many raw materials. Italian products, such as Fiat cars, Vespa motor scooters, footwear and fashions, wines, olive oil, and fruits are sought all over the world. Membership in the European Economic Community (Common Market) has strengthened the Italian economy.

Motor scooters being assembled at the Lambretta factory in Milan.

In the past 10 years the value of Italian trade with foreign countries has more than tripled.

Transportation and Communication

Transportation facilities have also greatly improved in the years since the war. New railroad lines have been developed, cars have been modernized, and stations repaired and rebuilt. A plan called the progressive scheme, which will cost the government close to 1,800,000,000 lire, has been in effect. This plan will continue to make rail transportation faster and more comfortable for Italians and tourists as well.

Although the merchant navy was badly damaged by the war, it is now the seventh largest in the world. The government has also given it financial support. Four new transatlantic liners, the *Leonardo da Vinci,* the *Cristoforo Colombo,* the *Michelangelo,* and the *Raffaello* have been built by the Italian Line.

Italy also has a superhighway system, the *autostrade,* which is being improved under a 10-year government plan. The national airline, Alitalia, flies to nearly all the major countries of the world. Rome's Leonardo da Vinci (Fiumicino) Airport is the largest of Italy's 25 major airports.

Communications services such as the telephone, telegraph, postal service, and radio and television are government-owned or government-supervised. The daily circulation of Italian newspapers has reached about 5,000,000. Most are published in northern and central Italy, with Milan and Rome as the two main centers.

GOVERNMENT

Italy is a republic governed by freely elected representatives of the people. Laws are passed by Parliament, which consists of the Chamber of Deputies and the Senate. There members of the various parties discuss their views before coming to a vote. Several parties represent different interests and opinions. Executive power is carried out by the Cabinet of Ministers, each minister having his own department, such as Agriculture and Forestry, Industry and Commerce, Transportation, Interior, Defense, and Merchant Navy. Ministers are led by a premier, who is chosen by the president of the republic. He forms his cabinet by consulting Parliament.

Italy is divided into 20 autonomous regions. Five of these—Sicily, Sardinia, Trentino-Alto Adige, Friuli-Venezia Giulia, and Val d'Aosta—have been autonomous for a number of years. The establishment of the remaining 15 autonomous regions, each with its own council and the right to make some of its own laws, was approved by the voters in 1970. Men and women over 21 can vote in elections for deputies; those over 25 can vote for senators.

HISTORY

Many myths surround the origin of civilization in Italy. According to one of the most famous, the city of Rome was founded by Romulus and Remus, twin sons of Mars, the god of war, in 753 B.C. When they were infants, their uncle separated them from their mother and left them in a basket on the Tiber River. A she-wolf found them and kept them alive. After they grew up and found out who they were, they left to found a new city, Rome.

Actually tribes such as the Villanovans, Sabines, Ligurians, and Etruscans had been living in Italy since the beginning of history. When the Romans established a republic in 509 B.C., they became friendly with many of the neighboring peoples and conquered others. By 270 B.C. Rome had taken all of Italy. It later developed an empire that included much of Europe, North Africa, and Asia Minor. This empire knew 2 centuries of peace and development in areas of government, architecture, and law. Julius Caesar (100?–44 B.C.) was the last dictator. Augustus (63 B.C.–A.D. 14) became the first emperor.

Jesus Christ, the founder of Christianity, was born in the time of Augustus. He died during the reign of Tiberius (42 B.C.–A.D. 37). The Christians believed in a God who had more power than the human emperors. They were forced to practice their religion in secret and were often executed for not worshiping the gods of Rome.

By A.D. 200 the Roman Empire began to weaken. One emperor, Diocletian (245–313), divided the kingdom into eastern and western halves to make the government stronger. Constantine (280?–337), his successor, moved the capital from Rome to the eastern city of Byzantium, which was renamed Constantinople. He accepted Christianity, and soon afterward the Christians were able to come out of hiding to practice their faith. The Roman Empire flourished in the east, but Germanic tribes had begun invading the western part. In A.D. 476 the leader of the Heruli, a northern tribe, seized control from the Roman emperor in the west.

After the fall of the empire in the west, Italy began its darkest age. There was no central government to keep order. The popes, who were the head of the Catholic Church in Rome, thought that they should rule at least in spiritual matters. The eastern emperors refused to recognize their rule, beginning the dispute between emperors and popes that was to last for centuries.

In the 6th century Pope Gregory the Great (540?–604) declared that he was the ruler of all Christendom. During the next 2 centuries many barbaric rulers were converted to Christianity. By the end of the 8th century the Franks, a tribe from Germany, had conquered territory that today would include France, Belgium, the Netherlands, Germany, and northern Italy, and a part of northern Spain, Czechoslovakia, and Yugoslavia. Pope Leo III (750–816) wanted Charlemagne (742?–814), the leader of the Franks, to be emperor because he had protected the church and converted heathen tribes to Christianity. When the Pope crowned Charlemagne emperor, he founded what was to become the Holy Roman Empire. After Charlemagne's death his empire was later divided among his three grandsons by the Treaty of Verdun (843). One grandson received most of France, the second received the remainder of France and part of Italy, and the third received Germany.

As the French writer Voltaire (1694–1778) said, the Holy Roman Empire was "neither holy, nor Roman, nor an Empire." It did not have the unity that its name implied. Popes and emperors quarreled over religious and political affairs for centuries. In the 12th century Frederick Barbarossa (1123?–90) came down to Italy from Germany and was crowned Holy Roman Emperor. Frederick was related to two warring families of Germany, known in Italy as the Guelphs and the Ghibellines. Later Frederick and the Pope became enemies. Frederick was defeated by an alliance of the Pope and a league of northern Italian cities, but his son captured Sicily. The Guelph-Ghibelline struggles continued for many years in nearly every major Italian city.

In the beginning of the 14th century Philip IV (1268–1314), King of France, helped a French clergyman to be elected pope. The papacy was moved to the French town of Avignon for over 70 years. In 1378 an Italian was elected pope, but some of the cardinals objected and named a Frenchman. A great schism, or break, occurred in the Catholic Church. A third pope was chosen at a meeting of the two groups of cardinals in 1409. However, at the Council of Constance (1414–1418), the rift was healed when one new pope was elected.

While the papal struggle was going on, a deep-reaching change was beginning. Cities in the Po valley region were becoming rich from the produce of the fertile soil. Communities like Florence, Siena, and Pisa in Tuscany; Milan, Cremona, and Pavia in Lombardy; Amalfi near Naples; and Venice and Genoa were slowly emerging from the dark period of the Middle Ages. Genoa and Venice were seagoing republics that monopolized all European commerce with the east. Most of the other cities were inland trading communities of bankers and merchants. They were democratically governed by a council of their citizens. Some of these communes, or city-states, became large and powerful by conquering their neighbors. Soon Florence had all of Tuscany under its control; Milan ruled much of Lombardy; and Venice, all of Venetia. In the 14th century the cities gave Italy its first major flowering of art since Roman times. By the 15th century some of the finest thinkers, painters, and architects had gathered in Florence at the court of the Medici family. One member, Lorenzo (1449–92), known as Lorenzo the Magnifi-

The Teatro Massimo in Palermo, the capital of Sicily.

A regatta (boating race) on the Grand Canal in Venice.

cent, supported these creative artists and brought wealth to the city. The Renaissance, or rebirth of culture, in Italy was one of the highlights of world history and produced such geniuses as Leonardo da Vinci and Michelangelo.

By this time the democratic form of government had been replaced by duchies. Dukes governed Florence, Milan, Mantua, Urbino, and Ferrara, and the pope ruled a large region around Rome (called the Papal States) for centuries. But the Italian states at the end of the 15th century, continually competing with one another for supremacy, were unable to hold back united foreign powers, such as France and Spain. These two nations began raiding Italy. By 1559 Spain ruled over most of Italy and continued to do so for almost 2 centuries.

The spirit of the Renaissance did not last very long. The popes in Rome became more and more interested in money and worldly goods. Martin Luther (1483–1546), a German priest, was so disturbed by the corruption in the church that he openly criticized it in his

95 theses and nailed them to a church door in Wittenburg, Germany. Luther was excommunicated, but this began the Protestant Reformation. Charles I (1500–58) of Spain, Holy Roman Emperor from 1519 to 1556, was opposed to the spreading of Lutheranism. Through many religious wars he was able to keep the Reformation from reaching Italy. Italy was a victim of political struggles, still under the control of Spain.

Italy was undergoing an economic crisis as well. Christopher Columbus, an Italian navigator in the Spanish service, had discovered America in 1492. The result was that the Italian states lost much of their sea trade to Europe's Atlantic seaboard nations, mainly Spain, France, and England. The Mediterranean was no longer the main avenue of commerce.

During the 16th and 17th centuries, Italy was less active in politics. In the wake of the French Revolution, Napoleon I (1769–1821) appeared and in 1796 shook Italy from its slumber. The people welcomed his ideas of freedom and equality for all classes. During his short reign he carried off the Pope to France, divided Italy into separate states, and made the Austrian emperor Francis II (1768–1835) drop the title Holy Roman Emperor. Even after Napoleon's downfall in 1815, the people continued to feel the spirit of freedom that had brought about the French Revolution.

Secret societies began plotting against the Austrians, who ruled most of northern Italy. Three leaders arose to drive out the foreign powers and unite Italy under its own rule—Giuseppe Mazzini (1805–72), Giuseppe Garibaldi (1807–82), and Count Camillo di Cavour (1810–61). Mazzini was exiled to Marseilles, France, for causing political unrest. While there in 1831 he organized the youth of Italy into a revolutionary movement called Young Italy. Garibaldi had been exiled for taking part in a revolt, and he corresponded with Mazzini from South America. After the Italian States declared their independence from Austria in 1848, Garibaldi returned. He formed a band of citizen-soldiers called redshirts. In 1860, 1,000 of them conquered Sicily and most of southern Italy. Cavour, the Premier of Piedmont and Sardinia, added the Piedmontese troops to the force. They added the regions of Umbria and the Marches in central Italy. King Victor Emanuel II (1820–78) of Sardinia used his alliances with France to drive the Austrian emperor out of Lombardy. Garibaldi joined his conquests to those of Cavour and Victor Emanuel, and Italy was unified politically in 1861. Victor Emanuel became king of Italy. A further campaign in 1866, with Germany as an ally against Austria, added Venetia. In 1870 the conquest of Rome as the capital completed the unification. Italy then began to grow as a major European power.

When World War I broke out in 1914, Italy declared itself to be neutral, but in 1915 it sided with the Allies against Germany. Although Italy helped the Allies to defeat Austria and Germany and gained Trieste and Trento, the effort was costly to the new Italian state. After the war the country was in a state of economic depression, beset by strikes, and without a strong government. The leader who emerged at this time was unlike the earlier men who brought about the unification of Italy. Benito Mussolini (1883–1945), founder of the Fascist Party, imposed strict order under a totalitarian form of government in 1922. Known as Il Duce (The Leader), Mussolini tried to stabilize the economic situation, drained the Pontine marshes, and signed the Lateran Treaty (1929), which gave the Pope complete authority over the Vatican. The Pope in turn recognized the authority of the Government of Italy and its right to govern the former Papal States. Mussolini became allied with the Nazi dictator Adolf Hitler. In 1940 the Fascist government led Italy into World War II on the side of Nazi Germany.

After enduring many defeats, Italians turned against Mussolini. They deposed him in 1943. A bitter civil war went on until the end of the general war in 1945. German and Allied armies, however, continued to battle in Italy until May, 1945. Mussolini was finally captured and shot. In 1946, a year after the end of the war, the Italians voted the King out and declared a republic.

A keen struggle between leftist and moderate parties ensued, but the Christian Democrats, under the leadership of Premier Alcide de Gasperi (1881–1954), managed to forestall a Communist revolution by urging many reforms on the war-torn nation. De Gasperi remained in office until 1953.

With aid from the European Recovery Plan, Italians were able to begin rebuilding their country. Malaria, which had plagued Italy for so long, was brought under control. The country also became active in the movement for European unity. Italy became a member of the North Atlantic Treaty Organization (NATO) in 1949, the United Nations in 1955, and the European Economic Community (EEC) in 1957.

The country has been called *L'Italia che cambia,* or "changing Italy." It has developed from a rural country into an industrial one and has taken its place as one of the major European powers.

GLAUCO CAMBON
University of Connecticut
Reviewed by MARIANITA GARGOTTA
Librarian, Italian Cultural Institute
New York City

See also FASCISM; POMPEII; RENAISSANCE; ROMAN EMPIRE; ROME; VATICAN CITY; articles on famous Italians.

ITALIAN ART AND ARCHITECTURE

Italy is like a vast museum. For more than 3,000 years the people of this boot-shaped peninsula have surrounded themselves with beautiful works of art.

▶ **EARLY CHRISTIAN ART**

In the 4th century A.D. Christianity became an official religion of the Roman Empire. The styles of art used in ancient Greece and Rome were then adapted to the needs of the Christian religion. Temples and palaces were replaced by churches. Most painting and sculpture were designed to decorate the walls of churches.

There was constant trade between Rome and its neighbor to the east, the Byzantine Empire. The Oriental style of Byzantine art had a great influence on early Christian art in the West. The Eastern style was less realistic than Greek and Roman art. Western art became flat and decorative, and by the 6th century, artists in Italy were no longer creating lifelike figures.

Early Christian churches were usually built in either the basilican or the central plan. The **basilican plan** was used for palaces and law courts in ancient Rome and became the model for most churches built in Italy after the 4th century. A basilican church is shaped like a rectangle. The wide section in the center, called the **nave**, is separated from aisles on both sides by rows of columns. At one end of the rectangle is a rounded section called the **apse**, where the altar is located. One of the finest early Christian churches built in this way is the church of St. Sabina in Rome. The marble columns used in this church were taken from the ruins of an ancient pagan temple.

The **central plan** was developed in the Near East. In Italy it was most commonly used in such cities as Ravenna and Venice, which had a great deal of contact with the Byzantine Empire. In central plan churches, all sections were built around the central dome.

Although the exteriors of the early Christian churches were plain, the interiors were elegant and colorful. The flat wooden ceilings were brightly painted, and marble decorated the interiors. Many-domed St. Mark's in Venice is a splendid example of a rich Byzantine interior. Colored marble and mosaic and an altar of gold set with enamels and jewels enrich the church. Silk robes, ivory carvings, enamel ornaments, and **illuminated manuscripts** (books written and illustrated by hand) were also used in many churches.

Art was used in churches for decoration and for teaching the stories of Christianity. In **mosaic**, an art that began in the East, tiny pieces of colored glass or stone are set in cement. In the church of San Vitale in Ravenna there is a mosaic panel of the emperor Justinian and his court. Against a brilliant gold background all the figures stand in line and stare straight ahead. Their robes flow from seemingly weightless bodies. They are so unaware of each other that they show no reaction to stepping on one another's toes.

Frescoes, another type of wall decoration, are paintings done on wet plaster. Frescoes are much less costly than mosaics. They had been used by the ancient Romans on the walls of their homes and **catacombs** (burial chapels).

In very early Christian art, figures were copied from realistic ancient Greek and Roman models. But by the 6th century Christian figures were made less lifelike. It took almost 1,000 years before there was interest in making figures look like real people again.

Most early Roman Christian sculpture was for **sarcophagi** (tombs). Crowded scenes from the Old and New Testaments decorated many tombs. One of the most beautiful is the Sarcophagus of Theodorus, a 5th-century tomb in Sant'Apollinare in Ravenna. On one wall the two Greek letters that stand for Christ are carved inside a circle. On either side of the letters is a peacock, symbol of eternity, and behind the peacocks are birds and vines.

▶ **THE EARLY MIDDLE AGES**

During the Middle Ages (the period from about the 6th to the 15th century) there were three main streams of art in Italy. One was the realistic style left over from ancient Rome. The second was a style based on decorative, simple, and religious Byzantine art. The third was barbarian art. This was largely geometric in design and was based on the style of the Germanic tribes who had invaded

Above: The church of St. Sabina was built in Rome in the 5th century A.D. Some of the parts of this early Christian church were taken from an ancient Roman temple. Below: The interior of San Marco's (St. Mark's) in Venice. The Byzantine church was begun in 1063 and completed in the 15th century.

The church of Sant'Ambrogio (1125–50) in Milan was built in the Romanesque style.

The Cathedral in Siena (1226–1380) is a good example of the Italian Gothic style.

Italy from the north. The combination of these three styles led to the development of Italian medieval art.

In the 10th through 12th centuries a style of architecture developed in Europe called **Romanesque**. Romanesque churches in Italy started with the basilican plan. But, realizing that they needed something more permanent than wooden ceilings, builders replaced them with rounded stone arches. Thick walls supported the arches. Windows were kept small to keep out the heat of the brilliant

Italian sun. This gave the Italian Romanesque churches a heavy and solid look. The somber, bare interiors had many apses and side aisles. A feature that the Italians added to Romanesque architecture was a separate **campanile** (bell tower), built beside the main church.

Painting during the 9th through 12th centuries was used mainly to decorate churches. In the south and in Venice and Ravenna, mosaics were common. Frescoes were popular near Rome. Illuminated manuscripts were also made.

The Doge's Palace in Venice (1309–1424). Elements of both Gothic and Byzantine architecture are combined in its design.

Above: *Flight Into Egypt* by Giotto. The painting is part of a series completed around 1309 in the Arena Chapel, Padua. Below: *Madonna and Child* by Duccio is on a portion of an altarpiece painted between 1308 and 1311 in Siena.

Above: The Cathedral of Florence. Designed in the Renaissance style by Brunelleschi, the dome was built between 1420 and 1436. Below: The courtyard of the Medici Palace (begun 1444) in Florence. The architect was Michelozzo.

THE LATE MIDDLE AGES

Beginning in the 12th century, France led the world in architecture with the elegant, soaring style known as **Gothic**. Gothic churches are high, light, and airy. The columns that support the vaults rise like trees, leading the eyes of the worshiper toward heaven. The diagonal, arched supports outside the church are called **flying buttresses**. The graceful Gothic style is in great contrast to the heavy, solid look of Romanesque. Although Gothic architecture influenced Italy, it never completely dominated as it did in France.

The architect Arnolfo di Cambio (1232?–1300?) designed the huge Florence Cathedral late in the 13th century. He planned the church in the French Gothic style. But the nave is much wider than those of French Gothic churches, and the effect is heavy rather than soaring. Other important Gothic cathedrals in Italy were built about the same time at Siena and Orvieto. Their exteriors were unlike any French church's. They had marble stripes of bright green, white, black, and pink.

The Gothic style was used until the 16th century. But the Cathedral of Milan, begun in 1386, was the last important Italian cathedral to be built in this manner. Designed with the advice of French architects, it took nearly 2 centuries to complete and is one of the largest cathedrals built during the Middle Ages. It is a gleaming mass of white marble with many buttresses and slender peaks piercing the sky.

The carvings on many Gothic cathedrals show a great change of attitude toward nature and toward human life. Throughout the Middle Ages, the church taught that man's life on earth was a punishment and that his only hope for happiness lay in salvation after death. But in the 12th century, life on earth became more important to men.

The 12th and 13th centuries brought recognition to individual artists. Before this, few artists had signed their names to their work. The facade of the Siena Cathedral is filled with carvings of leaves, prophets, and horses and other animals designed by the sculptor Giovanni Pisano (1245–1314). He designed his figures with graceful curves, and the faces wear the suggestion of a smile. The carvings at Orvieto of the creation of man and the Last Judgment show human suffering. The sculptor Lorenzo Maitani (1275?–1330) attempted to portray human proportions. These sculptures, still Gothic in their graceful curves and willowy bodies, express a new spirit. This spirit may be called **humanism**—concern with the individual qualities of men.

Nicola Pisano (1220–84), father of Giovanni, was influenced by the sculpture of ancient Rome. A famous group of pulpits, richly carved with scenes from the Bible, was made by Nicola and Giovanni for various Tuscan churches between 1260 and 1300. Nicola's panels were crowded with figures, many based on Roman models. His Virgin Mary receiving the visit of the three kings has the dignity of a Roman empress. In his use of ancient models Nicola forecast a great new age called the Renaissance.

The new spirit of humanism also appeared in the painting of the late Middle Ages. Many important artists of the 12th and 13th centuries came from the city of Siena. Siena was on the trade route to the East, and Sienese artists were influenced by the Byzantine style. The painter Simone Martini (1283–1344), however, was influenced as much by French Gothic art as by Byzantine.

The work of Duccio de Buoninsegna (1255?–1319?) added warmth and humanity to the decorative Byzantine style. In his painted altarpiece *Maesta* (*Madonna in Majesty*) the flat background is gold. The figures rise from the sides toward the towering central figure of the Virgin. The faces have wrinkled brows and eyes that express real emotion.

Giovanni Cimabue (1240?–1302?) was a 13th-century painter. His importance can be seen through the works of his pupil, Giotto di Bondone (1267?–1337). Giotto's scenes for the Arena Chapel reflect a new style in painting and a concern for **naturalism**—painting things as they really appear. He realized that the Virgin, like any wise mother, would have wrapped her child in her cloak on a dangerous journey. And she would have held him so close to her that they would seem to form a single body. As he led their donkey, Joseph would have turned back with a look of concern to the holy pair. Every scene that Giotto painted on the walls of the little chapel effectively tells a story from the life of the Virgin or Jesus. The citizens of Padua who

The Tempietto was designed in 1502 by Bramante and built in the courtyard of San Pietro in Montorio in Rome.

could not read the Bible could understand the simple dramatic message of these pictures. Giotto's saints were the same as the people who viewed them, ordinary men and women who looked at one another, not straight ahead, and whose faces showed joy and sorrow.

▶THE RENAISSANCE

The Renaissance began in Italy in about 1400. The sculpture of Nicola Pisano and the paintings of Giotto had led the way for the new age. It was an age inspired by ancient Greece and Rome. It was an age that found each man and his world to be as important as the church and its world. It was an age of scientific discovery and invention.

The art of the Italian Renaissance can best be seen in Florence, Rome, and Venice. These were the three main centers of artistic activity during the 15th and 16th centuries.

Florence during the early Renaissance was a place of many contrasts. This walled city with narrow streets and tall towers had joyous pageants and handsome palaces. Under such families as the Medici, who were bankers and great patrons of art, Florence's business and art flowered. It was also a city of violence, brutality, and constant wars. The church fought nobles for power, and noble families feuded among themselves. The rivalries

The Rotonda, a country home near Venice designed in 1550 by Palladio.

reached to art; each noble wished to be served by the best artist and to own the most beautiful objects. No other city in any other century produced so many great and famous artists.

Architecture in Florence and Rome

People of the Renaissance wanted to bring back the golden age of the faraway past. Men were encouraged to study the ancient Greeks and Romans and to learn from their art and architecture.

The Renaissance architect Filippo Brunelleschi (1377?–1446) spent several years in Rome studying the ruins of the great ancient buildings. When he returned to Florence in about 1417, he began to build in a different style. Instead of the Gothic pointed arch, Brunelleschi used a round Roman arch. He used very little carved decoration. The columns, **capitals** (crowns of the columns), and bases are simple imitations of Roman models. The dome of the Florence Cathedral is Brunelleschi's greatest monument.

Madonna and Child (1475), ceramic figures by Andrea della Robbia; Bargello Museum, Florence.

By the 15th century, architects were building as many palaces and civic buildings as cathedrals. The massive Florentine palaces were built of huge blocks of stone on narrow streets. The outsides still resembled fortresses. The Medici Palace by Michelozzo (1396–1472) is typical of the city palaces of the day. The heavy exterior formed a contrast to the graceful interior. Rooms were arranged around an unroofed court opening onto a walled garden with a sculptured fountain amid beds of flowers and shrubs. Delicate columns

The Gattamelata (1501–04) by Donatello was the first life-size equestrian (horse and rider) statue since the Classical Age. It is in the Piazza del Santo, Padua.

Madonna and Child Enthroned (1426) by Masaccio is now in the National Gallery, London.

The Virgin, Jesus and St. Anne (1508–12) by Leonardo da Vinci is in the Louvre, Paris.

Birth of Venus (1480?) by Botticelli is in the Uffizi Gallery, Florence.

and capitals were copied from Roman models.

Leon Battista Alberti (1404–72) was both a scholar and an architect. His buildings carried out what he proposed in his books: Florentine designs based on ancient Roman architecture, but better than their models. His ideas had a great influence on later architects.

Rome in the 15th century was a city of splendor and magnificence. Churches, palaces, villas, and formal gardens all reflected the tastes of the Renaissance. The Farnese Palace is the grandest palace of this period. Designed by Antonio Sangallo (1483?–1546), the palace is a rectangle broken by an entrance in the center and a balcony above. The windows, in 16th-century style, are separate units with their own columns. The palace has three stories of equal height made of brick and stucco covered with **travertine** (Roman limestone). The top story was designed later by Michelangelo.

The interiors of the palaces had gilded ceilings, frescoes, and luxurious furnishings of velvet and brocade. The **villa**—a country house nestled in the surrounding hills—and its formal gardens were an important part of the Roman scene.

Donato Bramante (1444–1514) was an outstanding architect of the Renaissance. Exiled from Milan around 1500, when French troops took the city, Bramante went to Rome. He fell in love with Rome's ancient monuments and with the Palazzo Venezia, which was a completely new building supervised by Alberti and built to fit in with the ancient style. By 1503 Bramante had built the gemlike Tempietto ("little temple") in the courtyard of the church of San Pietro in Montorio. The design of the temple is based on the rectangle and the circle—a circle of columns surrounds a round wall, which is broken by rectangular doors and windows.

In 1505 Pope Julius II decided to rebuild St. Peter's Basilica as a gigantic monument to himself. It was also to be the greatest church in Christendom. The Pope held a contest for a new design, and Bramante won. Bramante's design was in the shape of a Greek cross capped by a circular Renaissance dome. Work began in 1506, but the huge basilica was not finished for 120 years. The design was changed many times by different architects under the direction of many popes. Michelangelo spent the last years of his life working on St. Peter's and is responsible for much of its present design, especially the dome.

The Architecture of Venice

Venice is an island city in the Adriatic Sea. Throughout the Middle Ages, from the time when it was founded in the 5th century, Venice was an independent island protected from the troubles of other Italian cities. Venice was also on the main trade route to the East in the 15th century. Powerful and peaceful, Venice devoted much effort to commerce and art.

The Florence-born sculptor-architect Jacopo Sansovino (1486–1570) was the chief architect of the Republic of Venice. He built a handsome arcaded library with **friezes** (sculpted panels) of children holding garlands. He cleared and paved the central square of the Piazza San Marco. On the Grand Canal he built a palace that has a massive Roman look; it was the first house since Roman times to have running water.

Andrea Palladio (1518–80) was regarded for the following 300 years as the greatest Italian architect. Palladio designed many palaces, but his great contribution was the country villa. The Rotonda is the most famous. It stands on a low hill just outside Vicenza. The Rotonda is square in plan and is topped by a Renaissance dome. Each side is approached by a flight of stairs leading to a colonnaded porch. From each porch there is a view of the surrounding country. His other beautiful villas dot the Venetian countryside, and many are still in use. Their walls are decorated with frescoes by famous painters of the day. Surrounded by fountains and gardens, the villas still create a sense of quiet loveliness. Palladio's ideas influenced English and early American architecture.

Sculpture in Florence

About 1400 a young goldsmith named Lorenzo Ghiberti (1378–1455) won a contest in Florence. It was a design contest for a pair of gilded bronze doors for the Florence Baptistery. The doors in Ghiberti's design were to be decorated with **reliefs** (sculpture raised from a background). It was such a big undertaking that he did not finish the doors for 20 years. A second pair took him another 22 years. The earlier gate is still somewhat Gothic in style. The figures are modeled in graceful, curved Gothic lines, and their drapery flies off their shoulders in decorative folds. Ghiberti treated each of the many panels on the door as though it were a separate sculpture, each telling a new story. Copies of sculpture from classical times appear in his work. In many of his panels there are nude figures that appear to be copied from ancient pagan models.

Just as Brunelleschi sought new forms to express his ideas in architecture, Donatello (1386?–1466) gave new and dynamic life to

David (1502-04) by Michelangelo. The larger than life-size statue (18 feet) is in the Academy, Florence.

sculpture. He carved the first free-standing statues (those that can be seen from all sides) since ancient times. In his reliefs Donatello showed an understanding of perspective. He also studied ancient sculpture and nude models to understand how the human body looks and moves. His bronze *David,* his marble *Prophets,* and his portrait statue of the mounted soldier *Gattamelata* all reflect this knowledge.

The sculptor Luca della Robbia (1400?–82) introduced a new medium to Italian sculpture. This was *terra cotta* (fired clay), which was cheaper than stone or bronze and easily glazed in bright colors. Della Robbia's sweet and tender saints, colored in vivid blues, green, yellow, and purple and enclosed in garlands of lemons, grapes, or leaves, decorated doorways and altars.

Michelangelo Buonarroti (1475–1564) dominated 16th-century sculpture. During his long life he produced great works as architect, painter, and poet as well as sculptor. His sculpture combined the beauty of classical form with a deep religious concern for man's life and sin. One can see this in his famous statue *David.* It was carved between 1502 and 1504 in Florence out of a huge block of marble. The face shows the strength and calmness of a young Greek athlete. But the rest of the body seems tense and anxious as David awaits his battle with the giant Goliath. Michelangelo also created many works for several popes in Rome, especially in St. Peter's Basilica.

Painting in Florence and Rome

Masaccio (1401–28) completely overthrew the medieval tradition and established the new direction in Florentine painting for the next 200 years. The first great painter since Giotto, Masaccio, too, depicted human stories. In his frescoes for the Brancacci Chapel in Florence, the despairing figures of Adam and Eve are shown being driven in shame from the Garden of Eden. Masaccio's *Trinity* showed his admirable perspective technique. If you stand in the right spot in the church and close one eye, you feel as though you are looking into a real chapel instead of at a painted surface. Masaccio also studied ancient sculpture and copied live models in order to understand how the human body looks and works.

The painters who followed Masaccio helped Florence get and keep her reputation as the leader of artistic progress. Paolo Uccello (1397–1475) painted the *Rout of San Romano* showing horses from several angles and positions in order to depict perspective. Andrea del Castagno (1423–57), Andrea Mantegna (1431–1506), and Antonio Pollaiuolo (1429–98) studied anatomy and portrayed the human body as it looked in action. Piero della Francesca (1416?–92) was a mathematician as well as a painter. He wrote several books on perspective and geometry. Piero brought the scientific spirit of Florence to Arezzo, where he made a series of frescoes called the *Legend of the True Cross*. In these frescoes he used his knowledge of geometry. His figures are shaped like cylinders, their heads are like spheres, and they wear cones for hats.

The poetic and delicate paintings of Sandro Botticelli (1444?–1510) express the Renaissance longing for the ancient past. In works such as the *Birth of Venus* we see a cloudless, flower-filled world in which love and beauty seem eternal.

The life and the work of Leonardo da Vinci (1452–1519) summed up the goals of the entire 15th century. Painting and sculpture were only two of his many interests. He was also an outstanding writer, engineer, inventor, stage designer, musician, and astronomer. In Leonardo's paintings, gestures and facial expressions reveal the feelings of the subject. In his *The Virgin, Jesus and St. Anne*, a painting that influenced many younger artists, the monumental, almost sculptural figures also convey a great sense of motion.

Raphael Sanzio (1483–1520) of Urbino was influenced by Leonardo. Dividing his time between Florence and Rome, Raphael created several scenes of the Madonna and Child, which are his best-known works. His clear and delicate figures appear to have been made without effort. In 1508 Raphael was called to Rome to decorate several rooms in the Vatican. In the Stanza della Segnatura he painted four murals that show theology, law, philosophy, and art as they relate to the doctrine of the Catholic Church.

Michelangelo once said, "the nearer painting comes to sculpture the more beautiful it is." His frescoes for the Sistine Chapel in

Perseus (1545–54) by Cellini was cast in bronze. It is in the Loggia dei Lanzi, Florence.

the Vatican are as well-known as any of his sculpture. The Sistine ceiling was done in 1508–12 for Pope Julius II. It covers over 3,000 square feet. Michelangelo painted scenes describing the Creation, Sin, and Redemption of Mankind, and the majesty of God. His massive figures seemed to burst forth from their limited space. Color was not so important to Michelangelo as the power and energy of human form.

Painting in Venice

In the 15th century, artists such as Gentile Bellini (1429?–1507) and Carpaccio (1455?–1523?) painted scenes of Venetian rooms or landscapes in soft, subtle tones. By the 16th century the style of Venetian painting was quite different from that of Florence and Rome.

The popularity of Venetian painting was due chiefly to the talents of four painters: Giorgione (1478?–1510), Titian (1488?–1576), Jacopo Tintoretto (1518–94), and Paolo Veronese (1528–88). Like most Italian painters before them, they painted religious subjects for churches and public buildings. But they also painted more portraits and mythological scenes for private use than had been done before.

Giorgione was very skillful in the use of oil paint. His figures have no sharp outlines at all, and his landscapes seem bathed in mist. In his picture *The Storm,* Giorgione created a startling effect of a sudden flash of lightning in the dark sky above a town.

Giorgione died young. We do not know how great he might have become. But his friend Titian followed his lead in experimenting with oil paint. For more than 60 years Titian explored the possibilities of color in his paintings. He used only a few colors to create soft shading. Like Giorgione he used color instead of outlines to create form. Titian was a popular portrait artist because he painted what the client wished to look like rather than what he really was. Titian liked to paint scenes from classical myths. He called them poems, because he tried to put on canvas special beauty and deep feelings. Previously these qualities had been thought of as part of poetry rather than painting.

Titian's pupil Paolo Veronese was a great decorator. In such scenes as the *Feast in the House of Levi,* Veronese painted a glorified image of a luxurious Venetian banquet. In the background he painted arches from the architecture of Palladio and Sansovino.

Titian's follower Tintoretto was entirely different. While Titian took months to finish a single canvas, Tintoretto appeared to paint with the speed of light. His canvas, the *Last Supper,* hangs in the apse of Palladio's Church of San Giorgio Maggiore in Venice. The figure of Christ at the back of the room is lighted by the halo behind his head as he gives the symbolic bread to his disciples. The table is realistically lighted by a lamp hanging from the ceiling. After Tintoretto's death no major painters appeared in Venice for over 100 years.

Mannerism

Renaissance art described a joyous faith in man's perfection and in the beauty of the world. But in the 16th century, Italy was a battleground for foreign armies. A religious reformation was taking place in Europe, and the Catholic Church was fighting to remain powerful. A group of artists in Florence was no longer willing to make art that described the world as wonderful. Instead of stressing

The Piazza (Plaza) of St. Peter's in Rome. Begun in the 16th century, the structure was designed by many architects. Michelangelo helped design the dome of the church. The plaza was designed in the 1650's by Bernini.

Above: *Girl With a Bowl of Fruit (Lavinia)* by Titian; Gemälde Galerie, Berlin. Right: *St. George and the Dragon* by Raphael; National Gallery of Art, Washington, D.C.

Last Supper (1592–94) by Tintoretto; San Giorgio Maggiore, Venice.

Calling of St. Matthew (1597?) by Caravaggio; Contarelli Chapel, San Luigi dei Francesi, Rome.

subjects that glorified men, these artists emphasized style. In other words, the manner in which a picture was painted or sculpture was carved became more important than the subject matter. For this reason, these artists were called **mannerists**.

Mannerist architects did fanciful things such as turning a doorway into a dragon's mouth. The upper part of a building was more highly decorated than the lower part. Sections

Melancholy and Mystery of a Street (1914) by Giorgio di Chirico; private collection, Connecticut.

of buildings were distorted in small ways so that the visitor often felt he was losing his balance.

In sculpture, lithe forms like *Perseus* by Benvenuto Cellini (1500–71) took the place of the vigorous work of Donatello or the heroic, manly statues of Michelangelo. Cellini's jewelled vases reflect the elaborate tastes of the day.

The artist Antonio Allegri (1494?–1534) is always known by the name of his birthplace, the town of Correggio. Correggio's home was far from the artistic centers of his time. Yet when the great Titian saw Correggio's *Assumption of the Virgin* on the dome of the Parma Cathedral, he was overwhelmed. Titian is reported to have said that if the dome were filled with gold, it would not equal the worth of the fresco itself. The *Assumption of the Virgin* is filled with angels who appear to be constantly twirling around the figure of the Virgin Mary. Bathed in a radiant light, the angels give the impression of traveling upward and out of the dome. Correggio's work foreshadowed the painting methods of baroque artists. He also had a great influence on French artists.

▶ BAROQUE ART

During the baroque age (the 17th century) the Catholic Church launched a huge building program. Giovanni Lorenzo Bernini (1598–1680) cleared away the buildings near the completed St. Peter's Basilica and enclosed an oval space about ⅛ mile wide within 284 huge columns. Above these columns there were over 60 statues.

Seventeenth-century Rome had its face lifted by Bernini, the most outstanding sculptor-architect of his time. Bernini built many churches and palaces. His trademark, and a trademark of baroque art, was the oval, which he preferred to the geometric shapes used so much in the Renaissance.

The Romans loved the sound and sight of running water. Elaborate fountains, many of them designed by Bernini, decorated *piazze* (plazas) all over Rome. Gardens were beautified with pools and water organs, which make music from running water. There were even hidden fountains that could suddenly be turned on to drench an unsuspecting passerby. The gardens had few flowers, but could be enjoyed the year round because of their ever-green box hedges and avenues of cypress trees. Niches contained ancient statues.

Bernini's rival, Francesco Borromini (1599–1667), scorned Bernini's classical taste. His buildings were more lavish in design and ornament. He covered blank spaces with stars, spirals, or irregular shapes to create great movement in the design.

Although Rome was the leader of Italian baroque, the style spread to the whole of Italy and beyond the Alps. But few buildings elsewhere are so original as those of Bernini and Borromini.

The most revolutionary painter of the 17th century was Michelangelo da Caravaggio (1573–1609). Caravaggio did not choose noble and beautiful models for his holy figures as others had done. Turning his back on the classicism of the Renaissance in favor of the truth he found in the streets, he chose simple and poor people as models. The Christ who calls St. Matthew from a dark cellar is neither beautiful nor radiant. Yet the painting has a power and dignity that come largely from the composition. A shaft of light and several pointing hands lead the viewer's eyes toward the figure of the saint.

▶ **ITALY SINCE THE BAROQUE PERIOD**

Venice regained its importance as an artistic center in the 18th century. Giovanni Battista Tiepolo (1696–1770) gave a new life to fresco painting. He thought that the ceiling in a villa should be full of Greek gods just as a church ceiling was full of angels. Learning from Titian's discoveries, Tiepolo brushed luscious, light-toned colors onto big canvases to create charming saints and delightful characters from poetry. This gay style is called **rococo**. At the same time, painters like Antonio Canaletto (1697–1768) and Francesco Guardi (1712–93) composed detailed, jewel-like scenes of daily life in carefree Venice, the playground of Europe.

There were few architects of importance in 18th-century Italy. The most distinguished was a Sicilian, Filippo Juvara (1676–1736), who worked in Rome, Turin, and Madrid. His most imposing creation is the hunting lodge of the King of Piedmont at Stupinigi near Turin (begun in 1729).

The major 18th-century sculptor, Antonio Canova (1757–1822), was less affected by the gaiety of the rococo period than by the growing neoclassical enthusiasm. Neoclassicism was another movement that tried to equal the art of ancient Greece and Rome. Canova imitated antique sculptors. So closely did he copy them that two of his sculptures (*Perseus* and *The Pugilists*) were placed in the Vatican with the most cherished ancient sculptures of the pope's collections. After Napoleon conquered Italy he unsuccessfully tried to convince Canova to be his official artist. Canova refused, but he did some handsome marble portraits of Napoleon and his family. These sculptures depict the French family as though they were ancient Romans.

A few 19th-century Florentine painters, inspired by the French painters known as the impressionists and pointilists, formed a group called the Macchiaioli (spot painters). Their leader, Giovanni Fattori (1825–1908), was better than the rest. But even his work could not compare with the excellent French art of the same period.

Between 1910 and 1914 another group of Italian artists, the **futurists**, became internationally known. Rejecting the past, they sought new ways to portray feelings and tried especially to show movement. Their broken rhythms had a considerable impact on art. Umberto Boccioni's (1882–1916) *Dynamism of a Cyclist* (1913) illustrates the jagged forms of the futurists.

Aside from the paintings of the surrealist Giorgio di Chirico (1888–   ), Italy produced little work of interest until after World War II. A few artists, such as the sculptors Marino Marini (1901–) and Giacomo Manzù (1908–) and the painter Giorgio Morandi (1890–1964), have become well-known. It is in architecture that Italy is again moving toward what may be a distinctive national style. The use of reinforced concrete by the architects Pier Luigi Nervi (1891–   ) and Gio Ponti (1891–   ) is in keeping with international trends. But their buildings also contain unmistakable traces of their unique Italian heritage.

RUTH KENNEDY
Smith College

See also ARCHITECTURE; DECORATIVE ARTS; PAINTING; RENAISSANCE ART AND ARCHITECTURE; ROMANESQUE ART AND ARCHITECTURE; SCULPTURE.

ITALIAN LANGUAGE AND LITERATURE

The roots of Italian language and literature go back to the days of the long-dead Roman Empire, when Latin was the language of the people. Italy's literature and language have a history as distinguished as it is old.

▶ ITALIAN LANGUAGE

Latin is still very much alive in the language spoken today in Italy. Modern Italian, however, is not the same Latin that was written by Caesar, Cicero, and other Latin authors. Italian is a neo-Latin, or new Latin, language. It results from the changing forces of several centuries of history working upon the Latin spoken by the inhabitants of Italy.

From Latin to Italian

In the ancient Roman world there was a noticeable difference between the Latin spoken by the masses (called common or Vulgar Latin) and the Latin used in the schools and in literary works. The school Latin had, however, a certain standardizing influence upon the spoken Latin. When the barbarians invaded Italy and the power of Rome declined in the 5th century A.D., the influence of literary Latin became weaker. As a result, the common, spoken Latin, bound by fewer and fewer controls, became still more different from the literary form.

As this somewhat lawless spoken Latin moved away from the standard literary form, it broke up into the several kinds of speech used today in the regions of Italy. These local, or regional, kinds of speech are called dialects. Although they are all Italian, they are so different that it is not always possible for two Italians to understand each other if each speaks in his local dialect.

For many centuries the people of Italy spoke more than 18 principal Italian dialects. For two main reasons they felt no need for a common language. In the first place, Latin remained the official language, in a form somewhat changed from the classical language of the Roman Empire. The position of Latin was so strong that Italian was not used in a document until 960. Literary works in Italian finally appeared in the 1200's. Secondly, at the fall of the government of Rome, Italy had become divided into several small states. Because of the lack of a strong central government, there was no power that could set up and force a standard language upon all the Italians.

Florentine as Standard Italian. When the Italians chose one of the dialects as the basis for a standard language, they did it for cultural reasons. In the 14th century three men writing in the language of their native city, Florence, composed works that are still masterpieces of world literature. The works of these three—Dante, Petrarch, and Boccaccio—were read everywhere in Italy. The three were of such importance that they encouraged all other writers to imitate their language and style. Thus Florentine, the dialect of Florence, became the standard written Italian. As the centuries passed, it served also as the foundation upon which spoken Italian was built.

Many other languages also have left their mark on modern Italian. Its vocabulary has been enriched by words that have come from ancient Greek, Arabic, German, French, and English. It is difficult to recognize these words as strangers, for they soon acquire an Italian look and sound.

Spoken Italian is one of the world's most beautiful languages. In an Italian word almost every clearly pronounced consonant is followed by a pure vowel sound. The result is an extremely musical language that has always been a favorite of singers and poets.

▶ ITALIAN LITERATURE

Italian literature holds a special place among the literatures of the world. In it we find for the first time many of the ideas and movements that have shaped the culture of modern Europe. This is especially true of the movement called the Renaissance, the rebirth of art and learning.

Also, Italian literature holds a special place because of the beauty that its writers have been able to create.

The Beginnings—13th Century

For many centuries the language of literature in Italy was Latin. No author thought of writing anything in Italian. Not until the beginning of the 13th century were there enough compositions to form what could be called an Italian literature. This early litera-

Dante and His Book (1465), a painting by Domenico di Michelino, in the Cathedral (Santa Maria del Fiore), Florence.

ture, mostly poetry, deals with the basic things in human nature. It is generally about different kinds of love.

Saint Francis. One of the first figures of Italian literature was Saint Francis Bernardone of Assisi (1182–1226). St. Francis gave up a life of riches to dedicate all his love to God and to God's creatures. This great love is expressed in a hymn called the "Canticle of the Sun," written about 1224.

The Sonnet. Poetry that sang of the love between man and woman was developed at the court of Emperor Frederick II (1194–1250). The poets of this group copied older styles and did not often express their own feelings. The poetry, therefore, hardly ever reached the level of great art. But it gave Europe one of its most popular poetic forms, the 14-line poem called the sonnet.

Guinizelli. Guido Guinizelli (1230?–76?), a lawyer in Bologna, gave freshness and originality to the lifeless Sicilian poetry. In his writings he says that it is love and not birth that makes a man noble. Love is not only a thing of the senses. It is also a thing of the mind and spirit. A man who experiences love must therefore become more refined and ennobled.

Dante. The ideas of Guinizelli were further developed in Florence by a group of poets. The chief member of this group was Dante Alighieri (1265–1321). He invented the name given ever since to this poetry by calling it the *dolce stil nuovo,* or the "sweet new style." Some of his poems are among the best in this style.

Dante put a certain group of his poems together in a book and called it *The New Life*

A 16th-century illustration for Petrarch's *Trionfi.* Laura stands in the chariot.

(1292–93). This book tells of his love for Beatrice. Dante saw Beatrice for the first time when they both were about 9 years old. *The New Life,* in prose as well as in poetry, is an account of the growth of this love during the next 16 years. Dante tries to understand and to react properly to this new love. After Beatrice's death, Dante is confused for a time. He finally realizes that he must become more worthy in order to be able to write things about Beatrice that had never before been written about any other woman.

The Divine Comedy fulfills this promise. One of the greatest poems of world literature, it is divided into three parts: Hell, Purgatory, and Paradise. It tells how Beatrice, in heaven, sees that Dante has lost the way of divine love. She obtains a special favor for him so that he may find the proper relationship between love for the world and love for God. He must make a journey through Hell and Purgatory to arrive finally in Paradise. Here Beatrice leads him into the presence of God.

Renaissance—14th Century

In the 4th century the Church triumphed over the religion of ancient Rome. From that time one purpose held the attention of most learned men. The highest goal of every writer was to spread, explain, and defend the Christian religion. To do this it was necessary to give a Christian explanation to everything that had happened before Christ as well as after Christ. This explanation was religious rather than historical. History tells about man and his life on earth. Religion tells chiefly about God and man's soul. The Christian explanation of life, then, tended to pay less attention to the human being than to his soul. The period of which this interpretation is typical is called the Middle Ages.

Petrarch. For many years before the time of Francesco Petrarch (1304–74) the direction of European man's thoughts had been slowly changing. Writers and thinkers were giving more attention to man on this earth than to man's soul. It was Petrarch, however, who clearly expressed and organized this new way of thinking.

Petrarch's studies and writing, mostly in Latin, are the roots of the period called the Renaissance. The outstanding feature of this period is the importance given to the human being and what he can accomplish on earth with his intelligence. Sometimes, therefore, this period is called the age of humanism. It is the basis upon which our present civilization is built.

Petrarch is also famous for a collection of poems in Italian written for a woman called Laura. These poems differ from those of the "sweet new style." They are more personal and express Petrarch's own feelings of happiness and sorrow. Many later love poems and songs developed from this book of Petrarch's.

Boccaccio. Giovanni Boccaccio (1313–75) followed in the steps of his friend Petrarch. He, too, was a humanist. His greatest work, the *Decameron* (1353), contains 100 short stories, or *novelle*. In the *Decameron* 10 friends leave the city of Florence to escape a plague. For 10 days each of them tells a story a day.

Boccaccio did not make up all the stories,

but the way in which he tells them is most original. They represent very well the new spirit, for they are not concerned with religious or moral ideals. The subject is man and his daily life with all its humor, tragedy, beauty, and ugliness. The language, style, and subject matter of the *Decameron* inspired many European writers. In Italy Boccaccio's book set the pattern of storytelling for several centuries.

Renaissance—15th Century

The Italians of the first part of the 15th century found the classical world, discovered and in part created by the humanists, very attractive. It became fashionable to ignore the Italian language and to try to write in a Latin as close as possible to the ancient literary language.

Alberti. Leon Battista Alberti (1406–72) was one of the few writers to try his hand at Italian. In his best work, *Della Famiglia* ("On the Family") (1437, 1438, 1441), he deals with home economics, marriage, bringing up children, and friendship. Alberti is a "universal man," a type of man found fairly often in Italy at that time. Leon Battista was an elegant writer in Italian and Latin; he was a first-class architect, mathematician, and astronomer. He was also a very well-prepared student and teacher of painting and sculpture.

Lorenzo de' Medici. Italian returned as a literary language in the second half of the 15th century at the court of Lorenzo de' Medici (1449–92) in Florence. He was called the Magnificent and was lord of the city in fact if not in name. He used his power and wealth to gather about him a group of gifted writers, thinkers, painters, sculptors, and architects. Under his influence some of the highest artistic creations in the history of Europe were produced.

Lorenzo himself set the example by writing in Italian. His best poems are those that are near the spirit of the people. Among these are "Nencia da Barberino" ("Nencia from Barberino") and a carnival song, "The Triumph of Bacchus and Ariadne." "The Triumph of Bacchus and Ariadne" renews a very old theme. It invites man to enjoy his youth while it lasts, "for of tomorrow we have no guarantee." Such an attitude is typical of the Renaissance.

Poliziano and Pulci. Two poets are especially outstanding in the group that Lorenzo formed about him. Angelo Ambrogini (1454–94), who called himself Poliziano, had the greatest sense of beauty of his time. He was also an excellent humanist, skilled in Latin and Greek. Luigi Pulci (1432–84) excelled in poetry that closely imitated the taste and manners of the people.

Poliziano can be praised for the beauty of his compositions both in Latin and in Italian. When he was 26 years old, he wrote *La Favola di Orfeo* ("The Fable of Orpheus"). The unfinished *Stanze per la Giostra* ("Stanzas for the Tournament") (1475) is considered the most perfect art of Poliziano's century. In this work Poliziano proved that the Italian language was as suitable for poetry as the classical languages.

Luigi Pulci's masterpiece is the *Morgante* (1483). The long poem in 28 cantos, or chapters, is more than a retelling of the old French story of Charlemagne and Roland. Pulci has much to add. Two humorous characters are his own: Morgante and Margutte.

Renaissance—16th Century

After the efforts of Lorenzo's group, Italian as a language was seen to be the equal of Latin in elegance and literary power.

Sannazaro and Boiardo. Both Jacopo Sannazaro (1456–1530) and his *Arcadia* (1504) and Matteo Maria Boiardo (1441–94) with his *Orlando Innamorato* ("Roland in Love") (1482–83) helped the Italian cause. The language became a highly effective literary tool that showed much Latin influence in its structure and vocabulary. Writers of the later 16th century eagerly used this new tool in all types of writing. In many cases their works turned out to be beautifully elegant rather than great.

Machiavelli. Niccolò Machiavelli (1469–1527) wrote mostly about politics. Yet his comedy *La Mandragola* ("The Mandrake") (1513) is perhaps the best of the century. His most famous work is *The Prince* (1532). In it Machiavelli studies what a ruler must do to found and maintain a state. If he hopes to be successful, the only guide for the ruler or prince must be the good of his state.

The Prince is a fine example of still another part of the Renaissance spirit. Machiavelli's book clearly shows the separation that the

Renaissance made between the purely human and the spiritual. The prince must be guided by his human intelligence and strength to create as perfect a state as possible. The state, therefore, must not be judged by religious or moral values. In other words, human efforts must be directed and judged by earthly or human values. *The Prince* was one of the great artistic creations of 16th-century Italy.

The country itself was badly off. During the first part of the century the growing states of Europe used Italy as their battlefield and Italians as their troops. As a result, the Italians lost their freedom, and Spain and Austria came to control Italy completely.

Ariosto. Lodovico Ariosto (1474–1533) escaped the sad conditions of his country by creating his own world of humorous fancy and great beauty. His *Orlando Furioso* ("The Mad Roland") (1532) is a world masterpiece. The many characters move fancifully from one delightful adventure to another. These adventures take place everywhere—on the moon and in worlds invented by Ariosto. Emperors, kings, queens, strong knights, magicians, a magic ring, a flying horse, and many other people and things are masterfully mixed in a charming, happy, and satisfying tale.

Michelangelo and Cellini. Two famous artists composed works that are among the best of this period. Michelangelo Buonarroti (1475–1564) is known throughout the world as a painter, sculptor, and architect. His lyric poetry is perhaps the most personal and therefore the most interesting of his time. Benvenuto Cellini (1500–71), a goldsmith and sculptor, wrote a delightful account of his eventful life. This autobiography, called simply *Vita* ("Life") (1566), is a happy mixture of truth and fancy. In a fresh, engaging style it gives an excellent account of the customs of 16th-century society.

Tasso. During the second half of the 16th century, Italians seemed dissatisfied with one important phase of the Renaissance. The experimenting that marked the early years gave way to rigid rules for all kinds of literature. An official Christian tone made itself heard everywhere. Torquato Tasso (1544–95) shows in his life and in his writings the struggle existing between the dying Renaissance and the new movement. His *Aminta* (1573) tells of the love of the shepherd Aminta for the huntress Silvia. Its main purpose is to be beautiful in the Renaissance manner.

Another work by Tasso shows the spirit of the new return to Christian and moral writing.

WORDS IN EVERYDAY USE	PAROLE D'USO COMUNE
beautiful	bèllo
book	libro
bread	pane
child	bambino
church	chiesa
city	città
cold	freddo
daughter	figlia
day	giorno
father	padre
half	mèzzo
high	alto
house	casa
low	basso
mother	madre
people	gènte
school	scuola
son	figlio
sweet	dolce
time, weather, season	tèmpo
warm	caldo
way, road	via

DAYS OF THE WEEK	GIORNI DELLA SETTIMANA
Sunday	domenica
Monday	lunedì
Tuesday	martedì
Wednesday	mercoledì
Thursday	giovedì
Friday	venerdì
Saturday	sabato

NUMBERS	NUMERI
one	uno
two	due
three	tre
four	quattro
five	cinque
six	sei
seven	sette
eight	otto
nine	nove
ten	dieci
eleven	undici
twenty	venti
twenty-one	ventuno
one hundred	cento

MONTHS OF THE YEAR	MESE DEL'ANNO
January	gennaio
February	febbraio
March	marzo
April	aprile
May	maggio
June	giugno
July	luglio
August	agosto
September	settèmbre
October	ottobre
November	novèmbre
December	dicèmbre

It is called *Jerusalem Liberated*. Like Ariosto's poem, Tasso's is the story of knightly adventures. Tasso's theme, however, is a religious one. His poem tells about the first crusade and about the Christians who went to the Holy Land to free it from the hands of the Turks.

17th and 18th Centuries

The 17th century in Italy was a very showy one. It gave Italian cities, such as Rome and Naples, the grand appearance they still have. People's taste for the theatrical or showy was satisfied by artists and architects who were masters of pomp and splendor. In literature we find the same features as in other arts.

Poetry and Drama. Poetry became more and more elaborate. The poets took greater pride in the fancy way they wrote than in what they were saying. Giambattista Marino (1569–1625) is the most outstanding poet of this kind. His *Adonis* (1623), a long poem of about 45,000 lines, has a very weak plot about the love of Venus for Adonis. The greater part of the work is given to pompous, splendid descriptions. Yet it was most popular in all of Europe.

The theater was very popular, and many plays were written. Among these, *Queen of Scotland* (1628) by Federico Della Valle (1560–1628) is probably the best.

Galileo and Vico. The voice of Galileo Galilei (1564–1642) is by far the greatest in this period of grand sounds and little meaning. Galileo had great ideas to express, and he expressed them in a simple, plain style. He wrote of his important scientific discoveries in such books as the *Dialogue Concerning the Two Chief World Systems* (1632) and the *Dialogues Concerning Two New Sciences* (1638).

Giambattista Vico (1668–1744) was another man who had interesting things to say. His book, usually called *The New Science* (1725), is still very important today for its many ideas about history.

Arcadian Poetry. Writers began to fight against the pompous emptiness of work like Marino's. Their reaction against Marino's type of poetry, however, often tried to correct only the elaborate form. It did not fight against the lack of meaning. The result was a literature different in form but still without serious meaning. Its form pretended to be that of a simple shepherd's song. The name Arcadian was given this poetry because Arcadia in Greece was believed to be the land where shepherds lived and sang happily in the old days. Pietro Metastasio (1698–1782) is the best poet of this group.

The Risorgimento. In time many Italian writers felt they had to leave the graceful song-world of the Arcadians. They believed that Italians should restudy their great past and try to do things worthy of it. Above all they wanted to awaken a moral and civic spirit in Italy. With such a spirit Italians might be able to unite, drive out the foreigners, and form a united Italy. The dreams of this movement, called the Risorgimento, came true in 1871. Many years of hard work and fighting still lay ahead.

Giuseppe Parini (1729–99), Vittorio Alfieri (1749–1803), and Ugo Foscolo (1778–1827) are among the chief figures of the Risorgimento. Parini's main work is *Il Giorno* ("The Day"). The four parts of the poem appeared between 1763 and 1801. A satire, it tells of the worthless, daily actions of a young lord. Parini pretends to praise the lord's way of life, but he really criticizes it severely.

Vittorio Alfieri's poetry, prose, and plays all had a great part in creating the spirit of the new Italy. His autobiography, *Vita,* (1804) is still loved by Italians. *Saul* (1782) is considered his best play. Italy reveres Ugo Foscolo, especially for his *I Sepolcri* ("Tombs") (1807). In very beautiful poetry Foscolo encourages man to do great things. By so doing he will be remembered, and his tomb will encourage men to accomplish noble works.

Still another reformer lived at this time. The reforms of Carlo Goldoni (1707–93) were aimed at the theater and especially at comedies. Through his efforts actors learned and recited the lines of a comedy as they had been written by the author. Before, the actors followed the manner of the *commedia dell'arte*. They made up the lines of the comedy as they acted before the public. Some of Goldoni's plays hold up well.

19th and 20th Centuries

Throughout most of the 19th century, Italian efforts were given to freeing and uniting

The cover of a recent Italian edition of Collodi's *The Adventures of Pinocchio.*

Italy. Many authors, however, found time to produce outstanding works.

Leopardi and Manzoni. Giacomo Leopardi (1798–1837) wrote beautiful poems telling of the sadness of life. We have so many wonderful dreams, Leopardi's poems say, but how few of them come true! Two of his loveliest poems are "To Silvia" and "The Broom Plant."

Alessandro Manzoni (1785–1873) wrote the greatest novel of Italian literature. Manzoni worked some 21 years on this book. He wanted it to serve as an example of the language that the modern Italian should use. *The Betrothed* (1842) tells of the sufferings and dangers Lucia and Renzo undergo because of their love for each other. Italians are very fond of the humorous tone of this historical novel. Manzoni also wrote essays, poetry, and tragedies.

Carducci and Verga. One of the great voices of the Risorgimento was that of Giosuè Carducci (1835–1907). His patriotic poetry had enormous influence, but his best poems are the personal ones, such as "St. Martin's" and "At the Station on an Autumn Morning." He received the Nobel prize for literature in 1906, 2 months before he died.

The man who has had a most important influence on Italian prose in modern times is Giovanni Verga (1840–1922). He wrote exceptionally beautiful short stories and novels about the hard life of the poor, humble people of Sicily. The language he uses matches that of the books' characters. To the reader it seems that the characters themselves, and not Verga, tell the story. *The House by the Medlar Tree* (1881) and *Mastro Don Gesualdo* (1889) are his best novels. One of his stories, *Cavalleria Rusticana,* was made into an opera.

Collodi and Bertelli. Italy's gift to the children of the world is Carlo Lorenzini (1826–90), more commonly known as Collodi. His story of Pinocchio is a universal favorite. Luigi Bertelli (1858–1920), another children's author, also has a pen name: Vamba. His *Ciondolino* ("Shirttail") (1895) is the story of a little boy who becomes an ant and finally emperor of the ants. It contains precise information about the life of insects. In the *Giornalino di Gian Burrasca* ("Diary of Gian Burrasca") (1920), Gian himself tells of and draws pictures of the mischief he creates at home and at school. It is very amusing, and grown-ups like it as much as children.

Of the many other good 19th- and 20th-century authors, a few must be singled out. *Little World of the Past* (1895), as well as many other novels of Antonio Fogazzaro (1842–1911), relates the agonizing struggle between faith and reason. The exceptionally musical poems of Giovanni Pascoli (1855–1912) express a love for nature and for the simple and childlike. Gabriele D'Annunzio (1863–1938) wrote many novels, stories, and plays, but his outstanding contribution is his poetry. The best of his poetry, which glorifies the superman, can be found in the three books of *Lauds* (1903–04). Special mention should also be made of Benedetto Croce (1866–1952), one of Europe's greatest philosophers and critics.

Nobel prizes have been awarded to Luigi Pirandello (1867–1936) for stories and plays, Grazia Deledda (1871–1936) for novels, and Salvatore Quasimodo (1901–   ) for poetry.

The book jacket for the American edition of a world-wide best seller.

The poet Salvatore Quasimodo won the Nobel prize for literature in 1959.

Pirandello's plays and ideas remain important factors in the European and American theater. One of his best-known plays is *Six Characters in Search of an Author* (1921).

Several fine authors have been active both before and after World War II. Aldo Palazzeschi (1885–   ) shows an ironic, fanciful humor in his *Materassi Sisters* (1934) and *Roma* (1953). Another gifted storyteller is Alberto Moravia (1907–   ). His particular kind of realism is present in all his books, from *The Time of Indifference* (1929) to *The Empty Canvas* (1960). The novels of Cesare Pavese (1908–50) have both a realism and a dreamlike, poetic feeling about them. His treatment, as in *The Moon and the Bonfire* (1950), of the torment experienced in trying to realize oneself in a chaotic world has had great appeal to young writers since World War II. *A Tale of Poor Lovers* (1947) by Vasco Pratolini (1913–   ) became one of the most translated books of its time. His realistic novels deal mostly with the working class of his native Florence. He has given a historical view of the workers from the last decades of the 19th century to 1930 in *Metello* (1955) and in *Lo Scialo* (*The Squandering*) (1960).

Realism, then, was the main trend in Italy after World War II. Yet two major writers left this style to seek inspiration elsewhere. *The Baron in the Trees* (1957) by Italo Calvino (1923–   ) represents a turning to fancy. Calvino's flights of fancy, however, have a particular quality that stimulates the reader. Giuseppe Tomasi di Lampedusa (1896–1957) produced a worldwide best seller in his *Leopard* (1958) by writing of Sicily at the time it became a part of the Italian nation.

Besides the Nobel winner Quasimodo, there are two other major poets. They are Giuseppe Ungaretti (1888–   ) and Eugenio Montale (1896–   ). In Ungaretti's poetry there is the voice of human sorrow accompanied by religious fervor. Montale's poems treat the frightening and desperate conditions of man alone in a meaningless world.

ALFRED F. ALBERICO
San Francisco State College

ITALIAN MUSIC

Italy is often called the homeland of music. Musical instruments survive from the prehistoric tribes that inhabited Italy even before the appearance of the Etruscans, the people who came before the ancient Romans. When Rome was the center of civilization in the Western world, music occupied an important place in public and private life. It was used in warfare, religion, and public entertainment. Music was especially called for in the open-air arenas, called circuses, in which popular entertainments were held.

▶ MUSIC IN THE EARLY CHRISTIAN CHURCH

Before the end of the Roman Empire and the beginning of the Middle Ages, Christianity had struck roots deep into the Italian earth. The new religion spread from the Holy Land and settled in Rome, making that ancient city the capital of another, different empire, which has endured. At first, members of the early Christian churches met secretly underground in order to escape persecution. Gradually they came out into the sunlight and took a leading position in Italian life. Religious song became a chief means of devotion. It was pure, unadorned melody, which few music lovers today can understand or truly hear. For it consisted entirely of one melody at a time without the accompaniment of harmony, which we have grown accustomed to hearing with all melody.

This sung melody, called plainsong or plainchant, probably developed from chants sung in the Holy Land and other areas of the Near East. It was music that depended entirely upon the sacred texts that it decorated. The length, pitch, and stress of its tones reflected very closely the stresses and lengths of the text's vowels and syllables.

The Beginnings of Polyphonic Music

Gradually, however, the urge toward musical expressiveness became greater than the desire to keep the sacred texts clearly audible. Singers started using series of tones sung to a single syllable. At times two singers—perhaps a man and a boy—sang the same melody, but each started on a different pitch. As a result, one singer sang the melody higher than the other. Then over the centuries, two, three, and four different melodies were sung together.

A 16th century open-air concert with spinet, lute, recorder, and bass viol.

The result was polyphony. "Polyphony" is the word for music having several melodies sounding together. Sometimes each of the several distinct melodies was sung to different words. Understanding of the text became more and more difficult—and finally impossible. The Church ruled against this polyphonic music in its services. But it did not prevent its spread and development elsewhere.

The collection of sacred melodies approved by the Church was begun during the reign (590–604) of Pope Gregory the Great. It is therefore known as Gregorian chant. Little by little, however, Gregorian chant ceased to satisfy the creative urge of musicians. Song began to be accompanied and sometimes even replaced by music played on instruments. Meanwhile polyphony had almost completely replaced monophony, or music consisting of a single unaccompanied melody.

Throughout the early Middle Ages, Italian musicians moved across Europe, carrying the forms and practices of Italian music everywhere. Attracted by the rapidly growing fame of Italian music, students from all over Western Europe went to Italy to train in their art. As the end of the Middle Ages approached, music in Italy and elsewhere was breaking away from its dependence upon religious services. It was becoming an art in its own right, as we can still hear in the dance-songs of Francesco Landini (1325–97). Landini, who was blind since childhood, was the most famous Italian composer of his time. He was also a celebrated organist and lute player.

▶ THE RENAISSANCE

By the 15th century, vocal polyphony had become enormously complicated. Mastering its technique required years of hard study and practice. During the period of artistic flowering called the Renaissance ("rebirth"), the art of vocal polyphony was brought to a magnificent climax by one of the greatest of all composers. His name was Giovanni Pierluigi da Palestrina (1525?–1594). Palestrina's compositions and those of several of his talented contemporaries are appreciated by music lovers to this day.

But that great summing-up was also a farewell. For Italian music, like music almost everywhere in Europe, was moving further and further away from the Church. And it was ceasing to be almost entirely vocal. Some of the leading Italian musicians, such as Luca Marenzio (1553–99) and Carlo Gesualdo (1560?–1613), devoted themselves to the polyphonic, nonreligious vocal pieces called madrigals. Others, including Girolamo Frescobaldi (1583–1643), concentrated more on music for the organ and other instruments. Stringed instruments and some wind instruments already were being used apart from vocal music. In Venice, for example, Andrea Gabrieli (1510–86) and his nephew Giovanni Gabrieli (1557–1612) wrote some of the earliest great music for groups of brass instruments.

▶ MUSIC FOR VIOLINS

The early stringed instruments called viols began to be replaced by the more brilliant violins. Italy once again showed its musical leadership and produced great violinists and composers. Italian violin-makers set the standards of excellence for all of Europe. (Who today does not know the name of Antonio Stradivari (1644–1737), the famous maker of violins?) Arcangelo Corelli (1653–1713) created wonderful music in which violins took leading roles. The history of 17th- and 18th-century music is crowded with the names of Italian violinists, violin-makers, and composers of music for the violin.

▶ THE OPERA IS BORN IN ITALY

Meanwhile at Florence in about 1600 a small group of poets, musicians, and artists worked out a new form of musical dramatic entertainment. Believing that they were staging plays as the ancient Greeks had staged them—with music throughout—they accidentally produced something quite different. They brought forth the first true operas, which assured Italian leadership in another form of music for at least 2 centuries. Palestrina scarcely was dead before the triumph of homophony (melody supported by chords) over polyphony was certain.

The first composers of opera were eager experimenters rather than musicians with great talent. But their experiments attracted the attention of the foremost Italian composer of the generation after Palestrina's: Claudio Monteverdi (1567–1643). In 1607 at Mantua, Monteverdi produced an opera entitled *Orfeo*, a masterpiece that still is performed. Thereafter opera, combining the arts of drama, music, dance, and stage decoration, swept Italy and then the rest of the Western world.

The foremost composer of serious opera in the late 17th century and early 18th was Alessandro Scarlatti (1660–1725). Masterpieces of comic opera were composed by Giovanni Battista Pergolesi (1710–36) and Domenico Cimarosa (1749–1801). Both Pergolesi's *La Serva Padrona* (*The Maid as Mistress*) and Cimarosa's *Il Matrimonio Segreto* (*The Secret Marriage*) are performed widely to this day.

Alongside opera, a less theatrical form of homophony (often alternating with polyphonic choruses) became almost as widely popular. This was the oratorio, a sort of unstaged religious opera. The first great composer of oratorios was Giacomo Carissimi (1605–74). The oratorio has had as long but not so varied and exciting a career as opera.

Opera at first was an expensive plaything for princes, dukes, cardinals, and other aristocrats. But soon public opera houses were opened. It was found that nonaristocrats were eager to pay for the privilege of attending the opera. Schools of opera composers sprang up at Venice, Rome, and Naples. Opera theaters were built in every Italian city and town. To this day every center of Italian population bigger than a village has its opera house. Singers developed who were capable not only of intense expressiveness but also of feats of vocal acrobatics exciting in themselves. Operatic scenery became more and more complicated. Fountains of real water played upon the stage. Gods floated down upon banks of artificial clouds. Huge rooms full of furniture, with chandeliers ablaze, were lowered onto the stage and whisked up and away again when they were no longer wanted.

The Spread of Italian Opera

Again Italian composers spread across Europe, this time carrying operas with them. They traveled to France, England, Spain, Portugal, Germany, and distant Russia. Italian, the language of music, was sung on the stages of London, Paris, St. Petersburg, Madrid, and Lisbon. It was sung even in Philadelphia and New York in the young United States of America. The very directions telling musicians how to perform music were almost wholly in Italian, as they still are. They include such terms as *presto* ("quickly"), *moderato* ("moderately"), *ritardando* ("slowing down"), *forte* ("loud"), *piano* ("soft"), *sforzando* ("forced"), and many more. In order to be able to read music, a musician had to understand (as he still must) a hundred or so Italian words. In order to sing opera on the big international stages, he had to sing and speak Italian fluently.

▶ THE PIANO MAKES ITS APPEARANCE

The mightiest of musical instruments, the organ had roared and whispered in Italian churches from early times. Many Italian musicians had composed organ music in Italy and in other countries as well. But after the first big steps taken by opera and orchestral music, the organ lost some of its importance outside churches. However, Italians played a leading part in developing the most important keyboard instrument after the organ—the piano. Its name originally was *pianoforte* or *fortepiano* (Italian for "soft-loud" or "loud-soft"). Unlike earlier keyboard instruments such as the harpsichord or clavichord, the piano could produce sounds ranging from very soft to very loud.

Where the first pianos were made is a matter for argument among scholars. But two instruments labeled *piano e forte* were seen at Modena, Italy, in 1598. The man who manufactured the first practical piano was an Italian, Bartolommeo Cristofori (1655–1731). One of his pianos can be seen now in the Metropolitan Museum of Art in New York.

▶ INSTRUMENTAL MUSIC

The violin, the piano, and the orchestra all had their beginnings in Italy. But the richest developments in instrumental composition took place elsewhere. The devotion with which Italian composers and audiences gave themselves to opera in the 17th, 18th, and 19th centuries left little time for instrumental music. The brilliant harpsichord sonatas of Domenico Scarlatti (1685–1757) were an exception. Other exceptions were the works of the violinist-composers of the 18th century, such as Giuseppe Tartini (1692–1770),

Pietro Locatelli (1695–1764), and Antonio Vivaldi (1675?–1741). Vivaldi, a Venetian priest, was one of the leading composers for orchestra and solo instruments. His concertos were much admired by Johann Sebastian Bach. The leading 19th-century successor of these men was perhaps the greatest of all violinists, Nicolò Paganini (1782–1840).

Nevertheless, Germany, Austria, Bohemia, and France were to be the homes of the foremost instrumental composers. No Italian writer of orchestral and chamber music can be compared with Haydn, Mozart, or Beethoven. Perhaps the only chamber music composer who can be mentioned with them is Luigi Boccherini (1743–1805). Muzio Clementi (1752–1832) was an important early composer for the piano. He was one of the first to develop a piano music style that exploited the characteristics of the instrument. But no Italian writer of piano music can be compared with Chopin, Schumann, or Debussy. Neither did Italians devote themselves intensely to the art song. Again, no Italian song composer can be compared with Schubert, Schumann, or Brahms.

▶THE GREAT AGE OF ITALIAN OPERA

But in opera and opera singing, Italians were the masters. When opera began its greatest period, Wolfgang Amadeus Mozart (1756–91), an Austrian, composed three of his best operas to Italian texts: *Le Nozze di Figaro* (*The Marriage of Figaro*) (1786), *Don Giovanni* (1787), and *Così fan tutte* (1790). Mozart received some of his training in Italy, and his style was often very Italianate.

Il Barbiere di Siviglia (*The Barber of Seville*), the first opera to start the whole world singing and whistling, was heard at Rome in 1816. It was written by Gioacchino Rossini (1792–1868). For 19 years Rossini turned out opera after opera, until in many places his name and the word "opera" meant almost the same thing. After Rossini stopped composing operas in 1829, other Italian composers began to take their places in the world's opera houses. The most renowned of them at first were Gaetano Donizetti (1797–1848), composer of *Lucia di Lammermoor* (1835), and Vincenzo Bellini (1801–1835), who wrote *Norma* (1821). Italian operas by the hundreds filled the stages of theaters

Opera, a blending of music and drama, was born in Italy shortly before 1600.

across the world. The names of many of their composers now are found only in music encyclopedias.

Borrowing some of the special aspects of French opera, Italians also helped to develop what is called "grand opera." This is a pageantlike opera often based on episodes taken from history. Among the first true grand operas were Rossini's *Guillaume Tell* (*William Tell*) (1829) and Gasparo Spontini's *La Vestale* (1807). Both were composed to French texts and first sung at the Paris Opera, but they are both completely Italian in musical style.

In 1813 one of the greatest of all opera composers was born—Giuseppe Verdi (1813–1901). Verdi, who composed operas during 53 of his 87 years, crowned the whole history of Italian opera with a series of masterpieces. They include *Rigoletto* (1851), *La Traviata* (1853), *Il Trovatore* (1853), *Aida* (1871), *Otello* (1887), *Falstaff* (1893), and many others. *Aida* became the most popular opera—perhaps the most popular long musical work—ever created.

Before Verdi's death in 1901 a new form of Italian opera known as *verismo* appeared. These operas were usually based on a violent story from everyday life. The best of the *verismo* operas are *Cavalleria Rusticana* (1890), by Pietro Mascagni (1863–1945) and *Pagliacci* (1892), by Ruggiero Leoncavallo (1858–1919). The most gifted Italian composer after Verdi was Giacomo Puccini (1858–1924). It is difficult to imagine how opera houses anywhere could give full seasons without Puccini's *La Bohème* (1896), *Tosca* (1900), *Madama Butterfly* (1904), and *Turandot* (produced posthumously in 1926).

▶ ITALIAN MUSIC IN THE 20TH CENTURY

For the first time in perhaps a thousand years Italy does not lead the world in any aspect of music. The one exception might be the mere presentation of opera. The Teatro alla Scala at Milan, familiarly known as La Scala, is probably still the world's leading opera house. But not since the orchestral tone poems of Ottorino Respighi (1879–1936) has an Italian composer won a world-wide reputation. Since Puccini and Respighi no Italian composer has added to the world repertory of music. The works of Luigi Dal-lapiccola (1904–) and Goffredo Petrassi (1904–) are only occasionally performed outside Italy.

Though Italians no longer lead the world in music, musical activity in Italy is as widespread as ever. Since earliest times each little area of Italy has enjoyed a wealth of local folk music, both vocal and instrumental. Italian composers always have taken hints and ideas from their folk music, which is a treasury of melody, rhythm, and harmony. Sometimes they have borrowed directly from a folk source. Neapolitan songs, for example, have often been used by composers. Ever since the 18th century the words "Neapolitan song" have suggested not only a sensuous vocal piece, but also a certain type of popular song. Though true local folk music is often replaced by American jazz or Latin-American dance pieces, Italian folk music is still very much alive.

Italian composers, as well as those of other lands, today are working in modern experimental music. Perhaps when the present period of experimentation is over, master composers will appear, to add once more to Italy's unmatched musical history. Some of the most experimental musicians of the period since World War II have been Italians. Discussions of modern music always bring up the names of Bruno Maderna (1920–) and Luigi Nono (1924–).

The musical world would be indeed poorer without the music of Palestrina, Monteverdi, Corelli, Vivaldi, Scarlatti, Rossini, Donizetti, Bellini, Verdi, Puccini, and dozens more. The world of music would be poorer also without the instruments and performing skills developed by Italians. It would certainly be poorer without the opera or the thousands of Italian folk songs and dances. In fact the development of music as an art worthy to be classed with painting, sculpture, architecture, and literature may owe more to Italy than to any other land. It may owe more to Italians than even to Netherlanders, Austrians, Germans, Englishmen, and Frenchmen. It would scarcely be an exaggeration to say that music is, of all the arts, the most Italian.

HERBERT WEINSTOCK
Author, *Donizetti and the World of Opera in Italy, Paris, and Vienna in the First Half of the Nineteenth Century*

IVES, CHARLES (1874–1954)

Charles Edward Ives, a pioneer of 20th-century music, was one of America's most remarkable composers. He was born on October 20, 1874, in Danbury, Connecticut, where his father was conductor of the village band. His father taught him to play several instruments and to write music. Young Ives loved the band concerts on the village green. When he was 12 years old, he joined the band as a drummer. He composed some pieces for the band and played the organ at church.

After attending Yale University, where he studied with the composer Horatio Parker, Ives became a partner in an insurance business in New York City. But this did not end his musical career—quite the contrary. The business was so successful that he didn't have to depend on the sale of his music to earn a comfortable living. Moreover, his financial security enabled him to compose just as he wished. He did not have to worry about pleasing the public, the critics, or the music publishers. And in fact for many years he did not please them. His music had too many harsh sounds and odd rhythms for the taste of that day. Nevertheless, he continued to compose in his own way.

Nearly all of Ives's music is connected in some way with the life and literature of America. He often used American folk tunes, patriotic songs, and hymns in his music. The subtitle of his second piano sonata, perhaps his most famous work, is *Concord, Mass., 1840–1860*. It was inspired by several New England authors of the 19th century. Each of its four movements has a name: "Emerson," "Hawthorne," "The Alcotts," and "Thoreau." One of Ives's best-known orchestral works is *Three Places in New England*.

Ives sometimes wrote essays to explain his music. The dedication of *Essays Before a Sonata,* which appeared together with the *Concord* sonata, shows his characteristic wit. He wrote these essays "for those who can't stand his music—and the music for those who can't stand his essays; to those who can't stand either, the whole is respectfully dedicated."

In 1930 illness forced Ives to put down his pen. Many years were to pass before recognition finally came to him. His third symphony, published in 1911, was not performed until 1946. This symphony won the Pulitzer prize in the following year, and Ives's name at last became known. Works that he had written 30 or 40 years earlier now received public performance, often for the first time. When Ives died on May 19, 1954, in New York City, he was honored as one of the most important of American composers.

IVORY

Ivory is the dentin, or inner layer, of teeth. Most commercial ivory comes from the tusk of the elephant. Although the tusk is really a long, partly hollow tooth, the elephant uses it for fighting and grubbing out roots instead of for chewing its food. Some elephant tusks are as long as 8 feet and weigh up to 150 pounds. The teeth of other animals are also ivory, but the amount is too small to be of value. Also, the teeth of other animals are covered by a protective outer layer, or enamel, which makes the ivory more difficult to work with. The enamel almost completely wears off the tusk of the elephant while it is still young.

There are two characteristics that make ivory such a prized material. The first is its warm, glowing tone, caused by a fluid inside the tusk. When the tusk is rubbed, the fluid helps the tusk take on a high polish. The fluid also allows stains and dyes to soak in more easily. The second characteristic is the fine, closely set natural lines, or grain, in ivory. Ivory's clear, smooth appearance comes from the small size and structure of the grain. Since ivory does not have to be carved with the grain, it can be cut into any shape and into very thin slices. The slices stick firmly to most surfaces if they are properly glued.

The most valuable ivory comes from Africa, where the best ivory is a mellow white with almost no mottling (blotches of different colors).

Ivory taken from elephants that have recently been killed is called **green** ivory. So-

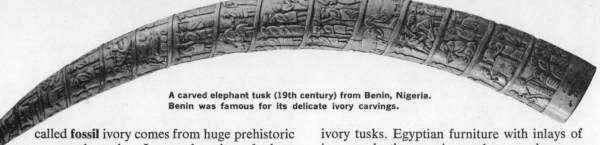

A carved elephant tusk (19th century) from Benin, Nigeria. Benin was famous for its delicate ivory carvings.

called **fossil** ivory comes from huge prehistoric mammoth tusks. Large deposits of these ancient tusks have been found in many northern countries, particularly Siberia. Some Siberian deposits have been worked for more than 200 years. This ivory is usually gray in color and not as good as green ivory.

The teeth of the hippopotamus, walrus, narwhal (a small member of the whale family), sperm whale, and some wild boars have also been used for ivory. Hippopotamus ivory is thick and hard. Until recently it was widely used for false teeth. Narwhal ivory is very dense and of good quality. But since the hollow tooth is spiral shaped, it is not used for large ornaments. During the Middle Ages the odd shape of the narwhal tooth made many people believe it had magical qualities. It was supposed to be the twisted horn of the imaginary white beast, the unicorn. After the Middle Ages everyone knew the tooth had no special powers and did not belong to the unicorn, but its strange shape continued to fascinate people. Sailors on whaling ships whiled away their free hours by carving whale teeth into fanciful shapes. These carvings are called scrimshaws. So few sperm whales, walruses, and wild boars are left that their teeth are no longer of much commercial importance.

Before ivory can be carved, the outer layer of the tusk must be stripped off and the inner layer left to season. In some places ivory is still carved by hand, as it has been for centuries. But cutting machines and a new flattening process are also used. To flatten the ivory into a larger, more workable piece, the ivory tusk is first peeled in a continuous strip. The long peel is then pressed into a flat sheet.

Ivory is now mainly used for ornaments and, surprisingly enough, for high-quality billiard balls. Only the finest tusks are made into billiard balls, since the balls must be even and not crack.

▶ **HISTORY OF IVORY**

Ivory has a rich, varied history. Cavemen carved pictures of reindeer and mammoths on ivory tusks. Egyptian furniture with inlays of ivory and other precious substances has survived over the centuries and can still be seen in museums. The Egyptians also carved ivory into a multitude of delicate shapes.

Boatloads of ivory, gold, peacocks, and monkeys were brought every 3 years to King Solomon. He is even said to have had an ivory throne covered with gold. Gold and ivory were often combined. Since ivory has such a lifelike tone, the Phoenicians, and later the Greeks, made statues with ivory skin and gold robes. Over the centuries ivory has continued to be carved into beautiful statues and boxes.

Until the late 19th century the African ivory trade was controlled by the Arabs. They were the only ivory traders who dared go into the heart of Africa. From the interior they brought their precious cargo to coastal trading centers, such as fabled Zanzibar. But the arrival of the European hunters with their powerful guns and fast transportation almost ended the ivory trade. The competing hunters destroyed so many elephant herds that elephants began to disappear from Africa.

Some elephants still roam freely in the deepest jungles, but most elephants today are on reservations. Since there is so little ivory, manufacturers try to waste none of it. The dust from a carving is carbonized—that is, changed to a black powder. The powder is used to make a special artists' paint known as ivory black. The scraps are used in inlays.

There are several substitutes that are used in place of ivory. Vegetable ivory is made from the dried seeds of a plant commonly called the ivory-nut palm. The seeds are used to make ivorylike buttons and other small objects. Imitation ivory has been made from Galalith (a substance made from milk) and several plastics. Celluloid, which was developed in the late 19th century, has been widely used as a substitute for ivory. Celluloid looks very much like ivory, but it does not have the fine grain of natural ivory.

Reviewed by THEODORE KAZIMIROFF
Fellow, New York Zoological Society

IVORY COAST

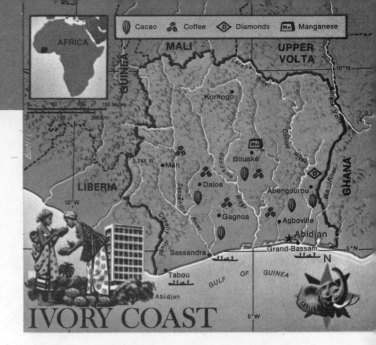

IVORY COAST

Although the name "Ivory Coast" makes us think of a country where many elephants are found, most of the people there never see one unless they visit a game preserve or a circus happens to come to town.

Nowadays, a better name for this nation would be "Coffee Coast"—it is the world's third largest exporter of coffee. But the old name has been kept, and the elephant is pictured on the country's coat of arms and on postage stamps. It symbolizes the qualities of strength and endurance, which are much admired by the people of this new African nation.

▶ THE PEOPLE

About 4,200,000 people live in the Ivory Coast. Because of its history, life in this country is a mixture of African and French cultures. The majority of the people still lead a traditional village life. An increasing proportion, however, live and work in modern cities.

Some ethnic groups are organized in tribes, headed by chiefs. The Baule (Baoulé), one of the largest groups in the country, make up about one fifth of the total population.

FACTS AND FIGURES

REPUBLIC OF IVORY COAST is the official name of the country.

CAPITAL: Abidjan.

LOCATION: Western Africa. **Latitude**—4° 21′ N. to 10° 45′ N. **Longitude**—2° 30′ W. to 8° 39′ W.

AREA: 124,503 sq. mi.

POPULATION: 4,200,000 (estimate).

LANGUAGE: French (official), local languages.

GOVERNMENT: Republic. Independent since August 7, 1960. **Head of Government**—president. **International Co-operation**—United Nations, Organization of African Unity (OAU).

NATIONAL ANTHEM: *L'Abidjanaise.*

ECONOMY: Agricultural products—yams, bananas, coffee, coconuts, cocoa, pineapples, cotton, palm nuts and kernels, rubber. **Industries and products**—textiles, timber, fishing, food processing, canning, vegetable oil, coffee, cocoa, bananas, fruit juices and preserves, tuna, pineapple. **Chief minerals**—diamonds, manganese. **Chief exports**—coffee, cocoa, wood, bananas, palm oil, diamonds. **Chief imports**—food, iron and steel products, cotton cloth, vehicles, machinery, petroleum products, building materials. **Monetary unit**—franc CFA (African Financial Community).

According to legend, they came to the Ivory Coast from Ghana in about 1750.

Another ethnic group with important chiefs is the Senufo. Many smaller groups live in the southwest. Among them are the Bete, Wobe, and Guere.

The Baule men wear colorful robes that look like ancient Roman togas. The Senufo and many other northerners wear *bubu*—long, loose shirts down to their ankles.

Most of the southern people live in rectangular houses, while in the north most houses are round. In the farm region the walls of houses are usually of mud or grass, and the roofs are of thatch. But in towns people who can afford them prefer houses of cinder block or cement, with corrugated tin roofs. Tin roofs last longer and are fireproof, but thatched roofs are cooler in the tropical climate.

There are many languages spoken in the Ivory Coast. But an Ivoirien (Ivory Coast citizen) usually speaks French. It is the official language of the country.

Young students in Abidjan, the capital, are taught arithmetic, spelling, history, and other subjects familiar to school children all over the world. During recreation period the Ivoirien boy plays games similar to those played by a French boy. Soccer is the big favorite. Since noon is the beginning of the hottest part of the day, the Ivoirien boy takes a 2-hour lunch and a nap—the *sieste*. The evening meal consists of an African dish, such

A Senufo village in northern Ivory Coast. The houses are made of mud or grass and have thatched roofs to protect their inhabitants against the hot sun.

as manioc and fish stew in tomato sauce. In the city everyone sits down together for supper. The village boy, on the other hand, seldom eats with his father, but has meals with his own mother, his father's other wives, and all their children. His school is smaller and not as modern as the one in the city. But if he does well, he may attend high school and later the new university in Abidjan.

One important holiday that everyone shares is Ivory Coast Independence Day, August 7, when the schoolchildren march in parades. Christmas and Tabaski (the Muslim feast of the lamb) are two major religious holidays. But the majority of Ivoiriens are neither Christian nor Muslim. They revere their creator and the spirits of their ancestors. Country people celebrate holidays such as the festival of yams, a sort of Thanksgiving Day, at harvest time.

Wood sculpture, gold and brass casting, and weaving have a long history in the Ivory Coast. The most favored sculptured objects are masks and statues that have a religious meaning. Their artistic qualities have made them world-famous. The Ivoiriens are also proud of their national theater and dance troupe. Ivoirien plays have been well received both in Africa and in Paris.

▶ THE LAND

The Ivory Coast is a square-shaped land about 300 miles north of the equator. It is bounded by Liberia and Guinea on the west, by Mali and Upper Volta on the north, by Ghana on the east, and by the Gulf of Guinea on the south. It has an area of 124,503 square miles, slightly larger than that of Italy. Although it is generally very hot in the Ivory Coast, there are some important differences between the northern and the southern regions.

The south is an area of dense rain forests. It is both hot and humid, with temperatures ranging from 72 to 90 degrees Fahrenheit. There is almost no difference between daytime and nighttime temperatures. During the long rainy season starting in mid-May, rain falls nearly every day for 2 months. A dry season follows, then a short rainy season, and another dry season. The total annual rainfall is about 90 inches. The southern climate is best suited for producing a type of coffee called robusta, which is used mainly for instant coffee.

The north is a grassy plain with hills in the western part. The north has one rainy season and an annual rainfall of only 54 inches. Temperatures in the north reach greater extremes than in the south.

There are four major rivers: the Comoe, the Bandama, the Sassandra, and the Cavally. They all run from north to south and provide fish for a large number of people. Unfortunately, many stretches of rapids make the rivers hard to navigate. To make them useful, the government is constructing dams to control flooding and to supply hydroelectric power.

The huge forests are the greatest natural resource of the country. Rubber trees, coconut palms, oil palms, banana trees, cacao trees, and pineapples have been planted. The Ivory Coast is also rich in diamonds and manganese.

▶ **INDUSTRIES AND PRODUCTS**

Ninety percent of the Ivoiriens are farmers. The coffee, rubber, coconuts, palm oil, bananas, pineapples, and cacao grown in the south supply products for export as well as for local use. Vegetables, such as okra, tomatoes, yams, taro, and cassava, supply most of the daily food needs. Rice, millet, corn, and yams are grown for local consumption in the north. Without a cash crop, the north is a poor region. It has fewer roads, schools, and hospitals than the south. The government has recently encouraged the planting of cotton and the raising of cattle in this region.

Ivory Coast factories produce palm oil, margarine, fruit preserves, and fruit juices. There are sawmills, soap and plywood factories, textile mills, and a French-owned automobile assembly plant.

Coffee is the major export. The Ivory Coast's huge forests supply thousands of tons of mahogany, African teak, and other woods for export to Europe and America. Minerals, such as diamonds and manganese, are also being exported. Imports to the Ivory Coast

Above: Abidjan, capital of Ivory Coast, is a modern city with tall buildings and well-paved streets. Below: Sea snails are sold at fish markets in the old section of Abidjan.

Ivory Coast magistrates in the lobby of the Abidjan Courthouse.

include textiles, machinery, and motor fuels and oils.

Cities. The Pearl of the Lagoon is the nickname for Abidjan, the beautiful capital city. It is situated on a lagoon along the eastern coast of the country. In 1910 Abidjan was only a small fishing village. Today it is a cosmopolitan city of some 450,000 people and a center of trade. It has one of the most modern harbors on the west coast of Africa. There are airports at Abidjan, Bouake, Korhogo, Sassandra, Man, and Tabou. Other important towns are Daloa, Agboville, and Abengourou. Each of these towns serves as the center of trade and local government for its surrounding region. Produce from farms is brought to the town and shipped to Abidjan by rail or truck, while goods from all over the world come to the town markets for the local consumer.

▶**GOVERNMENT**

The Ivory Coast is a republic. Its chief executive is the president. He is assisted in his work by a cabinet. The principal lawmaking body of the country is the National Assembly. The president and members of the assembly are elected by universal adult suffrage.

▶**HISTORY**

European explorers and traders first established posts along the southern coast of West Africa in the 18th century. They started to buy slaves, palm oil, and gold from the people who lived near the sea. In 1893 the French took control of the coast and penetrated into the hinterland. They created the colony of the Ivory Coast and ruled it through a governor.

In order to do the work that France wanted done, Africans were forced to work for low pay and under unpleasant conditions. The colonial government had to convince Africans to plant crops that would be useful to France. Those who did earned enough money to make it possible for their children to be educated.

Many of the Africans fought for France during World War I and World War II. When World War II ended in 1945, the educated Africans, in return for their loyalty, demanded some voice in government. Some of them were allowed to vote for two deputies (congressmen) to the French National Assembly. One of the deputies was Félix Houphouet-Boigny, an African doctor, who organized his followers into a national movement called R.D.A., which stands for Rassemblement Democratique Africain (African Democratic Rally).

In spite of opposition from French colonists, the Africans demanded more freedom. In 1958 France made the Ivory Coast an autonomous republic with full control over all internal affairs. Two years later the Ivory Coast became completely independent, and its flag—the orange, white, and green tricolor—was added to the flags of the United Nations.

VERA L. ZOLBERG
Oberlin College Peace Corps Project for the
Ivory Coast, Gabon, and Cameroon

Reviewed by ARSÈNE ASSOUAN USHER
Ambassador of Ivory Coast to the United Nations

I, ninth letter of the English alphabet   **I** 1
See also Alphabet
Iago, character in Shakespeare's *Othello*   **O** 236
Iambic (i-AM-bic), a metrical foot in poetry   **P** 354
Iambic pentameter (pen-TAM-et-er), meter in poetry   **P** 354
I and the Village, by Chagall, painting   **C** 184
IATA see International Air Transport Association
Ibadan (i-BA-don), Nigeria   **N** 255
Ibadan, University of, picture   **N** 253
Ibáñez, Vicente Blasco see Blasco Ibáñez, Vicente
I-beams, for building construction, picture   **I** 407

Iberian (i-BER-ian) **peninsula,** southwestern peninsula of Europe whose area of about 228,000 square miles includes Spain and Portugal. It is bounded by Atlantic Ocean on west and north, by Mediterranean on east and southwest, by Pyrenees on northeast, and by Strait of Gibraltar on south.

Iberians, ancient people of western Europe
Spain   **S** 350
Spanish art and architecture   **S** 360

Ibert (e-BARE), **Jacques** (1890–1962), French composer, b. Paris. He won the Prix de Rome in 1919. His popular symphonic suite *Escales* ("Ports of Call") was inspired by a Mediterranean cruise while he was serving in the French Navy during World War I. He was director of the French Academy in Rome (1937–55) and of the Paris Opéra and Opéra-Comique (1955–57). His compositions include operas, ballets, orchestral works, and vocal, chamber, and piano music.

Iberville (e-ber-VEEL), **Pierre Lemoyne, Sieur d'** (1661–1706), French-Canadian naval commander and explorer, b. Montreal. After serving in the French Royal Navy (1675–85), he participated (1686–97) in French attempts to expel the British from North America by attacks on English forts and Hudson's Bay Company fur-trading posts. When the French and English war ended (1697), he was commissioned (1698) by the French Government to found a colony in Louisiana. He established a colony at Biloxi Bay (1699) and was made governor of Louisiana (1704).

Ibex (I-bex), grayish-brown wild goat found high in the mountains of temperate Europe and Asia. The ibex has a short tail and a beard hanging from the middle of its lower jaw. Its horns curve upward, backward, and to the sides. Picture   **H** 218.
wild goats and hoofed mammals of the bovine family
G 244;   **H** 221

Ibis (I-bis), any of several wading birds found along shores and in marshes of temperate and tropical regions. Ibises are long-legged and have a long, thin bill that curves downward. In many the face (or entire head and neck) is bare of feathers, revealing black or brightly colored skin.

IBM see International Business Machines
Ibn, meaning in names   **N** 5
See also for those not listed below, first part of name, as Abdullah ibn Hussein
Ibn-Batuta, Moroccan writer   **A** 76d
Ibn Ezra, Moses, Hebrew poet   **H** 102–03
Ibn-Gabirol (ib'n-ga-BI-rol) **Solomon,** Hebrew poet
H 102–03
Ibn-Khaldun, Tunisian writer   **A** 76d

Ibn Saud (IB'n sa-OOD) (Abdul Aziz ibn Saud) (1880–1953), first king of Saudi Arabia (1932–53), b. Riyadh. He won control of most of Arabian peninsula and founded the kingdom of Saudi Arabia (1932). He established a considerable measure of law and order in a previously lawless land.   **S** 49

Ibn Sina see Avicenna
Ibo (E-bo), a people of Nigeria   **N** 253, 258
proverbs quoted   **A** 76a
Ibsen, Henrik, Norwegian poet and playwright   **I** 2
Grieg suites for *Peer Gynt*   **G** 376
realistic drama   **D** 297
Scandinavian literature   **S** 51
I came, I saw, I conquered, Caesar's victory message
C 6
Icarus (IC-a-rus), asteroid   **P** 274

Icarus, in Greek mythology, youth imprisoned by King Minos with his father, Daedalus, who contrived wings for them to escape. When Icarus flew too near sun, the wax holding his wings together melted and he fell into Icarian Sea (named for him). According to legend, Hercules buried his body, which had been washed ashore on island since called Icaria.
legendary flight of Icarus   **A** 36, 567; picture   **A** 568

ICBM's see Intercontinental ballistic missiles
ICC see Interstate Commerce Commission
Ice   **I** 3–12
glacial caves   **C** 156; picture   **C** 157
glaciers   **G** 223–25
How does an ice skate glide on ice?   **I** 4
how heat changes matter   **H** 92
iceboating   **I** 28–31
ice crystals formed into snowflakes   **R** 95–96
ice-particle theory of electricity in clouds   **T** 172–73
IGY studies in Antarctica   **I** 319–20
physics of ice skating   **I** 4
polar regions   **P** 366
sculpture, picture   **N** 159
sublimation of clouds   **C** 359, 360
water cycle   **W** 51, 53
water desalting   **W** 56a
See also Dry Ice; Icebergs
Ice ages   **I** 13–24
Agassiz's findings   **A** 80
Canadian Shield, Canada   **Q** 10
caves, formation of   **C** 156
distribution of animal life   **L** 237
earth's history   **E** 9, 21
glacial geology, studies in   **G** 115
Glacier National Park   **G** 222
ice sheets of the earth   **I** 8–12
prehistoric art   **P** 439–41
prehistoric man   **P** 442–46
Icebergs   **I** 25–27
ablation processes (calving), in glaciers   **I** 6–7
Antarctic regions   **P** 366
Greenland, picture   **G** 370
looming mirage, picture   **M** 342
Titanic disaster   **O** 24
why they float   **I** 5
Iceboating   **I** 28–31
Ice boxes see Refrigeration

Icebreaker, ship with special hull designed to force path through ice. Such ships are used in Arctic and Antarctic exploration. First nuclear-powered icebreaker was built (1959) by Soviet Union.
IGY studies, use of an icebreaker in, picture   **I** 316

Ice cream   **I** 31–34
Dr. Coles Trust Fund   **F** 390

Ice Cream (continued)
  introduced to U.S. by Thomas Jefferson **F** 340
  stain removal **L** 84
  sundae, origin **F** 335
Ice crystal clouds **C** 359, 360
Iced tea **T** 38
Ice-glass, Venetian glassmaking process **G** 229
Ice hockey **I** 35–40
  Canada **C** 67
  Olympic Games **O** 109; pictures **O** 113, 116c
  See also Field hockey; Stanley Cup
Iceland **I** 41–45; **S** 49
  center of mid-ocean rift **E** 15
  Ericson, Leif **E** 275
  flag **F** 239
  geysers and hot springs **G** 192
  Icelandic literature **S** 50–51
  pagan Norse culture kept alive **N** 277
  Viking migrations to **V** 339
Icelanders, immigrants to Manitoba **M** 77
Icelandic literature **S** 50–51
Iceland moss **F** 95
Iceland spar, mineral **R** 271–72
Ice milk, frozen dessert **I** 34
Ices, frozen desserts **I** 34
Ice sheets **I** 8–12
Ice skating **I** 46–53
  high standard required for ice hockey **I** 37
  How does an ice skate glide on ice? **I** 4
  physics of **I** 4
  racing in the Netherlands **N** 116
  See also Ice hockey; Roller-skating
Ichabod Crane, character in *Legend of Sleepy Hollow, The* **A** 199–200
Ichthyology (ic-thi-OL-ogy), study of fishes **F** 181
Ichthyornis (ic-thi-OR-nis), prehistoric bird **B** 207, 209
Ickelsamer (ick-el-ZA-mer), **Valentin**, German teacher **P** 193

Ickes (ICK-es), **Harold L.** (1874–1952), American politician, b. Frankstown Township, Pa. After active participation in Chicago political reform movements, he became one of the principal New Dealers under Franklin D. Roosevelt. While secretary of interior (1933–46), he was administrator of public works (1933–39), co-ordinator of fisheries (1942–46), and hard-fuels administrator (1943–46).

Iconoclasts (i-CON-o-clasts) (from Greek word meaning "image-breaking"), originally, group in 8th- and 9th-century Byzantine Empire who opposed use of images in religious worship on grounds that this practice led to idolatry. The movement was outlawed by ecumenical council of Nicaea (787), which advocated veneration, but not adoration, of statues and pictures in churches. Term is now used to refer to anyone who departs from traditionally accepted views.
  Byzantine art, period of iconoclasm in **B** 487

Iconostastis (i-con-OS-ta-sis), screen in churches **U** 54
Icons (I-cons), religious images and holy pictures **O** 229
  Byzantine art form, pictures **B** 485, 490
  Russian art **U** 55; pictures **U** 56
Icterus *see* Jaundice

Ictinus (ict-I-nus) (mid-5th century B.C.), Greek architect. He was the chief designer of the Parthenon (construction begun 447 B.C.) and designed the Temple of Demeter and Persephone at Eleusis and the Temple of Apollo at Bassae.

Idaho **I** 54–68
  Sawtooth National Forest, picture **N** 36
Idaho, University of **I** 63
Idaho Falls, Idaho **I** 66
Id-Al-Adha, religious holiday **R** 154
Id-al-Fitr, religious holiday **R** 155
Ideal states *see* Utopias
Identical twins **G** 86; picture **G** 78
Identification
  by fingerprints **F** 129
  by laundry marks **L** 85
Identification bracelets **J** 99
Identification cards, carried by aliens **A** 166
Identity element for addition, or zero **N** 388
Identity element for multiplication, or one **N** 388
Ideographs (I-de-o-graphs), characters in Chinese writing **C** 431
  writing, development of **W** 317

Ides, in Roman calendar, 15th day of March, May, July, and October and 13th day of any other month. It was used by Romans as fixed point (along with calends and nones) from which to designate the days of the months. It is referred to in Shakespeare's *Julius Caesar*—"Beware the ides of March."
  Caesar's assassination **C** 6

Idler, The, essays by Samuel Johnson **E** 293
Idlewild Airport *see* John F. Kennedy International Airport
Idols, images representing gods **R** 145–46
Idris I (id-REES), king of Libya **L** 205
Idris, Moroccan ruler **M** 461
Idun (E-dun), Norse goddess **N** 280
Idylls of the King, by Tennyson **E** 262; **T** 101
Iemitsu (e-ye-MI-tsu), Japanese shogun **J** 46
Ieyasu (e-AY-a-su), Japanese statesman and shogun **J** 45, 46
If, poem by Rudyard Kipling **K** 261
Ifé (E-fe), ancient kingdom in Africa
  early art achievements **A** 71–72; picture **A** 73
Ifé, Nigeria **N** 258

Ifni (IF-ni), small area on southwestern coast of Morocco having dry land and climate. It was occupied by Spain in 1934 and remained a Spanish overseas territory after Moroccan independence (1956). It was ceded to Morocco (1969) after 11 years of negotiation. Its principal city is Sidi Ifni.
  Morocco and Spain **M** 461; **S** 356

IFR *see* Instrument Flight Rules
Igloos, Eskimo homes and shelters **E** 290; picture **E** 287
  anthropologists study family and homes **A** 302–03
  houses of snow **H** 172–73

Ignatius (ig-NAI-tius) (50?–107?), third bishop of Syrian Antioch, Christian martyr, and saint, b. Syria. He is believed to be disciple of St. John the Evangelist. While en route to Rome, where he was martyred, he wrote seven letters now included in book *Apostolic Fathers*.

Ignatius of Loyola, Saint *see* Loyola, Saint Ignatius
Igneous (IG-ne-ous) **rock** **R** 263–66
  mountain building **M** 493
  studies by early geologists **G** 111
Ignimbrite, rock **V** 382

Igorots (ig-o-ROTS), several ethnic groups inhabiting parts of the Philippine Islands. The Igorots are now engaged in agricultural pursuits, mainly rice-growing. Most of them live in villages on the island of Luzon.

Iguanas (i-GUA-nas), kind of lizard
  Galápagos Islands, Ecuador **E** 56
  marine iguana **L** 319
Iguanodon (i-GUA-no-don), dinosaur **D** 172, 177–79
Iguazú (i-gua-SU) **Falls,** or **Iguacu** (Iguassu) **Falls,** South America **A** 392, 393; picture **S** 274
  famous waterfalls **W** 56b
IGY see International Geophysical Year
I Had a Dove, poem by John Keats **K** 200
I have a little shadow that goes in and out with me, from *My Shadow* by Robert Louis Stevenson **S** 424
I have not yet begun to fight, words of John Paul Jones **J** 135
Ijsselmeer (I-sel-mare), lake in the Netherlands **L** 31; **N** 118
Ikebana, Japanese flower arranging **J** 49

Ikeda (e-KED-a), **Hayato** (1899–1965), Japanese political leader, b. Yamaguchi Prefecture. He began government service as an administration officer in Ministry of Finance (1925) and served as vice-minister of finance (1947–48), minister of finance (1949–52, 1956–57), minister of international trade and industry (1959–60), and prime minister of Japan (1960–64). During the occupation (1945–52) he worked with American authorities on anti-inflationary policies that guided Japan to new prosperity.

Ikhnaton see Akhnaton
I Know Where I'm Going, folk song **F** 320
Ile de la Cité, (ELE d'la ci-TAY), Paris **P** 73
Ile Saint Jean (san JON), now Prince Edward Island, Canada **P** 456b–456h
Ile Saint-Louis, Paris **P** 69
Iliad (IL-i-ad), epic poem by Homer **I** 69
  Aeneid compared with **A** 35
  dancing described **D** 23
  early form of fiction **F** 110
  early Greek literature **G** 350
  Homer **H** 167
  Trojan War **T** 293–94
Iliamna Lake, Alaska **A** 133
Ilium, or **Ilion,** Greek name for Troy **T** 293

Illampú (ee-yam-PU), mountain of the Cordillera Real range of the Bolivian Andes. Glacier-covered and perpetually snow-capped, it rises to a height of 21,275 feet—about 200 feet less than its twin peak, Ancohuma. It is often given the name Sorata, after the village located high on its slopes.

Illimani (ee-yee-MA-nee), volcanic mountain in the central Andes. Situated in Bolivia southeast of La Paz, the mountain rises to a height of more than 21,000 feet, making it one of the highest peaks in the country. Its perpetual snow line begins at about 15,000 feet.

Illinois (ill-in-OI) **I** 70–86
  Chicago **C** 227–30
  Lincoln, Abraham **L** 292
  modern public library in Skokie, picture **L** 200
  places of interest in Negro history **N** 94
Illinois, University of **I** 79; picture **I** 74
Illiteracy see Literacy
I'll Tell You How the Sun Rose, poem by Emily Dickinson **D** 164
Illuminated (il-LU-min-ated) **manuscripts** **I** 87–88
  art, the meanings of **A** 438
  Berthold Missal, picture **G** 167
  how medieval books were made **B** 320
  illustration of books **I** 89–90
  important art form for early Germany **G** 165–66

Islamic art **I** 417
Kells, Book of **K** 202–03
Limburg brothers **D** 349
medieval painting **P** 17–18; picture **P** 19
Middle Ages, art of **M** 297
Illuminating Engineering Society of America **L** 289
Illumination see Lighting
Illusions, incorrect perceptions **P** 488–91
  magic tricks **M** 18
Illustration and illustrators **I** 89–97
  art departments of magazines **M** 15–16
  book illustration **B** 330
  Caldecott medal for children's books **B** 309–10
  children's books **C** 242–43
  comic books **C** 422–23
  commercial art **C** 424–27
  early bookmaking **B** 321
  Islamic books **I** 421; picture **I** 418
  mechanical drawing **M** 197
  photography **P** 205
  See also Illuminated manuscripts

Illustrators, Society of, association to advance the art of illustration. It conducts classes, grants scholarships, and holds exhibits of the year's best illustrations. Founded in 1901, it maintains headquarters in New York, N.Y., and publishes an annual entitled *Illustrators*.

ILO see International Labour Organisation
Il Penseroso (il-pen-ser-O-so), poem by Milton **M** 311
Imagemaker, or variable image reflector, a criminal identification tool **P** 376
Imagery, in writing
  Beowulf **B** 141
Images, in psychology **P** 500–500a
Images, optical
  light reflection **L** 261
  real and virtual of lenses **L** 144–46
Imaginary numbers, as the square root of a negative number **N** 386
Imagination
  use of images in thinking **P** 500–500a
Imagists, group of poets **A** 209
Imam (e-MOM), Muslim leader **I** 416
  Yemen (Sana) ruler **Y** 348
Imhotep (im-HO-tep), ancient Egyptian counselor to King Zoser **E** 95
  tombs and temples in ancient Egypt **A** 221

Immaculate Conception, Roman Catholic doctrine that states that the Virgin Mary, although born of human parents, was conceived free from original sin. Catholics believe that all other human persons, from the very beginning of life, inherit a human nature that has a strong inclination to sin. Mary was especially privileged to be conceived immaculate because she was to be the mother of Christ. The doctrine of the Immaculate Conception should not be confused with that of the Virgin Birth—the belief that Jesus Christ was born of a virgin mother.

Immaculate Conception, Feast of the, religious holiday **R** 155, 290

Immanuel, or **Emmanuel** (Hebrew word meaning "God is with us"), in Old Testament (Isaiah 7:14) symbolic name of son who Isaiah said would be a sign that God was with his people, protecting them against Syria and Ephraim. This passage is often interpreted as promise of a messiah by Christians.

Immigration and emigration   I 98–103
  Addams, Jane, aided immigrants   A 19
  aliens and registration of aliens   A 166
  American Museum of Immigration with Statue of Liberty   L 168
  Australia   A 499
  Brazil   B 372–74
  Canada   C 49
  Chinese restricted, Hayes administration   H 81
  folklore of immigrant groups   F 309–10
  immigrant visas   P 95
  Jews to Palestine and later to Israel   J 112–13
  Liberty, Statue of   L 168
  population and census taking   P 394
  segregation   S 114
  United States   U 133
  Westward movement in U.S. history   W 142–46
  See also Citizenship; Naturalization, and people section of state and province articles
Immigration and Nationality Act of 1952, or McCarren-Walter Act, 1952   I 101
  citizenship   C 312, 313
Immigration and Naturalization Service, U.S.   I 102; N 58
  Investigations Division   F 76

Immortality, endless or perpetual life. Belief in immortality of the soul is common in many religions, such as Islam and Christianity.

Immune responses, in immunology   I 104
Immunization, medical techniques of   M 209–10
Immunology (im-mu-NOL-ogy)   I 104–07
  active and passive immunity   A 317
  antibiotics   A 310–16
  disease, prevention of   D 219–21
  Pasteur, Louis   P 97
  vaccination and inoculation   V 260–61
  vectors   V 282–85
Impalas (im-PA-las), Africa's antelopes, picture   A 51
Impeachment, legal action against a public official   I 108
  Johnson, Andrew   J 125–26; R 119
  limitation on presidential pardoning power   P 454
  recall   O 205
Imperfect flowers   P 296
Imperial City, Peking, China   P 118
Imperial gallons, liquid measures   W 114
Imperial Hotel, Tokyo, Japan
  designed by Frank Lloyd Wright   W 315
Imperialism   I 109
  British in Asia and Africa   E 227–28
  McKinley administration in United States   M 189–90
  policy of increasing power of a nation over other nations   I 322–23
Imperial Valley, California   C 19; picture   G 106
  a vast oasis   O 3
Impetigo (im-pe-TY-go), skin disease   D 199
Implements see Farm machinery; Tools
Imports   T 243
  international trade   I 326–27, 330
  tariff discourages imports   T 25
  See also country, province, and state articles
Imposition, arrangement of pages of a book for printing   B 327; pictures   B 328, 333
Impressionism, in art   P 29
  art of the artist   A 438g
  Degas, Edgar   D 84
  France   F 426, 431, 447
  Manet, Édouard   M 73
  modern art   M 387–88
  Monet, Claude   M 408
  See also Pissarro, Camille

Impression: Sunrise, painting by Monet   M 386
Impressment, of seamen
  Jefferson and the embargo   J 68–69
  War of 1812   W 10–11
Imprint, of a book   L 181
Imprints, fossil   F 110
Impromptu, a musical form   M 536
Impromptu speech delivery   P 510
Improper fractions   F 398
Improvisation (im-pro-vi-ZAY-tion), composition on the spur of the moment
  acting   T 160
  African and American folk music   A 78
  jazz   J 57, 62
  music   M 402
  Negro spirituals   N 106
  Oriental music   O 220d
Impulse engines   E 209
Impulses, nerve   B 283, 288
Impulse turbines   E 210
Inauguration, of a United States president   P 447
  Eisenhower's inaugural parade, picture   E 110
  Polk's, in the rain, picture   P 385
  oath of office   P 447
  Twentieth Amendment to the U.S. Constitution   U 157
Incandescence (in-can-DES-cence), emission of light from intense heat   I 333–34
  cold light, or bioluminescence   B 197
Incandescent filament lamps   L 284–85
Incas, Indians of South America   I 203–07
  development of arts   I 155–56
  earliest roads in the Americas   T 259
  Ecuador   E 52, 57
  exploration, methods of the conquerors   E 386
  influence on Latin-American art and architecture   L 64
  knotted ropes as records   K 289; picture   C 451
  Machu Picchu ruins, pictures   A 354; W 219
  Peru   P 165
  Pizarro, Francisco   P 266
  pre-Columbian dance   L 68
  quipu (knotted rope), counting device, picture   C 451
  South America unified over a huge area   S 293
Incense   P 154
  resins used for incense   R 184
  Somalia, leading exporter of   S 253
Inch, measure of length   W 111
Inchon, Korea   K 303
Incinerators (in-CIN-er-ators), to burn refuse   S 34
Incisors (in-CY-sors), teeth   T 47
Inclined planes, simple machines   W 246–47
  first inventions   I 335
Income   E 51
  budgets, family   B 425–26
  consumer education   C 494, 494a
  how to divide between labor and management   L 11
  per capita income   I 327
  poverty, assured annual income as cure for   P 424b
Income tax   I 110–11
  principle of a good tax   T 26, 27
Incubation, hatching of eggs   E 90–90a
  birds   B 214–15
Incubators (IN-cu-bators), for chicks, picture   P 421
Incunabula (inc-u-NAB-u-la), term used for earliest printed books   B 321
Indefinite pronouns   P 91

Indemnity (from Latin in plus damnum, meaning "hurt"), an assurance of compensation in case of loss or damage.

Indentured servants, in colonial America   C 386–87
  Negro history   N 91

Independence Day F 156; I 112
  July holidays J 148
Independence Hall, Philadelphia, Pennsylvania I 113
  Liberty Bell L 169
  places of interest in Philadelphia P 182
  signing of Declaration of Independence D 59
Independence National Historical Park, Philadelphia
  P 182
Independent Man, statue dedicated to Rhode Island
  R 212; picture R 223
Independent Treasury Act, 1846 P 385

Index librorum prohibitorum (Latin for "index of forbidden books"), catalog of books judged dangerous to faith or morals by Roman Catholic Church. Members of the Church are forbidden to read any of these books except with special permission. The Index, as it is popularly called, includes very few books in English. The list was first published in 1559 during the pontificate of Pope Paul IV and has been revised periodically since then. In 1966, The Congregation for the Doctrine of the Faith declared that there would be no more editions of the Index.

Indexes, periodical I 115
Indexes and indexing I 114–15
  encyclopedias E 197
  how to use the index of this encyclopedia A 575–81
  maps, use of grids M 90
  parts of books L 182
  reference books R 130
  research methods R 183
Index fossils, used to trace strata of rock G 113
India I 116–35
  Alexander the Great invades A 152–53
  art and architecture O 212–13, 215
  art as a record A 438f
  Asia's population, concentration of A 453
  Bangladesh B 44–44c; P 41
  Bombay B 307–08
  Calcutta C 9–11
  civil and human rights conflicts C 316
  costumes, traditional, pictures C 350; D 264
  cotton, early use of C 519
  dance combined with religion D 31
  Delhi D 101–03
  dyed cloth drying, picture D 368
  early Hindu drama D 293
  East India companies E 43
  fables F 3
  favorite foods F 340
  flag F 237
  funeral customs F 493
  Gama, Vasco da, opens trade with Europe E 379;
    G 7
  Gandhi, Mohandas Karamchand G 24
  Ganges River G 25
  Girls High School, picture E 81
  Himalayas H 128–29
  Hinduism H 130–32
  holidays H 155, 158
  jute preparation, picture A 464
  Kashmir dispute K 198–99
  legend "The Mallard That Asked for Too Much" L 135
  literature O 200d–220e
  Madras, capital of Tamil Nadu M 10
  music O 221; picture O 220d
  national anthem N 21
  Nehru, Jawaharlal N 107
  New Delhi D 101–03
  poverty P 424a, 424b
  Sikkim, a protectorate of India S 177

Taj Mahal T 14
  Tamil Nadu, formerly Madras state M 10
  theater T 163
  Victoria made empress of India E 227
  voting, picture E 115
  Zoroastrianism Z 380
India ink I 256
Indiamen, trading vessels of East India Company E 43
Indian, or Bengal, **tigers** T 186
Indiana I 136–51
  holiday, Discovery Day H 149
Indiana, Robert, American artist
  American Dream #1, painting U 120

Indian Affairs, Bureau of, agency of U.S. Department of War until creation of Department of Interior (1849). It works toward giving full citizenship to American Indians and natives of Alaska through better education and economic independence. It was founded in 1824. Its headquarters is in Washington, D.C.

Indianapolis (indian-AP-o-lis), capital of Indiana I 147–48
  automobile racing A 539
Indianapolis Children's Museum, Indiana I 145
Indianapolis Motor Speedway, Indiana I 147
Indian art, of North and South America I 152–57
Indiana University I 143; picture I 142
Indian beadwork I 157–59
  Chimu collar, picture I 203
Indian brave makeup, picture P 340
Indian Chief, group game I 226
Indian City, U.S.A., Oklahoma O 88
Indian Cliff Palace, Mesa Verde, Colorado, picture A 353
Indian corn see Corn
Indian music, of India O 221; picture O 220d
  rock music R 262d
Indian music, of North America I 160–61
Indian music, of South America L 73–74
  Ecuador E 52–53
Indian Mutiny see Sepoy Mutiny, 1857
Indian National Congress, political party N 107
Indian Ocean O 47
  ocean floor explored by geologists G 115
Indian paintbrush, plant
  state flower of Wyoming W 322
Indian Reorganization Act, 1934 I 200
Indian reservations I 176–77, 196
  Arizona A 413–14
  boarding school cafeteria, picture I 200b
  first one at Brotherton, New Jersey I 199
  North Dakota N 327–28
  Sioux of the present day I 169
  South Dakota S 323
Indian rice, or wild rice M 329
Indians of North America I 162–200b
  arts, development of I 156
  Arizona's population largest in United States A 408
  Athapascans, in Canada Y 364
  Brant, Joseph B 371
  Buffalo Bill, Indian fighter and scout B 428
  Canadian folk art C 64
  Canadian population C 49
  canoes C 99–100
  cave paintings C 158
  communication by smoke signals C 437
  corn C 506; I 183, 189
  first Americans U 131
  Five Civilized Tribes O 80, 84, 95
  folklore F 313–14
  French and Indian War F 458–62
  funeral customs F 494
  fur trade F 520

Indians of North America (continued)
Geronimo, Apache leader **G** 189
Haskell Institute, Lawrence, Kansas **K** 183
hieroglyphic writing **C** 431
horses **H** 241
Hurons **C** 69
Indian Cliff Palace, Mesa Verde, picture **A** 353
Indian Wars **I** 212–15
Iroquois **C** 69–70
Jackson's resettlement program **J** 6
lacrosse **L** 20–21
leather tanners **L** 110–11
"Legend of the White Deer" **L** 134
missionary work in early Massachusetts **M** 149
myth of origin of potlatch **M** 559–60
Oklahoma, former Indian capitals in **O** 92–93
paintings of George Catlin **U** 120–21
Plymouth Colony **P** 345
Pontiac **P** 391
potlatch custom **I** 181; **M** 559–60
pueblos, pictures **A** 302; **N** 186
Quebec, present-day life in **Q** 10a
reservations see Indian reservations
Sequoya **S** 124
Sun Dance religion of Plains tribes **M** 563–64
sweet potatoes discovered by **P** 307
Tecumseh **T** 47
wampum **C** 374; **M** 411
See also history section of province, and state articles;
names of families and tribes
Indians of South America **I** 201–11; **S** 293
arts, development of **I** 155–56
Alakaluf studied by anthropologists **A** 306–07
Bolivia, most Indian South American nation **B** 302
corn **C** 506
farmers market in Bogotá, picture **C** 379
folklore **F** 313–14
Latin-American languages **L** 49
life in Latin America **L** 50–51
Peru **P** 161
pre-Columbian dance **L** 68
See also country articles; names of tribes
Indian summer **H** 159
Indian Territory, Oklahoma **O** 80, 94–95
Indian wars **I** 212–15
Apache leader Geronimo **G** 189
Champlain helps defeat Iroquois **C** 187
French and Indian War **F** 458–62
garrison houses for places of refuge **N** 163
gold discoveries led to war **G** 253
Pontiac **P** 391
Tecumseh **T** 47
War of 1877 **I** 176
westward movement **W** 142–44
Indictment (in-DITE-ment), in law **C** 527
Indies, Council of the, colonial Latin America **L** 52
Indigo, plant
dyestuff, source of **D** 367
dying cloth, Nigeria, picture **N** 257
early commercial crop in South Carolina **S** 296
Indigo snake, picture **S** 212
Indirect taxes **T** 26
Indium, element **E** 154, 161
Individual differences **C** 232
family life influences **F** 43
Individualized instruction see Programed instruction
Indo-America, Indian culture in Latin America **L** 51
Indo-Aryan, language group of Asia **A** 460
Bangladesh **B** 44
India **I** 117, 119
Indochina, former name for area of Southeast Asia
comprising Vietnam, Cambodia, and Laos **S** 328

Indochina War, 1946–54 **V** 334d
Indochina War, Second see Vietnam War, 1958–
Indo-European languages **L** 38–39
anthropological studies **A** 308
in historical linguistic studies **L** 303
Indo-Iranian (i-RAY-nian) languages **L** 39
Indonesia (in-do-NE-sia) **I** 216–22
batik cloth, hand-dyed, picture **D** 368
Djakarta **D** 236–37
flag **F** 237
orchestral music **O** 221; picture **O** 220d
picking tea, picture **T** 40
typical meal, the rice-table **F** 341
West Irian in New Guinea **N** 147
Indoor activities **I** 223–26
airplane models **A** 104–07
automobile models **A** 535–37
card games **C** 106–15
charades **C** 188
checkers **C** 191–92
chess **C** 221–26
clay modeling **C** 336–37
darts **D** 38–39
dolls **D** 263–69
dominoes **D** 284
dressmaking **D** 311–15
finger painting **F** 126–28
gift wrapping **G** 206–09
Indian beadwork **I** 157–59
jewelry making **J** 100
jokes and riddles **J** 132–33
leathercraft **L** 112–13
linoleum-block printing **L** 304–06
magic **M** 18–21
mosaic, how to make **M** 463
number games and puzzles **N** 372–77
origami **O** 222–26
papier-mâché, how to make **P** 58b–59
parties **P** 87–89
puppets and marionettes **P** 534–39
putting on plays **P** 335–41
railroading, model **R** 91–92
soap sculpture **S** 216–17
tops **T** 226
toys, how to make **T** 230–35
tricks and puzzles **T** 288–89
valentines, how to make **V** 266–68
ventriloquism **V** 301–03
weaving **W** 97–98
word games **W** 236–38
See also Games; Hobbies
Indoor games see Games
Induced tolerance, type of immunization **I** 107
Induction, magnetic see Magnetic induction
Induction motors, electric **E** 139
Indulgences (in-DUL-gen-ces), papal grants **C** 285;
R 133, 294
Luther's theses against **L** 378
Indus River, Asia **R** 244
ancient civilization **A** 223–25; **I** 116
land of India, north Indian alluvial plains **I** 125
Tarbela Dam **D** 21
Industrial alcohol **A** 147; **G** 286
Industrial arts **I** 227–28
machine-made decorative arts **D** 78
printing **P** 457–67
woodworking **W** 229–34
Industrial design **I** 229–32
Bauhaus school, Germany **B** 103–05
commercial art **C** 424–27
Industrial diseases see Occupational diseases
Industrial geography **G** 108

Industrial painting see Painting, industrial
Industrial Revolution I 233–41
  advertising begins **A** 34
  building construction, effect on **B** 435
  capitalism became a great force **C** 104
  chemical industry **C** 194
  cities, greatest growth during **C** 307–08
  England **E** 226; **U** 65
  farm machinery **F** 55
  industrial growth **I** 244–45
  inventions, selected list **I** 339–45
  labor movement, history of **L** 2
  machine-made decorative arts **D** 78
  manufacturing **M** 83–84
  mining expanded rapidly **M** 320
  socialism, history of **S** 220
  technology, development of **T** 46
  unemployment for first time **U** 25
  wheels, part played by **W** 158
Industrial spies **S** 389
Industrial unions **L** 8–9
Industrial wastes
  water pollution **E** 272e; **W** 58, 59; picture **E** 272d
Industrial Workers of the World (I.W.W.) **L** 6
Industry I 242–51
  air pollution **A** 108–11; **E** 272f–272g
  agriculture a business enterprise **A** 92, 100
  automation **A** 528–34
  big business in United States **U** 130–31
  captains of industry **U** 131
  control and development of natural resources **N** 60
  detergents and soaps, uses in **D** 146
  environment, problems of **E** 272a–272h
  factories changed by electric motors **E** 141
  growth affects labor-management relations **L** 11–12
  how shown on maps, picture **M** 90
  Industrial Revolution I 233–41
  international trade **I** 326–30
  Japan's rapid industrial development **J** 35, 37
  jewelry **J** 101
  manufacturing **M** 83–85
  mass production **M** 151
  monopolies permitted to encourage industry **T** 305
  museums **M** 513
  New Jersey, concentration in **N** 169
  noise, protection from **N** 270
  nursing in industry **N** 410
  public relations **P** 507–08
  retailing second largest business in U.S. **R** 188
  rivers, uses of **R** 242
  safety measures **S** 7
  Soviet method of locating heavy industry **U** 38
  special libraries for industry **L** 176–79
  steel industry, importance of **I** 407–08
  tariff adopted to protect home industry **T** 25
  technology **T** 45–46
  unemployment **U** 25–26
  UN Industrial Development Organization **U** 86
  waste, a conservation problem **C** 483
  women, role of **W** 212
  woodworking industries **W** 229
  work methods, changes in **W** 251
  world industrial areas **W** 266–67
  X-ray photography **P** 206
  See also country, province, and state articles, and
    names of industries
Indy (an-DI), **Vincent d'**, French composer **F** 446
Inequalities, in mathematics **M** 165–66
Inert, chemical term **C** 219
Inert gases see Noble gases
Inertia (in-ER-sha), (physics) **M** 171; demonstration **E** 37
  motion, Newton's laws of **M** 469

  satellites **S** 39
  seismograph **E** 37–38
Inertial guidance, navigation system **N** 68, 69
  gyroscope **G** 435–36
  missiles **M** 344
  rockets **R** 261
  space navigation **S** 340f

Infallibility, Roman Catholic doctrine that states that the
pope, or the bishops acting jointly, cannot err when they
define a doctrine concerning faith or morals. Such a
definition, however, may later require refinement or
clarification.

Infantile paralysis see Poliomyelitis
Infantry
  United States Army **U** 168
Infants see Baby
Infant schools **K** 242
Infectious diseases, or communicable diseases **D** 186
  early studies of **M** 208
  number of hospitals in various countries compared
    H 252
  Public Health Service in checking epidemics **P** 503
  vectors, carriers of disease **V** 282–85
Infectious mononucleosis (mon-o-nu-cle-O-sis), disease
  D 199

Inferiority complex, in psychology, term used by Alfred
Adler to describe an individual's sense of real or fancied
inferiority. He believed that striving for superiority is the
strongest human impulse and, if thwarted, results in
feeling of inferiority. An individual reacts, according to
Adler, either by withdrawing from society or by overcom-
pensating (as in achievements of genius).

Infielder, in baseball **B** 74
Infinite sets, in mathematics **S** 126
Infinity **M** 160
  mathematical symbol for **M** 154
Inflation and deflation, of prices **I** 252–53
  economic cycles **E** 50, 51
  financial panic and bank failures **B** 47–48
  Nixon's wage-price freeze **N** 262f
  problems of old age insurance **O** 97
  See also Banks and banking
Inflections, in language **E** 244
  Latin declensions **L** 76
In-flight motion pictures, picture **M** 486

Inflorescence, natural arrangement of flowers on a plant.
The flowers or flower clusters are supported by a part of
the plant called the floral axis, which is a part of a
branch or of a stem. Inflorescences take on a great
variety of forms and structures. They are very important
in the classification of plants.

Influenza, virus disease **D** 200
  vaccination **V** 261
  virus, picture **V** 361
Information storage and retrieval systems
  computers **C** 449–57
  punched-card machines and computers **O** 58
  use in libraries **L** 174, 177
Infrared microscopes (in-fra-RED MY-cro-scopes) **M** 283
Infrared radiation **R** 44
  light, spectrum analysis of **L** 269–70
  missile guidance **M** 345
  photography **P** 207
  solar energy **S** 235
Infusorians (in-fu-SO-rians), microscopic organisms
  B 193

Inge, William (1913–73), American playwright, **b.** Independence, Kans. Plays of his that have been made into movies include *Bus Stop, Picnic* (Pulitzer prize, 1953), *The Dark at the Top of the Stairs*, and *Come Back, Little Sheba*.

American drama **A** 216

Ingersoll (ING-er-soll), **Jared** (1749–1822), American lawyer, b. New Haven, Conn. One of the most distinguished lawyers in Philadelphia, he was a delegate to the Continental Congress (1780 and 1781) and to the Constitutional Convention (1787). He was also city solicitor (1798–1801), attorney general of Pennsylvania (1790–99, 1811–17), Federalist candidate for vice-president (1812), and presiding judge of the district court of the county and city of Philadelphia (1821–22).

Ingersoll, Robert Green (1833–1899), American orator, b. Dresden, N.Y. He is celebrated for his speech nominating James G. Blaine for Republican presidential candidate (1876). Called the great agnostic, he was a popular speaker and published his lectures in *The Gods* and *Some Mistakes of Moses*.

In God We Trust, motto on United States coins **M** 338
Ingots
steel **I** 399; picture **I** 405

Ingres (ANGR-ra), **Jean Auguste Dominique** (1780–1867), French artist, b. Montauban. A student of David, he was a noted classicist and conservative member of French Academy. He shows attention to line in works such as *The Turkish Bath* and *Odalisque*. His other paintings include *The Painter Granet, Madame Rivière*, and *Madame de Senonnes*.
neoclassical style in French art **F** 425; **P** 29

Ingstad (ING-stad), **Helge,** Norwegian explorer
V 339–40
Inherited characteristics **G** 85–88
Inherited diseases **D** 188
Inhibitors, in chemistry
plastics **P** 327
Initials, commonly used as abbreviations **A** 4–6
Initial Teaching Alphabet **I** 254
reading aid **R** 109
Initiative, referendum, and recall, legislative processes in goverment, the Oregon system **O** 205

Injunction, written court order either prohibiting a person or group from performing, or requiring them to perform, a certain act. Injunctions are often used in labor disputes and in instances of restraint of trade. Excessive use of the injunction against strikers led to the Norris-LaGuardia Act of 1932.

Injuries see First Aid
Ink **I** 255–56
ball-point pens **P** 147
communication advanced by **C** 432
drawing inks **D** 303
Gutenberg discovers an ink for metal type **P** 457
magnetic ink for computer input **C** 452
Ink-blot tests **T** 118
Inland Sea, Japan **J** 34; picture **J** 47
Inland seas, lakes **L** 25
Inland waterways
Great Lakes-St. Lawrence system **G** 326; **S** 15, 16–17
Ontario **O** 121–22
section at Fort Lauderdale, Florida, picture **U** 107
Inlaying, or marquetry, of furniture **D** 77; **F** 508

Inman, Henry (1801–46), American painter, b. Yorkville, New York. Well-known during his lifetime as a portrait painter, he included among his subjects such celebrities as Martin Van Buren and William Wordsworth. He also painted landscapes and familiar scenes of everyday life. Many of his works, including *The Young Fisherman* and *Picnic in the Catskills*, hang in American museums.

Inner Asia **A** 449, 452
Inner Mongolia, a region of China **M** 413
Inner Six, of the European Economic Community (Common Market) **E** 334–35
Inner Temple see Inns of Court

Inness (INN-ess), **George** (1825–94), American artist, b. Newburgh, N.Y. In his youth he was apprenticed to an engraver and showed considerable artistic talent. After painting in Rome and in Paris, he opened a studio in New York City and became well known for his landscapes, several of which hang in American museums. He died in Scotland. His son, **George Inness, Jr.,** (1854–1926), gained a wide reputation as a painter of landscapes and animals.
landscape painting in the United States **U** 121

Innings, in baseball **B** 70

Innis, Roy (1935–), American civil rights leader, b. St. Croix, Virgin Islands. He is National Director of the Congress of Racial Equality (CORE). He drafted for introduction to the United States Congress a bill called the Community Self-Determination Act of 1968, which proposed the establishment of community development corporations in which the members of poor black and white communities could purchase shares. In October, 1970, he submitted a brief to the United States Supreme Court concerning community-controlled schools and the busing of pupils.

Innisfallen (IN-nish-FALL-en), island in Loch Leane, Ireland **L** 31

Innisfree (IN-nish-FREE), a tiny, picturesque island in Lough Gill, County Sligo, Ireland. Many visitors have been captivated by its tranquil beauty. The Irish poet William Butler Yeats described the island in his famous poem "The Lake Isle of Innisfree."

Innisfree, Lake Isle of, poem by Yeats
Y 344
Innocent III, pope **M** 294
abolished trial by ordeal **J** 159
Albigensian heresy stamped out **R** 292
Jews persecuted by **J** 108
world domination of papacy **R** 292

Inn River, tributary of the Danube in central Europe. Rising in Switzerland, the river flows for over 300 miles through Austria and Germany before emptying into the Danube. Part of its length forms the Austro-German border.

Inns see Hotels; Motels

Innsbruck (INNS-brook), Austrian city. Situated on the Inn River in the Austrian Alps, it is a popular winter and summer resort. Among its tourist attractions are a botanical garden that houses a large variety of Alpine plants, a 15th-century castle, and a 16th-century church. Innsbruck, the fifth largest city and the capital of the province of Tyrol, has a population of approximately 100,000.

Inns of Court, name given to the group of buildings that house London's four legal societies. These societies—Gray's Inn, the Inner Temple, Lincoln's Inn, and the Middle Temple—were founded in the late 13th and early 14th centuries. The buildings were the original homes and schools of young legal apprentices. Today the societies exercise complete control over permission to practice law in England.

Innuit (or **Inuit**), Eskimo word for "the people" E 284

Ino (I-no), Greek goddess, daughter of Harmonia and Cadmus. The second wife of Athamas, she was the mother of Learchus and Melicertes. When Athamas went mad and tried to kill her, she plunged into the sea and was transformed into the sea goddess Leucothoe.

Inoculation see Vaccination and inoculation

Inonu (ee-no-NU), **Ismet** (1884–1973), Turkish statesman. He fought in World War I and played an active role in Turkey's struggle for independence from Greece. In 1923 he became prime minister of the new republic and served as its president (1938–50). After leaving office, he was a leading figure in the political life of Turkey, heading two unsuccessful coalition cabinets.

Inorganic chemistry see Chemistry, inorganic
Inorganic fertilizers F 97
Inorganic substances C 219

Inouye (in-o-OO-yeh), **Daniel Ken** (1924–), American politician, b. Honolulu, Hawaii. He has been majority leader of the Territorial House of Representatives (1954–58), member of the Territorial Senate (1958–59), member of the U.S. House of Representatives (1959–62), and U.S. senator from Hawaii (since 1963).

Input and output units, of computers C 450, 451–52

Inquest, in law, a judicial inquiry, by a jury, especially one conducted by coroner into a cause of death. The term also refers to the findings of such a jury. A grand jury investigation is sometimes called a grand inquest.

Institute for Advanced Study, organization founded (1930) at Princeton, N.J., for postdoctoral research in the humanities, mathematics, mathematical physics, and historical studies. It publishes (with Princeton University) *Annals of Mathematics.*
  Einstein, Albert E 105
  Princeton University N 173

Instrumental conditioning, in learning **L** 100
Instrumental music
    baroque music **B** 65–66
    Renaissance music **R** 173–74
Instrument Flight Rules (IFR), of airplanes **A** 564
Instruments, musical see Musical instruments
Insular Mountains, submerged chain off Canada **C** 51
Insulation and insulating materials **I** 290–92
    poor conductors of heat **H** 94–95
    refrigeration necessity **R** 137–38
    wood a good heat insulator **W** 222
Insulators, electric **E** 126, 128, 144
Insulin, pancreatic hormone used in treatment of dia-
        betes **D** 195–96
    Banting's discovery **B** 52
    chemical messenger in the body **B** 279
    discovery important to biochemistry **B** 183
    produced from animal glands **M** 196
Insurance **I** 293–97
    banks and banking, deposit insurance **B** 48
    Hartford, Conn., U.S. Insurance Capital **C** 476
    health insurance in four countries **O** 99
    hospital insurance **H** 251
    old-age health plans **O** 99
    probability theory used in mortality and accident ta-
        bles **P** 474
    social insurance **S** 221–22
    social insurance for labor **L** 14
    trade and commerce **T** 243
    unemployment insurance **U** 25–26
    workmen's compensation **W** 253
Insurance, accident **I** 295
Insurance, automobile **I** 294
Insurance, casualty **I** 293–94
Insurance, fire **I** 294
Insurance, group **I** 295
Insurance, health **I** 295
Insurance, liability **I** 294
Insurance, life **I** 294
    force of mortality, basis of rates **A** 81
    true interest rates on loans **I** 289
Insurance, social see Social security
Insurance, unemployment see Unemployment insurance

Intaglio (in-TAL-yo), in art, a concave design cut into
surface of material (glass, stone, etc.), rather than
raised, as in relief. The term also refers to a jewel so
executed. The Intaglio process is used in making seals
and signet rings, which then stamp their impression in
relief, and also in etching.

Intaglio printing **P** 460
    engraving **E** 272
    graphic arts **G** 302
    lithography **L** 315
Intarsia (in-TAR-sia), inlaying of wood furniture **D** 77
Integers (IN-te-gers), positive and negative numbers and
        zero **N** 384
Integration
    United States Supreme Court ruling, 1954 **S** 115
    See also Segregation
Intelligence
    defined **A** 282
    Does a larger brain mean greater intelligence?
        B 366
Intelligence, governmental
    Federal Bureau of Investigation **F** 76–77
    spies and espionage **S** 389–90
    See also Central Intelligence Agency
Intelligence, military see Military intelligence
Intelligence of animals see Animals: Intelligence and be-
        havior

Intelligence Quotient, or IQ, score made on an intelli-
        gence test **T** 117
    retardation level **R** 190
Intelligence tests **P** 489
    how developed and used **T** 117–18
Intelsat (International Telecommunications Satellite
        Consortium) **E** 142e–142f
    television **T** 67
Intensifiers, in grammar **G** 289
Intensity, in physics
    light **L** 267
    sound waves **S** 259
Intensity, of color, in art **D** 143
Intensive agriculture **A** 89
Intensive care unit, of a hospital, picture **E** 142
Inter-American Highway **P** 50
    Costa Rica **C** 517
    El Salvador **E** 183
    Honduras **H** 197
    Nicaragua **N** 247
    Panama **P** 45
    See also Pan American Highway
Inter-American Treaty of Reciprocal Assistance, 1947
    O 211
    Cuba, why Monroe Doctrine was not invoked, 1960
    M 427
Intercession, prayer for others **P** 435

Intercollegiate (in-ter-col-LE-gi-ate) **Association of Amateur Athletes of America** (ICAAA), association of 66 colleges whose track-and-field teams compete in annual
cross-country, indoor, and outdoor championships.

Intercollegiate Cycling Association **B** 171
Intercontinental ballistic missiles **M** 346
Intercropping, of seeds **G** 52
Interest, money paid for use of money **P** 149–50
    installment buying finance charges **I** 288–89
    savings accounts in banks **B** 49
Interference, of light **L** 272
Interference, of sound waves **S** 262
Interference microscopes **M** 288
Interferometers (in-ter-fer-OM-et-ers), measuring instru-
        ments using principle of light interference **L** 272
    optical instruments **O** 172
    radio telescopes **R** 72
Interglacial (In-ter-GLAY-cial) **stages,** between ice ages
    I 13, 20
    Ewing-Donn theory **I** 24
Inter-Governmental Maritime Consultative Organization
    (IMCO) **U** 86
Intergovernmental relations
    city, state, and federal authority **M** 506
Interior, United States Department of the
    conservation bureaus **C** 486, 488
Interior decorating **I** 298–303
    furniture design **F** 505–10
Interior Plains, landform region of Canada **C** 51, 55
    Prairie Provinces **A** 146a; **M** 76; **S** 38a
Interjections, words of exclamation **P** 92
Interlibrary co-operation **L** 173
Interlingua, a constructed language **U** 195
    how languages change **L** 40
Interlochen (IN-ter-lock-en), Michigan
    National Music Camp **M** 267
Intermediate schools, or middle schools **S** 58
    education, history of **E** 74
Intermolecular bonding, adhesive process **G** 242
Intermountain Plateaus, North America
    United States **U** 91

Intermural games (from Latin *inter,* meaning "between," and *muralis*, "of a wall"), competitive sports between teams representing different schools.

Internal-combustion engines I 303–08
  automobiles **A** 542–43
  aviation **A** 557, 568
  construction equipment **B** 446
  diesel engines **D** 168–71
  diesel locomotives **L** 328
  engines, types of **E** 210–11
  ethyl gasoline reduces engine knock **G** 63
  fuels **F** 486
  gas turbines **T** 321–22
  industrial growth **I** 245
  invention replaces steam engine **I** 336
  mechanical energy **E** 203
  Wankel engine **I** 303, 308, 309
Internal energy, in physics **H** 87
Internal Revenue Code, United States **I** 110
Internal Revenue Service, United States **I** 110
  Alcohol and Tobacco Tax Division **F** 76
  Intelligence Division **F** 76

International, The, federation of working-class parties organized to change capitalist societies into socialist commonwealths and unify them in a world federation. The First International, or International Workingmen's Association (1864–74), founded in London, was led by Karl Marx. The Second International (1889–1914), founded in Paris, urged prevention of war. The Third International (1919–43) (Communist International, or Comintern), founded in Berne, Switzerland, to promote world revolution against capitalism, was reorganized as the Cominform (1947).

International, The, original anthem of Soviet Russia **N** 19

International Air Transport Association (IATA), organization of most international airlines. Founded in 1945, it regulates fares and appoints travel agents. Its headquarters is in Montreal.
  Canada's airways **C** 61

International Amateur Athletic Federation (IAAF), body that governs international track-and-field events. It was founded in 1913. The Marquis of Exeter is its president.

International Association of Automotive Modelers **A** 537
International Atomic Energy Agency (IAEA) **U** 85
  disarmament **D** 184
International Badminton Federation **B** 13
International Bank for Reconstruction and Development (World Bank) **U** 86
  international banks **B** 51
International Bobsleigh and Tobogganing Federation **B** 266

International Boundary and Water Commission, United States and Mexico, commission that deals with boundary and water matters between United States and Mexico. It constructs and operates international storage dams and power plants on the Rio Grande and supervises Rio Grande Rectification and Canalization Projects and Lower Rio Grande flood control project. It was founded in 1889 and has headquarters in El Paso, Tex., and Ciudad Juárez, Mexico.

International Boundary Commission, United States and Canada, commission in charge of demarcation of boundary line between United States and Canada. Founded (1906) by treaty with Great Britain, it has headquarters in Washington, D.C.

International Brotherhood of Teamsters (I.B.T.) **L** 7
International Bureau of Expositions **F** 16

International Bureau of Weights and Measures, scientific organization, of approximately 31 countries, that has established international standards for metric system and for measurement of units of electricity; it was founded in 1875 and has headquarters at Sèvres, France.

International Business Machines Corporation (IBM)
  laboratories at Poughkeepsie, picture **N** 216
International Canoe Federation **C** 101
International Civil Aviation Organization (ICAO) **U** 86
  Canada **C** 61
International Code
  signal flags **F** 245
International Committee of the Red Cross **R** 126
International Confederation of Free Trade Unions (I.C.F.T.U.) **L** 10
International co-operation
  Antarctic regions **P** 368, 370–71
  postal service **P** 405–10
  Red Cross **R** 126–27
  United Nations **U** 80–88
International Cooperative Alliance **C** 500

International Council of Scientific Unions (ICSU), federation of scientific unions formed to promote and coordinate activities in the fields of natural and exact sciences. It was formed (1931) to succeed the International Research Council. It directed International Geophysical Year activities (1957–58). Headquarters is in London, England.
  International Geophysical Year **I** 310–20

International Council of Women (ICW), union of women's organizations of all races and creeds. Founded in Washington, D.C. (1888), it aims to promote the welfare of all peoples and to support international peace and the establishment of equal rights for women. Headquarters is in Zurich, Switzerland. Its publications include the *Bulletin*.

International Court of Justice, The Hague **U** 85
  Coolidge favored **C** 497
  international relations **I** 321

International Criminal Police Organization (Interpol), association of police forces from 90 countries working in a co-operative effort to prevent crime. Founded in 1923, headquarters is in Paris, France. It publishes *International Criminal Police Review*.
  duties of Interpol and its organization **P** 377

International date line **I** 309–10
  Alaska **A** 128
  180th meridian **L** 83
  where time begins **T** 190–92
International Development Association (IDA) **U** 86
  international banks **B** 51
International Exhibition, 1862, London, picture **F** 14
International Exposition of 1851, London **F** 13
International Federation of Trade Unions (I.F.T.U.) **L** 10
International Fencing Federation **F** 86
International Finance Corporation (IFC) **U** 86
  international banks **B** 51
International Geophysical Year (IGY) **I** 310–20
  jet streams studied **J** 91
  polar regions **P** 368, 370

International Gymnastics Federation (F.I.G.) **G** 431–32
International Ice Hockey Federation **I** 35
International Ice Patrol **I** 27
    United States Coast Guard duties **U** 176

International Joint Commission (IJC), council of six U.S. and Canadian delegates who settle cases involving boundary waters and common frontier between United States and Canada. Organized in 1911, it has headquarters at Washington, D.C., and Ottawa, Canada.

International Kennel Club **D** 261
International Labor Day see May Day
International Labour Organisation (ILO) **L** 10
    a specialized agency of the United Nations **U** 85
International Ladies' Garment Workers' Union **C** 354
International Languages see Universal languages
International law **I** 320–21
    aliens **A** 166
    codes developed by peace congresses **P** 104
    copyright **T** 245
    naturalization **N** 58
    passports and visas **P** 94–95
    patent owners, rights of **P** 98
    treaties **T** 270–73
    war crimes trials **W** 9–10
    World Court an umpire in international relations **I** 325
International Lawn Tennis Federation (ILTF) **T** 90
International Livestock Exhibition, Chicago **C** 230
International Missionary Council **P** 486
International Monetary Fund (IMF) **U** 86
    international banking **B** 50–51
International Morse Code see Morse Code, International
International News Service **N** 201
International Olympic Committee (I.O.C.) **O** 107–08
International Organization of Consumers Unions (IOCU) **C** 494a
International Peace Bridge see Peace Bridge International
International Peace Garden, North Dakota–Manitoba **M** 79; **N** 333
International Periodicals Directory **M** 15

International Phonetic Alphabet (IPA), series of symbols designed by International Phonetic Association (1888) to represent speech sounds of languages. In transcription of speech, each symbol denotes one sound.
    alphabetic systems of writing, problems of speech sounds **L** 38

International Polar Years (IPY-1 and 2) **I** 310–11
    polar regions **P** 368
International Quiet Sun Year (IQSY) **I** 320

International Reading Association (IRA), association of reading teachers interested in research and study of reading problems. Founded (1956) when International Council for the Improvement of Reading Instruction merged with National Association for Remedial Teaching, it has headquarters in Newark, Del.

International Red Cross see Red Cross

International Refugee Organization (IRO), temporary specialized UN agency organized in 1948 (discontinued 1951) to aid, protect, and resettle refugees and displaced persons. Its headquarters was at Geneva, Switzerland.

International relations **I** 322–25
    between the world wars **W** 282–87
    Bismarck's unification of Germany **B** 250
    disarmament **D** 184–86
    foreign aid programs **F** 368

    foreign service **F** 369–70
    grant money from foundations **F** 393
    imperialism **I** 109
    international law **I** 320–21
    international trade **I** 326–30
    League of Nations **L** 96–97
    Monroe Doctrine **M** 425, 426–27
    narcotics traffic **N** 14
    Open Door Policy for China **M** 189–90
    Organization of American States **O** 210–11
    patent owners, rights of **P** 98
    Peace Corps **P** 101–03
    peace movements **P** 104–05
    powers in foreign affairs of U.S. president **P** 454
    treaties **T** 270–73
    United States **U** 136–37
    Washington, George, administration of **W** 43
    What is the Bamboo Curtain? **I** 323
    What is the Iron Curtain? **I** 323
International Rice Research Institute, Philippines **R** 231
International road signs, picture **D** 320
International Skeeter Association **I** 29
International Society for Contemporary Music **M** 550
International Telecommunications Satellite Consortium see Intelsat
International Telecommunications Union (ITU) **U** 86
    control of air space and broadcasting rights **R** 54
International trade **I** 326–30
    cartels, international monopolies **T** 306
    Europe and the Common Market **E** 329–30, 334–35
    free ports **I** 330
    selling **S** 116–17
    ships and shipping **S** 155–61
    tariff **T** 25
    trade and commerce, history of **T** 242–43
    triangular trade, New England, West Indies, Africa **S** 198
    United States **U** 109
    What is a free port? **I** 330
International Typographical Union **N** 205
International Whaling Commission **W** 151

International Year for Human Rights (1968), observance marking the 20th anniversary of the adoption, by the United Nations, of the Universal Declaration of Human Rights. The president of the General Assembly officially opened the year-long celebration on January 1. The theme was "greater recognition and full enjoyment of the fundamental freedoms of the individual and of human rights everywhere."

International Youth Hostel Federation **H** 253
Internist, physician **D** 239

Internment, in international law, the confining of property, enemy aliens, or suspicious persons within prescribed limits. It was used, for example, by United States during World War II to detain Japanese aliens and their native-born children. **A** 166

Interns, in hospitals **D** 241; **H** 250
    dental interns **D** 115
Internuncios, ambassadors of the popes **V** 281
    Pius XII, service to Bavaria **P** 266
Inter-Parliamentary (in-ter-par-li-MENT-ry) **Union**, representatives of national legislative bodies **P** 82
Interplanetary space see Space, outer
Interpol see International Criminal Police Organization
Interrogative pronouns **P** 90
Interrupted projections **M** 93; picture **M** 94
Interstate commerce **I** 331–32
    Marshall's ruling for federal government **M** 112

Interstate Commerce Act, 1887 **I** 332
Interstate Commerce Commission (ICC) **I** 332
Inter-Testament, apocryphal books of the Bible **B** 152
Intertidal areas
   life, plant and animal adaptations **L** 222–23
Intertype, slug-casting machine in printing **P** 465
   type casting **T** 344–45

Interventionists, persons favoring interference by force or threat of force, in affairs of another state, usually to further political ends or to protect life or property.

Interviewing
   opinion surveys **O** 159
   tools of research **R** 182–83
Intervision, television network of eastern Europe **T** 71
Intestate, one who dies without a will **W** 174
Intestinal cancer **C** 92, 95
Intestines
   digestive function in human body **B** 275; diagram **B** 274
In the pond, line game **G** 23
Intolerable Acts, 1774, British reprisals against American colonies **D** 60
   events leading to Revolutionary War **R** 196–97
   Quebec Act listed with them **C** 71
Intoxication see Alcoholism
Intracoastal Waterway, eastern and Gulf coasts, United States **N** 313–14
   Florida section **F** 267
   South Carolina **S** 302
   Texas **T** 125

Intramural games (from Latin *intra*, meaning "within" and *muralis*, "of a wall"), athletics in which competition is confined to teams within an individual school.

Intransitive verbs **P** 91
   grammar **G** 289
Introductions, in etiquette **E** 301
Inuit, Eskimo word meaning "the people" **E** 284
Invalides see Hôtel des Invalides
Invalids
   home nursing **N** 413–15
   nurses and nursing **N** 409–13
Invariants, in topology **T** 220
Inventions **I** 333–48
   agricultural tools **A** 96
   aided growth of industry **I** 245
   air conditioning **A** 102
   alphabet **A** 170–73
   Archimedes **A** 369
   automobiles **A** 541–42
   aviation **A** 567–574
   Bessemer's steel process and other inventions **B** 149
   cotton gin **C** 521, 523
   diving equipment **D** 79
   Edison, Thomas A. **E** 59–60
   farm machinery **F** 55–62
   Franklin's **F** 453–54
   Industrial Revolution **I** 234–39
   Langmuir, Irving **L** 35
   Leonardo da Vinci **L** 152–55
   McCormick's reaper **M** 186
   patents **I** 347; **P** 97–98
   printing **P** 457–58
   spinning jenny **I** 235
   technology and inventions **T** 45–46
   telephone **T** 56
   Watt, James **W** 68–69
   wax paper **W** 70
   weaving loom **I** 235

Westinghouse, George **W** 125
What is a patent? **I** 347
What is the difference between an invention and a discovery? **I** 336
What president of the United States was also an inventor? **I** 335
Why has no one invented a perpetual-motion machine? **I** 333
Why were electric irons invented? **E** 118
writing **W** 317–18
See also Farm machinery; Patents; Technology; and inventions and inventors by name

Inverness (in-ver-NESS), capital of Inverness county, Scotland. A seaport on the Ness River, its population numbers about 30,000. Inverness castle, built in 1835, is said to be on the site where Macbeth murdered Duncan.

Inverse-square law, rule of electric forces between two particles **N** 367
Inversion, temperature **F** 289
   air pollution **A** 109; **E** 272g
Invertebrates (in-VER-teb-rates), animals without backbones **A** 264
   jellyfishes and other coelenterates **J** 70–75
   kingdoms of living things **K** 251
   learning ability **L** 104
   prehistoric animals, development of **P** 437
   starfishes **S** 402–03
Investment banks **B** 49–50
Investments, economic activities
   depressions and recessions **D** 122
   insurance **I** 297
   investment banks **B** 49–50
   real estate **R** 112–13
   stocks and bonds **S** 427–33
Investment trusts, in which property or money is held for safekeeping **T** 303
Investors, people who buy securities **S** 427
Invincible Armada see Armada, Spanish
Invisible inks **I** 255–56
Invitations, letters **L** 159
   for parties **P** 87–88
   to Halloween parties **H** 15
Invocation, a calling prayer **P** 434
Involuntary muscles, diagram **B** 272
Involute curve, picture **G** 131
In winter I get up at night, from *Bed in Summer* by Robert Louis Stevenson **S** 424

Io, in Greek mythology, a mortal whom Zeus loved and turned into a white heifer to protect her from Hera's jealousy. In some versions it was Hera who transformed Io, torturing her with gadfly until she jumped into sea (named Ionian after her), swam to Egypt, was restored to human form, and became mother of Epaphus.

Iodine, element **I** 349
   elements, some facts about **E** 154, 161
   nutrition, use in **N** 417
   tincture of **M** 202
Iodized salt **S** 21
Iolani Palace, Honolulu, Hawaii **H** 66, 69
Iolanthe (i-o-LANTH-e), operetta by Gilbert and Sullivan **G** 210

Ionesco (yon-ES-ko), Eugene (1912–), French playwright, b. Bucharest, Rumania. He is a controversial, avant-garde playwright whose characters are often considered eccentric and grotesque. He writes about hopelessness of human communication in *Rhinoceros*.

Ionian (i-O-nian) **Islands,** west of Greece **I** 430, 434
 landforms of Greece **G** 333
Ionian School, of Greek philosophers **S** 61–62
Ionian Sea **O** 47
Ionic (i-ON-ic), Greek style of architecture **G** 346; picture **G** 347
 architectural orders **A** 375; picture **A** 376
I only regret that I have but one life to lose for my country, last words of Nathan Hale **H** 12
Ionosphere (i-ON-o-sphere), upper layer of earth's atmosphere **A** 481; **E** 17
 effect of solar radiation **S** 235–36
 ions and ionization **I** 352
 magnetic storms in **E** 27
 radio **R** 52
 weather in the ionosphere **W** 72
 Why can you hear radio stations from farther away at night? **R** 50
Ion propulsion, for rockets **R** 261
Ions and ionization **C** 219; **I** 350–55
 chemistry of ions **C** 202
 crystals **C** 542
 electron emission **E** 144–45
 electroplating **E** 149–50
 International Geophysical Year findings **I** 317
 ion-exchange resins to purify water **R** 185
 lightning **T** 170–71
 physical chemistry, development of **C** 215
 water desalting **W** 56a

I.O.U. (IOU), colloquial term for "I owe you"; a piece of paper with the letters IOU, a signature admitting the debt, and the amount of money owed; an informal promissory note.

Iowa (I-o-wa) **I** 356–71
Iowa University of **I** 364; picture **I** 367
Iowa, State University of Science and Technology, at Ames **I** 364, 366
Iowa City, former capital of Iowa **I** 367
Iowa Test of Basic Skills, sample **T** 118
Iowa Wesleyan (WES-le-yan) **College** **I** 366
Ipecac (IP-e-cac), plant **P** 314
Iphigenia (iph-i-ge-NY-a), in Greek mythology **G** 365
IPY-1 and 2 see International Polar Years
IQ see Intelligence Quotient
Iqbal, Indian poet **O** 220e
IQSY see International Quiet Sun Year
Iquitos (ee-KI-tose), Peru **P** 164
I.R.A. see Irish Republican Army
Iran (ir-AN) **I** 372–77
 archeological site at Tepe Sarab, picture **A** 357
 Azerbaijan **U** 45
 flag **F** 237
 rug weaving industry, Persian rugs **R** 354
 Teheran **T** 49–50
 See also Persia
Iraq (ir-OK) **I** 378–83
 archeological site at Jarmo, picture **A** 357
 flag **F** 237
Irazú (ir-a-ZU), volcano in Costa Rica **C** 516
Irbid, Jordan **J** 139
Ireland **I** 384–91
 agriculture, picture **A** 97
 ancient Irish blessing **P** 435
 Christianity, history of **C** 283, 284
 England, history of **E** 222, 228, 232
 flag **F** 239
 Gaelic football **F** 366
 gardens, pictures **G** 32
 Gladstone's reform programs **G** 225
 harp playing **H** 43

 holiday, Saint Patrick's Day **H** 148
 literature see Irish literature
 national anthem **N** 21
 Northern Ireland **U** 73
 O'Conneil, Daniel **O** 51
 Patrick, Saint **P** 98
 peat used for fuel, picture **F** 486
 potato famine, 1845, 1846 **P** 411
 Roman Catholic Church **R** 290
 theater **T** 161
 Viking era **V** 338
 Yeats, William Butler, a senator **Y** 345
 See also Northern Ireland
Ireland, National University of **U** 207
Ireland, Northern see Northern Ireland
Irene, Goodnight, folk song **F** 321
Iriarte see Yriarte, Tomas de
Iridium (i-RID-ium), element **E** 154, 161
 alloyed with platinum **J** 92
 metals, chart of ores, location, properties, uses **M** 227

Iris (I-ris), Greek goddess of the rainbow. A handmaiden of Zeus and Hera, she served as messenger for the gods. The familiar colorful garden flower is named for her.

Iris, of the eye **B** 284; **M** 208g
Irises, flowers **G** 41; picture **T** 206
 Japanese Iris Festival **J** 31
 state flower of Tennessee **T** 75
Irish harp, picture **H** 44
Irish literature **I** 392–95
 arts in Ireland **I** 386
 drama **D** 298–99
 Irish Renaissance in English literature **E** 266
 Kells, Book of **K** 202–03
 Yeats, William Butler **Y** 344
Irish moss, a seaweed **N** 344b
 in ice cream **I** 33
Irish potatoes **P** 411–12
Irish Republican Army (I.R.A.) **I** 391; **U** 73
Irish Sea **O** 47
Irish setter, dog, picture **D** 253
Irish system, of reforming criminals **P** 469
Irish Volunteer movement, of nationalists **I** 391
Irish wolfhound, dog, pictures **D** 250, 254

Irkutsk (ir-KUTSK), industrial city of Siberia. Situated on the Angara and Irkut rivers near Lake Baikal, this busy port is the site of a hydroelectric plant. Known also as a cultural center, the city is the home of a leading university and several colleges. A major port on the Trans-Siberian Railroad, Irkutsk has a population of about 400,000 people.

Irminger Current, North Atlantic
 diagram **G** 411
IRO see International Refugee Organization
Iron **I** 396–408
 antique ironwork **A** 321
 armor, chain mail **A** 433
 Assyrians used for weapons **A** 225
 building material **B** 438
 carbon added to make steel **C** 106
 chemical symbol from its Latin name **C** 198
 decorative arts **D** 77
 elements, some facts about **E** 154, 161–62
 ferrous alloys **A** 168
 filings used to show magnetic lines of force **E** 130; **M** 25–26
 galvanized iron **Z** 370
 how radiation changes form **R** 41

importance to Industrial Revolution   I 236–37
Lapland's deposits   L 45
magnetic qualities   M 26–28
Mesabi Range in Minnesota   M 329–30, 337
metals, chart of ores, location, properties, uses
   M 227
mordant in dyeing   D 369
nutrition, use in   N 416–17
ore formations in Labrador   N 141
Quebec, Canada, a leading producer   Q 11
rusting, slow oxidation   O 268
wrought iron and cast iron plows   F 57
See also Steel
Iron age   P 446
metallurgy   M 233
tools, Roman   T 211
Iron Chancellor, nickname for Otto von Bismarck   B 250
Ironclads, Confederate and Union warships   C 323
Iron Cross, German award, picture   M 200
Iron Curtain, imaginary barrier dividing Eastern Europe
   from the West   I 323
origin of the phrase   C 298; M 375
Iron Duke, nickname of the Duke of Wellington   W 122
Iron filings, how to make and use for experiments
   E 130; M 25–26
Iron industry and trade   I 404–05
Ironing, laundry   L 85

Iron lung, metal tank used as an apparatus of artificial respiration. Patient's head protrudes from the tank, and a rubber collar around neck prevents leakage of air. Air pressure in tank, electrically controlled, decreases and increases, resulting in expansion and contraction of chest. The lung is used for those paralyzed by polio, poisoning, or asphyxia. It is also called a Drinker Respirator, after its designer, Philip Drinker (1928).

Iron Mask, Man in the (?–1703), an unidentified French prisoner of state, said to have worn a velvet mask, who died in Bastille and was buried under name of Marchioli in St. Paul Cemetery, Paris. Title was given to him by Voltaire, who described him as wearing an iron mask. He was subject of much speculation and romantic literature, including novel of same name by Alexandre Dumas, who characterized prisoner as twin brother of Louis XIV.

Iron metals   E 158
Iron Mountain, Michigan
   ski area, picture   M 271
Iron ore   I 403–04
Europe   E 315
Mesabi Range, Minnesota   M 329–30, 337
North America world's greatest source   N 292–93
Sweden   S 485
world distribution, diagram   W 261
Iron pyrites, mineral nicknamed "fool's gold"   G 249
Irons, for pressing clothes   E 118
Why were electric irons invented?   E 118
Irons, golf clubs, picture   G 254
how to use, pictures   G 258
Ironsi, Johnson Aguiyi- see Aguiyi-Ironsi, Johnson
Iron Triangle, Korea   K 304
Ironwood, Michigan   M 270
Ironwork
Spain   S 364
welding   W 118–19
wrought iron   I 405
Irony (I-ro-ny), a form of humor   H 281
Iroquois (IR-o-quoi), Indians of North America   I 186–87
carved masks   I 156
Champlain makes bitter enemies of   C 187
early conflicts with Algonkians in New York   N 224

family life   A 302–03
Indian wars   I 212
League of Six Nations   I 184
New France almost destroyed by   C 69–70
present-day life in Quebec   Q 10a
Irradiation
meat preservation process   M 195
Irrational numbers, those that cannot be expressed as
   quotient of two integers   N 385
Irrawaddy (ir-ra-WA-dy) **River,** southeast Asia   R 244
largest river in Burma   B 456
Irregular verbs, principal parts   P 91
Irrigation   I 408–10
Arizona desert, picture   D 126
California projects   C 19
care of cotton crop   C 524
dams   D 16
deserts, future of   D 129, 130
ditches, picture   F 256
how rivers provide water   R 241–42
India, picture   I 123
Middle East   M 302–03
Nebraska's Platte River   N 76–77
oases   O 2–3
orchards   F 482
prairie farming   P 432
Reclamation Act, 1902   C 485
soil management in agriculture   A 93
sugar beet field, picture   U 108
vegetable gardening   V 288
water power   W 61
waterwheel, picture   A 63
See also Dams

Irving, Sir Henry (John Henry Brodribb) (1838–1905), English actor, b. Keinton Mandeville. With Ellen Terry as his leading lady, he formed (1878) his own company in his own theater, the Lyceum. In 1883 he made the first of eight tours in America. One of his greatest triumphs, Tennyson's *Becket* (1893), was performed by command before Queen Victoria at Windsor Castle. Hamlet was his finest Shakespearean role. The first actor to be knighted (1895), he was buried in Westminster Abbey.

Irving, Washington, American writer   I 410–11
American literature   A 199–200
children's literature   C 238
essays   E 293
"Rip Van Winkle," excerpt   I 411–12
short stories   S 166
Irwin, James B., American astronaut   S 345, 347

Irwin (ER-win), **Will** (William Henry Irwin), (1873–1948), American journalist and author, b. Oneida, New York. He first gained prominence for his report in *The Sun* of the San Francisco earthquake and fire in 1906. This story was later published in book form as *The City That Was.* During World War I he was a correspondent for the London *Daily Mail* and several American publications. He also wrote poetry, biographies, and collaborated on two plays, *The Thirteenth Chair* and *Lute Song.*

Isa Town, Bahrain   B 18
Isaac (I-zac), Hebrew patriarch   I 413
Abraham's sacrifice   A 7
Isaac (E-zoc), **Heinrich,** Flemish composer   D 364
Renaissance music   R 172–73
Isaacs (E-socs), **Jorge,** Colombian writer   C 380
Isabella I, Spanish queen, aided Columbus   F 87
art, patron of   S 361
Caribbean islands, colonization of   C 118
Columbus and Isabella   C 417

Isabelline, Spanish art style S 361
Isafjordur (E-sof-yur-dur), Iceland, picture I 41
Isaiah (i-SAI-ah), book of the Bible B 154, 155
Isaiah, Hebrew prophet I 413
  history of the Jews J 105
  Michelangelo painting B 158
Ise (E-say), Japan, site of shrine to sun goddess J 42
Isenheim altarpiece, painted by Grünewald G 167, 169
Isfahan (is-fa-HON), Iran I 376
  mosque, picture I 372
I shall find a way or make one, words of Robert E.
  Peary P 116
I shall return, words of Douglas MacArthur M 2

Ishmael (ISH-may-el), in Old Testament, son of Abraham
and Hagar. Ishmael was exiled with Hagar from Abraham's house and was miraculously found in the wilderness and saved. He married an Egyptian and according
to tradition founded the Arab race. His name is now used
to denote an outcast or misfit.
  Abraham's son A 7
  Muslim traditions I 414–16; M 196

Ishmaelites (ISH-may-el-ites), nomadic peoples, descended from Ishmael, who pitched their tents in
northern Arabia and traded with Egypt. They are
mentioned in several places in the Bible.

Ishtar Gate, picture A 243

Isis (I-sis), chief goddess of the early Egyptians, sister-
wife of Osiris and mother of Horus. Isis ruled over all matters concerning fertility and motherhood. Her worship
began around Memphis centuries before the birth of
Christ.

Islam, religion of Muslims I 414–16
  Africa A 56
  Arabic language L 39
  art and architecture see Islamic art and architecture
  Asia, chief religions of A 460
  Azerbaijan U 45
  Bangladesh B 44, 44b
  customs being revised by civil law in Tunisia
    T 309
  divorce D 234
  funeral customs F 493
  holy war against Christian world R 290–91
  Judaism and founding of Islam J 107
  Koran K 294–95
  lunar calendar T 194
  marriage rites W 102
  Mauritania M 179
  Mecca, holy city of M 196
  Mohammed M 404–05
  Muslims at prayer, picture R 150
  prayer from the Koran P 435
  religion of the Middle East M 305
  religious holidays R 154
  Saudi Arabia, site of the holy cities S 48
  science, advances in S 64
  Southeast Asia S 330
  Soviet Central Asia U 46
  two sects, the Sunnites and the Shi'ites R 150–51
Islamabad (is-LA-ma-bod), capital of Pakistan P 40
Islamic art and architecture I 417–22
  Blue Mosque, Istanbul, picture T 323
  Court of the Lions, Alhambra, picture S 363
  illuminated manuscripts I 88
  in Spain S 360–61
  Taj Mahal T 14
  tapestry T 22

Islands I 423–37
  Caribbean C 116–19
  how coral islands were formed O 39
  Indonesia's major groups I 218–20
  life, distribution of animals and plants L 236
  Mediterranean Sea M 213
  mid-Atlantic ridge, islands of A 478
  New York, a city of islands N 227–28
  North American continent, those islands considered
    part of N 282
  Pacific Ocean and islands P 2–10
  Southeast Asia S 328–35
  See also islands by name, as Liberty Island
Islas Malvinas (Falkland Islands) I 430; S 278
Isle of Man, in the Irish Sea I 435

Isle of Pines, mountainous, densely forested island in
the South Pacific, a dependency of New Caledonia,
administered by France. A former penal colony, the
island is now a tourist resort.

Isle of Spice, nickname of Grenada G 374b
Isle of Wight, in English Channel I 437
Isle Royale National Park, Lake Superior, Michigan M 268
  a few surviving wolves live in the park D 245
Ismay, Thomas H., English ship owner O 24
Isobars (I-so-bars), lines of weather maps indicating
  equal barometric pressures W 78–79

Isocrates (i-SOC-ra-tese) (436–338 B.C.), Athenian educator. A great speech writer and teacher, he opened a
school where he taught politics and the art of speech-
making. Although he himself never made speeches, he
wrote many for Athenian statesmen to deliver. He was
a strong believer in the unification of the Greek city-
states under the leadership of Athens.

Isodorus of Miletus (is-o-DOR-us of mi-LE-tus), Byzantine
  architect B 485
Isolationism, a policy in international relations I 322
  American colonies and later U 136
  Jefferson's policies J 67
Isomers (I-so-mers), in chemistry C 200, 219

Isometrics (i-so-MET-rics) (from Greek *isos,* meaning
"equal," and *metron,* meaning "measure"), system of
exercises based on the action of muscles against strong
resistance. This results in muscular contraction with
little shortening of the muscle fibers. Isometric exercises
increase muscle tone.

Isoniazid (i-so-NY-a-zid), drug D 212
Isoprene (I-so-prene), liquid hydrocarbon R 345–46
Isosceles (i-SOS-cel-ese) **trapezoids,** geometric forms
  G 126
Isosceles triangles, diagram G 125
Isostasy (i-SOS-ta-sy), theory of the balance of earth's
  crust G 114–15
Isotherms (I-so-therms), diagram Z 373
Isotopes (I-so-topes), of chemical elements E 153–54
  atomic weight A 487–88
  cancer treatment C 91, 95
  chemistry of isotopes C 203–05
  defined C 219
  nuclear energy N 356
  radioactive elements and isotopes R 67–68
  uranium 235 and 238 U 231

Isotype, picture symbol representing a fixed number or
quantity of the thing symbolized, such as a stick figure
of a man to represent 10,000 people. Isotypes are used
for statistical charts and in visual education.

Israëls (E-sra-els), **Jozef** (1824–1911), Dutch painter, b. Groningen. When ill health forced him to live in the fishing village of Zandvoort, near Haarlem, he turned from portrait paintings to the paintings of Dutch fisherfolk and peasants that made him a leader of The Hague school of genre painting (flourished 1870–90). His gray-brown, almost monochrome paintings express great compassion for the inhabitants of Dutch fishing villages and of the Jewish quarter of Amsterdam.

Israfil, or **Israfeel** (ees-ra-FEEL) (probably from Hebrew *Serāfim*, the highest order of angels), Muslim angel of music. According to the Koran, Israfil, Gabriel, and Michael were the angels who warned Abraham of Sodom's destruction. Israfil was Mohammed's companion for 3 years until Gabriel replaced him. Israfil is enormous, has four wings, and is covered with hair, mouths, and tongues. Called Lord of the Trumpet, he will blow the trumpet on Judgment Day.

Istria (IS-tree-a), peninsula in the Adriatic Sea. Often a source of conflict among Yugoslavia, Italy, and Austria, most of the area was ceded to Yugoslavia in 1947. The population is mostly Yugoslav and Italian; the chief city is Pola. The peninsula covers about 2,000 square miles.

Iturbi, (e-TOUR-be), **José** (1895–   ), Spanish pianist and conductor, b. Valencia. He graduated (1912) from the Paris Conservatory with honors and began his career as a virtuoso after teaching in the Geneva Conservatory (1919–23). He went to the United States (1938) and was conductor of the Rochester Philharmonic Orchestra (1936–44). He has been guest conductor with major world orchestras and has appeared in movies.

Ivan the Terrible (Ivan IV Vasilievich) (1530–1584), czar

Ivan the Terrible (continued)
of Russia (1533–84). He succeeded his father, Basil III (1533), and at age 17 was crowned czar of All the Russias—the first to use the title officially. During his reign he introduced a new code of law and established diplomatic and commercial relations with England. But after 1560 he developed a deep distrust of all with whom he came in contact. He created a special royal domain that eventually included half the territory of the state, with a special police force that committed great cruelties in order to prevent treason. He used his immense powers, unlimited by any form of control, to torture and execute a vast number of people. He even murdered his son and heir, Ivan, in a fit of anger (1581).

Moscow, the state, in Russian history **M** 467; **U** 48

Ivan V, Russian ruler **P** 168

Ives, Burl (Burl Icle Ivanhoe Ives) (1909–), American folk singer, b. Hunt, Ill. He has made many world tours, singing American folk songs. He has published collected folk music in *Burl Ives Song Book* and also recorded series *Historical America in Song* for *Encyclopædia Britannica*. He starred in movies *So Dear to My Heart* and *The Big Country* (won 1959 Oscar).

Ives, Charles, American composer **I** 487; **U** 126
modern music **M** 401

Ives, Joseph Christmas (1828–1868), American soldier and explorer, b. New York, N.Y. He was put in command of an expedition to explore the Colorado River (1857–58), and his detailed report added greatly to the knowledge of that little-known region. He was also engineer and architect of the Washington national monument (1859–60), astronomer and surveyor for a commission surveying the California boundary (1860–61), and an engineering officer in the Confederate Army during Civil War.

Ivoiriens, Ivory Coast citizens **I** 489
Ivory **I** 487–88
Byzantine carvings **B** 486–87, 489–90
decorative arts **D** 68, 70
elephant tusks **E** 169
Ivory-billed woodpeckers, birds **B** 232; picture **B** 230
Ivory Coast **I** 489–92
flag **F** 235
thatched houses, pictures **A** 303, **I** 490

Ivy League, term referring to a group of colleges and universities located in the northeastern part of the United States, and to the athletic league in which these schools compete. The schools include Harvard, Yale, Columbia, Princeton, Brown, Cornell, Dartmouth, and Pennsylvania. The term "Ivy League" connotes such characteristics as high scholastic achievement, prestige, and sophistication.

Iwanowski, Dmitri, Russian scientist **V** 362
I Wish That My Room Had a Floor, poem by Gelett Burgess **N** 274

Iwo Jima (E-wo JI-ma), an island in northwestern Pacific, largest of the Volcano group. Formerly under Japanese rule, it was occupied by United States Marines during World War II. Administered by the United States 1945–68, it was then returned to Japan.
Volcano Islands **P** 8

Iwo Jima, battle of (1945), important engagement for United States forces before the occupation of Japan. Iwo Jima, a volcanic island heavily fortified by the Japanese, was bombarded from sea and air before it was assaulted by U.S. Marines (Feb. 19, 1945). A famous photograph shows a group of Marines, after fierce fighting and heavy losses, raising the U.S. flag on Mt. Suribachi.
World War II **W** 305

I.W.W. see Industrial Workers of the World

Ixion (IX-e-on), in Greek mythology, King of the Lapiths, and father of the centaur monsters. For daring to love Hera, queen of the gods and wife of Zeus, he was banished to Tartarus to burn forever on a fiery, revolving wheel.

Ixtacihuatl (i-sta-CI-hua-tel), extinct volcano, Mexico **M** 242

Izaak Walton League of America, private conservation organization with nationwide membership. It was founded (1922) for preservation of wildlife and soil and water resources. It has headquarters in Glenview, Ill., and publishes *The Izaak Walton Magazine*.

Izalco (i-ZOL-co), volcano in El Salvador **E** 181
Izmir (eez-MERE), formerly Smyrna, Turkey **T** 326
Izvestia (eez-v'YEST-ya) Soviet newspaper **U** 41

ILLUSTRATION CREDITS

The following list credits, by page, the sources of illustrations used in Volume I of THE NEW BOOK OF KNOWLEDGE. Credits are listed illustration by illustration —left to right, top to bottom. Wherever appropriate, the name of the photographer or artist has been listed with the source, the two being separated by a dash. When two or more illustrations appear on one page, their credits are separated by semicolons.

3– Wesley B. McKeown
5
6 U.S. Coast Guard
7 Wesley B. McKeown
8 Bob & Ira Spring; Wesley B. McKeown.
9 U.S. Coast Guard; Wesley B. McKeown
10 Science Service; U.S. Forest Service.
11 National Academy of Sciences
12 Bob & Ira Spring
14 Bob & Ira Spring; Wisconsin Conservation Department; Macs Foto; A. F. Buddington—U.S. Geological Survey; William S. Cooper.
15 W. C. Alden—U.S. Geological Survey; Annan.

16 Geological Survey of Canada; Bob & Ira Spring; U.S. Coast Guard.
17 F. C. Calkins—U.S. Geological Survey
18 Bradford Washburn; Monkmeyer.
19 Harry Scott
21 Contributions from Cushman Foundation for Foraminiferal Research, Foraminifera of Martha's Vineyard, Todd and Low.
23 U.S. Naval Oceanographic Office
25 U.S. Coast Guard
26 Chuck McVicker
27 U.S. Coast Guard
28 Niels Lauritzen—*Sports Illustrated*
30 N. C. Potter

32– Kenneth Longtemps
34
35 Mimi Forsyth—Monkmeyer Press
36 Edward Vebell
38 Edward Vebell
39 Edward Vebell
41 George Buctel; Solarfilma—Icelandic Airlines.
42 Tom Hollyman—Photo Researchers
43 Solarfilma—Icelandic Airlines
44 Tom Hollyman—Photo Researchers
45 Grethe Buhl—PIP
46 Pictorial Parade
47 Edward Vebell
49 Edward Vebell

262 Gaetano Di Palma; Louis Quitt—Photo Researchers; Walter Rohdich—Annan; John H. Gerard; Hermann Eisenbeiss—Annan.
263 N. E. Beck, Jr.—National Audubon Society; H. A. Thornhill—National Audubon Society; John H. Gerard; John H. Gerard; John H. Gerard.
264 Gaetano Di Palma
265 Hugh Spencer; Green—Annan; Robert Hermes—Annan; Lynwood M. Chace; Lynwood M. Chace; Robert Hermes—National Audubon Society; Hugh Spencer.
266 Gaetano Di Palma; Ross E. Hutchins; Hermann Eisenbeiss—Photo Researchers; Ross E. Hutchins.
267 Gaetano Di Palma
268 Gaetano Di Palma
269 Ross E. Hutchins; Ross E. Hutchins; Wexler—Annan; Ross E. Hutchins.
270 Gaetano Di Palma
271 Gaetano Di Palma; Fran Hall—National Audubon Society.
272 Hermann Eisenbeiss—Photo Researchers; Hugh Spencer; Ross E. Hutchins; Ross E. Hutchins; Gaetano Di Palma.
273 Gaetano Di Palma
274 Gaetano Di Palma
275 Karl Maslowski—Photo Researchers; Ross E. Hutchins; Lynwood M. Chace; John H. Gerard; Robert Fink—National Audubon Society; Louis Quitt—Photo Researchers.
276 W. J. Jahoda—National Audubon Society; Ross E. Hutchins; Lynwood M. Chace; Lynwood M. Chace; Grace A. Thompson—National Audubon Society; Grace A. Thompson—National Audubon Society.
277 Lynwood M. Chace—National Audubon Society; Treat Davidson—National Audubon Society; Hugh Spencer; Stephen Collins—Photo Researchers; L. G. Kesteloo—National Audubon Society; John H. Gerard.
278 Lynwood M. Chace; Lynwood M. Chace; Ross E. Hutchins; Ross E. Hutchins; Noble Proctor—Photo Researchers; V. E. Ward—National Audubon Society; Stephen Collins—Photo Researchers; Norman R. Lightfoot—Photo Researchers.
280 U.S. Department of Agriculture
281 Herbert Hanks—Monkmeyer; John H. Gerard; Ross E. Hutchins; Walter Rohdich—Annan; Ross E. Hutchins; Annan; Annan; Ross E. Hutchins; John H. Gerard.
282 Allan D. Cruickshank—National Audubon Society; Karl Maslowski—Photo Researchers; John H. Gerard—National Audubon Society; Norman R. Lightfoot—Photo Researchers; Alexander Klots.
283 N. E. Beck, Jr.—National Audubon Society; Courtesy of American Museum of Natural History.
284 Gordon Smith—National Audubon Society; Hal Harrison—National Audubon Society.
285 R. C. Hermes—National Audubon Society
286 Hermann Schunemann—Annan; Leonard Lee Rue III—Annan.
291 Gerald McConnell
293 Courtesy of Lloyd's of London
299– Chuck McVicker
302
304– Gregori-Gelb Associates
308
309 Harry Scott
310 Culver
311 State University of Iowa; High Altitude Observatory, Boulder, Colorado; Blackstone Studios.
312 U.S. Coast and Geodetic Survey
313 Alex Ebel; National Bureau of Standards, Department of Commerce.
314 Jet Propulsion Laboratory, California Institute of Technology; British Information Services.
315 Victor Peter Hessler
316 U.S. Navy
317 National Academy of Science—I.G.Y. Photo
318 U.S. Coast Guard; U.S. Coast Guard; Woods Hole Oceanographic Institution.
319 University of Wisconsin
324 Gerald McConnell
326 Rene Burri—Magnum
329 The Coca-Cola Export Corp., New York
339– Gerald McConnell
345
350– Miller Pope
352
353 Brookhaven National Laboratory; University of California Lab.
355 Miller Pope
357 Color Illustration Inc.; J. C. Allan; Dyer; Gottscho-Schleisner.
358 Shostal
359 Diversified Map Corp.
361 Shostal
362 Shostal
365 Diversified Map Corp.
366 Graphic Arts International
367 University News Service, the University of Iowa
368 Diversified Map Corp.
369 Des Moines Chamber of Commerce
372 Inge Morath—Magnum
373 George Buctel; Shostal.
374 Inge Morath—Magnum
377 De Biasi—Rapho Guillumette
378 Monkmeyer
379 George Buctel
380 C. J. Coulson—Shostal
381 Inge Morath—Magnum
382 ZFA—PIP
383 John Lewis Stage—Photo Researchers
384 Irish Tourist Board
385 George Buctel
387 Shostal; Fritz Henle—Photo Researchers.
388 Fritz Henle—Photo Researchers; Tom Hollyman—Photo Researchers.
393 Graphic House
394 Jane Brown—Camera Press Ltd.
395 Irish National Tourist Office
397 Howard Koslow
399– Howard Koslow
402
405 Howard Koslow
407 Howard Koslow
409 Bureau of Reclamation, U.S. Department of the Interior; Jules Bucher—Photo Researchers.
412 Avery Peters
415 Alpha; Marc & Evelyne Bernheim—Rapho Guillumette
416 Tom Hollyman—Photo Researchers; William G. Froelich, Jr.
417 Duncan Edwards—FPG
418 Metropolitan Museum of Art, Bequest of Edward C. Moore, 1891; From *Arab Painting,* published by Skira, Geneva-New York; Art Reference Bureau; From *Arab Painting,* published by Skira, Geneva-New York.
419 Photo Researchers
420 Tom Hollyman—Photo Researchers
421 Inge Morath—Magnum
423 Paris Match—Pictorial Parade
424 R. Leahey—Shostal; George Hunter—Shostal; Shostal.
425 Shostal
426 Port of New York Authority; Ray Manley—Shostal.
431 Mac's Foto; Renda—Alpha; Tom Hollyman—Photo Researchers.
432 William G. Froelich, Jr.; Max Tatch—Shostal.
433 Edmund Stockius—Shostal; Ray Manley—Shostal.
434 David Pratt—Rapho; Shostal.
438 Erich Hartman—Magnum
439 George Buctel
440 A. L. Goldman—Rapho Guillumette
441 A. L. Goldman—Rapho Guillumette
442 Erich Hartman—Magnum; David Seymour—Magnum.
445 A. L. Goldman—Rapho Guillumette; A. L. Goldman—Rapho Guillumette.
446 Ray Manley—Shostal
447 George Buctel
449 Ronny Jacques——Photo Researchers; Gaetano Barone, Firenze.
450 Ray Manley—Shostal; Bernard G. Silberstein—Rapho Guillumette.
453 Lambretta Division, Innocenti Corp.
455 Gaetano Barone, Firenze
456 Fritz Henle—Photo Researchers
459 Shostal; Scala—Shostal.
460 Art Reference Bureau; Gaetano Barone, Firenze; Gaetano Barone, Firenze.
461 Art Reference Bureau; Aldo Martello, Editore, Milano.
462 Gaetano Barone, Firenze; Art Reference Bureau.
464 Georgina Masson from *Rome Revealed,* published by Thames Hudson, Ltd.; Rollie McKenna.
465 Louis H. Frohman; Art Reference Bureau.
466 Reproduced by Courtesy of the Trustees of the National Gallery, London—Art Reference Bureau; Art Reference Bureau.
468 Louis H. Frohman
469 Brogi—Art Reference Bureau
470 Fotocielo, Rome
471 Staatliche Museum, Gemälde Galerie, Berlin-Dahlem—Art Reference Bureau; Courtesy of National Gallery of Art, Andrew Mellon Collection, Washington, D.C.; Art Reference Bureau.
472 Art Reference Bureau; Lee Boltin—Courtesy of Mrs. Stanley Resor.
475 Art Reference Bureau
476 From a 16th-century manuscript *Ticiducticn des Tuamphes de Petrarque,* Bibliothèque Nationale, Paris.
480 Cover by Attilio Mussino from *Le Avventure di Pinocchio* by C. Collodi, issued in a 1965 edition by Bemporad Marzocco, Firenze, which first published Collodi's masterpiece.
481 Reprinted from the jacket of *The Leopard* by Guiseppe Lampedusa, by permission of Pantheon Books, a division of Random House, Inc.; Courtesy of Farrar, Straus & Cudahy.
482 Museum Bourges—Giraudon, Art Reference Bureau
485 James Cooper
488 Brooklyn Museum
489 George Buctel
490– Marc & Evelyne Bernheim—Rapho Guillumette
492